SOLVENCY REQUIREMENTS FOR EU INSURERS

SOLVENCY REQUIREMENTS FOR EU INSURERS

Solvency II is Good for You

Karel VAN HULLE

intersentia
Cambridge – Antwerp – Chicago

Intersentia Ltd
Sheraton House | Castle Park
Cambridge | CB3 0AX | United Kingdom
Tel.: +44 1223 370 170 | Fax: +44 1223 370 169
Email: mail@intersentia.co.uk
www.intersentia.com | www.intersentia.co.uk

Distribution for the UK and Ireland:
NBN International
Airport Business Centre, 10 Thornbury Road
Plymouth, PL6 7PP
United Kingdom
Tel.: +44 1752 202 301 | Fax: +44 1752 202 331
Email: orders@nbninternational.com

Distribution for Europe and all other countries:
Intersentia Publishing nv
Groenstraat 31
2640 Mortsel
Belgium
Tel.: +32 3 680 15 50 | Fax: +32 3 658 71 21
Email: mail@intersentia.be

Distribution for the USA and Canada:
Independent Publishers Group
Order Department
814 North Franklin Street
Chicago, IL 60610
USA
Tel.: +1 800 888 4741 (toll free) | Fax: +1 312 337 5985
Email: orders@ipgbook.com

Solvency Requirements for EU Insurers. Solvency II is Good for You

ISBN 978-1-78068-177-1
D/2019/7849/59
NUR 820

British Library Cataloguing in Publication Data. A catalogue record for this book is available from the British Library.

*"Not everything that can be counted,
counts, and not everything that
counts can be counted"*

Albert Einstein

FOREWORD

On 1 December 2004, I met Karel Van Hulle for the very first time at a meeting of the so-called Insurance Committee in Brussels. Shortly before – in November 2004 – Karel became the Head of the Insurance and Pensions Unit of the European Commission's Directorate General for Internal Market and Services.

It was also the penultimate meeting of the Insurance Committee before the European Insurance and Occupational Pensions Committee (EIOPC) – the Level 2 committee of the Lamfalussy process – replaced it on 13 April 2005. I was representing Portugal.

The meeting agenda was rich and full: introducing the draft Work Program for 2005, Karel (the Chairman of the Committee) stressed that Solvency II would be the Committee's main work focus in 2005. The need for an impact assessment meant that formally, it would not be possible to table a proposal of Solvency II in 2005, but a draft proposal would be prepared by the end of the year.

Furthermore, Karel announced that 2006 was the target date for any proposal on insurance guarantee schemes. All delegations who took to the floor stressed the importance, scale and ambition of the Solvency II project, the complexity even exceeding that of Basel II, the project of the banking sector.

In fact, what I remember most of Karel from that meeting was the impression he made on the insurance experts from the very first day, by mentioning that in his first contact with insurance, one thing is taken for granted: insurance is by far more complex than banking.

From that day in December 2004, until February 2013 when Karel left the European Commission, I had the privilege of working very closely with him in various capacities.

On 10 July 2007, the European Commission presented its proposal for the Solvency II Directive. At that time, Portugal held the European Union Presidency and the Portuguese government asked me to chair the Council working group in charge of the Member State negotiations.

The headline of the European Commission's press release read: "Solvency II: European Union to take global lead in insurance regulation". The European Commission proposed a ground-breaking revision of European Union insurance law to improve consumer protection, modernise supervision, deepen market integration and increase the international competitiveness of European insurers. Under the new system, insurers would be required to take account of all types of risk to which they are exposed and to manage those risks more effectively. In addition, insurance groups would have a dedicated "group supervisor" that would enable better monitoring of the group as a whole. The European Commission aimed to have the new system in operation by 2012, which was good news for consumers, for the insurance industry and for the economy of the European Union as a whole.

During the second half of 2007, Karel and I worked very closely to ensure that good progress was made during the Solvency II discussions. After intensive negotiations between the European Commission, the European Parliament and the European Council, the three European legislative institutions agreed on a compromise text for the Solvency II Framework Directive. On 22 April 2009, the European Parliament's plenary session adopted the Directive, which finally became Directive 2009/138/EC of 25 November 2009 on the taking-up and pursuit of the business of Insurance and Reinsurance (Solvency II).

Over the years, I learned to trust and respect Karel. Karel represented the European Commission in the Committee of European Insurance and Occupational Pensions Supervisors (CEIOPS) and in the International Association of Insurance Supervisors (IAIS). Most of the time, we agreed and were of the same opinion. And, when we disagreed, I always appreciated Karel's pragmatic way of finding a good compromise and moving forward.

This book tells the story of Solvency II through the lens of one of its major architects. Karel always understood that a major reform like Solvency II had to be built on extensive consultation and debate, and ultimately benefits from the contributions of many dedicated people from both the public and the private sectors. This is what makes Solvency II a unique piece of legislation in the financial sector.

History will look positively on Karel's commitment and passionate work in the area of insurance regulation. He was instrumental in driving Solvency II through difficult waters in times of crisis. He did so because he essentially believed in sound principle- and risk-based regulation. I am sure that at the end of the book, which makes for pleasant reading, the reader will agree: "Solvency II is good for you!"

Gabriel Bernardino
Chairman, European Insurance and
Occupational Pensions Authority (EIOPA)

PREFACE

One might be alarmed, looking at the length of this book: so many pages to convey the message that "Solvency II is good for you". Can this be right? I think it is. It is precisely because I believe that "Solvency II is good for you" that I decided to write this book. I had not expected it to be so long, but the length of the book is the result of complexity added to the initial principles-based text, because of both the financial crisis and the reluctance in the insurance world and in the supervisory community to leave too many questions unanswered.

I was privileged to have been made responsible for the development of a new, risk-based solvency capital regime for (re)insurance undertakings in the EU. However, at the start, it seemed an almost impossible task. Carrying out such a profound change in a naturally conservative sector sounded like a daring proposition. However, I was wrong. The enthusiasm with which the insurance industry, the supervisory community, finance ministries and stakeholders in general approached this project was impressive. The support for this project was such that it led me to conclude my presentation on the objectives of Solvency II at a conference organised by Confrontations Europe in the European Economic and Social Committee in Brussels on 8 March 2007 with the words: "Solvency II is good for you".

Solvency II is good because it moves risk management to the forefront. It fosters a holistic and forward-looking appreciation of risk and enhances market forces by increasing transparency and disclosure. Solvency II has created a more transparent, more professional and thus more secure insurance market. That became clear when the financial crisis also hit the insurance industry. The importance attached to risk management and the careful preparation of the project, with consultations, quantitative impact studies, workshops and seminars, created an environment that helped the insurance industry to survive one of the worst possible scenarios that could have been imagined: a prolonged low interest rate environment, which hits both sides of the balance sheet and makes it difficult to continue to offer long-term guarantees. As can be seen from the last stress test carried out by EIOPA, the insurance industry is not only well capitalised, but it is also capable of withstanding very severe natural catastrophe scenarios.

Solvency II is not only good, it is also good *for you*: as a *policyholder or beneficiary*, because it increases the level of security, making it less likely that an insurer will fail; as a *(re)insurer*, because it rewards professionalism, making the industry more attractive to young professionals; as a *supervisor*, because it delivers the right supervisory tools, making it easier to carry out forward-looking supervision; as an *actuary*, because it puts the actuarial function on the map, making full use of the actuarial profession's expertise; as a *risk manager*, because it adopts the newest techniques in risk management, giving proper recognition to the importance of risk management; as an *insurance intermediary*, because it brings transparency and a customer focus, making it easier to advise clients on the best insurance solution; as an *academic*, because it provides detailed data on the insurance industry, allowing for evidence-based research; and as a *consumer*, because it delivers better-designed products, making life easier by better responding to customer demands.

Solvency II is good for society as a whole because it strengthens an industry the importance of which is probably the best-kept secret in the world. However, without an insurance industry that is strong and well managed, our society will not be able to meet the challenges that face us, such as climate change, increased longevity, health care, pension financing, and so on.

Of course, Solvency II is not perfect. It was never meant to be. And Rome was not built in a day. A review is planned for 2020/2021. This review should be carried out very carefully. It should provide better treatment for long-term business, with appropriate recognition of the insurance business model. Learning from our experience and from that in other parts of the world, we should improve the system where we can, but do so with full respect for the principles of a risk-based solvency regime, which creates a link between risk and capital and which aims at protecting policyholders and beneficiaries.

In the first part of this book, I explain the origins of Solvency II. The project was inspired by developments both within Europe, particularly in Germany, the Netherlands, Switzerland and the UK, but also outside Europe, in countries such as Australia, Canada and the USA, and in international bodies, such as the Basel Committee, the IASB and the IAIS. Valuable input was obtained from the actuarial profession and from the risk management community.

Like all EU legislation, Solvency II is not the work of anonymous "Brussels". The Solvency II framework was extensively consulted on and debated. It took more time than expected, in part because of the financial crisis. Many people contributed to the project: a small team of civil servants and national experts at the EC, in close cooperation with supervisors organised within CEIOPS/ EIOPA and with experts from the (re)insurance industry. They were helped by actuaries, chief risk officers, policy advisers, experts in finance ministries, consumers and civil society in general. The ultimate decisions were taken by the EC and by the co-legislators: the EP and the Council. Although the negotiations were sometimes difficult and challenging, one should not forget that Solvency II is a European project and that – by producing Solvency II – we Europeans showed that we are capable of carrying out a major reform that is in the interest of the EU, its undertakings and its citizens, and that has, right from its inception, influenced similar reforms in many other parts of the world, as well as within the IAIS.

The second part of this book contains a detailed description of the Solvency II regulatory framework. It shows that solvency is not just about capital. It is about people, about risk management and about a dialogue between supervisors and supervised entities in an atmosphere of trust. This second part has been written without too much technical detail. I have tried to give a holistic picture of Solvency II, how it fits into the European single market, what its main characteristics are and how it relates to other parts of EU legislation that are relevant for the (re)insurance industry. I have also provided some examples and identified good practices. As insurance is technically complex, solvency regulation is not easy to understand. Nevertheless, I have written this book so that non-experts can also understand what this is all about. That may be a disappointment for experts, who might have wanted more technical detail. I have however learned from experience that even experts sometimes lose their way. This book might help them to get back on the right track.

I have not covered a number of topics that certainly merit more attention, such as a comparison between the US Risk-Based Capital model and Solvency II, and between Solvency II and the International Capital Standard that is being developed by the IAIS and that will hopefully see the light of day as planned by the end of 2019. A discussion of these topics would have made the book even longer.

I could not have written this book without the help of many people. As a non-expert in insurance, most of what I know I have learned from others: my colleagues at the EC, especially the national experts seconded to the EC, my colleagues at KU Leuven and at Goethe University in Frankfurt, and my many friends in the supervisory community, in EIOPA, in the actuarial profession, in the communities of risk managers and insurance intermediaries, and in the (re)insurance industry. I would like to thank so many people by name, but I am afraid that if I do so, I might miss out people who deserve to be mentioned.

However, I would like to make a few exceptions. I want to thank in particular Lieve Lowet (Schuman European Affairs), who has not only been a source of inspiration but also agreed to read and reread many of my drafts and whose comments have been very valuable. I would also like to thank Ben Carr (Aviva), former national expert in my Solvency Technical Team at the EC, who reviewed the Pillar 1 chapter of this book, and Ivo van Es (member of the ECON Secretariat), former member of the Solvency Technical Team at the EC, who provided insights from a EP perspective.

Finally, I want to thank my wife, Greta, for her patience and understanding. It has at times been difficult, but she knew that this book was important to me and she gave me the time and the support to finish it.

Karel Van Hulle
30 April 2019

CONTENTS

LIST OF ABBREVIATIONS

AAE	Actuarial Association of Europe
AD	Accounting Directive
AIFM	alternative investment fund managers
ALDE	Alliance of Liberals and Democrats for Europe (EP)
AMSB	administrative, management or supervisory body
AR	Audit Regulation
BCBS	Basel Committee of Banking Supervisors
BIS	Bank for International Settlements
BMA	Bermuda Monetary Authority
BoS	Board of Supervisors (EIOPA)
BSCR	basic solvency capital requirement (basic SCR)
CEA	Comité Européen des Assurances (now Insurance Europe)
CEBS	Committee of European Banking Supervisors
CEIOPS	Committee of European Insurance and Pensions Supervisors
CEO	Chief Executive Officer
CESR	Committee of European Securities Regulators
CFO	Chief Financial Officer
Co-Co	Coordinating Committee
COM	(European) Commission (Services)
ComFrame	Common Framework for the Supervision of IAIG
COMP	Directorate-General for Competition (EC)
CoR	European Committee of the Regions
COSO	Commission of Sponsoring Organizations (Treadway Commission)
Council	Council of Ministers of the EU
CQS	credit quality step
CRA	Credit Rating Agency
CRD	Capital Requirements Directive
CRO	Chief Risk Officer
CRR	Capital Requirements Regulation
DA	Delegated Act

DG	Directorate-General (European Commission)
EBA	European Banking Authority
EC	European Commission
ECAI	External Credit Assessment Institution
ECB	European Central Bank
ECFIN	Directorate-General for Economic and Financial Affairs (EC)
ECIROA	European Captive Insurance and Reinsurance Owners Association
ECON	Economic and Monetary Affairs Committee (EP)
ECR	European Conservatives and Reformists (EP)
EEA	European Economic Area
EEC	European Economic Community
EESC	European Economic and Social Committee
EFR	European Financial Services Roundtable
EIB	European Investment Bank
EIF	European Investment Fund
EIOPA	European Insurance and Occupational Pensions Authority
EIOPC	European Insurance and Occupational Pensions Committee (EC)
EMAC	Economic and Monetary Affairs Committee (EP)
EMIR	European Market Infrastructure Regulation
EMPL	Directorate-General for Employment, Social Affairs and Inclusion (EC)
ENTR	Directorate-General for Enterprise and Industry (EC)
EP	European Parliament
EPIFP	expected profits in future premiums
EPP	European People's Party (EP)
ESCB	European System of Central Banks
ESFS	European System of Financial Supervision
ESMA	European Securities and Markets Authority
ESRB	European Systemic Risk Board
EU	European Union
FD	Solvency II Framework Directive
FICOD	Financial Conglomerates Directive
FINMA	Swiss Financial Market Supervisory Authority
FISMA	Directorate-General for Financial Stability, Financial Markets and Capital Markets Union (EC)

FIN-USE	Forum of User Experts in the Area of Financial Services
FIO	Federal Insurance Office (Treasury Department USA)
FoE	freedom of (cross-border) establishment
FoS	freedom to provide (cross-border) services
FSA	Financial Services Authority (UK)
FSAP	Financial Sector Assessment Program
GAAP	generally accepted accounting principles
GDV	German Insurance Association
GNAIE	Group of North American Insurance Enterprises
GREENS	The Greens/European Free Alliance (EP)
G-SII	global systemically important insurer
GSP	group-specific parameters
GUE/NGL	European United Left/Nordic Green Left (EP)
IAA	International Actuarial Association
IAASB	International Auditing and Assurance Standards Board
IAD	Insurance Accounts Directive
IAIG	internationally active insurance group
IAIS	International Association of Insurance Supervisors
IAS	International Accounting Standards
IASB	International Accounting Standards Board
ICAS	Individual Capital Adequacy Standards (UK)
ICP	Insurance Core Principle (IAIS)
ICS	International Capital Standard (IAIS)
IDD	Insurance Distribution Directive
IFRS	International Financial Reporting Standards
IGD	Insurance Groups Directive
ILS	insurance-linked securities
IMD	Insurance Mediation Directive
IORP	institutions for occupational retirement provision
IORP I	IORP Directive (2003)
IORP II	IORP Directive (recast) (2016)
IRSG	Insurance and Reinsurance Stakeholder Group (EIOPA)
ISA	international standards on auditing
ITS	implementing technical standards
JLS	Directorate-General for Justice, Freedom and Security, Private Law and Criminal Law (EC)
JURI	Legal Affairs Committee (EP)

LAC-DT	loss-absorbing capacity of technical provisions and deferred taxes
LGD	loss-given-default
LTG	long-term guarantees
MA	matching adjustment
MARKT	Directorate-General for Internal Market and Services (EC)
MCR	minimum capital requirement
MiFID	Market in Financial Instruments Directive
MS	Member State
NAIC	National Association of Insurance Commissioners (USA)
NCB	national central bank
NSA	national supervisory authority
NSLT	health not similar to life techniques
NTNI	non-traditional non-insurance
OECD	Organisation for Economic Cooperation and Development
OEEC	Organisation for European Economic Cooperation
OJ	Official Journal of the European Union
ORSA	own risk and solvency assessment
PD	probability of default
PEIF	Pan-European Insurance Forum
QIS	quantitative impact study
QRT	quantitative reporting template
RSR	regular supervisory report
RTS	regulatory technical standards
S&D	Progressive Alliance of Socialists and Democrats (EP)
SANCO	Directorate-General for Health and Consumers (EC)
SCE	European Cooperative Society
SCR	solvency capital requirement
Sec Gen	General Secretariat (EC)
SFCR	solvency and financial condition report
SII	systemically important insurer
SLT	health similar to life techniques
SME	small and medium-sized enterprise
SPE	special-purpose entity
SPV	special-purpose vehicle
SRP	supervisory review process
SST	Swiss Solvency Test

STS	simple standardised and transparent securitisations
TFEU	Treaty on the Functioning of the European Union
UCITS	undertakings for collective investment in transferable securities
UK	United Kingdom
USA	United States of America
USP	undertaking-specific parameter
VA	volatility adjustment
VaR	value-at-risk

PART I
EU INSURANCE REGULATION AND THE BIRTH OF SOLVENCY II

CHAPTER 1
INTRODUCTION

1. WHAT IS INSURANCE?

Insurance is based upon a contract under which one party, the insurer, promises another party, the policyholder, cover against a specified risk in exchange for a premium.[1] The objective of insurance is to transfer risks from private individuals, organisations, such as public administrations or schools, or undertakings to an insurance undertaking, which manages those risks. Through insurance, private individuals, organisations or undertakings can protect themselves from financial loss or from loss that can mostly be expressed in financial terms. Sometimes insurance provides a service in kind, such as assistance insurance. Insurance also provides financial security in the event of death or disability.

The insured must have an insurable interest, i.e. the individual or undertaking must stand to suffer a direct financial loss if the event against which the insurance cover was bought does occur. The risk of occurrence must be beyond the control of the policyholder and may not be systematic, i.e. it must be subject to a defined and observed law of large numbers or at least to a known maximal loss. It must also be non-financial in the sense that it cannot be directly related to the economic and financial cycle.[2]

Insurance is complex because it deals with the future. The future is uncertain and an insurance undertaking will have to estimate the probability of a risk materialising. Insurance is a promise to pay claims in the future in exchange for premiums today. Confidence in the insurance industry rests upon the foundation that these claims will be paid. Calculating the risk relating to an insurance contract will usually involve the intervention of an actuary, who

---

1 COUSY, H., Changing Insurance Contract Law: An Age-Old Slow and Unfinished Story, in MARANO, P. and SIRI, M. (Eds.), *Insurance Regulation in the European Union*, Palgrave Macmillan, Cham, 2017, p. 32, who describes how insurance has evolved from a highly suspect aleatory operation, similar to games and gambling, to a fully regular financial transaction that has become a normal and indeed indispensable ingredient of modern economic and social life.

2 KESSLER, D., DE MONTCHALIN, A. and THIMANN, C., The Macroeconomic Role of Insurance, in HUFELD, F., KOIJEN, R.S.J. and THIMANN, C. (Eds.), *The Economics, Regulation and Systemic Risk of Insurance Markets*, Oxford University Press, New York, 2017, pp. 27–28.

will calculate the insurance liability (technical provision or reserve), which the insurance undertaking has to set up as soon as the contract has been signed. The calculation of the insurance liability takes account of prior experience and reflects the expected risk. When the duration of the contract extends over many years, the calculation of the risk becomes very difficult.

The contractual relationship between a policyholder and an insurance undertaking is the subject of insurance contract law, which is heavily regulated in all Member States of the EEA.[3] As insurance is a service, it is important to protect the rights of policyholders because of the information asymmetry between the insurance undertaking and policyholders. This is particularly true for retail insurance (B-to-C), which is therefore more heavily regulated than commercial insurance (B-to-B) or reinsurance.

Insurance is not popular because people are naturally risk-averse.[4] They are not always conscious of the risks to which they might be exposed and they do not like to be reminded of this. This is the reason why insurance is sold and not bought, i.e. insurance undertakings will have to go to the market to offer their services. It is not common for consumers to contact an insurance undertaking at their own initiative.[5] As insurers must attract their customers, it is important to ensure that potential customers are well informed about the insurance service that is being proposed. This matter has become more important in recent years, particularly after the financial crisis in 2007/2008, when it appeared that many people had bought investment products linked with an insurance contract where it was not always clear which risk they were incurring or which part of the premium was actually invested.

Insurance distribution is being subject to more and more regulation. Insurance can be sold through an intermediary (agent or broker) or directly by the insurance undertaking. Regulation requires transparency from intermediaries about the remuneration (fee, commission or other benefit), which they receive for their services. It also requires intermediaries to act in the best interest of their clients. Similar requirements are also imposed upon insurance undertakings when they sell insurance directly to consumers, often through the internet.[6]

---

3 This book describes the insurance solvency regulation developed by the EU, which comprises 28 Member States. This regulation also applies to three countries (Iceland, Liechtenstein and Norway) which together with the 28 EU Member States form the European Economic Area (EEA).

4 The lack of popularity of insurance is also related to the behaviour of insurance undertakings which are sometimes slow in settling claims. This is particularly true in travel insurance. See, EIOPA, *Seventh Consumer Trends Report*, Luxembourg, Publications Office of the EU, 2018, pp. 29–30.

5 Except for cases of mandatory insurance, such as third-party liability insurance in motor insurance.

6 See Directive (EU) 2016/97 of the EP and of the Council of 20 January 2016 on insurance distribution (recast), *OJ* L 26, 2.2.2016, p. 19 and DE MAESSCHALCK, N., The Insurance Distribution Directive: What Does It Change for Intermediaries and for Others?, in

Technological innovations (for instance, direct sales channels such as the internet or mobile devices) are breaking up the traditional insurance distribution process and re-configuring standard intermediary functions. This is particularly the case in retail insurance.[7]

2. THE INSURANCE BUSINESS MODEL

The insurance business model is rarely understood outside the insurance community.[8] Most people, who are not experts in insurance, do not realise that there is a link between a risk and a premium. The higher the risk, the higher the premium has to be. In order to be profitable, an insurer must collect more in premiums and investment income than is paid out in losses or claims. Insurers make money through underwriting,[9] i.e. the process whereby an insurer selects which risks to insure and decides what premium to charge for the covered risks, and through investing the premiums collected from policyholders.

The profitability of an insurer is often measured by reference to the combined ratio. The combined ratio is usually expressed as an equation: the sum of incurred losses (including changes in loss provisions) and expenses divided by earned premiums. A ratio below 100% indicates that the insurer is making an underwriting profit, while a ratio above 100% means that the insurer is paying out more money in claims than it is receiving from premiums. An insurer can still be profitable with a combined ratio above 100% because of investment income. However, a combined ratio below 100% is usually a sign of good risk management. The success of an insurer starts with good underwriting management.

Insurance risks are spread or shared between a group of people or undertakings (pooling of risks) using the law of large numbers (connecting the misfortunes of the few to the fortunes of the many), which helps insurers to more accurately estimate the value and frequency of future claims paid out to insured parties. The law of large numbers stems from probability theory in statistics: when a sample of observations increases, variation against the mean (average) observation declines. In other words, the average value gains predictive power

MARANO, P. and SIRI, M. (Eds.), *Insurance Regulation in the European Union*, Palgrave Macmillan, Cham, 2017.

7 See, Swiss Re, Digital distribution in insurance: a quiet revolution, *Sigma*, 2014, No 2, 37 p; See also, EIOPA, *Big data analytics in motor and health insurance: a thematic review*, Publications Office of the EU, Luxembourg, 2019, 65 p.

8 See also THIMANN, C., What Is Insurance and How Does It Differ from General Finance?, in HUFELD, F., KOIJEN, R.S.J. and THIMANN, C. (Eds.), *The Economics, Regulation and Systemic Risk of Insurance Markets*, Oxford University Press, New York, 2017, p. 17: "Insurance is seen as notoriously difficult to understand."

9 This includes three sources of profit: the technical profit (on the tariff part of the premium), the loading profit (on the administrative and distribution part of the premium) and a margin on top of these.

and is more likely to represent the expected value. In practical terms, the larger the pool, the more predictable the amount of losses will be in a given period.

The traditional business model of insurance builds on the underwriting of large diversified pools of mostly idiosyncratic[10] and uncorrelated risks.[11] Through diversification, insurers reduce their risk. Risk diversification can be achieved in different ways: pooling policyholders' risks, insuring a wide variety of policyholder pools, underwriting in different geographical areas or diversifying across different risk types, such as underwriting and investment risk. Other techniques to mitigate an insurer's risks are reinsurance, hedging, insurance linked securities and the use of separate accounts for certain life insurance products where the policyholder bears most or all of the investment risk (ring-fenced funds).[12]

Even though insurance may be concluded for a time period not exceeding one year, insurance is usually regarded as long-term business. This is of course particularly true for life insurance, where the term of the contracts may vary from seven to 40 years, or even longer, but is also true for insurance against natural catastrophes or for professional indemnity insurance. Even for short-term insurance business, such as motor insurance or home insurance, which is usually renewable on an annual basis, insurance undertakings will try to prolong the insurance contract.

One characteristic of the insurance business is its inverted production cycle: policyholders pay premiums upfront and claims payments are generally made only if and when an insured event has occurred. This means that insurance undertakings usually have a large amount of cash as a result of the premiums they receive, which they invest in various types of assets (government bonds, corporate bonds, equity, real estate, securitisations, infrastructure, venture capital, wine, etc.). In order to ensure that there is enough liquidity when payments are due, it is important for an insurer to correctly match the term of the investment with the length of the insurance liability. Long-term guarantees must be matched with long-term investments. For non-life insurance, short-term investments may be appropriate, depending on the type of insurance. For instance, for liabilities resulting from home or fire insurance, which is usually renewable every year, premiums may be invested for a short term, whilst for natural catastrophe insurance or professional indemnity insurance, long-term investment of the premiums would be more appropriate.

The inverted production cycle and the contractual premium payments of policyholders allow for a stable cash flow to insurers.[13] This is one of the reasons

---

10 Unsystematic risk, i.e. a risk that is related to a particular person, asset or event.

11 IAIS, *Insurance and Financial Stability*, November 2011, p. 6.

12 BRAUMÜLLER, P. and WARZILEK, A., Insurance and Financial Stability, in LIEDTKE, P.M. and MONKIEWICZ, J. (Eds.), *The Future of Insurance Regulation and Supervision: A Global Perspective*, Palgrave Macmillan, Basingstoke, 2011, p. 126.

13 IAIS, *Insurance and Financial Stability*, November 2011, p. 6.

why it is often argued that traditional insurance does not cause financial stability problems, as opposed to banking, and that insurance is a stabilising factor in the economy:

> "Insurers can be seen as 'future-oriented': they collect the current liquidity of individuals and organizations to fund their future lifestyles and projects. In contrast, banks can be seen as 'present-oriented': through credit, they fund today's projects and lifestyles by prefunding future liquidity."[14]

Particularly after the financial crisis, when new regulation was introduced in the banking sector, especially for systemically important financial institutions, there was a fear that similar rules would also be adopted for (re)insurers. Several publications were issued by (re)insurance undertakings or by associations of (re)insurers in which the particularities of the insurance business model were highlighted. The core activity of (re)insurers is risk pooling and risk transformation, while that of banks is the collection of deposits and maturity transformation. The balance sheet of (re)insurers is economically stable, as fairly long-term policyholder liabilities are matched with assets of corresponding duration. In the case of banks, assets and liabilities are not matched, and the average duration of most bank assets is generally longer than the average duration of their liabilities. Furthermore, the risk profiles of (re)insurers and banks are fundamentally different. (Re)insurance undertakings are mainly exposed to underwriting risk, market risk and the risk of mismatch between assets and liabilities, whereas the most significant risks to which banks are exposed are credit risk, liquidity risk and market risk. The main conclusion was that from a macro-prudential point of view, the core insurance business model, as described above, does not generate systemic risk that is directly transmitted to the financial system.[15]

However, (re)insurers also engage in other non-core business,[16] which is often referred to as NTNI (non-traditional non-insurance), such as variable annuities, certain types of guarantees or speculative derivative transactions. These activities, together with size, were initially seen as the most likely drivers

---

14 KESSLER, D., DE MONTCHALIN, A. and THIMANN, C., The Macroeconomic Role of Insurance, in HUFELD, F., KOIJEN, R.S.J. and THIMANN, C. (Eds.), *The Economics, Regulation and Systemic Risk of Insurance Markets*, Oxford University Press, New York, 2017, p. 39.

15 See CEA, Why insurers differ from banks, October 2014, pp. 6–7. See also THIMANN, C., What Is Insurance and How Does It Differ from General Finance?, in HUFELD, F., KOIJEN, R.S.J. and THIMANN, C. (Eds.), *The Economics, Regulation and Systemic Risk of Insurance Markets*, Oxford University Press, New York, 2017.

16 Some insurers have become pure asset managers. See, for instance, Standard Life in the UK, which sold its insurance business to the Phoenix Group and now calls itself a pension savings company.

for insurers potentially becoming systemically important.[17] However, the inability to agree on an exact definition of what is not the core business of insurance and the realisation that traditional insurance business might also have some systemic implications led the International Association of Insurance Supervisors (IAIS) to change its approach towards systemically important insurers (SIIs), moving away from a so-called entity-based approach, whereby certain undertakings were designated as global systemically important insurers (G-SIIs),[18] towards an activity-based approach, whereby more attention is paid to the business carried out by an insurer and the way it affects the broader economy.[19]

Insurance is changing profoundly because of digitalisation, although it is generally recognised that digitalisation is moving more slowly in insurance than in banking.[20] This may have to do with the fact that insurance is more than just a product. It is a service and policyholders may still prefer personal contact over dealing with their problems through bots. The complexity of insurance may be another reason. On the other hand, recent studies indicate that the greatest source of value creation through the digitalisation of insurance lies in the ability to develop new and more customer-centric products and solutions. By lowering the cost of information gathering and processing (data analytics), digital technology and automation will enable insurers to increase the efficiency of administering, underwriting and pricing risk, and settling claims. This should lead to lower premiums, boosting affordability and coverage.[21] Digitalisation might also help the insurance industry to move away from compensation to prevention and protection, thereby increasing its importance as a service industry.

---

17 See ESRB, *Report on systemic risks in the EU insurance sector*, November 2015, p. 14. See also the Geneva Association, *Systemic Risk in Insurance*, March 2010, 118 p. and *Insurance and Resolution in Light of the Systemic Risk Debate*, February 2012, 62 p.

18 See the annual designation by the FSB of certain insurers as G-SIIs. The FSB decided not to continue this approach, awaiting further research and input by the IAIS on its activity-based approach. The last designation of insurers as G-SIIs occurred in 2016. See the announcement by the FSB on 21 November 2017. The policy measures applicable to G-SIIs continue to apply to the nine insurers that were designated as G-SIIs in 2016.

19 See IAIS, *Systemic Risk from Insurance Product Features (previously referred to as Non-Traditional Non-Insurance activities and products)*, 16 June 2016, 28 p. See also HUFELD, F., A Regulatory Framework for Systemic Risk in the Insurance Industry, in HUFELD, F., KOIJEN, R.S.J. and THIMANN, C. (Eds.), *The Economics, Regulation and Systemic Risk of Insurance Markets*, Oxford University Press, New York, 2017, pp. 194–207. This is also the approach in the USA, where the Financial Stability Oversight Council (FSOC) has proposed on 6 March 2019 to introduce a new activities-based approach to monitor the systemic risk that insurers pose to the US economy (https://home.treasury.gov/system/files/261/Notice-of-Proposed-Interpretive-Guidance.pdf).

20 Digital technologies in insurance continue to grow, particularly in motor insurance. See EIOPA, *Seventh Consumer Trends Report*, Publications Office of the EU, Luxembourg, 2018, 68 p.

21 The Geneva Association, *Insurance in the Digital Age: a view of key implications for the economy and society*, September 2018, 20 p. The report also indicates that digital technology can give rise to issues of fairness as individual risk-based insurance will be possible and might mean that some high-risk individuals might be denied cover or would face prohibitively high insurance costs.

3. WHY DO INSURERS NEED TO BE REGULATED?

3.1. OBJECTIVES OF INSURANCE REGULATION AND SUPERVISION

As insurers work with other people's money, it is important that they are authorised before they can start their business and that they are subject to supervision.

Because of the inverted production cycle, policyholders pay their premium upfront before they receive any service. It is therefore important to make sure that the insurance promise is kept. Technically, this is achieved by requiring insurers to set up a technical provision for the expected risk (potential liability) arising from the insurance contract and to create a capital buffer (own funds) over and above the technical provisions to ensure the delivery of the insurance promise in situations of stress. Stress might result from unexpected risks, such as an increase or a decrease of interest rates.

In economic theory, regulation of insurance is justified in order to resolve market imperfections: insurers can change their risk profile after the contract has been signed, customers are unable to analyse an insurer's financial soundness, and in the case of mandatory insurance, insurers may be incentivised to price their products too low. With market imperfection being the rationale for insurance regulation, the objective of insurance regulation should be to mimic perfect market conditions as closely as possible.[22]

In all EEA Member States, insurance has been the subject of regulation for a long time. This should not come as a surprise because of the important socio-economic role of insurance. Insurance contributes to the economic security and protection of households, undertakings and communities. Some types of insurance, such as health insurance, life insurance and pensions, are closely linked to social security. Insurance also allows individuals and undertakings to develop their talents and business despite the presence of risk, which is an essential condition for economic development and growth.[23] From a business perspective, insurance was also regulated because Member States favoured the creation of national champions in order to protect their domestic market against competition from foreign (re)insurers.

Other considerations also played a role. From a macro-economic perspective, the insurance industry has traditionally been regarded as an important institutional investor. A large part of the national public debt was (and still is) held by

22 DOFF, R., The final Solvency II framework, *The Geneva Papers on Risk and Insurance – Issues and Practice*, Vol 41, No 4, October 2016, p. 589.

23 THIMANN, C., What is insurance and how does it differ from general finance?, in HUFELD, F., KOIJEN, R.S.J. and THMANN, C. (Eds.), *The Economics, Regulation and Systemic Risk of Insurance Markets*, Oxford University Press, New York, 2017, p. 11.

insurance undertakings. Much of the insurance regulation in the past therefore dealt with investment policy, prescribing in which assets insurers could invest. Investment in sovereign bonds was particularly stimulated and still is under the new solvency regime, whereby an investment in sovereign bonds is considered risk-free and therefore carries no capital charge.[24] The role of insurers as institutional investors has received more attention recently and has resulted in amendments to the regulatory regime, favouring investment in infrastructure projects or in securitised loans to small and medium-sized enterprises (SMEs).[25]

The main objective of insurance regulation and supervision was and is the protection of policyholders and beneficiaries.[26] This was already stated in earlier EU legislation and has been repeated after the recasting of that legislation in Art. 27 Solvency II Framework Directive (FD).[27] The reference to "beneficiaries" covers situations in which, for instance, a life insurance contract is concluded in the interest of another party. As stated in recital 16 FD: "the term beneficiary is intended to cover any natural or legal person who is entitled to a right under an insurance contract".

As views about the role of insurance are evolving, the protection of policyholders should not be looked at too narrowly. Supervisory authorities must also pay attention to the long-term interests of policyholders. To the extent that an insurance undertaking is not delivering a service that is of benefit to existing and potential policyholders in the long term, i.e. is not carrying out an activity that is sustainable in the long term, it may not be acting in the interest of policyholders. Supervisory authorities should be mindful of this: the discussions about sustainable finance[28] and macro-prudential supervision[29] are likely to

---

24 See further, Chapter 6, section 4.2.2.2.4.

25 KESSLER, D., DE MONTCHALIN, A. and THIMANN, C., The Macroeconomic Role of Insurance, in HUFELD, F., KOIJEN, R.S.J. and THIMANN, C. (Eds.), *The Economics, Regulation and Systemic Risk of Insurance Markets*, Oxford University Press, New York, 2017, p. 22.

26 Information asymmetry and market imperfection are some of the economic reasons advanced for justifying insurance regulation. See, KWON, W.J., The Economic Rationale for Insurance Regulation, in LIEDTKE, P.M. and MONKIEWICZ, J. (Eds.), *The Future of Insurance Regulation and Supervision: A Global Perspective*, Palgrave Macmillan, Basingstoke, 2011, pp. 23–40.

27 Directive 2009/138/EC of the EP and of the Council of 25 November 2009 on the taking-up and pursuit of the business of insurance and reinsurance (Solvency II) (recast), *OJ* L 335, 17.12.2009, p. 1.

28 EC, *Financing a sustainable European economy: Final Report by the High-Level Expert Group on Sustainable Finance*, January 2018, pp. 70–72 and EC, Communication to the EP, the European Council, the ECB, the EESC and the CoR – Action Plan: Financing Sustainable Growth, COM (2018) 97 final, 8 March 2018, 20 p.

29 See EIOPA, *Systemic risk and macro-prudential policy in insurance*, Publications Office of the EU, Luxembourg, 2017, 77 p.; *Solvency II tools with macro-prudential impact*, Publications Office of the EU, Luxembourg, 2018, 62 p.; *Other potential macro-prudential tools and measures to enhance the current framework*, Publications Office of the EU, Luxembourg, 2018, 72 p. See also ESRB, *Report on systemic risks in the EU insurance sector*, November 2015, 39 p. with annexes.

have a growing impact on how insurance supervision will take place in the years to come.

Another objective of insurance regulation that is particularly stressed in some Member States, such as the UK, but also in the IAIS's Insurance Core Principle (ICP) 1, is ensuring fair and stable markets for insurance products.[30]

Financial stability has been added recently as an important second objective of insurance regulation and supervision, after the financial crisis in 2007/2008. In accordance with Art. 28 FD, Member States must ensure that, in the exercise of their general duties, supervisory authorities duly consider the potential impact of their decisions on the stability of the financial systems concerned in the EU, in particular in emergency situations, taking into account the information available at the relevant time. In times of exceptional movements in the financial markets, supervisory authorities must take into account the potential pro-cyclical effects of their actions.

Although financial stability is another objective of insurance regulation and supervision, this should not undermine the main objective, which remains policyholder protection (recital 16 FD). Sometimes the objectives of policyholder protection and financial stability might come into conflict with one another. Supervisors may want to give priority to financial stability when dealing with systemic problems in the insurance sector. This has been the case in the life insurance sector, where, as a result of the low interest rate environment, insurers were "asked" by supervisors to set aside part of their profits rather than to make all profits directly available to policyholders and shareholders.[31] The stability of the sector in the long term was thereby regarded as more important than safeguarding the short-term interest of policyholders and shareholders.

It is interesting to observe that insurance regulation and supervision developed more slowly than banking regulation and supervision. An important reason for this might be the general lack of interest from policymakers. As stated before, the insurance business model is not well known outside the insurance sector. Insurance is considered to be complex and regulating the insurance sector is rarely considered an attractive proposition or an easy win in political terms. This was further aggravated by the fact that the insurance industry preferred to be scoped out from new regulation (for instance in accounting) because of its special nature, which required derogation from the general rules.

The absence of a lender of last resort in the insurance sector also played a role. Central banks have a natural interest in proper regulation and supervision of the banking sector. Because of the nature of the banking activity (maturity transformation), banks are more vulnerable to shocks in the financial system.

---

30 IAIS, ICP 1 – Objectives, Powers and Responsibilities of the Supervisor, para. 1.3. See also the reference in recital 16 FD to fair and stable markets as another objective of insurance regulation and supervision.

31 This has, for instance, been the case in Belgium and in Germany.

The successive financial crises have produced tougher banking regulation and supervision. In order to establish a level playing field, pressure increased to also introduce a more developed regulatory regime for insurance.[32]

3.2. INSURANCE REGULATION IN THE EU

A detailed description of EU insurance regulation[33] would go beyond the scope of this book, which concentrates on the new risk-based solvency regime. A quick recapitulation of important parts of EU insurance regulation is however necessary to facilitate a good understanding of the new regime, which was built on top of the legal framework that existed before Solvency II. Although that legal framework was incorporated in the European Commission's (EC) proposed Solvency II FD, an interinstitutional agreement was concluded in 2007 between the EC, the European Parliament (EP) and the Council not to amend any other part of EU insurance regulation than that which specifically related to the solvency regime, with the exception of consequential changes that followed from the introduction of the new solvency regime. Any other decision would have created the risk of a re-negotiation of other parts of EU insurance regulation, which had nothing to do with the new solvency regime.

3.2.1. Principle of Authorisation

All (re)insurance undertakings in the EU must be authorised before they can take up the business of direct insurance or reinsurance (Art. 14 (1) FD).[34] Authorisation is also required if an insurance undertaking that has already been authorised wishes to extend its business to an entire insurance class or to insurance classes other than those already authorised (Arts. 14 (2) and 18 (2) and (3) FD). The classes of non-life insurance and of life insurance are listed in Annexes I and II FD respectively.

---

32 EC, Communication on Implementing the framework for financial markets: action plan, COM (1999) 232 final, 11 May 1999. Initially, the idea was to copy and paste Basel II and the CRD and to introduce this as the solvency regime for (re)insurance undertakings. It quickly became clear, however, that the business models of insurance and banking were very different. In many Member States, (re)insurers are now supervised by central banks.

33 All insurance supervisory authorities in the EU are members of the IAIS and have committed themselves to applying the Insurance Core Principles (ICPs) of the IAIS, which were last coordinated in November 2018. The ICPs are not systematically repeated in EU legislation, which is in many areas (such as solvency) more detailed and aims at facilitating cross-border operations by (re)insurance undertakings in the EU. For matters not specifically dealt with in EU legislation, it is important to keep in mind that there are other regulatory measures that can be found in the ICPs and in provisions of national law that go beyond EU legislation, in those areas were a uniform treatment has not been prescribed by EU law.

34 See also IAIS, ICP 4 – Licensing.

Authorisation is given by the supervisory authority of the home MS, which must require the following for every undertaking for which authorisation is sought (Art. 18 (1) FD):

- for insurance undertakings, limitation of their activity to the business of insurance and operations arising directly therefrom, to the exclusion of all other commercial business;
- for reinsurance undertakings, limitation of their activity to the business of reinsurance and related operations, which might include a holding company function and financial sector activities within the meaning of Art. 2 (8) Financial Conglomerates Directive (FICOD);
- submission of a scheme of operations, which must include the details referred to in Art. 23 FD;
- holding of eligible basic own funds to cover the absolute floor of the MCR[35] (Art. 129 (1) (d) FD);
- provision of evidence that the undertaking will be in a position to hold eligible own funds to cover the solvency capital requirement (SCR)[36] going forward (Art. 100 FD);
- provision of evidence that the undertaking will be in a position to hold eligible basic own funds to cover the minimum capital requirement (MCR)[37] going forward (Art. 128 FD);
- provision of evidence that the undertaking will be in a position to comply with the governance requirements in Chapter IV, section 2 FD;
- if the undertaking intends to pursue motor vehicle insurance, communication of the name and address of all claims representatives in each MS other than the MS in which the authorisation is sought.

The head office of the (re)insurance undertaking must be situated in the same MS as its registered office (Art. 20 FD).

Where close links exist with other natural or legal persons, authorisation can only be granted if those links do not prevent effective supervision (Art. 19 FD). Member States may not require prior approval of general and special policy conditions and premiums (Art. 21 FD) nor link the authorisation with economic requirements of the market (Art. 22 FD). The supervisory authorities must be informed about the identities of the shareholders or members with qualifying holdings and must be satisfied with the qualifications of these shareholders or members (Art. 24 FD).

35 See further, Chapter 6, section 4.3.
36 See further, Chapter 6, section 4.2.
37 See further, Chapter 6, section 4.3.

Every authorisation or withdrawal of authorisation must be notified to the European Insurance and Occupational Pensions Authority (EIOPA), which publishes the names of each (re)insurance undertaking to which authorisation has been granted on a list that is kept up to date on its website (Art. 25a FD).

The supervisory authority must, before granting authorisation to a (re)insurance undertaking, consult the supervisory authority of another MS where the (re)insurance undertaking is (Art. 26 (1) FD):[38]

- a subsidiary of a (re)insurance undertaking authorised in that other MS;
- a subsidiary of the parent undertaking of a (re)insurance undertaking authorised in that other MS;
- controlled by the same natural or legal person who controls a (re)insurance undertaking authorised in that other MS.

The supervisory authority must, before granting authorisation to a (re)insurance undertaking, consult the supervisory authority that is responsible for the supervision of credit institutions or investment firms in the MS concerned, where the (re)insurance undertaking is (Art. 26 (2) FD):

- a subsidiary of a credit institution or investment firm authorised in the EU;
- a subsidiary of the parent undertaking of a credit institution or investment firm, authorised in the EU;
- controlled by the same natural or legal person who controls a credit institution or investment firm authorised in the EU.[39]

The consultation covers, in particular, the assessment of the suitability of the shareholders and the fit and proper requirements of all persons who effectively run the undertaking or have other key functions and who are involved in the management of another entity of the same group. The authorities concerned must inform each other of any information regarding the suitability of shareholders and the fit and proper requirements of all persons who effectively run the undertaking or have other key functions that are of relevance to the other supervisory authority concerned for the granting of an authorisation or for the ongoing assessment of compliance with operating conditions (Art. 26 (3) FD).

Prior authorisation is also required for any insurance undertaking with a head office outside the EU (third-country insurer), that wants to carry out *insurance*

---

[38] For the exchange of information with other financial supervisory authorities, see also EIOPA, Decision on the collaboration of the insurance supervisory authorities, EIOPA-BoS-17/014, 30 January 2017, pp. 7–12.

[39] A similar provision is included in Art. 16 (2) CRD.

business in a MS. Member States may only grant an authorisation where the undertaking fulfils at least the following conditions (Art. 162 FD):

- it is entitled to pursue insurance business under its national law;
- it establishes a branch (a permanent presence) in the territory of the MS in which authorisation is sought;
- it undertakes to set up at the place of management of the branch accounts specific to the business which it pursues there, and to keep there all the records relating to the business transacted;
- it designates a general representative, to be approved by the supervisory authority;
- it possesses in the MS in which authorisation is sought assets of an amount equal to a least one half of the absolute floor of the MCR (Art. 129 (1) (d) FD) and deposits one quarter of that absolute floor as security;[40]
- it undertakes to cover the SCR and the MCR;[41]
- it communicates the name and address of the claims representative appointed in each MS other than the MS in which authorisation is sought when it pursues motor vehicle insurance;
- it submits a scheme of operations in accordance with Art. 163 FD;
- it fulfils the governance requirements laid down in Chapter IV, section 2 FD.

Authorisation of a branch does not grant the right to conduct business across the EEA, but only in the MS that has granted the authorisation.

If a third-country insurer has requested or obtained authorisation from more than one MS, it can benefit from certain advantages. For instance, the SCR may be calculated in relation to the entire business which it pursues within the EU (which allows for diversification benefits to be taken into account) (Art. 167 FD).

The FD treats third-country branches almost as subsidiary undertakings that must fully comply with the Solvency II requirements. This is further clarified in the EIOPA Guidelines on the supervision of branches of third-country insurance undertakings.[42] For instance, in terms of the capital requirements, Guideline 22 states that the host supervisory authority must ensure that the branch SCR and the branch MCR are calculated based on the branch balance sheet as if the branch operations constituted a separate insurance undertaking.

---

40 Art. 166 FD sets further requirements to ensure that the MCR is composed of strong capital and that the assets representing the SCR are kept within the EU (up to the amount of the MCR within the MS where the activities are pursued).

41 See further, Chapter 6, sections 4.2 and 4.3.

42 EIOPA, Guidelines on the supervision of branches of third-country insurance undertakings, EIOPA-BoS-15/110, 36 p.

The third-country insurance undertaking must ensure that the branch complies with the governance requirements, including the key functions, the fit and proper requirement and the own risk and solvency assessment (ORSA) requirement. The branch does not have to publish a solvency and financial condition report (SFCR) unless the third-country prescribes such disclosure. The third-country insurance undertaking must submit extensive information on the activities of the branch for supervisory purposes and must apply for that purpose the templates included in the EIOPA Guidelines.[43]

The EIOPA Guidelines cover branches of insurance undertakings from third countries, regardless of whether the solvency regime of the third country has been considered equivalent with Solvency II (see further, Chapter 10). However, supervisory authorities may want to take account of equivalence decisions taken by the EC, which are relevant to assessing the solvency of the whole third-country insurance undertaking, including its branch. Although no specific examples are given in the Guidelines, one would assume that, for instance, the requirement in Guideline 2 to include in the scheme of operations of the branch an analysis of the differences between the home-country solvency rules and the rules of Solvency II can be waived if the solvency regime of the third country has been considered equivalent with Solvency II.

For third-country (re)insurance undertakings that want to conduct *reinsurance business* in the EU, the FD does not provide specific authorisation requirements. That means, for instance, that there is no EU requirement for third-country reinsurance undertakings to set up a branch in the EU for conducting reinsurance business in the EU.[44] This is a matter dealt with under national law. However, the FD includes a special regime for equivalence in relation to reinsurance undertakings (Art. 172 FD). If the supervisory regime of a third country applying to reinsurance activities of undertakings with their head office in that third country has been considered equivalent with the supervisory regime in the EU, reinsurance contracts concluded by that undertaking with (re)insurance undertakings in the EU will receive a similar treatment as reinsurance contracts concluded with EU reinsurance undertakings (see further Chapter 10, section 4).

Art. 175 FD provides for the possibility for the EU to conclude an agreement with third countries regarding reinsurance. Only one such agreement has been

---

43 EIOPA, Guidelines on the supervision of branches of third-country insurance undertakings, EIOPA-BoS-15/110, Guidelines 44, 45 and 47.

44 Austria, Germany and Poland provide that reinsurers headquartered in a third country deemed equivalent (see Chapter 10, section 4) may pursue reinsurance business on the local market through direct provision of cross-border services. Reinsurers established in non-equivalent third countries are, however, treated similarly to third-country insurers and may only conduct reinsurance business through a local branch and subject to an authorisation from the NSA. See US Reinsurers face unexpected EU market access restrictions, *Insurance Day*, 26 October 2016, https://www.insuranceday.com/news_analysis/legal_focus/us-reinsurers-face-unexpected-EU-market-access-restrictions.

concluded so far, i.e. the bilateral agreement between the EU and the USA on prudential measures regarding insurance and reinsurance, which was signed on 22 September 2017[45] (see further Chapter 10, section 4).

Any decision to refuse an authorisation must be notified to the undertaking concerned and duly justified. It must be subject to a right of appeal or to a right of recourse with a court in the case where the supervisory authority has not acted on the application for authorisation within six months of the date of its receipt (Art. 25 FD).

3.2.2. *Supervisory Authority*

The supervisory authority[46] is defined in Art. 13 (10) FD as the national authority or the national authorities empowered by law or regulation to supervise (re)insurance undertakings. In practice, there may be multiple authorities responsible for different aspects of supervision, for example separate authorities for prudential and market conduct supervision (so-called "twin peaks" model), for macro- and micro-prudential supervision, for authorisation and ongoing supervision or for supervision and resolution. Where there are multiple authorities, national law must clearly set the responsibilities of the respective authorities and must ensure coordination between them (Article 247 (8) FD).[47] In order to ensure that all requirements of the FD are met, the FD consistently uses the plural word "supervisory authorities", even if there is only one single supervisory authority in the MS.[48]

ICP 2[49] requires the supervisory authority to be operationally independent, accountable and transparent. It must protect confidential information, have appropriate legal protection, have adequate resources and must meet high professional standards.

45 Bilateral agreement between the EU and the USA on prudential measures regarding insurance and reinsurance, *OJ* L 258, 6.10.2017, p. 4. A similar agreement was concluded between the USA and the UK, as a result of Brexit, on 11 December 2018.

46 Throughout the book, the term "supervisory authority" is used, even though there might be more than one supervisory authority in a particular MS. The EIOPA Regulation uses the term "competent authority", as this is the term that is used in the Insurance Mediation Directive (IMD)/Insurance Distribution Directive (IDD) and in IORP I and IORP II.

47 The website of EIOPA includes a list of its members. That list does not however include all supervisory authorities responsible for insurance supervision. For instance, it does not include all supervisory authorities that are responsible for market conduct supervision.

48 The economic rationale for organising the supervisory setting is not always evident. Politics often matter as well. This was clearly visible after the global financial crisis (2007–2008). See MASCIANDARO, D. and QUINTYN, M., The Architecture of Insurance Supervision Before and After the Financial Crisis, in LIEDTKE, P.M. and MONKIEWICZ, J. (Eds.), *The Future of Insurance Regulation and Supervision: A Global Perspective*, Palgrave Macmillan, Basingstoke, 2011, p. 126.

49 IAIS, ICP 2 – Supervisor.

Most of these requirements are also included in the FD:
- transparency and accountability (Art. 31 FD);
- adequate resources (Art. 27 FD);
- high professional standards (Art. 27 FD);
- confidentiality (Art. 64 FD).[50]

There is no specific provision in the FD which requires supervisory authorities to be independent.[51] ICP 2 states in this regard that the supervisory authority and its staff must be free from undue political, governmental and industry interference in the performance of supervisory responsibilities.[52] The financing must be such that it does not undermine the independence of the supervisory authority. The supervisory authority must also have the discretion to allocate its resources in accordance with its mandate and objectives and the risks it perceives.

Decisions taken by the supervisory authority in respect of (re)insurance undertakings are subject to a right of appeal to the courts (Art. 297 FD). This is in line with ICP 2, which requires that there be processes to appeal against supervisory decisions, including using judicial review.[53] These processes must be specific and balanced to preserve supervisory independence and effectiveness. They may not however unduly impede the ability of the supervisory authority to make timely interventions in order to protect the interests of policyholders.

3.2.3. Freedom of Establishment and Freedom to Provide Services

An important objective of the EU is the creation of an internal market (single market) between the 28 Member States[54] based upon four freedoms: free movement of people, capital, goods and services. As operators within the internal market, (re)insurers benefit from freedom to provide (cross-border) services (FoS) and from freedom of (cross-border) establishment (FoE).

FoS allows (re)insurance undertakings that have received prior authorisation in one MS to provide (re)insurance services in another MS directly, without

---

50 See also IAIS, ICP 3 – Information Exchange and Confidentiality Requirements.

51 This may also be the case in national law, although the independence requirement can be stated indirectly. For example, section 2 of the Act of 22 April 2002 establishing the Federal Financial Supervisory Authority (Bafin) in Germany states: "The Supervisory Authority is subject to legal and technical supervision by the Federal Ministry of Finance": Federal Law Gazette I, p. 1310. This suggests that there is no political interference. Independence will normally be guaranteed if the supervision is carried out by the central bank, as is the case in many Member States.

52 IAIS, ICP 2 – Supervisor, para. 4.

53 IAIS, ICP 2 – Supervisor, para. 8.

54 As indicated before, the three EEA countries – Iceland, Norway and Liechtenstein – are also part of the internal market even though they are not Member States of the EU. Together with the 28 EU Member States, they make up the 31 EEA Member States.

opening a branch, a representative office or a similar establishment. FoE allows (re)insurance undertakings that have received prior authorisation in their home MS to create a subsidiary or to open a branch in another MS and to provide (re)insurance services in that MS through that subsidiary or branch.

When a (re)insurance undertaking operates in another MS than that in which it has its head office, through the provision of cross-border services (FoS) or through the establishment of a branch, it automatically enters into the legal space of that other MS. FoE and FoS cannot work without close cooperation between the supervisory authorities of home and host Member States. The principles of this cooperation are included in the FD. They are further refined in a Decision adopted by EIOPA in 2017 that takes stock of the experience gathered in practice.[55] If there are difficulties in the cooperation between supervisory authorities in cross-border situations, one of the authorities concerned can call upon EIOPA for mediation. Such mediation is foreseen in a number of specific cases,[56] but can also be extended to other situations (Art. 19 EIOPA Regulation).[57]

Mutual recognition plays an important role in allowing undertakings to operate cross-border under a single regulatory regime, that of the home jurisdiction.[58]

In order to define the respective powers and responsibilities of the Member States and their supervisory authorities concerned, EU law uses the concepts of "home Member State" and "host Member State", which are defined in Art. 13 FD. The definitions are somewhat complex because they cover various situations.

"Home Member State" is defined in Art. 13 (8) FD as:

- the MS in which the head office of the insurance undertaking covering the risk is situated (in the case of non-life insurance);

---

55 See, EIOPA, Decision on the collaboration of the insurance supervisory authorities, EIOPA-BoS-17/014, 30 January 2017, 59 p.

56 For instance, on-site inspections by the supervisory authority of the home MS in the host MS in the context of the supervision of a branch (Art. 33 FD).

57 The system does not always work well because of a lack of communication between home and host supervisory authorities. See European Court of Auditors, *Special Report: EIOPA made an important contribution to supervision and stability in the insurance sector, but significant challenges remain*, Publications Office of the EU, Luxembourg, 2018, pp. 23–36.

58 See WYMEERSCH, E., How to make Europe's financial regulatory and supervisory system more efficient?, *Revue trimestrielle de droit financier*, 2016, No 2, pp. 18–30. The author believes that there should be a single supervisor in insurance, as is already the case in banking, where the ECB carries out direct supervision over the largest EU banking groups. EIOPA is struggling with cross-border supervision, as can be seen from its latest report on group supervision, in which it pleads in favour of more powers to carry out effective supervision in cross-border situations. See EIOPA, Report to the EC on group supervision and capital management with a group of insurance or reinsurance undertakings, and FoS and FoE under Solvency II, EIOPA BOS-18-485, 14 December 2018, pp. 17–18.

- the MS in which the head office of the insurance undertaking covering the commitment is situated (in the case of life insurance);
- the MS in which the head office of the reinsurance undertaking is situated (in the case of reinsurance).

"Host Member State" is defined in Art. 13 (9) FD as the MS, other than the home MS, in which a (re)insurance undertaking has a branch or provides services. For life and non-life insurance, the MS of the provision of services means, respectively, the MS of the commitment or the MS in which the risk is situated, where that commitment or risk is covered by an insurance undertaking or a branch situated in another MS.

"Member State in which the risk is situated" is defined in Art. 13 (13) FD as:
- the MS in which the property is situated, where the insurance relates either to buildings or to buildings and their contents, in so far as the contents are covered by the same insurance policy;
- the MS of registration, in the case of motor vehicle insurance;
- the MS where the policyholder took out the policy in the case of policies of a duration of four months or less covering travel or holiday risks, whatever the class of insurance concerned;
- in all cases not explicitly covered above, the MS in which the habitual residence of the policyholder or – in the case of a legal person – the policyholder's establishment to which the contract relates is situated.

"Member State of the commitment" is defined in Art. 13 (14) FD as the habitual residence of the policyholder or, if the policyholder is a legal person, that policyholder's establishment to which the contract relates.

If an insurance undertaking intends to pursue business for the first time in one or more Member States under the freedom to provide services, it must first notify the supervisory authority of its home MS, indicating the nature of the risks or commitments it proposes to cover (Art. 147 FD).

Within one month of the notification, the supervisory authority of the home MS communicates to the supervisory authorities of the MS in which the insurance undertaking intends to pursue business (host MS) under FoS (Art. 148 FD):

- a certificate attesting that the undertaking covers the SCR and the MCR;[59]
- the classes of insurance which the undertaking has been authorised to offer;
- the nature of the risks or commitments which the undertaking proposes to cover in the host MS.

---

59 See further, Chapter 6, sections 4.2 and 4.3. For an example of such a certificate, see EIOPA, Decision on the collaboration of the insurance supervisory authorities, EIOPA-BoS-17/014, 30 January 2017, Annex I, pp. 58–59.

At the same time, the supervisory authority of the home MS informs the insurance undertaking of that communication. The undertaking may start business as from the date on which it is informed of that communication.[60]

In cases where an insurance undertaking applying for authorisation has clearly indicated, for instance in the scheme of operations, that it intends to operate exclusively or almost exclusively in one or more other Member States on an FoS basis, EIOPA requires the authority of the home MS to ask the undertaking for the reasons supporting that strategy and to engage as soon as possible with the supervisory authority of the host MS in order to avoid any misunderstanding.[61]

If an insurance undertaking[62] proposes to establish a branch[63] within the territory of another MS, it must first notify the supervisory authority of its home MS (Art. 145 (1) FD). The notification must include the following information:[64]

- the host MS within the territory of which it proposes to establish a branch;
- a scheme of operations setting out, at least, the types of business envisaged and the structural organisation of the branch;
- the name of the authorised agent, i.e. a person who possesses sufficient powers to bind, in relation to third parties, the insurance undertaking and to represent it in relation with the authorities and courts of the host MS;
- the address in the host MS from which documents may be obtained and to which they may be delivered, including all communications to the authorised agent.

Unless the supervisory authority of the home MS has reason to doubt the adequacy of the system of governance or the financial situation of the insurance undertaking or the fit and proper requirements of the authorised agent, taking

60 See also EIOPA, Decision on the collaboration of the insurance supervisory authorities, EIOPA-BoS-17/014, 30 January 2017, pp. 26–31.

61 EIOPA, Decision on the collaboration of the insurance supervisory authorities, EIOPA-BoS-17/014, 30 January 2017, p. 13.

62 The FD does not deal specifically with the establishment of a branch by reinsurance undertakings. It can however be presumed that this omission is not intentional and that the same conditions apply in the case of reinsurance. See also EIOPA, Decision on the collaboration of the insurance supervisory authorities, EIOPA-BoS-17/014, 30 January 2017, pp. 24–25. The fact that reinsurance undertakings can set up a branch in another MS is explicitly recognised in Art. 158 (1) FD. Reinsurance undertakings may however prefer to offer their services directly cross-border without setting up a branch.

63 A branch is defined in Art. 13 (11) FD as an agency or a branch of a (re)insurance undertaking which is located in the territory of a MS other than the home MS. See also IAIS, *Issues Paper on supervision of cross-border operations through branches*, October 2013, 28 p. which includes an annex describing the system of FoE and FoS in the EU.

64 See also EIOPA, Decision on the collaboration of the insurance supervisory authorities, EIOPA-BoS-17/014, 30 January 2017, pp. 18–19.

into account the business planned, it must, within three months of receiving the information, communicate that information to the supervisory authority of the host MS and at the same time inform the insurance undertaking thereof (Art. 146 (1) FD).

Before the branch can start business, the supervisory authority of the host MS must, where applicable, within two months of receiving the information, inform the supervisory authority of the home MS of the conditions under which, in the interest of the general good, that business must be pursued in the host MS.[65] The supervisory authority of the home MS must communicate this information to the insurance undertaking concerned, which can then establish the branch and start business (Art. 146 (3) FD).[66]

3.2.4. European Passport

(Re)insurance undertakings authorised in one MS enjoy a European passport (Art. 15 (1) FD). Once they have been authorised, they can sell their products in another MS without prior approval of those products by that MS. They are subject to home country control; in other words, the financial supervision (solvency) of (re)insurance undertakings, including that of the business they pursue either through branches or under FoS, is the sole responsibility of the home MS that has authorised them (Art. 30 FD). The host MS is responsible for market conduct supervision (Arts. 154 and 155 FD) and might prohibit a product that it considers contrary to its "general good" (Art. 180 FD).[67]

Home MS supervisory authorities who are responsible for prudential supervision may not always have the same deep knowledge of the host market or products. There may also be a language issue. This might make it more difficult for them to understand the risks borne by the insurance undertaking in the host MS. This challenge becomes even more relevant when the amount of business written in the host MS is significant relative to that written in the home market and/or when the insurance undertaking, through writing cross-border business, grows to a size much larger than the typical-sized domestic undertaking supervised by the home supervisory authority. The home supervisory authority of such cross-border undertakings needs to be able to adequately resource the supervision of such undertakings and have access to knowledge of the relevant host market. This does not always work well in practice. Home Member States might not pay as much attention to business operations concluded by their

---

65 See also EIOPA, Decision on the collaboration of the insurance supervisory authorities, EIOPA-BoS-17/014, 30 January 2017, pp. 21–22.

66 See also EIOPA, Decision on the collaboration of the insurance supervisory authorities, EIOPA-BoS-17/014, 30 January 2017, pp. 22–23.

67 See EC, Interpretative Communication on Freedom to provide services and the general good in the insurance sector, *OJ* C 43, 16.2.2000, p. 5.

(re)insurance undertakings in host Member States as they do to business operations concluded by these undertakings on the domestic market. This has led to difficulties.[68] EIOPA has therefore asked in the context of the reform of the ESFS to obtain the power to arbitrate between the NSAs of home and host countries in cases where the co-operation between NSAs in cross-border business does not function well (see further Chapter 11, section 2.2.3).

One of the unresolved difficulties with cross-border business is the lack of consistency in the scope of national compensation schemes in the event of an insurance undertaking being wound up. In the EU, there are different sources of resolution funding available for failing insurance undertakings. The landscape of insurance guarantee schemes is also significantly fragmented, with the existing schemes differing quite substantially in terms of financing, functions, mandate and coverage. A policyholder living in a host country might or might not be covered by any scheme in that country.

In July 2018, EIOPA published a discussion paper on resolution funding and national insurance guarantee schemes[69] as a follow-up to its 2017 opinion on this issue.[70] The discussion paper proposes a minimum degree of harmonisation in the EU that would benefit policyholders, the insurance market and more broadly financial stability in the EU. Feedback was sought from stakeholders by October 2018 regarding their assessment and the potential design features of insurance guarantee schemes such as their scope, funding and coverage. A well-functioning internal market for insurance products requires a level playing field for consumers too. Consumers should not be trapped as a result of the non-existence of an insurance guarantee scheme in the country in which they buy their insurance. On the other hand, Member States should not be required to set up an insurance guarantee scheme that would be too onerous. The cost of such a scheme will in the end be borne by policyholders (see further Chapter 12).

3.2.5. Brexit

One of the best examples for understanding how the internal market with its freedom of establishment, freedom to provide cross-border services and the European passport operates in practice is Brexit.[71]

---

68 See, EIOPA, Decision on the collaboration of the insurance supervisory authorities, EIOPA-BoS-17/014, 30 January 2017, pp. 35–40 and EIOPA, Report to the EC on Group Supervision and Capital Management with a Group of Insurance or Reinsurance Undertakings, and FoS and FoE under Solvency II, EIOPA BOS-18-485, 14 December 2018, pp. 108–119.

69 EIOPA, Discussion paper on resolution funding and national insurance guarantee schemes, EIOPA-BoS-18-003, 30 July 2018, 61 p.

70 EIOPA, Opinion to the institutions of the EU on the harmonisation of recovery and resolution funds for (re)insurers across the MS, EIOPA-BoS/17-148, 5 July 2017, 88 p.

71 See also EC, Communication to the EP, the European Council, the Council, the ECB, the EESC, the COR and the EIB on Preparing for the withdrawal of the UK from the EU on 30 March 2019: a Contingency Action Plan, COM (2018) 880 final, 13 November 2018, with annexes.

On 29 March 2017, the UK submitted the notification of its intention to withdraw from the EU pursuant to Art. 50 TEU. This means that, unless a ratified withdrawal agreement establishes another date, all EU primary and secondary law will cease to apply to the UK from 30 March 2019.[72] After the withdrawal date, the UK will become a third country. From the EU side, both the EC and EIOPA reminded the insurance industry and national supervisory authorities (NSAs) at an early stage about the possible consequences of Brexit and the actions that might need to be taken.[73]

Upon withdrawal from the internal market and in the absence of a political agreement between the EU and the UK to the contrary, UK (re)insurance undertakings lose their right to conduct business in the EEA30 Member States by way of FoE and FoS, having become third-country (re)insurance undertakings. They must re-apply for authorisation in each individual EEA30 MS if they want to continue to carry out business there, either by creating a subsidiary or branch or by offering cross-border services (in the case of reinsurance).[74] Existing branches of UK (re)insurance undertakings will need an authorisation in the MS of their activity in order to be able to continue to do business there and they must comply with the conditions for authorisation in Art. 162 FD.

There was a risk that UK (re)insurance undertakings relocating to an EEA30 MS might have tried to exploit any remaining differences between regulatory frameworks and supervisory attitudes between EEA30 Member States (regulatory arbitrage). EIOPA had to remind NSAs about EU requirements in terms of authorisation and outsourcing back to the UK.[75]

UK reinsurance undertakings must comply, for their business in the EU, with the conditions set by the MS in which they carry out their activity. These conditions have not been harmonised. They cannot be more favourable than

72 This date could be later if there is a withdrawal agreement with a transitional period. In that case, the situation will only change after the end of the transitional period. At the time of finishing this book, it was still unclear whether, how and when Brexit would happen. The EU and the UK negotiated a draft withdrawal agreement including a transitional period after the withdrawal, during which the UK would remain part of the internal market. The endorsement of this draft agreement was still uncertain at the time of finishing this book. After a first postponement of the withdrawal date until 12 April 2019, the EU27 leaders agreed on 10 April 2019 to delay Brexit until 31 October 2019.

73 See EIOPA, Opinion on supervisory convergence in light of the UK withdrawing from the EU, EIOPA-BoS-17/141, 11 July 2017, 7 p.; EIOPA, Opinion on service continuity in insurance in light of the withdrawal of the UK from the EU, EIOPA-BoS-17/389, 21 December 2017, 5 p.; EC Directorate-General for Financial Stability, Financial Services and Capital Markets Union (DG FISMA), *Notice to Stakeholders: Withdrawal of the UK and EU rules in the field of insurance/reinsurance*, 8 February 2018, 4 p.

74 This authorisation cannot be considered a formality and must be examined by EU NSAs on its merits. The undertaking established in the EU may not be an empty shell and the members of the AMSB and key function holders must dedicate sufficient time to fulfil their duties.

75 See EIOPA, Opinion on supervisory convergence in light of the UK withdrawing from the EU, EIOPA-BoS-17/141, 11 July 2017, 7 p. Similar actions were taken by EBA and ESMA.

those applying to EEA reinsurance undertakings, but they may be less favourable and may well differ between Member States: for example, Member States are free to require the pledging of assets (collateral) or the establishment of a branch by the UK reinsurance undertaking.[76]

In order to avoid this situation, which could be quite burdensome, some UK (re)insurance undertakings have either relocated to or set up a subsidiary in an EU country, mainly in Belgium, Ireland and Luxembourg, in order to maintain access to the EEA internal market. Once the subsidiary has been established, it can benefit from freedom of establishment and freedom to provide cross-border services into other EEA Member States. It enjoys the European passport.

A similar situation arises for EEA (re)insurance undertakings that are offering cross-border services into the UK. They will also need to re-apply for authorisation once the UK leaves the EU, as all EEA Member States will have become third countries for the UK. Fortunately, the UK has adopted a temporary permissions regime. Under this regime, an EEA (re)insurance undertaking that is authorised to carry on regulated activities in the UK through FoE or FoS passporting can obtain a (deemed Part 4A) permission to carry on those activities for a maximum of three years, subject to HM Treasury's power to extend the duration of the regime by increments of twelve months. This permission means that the EEA (re)insurance undertaking will continue to be an authorised person for the purpose of UK law. The permission will cover those activities that the EEA (re)insurance undertaking was permitted to carry on in the UK via passporting immediately before the withdrawal date.[77] A similar transitional arrangement does not exist for UK (re)insurance undertakings offering cross-border services into the EEA.

UK (re)insurance undertakings that have no establishment in the EEA, may – depending on applicable national rules – no longer be able to ensure service continuity with regard to existing contracts,[78] although the contracts remain in principle valid after the withdrawal date. In accordance with Arts. 41 (4) and 46 (2) FD, all insurance undertakings must take measures to ensure that contracts can continue to be serviced. (Re)insurance undertakings must therefore assess the impact of Brexit on their operations and contract portfolios and, in cooperation with the relevant NSAs, identify and mitigate possible risks. This may not be an issue for one-off or short-term annual contracts such as travel insurance. However, even contracts that will have terminated on the

---

76 Unless there has been an equivalence decision by the EU for the UK, in which case reinsurance contracts concluded with (re)insurance undertakings from the UK must be treated by Member States in the same manner as reinsurance contracts concluded with undertakings authorised under the FD (Art. 172 FD). See further, Chapter 10, section 4.

77 See Bank of England, *Temporary permissions regime*, https://www.bankofengland.co.uk/eu-withdrawal/temorary-permissions-regime.

78 EU (re)insurance undertakings that have no establishment in the UK may continue to offer their services as long as they are covered by the temporary permissions regime.

withdrawal date might be affected when there are open claims or when claims are reported after the withdrawal date. Problems could in particular arise for life insurance contracts.

In order to ensure service continuity, EIOPA has identified a number of options, which may need to be combined for some portfolios:

- the transfer of insurance contracts of UK undertakings with policyholders in the EEA30 Member States to an insurance subsidiary established in an EEA30 MS;
- the transfer of insurance contracts of EEA30 undertakings with UK policyholders to an insurance subsidiary established in the UK (this may be less urgent as long as the temporary permissions regime applies);
- the establishment of a third-country branch in the UK or in the EEA30 MS of the policyholder;
- with regard to UK undertakings in the legal form of a European company (SE),[79] the change of domicile of the company to an EEA30 MS.

EIOPA has advised NSAs to use their powers on the basis of Art. 41 (5) FD to review the system of governance of the insurance undertakings authorised in their jurisdiction which are impacted by Brexit and to require these undertakings to improve and strengthen their system of governance to ensure compliance with legal requirements:

- insurance undertakings must assess, on an ongoing basis, the impact of the withdrawal of the UK from the EU on their business, including for the service continuity of insurance contracts concluded by UK insurance undertakings in the EEA30 Member States and by EEA30 insurance undertakings in the UK by way of FoE and FoS;
- insurance undertakings with such cross-border insurance contracts must develop contingency plans that set out measures to prevent insurance activity without authorisation and ensure service continuity after the withdrawal date;
- contingency plans must include the scenario that on the withdrawal date the UK becomes a third country and leaves the internal market;
- undertakings may not rely in their contingency plans on any arrangement between the EU and the UK to continue after the withdrawal date concerning the access of UK insurance undertakings to the EEA30 insurance market or the access of EEA30 insurance undertakings to the UK insurance market, unless and until such an arrangement is agreed between the two parties;
- the implementation of the contingency plans must be realistic;

[79] Council Regulation (EC) No 2157/2001 of 8 October 2001 on the Statute for a European company (SE), *OJ* L 294, 10.11.2001, p. 1. For instance, Amlin Insurance SE.

- insurance undertakings must take the necessary measures to prevent them from carrying out an insurance activity without authorisation and to ensure that there is service continuity after the withdrawal date.

Customers who have already concluded an insurance contract, as well as beneficiaries of insurance contracts, should be appropriately informed by insurance undertakings about how the relevant contingency measures taken by their insurance undertaking impact their contractual relationship and services to them. The impact will depend on the contingency measures envisaged by the individual insurance undertaking. EIOPA has identified the following examples of possible impacts:[80]

- change of the contractual counterparty following a transfer of insurance contracts to another insurance undertaking;
- continuity of services and validity of insurance contracts;
- change or loss of protection provided by any existing national compensation scheme due to the transfer of insurance contracts to an insurance undertaking located in another jurisdiction;[81]
- tax implications of insurance contracts, for example insurance premium tax or changes to the claims management procedure or to other customer services following the relocation of an entity to another jurisdiction;
- additional organisational arrangements to deal with customer inquiries related to the withdrawal of the UK from the EU, for example publication of frequently asked questions for customers, contact details, helplines, etc.;
- jurisdiction and contact details of the NSA following a transfer of insurance contracts to another insurance undertaking or the relocation of an entity;
- change of the law applicable to the insurance contract.

By November 2018, most insurers had taken the necessary measures to ensure the continuity of services. However, in an urgent message, dated 5 November 2018, EIOPA noted that 124 undertakings from the UK and Gibraltar with cross-border business in EEA30 jurisdictions had still no or insufficient contingency plans in place to ensure service continuity.[82] EIOPA was working

---

80 EIOPA, Opinion on disclosure of information to customers about the impact of the withdrawal of the UK from the EU, EIOPA-BoS-18/119, 28 June 2018, p. 3 and Frequently asked questions, EIOPA-BoS-18/217, 28 June 2018, 3 p.

81 Because insurance guarantee schemes do not exist in all MS.

82 In its message, EIOPA indicates that in case of a withdrawal without agreement, 9.1 million EEA30 policyholders might face uncertainty and delays in receiving payments. This is significantly down from the total of 38 million EEA30 policyholders with a cross-border contract. Only 3% of the potentially affected policyholders have a contract with life insurers. The majority of the contracts are with non-life insurers. These contracts were short-term and with a low premium (less than €100). No action was needed in that case.

with the NSAs concerned to address this residual risk. On 19 February 2019, EIOPA adopted a number of recommendations[83] addressed to the NSA in EEA30 jurisdictions which should apply from the date following that on which the Treaties cease to apply to and in the UK. The objective of these recommendations is to minimise the detriment to policyholders and beneficiaries:

- NSAs should facilitate the orderly run-off of business which became unauthorised or should require the insurance undertakings to immediately take all necessary measures to become authorised under EU law: UK insurance undertakings should be prevented from concluding new insurance contracts or from establishing, renewing, extending, increasing or resuming insurance cover under existing insurance contracts as long as they are not authorised for such insurance activities under EU law;
- when UK insurance undertakings seek authorisation to carry out cross-border business through a branch in a MS, NSAs should apply the principle of proportionality and take into account that the UK insurance undertaking was subject to Solvency II requirements before the UK's withdrawal;
- NSAs should apply existing provisions on lapse of authorisation to UK insurance undertakings in their jurisdiction and effectively enforce these provisions in co-operation with the supervisory authorities in the UK;
- NSAs should allow the finalisation of portfolio transfers from UK insurance undertakings to EU27 insurance undertakings, provided that the transfer was initiated before the withdrawal date;
- where a policyholder established in the UK concluded a life insurance contract with a UK insurance undertaking and afterwards changed its habitual residence or place of establishment to a EU27 MS, NSAs should take into account in the supervisory review that the insurance contract was concluded in the UK and that the UK undertaking did not provide cross-border services for the EU27 for this contract;
- where a UK insurance undertaking has cross-border business in more than one MS, the NSAs of those Member States should co-operate with regard to supervising that business, in particular by exchanging information. Where deemed necessary, EIOPA may establish a cooperation platform for a specific undertaking;
- UK insurance undertakings should disclose the consequences for their rights and obligations to the policyholders and beneficiaries of contracts affected by the UK's withdrawal.

---

[83] EIOPA, Recommendations for the insurance sector in light of the UK withdrawing from the EU, EIOPA-BoS-19/040, 19 February 2019, 7 p. See also, FCA, *Brexit: information for general insurers and intermediaries in the UK*, 11 March 2019, https://www.fca.org.uk/firms/preparing-for-brexit/uk-general-insurers-intermediaries.

There is a clear intention both from EEA 30 supervisory authorities and from the UK supervisory authorities to continue the good cooperation that has existed before the Brexit discussions started. On 5 March 2019, EIOPA announced that – in the case of a hard Brexit, i.e. a withdrawal without an agreement, two Memoranda of Understanding will be concluded with the Bank of England in its capacity as the Prudential Regulation Authority (PRA) and the Financial Conduct Authority (FCA): one Multilateral Memorandum of Understanding on supervisory cooperation, enforcement and information exchange between the EEA NSAs and the UK authorities and one Bilateral Memorandum of Understanding between EIOPA and the UK authorities on information exchange and mutual assistance in the field of insurance regulation and supervision.[84]

A number of EU Member States (Belgium, France, Germany, Ireland, Italy, the Netherlands) have adopted specific legislation in order to protect their policyholders, for instance by granting passporting rights for a specific period of time after the withdrawal.

3.2.6. Liberalisation and Coordination

Establishing a single market for (re)insurance, allowing unimpeded cross-border sales and establishment, did not come about easily. It required the adoption of measures dealing with liberalisation[85] and coordination in the areas of direct insurance (including life and non-life insurance), reinsurance, co-insurance[86] and insurance mediation.

Coordination was achieved through the adoption of a number of directives. A directive is a legal instrument, proposed by the EC and adopted by the Council and the EP (the co-legislators), that must be implemented by Member States within a given period of time. The objectives of the coordination are to facilitate the taking up and pursuit of (re)insurance by (re)insurance undertakings, to harmonise financial supervision by agreeing on a set of technical rules to ensure the solvency of (re)insurance undertakings and to establish minimum rules on insurance contracts.

Liberalisation and coordination in the direct insurance sector (life and non-life) took place separately from reinsurance and co-insurance with the assistance of three generations of directives. The following directives constituted

84 EIOPA, *EIOPA and its Members agree on No-deal Brexit Memoranda of Understanding with the Bank of England and the Financial Conduct Authority*, Press release, 5 March 2019, https://eiopa.europa.eu/Pages/News/EIOPA-No-deal-Brexit-Memoranda-of-Understanding-with-the-Bank-of-England.aspx.

85 General Programme for the abolition of restrictions on freedom to provide services, *OJ Spec Ed.* 3, 15.1.1962, p.3 and General Programme for the abolition of restrictions on freedom of establishment, *OJ Spec. Ed.* 7, 15.1.1962, p. 7.

86 Insurance where the cover is shared between two or more insurers in order to spread the potential liability in the case of very large risks.

the EU harmonisation programme in the areas of direct insurance, reinsurance and co-insurance, before they were recast in the Solvency II FD:

- Council Directive 64/225/EEC of 25 February 1964 on the abolition of restrictions on freedom of establishment and freedom to provide services in respect of reinsurance and retrocession;[87]
- First Council Directive 73/239/EEC of 24 July 1973 on the coordination of laws, regulations and administrative provisions relating to the taking-up and pursuit of the business of direct insurance other than life assurance;[88]
- Council Directive 73/240/EEC of 24 July 1973 abolishing restrictions on freedom of establishment in the business of direct insurance other than life insurance;[89]
- Council Directive 76/580/EEC of 29 June 1976 amending Directive 73/239/EEC of 24 July 1973 on the coordination of laws, regulations and administrative provisions relating to the taking-up and pursuit of the business of direct insurance other than life assurance;[90]
- Council Directive 78/473/EEC of 30 May 1978 on the coordination of laws, regulations and administrative provisions relating to Community co-insurance;[91]
- Council Directive 84/641/EEC of 10 December 1984 amending, particularly as regards tourist assistance, the First Directive (73/329/EEC) on the coordination of laws, regulations and administrative provisions relating to the taking-up and pursuit of the business of direct insurance other than life assurance;[92]
- Council Directive 87/344/EEC of 22 June 1987 on the coordination of laws, regulations and administrative provisions relating to legal expenses insurance;[93]
- Second Council Directive 88/357/EEC of 22 June 1988 on the coordination of laws, regulations and administrative provisions relating to direct insurance other than life assurance and laying down provisions to facilitate the effective exercise of freedom to provide services;[94]
- Council Directive 92/49/EEC of 18 June 1992 on the coordination of laws, regulations and administrative provisions relating to direct insurance other than life assurance (third non-life insurance Directive);[95]

---

87 *OJ* L 56, 4.4.1964, p. 878.
88 *OJ* L 228, 16.8.1973, p. 3.
89 *OJ* L 228, 16.8.1973, p. 20.
90 *OJ* L 189, 13.7.1976, p. 13.
91 *OJ* L 151, 7.6.1978, p. 25.
92 *OJ* L 339, 27.12.1984, p. 21.
93 *OJ* L 185, 4.7.1987, p. 77.
94 *OJ* L 172, 4.7.1988, p. 1.
95 *OJ* L 228, 11.8.1992, p. 1.

- Directive 98/78/EC of the EP and of the Council of 27 October 1998 on the supplementary supervision of insurance undertakings in an insurance group;[96]
- Directive 2001/17/EC of the EP and of the Council of 19 March 2001 on the reorganisation and winding-up of insurance undertakings;[97]
- Directive 2002/13/EC of the EP and of the Council of 5 March 2002 amending Council Directive 73/239/EEC as regards the solvency margin requirements for non-life insurance undertakings;[98]
- Directive 2002/83/EC of the EP and of the Council of 5 November 2002 concerning life assurance;[99]
- Directive 2005/68/EC of the EP and of the Council of 16 November 2005 on reinsurance.[100]

These 14 Insurance Directives were recast as part of the Solvency II reform. They are now incorporated into the Solvency II FD.

Further directives deal with motor insurance,[101] insurance accounting[102] and insurance mediation (distribution).[103] These directives are not included in the Solvency II FD.

---

96 *OJ* L 330, 5.12.1998, p. 1.
97 *OJ* L 110, 20.4.2001, p. 28.
98 *OJ* L 77, 20.3.2002, p. 17.
99 *OJ* L 345, 19.12.2002, p. 1.
100 *OJ* L 323, 19.12.2005, p. 10.
101 The five Motor Insurance Directives were recast in 2009 into one single legal document: Directive 2009/103/EC of the EP and of the Council of 16 September 2009 relating to insurance against civil liability in respect of the use of motor vehicles, and the enforcement of the obligation to insure against such liability, *OJ* L 263, 7.10.2009, p. 11.
102 Council Directive of 19 December 1991 on the annual accounts and consolidated accounts of insurance undertakings, *OJ* L 374, 31.12.1991, p. 7.
103 Directive 2002/92/EC of the EP and of the Council of 9 December 2002 on insurance mediation, *OJ* L 9, 15.1.2003, p. 3. The scope of this Directive was extended in 2016 to other forms of insurance distribution: Directive (EU) 2016/97 of the EP and of the Council of 20 January 2016, on insurance distribution, *OJ* L 26, 2.2.2016, p. 19.

CHAPTER 2
INSURANCE SOLVENCY

A (re)insurance undertaking is solvent when it has sufficient financial resources. The financial resources (own funds) of a (re)insurance undertaking are in essence the difference between the assets and the liabilities. That difference constitutes a kind of safety capital or buffer that is necessary for the protection of the (re)insurer against unforeseen events. These events may be the result of higher than expected claims levels or unfavourable investment results.

The question then arises as to how large that buffer should be. For what time horizon should it be calculated and what kind of assets could be included in the buffer? These questions have received different answers over time.[1] In the IAIS glossary, insurance solvency is defined as "the ability of an insurer to meet its obligations to policyholders when they fall due".

1. SOLVENCY I

Under Solvency I, the safety capital or capital buffer was referred to as the solvency margin. It had to be calculated so that an insurance undertaking covering this margin with admissible own funds would most likely be able to fulfil its obligations during the years to come. If the own funds fell below the required amount, the supervisory authority would intervene and prescribe measures to restore the sound financial situation of the undertaking concerned. If the restoration measures appeared unsuccessful, the undertaking would be required to apply other measures in order to safeguard, to the greatest extent possible, the interests of the policyholders.

Technical provisions had to be calculated on a prudent basis and had to be covered by assets that were considered of good quality to safeguard commitments to policyholders. The solvency margin was defined based upon premiums and claims in non-life insurance and on technical provisions and capital at risk in life insurance. The solvency margin had to be covered by assets of good quality.

1 For an overview, see SANDSTRÖM, A., *Solvency: Models, Assessment and Regulation*, Chapman & Hall, Boca Raton, 2006, pp. 7–12.

The Solvency I requirements introduced in 1973 (for non-life insurance) and in 1979 (for life insurance) were largely based upon the research conducted by Prof. Cornelis Campagne, the chairman of the supervisory authority in the Netherlands.[2] In 1948, Prof. Campagne wrote a report on solvency assessment for life assurance undertakings based on data from 10 Dutch insurance undertakings for the years 1926–45. In 1957, he produced a report for non-life insurers based on the data from 10 Swiss insurance undertakings for the years 1945–54. These reports were written at the request of the Insurance Committee of the Organisation for European Economic Cooperation (OEEC), the predecessor of the Organisation for Economic Cooperation and Development (OECD). A final report was presented in 1961.

After discussions with the Conference of Insurance Supervisory Authorities of the Member States of the EEC[3] (the predecessor of CEIOPS[4] and now EIOPA), the slightly modified approach proposed by Campagne was introduced in the four life directives and four non-life directives adopted between 1973 and 2002. Strictly speaking, only the directives adopted in 2002 are considered the "Solvency I Directives". However, since the start of the Solvency II project, the whole system built up by these eight directives has come to be known as Solvency I.[5]

2. DEFICIENCIES OF SOLVENCY I

Although the solvency regime was updated in 2002, after the capital market crisis, a number of structural weaknesses remained. These are described in the Impact Assessment Report that accompanied the EC's 2007 proposed Solvency II FD.[6]

---

2 Called "Verzekeringskamer" at that time. The supervisory authority is now de Nederlandsche Bank (DNB).

3 This organisation was established in Paris in 1958 and became later the Conference of Insurance Supervisory Authorities of the EU.

4 The Committee of European Insurance and Pensions Supervisors (CEIOPS) was established in 2003 by Commission Decision 2004/6/EC of 5 November 2003, *OJ* L 3, 7.1.2004, p. 3, which was repealed by Commission Decision 2009/79/EC of 23 January 2009, *OJ* L 25, 29.1.2009, p. 28. That decision enlarged the competences of CEIOPS. CEIOPS was, and its successor EIOPA is, located in Frankfurt.

5 For a detailed description of the background and development of Solvency I, see SANDSTRÖM, A., *Handbook of Solvency for Actuaries and Risk Managers. Theory and Practice*, Chapman & Hall/CRC, Boca Raton, 2011, 1055 p. See also, SCHLUDE, H., The EEC solvency rules for non-life insurance companies, *Nordisk Försäkrings Tidskrift*, 1979, No 1, pp. 24–30.

6 EC Commission Staff Working Document: Accompanying document to the Proposal for a Directive of the EP and of the Council on the taking-up and pursuit of the business of Insurance and Reinsurance. Solvency II: Impact Assessment Report, SEC (2007) 871, 10 July 2007, pp. 9–14.

Under Solvency I, the capital buffer mainly looked at underwriting risk. The disadvantage of this limited approach to risk became apparent during the capital market crisis at the beginning of the 21st century. The capital buffer did not require insurers to hold sufficient capital for market risk, and there were no specific rules dealing with concentration risk. As a result, insurers that were heavily invested in equity suffered major losses when the value of their investments diminished as a result of the capital market crisis.

Besides market risk and concentration risk, other key risks, such as credit and operational risk were either not captured at all in the required solvency margin or were not properly taken into account.

Lack of risk sensitivity was also shown in the lack of recognition of risk mitigation tools, such as reinsurance, securitisation and derivatives. In addition, Solvency I did not give insurers credit for diversification effects across lines of business or between legal entities, even though the diversification of risks is a key characteristic of the insurance business model.

In general, Solvency I did not contain an incentive for insurers to manage their risks properly. As a result, some insurers were operating with too much capital, while other insurers were underwriting business for which they did not have the right amount of capital.

Furthermore, the required solvency margin calculation under Solvency I was based on past data. For instance, Member States had the option to value assets at their historic cost and to apply a discount rate to life insurance liabilities consistent with the conditions of the government bond market at the time the contract was concluded. By mainly looking at underwriting risk, Solvency I very much focused on the past situation of the insurer.

Under Solvency I, attention was exclusively paid to the quantitative aspects of solvency, thereby overlooking the importance of qualitative aspects, such as proper governance of the institution. However, studies such as the Müller Report[7] and the Sharma Report[8] had shown that when insurers failed, it was less likely due to an insufficient amount of capital, but more likely to a lack of proper governance.[9] This qualitative aspect of prudential supervision, already recognised in Basel II, was absent under the Solvency I regulatory regime.

---

7 Conference of Insurance Supervisory Services of the Member States of the EU, *Report on Solvency of Insurance Undertakings*, April 1997, 101 p., carried out under the chairmanship of Helmut Müller, Vice-President of the Bundesaufsichtsamt für das Versicherungswesen, commonly referred to as the "Müller Report".

8 Conference of Insurance Supervisory Services of the Member States of the EU, *Report on Prudential Supervision of Insurance Undertakings*, December 2002, 112 p., prepared under the chairmanship of Paul Sharma, Head of the Prudential Risks Department of the UK's FSA, commonly referred to as the "Sharma Report".

9 For an analysis of some notorious insurance failures, such as Equitable Life, HIH and AIG, see CURTIS, R., Solvency as a Focal Point of Prudential Regulation, in LIEDTKE, P. M. and MONKIEWICZ, J. (Eds.), *The Future of Insurance Regulation and Supervision: A Global Perspective*, Palgrave Macmillan, Basingstoke, 2011, pp. 92–97.

One of the main conclusions of the Sharma Report (2002), which analysed failures and "near misses" in the EU between 1996 and 2001, was that the primary causes were poor management and inappropriate risk decisions.[10] The analysis also showed that the required solvency margin did not act as a useful early-warning indicator that the insurance undertaking was getting into financial difficulties.

The findings of the Sharma Report were confirmed in CEIOPS' survey on failed insurers and "near misses" in 2005.[11] In more than 75% of cases examined by CEIOPS, the reported solvency ratio up to one year before failure was more than 100%, and in 20% of cases, the reported ratio was over 200%. A more recent study by EIOPA of 180 cases in the period from 1999 to 2016 came to similar conclusions: management and staff competence risk was one of the top five primary causes of failures and near misses for EU life and non-life undertakings.[12]

Solvency I is a good example of the disadvantage of minimum harmonisation. Most Member States operated an "EU-minimum plus" regime whereby insurers were subject to more stringent requirements than those set out in the Insurance Directives. Member States had indeed updated their regulatory regime in order to bring it into line with developments in financial markets, actuarial science and risk management techniques and technology.

Key differences between the approaches adopted by Member States when supplementing the rules laid down in the Insurance Directives related to the importance attached to technical provisions and capital requirements, the eligibility and valuation of assets as well as the quantitative limits applied to investments.

Examples of the different approaches followed by Member States can be found in the KPMG Report,[13] which was produced as part of the preparatory work on Solvency II. The Report concludes that:

> "Member States are allowed a high degree of freedom to establish more stringent rules for the undertakings they authorise. In some areas the Directives do not lay down any prescriptive requirements.

---

10 See also the study produced in Canada by LEADBETTER, D. and SYODOLAK, P., *Why insurers fail: inadequately pricing the promise of insurance*, Property and Casualty Insurance Compensation Corporation, Toronto, 1999, 30 p., which puts the emphasis on inadequate pricing as part of poor risk management.

11 CEIOPS, Answers to the EC on the second wave of Calls for Advice in the framework of the Solvency II project, CEIOPS-Doc-07/05, 31 October 2005, p. 263, https://eiopa.europa.eu/CEIOPS-Archive/Documents/Advices/Doc07_05-AnswersEC2ndwaveSII.pdf.

12 See EIOPA, *Failures and near misses in insurance*, Publications Office of the EU, Luxembourg, 2018, 46 p.

13 EC, *Study into the methodologies to assess the overall financial position of an insurance undertaking from the perspective of prudential supervision*, May 2002, 243 p. This study is commonly referred to as the "KPMG Report" as it was carried out by KPMG on behalf of the EC.

> The flexibility allowed has resulted in some countries having a solvency regime that is super equivalent, i.e. implementation of rules over and above the minimum required by the EC Directives. The ability to set additional capital requirements, combined with the freedom to determine the rules governing the valuation of assets and liabilities for regulatory purposes, has led to significant differences in approach adopted towards prudential supervision between Member States."[14]

Differences between solvency regulation in Member States made it difficult to operate cross-border and hindered the proper functioning of the internal market.

Another important weakness of Solvency I that affected the internal market was that insufficient attention was paid to group supervision. Most supervisors in the EU were in favour of solo supervision and looked at group supervision as a form of supplementary supervision, rather than as a form of supervision in its own right. In fact, supervisors felt responsible only for those insurance undertakings that they had authorised, and failed to realise that the financial solvency of an insurance undertaking can be heavily affected by its position in a group (for instance, as a parent undertaking or a subsidiary).

The main deficiencies of Solvency I can be summarised as follows:[15]

- The capital buffer under Solvency I mainly looked at insurance risk (underwriting risk), thereby failing to draw attention to other risks which an insurer might incur, such as market risk, credit risk or operational risk.
- The Solvency I regime did not include an incentive for good risk management. There was no direct relationship between risk and capital. Insurers could therefore operate successfully under the solvency regime without proper risk management. A good example is life insurance. Many insurers continued to offer fixed guarantees at rates which were higher than the market rate. Under Solvency I, they could nevertheless show an attractive solvency margin.
- The Solvency I regime did not contain an early-warning signal. The system would not show that an insurer was becoming insolvent. As insurance is often a long-term business, problems will only appear gradually, and when they become clear, it is often too late to do something about it. Supervisors did not have sufficient information nor the tools to intervene when there was still time to deal with the problems.
- As Solvency I mainly focused on underwriting risk, it very much looked at the past situation of the insurer. In order to understand the solvency position of an insurance undertaking, it is however important to look at its business model over a number of years. A forward-looking approach was therefore lacking.

---

14 EC, *Study into the methodologies to assess the overall financial position of an insurance undertaking from the perspective of prudential supervision*, May 2002, pp. 7–8.

15 See also STEFFEN, T., Solvency II and the work of CEIOPS, *The Geneva Papers*, 2008, No 33, p. 61.

- Solvency is not just about capital, it is very much also a question of good risk management and proper governance. If an insurance undertaking is properly managed, it will match the risks that it underwrites with the right amount of capital. Under Solvency I, too much attention was being paid to the volume of the business (an increase in written premiums) rather than to the quality of the business (have the right risks been underwritten). Actuarial or risk management expertise was not always present at the right level in the organisation. Insufficient attention was being paid to the qualitative aspects of solvency.
- Public disclosure and supervisory reporting were minimal under Solvency I. In addition, the linkage of the supervisory data to the accounting data and the lack of harmonisation of the accounting data produced a situation whereby data relating to insurance undertakings were not comparable. This made it impossible to really compare the financial situation and the solvency situation of insurance undertakings belonging to different Member States.

3. ORIGINS OF SOLVENCY II

A lot of work was carried[16] out before the project really started in 2004.[17] The preparatory work commenced in 1999 with a paper prepared by the Insurance Unit within Directorate-General (DG) Markt,[18] which outlined the new project for the first time. In that paper, reference was made to six areas that required further examination: technical provisions, assets/investment risk, asset–liability management, reinsurance, a solvency margin reflecting more accurately the true risks, and the accounting regime. The Commission Services produced several internal notes for discussion within the Solvency Subcommittee of the Insurance Committee.

---

16 For a good overview of the development of the Solvency II project, see SANDSTRÖM, A., *Handbook of Solvency for Actuaries and Risk Managers. Theory and Practice*, Chapman & Hall/CRC, Boca Raton, 2011, pp. 575–627. See also LINDER, U. and RONKAINEN, V., Solvency II – towards a new insurance supervisory system in the EU, *Scandinavian Actuarial Journal*, 2004, No 6, pp. 462–474; Swiss Re, Solvency II: an integrated risk approach for European insurers, *Sigma*, 2006, No 4, pp. 5–18; VAN HULLE, K., Regulatory challenges in the European Union, in LIEDTKE, P. and MONKIEWICZ, J. (Eds.), *The Future of Insurance Regulation and Supervision: A Global Perspective*, Palgrave Macmillan, Basingstoke, 2011, pp. 300–309.

17 The Solvency II project was started in DG Markt under the leadership of David Deacon, Head of Unit (1999–2004). He was assisted by Ulf Linder, Mike Thom, Manuel de Frutos, Ivo van Es and Vesa Ronkainen.

18 DG Markt, *The review of the overall financial position of an insurance undertaking (Solvency II review)*, 1999.

The objective of the project was clearly stated in the foreword signed by Jean-Claude Thébault, a director of DG Markt responsible for banking and insurance, in the KPMG Report (see below, section 3.2):

> "This project is to establish a solvency system that is better matched to the true risks of an insurance company. A future solvency system in the EU should also not be overly prescriptive, avoid undue complexity, reflect market developments (such as derivatives and alternative risk transfer) and, where possible, be based on common accounting principles."

The work was carried out in two phases; the first phase was devoted to an analysis and discussion of the issues and the second phase concentrated on the development of the new solvency regime. A number of studies[19] were carried out and discussions were held with industry experts, the actuarial profession, supervisory authorities and experts from Member States.

Although Solvency II was a European project with the input of experts from a number of Member States,[20] there can be no doubt that the UK played a crucial role in the development of Solvency II.[21] Because the UK had already moved away from Solvency I by developing its Individual Capital Adequacy Standard (ICAS) regime in 2002, it had experience with a solvency regime that contained both quantitative (Pillar 1) and qualitative (Pillar 2) requirements.[22] Experts from the Financial Services Authority (FSA)[23] and from the UK insurance industry were very vocal and influential throughout the development of Solvency II.

The discussions also looked at developments in the banking sector and at the situation in other countries outside the EU, notably the USA (the Risk-Based Capital regime), Australia (the new risk-based solvency regime developed by the

---

19 See, for instance, Conference of the Insurance Supervisory Authorities of the Member States of the European Union, *Report on technical provisions in non-life insurance*, 2000, 42 p., prepared under the chairmanship of Giovanni Manghetti, President of the Italian Insurance Supervisory Authority (ISVAP), commonly referred to as the "Manghetti report".

20 For an overview of the technical input and the academic literature that served as a basis for the development of the standard formula in Solvency II, see SANDSTRÖM, A., *Handbook of Solvency for Actuaries and Risk Managers. Theory and Practice*, Chapman & Hall/CRC, Boca Raton, 2011, pp. 3–558.

21 This is particularly underlined by QUAGLIA, L., The politics of insurance regulation and supervision in the European Union, *Comparative European Politics*, 2011, No 9, pp. 100–122. It was quickly forgotten by the UK government. Reacting to Prudential's threat to relocate to Hong Kong to escape Solvency II's punitive capital charges, the UK Prime Minister, David Cameron, referred in March 2012 during a debate in the UK House of Commons to Solvency II as "a good example of ill thought-out EU legislation".

22 See HUMPHRY, D., Solvency II in the UK: Evolution rather than Revolution, in MARANO, P. and SIRI, M. (Eds.), *Insurance Regulation in the European Union*, Palgrave Macmillan, Cham, 2017.

23 For instance, Paul Sharma within CEIOPS/EIOPA, and Rob Curtis within the IAIS.

Australian Prudential Regulation Authority after the collapse of HIH Insurance), Canada (the Minimum Capital Test for property and casualty insurers, and the Minimum Continuing Capital and Surplus requirements for life insurers) and Switzerland (the Swiss Solvency Test). Account was also taken of the work carried out at international level by the IAIS, the International Actuarial Association (IAA) and the International Accounting Standards Board (IASB).

3.1. MÜLLER REPORT

The Müller Report,[24] produced by the Conference of the Insurance Supervisory Services of the Member States of the EU,[25] under the chairmanship of Helmut Müller, Vice-President of the Insurance Supervisory Federal Authority of Germany,[26] considered the present solvency regime as generally satisfactory, although it recognised certain weaknesses in the methodology (for instance the lack of importance attached to investment risk) and made a number of recommendations for improvement. It looked at the risk-based capital approach applied in the USA, as well as at the solvency rules applicable to credit institutions. It also examined financial difficulties in insurance undertakings in the Member States of the EU and concluded that the problem was mostly not a question of a lack of capital but of management failure.

3.2. KPMG REPORT

The KPMG Report,[27] which was carried out on behalf of the EC, analysed the main risks facing insurers, as well as the techniques used by insurers to measure and manage those risks. In addition, it looked at the various regulatory approaches used in the determination of technical provisions, the methods used to value assets and the regulatory tools designed to take account of or reduce investment risk. The study also looked at the treatment of reinsurance and other risk mitigation techniques, the impact of future accounting changes, the use of rating agencies and market mechanisms, Basel II and the pros and cons of applying a three-pillar structure to insurance regulation. The study finished with a comparative analysis of solvency margin methodologies in the USA, Australia and Canada.

---

24 Conference of the Insurance Supervisory Authorities of the Member States of the European Union, *Report on solvency of insurance undertakings*, April 1997, 102 p.

25 The predecessor of CEIOPS.

26 The Bundesaufsichtsamt für das Versicherungswesen.

27 EC, *Study into the methodologies to assess the overall financial position of an insurance undertaking from the perspective of prudential supervision*, May 2002, 243 p.

The report concluded that there was a need to reform the current EU regime in favour of an approach that produced greater consistency in measurement, took account of all significant risks, and did not impose an overly prudent capital requirement on insurers. In addition, it recommended that the Basel II three-pillar structure should be adopted for the new solvency regime and highlighted the importance of ensuring consistent implementation. However, the report also noted that the solvency regime would need to be sufficiently flexible to recognise the considerable heterogeneity in the European insurance industry.

3.3. SHARMA REPORT

The Sharma Report,[28] produced by the Conference of the Insurance Supervisory Services of the Member States of the EU under the chairmanship of Paul Sharma, Head of the Prudential Risks Department of the UK's FSA, analysed the risks that European insurers face and tried to identify those risks that have led to actual solvency problems. It also looked at how effective the current EU regime was at detecting solvency problems in advance, as well as the effectiveness of a variety of supervisory tools designed to detect and prevent problems. The analysis was based on a survey of actual failures and near misses between 1996 and 2001, a questionnaire looking at the diagnostic and preventative tools used by supervisors, and 21 detailed case studies.

The report observed that the main causes for insurance failures were clustered around the broad themes of management quality and inappropriate risk decisions, rather than inadequate capitalisation per se. Therefore, not only should the new solvency regime be based on more risk-sensitive capital requirements, but there should also be a greater focus on risk management.

4. THE THREE-PILLAR APPROACH

It was clear from the outset that Solvency II would have to adopt the three-pillar approach introduced by Basel II. Experience in the banking sector with Basel I had shown that a capital adequacy regime that only focused on capital was incapable of ensuring bank solvency, as banks were inclined to treat the capital requirements as a regulatory formality and did not integrate the supervisory requirements in their internal capital management.

It was therefore important to have a capital regime that would not be limited to quantitative aspects (Pillar 1 – minimum capital requirements) but

28 Conference of the Insurance Supervisory Authorities of the Member States of the European Union, *Report on prudential supervision of insurance undertakings*, December 2002, 112 p.

would also include qualitative requirements (Pillar 2 – governance, including internal capital assessment and supervisory review) and rules on transparency (Pillar 3 – reporting). As pointed out by the Basel Committee of Banking Supervisors (BCBS) upon the review of the 1988 Basel Accord (Basel I) in 2004:

> "[B]anks and supervisors need to give appropriate attention to the second (supervisory review) and third (market discipline) pillars of the revised framework. It is critical that the minimum capital requirements of the first pillar be accompanied by a robust implementation of the second, including efforts by banks to assess their capital adequacy and by supervisors to review such assessments. In addition, the disclosures provided under the third pillar of the revised framework will be essential in ensuring that market discipline is an effective complement to the other two pillars."[29]

The work on Solvency II evolved around the three-pillar system introduced at international level for internationally active banks, which had been adopted in the EU for credit institutions and investment firms.[30]

The *first pillar* would comprise two capital requirements: a solvency capital requirement (SCR), i.e. a desired or target capital reflecting the economic capital a (re)insurance undertaking would need in order to operate with a low probability of failure, and a minimum capital requirement (MCR), i.e. a safety net that would constitute a basic trigger level for ultimate supervisory action. The new regime would allow undertakings to use internal risk models to calculate the SCR. The first pillar would also include the solvency balance sheet with the rules for the valuation of assets and liabilities (technical provisions) and for the definition of own funds.

The *second pillar* would include the rules on governance and risk management, as well as the tools (such as intervention powers) for the supervisory review process. Risks, such as liquidity risk, for which no capital requirements would be set in Pillar 1, would have to be assessed under Pillar 2.

The *third pillar* would include the rules on supervisory reporting and public disclosure, with the aim of providing supervisory authorities with the necessary information to carry out their supervisory role and to establish market discipline. As transparency was not a characteristic under Solvency I, care would have to be taken not to overburden the insurance industry with too-onerous reporting requirements.

---

29 BCBS, *International Convergence of Capital Measurement and Capital Standards. A Revised Framework*, BIS (Ed.), Basel, June 2004, p. 15.

30 See Directive 2006/48/EC of the EP and of the Council of 14 June 2006 relating to the taking up and pursuit of the business of credit institutions (recast), *OJ* L 177, 30.6.2006, p. 1, and Directive 2006/49/EC of 14 June 2006 on the capital adequacy of investment firms and credit institutions (recast), *OJ* L 177, 30.6.2006, p. 201.

This three-pillar approach has led to the "house" of Solvency II, which is composed of three pillars and a roof, the roof representing the requirements on group supervision, which – under Solvency II – have equal importance to the rules on solo supervision.

Figure 1. Solvency II: three pillars and a roof

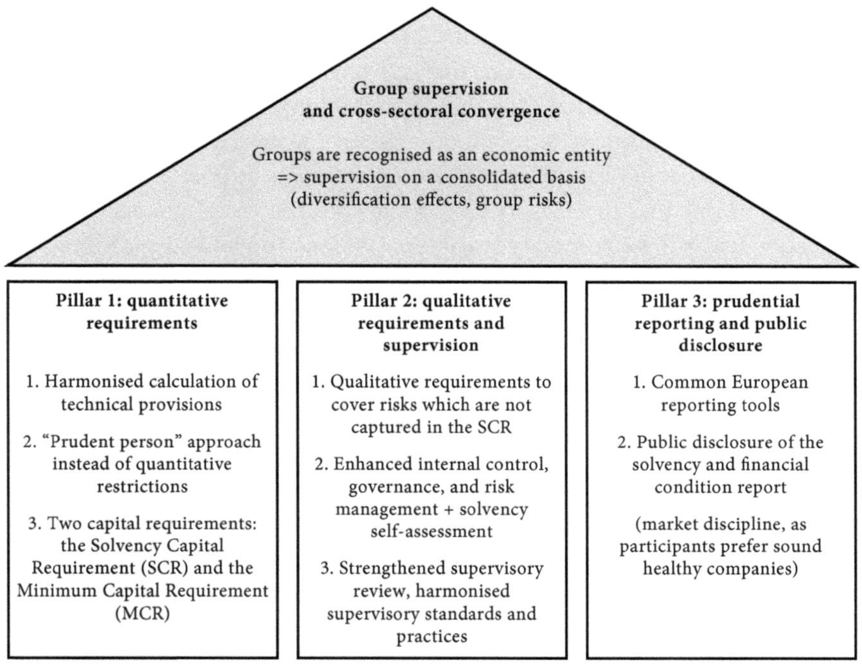

Source: Produced by the author.

Under Solvency II, each of the three pillars are of equal size, i.e. they are of equal importance. They are also interlinked: if proper risk management is exercised (Pillar 2), the undertaking is unlikely to operate without sufficient capital (Pillar 1). If the undertaking is well managed (Pillar 2) and operating with the capital that it needs (Pillar 1), there is no problem with being transparent about it to the supervisory authority and to the public (Pillar 3).

5. A PROJECT IN STAGES

The Solvency II project was the first initiative in the area of insurance that followed the so-called Lamfalussy approach. Baron Alexandre Lamfalussy chaired a Committee of Wise Men, which was asked by the EC to develop proposals for a more efficient procedure of European law making in the area of securities regulation. The Committee presented its report on 15 February 2001.[31] The approach proposed by the Committee, which is commonly referred to as the Lamfalussy approach, was progressively extended to all areas of financial services.

Based upon experience from the past, the Committee of Wise Men proposed fundamentally changing the way in which EU legislation in the area of financial services was developed. Past experience had shown that too-detailed legislation in an area (such as financial services) that is so often subject to important changes very soon becomes outdated such that it can no longer serve its very purpose. It must therefore be possible to adopt legislative measures at different levels: basic legislation at level 1 and implementing measures at level 2. Furthermore, the eminent role that supervisors play in the enforcement of financial services legislation needs to be properly recognised. Guidance on how to apply the rules should therefore be developed at level 3.

The Lamfalussy Report also refers to a level 4, which relates to the enforcement action taken by the EC. It is the role of the EC to ensure that Member States comply with the measures agreed at levels 1 and 2.

The development of a legislative project in different stages has advantages and disadvantages. The main advantage is flexibility. If the level 1 text is developed as a framework directive that only contains basic principles, there is no need to regularly amend the level 1 text so as to adapt its provisions to changed circumstances. Adaptation can take place at levels 2 and 3, which should be easier as it does not imply a full legislative procedure.

The Lamfalussy approach forced the EC and the co-legislators (Council and EP) to concentrate on the basic principles. However, a significant disadvantage was that the co-legislators soon developed a tendency to push the problems to levels 2 or 3, thereby postponing a solution to difficult questions. Another disadvantage was the limited role given to the EP. The level 2 measures, which were based upon a delegation of powers given in the level 1 text by the co-legislators to the EC, were developed in close cooperation between the EC, Member States and their NSAs. The EP was essentially absent from the procedure at level 2. It received a right of scrutiny that was extended progressively until it reached its climax in the Lisbon Treaty (2007). This Treaty replaced the Lamfalussy approach with a different procedure that gives more powers to the EP and to the European supervisory authorities (ESAs). This led to the "Lisbonisation" of Solvency II, which was introduced by Omnibus II (see further, Chapter 3, section 4.2.3).

---

31 EC, *Final Report of the Committee of wise men on the regulation of European securities markets*, 15 February 2001, 117 p.

Solvency II is a good example of a project where a real attempt was made to make the Lamfalussy approach work in practice. However, it clearly suffered from the disadvantages listed above. In addition, the financial crisis and the low interest rate environment interfered with the introduction of the new solvency regime. As Sharon Bowles (ALDE, UK) pointed out during the debate on Omnibus II (see further, Chapter 3, section 4.2.3):

> "We have learned a lot about kicking the can down the road, it is not a good idea because it comes back to bite you. Using a level 2 fix to get you through a trilogue is not a good solution and it is important to be careful about the pointers you set at level 1."[32]

The Lamfalussy approach involved intense cooperation between the EC, Member States (finance ministries or other ministries competent for insurance), NSAs and the EP (to a lesser extent).

Finance ministries or other ministries responsible for insurance of Member States[33] regularly met with the EC within the so-called level 2 regulatory committees: the European Insurance and Occupational Pension Funds Committee (EIOPC)[34] for insurance and pensions, the European Banking Committee (EBC)[35] for banking, and the European Securities Committee (ESC)[36] for securities regulation. These committees were consulted by the EC before and during the development of implementing measures (level 2). These measures could only be adopted if they were agreed to by a qualified majority of Member States. In order to promote cross-sectoral convergence between the three sectors, guidance was received from the Financial Services Committee (FSC), which met regularly and was composed of senior policymakers of the finance ministries.

NSAs were organised at EU level in so-called level 3 committees: the Committee of European Insurance and Occupational Pensions Supervisors (CEIOPS),[37] the Committee of European Banking Supervisors (CEBS)[38] and the Committee of European Securities Regulators (CESR).[39] These committees were

---

32 Quoted in Solvencyiiwire.com, *Omnibus II trialogue agreement calls for impact assessment on long-term guarantee measures*, 13 July 2012.

33 The system did not always function as intended: very often Member States were represented in the EIOPC by experts from NSAs which created a confusion between levels 2 and 3.

34 Commission Decision 2004/9/EC of 5 November 2003, *OJ* L 3, 7.1.2004, p. 34.

35 Commission Decision 2004/10/EC of 5 November 2003, *OJ* L 3, 7.1.2004, p. 35.

36 Commission Decision 2001/528/EC of 6 June 2001, *OJ* L 191, 13.7.2001, p. 45.

37 CEIOPS was established in 2003 by Commission Decision 2004/6/EC of 5 November 2003, *OJ* L 3, 7.1.2004, p. 3, which was repealed by Commission Decision 2009/79/EC of 23 January 2009, *OJ* L 25, 29.1.2009, p. 28. That decision enlarged the competences of CEIOPS. CEIOPS and its successor, EIOPA, were located in Frankfurt.

38 Commission Decision 2009/78/EC of 23 January 2009, *OJ* L 25, 29.1.2009, p. 23.

39 Commission Decision 2001/527/EC of 6 June 2001, *OJ* L 191, 13.7.2001, p. 43.

closely associated with the development of EU legislation through mandates which they received from the EC. They were also responsible for developing supervisory guidance (level 3). A great deal of attention was paid to a close cooperation between the three committees in order to achieve a high degree of cross-sectoral consistency.

The EP is a co-legislator for level 1 legislation. Under the Lamfalussy approach, the EP had a right of scrutiny concerning implementing measures proposed by the EC. The EP engaged in a regular dialogue with the commissioner responsible for financial services legislation[40] and with the chairs of each of the level 3 committees. A practice developed whereby the Commission Services would communicate to the secretariat of the responsible committee in the EP (the Economic and Monetary Affairs Committee, ECON) all documents that were discussed in the level 2 committees. It was not uncommon for a member of the secretariat of ECON to participate as an observer in meetings of the level 2 committees.

The Solvency II proposal followed this approach. It was construed as a Framework Directive that only contained the basic principles for the new solvency regime (level 1). The proposal, to be adopted by the Council and the EP, indicated the areas where further implementing measures were necessary. These measures would be adopted by the EC (level 2). In adopting these measures, the EC had to consult CEIOPS. The draft measures were submitted for discussion to MS experts in the EIOPC before being adopted by the EC under the scrutiny of the EP. In order to ensure the harmonised application of the rules, CEIOPS would develop further guidance (level 3) which was not legally binding but which all NSAs had agreed to apply on a best-effort basis.

Under the Lamfalussy approach, much importance was attached to consultation with interested parties and to transparency. Consultation of a wide range of stakeholders and transparency about the procedure and the issues at stake were important guiding principles in the development of Solvency II.

Consultation with Member States occurred in the context of the EIOPC.[41] Within the EIOPC, a Solvency subcommittee was set up to discuss the development of Solvency II. Meetings of the Solvency subcommittee were also attended by a representative of CEIOPS and of the secretariat of ECON.

---

40 For Solvency II, the responsible commissioners were Charlie McCreevy (Ireland), from 2004 to 2010, followed by Michel Barnier (France), from 2010 to 2014, Jonathan Hill (UK), from 2014 to 2016 and Valdis Dombrovskis (Latvia), from 2016 to 2019.

41 Established by Commission Decision 2004/9/EC of 5 November 2003, *OJ* L 3, 7.1.2004, p. 34, which replaced the Insurance Committee, established by Council Directive 91/675/EEC of 19 December 1991, *OJ* L 374, 31.12.1991, p. 32.

Intense consultation took place with a number of organisations that represented various stakeholder groups:

- insurance industry: the Comité Européen des Assurances (CEA),[42] which became Insurance Europe in 2012,[43] and the Pan-European Insurance Forum (PEIF);
- mutual insurers: the Association internationale des sociétés d'assurance mutuelle (AISAM) and the Association des assureurs coopératifs et mutualistes européens (ACME), which merged into the Association of Mutual Insurers and Insurance Cooperatives in Europe (AMICE) in 2008;
- chief risk officers: the Chief Risk Officers Forum (CRO Forum);
- chief financial officers: the Chief Financial Officers Forum (CFO Forum);
- actuarial profession: Groupe Consultatif,[44] which later became the Actuarial Association of Europe (AAE);
- users: the Forum of User Experts in the Area of Financial Services (FIN-USE).

Other parties, such as the European Federation of Accountants (FEE), the Federation of European Risk Management Associations (FERMA), the European Captive Insurance and Reinsurance Owners Association (ECIROA) and the European Federation of Insurance Intermediaries (BIPAR) also intervened in the process when issues were discussed that were particularly relevant to them.

Many of the organisations listed above are now directly or indirectly represented in the Insurance and Reinsurance Stakeholder Group (IRSG) of EIOPA, which succeeded CEIOPS in 2011 (see further, Chapter 11, section 1).

Input was also delivered by organisations from countries outside the EEA, particularly from Bermuda (Association of Bermuda Insurers and Reinsurers (ABIR)), Japan (General Insurance Association of Japan (GIAJ) and Life Insurance Association of Japan (LIAJ)), Switzerland (Swiss Insurance Association (ASA/SVV)) and the USA (Group of North American Insurance Enterprises (GNAIE), American Council of Life Insurers (ACLI), Property Casualty Insurers Association of America (PCI), American Insurance

[42] Established in Paris in 1953 to represent the insurance industry in the Insurance Committee of the OEEC, later OECD. It later moved its seat to Brussels.

[43] Besides Insurance Europe, the European Federation of Insurers and Reinsurers, several of its member bodies played a very active role in the negotiations and intervened regularly in the consultation process. For a list of these member bodies, see the website of Insurance Europe.

[44] The Groupe Consultatif was established in 1978 to bring together the actuarial associations in the EU to represent the actuarial profession in discussions with the EU institutions. Its original name was: Groupe Consultatif des Associations d'Actuaires des Etats-Membres des Communautés Européennes. In 2002, its name was changed to Groupe Consultatif Actuariel Européen and in 2014 to AAE.

Association (AIA), Reinsurance Association of America (RAA), and National Association of Mutual Insurance Companies (NAMIC)).[45]

Several organisations listed above produced numerous documents on specific aspects of Solvency II.[46] This was especially so for the CEA (now Insurance Europe), which drafted a large number of papers that were made available on its website.[47] Particularly interesting is the Solvency II glossary, which was developed by the CEA and the Groupe Consultatif, which helped a great deal in the discussions.[48]

In terms of transparency, all documents under discussion were made available on the EC's website. Before decisions were taken, all drafts were circulated for comments both by the EC and by CEIOPS. Important letters addressed by the EC to CEIOPS or by CEIOPS to the EC were made available to the public on the Commission's website and on that of CEIOPS. The EC regularly suggested to CEIOPS that it make official letters from the EC available on its website. It is fair to say that in these initial stages of the development of Solvency II, all persons who were interested in the development of the new solvency regime had easy access to all relevant material and were able to find a listening ear with the EC and CEIOPS.

The EC also engaged in a regular dialogue with the EP during the preparation of the Solvency II project, particularly with the Chair of ECON (Pervenche Berès, S&D/France) and with the Solvency II Rapporteur (Peter Skinner, S&D/UK). It was not uncommon for the EC to send consultation documents that were put on its website to the Chair of ECON for information purposes.[49]

---

45 Many comments were also received from individual (re)insurance undertakings both from within and from outside the EEA.

46 During the development of the proposal, but also during the negotiations in the Council and in the EP, many discussions took place between experts on various aspects of Solvency II. Particularly useful were the annual meetings organised by Esko Kivisaari from the Finnish Insurance Association (later Finance Finland) in Finland where experts from the EC, the Groupe Consultatif, CEIOPS/EIOPA, NSAs, Ministries of Finance, the CRO Forum, CEA/Insurance Europe, AISAM/AMICE and from (re)insurance undertakings discussed possible solutions for the many complex issues that were on the table, in a friendly and musical atmosphere.

47 See, for instance, CEA, *Solvency II – Frequently asked questions*, February 2007, 19 p. Many interesting documents were also published by member bodies of Insurance Europe. The list of these members can be found on Insurance Europe's website.

48 CEA and Groupe Consultatif, *Solvency II Glossary*, March 2007, 68 p.

49 See, for instance, the letter of 18 May 2005 by the Director-General of DG Markt to Pervenche Berès concerning the third wave of specific calls for advice, in which the EC explained the approach it intended to follow in preparing the Solvency II project.

CHAPTER 3

DEVELOPMENT AND ADOPTION OF SOLVENCY II

1. DEVELOPMENT OF SOLVENCY II

The Solvency II project[1] was prepared on the basis of a Roadmap that was continuously updated by the Commission Services, in close cooperation with MS representatives in the Insurance Committee.[2] The Roadmap was adopted on 30 June 2004[3] and initially provided for the preparation of a Framework Directive by the end of 2005 and for the adoption of detailed legislation by means of implementing measures in the period 2005–2008. The Roadmap was put on the Commission's website and was communicated to CEIOPS and to the Chair of the Economic and Monetary Affairs Committee (EMAC)[4] of the EP.[5]

In order to prepare the FD, the Roadmap proposed the adoption of a general Framework for Consultation. This framework set out the main principles of the new solvency regime and served as a basis for further consultation of CEIOPS (and other stakeholders) and for three waves of specific calls for advice addressed to CEIOPS.

1.1. FRAMEWORK FOR CONSULTATION

Preparatory work for Solvency II really started with the adoption of a "Framework for Consultation on Solvency II", which built on the main design

---

1 For a description of the early stages of the Solvency II project and the input of the actuarial profession, see STÖLTING, R., *Auf dem Weg zu Solvency II: Aktueller Stand*, 8 November 2004, 16 p., http://www.mi.uni-koeln.de/~jost/stoelting2.pdf.

2 The Insurance Committee was a regulatory committee composed of MS representatives and chaired by a representative of the EC. It was created by Council Directive 91/675/EEC of 19 December 1991, *OJ* L 374, 31.12.1991, p. 32.

3 See EC, DG Markt, Note to the members of the EIOPC: Solvency II Roadmap towards a Framework Directive, Markt/2506/04, June 2004.

4 Now the Committee on Economic and Monetary Affairs (ECON).

5 See EC, DG Markt, Note to the members of the EIOPC, Solvency II Roadmap towards a Framework Directive, Markt/2502/05-rev. 2, July 2005.

features and architecture of the new Solvency II system that had been agreed between the EC and interested parties (including Member States and insurance supervisors).

It was agreed that the new solvency regime should:
- assess "overall solvency";
- be based on a Basel II-type three-pillar structure, adapted to insurance;
- build on a more risk-oriented approach, with incentives for proper risk management;
- increase harmonisation of quantitative and qualitative supervisory methods;
- seek more efficient supervision of insurance groups and financial conglomerates;
- employ "Lamfalussy" or comitology techniques to adopt/adapt legislation efficiently;
- ensure consistency between financial sectors;
- be developed in parallel with international developments at the IAIS, and in particular be compatible with the estimated outcome of the IASB's work (insurance contracts – Phase II).

The Framework for Consultation, prepared by the Commission Services on 14 July 2004, in close cooperation with MS experts, with CEIOPS and with other interested parties, served as a basis for the development of the new solvency regime. It was published on the EC's website and only comprised five pages.[6]

As stated in the document, the Framework for Consultation "provides a framework for CEIOPS and other stakeholders in connection with the development of a new solvency system (Solvency II) for life insurance, non-life insurance and reinsurance undertakings".

Anybody interested in the development of Solvency II should go back to this document, which covered the totality of the Solvency II project. It set out the policy principles and guidelines within which CEIOPS was asked to develop its advice. The advice to be delivered by CEIOPS was partly organised through "specific calls for advice" to CEIOPS launched by the EC, after consultation of the Insurance Committee, and partly initiated by CEIOPS itself, as CEIOPS was expected to carry out work on specific topics, on its own initiative, inspired by the policy principles and guidelines of the Framework for Consultation and by papers developed by the Commission Services.

In line with the principle of transparency, all interested parties were invited to contribute to the development of the new solvency system within the lines drawn by the Framework for Consultation. Their input was communicated by

---

6 EC, DG Markt, Framework for consultation on Solvency II, Markt/2509/03, 14 July 2004, 5 p.

the EC to CEIOPS. Interested parties could also address themselves to CEIOPS directly, with a copy to the Commission Services.

It was expected that the Framework for Consultation would be regularly updated and that it would serve as a dynamic reference document for the development of Solvency II. CEIOPS was invited to inform the EC if it felt that the Framework should be revised or that a choice should be made between several possible alternatives, analysing the advantages and disadvantages of the alternatives.

In fact, the Framework document was only updated twice, the first time in July 2005[7] and a second time in April 2006.[8] The second amendment took place at the request of CEIOPS and after discussions within the Solvency Working Group of the EIOPC, the successor of the Insurance Committee.[9] The document was still relatively short (nine pages). The most important change related to paragraph 16 dealing with technical provisions. The question had arisen during a members' meeting of CEIOPS as to whether a market-consistent valuation of technical provisions implied that technical provisions would have to be discounted. One CEIOPS member believed that this was not the case as this did not follow clearly from the text of the Framework for Consultation. The Commission observer, present at the meeting, agreed with the majority of the members of CEIOPS that discounting was the only possible interpretation and promised to update the Framework so as to clarify this point. Paragraph 16 of the Framework was redrafted to explain how technical provisions would have to be measured in the solvency balance sheet, i.e. as the sum of the best estimate and a risk margin and that the best estimate equalled the expected present value of future cash flows, using the relevant risk-free yield curve, based upon current and credible information and realistic assumptions (discounting).

The main elements of the Amended Framework for Consultation can be summarised as follows:

1. *General Features of the New Solvency Regime*
   (a) The new solvency regime should provide supervisors with the appropriate tools and powers to assess the "overall solvency" of (re)insurance undertakings based on a prospective and risk-oriented approach.
   (b) The solvency system should take as its starting point the three-pillar structure developed by Basel II and included in the Capital

7 The document was sent by the Commission Services to the Chair of CEIOPS on 15 July 2005, following discussions in the Insurance Committee.

8 EC, DG Markt, Amended Framework for Consultation on Solvency II, Markt/2515/06, April 2006, 9 p.

9 The Insurance Committee was an advisory committee to the EC composed of MS experts, usually from the ministries of finance. It was replaced by the EIOPC as part of the Lamfalussy reform. See below, section 1.4.

Requirements Directive (CRD). However, the individual pillars did not have to be identical to Basel II.

(c) There should be two capital requirements with different purposes: the solvency capital requirement (SCR) and the minimum capital requirement (MCR). The SCR should not be lower than the MCR.

(d) The solvency system should provide an incentive to insurers to measure and manage their risks. The SCR should cover the quantifiable risks. Internal models should be allowed, provided they improved an insurer's risk management, better reflected its true risk profile than under the standard formula and could be appropriately validated.

(e) An internal model could result in a higher or lower amount of the SCR than the amount calculated on the basis of the standard formula. Supervisors should be able to require undertakings for which the activities deviated substantially from the assumptions underlying the standard formula to develop an internal model.

(f) Appropriate attention should be paid to group supervision (group internal model, recognition of diversification benefits, appropriate split of responsibilities between supervisors, sufficient capital at solo level but possibility to streamline the capital).

(g) Valuation rules for assets and liabilities in the solvency balance sheet should be compatible with International Accounting Standards/International Financial Reporting Standards (IAS/IFRS), although there could be additions or adjustments. There should however be no requirement for all insurance undertakings to prepare their financial statements in accordance with IAS/IFRS. Simplifications could be justified for certain types of insurance undertakings.

(h) There should be a high level of harmonisation of the solvency requirements with uniform application and sufficient consumer protection whilst supporting fair competition.

(i) There should be a uniform level of prudence for the calculation of the technical provisions and the SCR.

(j) Regulatory arbitrage between the solvency rules for banks and for insurance undertakings should be avoided.

(k) Compatibility should be insured with the solvency work carried out by the IAIS, the Groupe Consultatif and the IAA.

(l) In order to evaluate the impact of the new solvency regime, quantitative impact studies (QIS) should be carried out by CEIOPS in cooperation with the insurance industry and the EC's proposal should be accompanied by an impact assessment that should have a broader scope and be less detailed than a QIS.

(m) The calibration of the new solvency regime should not take into consideration the existence of an insurance guarantee scheme (protection of last resort for policyholders). The new solvency regime should provide enough safety and confidence in the insurance industry without relying on guarantee schemes.

(n) Solvency II should not be overly costly to small insurance undertakings. Small undertakings should respect the same principles as all other undertakings but there could be reasons to provide for specific rules for them.

(o) Solvency II should take due account of the particularities of reinsurance undertakings.

2. *Quantitative Requirements (Pillar 1)*

(a) Technical provisions should be prudent, reliable and objective and allow comparisons between insurance undertakings. They should make optimal use of and be consistent with information provided by the financial markets and generally available data on insurance technical risks.

Technical provisions should be the sum of a best estimate and a risk margin. The best estimate should equal the expected present value of future cash flows, using the relevant risk-free yield curve, based upon current and credible information and realistic assumptions. No surrender value floors should be applied to the calculation of technical provisions.

The risk margin should cover the risks linked to the future liability cash flows over their whole time horizon. Two possible ways to calculate the risk margin should be considered as working hypotheses: a calculation as the difference between the 75th percentile of the underlying probability distribution until run-off and the best estimate, whereby the risk margin should at a minimum be equal to half a standard deviation in order to take account of strongly skewed distributions or a calculation based on the cost of providing SCR capital to support the business in force until run-off. The specificities of life and non-life insurance might require different treatments.

(b) The SCR should reflect a level of capital that enables an undertaking to absorb significant unforeseen losses and that gives reasonable assurance to policyholders and beneficiaries. The confidence level should be set at a ruin probability of 0.5% (value at risk of 99.5%) with a one-year time horizon as a working hypothesis. The SCR should be calculated on a going-concern basis. The principles underlying the calculation of the SCR should be the same under the standard formula and under an internal model. When an undertaking does not meet the SCR, it should re-establish the amount of capital covering the SCR in due time, based on a concrete and realisable plan submitted to the supervisor for approval.

(c) The standard formula for the calculation of the SCR could be based on a variety of methods, for example a factor-based formula, a probability-distribution-based formula, scenarios or combinations thereof. The specificities of life, non-life and reinsurance business should be recognised.
(d) The MCR should reflect a level of capital below which ultimate supervisory action would be triggered. The level of the MCR should be set after carrying out quantitative impact studies. It should be calculated in a more simple and robust manner than the SCR. In order to facilitate the transition to the new overall solvency system, the MCR should be construed in a straightforward manner as under Solvency I, while maintaining a sufficient level of prudence. It should have an absolute floor.
(e) The SCR should include the following quantifiable risks based upon the IAA risk classification: underwriting risk, credit risk, market risk, operational risk and liquidity risk. To the extent that these risks were not quantifiable, they should be taken into account in Pillar 2.
(f) Internal models should be allowed to replace the standard formula, subject to validation. The validation criteria should be developed and harmonised. Partial internal models should also be allowed, subject to validation and compatibility with the standard formula.

3. *Supervisory Activities (Pillar 2)*
(a) Supervisory action should aim at identifying undertakings with financial, organisational or other features susceptible to producing a higher risk profile. Such institutions should be required to hold more capital and/or to take measures to reduce the risks incurred.
(b) Supervisory methods, tools and powers should be harmonised.
(c) Supervisory activities should include increased cooperation between supervisors combined with peer reviews.

4. *Supervisory Reporting and Public Disclosure (Pillar 3)*
(a) Reporting from insurance undertakings to their supervisors should be an important part of the future regulatory architecture in the EU. Such reporting should go beyond financial reporting and include different types of information that a supervisor needs in order to perform his tasks.
(b) Transparency and disclosure of information to the public should serve to reinforce market mechanisms and discipline.
(c) Supervisory reporting and public disclosure requirements should be in line with those developed by the IAIS and by the IASB in order to reduce the administrative burden. They should also be compatible with disclosure requirements in the banking sector. It should be

possible to make additions and adjustments, as long as specific reasons are given. Proper consideration should be paid to confidentiality issues.

5. *Role to be Played by CEIOPS*[10]

The Amended Framework for Consultation recognised the important role CEIOPS had to play in developing the new solvency regime. CEIOPS was asked to provide regular progress reports at four-monthly intervals, to assist the EC in the preparation of potential mandates for the development of measures implementing the FD and to develop supervisory recommendations.

Six progress reports on the Solvency II Project were submitted by CEIOPS to the EC during the preparatory stage: the reports were dated 3 November 2004,[11] 25 February 2005,[12] 30 June 2005,[13] 9 December 2005,[14] 3 March 2006[15] and 4 July 2006.[16]

In order to deal with the various requests from the EC, CEIOPS set up an ad hoc structure with a number of expert groups. The most important expert group was the Pillar 1 expert group, split into a Pillar 1 Life expert group and a Pillar 1 Non-Life expert group. Other expert groups dealt with Pillar 2 issues, with Pillar 3 and accounting issues, and with group/cross-sectoral issues. Data collection (including QISs) was dealt with within CEIOPS' financial stability committee. These experts groups became later the Financial Requirements Expert Group (FinReq), the Internal Governance, Supervisory Review and Reporting Expert Group (IGSRR), the Internal Models Expert Group (IntMod), the Insurance Groups Supervision Committee (IGSC), and the Financial Stability Committee (FSC).

---

10 More information about CEIOPS' work in the context of Solvency II can be found in the Annual Reports which were published by CEIOPS and later by its successor, EIOPA.

11 CEIOPS, First Progress Report to the EC on CEIOPS' work in the field of the Solvency II project, CEIOPS-SEC-22/04, 4 p.

12 CEIOPS, Second Progress Report to the EC on CEIOPS' work in the field of the Solvency II project, CEIOPS-SEC-17/05, 21 p.

13 CEIOPS, Third Progress Report to the EC on CEIOPS' work in the field of the Solvency II project, CEIOPS-SEC-53/05, 11 p.

14 CEIOPS, Fourth Progress Report to the EC on CEIOPS' work in the field of the Solvency II project, CEIOPS-SEC-115/05, 3 p.

15 CEIOPS, Fifth Progress Report to the EC on CEIOPS' work in the field of the Solvency II project, CEIOPS-SEC-07/06, 4 p.

16 CEIOPS, Sixth Progress Report to the EC on CEIOPS' work in the field of the Solvency II project, CEIOPS-SEC-47/06, 3 p.

1.2. SPECIFIC CALLS FOR ADVICE

The EC sent three waves of specific calls for advice to CEIOPS asking questions on various topics that were crucial for the development of the new solvency regime. The specific calls for advice imposed tight deadlines on CEIOPS. It is remarkable that CEIOPS managed to respect these challenging deadlines. This was only possible because of the dedicated efforts from NSAs and from a small secretariat based in Frankfurt under the successive chairmanships of Henrik Bjerre-Nielsen (Denmark), Thomas Steffen (Germany) and Gabriel Bernardino (Portugal), assisted by Alberto Corinti (Italy) and Carlos Montalvo (Spain) as successive Secretaries-General.

The draft responses from CEIOPS were published for comments. CEIOPS also organised public hearings on the calls for advice in Frankfurt for interested parties.

The calls for advice to CEIOPS were published as annexes to the Framework for Consultation.

The *first wave* of specific calls for advice was published in July 2004 and dealt primarily with Pillar 2 issues:

- internal control and risk management;
- supervisory review process (in general);
- supervisory review process (quantitative tools);
- transparency of supervisory action;
- investment management rules;
- asset–liability management.

The advice from CEIOPS was delivered on 30 June 2005.[17]

The *second wave* of specific calls for advice was published in December 2004 and dealt mainly with Pillar 1 issues:

- technical provisions in life assurance;
- technical provisions in non-life assurance;
- safety measures;
- SCR: standard formula (life and non-life);
- SCR: internal models (life and non-life) and their validation;
- reinsurance (and other risk mitigation techniques);
- quantitative impact study and data-related issues;
- powers of the supervisory authorities;
- solvency control levels;

[17] See CEIOPS, Answers to the EC on the "First Wave" of Calls for Advice in the framework of the Solvency II Project, CEIOPS-DOC-03/05, 40 p.

- fit and proper criteria;
- peer reviews;
- group and cross-sectoral issues.

The advice from CEIOPS was delivered on 31 October 2005.[18]

The *third wave* of specific calls for advice was published in April 2005 and dealt mainly with Pillar 3 issues:

- eligible elements to cover the capital requirements;
- cooperation between supervisory authorities;
- supervisory reporting and public disclosure;
- pro-cyclicality;
- small undertakings.

A public hearing was organised by the EC on 11 January 2006 on this third wave of Specific Calls for Advice. The advice from CEIOPS was delivered on 31 May 2006.[19]

Besides these specific calls for advice, CEIOPS delivered a great deal of other advice, very often on its own initiative, which was helpful in the drafting of the Proposal for the Solvency II FD:

- Advice on sub-group supervision, diversification effects, cooperation with third countries and issues related to the MCR and SCR in a group context[20] (3 November 2006);
- Advice on insurance undertakings' Internal Risk and Capital Assessment requirements, supervisors' evaluation procedures and harmonised supervisors' powers and tools[21] (3 November 2006);
- Advice on safety measures (Limits on Assets)[22] (20 March 2007);
- Advice on supervisory powers – Further advice[23] (20 March 2007);
- Advice on Pillar II Capital add-ons for solo and group undertakings[24] (20 March 2007);
- Advice on Pillar II issues relevant for reinsurance[25] (20 March 2007);

---

18 See CEIOPS, Answers to the EC on the "Second Wave" of Calls for Advice in the framework of the Solvency II Project, CEIOPS-DOC-07/05, 279 p.

19 See CEIOPS, Answers to the EC on the "Third Wave" of Calls for Advice in the framework of the Solvency II Project, CEIOPS-DOC-03/06, 155 p.

20 CEIOPS-DOC-05/06, 31 p.

21 CEIOPS-DOC-06/06, 12 p.

22 CEIOPS-DOC-07/07, 21 p.

23 CEIOPS-DOC-06/07, 28 p.

24 CEIOPS-DOC-05/07, 15 p.

25 CEIOPS-DOC-04/07, 16 p.

- Advice on supervisory reporting and public disclosure[26] (20 March 2007);
- Advice on Pillar I issues – Further advice[27] (26 March 2007).

Article 5 of the EC's Decision 2004/6/EC,[28] which established CEIOPS, required CEIOPS to consult extensively and in an open and transparent manner with market participants, consumers and end-users, before transmitting an opinion to the EC. The consultation period was normally three months, unless the tight deadlines imposed by the EC made this impossible. In that case, CEIOPS tried to accommodate stakeholders by organising public hearings. Comments received were published on CEIOPS' website unless the respondents requested otherwise.[29]

1.3. QUANTITATIVE IMPACT STUDIES

As indicated in the Framework for Consultation, it was the intention to carry out a number of quantitative impact studies (QISs), which would help in the design and calibration of the new solvency regime. Five QISs were carried out by CEIOPS and, as of 2011, by EIOPA at the request of the EC, based upon technical specifications that were developed by CEIOPS/EIOPA and were agreed in advance between the EC and MS experts in the EIOPC's Solvency Working Group. The drafts of the technical specifications for each QIS were published for consultation before their finalisation. The QIS exercises were very useful and contributed a lot to preparing both the industry and supervisory authorities for Solvency II.

Each NSA that wished to participate in the QIS invited a range of different types and sizes of undertakings to carry out the exercise and submitted its country report to CEIOPS/EIOPA. The EC always asked for a certain minimum coverage, including a representative sample of small and medium-sized (re)insurance undertakings and captives.

The first two QISs were carried out before the EC presented its proposal for a FD. QIS 3 and QIS 4 took place during the negotiation of the Solvency II FD in the Council and in the EP. QIS 5 was carried out after the adoption of the FD and served as the preparation for the implementing measures. The number of participating undertakings increased with each QIS.

---

26 CEIOPS-DOC-03/07, 20 p.

27 CEIOPS-DOC-08/07, 206 p.

28 Commission Decision 2004/6/EC of 5 November 2003 establishing CEIOPS, *OJ* L 3, 7.1.2004, p. 34.

29 CEIOPS, Public Statement of Consultation Practices, CEIOPS-DOC-01/05, February 2005, 4 p. See also EIOPA, Public Statement of Consultation Practices, EIOPA-BoS-11-016, July 2011, 3 p.

QIS 1 was carried out between October 2005 and March 2006. It was preceded by a preparatory field study[30] covering a representative sample of life insurance undertakings.

The objective was to test the level of prudence in technical provisions under several hypotheses. The calculations were generally based on data as at the end of the financial year 2004. 312 undertakings from 19 countries participated in QIS 1. For the 259 undertakings for which the size category (based on national definitions) was provided, 68 were classified as small, 90 as medium-sized and 101 as large.

In its report of 17 March 2006,[31] CEIOPS concluded that – even though the data may not have been representative of the whole EEA – the first QIS gave valuable information on the impact of the best estimate and the risk margin, on the required technical provisions and on the ability of undertakings to perform the requested calculations. An important conclusion was that the amount of the best estimate plus the risk margin tended to be lower than the current level of technical provisions.[32]

QIS 2 was carried out between June 2006 and October 2006. The calculations were generally based on data as at the end of the financial year 2005. The objective was to further test the approach for the calculation of technical provisions and to provide a first test for the development of the SCR and the MCR. In total, 514 undertakings from 23 countries participated in QIS 2, an increase of 65% over QIS 1. To the extent that the size classification was indicated, 155 undertakings were classified as small, 220 as medium-sized and 132 as large.

In its report of 8 December 2006,[33] CEIOPS concluded that, in terms of the calculation of the technical provisions, most respondents had a clear preference for the cost-of-capital approach (proposed by the CEA and the CRO Forum and also applied in the Swiss Solvency Test) over the 75th-percentile approach for the calculation of the risk margin, because of the former's simplicity. As for the method of calculating the SCR, a preference was expressed for a scenario-based approach for market interest rate risk and for life underwriting risk. The interplay between the SCR and the MCR needed to be revised as there was a risk that in some instances the MCR could exceed the SCR or that the two control levels would be too close to each other. In general, participants felt that too many hypotheses had been tested and that more guidance was necessary.

In terms of the overall financial impact, using the QIS 2 methodology and parameters, the technical provisions generally decreased and the capital

30 CEIOPS, Preparatory Field Study for Life Insurance Firms – Summary Report, CEIOPS-FS-08/05, 15 p.

31 CEIOPS, QIS 1 – Summary Report, CEIOPS-FS-01/06, 38 p.

32 An important reason for this was, of course, that technical provisions were generally not discounted under Solvency I.

33 CEIOPS, QIS 2 – Summary Report, CEIOPS-SEC-71/06S, 61 p.

requirements increased. However, the available capital represented by the excess of the value of assets over liabilities also increased (because of the decrease in technical provisions as a result of discounting).

QIS 3 was conducted between April 2007 and June 2007. The key objectives of QIS 3 were to gather information about the practicability and suitability of the calculations involved, about the impact on balance sheets and the amount of capital needed to cover the SCR, about the suitability of the calibration for the SCR and the MCR and about the effect of applying the QIS 3 specifications to insurance groups. The calculations were generally based on data as at the end of the financial year 2006.

Both the number of (re)insurers and the number of participating countries increased in comparison to the preceding QIS exercises.[34] In total, 28 out of 30 EEA countries participated in the study. New in the sample were Bulgaria, Cyprus, Greece, Latvia and Slovakia. The total number of solo undertakings was 1,027, i.e. an increase of almost 100% over QIS 2. In terms of size, 422 undertakings were classified as small, 418 as medium-sized and 187 as large. 51 groups also participated in the study.

In its report of 21 November 2007,[35] CEIOPS concluded that the new regime did not appear to require extra capital in the European market as a whole, although there would be a redistribution process as a consequence of introducing a risk-based capital regime, where capital requirements would be in line with the risks assumed by the undertaking and the way in which these risks were managed and controlled. Technical provisions tended to decrease, thereby increasing available capital, as the implicit prudence in the current regime was removed. As for the capital requirements, the vast majority (98%) of companies would not need additional capital to meet the MCR. For most participating undertakings, the SCR ratio under Solvency II was lower than the current solvency ratio under Solvency I.

QIS 3 was particularly important for the design of the MCR. This matter had been left open in the proposed FD: a choice had to be made between the option of the MCR being a stand-alone capital requirement and the option of taking the MCR as a percentage of the SCR (the so-called compact approach, favoured by the industry). QIS 3 was also the first test on group solvency. Particularly important in this context was the issue of diversification benefits.

In the meantime, the EC had submitted its proposal for the Solvency II FD on 10 July 2007 (see further, section 1.4).

---

34 For a table showing the increasing participation in the QIS, see PRADIER, P.-C. and CHNEIWEISS, A., *The evolution of insurance regulation in the EU since 2005*, Documents de travail du Centre d'Economie de la Sorbonne, 2016, p. 11, https://halshs.archives-ouvertes.fr/halshs-01390899/documents.

35 CEIOPS, Report on its third Quantitative Impact Study (QIS) for Solvency II – Public report, CEIOPS-DOC-07/19, 191 p.

QIS 4 was carried out between April 2008 and June 2008. The key objectives of QIS 4 were to design the technical specifications in such a manner that they were aligned with the principles and calibration target in the proposed FD, to provide all stakeholders with information on the detailed quantitative impact of Solvency II and to encourage all stakeholders to begin preparations for the implementation of Solvency II. There was particular focus on the proportionality principle for smaller undertakings and the test of simplified methods for the calculation of technical provisions, on the calculation of the group capital requirements with respect to intra-group diversification and intra-group transactions, the comparability of results derived from the standard formula, partial and full internal models and the design and calibration of the new MCR formula.

In its call for advice, the EC had set out a target participation rate of 25% of solo undertakings and 60% of cross-border groups. This participation target was largely met and all 30 EEA countries participated in the study. In total, 1,412 companies participated, of which 667 were small, 522 medium-sized and 220 large.[36] 111 groups from 16 EEA countries plus Switzerland participated in the group part of the study. This figure included more than 60% of cross-border groups and a significant number of mutual groups. Captives were introduced as a separate category. This was a specific request from the EC. Captives had so far not been much involved in the discussions and the EC wanted to know how Solvency II would affect them and whether specific measures were needed for this sector. The data used were end 2007 data.

In its report of 19 November 2008,[37] CEIOPS concluded again that for the European insurance industry as a whole, Solvency II would not require additional capital. With respect to the solvency levels, the vast majority (98.8%) of undertakings were able to meet the MCR as tested in QIS 4. The situation was worse for captives, where almost 7% of the participating captives did not meet the MCR. Almost 11% of the participating undertakings did not meet the SCR under QIS 4 compared to 16% under QIS 3. For captives, the number was higher: 28.3%.

The results of QIS 4 were particularly important for the development of the implementing measures of the Solvency II FD. They were published in the middle of the financial crisis. It was therefore no surprise that questions were raised concerning the measurement of assets and liabilities at fair value. Although most participants continued to favour an economic balance sheet,[38]

---

36 Three undertakings could not be classified according to their size class.

37 CEIOPS, Report on its fourth Quantitative Impact Study (QIS) for Solvency II, CEIOPS-SEC-82/08, 398 p.

38 A balance sheet based on an accounting approach using market-consistent values for all current assets and liabilities. See further, Chapter 6, section 1.

it was recognised that there was a need to avoid pro-cyclical effects, in particular in times of severe market stress.

QIS 5 was conducted between August and November 2010. It was the first field test of Solvency II, based upon data from the financial year 2009. The draft technical specifications prepared by CEIOPS in 2010 were heavily criticised by the industry.[39] An article in the *Financial Times* alleged that if this were to be the final calibration, Solvency II would involve a considerable increase in capital for the European insurance industry. A figure of €500 billion in additional capital was suggested.

Whilst CEIOPS argued that the financial crisis urged them to follow a more restrictive approach on issues such as capital, technical provisions, own funds, calibration and correlation between risks, the industry complained that CEIOPS failed to look at the overall impact of its advice and that the CEIOPS proposals would lead to excessive capital requirements for an industry that was not the cause of the financial crisis.[40]

The controversies surrounding the expected impact of CEIOPS' advice led the Commission Services to ask CEIOPS to compare the impact of its final advice with the results of QIS 4. In CEIOPS' letter of 8 April 2010 to the EC, in which it presented its final advice on the implementing measures, CEIOPS indicated that a preliminary analysis showed that its final advice would on the one hand lead to an increase in the SCR compared with QIS 4 but on the other hand to a decrease in the level of technical provisions as a result of the inclusion of an illiquidity premium in the risk-free discount rate.

Regarding QIS 5, the Commission Services carried out a targeted consultation on the draft technical specifications between 15 April and 20 May 2010, including a QIS 5 stakeholder meeting on 30 April 2010 and a public hearing on 4 May 2010. In its note to the EIOPC of 24 June 2010, the Commission Services explained the changes which they proposed after the consultations. These changes resulted in a reduction of the capital requirements for a number of risks. This was not welcomed by CEIOPS, and the Commission observer was severely criticised at a CEIOPS members' meeting looking at the final text of the technical specifications. Many members of CEIOPS were of the view that the

---

39 See, for instance, the letter from PEIF of 9 December 2009 to Gabriel Bernardino, Chairman of CEIOPS, in which the Chairman of PEIF, Henri de Castries, asked "why the European insurance industry would have to increase its capital by hundreds of billions of euros when it did not need any additional capital in the face of the crisis". See also the letter from the CEA of 2 September 2009 to Thomas Steffen, Chairman of CEIOPS, which argued that "the concerns of the European industry are amplified by the impossibility of using the solutions proposed by CEIOPS, which are radically different from the tentative solutions tested in the past four rounds of QIS, as a basis for the specifications of QIS 5".

40 See CEA, *Why excessive capital requirements harm consumers, insurers and the economy*, March 2010, 36 p.

lower capital requirements were not in line with the confidence level that had been agreed to in the Solvency II FD.

In its letter to CEIOPS of 5 July 2010, the EC underlined that QIS 5 was a test which aimed at collecting additional empirical data that might help to improve the final calibration. In several cases, it was not possible to identify one single method or calibration to be tested. In a number of cases, the technical specifications therefore included multiple calculations. Undertakings were asked to carry out both calculations in order to ensure that a comparison of the results could be made.

As QIS 5 was the last major test, the results were crucial for the final calibration and for other elements of the level 2 implementing measures (the calculation of own funds and of technical provisions). CEIOPS was therefore urged to ensure a high participation rate from the industry (at least 60% of solo undertakings, which meant about 2,000 undertakings, and 75% of insurance groups, which meant about 100 groups). In order to stimulate participation by small and medium-sized insurers, CEIOPS was asked to make the spreadsheets user-friendly and to develop a QIS 5 manual. CEIOPS managed to outperform these targets. Whilst 33% of undertakings participated in QIS 4 (the target set by the EC was 25%), 77% of solo undertakings participated in QIS 5 (the target set by the EC was 60%). All 30 EEA member countries participated in the test. In total, 2,520 (re)insurers, as well as 167 groups,[41] participated. In total, more than 95% of technical provisions and 85% of premiums of the insurers subject to Solvency II were covered by the test.[42]

In its report of 14 March 2011,[43] EIOPA, the successor to CEIOPS set up in 2011, welcomed the high participation rate:

> "This shows that EIOPA has succeeded in engaging with supervisors and industry in the regulatory and supervisory discussion, which will continue to benefit the implementation efforts in the future months. It indicates that Solvency II has become a priority to all insurers, regardless of size, and that (re)insurance undertakings and groups are striving to be ready for the implementation date of 1st January 2013."[44]

In terms of the financial impact of the new solvency regime, EIOPA started its report by pointing out the differences between Solvency I and Solvency II. Because of the market-consistent valuation of assets and liabilities under

41 As opposed to 106 groups under QIS 4.

42 The participation increased remarkably from QIS 4.

43 EIOPA, Report on the fifth Quantitative Impact Study (QIS 5) for Solvency II, EIOPA-TFQIS5-11/01, 153 p.

44 The EC had just published its Omnibus II proposal, in which it had proposed postponing the application date for Solvency II from 1 November 2012 to 1 January 2013 (see below, section 4.1).

Solvency II, the immediate difference was an average increase in the level of own funds as compared to Solvency I due to a simultaneous decrease of technical provisions and, depending on the accounting rules applied in participating countries, an increase in the value of assets. At European level, the SCR increased when compared to the current required solvency margin under Solvency I, with the MCR in Solvency II being below or close to the required solvency margin under Solvency I. On the other hand, because of the financial crisis, the financial surplus of the insurance sector, calculated under Solvency I rules, had decreased markedly from €600 billion at the end of 2007 to €500 billion at the end of 2009. In the view of EIOPA, this overall reduction in terms of surplus was not likely to endanger the sustainability of the sector.

At European level, 15% of participants did not fully cover the SCR, and just under 5% of the participants did not meet the MCR.

EIOPA concluded that the design of Solvency II had received broad support and that the calibrations had been generally accepted as appropriate. There were however specific areas where more work was needed, for instance natural catastrophe risk and the non-life underwriting risk, particularly for very specialised insurers.[45]

Finally, EIOPA pointed to the need to have anti-cyclical mechanisms, such as Pillar 1 and Pillar 2 dampeners, to address the volatility inherent in a market-consistent valuation and concluded with some critical observations concerning the transitional measures proposed by the EC (see below, section 4.1) in Omnibus II:

> "Transitional measures, per essence limited, are needed, particularly to ensure sound competition based on a level playing field and to allow for a smooth transition from Solvency I to Solvency II. But such measures should not be prolonged in time unduly ... Too many transitional measures on too many topics as well as too much time will strongly disincentivise the shift towards Solvency II and risk-based supervision or have adverse effects on competition."

The EC very much welcomed the results of QIS 5, which were made public when the discussions on Omnibus II started. The EC was particularly pleased that the results of QIS 5 showed, against expectations from industry,[46] that the vast majority of European (re)insurers would be in a position to meet the new

45 This was particularly an issue for French mutual non-life insurers specialising in professional liability insurance, who could not benefit from diversification effects as they were specialised in one particular type of insurance.

46 The industry was still unhappy about the complexity and the exaggerated level of prudence in the draft implementing measures prepared by EIOPA and particularly about EIOPA's reluctance to accept a treatment of expected profits in future premiums as Tier 1 capital (see further, Chapter 6, section 3). See CEA, *Solvency II: Making it workable for all*, January 2011, 12 p.

Solvency II capital requirements. It was however agreed that the concerns about volatility had to be taken seriously and that more work was needed to reduce the complexity of the regime, particularly for SMEs.

1.4. DEVELOPMENT OF THE COMMISSION PROPOSAL

The EC's proposal was developed[47] in close cooperation with MS experts in the Solvency subcommittee of the EIOPC, based upon the advice received from CEIOPS. A member of the CEIOPS staff attended the meetings. The drafting team within the EC was very small and was mainly composed of national experts who were seconded from NSAs to the EC.[48]

The first challenge that had to be met was a decision on the timing of the proposal. There had been a political agreement[49] that the EC would submit its proposal by the end of 2005. As the preparatory work had not sufficiently advanced by the end of 2004,[50] it was decided to postpone the submission until the end of 2006, in order to allow CEIOPS to come forward with its advice taking into account the comments received from stakeholders. This delay was regretted by Member States and by the insurance industry, as there was a lot of support for quickly moving away from the old Solvency I regime, which was generally agreed to be outdated. However, the EC wanted to proceed prudently and to ensure that the proposal was based upon sound evidence and thorough consultation. When Member States in the EIOPC asked the EC to recast all the existing Insurance Directives (13) into the proposal so as to have one single document that would contain most of the European insurance

47 A detailed description of the preparatory process can be found in SANDSTRÖM, A., *Handbook of Solvency for Actuaries and Risk Managers. Theory and Practice*, Chapman & Hall/CRC, Boca Raton, 2011, pp. 575–627.

48 The drafting team was part of the Insurance and Pensions Unit within DG Markt, under the leadership of Karel Van Hulle, Head of Unit (2004–2013). The following people participated in the work: Susanne Rosenbaum and Paulina Dejmek (the recast); Ben Carr, Pauline de Chatillon, Evelyne Massé, Teresa Rubino and Ines Alpert (Pillars 1 and 2); Dominique Thienpont and Jung-Duk Lichtenberger (Pillar 3 and group supervision); and Joao de Abreu, Manuel Altemir Mergelina, Janne Lipponen and Kristina Summanen (coordination). Susanne Rosenbaum, Ines Alpert, Pauline de Chatillon, Evelyne Massé and Ben Carr were later replaced by Lars Dieckhoff, Benoît Hugonin, Alessia Angelilli, Ramon Carrasco, Kathrin Blanck-Putz and Rogier Wezenbeek. Ulf Linder, Mike Thom and Manuel de Frutos, who started the project, left the Unit in 2005. Ulf Linder came back later as Deputy Head of Unit and was succeeded by Steve Ryan. Omnibus II was finalised by Klaus Wiedner, who became Head of Unit in 2013. The DA was finalised by Nathalie Berger, who became Head of Unit in 2015.

49 See EC, Communication on implementing the framework for financial markets: action plan, COM (1999) 232 final, 11 May 1999.

50 The Framework for Consultation on which the calls for advice to CEIOPS were based was only finalised in July 2004.

regulation, it was decided to further postpone the submission deadline until 15 July 2007. Recasting existing legislation is a difficult exercise and involves close cooperation with the Legal Service of the EC. Care had to be taken to ensure that a rewording or a replacement of articles in the text would not change the meaning of the text, which had become law in all Member States. On the other hand, MS experts had to be reminded time and time again that a recast could not be used as an excuse to renegotiate the text of the existing directives.

The second challenge was the drafting of the text itself. More than 1,000 pages of detailed technical advice had been received from CEIOPS. These pages had to be turned into legal provisions. The objective was to take out of the advice the basic principles of the new solvency regime, leaving much of the detail for further elaboration at levels 2 and 3.

The third challenge was the preparation of a detailed impact assessment that would accompany the EC's proposal. This required a clear definition of why Solvency II was necessary and of the policy options examined and their impact, and a description of the overall expected impact of Solvency II, including the benefits for stakeholders, the potential short-term side effects and the administrative cost. As part of the impact assessment, representatives of a number of small, medium-sized and large insurance undertakings (whose names had been suggested by members of the EIOPC) were invited to meet with the drafting team in the EC in order to discuss the potential impact of the proposal for their undertaking. In order to broaden the impact assessment, specific reports were requested from the Economic and Finance Department (ECFIN) of the EC on the potential macro-economic impacts of Solvency II, from the ECB on the potential impact of Solvency II on financial stability, from the insurance industry (CEA/AISAM/ACME) on the impact of the introduction of Solvency II on insurance products and markets and on the administrative costs associated with the introduction of Solvency II, from FIN-USE on Solvency II from a consumer perspective, and from CEIOPS on the expected impact of Solvency II on NSAs. The impact assessment was presented to the Impact Assessment Board,[51] which made a few recommendations but also congratulated the drafting team on their excellent work.

The fourth challenge was the translation of the text into all (23) official languages of the EU. This was particularly difficult because the proposal contained 300 articles and the subject matter was highly complex.

As part of the Better Regulation agenda, an Inter-Service Steering Group was set up with participation from a wide number of other EC departments,

---

51 A body set up within the EC as part of the Better Regulation agenda, composed of leading officials from different EC departments. Solvency II was the first financial services proposal that had to be submitted to this newly created body.

including ECFIN, EMPL, COMP, JLS, ENTR, SANCO, the Joint Research Centre and Sec Gen. The draft proposal was discussed with colleagues from these other departments, who provided their input. Similarly, the Insurance and Pensions Unit ran an intra-DG Markt focus group to discuss the Solvency II project.

On 21 June 2006, a public hearing was organised in Brussels. Some 250 people attended the hearing, which included four panel discussions[52] and a general debate. There was unanimous support for the new risk-based solvency regime. Some of the issues raised concerned the treatment of specialised insurers, for instance professional liability insurers, whose treatment under the standard formula was rather severe as they could not invoke any diversification benefits, the link between the solvency rules and IAS/IFRS, the importance of Pillar 2 and the impact for consumers (need for better communication).

The official proposal was presented by Commissioner Charlie McCreevy at a press conference in the EP in Strasbourg on 10 July 2007, one week before the agreed deadline. The proposal[53] contained 305 articles and was accompanied by an impact assessment (60 pages), which included several annexes as well as the various reports that had been requested by the EC.[54]

In the press release issued the same day, Commissioner Charlie McCreevy said:[55]

> "This is an ambitious proposal that will completely overhaul the way we ensure the financial soundness of our insurers. We are setting a world-leading standard that requires insurers to focus on managing all the risks they face and enables them to operate more efficiently. It's good news for consumers, for the insurance industry and for the EU economy as a whole."

After the EC had introduced its proposal, a new directive[56] amending some of the provisions that were included in the recast part of the Solvency II Directive proposal was published in the Official Journal. It had been impossible to include these changes in the Solvency II Directive proposal as this amending directive

---

52 CEIOPS Update; Policyholders and other stakeholders; Insurance products and markets; International developments.

53 EC, Proposal for a Directive of the EP and of the Council on the taking-up and pursuit of the business of Insurance and Reinsurance (Solvency II) (recast), COM (2007) 361, 10 July 2007.

54 EC, Commission Staff Working Document: Accompanying document to the Proposal for a Directive of the EP and of the Council on the taking-up and pursuit of the business of insurance and reinsurance (Solvency II) (recast), COM (2007) 361 final, 10 July 2007.

55 EC, *Solvency II: EU to take global lead in insurance regulation*, Press Release, 10 July 2007. See also EC, *Solvency II: Frequently Asked Questions*, 10 July 2007.

56 Directive 2007/44/EC of the EP and of the Council of 5 September 2007 amending Council Directive 92/49/EEC and Directives 2002/83/EC, 2004/39/EC, 2005/68/EC and 2006/48/EC as regards procedural rules and evaluation criteria for the prudential assessment of acquisitions and increase of holdings in the financial sector, *OJ* L 247, 21.9.2007, p. 1.

had not yet been officially published in July 2007. Another problem arose with the political agreement reached in December 2007 on the so-called Rome I Regulation,[57] which deals with the law applicable on contractual obligations. This also affected provisions on applicable law and conditions of direct insurance contracts in the recast part of the Solvency II proposal. In order to avoid difficulties during the negotiation of the proposal in the Council and in the EP, the EC decided to introduce an amended proposal in February 2008, which included the latest changes in the recast part of the original proposal. This is the reason why all references to the Solvency II proposal during the negotiations are references to the amended Solvency II proposal.

2. NEGOTIATION IN THE COUNCIL AND IN THE EUROPEAN PARLIAMENT

2.1. DISCUSSIONS IN THE COUNCIL

The discussions in the Council Financial Services Working Party started as early as July 2007, under the Portuguese Presidency (1 July–31 December 2007).[58] The Working Party was chaired by Gabriel Bernardino.[59] Although the text was only available in a few official languages, all delegations were eager to start the discussion as soon as possible. After an initial introduction of the proposal by the EC Services and a first round of questions and answers, delegations were asked to provide their comments in writing by September 2007. Although all Member States had indicated that they were supportive of the proposal, about 1,000 pages of comments were received.

During the Portuguese Presidency, much of the debate concentrated on proportionality (see further Chapter 5), on the scope of the Directive (exclusion of small insurers), and on group supervision (see further Chapter 9).

The Portuguese Presidency was followed by the Slovenian Presidency (1 January 2008–30 June 2008). The Council Working Party was co-chaired by Jurij Gorisek and Mihael Perman.[60] Under the Slovenian Presidency, the debate focused on surplus funds (see further Chapter 6, section 3.1.3), on the relationship between MCR and SCR, and on group supervision and group support (see further Chapter 9, section 2).

---

57 Regulation (EC) No 593/2008 of the EP and of the Council of 17 June 2008 on the law applicable to contractual obligations (Rome I), *OJ* L 177, 4.7.2008, p. 6.

58 For an overview of the political process, see EID, T.K., *Solvency II: The Political Process*, Master's Thesis, Department of Political Science, University of Oslo, autumn 2014, 131 p., http://urn.nb.no/URN:NBN:no-47897.

59 At that time General Director of the Instituto de Seguros de Portugal (ISP).

60 Respectively, President and Director at the Insurance Supervision Agency in Slovenia.

On 29 May 2008, the European Economic and Social Committee (EESC) delivered its opinion on the Proposed Directive.[61] It broadly welcomed the Proposed Directive and "saluted" the extensive consultation that had preceded the presentation of the proposal. The EESC urged the EC to preserve the diversity of the insurance market by taking into account the role of small and medium-sized insurers, as well as of mutual and cooperative insurance societies. Since many of these operated in niche markets, the EESC considered it of great importance that some flexibility be allowed in the standard formula for the SCR and that recognition be given, for example, to the use of undertaking-specific parameters (USPs) and to generally accepted methodologies, without, however, disturbing fair competition between insurance undertakings. Due analysis and consideration had to be given to the possibility of mutual insurance companies calling on their members to shore up their solvency status, as had been seen in practice.

After about a year of discussions on the 350-page proposal during these two Presidencies, an agreement was reached in the Council on almost all aspects of the proposal at the beginning of the French Presidency (1 July 2008–31 December 2008). Under the French Presidency, the Council Working Party was chaired by Antoine Saintoyant.[62] This Presidency took place in the middle of the financial crisis and much time was therefore spent on issues such as pro-cyclicality and financial stability.

Indeed, in October 2008, the EC asked Member States and the EP whether they felt that any changes were needed to the proposal in order to take account of the lessons learned from the financial crisis. The discussion that followed this request led to the introduction of a new Article 28 in the proposal referring to financial stability as one of the objectives of insurance supervision and including a requirement for supervisory authorities to give proper consideration to financial stability concerns and to the potential pro-cyclical effects of their actions in times of exceptional movements in the financial markets. Other amendments made to the proposal included:

- introduction of a symmetric adjustment mechanism (equity dampener) in the equity risk sub-module in the standard formula in order to take account of the volatility in financial markets;
- extension of the period for recovering the SCR in the case of an exceptional fall in financial markets (level 2 dampener).

61 EESC, Opinion (2008/c224/03) of 29 May 2008 on the Proposal for a directive of the EP and of the Council on the taking-up and pursuit of the business of Insurance and Reinsurance – Solvency II, *OJ* C 224, 30.8.2008, p. 11. The draft opinion was written by Wauthier Robyns de Schneidauer.

62 An official at the French Treasury Department.

CEIOPS had also been asked to examine the possible consequences of the financial crisis for the Solvency II regulatory regime. In its paper of 19 March 2009,[63] CEIOPS stated that the most important lesson to be learned from the financial crisis was the urgent need to adopt Solvency II. The level 1 text did not need to be changed, but some suggestions were made for amending its earlier advice for levels 2 and 3:

- Pillar 1: more attention should be paid to the quality of capital, alternative risk transfers, market risk and the correlation between different risks;
- Pillar 2: reduction of reliance on credit rating agencies, consideration of liquidity risk and stricter conditions for the use of internal models;
- Pillar 3: attention should be paid to the possible pro-cyclical effects of market-value-based disclosures.

The main focus of the French Presidency was on the two outstanding issues: group supervision, including group support (see further Chapter 9, section 2), and the treatment of equity risk (see further Chapter 6, section 4.2.2.2.4).

As regards group support, the French Presidency proposed deleting the subsection on this topic, as there seemed to be no possibility of arriving at an agreed position on this issue in the Council, where a blocking minority led by Poland and Spain strongly opposed group support.

On equity risk, two proposals were put on the table: first of all, the introduction of an equity duration approach, which would lead to a lower capital charge for long-term equity investments in the context of pension financing;[64] secondly, in order to prevent fire sales in the case of short-term movements in financial markets, the introduction of an equity dampener mechanism (referred to as a Pillar 1 dampener), which would protect the equity portfolio against short-term movements in equity prices.

Finally, the French Presidency also proposed a so-called Pillar 2 dampener, i.e. an extension of the period for recovering the SCR in the case of an exceptional fall in financial markets in order to avoid pro-cyclicality.

---

63 CEIOPS, Lessons learned from the crisis (Solvency II and beyond), CEIOPS-SEC-107/08, 19 March 2009, 27 p.

64 France argued that it was unfair to "punish" French insurance undertakings, which – in the absence of occupational pension funds in France – were investing a lot in equity as part of their pension business, as opposed to other countries, such as the UK or the Netherlands, where pension business was carried out primarily by occupational pension funds, which were not subject to Solvency II. There was the additional issue that the French government pushed insurance undertakings in France to invest more in (French) equities. As a result, insurance undertakings in France held more equities in their portfolios than insurance undertakings in other Member States. See SPITZ, B., Europe's Risky Insurance Regulation, *The Wall Street Journal Europe*, 18 March 2009. In this article, the Chairman of the French Federation of Insurance Companies explains the French point of view.

After difficult negotiations, a compromise on these proposals was agreed by the Council as a "general approach"[65] on 2 December 2008: the group support regime was excluded from the text and the equity duration approach and the two dampener mechanisms proposed by France and supported by a large majority in the Council were introduced. Only the UK and the Netherlands opposed the removal of the group support regime. The EC did not support the compromise proposal as it did not consider the equity duration approach prudentially sound and as the group support regime was carved out.

2.2. DISCUSSIONS IN THE EUROPEAN PARLIAMENT

In the EP, Peter Skinner (S&D, UK), who had been the Rapporteur for the Reinsurance Directive, was appointed as Rapporteur for the Solvency II Proposal in ECON, which was chaired by Pervenche Berès (S&D, France). The legal affairs committee (JURI) had appointed Sharon Bowles (ALDE, UK) as its Rapporteur. The two Rapporteurs submitted their reports with draft amendments[66] on 13 March 2008[67] and on 2 July 2007[68] respectively.

There was a lot of interest in the EP on Solvency II. The discussions focused on the scope of the Directive, the treatment of mutual insurers, mutual groups, captives and institutions for occupational retirement provisions (IORPs), proportionality, surplus funds, the capital charge for investment in equity, the relationship between the SCR and the MCR, group supervision, and group support.

The EP was particularly interested in group supervision. It wanted to improve the efficiency of the supervision of financial groups in the EU. Several members of ECON had a strong interest in this issue.[69] Group support was seen as a major improvement that would allow more efficient capital management within groups. Several debates took place within ECON.

---

65 A "general approach" is an informal agreement within the Council, awaiting the opinion of the EP. By not adopting a formal position, the Council leaves the door open for a negotiation with the EP.

66 There were more than 800 proposed amendments, with some articles receiving more than 10–15 amendments each.

67 SKINNER, P., Draft Report on the amended proposal for a directive of the EP and of the Council on the taking-up and pursuit of the business of insurance and reinsurance (recast), ECON, 2007/0143 (COD).

68 BOWLES, S., Draft Opinion of the Committee on Legal Affairs for the Committee on Economic and Monetary Affairs on the amended proposal for a directive of the EP and of the Council on the taking-up and pursuit of the business of insurance and reinsurance (recast), JURI, 2007/0143 (COD).

69 For instance, Ieke van den Burg (S&D, Netherlands), who tabled a Report with recommendations to the Commission on Lamfalussy follow-up: future structure of supervision, A6-0359/2008, 18 September 2008.

The draft report submitted by Peter Skinner received 820 amendments. The ECON vote took place on 7 October 2008, and the Skinner Report with the adopted amendments was published on 16 October 2008.[70] At the CEIOPS annual conference in Frankfurt on 19 November 2008, Peter Skinner warned that the Council and EP needed to agree on Solvency II, preferably in 2008, to avoid the risk that the project would be derailed after the June 2009 elections for the EP.

The vote by ECON was well received by the insurance industry. In a press release issued on 7 October 2008,[71] CEA welcomed the text approved by ECON: "The compromises reached by MEPs across parties, on the basis of an excellent text prepared by the EC, will create a sophisticated, economic risk-based approach to the supervision and capital assessment of insurers". CEA was particularly pleased with the compromises reached on group support, on the role of the group supervisor and on the treatment of the MCR, for which ECON had adopted the so-called "combined approach", whereby the MCR would be situated within a corridor of 25–45% of the SCR.

2.3. TRILOGUE NEGOTIATIONS

The trilogue[72] negotiations were started under the Czech Presidency (1 January–30 June 2009) on 22 January 2009.[73] The negotiations became very difficult because each of the institutions involved in the trilogue had different positions:

- the EC wanted group support but could compromise on the equity proposal submitted by the Council;
- the EP wanted group support but not the equity proposal;
- the Council wanted the equity proposal but not group support.

---

70 EP, Report on the amended proposal for a directive of the EP and of the Council on the taking-up and pursuit of the business of insurance and reinsurance (recast), ECON, Rapporteur Peter Skinner, A6-0413/2008, 16 October 2008, 125 p.

71 CEA, *CEA welcomes European Parliament committee vote on Solvency II*, Press Release, 7 October 2008.

72 The trilogue is a negotiation between the co-legislators with the objective of agreeing on a final text. The EC participates actively in this negotiation and helps the EP and the Council in their search for a compromise. Once the co-legislators have agreed on a common position, the EP puts that position to a vote, after which the Council confirms its position in a formal decision.

73 The trilogue negotiations were led by Jiri Krol, the Financial Markets Policy Director at the Czech Ministry of Finance. The Council Working Party was chaired by Daniel Tosner from the Czech Ministry of Finance.

The members of the EP delegation – which was composed of Pervenche Berès (S&D, France), Chair of ECON; Peter Skinner (S&D, UK), Rapporteur; and the two Shadow Rapporteurs, Sharon Bowles (ALDE, UK) and Karsten Hoppenstedt (EPP, Germany) – were not entirely on the same page. While the Chair of ECON was inclined to support the Presidency compromise, the other members of the delegation were strongly opposed to the removal of the group support regime and the introduction of the equity duration approach, a position closer to the EC's position.

Meanwhile, the De Larosière Group, which had been mandated by the EC to look into the causes of the financial crisis that had broken out in 2008 and to come up with a number of recommendations for an improvement of the European supervisory architecture, came out with its report, which contained recommendations that were also relevant for Solvency II. In its Report, the De Larosière Group recommended the speedy adoption of the Solvency II FD,[74] particularly because it would foster risk assessment and rationalise the management of large insurance undertakings, and because it would facilitate the management and supervision of cross-border insurance groups. Recognising the differences of views between "home" and "host" Member States on the operation of the group support regime, the Group pleaded in favour of a balanced group support regime, coupled with sufficient safeguards for host Member States, a binding mediation process between supervisors and the setting-up of harmonised insurance guarantee schemes.

Seven trilogue meetings were held between 22 January and 18 March 2009. The discussions were difficult. Alternative proposals were put on the table by the Czech Presidency, by the EP delegation and by the EC. The EP delegation became desperate, as the Council was not ready to compromise, either on group support, or on equity risk.[75] The last trilogue meeting lasted almost a day and a half. At that meeting, a compromise was finally reached after the EP delegation threatened the Council that the EP might want to adopt its position in a first reading.[76]

On group support, the EP accepted the offer from the Council to replace the group support sub-section with a set of articles limited to increased cooperation between supervisors involved in groups with centralised risk management. In exchange, the Council accepted the introduction of a review clause, prescribing a review of group supervision arrangements three years after implementation of the FD. The Council also agreed that a reference be included in the review

74 EC, *Report of the High-Level Group on Financial Supervision in the EU*, 25 February 2009, Recommendation 5, p. 23.

75 Other issues on the table concerned the level of the MCR and the treatment of participations.

76 This would have implied a second reading with new negotiations.

clause (Art. 142 (2) FD) to the EC's group support proposal and to the (positive) comments on that proposal in the Skinner report.[77]

On equity risk, the EP accepted the introduction, as an MS option, of the duration approach (not only for occupational retirement business, but also for individual retirement business), the introduction of a Pillar 1 dampener (i.e. a mechanism whereby the equity risk charge is no longer a fixed amount, but is modulated in function of the evolution of markets over a number of months), and the introduction of a Pillar 2 dampener (i.e. a mechanism whereby a breach of the SCR does not have to be resolved within a maximum of nine months, but within a potentially much longer period in the event of an exceptional fall in financial markets). The Council accepted the restrictions on the duration approach (such as 'ring-fencing' for the assets and liabilities subject to the approach) insisted upon by the EP.

2.4. POLITICAL AGREEMENT

Based on the compromise reached with the EP, the Council agreed its formal position on 1 April 2009.[78] The Solvency II FD was adopted by the EP on 22 April 2009 with 593 votes in favour, 80 opposed and three abstentions.[79] In the plenary session, both the Rapporteur and Sharon Bowles regretted the absence of group support in the final text and asked the Commissioner not to wait until October 2015 before starting the review. Commissioner Charlie McCreevy thanked the Rapporteur and the EP for their work and their willingness to compromise, and indicated that he believed that the outcome would be widely welcomed by the EU insurance industry, by supervisors and by stakeholders in general. He did, however, express his disappointment with certain aspects of the compromise, in particular the removal of the group support regime and the introduction of the duration approach, which he considered an imprudent regime for investment in risk-based capital.

---

77 Any reference to the group support regime was heavily opposed by Spain. The only reference to group support can be found in recital 141 FD.

78 In a statement for the minutes, the EC regretted that the Council and the EP were not able to agree on the inclusion of the group support regime and indicated that it would pay particular attention to ensuring that the implementing measures would bring forward solutions that were prudentially sound and that would not be unduly burdensome for small and medium-sized (re)insurance undertakings, as well as for captive (re)insurance undertakings. The last message was made in order to help Malta sign up to the deal.

79 At the meeting, flyers were distributed by a French organisation, FAIDER (Fédération des Associations Indépendantes de Défense des Epargnants de la Retraîte), urging MEPs to vote against a proposal that was a bad imitation of Basel II and that did not take account of the interests of policyholders. See also the article published in the *Handelsblatt* on 27 April 2009 by the former CEO of Groupama, Jean Azéma, expressing similar ideas. See also: https://www.lemonde.fr/idees/article/2010/05/03/solvabilite-ii-menace-la-reprise-economique-aux-politiques-de-reprendre-la-main-par-jean-azema_1346078_3232.html.

He stressed that Solvency II was needed more than ever as an initial response to the financial crisis and that the new solvency regime could serve as a model for similar reforms internationally.[80]

The final text of the FD was generally welcomed by the insurance industry,[81] although the removal of the group support regime was regretted. CEA felt that this was a missed opportunity for a more efficient and effective supervision of multinational groups. After review of the text by the jurists-linguists and formal (unanimous) adoption of the final version by the Council on 10 November 2009, the final text was published in the Official Journal of 17 December 2009.[82] The Directive entered into force on 5 January 2010 and was supposed to become applicable from 1 November 2012.

2.5. REVIEW CLAUSES

The Solvency II FD contains a number of review clauses. Review clauses are often included in EU legislation as part of a compromise on issues that were highly controversial during the negotiations. They reflect the uncertainty of the co-legislators about the outcome of the negotiations. They require the EC to look again into a particular issue before a certain date and to report back to the EP and to the Council, possibly with proposals for change. Technically speaking, these review clauses are not necessary, as the EC can always come up with proposals for change. They do however send an important political message. The most significant review clauses relate to the standard formula (Art. 111 (2) FD), the cooperation between supervisory authorities (Art. 242 (1) FD), capital management within groups (Art. 242 (2) FD) and the duration-based equity risk sub-module (Art. 304 (2) FD).

Of particular interest is the review clause relating to capital management within groups, which requires the EC to look again at the group support regime

---

80 See also EC, *Solvency II: European Parliament's approval of proposed directive brings modern insurance regulation nearer*, Press Release, 22 April 2009.

81 See, for instance, the CEA's statement: "From the beginning, the CEA has strongly endorsed and fully supported the development of the Solvency II regulatory regime. Solvency II is seen by the insurance industry as a positive step forward in insurance sector regulation that moves away from a Solvency I approach of simply imposing crude capital requirements towards enhancing policyholder protection through a more sophisticated approach that combines both quantitative and qualitative elements of supervision. As it also promotes greater transparency to boost investor and consumer confidence, it fosters overall cost-effective and capital-effective product and service innovation". CEA, *Why excessive capital requirements harm consumers, insurers and the economy*, March 2010, p. 5. As stated publicly by the CEO of a major insurance group at a conference in 2009: "I am married to Solvency I but I am in love with Solvency II".

82 Directive 2009/138/EC of the EP and of the Council of 25 November 2009 on the taking-up and pursuit of the business of insurance and reinsurance (Solvency II) (recast), *OJ* L 335, 17.12.2009, p. 1. A corrigendum was published in *OJ* L 219, 25.7.2014, p. 66.

in its initial proposal (2007) and at the comments of the EP on this issue in the report of ECON (2008). This review clause is also interesting because it does not require the EC to assess the application of the FD but to look into ways and means to reintroduce group support, i.e. to reopen the debate on an issue on which no agreement could be reached in 2009. The review clause in Art. 242 (2) FD is linked with the review clause in Art. 304 (2) FD as the issues of group support and the duration-based approach were politically interlinked. The review clauses on both issues therefore had the same date, i.e. 31 October 2015.[83]

As soon as the level 1 text had been agreed, the level 2 preparations started, based upon a roadmap that had been agreed between the EC and CEIOPS and a work plan set up by the EIOPC (see further, section 5.1).

3. REFORM OF THE EUROPEAN SUPERVISORY ARCHITECTURE

The financial crisis in 2007/2008 exposed important shortcomings in the European supervisory architecture that had been set up in 2001 on the basis of the Lamfalussy Report with the creation of three regulatory committees – the EBC, ESC and EIOPC – and three committees of supervisors – the CEBS, CESR and CEIOPS. The crisis showed, in particular, significant shortcomings in the cooperation and coordination between NSAs, in the consistent application of EU law and in the trust between NSAs.

This was an important reason why the EC asked a group of high-level experts, chaired by Jacques de Larosière, to develop a blueprint for a new EU supervisory architecture. The group presented its report on 25 February 2009.[84] Building on its recommendations, the EC endorsed the report and set out proposals for a new European financial supervisory architecture in its Communication of 4 March 2009.[85] These proposals were presented in more detail in a Communication of 27 May 2009[86] and formally presented on 23 September 2009:

- establishment of a European System of Financial Supervision (ESFS), consisting of a network of national financial supervisors working in tandem with

83 This was changed by Omnibus II. The assessment of the benefit of enhancing group supervision and capital management within a group must now be carried out by the EC by 31 December 2018, whilst the report on the duration-based equity approach must be submitted by the EC by 31 December 2020.

84 EC, *Report by the High-Level Group on Financial Supervision*, chaired by Jacques de Larosière, 25 February 2009, 78 p.

85 EC, Communication to the EP and to the Council on Driving European recovery, COM (2009) 114 final, 4 March 2009, 19 p.

86 EC, Communication to the EP and to the Council on European financial supervision, COM (2009) 252 final, 27 May 2009.

new ESAs. The ESAs were to be created by transforming the existing European supervisory committees into authorities. This combined the advantages of an overarching European framework for financial supervision with the expertise of local micro-prudential supervisory bodies that are closest to the institutions operating in their jurisdictions;
- establishment of a European Systemic Risk Board (ESRB) in order to monitor and assess potential threats to financial stability that arise from macro-economic developments and from developments within the financial system as a whole. To this end, the ESRB provides an early warning of system-wide risks that might be building up and, where necessary, issues recommendations for action to deal with these risks.

Just a year later, the three ESAs were established by three separate regulations adopted on 24 November 2010.[87] The seat of the three ESAs remained the same as that of their predecessor: London for EBA, Paris for ESMA and Frankfurt for EIOPA. The ESRB, which is chaired by the President of the ECB, who also directs its Secretariat, was established by a regulation adopted on the same day.[88]

The three ESAs took over all of the functions of the existing committees of supervisors and received additional competences:

- the ability to develop proposals for technical standards following the principles of better regulation (with a view to arriving at a single European rulebook);
- the right to resolve cases of disagreement between NSAs, where legislation requires them to cooperate or to agree (binding mediation);
- the right to contribute to ensuring the consistent application of EU law, including through peer reviews (with a view to arriving at a uniform application of EU law);
- the power to play a coordination role in emergency situations.

---

87 Regulation (EU) No 1093/2010 of the EP and of the Council of 24 November 2010 establishing a European Supervisory Authority (European Banking Authority), amending Decision No 716/2009/EC and repealing Commission Decision 2009/78/EC, *OJ* L 331, 15.12.2010, p. 12; Regulation (EU) No 1094/2010 of the EP and of the Council of 24 November 2010 establishing a European Supervisory Authority (European Insurance and Occupational Pensions Authority), amending Decision No 716/2009/EC and repealing Commission Decision 2009/79/EC, *OJ* L 331, 15.12.2010, p. 48; Regulation (EU) No 1095/2010 of the EP and of the Council of 24 November 2010 establishing a European Supervisory Authority (European Securities and Markets Authority), amending Decision No 716/2009/EC and repealing Commission Decision 2009/77/EC, *OJ* L 331, 15.12.2010, p. 84.

88 Regulation (EU) No 1092/2010 of the EP and of the Council of 24 November 2010 on macro-prudential oversight of the financial system and establishing a European Systemic Risk Board, *OJ* L 331, 15.12.2010, p. 1.

In order for the ESFS to work effectively, changes were necessary to existing EU legislation:[89]

- definition of the appropriate areas in which the ESAs are able to propose technical standards as an additional tool for supervisory convergence and with a view to developing a single rulebook;
- incorporation in an appropriate manner of the possibility for the ESAs to settle disagreements between NSAs in a balanced way, in those areas where common decision-making processes already exist in sectoral legislation;
- general amendments that were necessary for the relevant Directives to operate in the context of new authorities, for example renaming the level 3 committees to the new authorities and ensuring that the appropriate gateways for the exchange of information are present.

The consequential changes in EU financial regulation were proposed by the EC on 26 October 2009. Because the proposal involved changes to 11 Directives, it was commonly referred to as Omnibus I. The Omnibus I Directive[90] did not include the consequential changes in the Solvency II FD, as the FD had not yet been formally adopted at the time of the presentation of the Omnibus I proposal.

4. OMNIBUS II

4.1. OBJECTIVES

In its press release accompanying the presentation of Omnibus I, the EC indicated that it would present the sectoral changes in the insurance sector "early in 2010".[91] These changes were only proposed by the EC one year later, on 19 January 2011. The proposal[92] included a limited set of amendments to the

---

89 These changes were set out in a Commission Staff Working Document (SEC (2009) 1233, 23 September 2009). Annex 1 to that document included the likely changes to the Solvency II FD.

90 Directive 2010/78/EU of the EP and of the Council of 24 November 2010 amending Directives 98/26/EC, 2002/87/EC, 2003/6/EC, 2003/41/EC, 2003/71/EC, 2004/39/EC, 2004/109/EC, 2005/60/EC, 2006/48/EC, 2006/49/EC and 2009/65/EC in respect of the powers of the European Supervisory Authority (European Banking Authority), the European Supervisory Authority (European Insurance and Occupational Pensions Authority) and the European Supervisory Authority (European Securities and Markets Authority), *OJ* L 331, 15.12.2010, p. 120.

91 See EC, Press Release IP/09/1582, 26 October 2009.

92 EC, Proposal for a Directive of the EP and of the Council amending Directives 2003/71/EC and 2009/138/EC in respect of the powers of EIOPA and ESMA, COM (2011) 8 final, 19 January 2011.

Prospectus Directive[93] and several amendments to the Solvency II FD. Because of its amendment of two legislative acts, the proposal was also commonly referred to as Omnibus II.

There were two reasons for the delay in the presentation of Omnibus II. First of all, Omnibus I had been adopted later than expected. As Omnibus II was building on what had been agreed for the banking and securities sectors in Omnibus I, the presentation of the proposal had to await the official publication of Omnibus I (15 December 2010). Secondly, it had become clear, particularly during the preparation and execution of QIS 5, that it was necessary to include in the Solvency II FD a number of transitional measures in order to smooth the transition from Solvency I to Solvency II, to avoid market disruption and to take account of the impact of Solvency II on a number of insurance products. The problem was that it was unclear to all parties concerned which transitional measures were necessary. The EC therefore included in its proposal broad powers for the introduction of transitional measures by way of delegated acts. This was a legal nightmare.[94] It was done by specifying in the FD a maximum period for transitional measures in a large number of areas and by giving power to the EC to reduce these maximum periods by way of delegated acts. Many readers of the proposal misunderstood the approach and believed that the EC was now proposing to postpone large parts of Solvency II for a long period of time (for instance, 10 years for the Pillar 1 requirements and three years for the Pillars 2 and 3 requirements).

Besides amendments similar to those in Omnibus I, i.e. defining the scope of technical standards to be drafted by EIOPA and the cases of binding mediation and changing all references to CEIOPS, some further amendments to the FD were proposed:

- adaptation of the procedure for the existing level 2 empowerments following the entry into force of the Lisbon Treaty (so-called "Lisbonisation");
- possibility to introduce transitional measures in relation to valuation, governance, supervisory reporting and public disclosure, the determination and classification of own funds, the standard formula for the calculation of the SCR and the choice of methods and assumptions for the calculation of technical provisions, including the determination of the relevant risk-free interest rate term structure;
- possibility to specify transitional arrangements in relation to the treatment of third-country solvency regimes in order to acknowledge that some third countries might need more time to adapt and implement a solvency regime that would fully satisfy the criteria for being recognised as equivalent;

93 Directive 2003/71/EC of 4 November 2003 on the prospectus to be published when securities are offered to the public or admitted to trading, *OJ* L 345, 31.12.2003, p. 64.

94 As it was unclear which transitional measures would eventually emerge and when.

- adaptation of existing level 2 empowerments concerning USPs, model change policies, special-purpose vehicles (SPVs) and the setting and removal of capital add-ons;
- ensuring cross-sectoral consistency by enabling level 2 measures in the context of investments in repackaged loans not only to specify requirements for such types of investment, but also to specify the consequences of breaching those requirements;
- inclusion of the European cooperative society (SCE)[95] in the list of permissible forms of (re)insurance undertakings;
- adaptation of the euro amount of the absolute floor of the MCR in order to take account of inflation;
- extension by two months (until 31 December 2012) of the date for the implementation of the FD in order to make the date for the first application of Solvency II coincide with the year-end date for most (re)insurance undertakings.

The EESC welcomed the Omnibus II proposal in its opinion of 5 May 2011. It expressed support for the introduction of transitional measures that would smooth the transition from Solvency I to Solvency II. It cautioned against transferring too much power to EIOPA, which had "to act as an autonomous body within the mandates set by the legislative institutions with a political responsibility".[96]

4.2. NEGOTIATION IN THE COUNCIL AND IN THE EUROPEAN PARLIAMENT

4.2.1. Discussions in the Council

The Council started the negotiations on Omnibus II quickly under the Hungarian Presidency and arrived at an agreement (general approach) in September 2011, under the Polish Presidency. Much of the debate in the Council concentrated on the so-called long-term guarantee (LTG) package, which had been developed by a special LTG Working Group established and chaired by the EC and composed of experts from Member States, from EIOPA, from the (re)insurance industry, from the CRO Forum and from the actuarial profession, following the release by EIOPA of the QIS 5 results on 14 March 2011.[97] These results showed a high

---

95 Council Regulation (EC) No 1435/2003 of 22 July 2003 on the Statute for a European Cooperative Society (SCE), *OJ* L 207, 18.8.2003, p. 1.

96 Opinion (2011/C218/15) of the EESC of 5 May 2011, *OJ* C 218, 23.7.2011, p. 82. The Rapporteur was Joachim Wuermeling.

97 See EIOPA, Report on the fifth Quantitative Impact Study (QIS 5) for Solvency II, EIOPA-TFQIS5-11/001, 14 March 2011, 153 p.

volatility in the calculation of own funds and technical provisions, as a result of market turbulence caused by budgetary difficulties in a number of Member States. It was clear that the Solvency II approach could not work without some adaptations to the calculation of the technical provisions, particularly in relation to long-term guarantees offered by life insurance undertakings.

The discussions showed very quickly that a one-size-fits-all solution was not possible because of the existence of a wide variety of life insurance products in Member States, for instance annuity products in the UK and Spain, very long-term guaranteed contracts in Germany and mainly savings products in Italy and France. On the other hand, a European solution was necessary to avoid creating distortions in the internal market and to prevent a move away from a unified approach to solvency.

The Working Group developed a package of measures, introducing solutions that took account of the different life insurance products available in Member States:

- *matching premium*: premium to be included in the interest rate to discount technical provisions of specific insurance products, for instance annuities, on the condition that the liabilities are illiquid (no surrender option and thus no lapse risk) and that annuities are backed by bonds that are held to maturity, so that the insurer is not exposed to full spread risk. The premium would prevent spread volatility leading to capital volatility. Strict requirements would need to be included in the implementing measures concerning application, calculation and risk management;
- *counter-cyclical premium*: this measure aimed at preventing pro-cyclical investment behaviour by insurers. It involved an adaptation of the discount rate in periods of stressed markets. EIOPA would determine whether there was a stressed financial market and would also calculate the premium. The criteria for the determination of a stressed financial market situation and for the calculation of the premium would be set out in the implementing measures and would be further detailed in technical standards;
- *extrapolation*: the interest rate curve for the discounting of technical provisions in the case of long-term contracts must be extrapolated. Because the volatility of the discount rate and the technical provisions depends on the starting point of the extrapolation and the extrapolation method, implementing measures would have to contain the necessary requirements for the extrapolation in order to stabilise the discount rate;
- *other measures* would have to deal with the symmetric adjustment of the equity risk sub-module, the capital requirement for spread risk of long-term bonds and the capital requirement for catastrophe risk of liability insurance.

This package showed the problems resulting from Solvency I: life insurance undertakings could still be very solvent under Solvency I, with solvency margins well above 100%, but insolvent under Solvency II because of the requirement to also take account of market risk. This "comfortable" position under Solvency I led a number of insurance undertakings to publicly state that the Solvency II reform was not needed, as they had managed to survive the financial crisis without major difficulties. Solvency II could even be dangerous because it would make it impossible for insurance undertakings to offer long-term guarantees in the future.

Supervisors looked at this situation very differently and were worried about the ability of life insurance undertakings to continue delivering on their promises. It is therefore no surprise that EIOPA urged NSAs in 2013 to monitor carefully the impact of the low interest environment on the (re)insurance industry,[98] in the absence of detailed solvency information under Solvency I.

In order to avoid a large number of insolvencies, it was necessary to accommodate insurance undertakings, particularly with regard to their back book, i.e. life insurance contracts concluded under a different regulatory regime, and to provide for a mechanism that would still allow life insurance undertakings to offer long-term guarantees under a market-consistent valuation approach in a low interest rate environment. From a public policy point of view, it was important to avoid insurance undertakings in the end being able to continue to offer the same products in a completely changed economic environment without taking into account the risks for policyholders. On the other hand, it was also important to make it possible for life insurance undertakings to offer (long-term) guarantees in the context of pension financing and to allow the insurance industry to continue its role as an institutional investor.

Member States (supported by the insurance industry) wanted to include part of the LTG package in the FD via Omnibus II because they were afraid that they might not get what they wanted if this matter were left to level 2. The package agreed in the general approach adopted by the Council in September 2011 included the counter-cyclical premium to be calculated by EIOPA, with formulas to be provided in the implementing measures (a solution not very popular in the industry as it was considered too uncertain). There was no specific reference to the extrapolation (only in a recital), nor to the matching premium in the text agreed for the general approach, but there was a political agreement to stick to the LTG package that had been agreed in the context of the EC's LTG Working Group and to introduce the measures at level 2.

4.2.2. Discussions in the European Parliament

Contrary to what might have been expected, the EP was not eager to quickly adopt its position on the EC's proposed Omnibus II Directive, which – besides

98 See EIOPA, Opinion on Supervisory Response to a Prolonged Low Interest Rate Environment, EIOPA-BoS-12/110, 28 February 2013, 6 p.

the important issue of transitional measures, which had not been considered in the Solvency II FD – mainly included the formal changes that resulted from the replacement of CEIOPS by EIOPA, with the consequential addition of new powers and the changes following from the Lisbon Treaty (as the LTG package was not part of the EC's proposal).

The Rapporteur in ECON, Burkhard Balz (EPP, Germany), struggled with the EC's proposal, and especially with the transitional measures and the powers for the EC to regulate these measures through delegated acts. He wanted to make more of Omnibus II. He thought that the debate should not only concentrate on procedural issues but should also deal with matters of substance. The Rapporteur presented his draft report on 27 July 2011, which included the following points:

- Omnibus II should introduce specific exemptions from supervisory reporting with application of the proportionality principle;
- the empowerments of the EC and to EIOPA for level 2 measures should be brought in line with changes resulting from the Lisbon Treaty ("Lisbonisation");
- the transitional measures should be spelled out more clearly;
- transitional equivalence should be introduced in the case of EU insurance groups with subsidiaries in third countries;
- the issues relating to long-term guarantees should be dealt with in the FD, as the proposed solutions could have significant effects for policyholders, for the insurance industry and for the internal market.

Burkhard Balz refused to accept the LTG package as such because he did not believe that it was in the interest of policyholders and that it introduced too many national options. He particularly disliked the matching premium, which he considered a present to the UK and which he wanted to limit both in substance and in time, renaming it the "matching adjustment" (MA). He also had difficulties with the counter-cyclical premium, as he could not see how it could be made workable. In terms of an LTG package, he only wanted a solution for the extrapolation of the relevant risk-free interest rate term structure, which was a particular German concern, as German life insurance contracts have long maturities, and a possibility for NSAs to extend the period for a recovery of the SCR in extreme market conditions (such as a prolonged low interest rate environment).

Intensive discussions took place within ECON, as can be seen from the 472 amendments that were tabled on the Balz Report. Several meetings were held with experts from the EC. When discussing Omnibus II, MEPs were also interested in the implementing measures of the FD. They therefore asked the EC to brief them on the state of progress and to submit the draft implementing measures to the EP.[99] The ECON vote, initially scheduled for 22 November 2011, was postponed until 19 December 2011 because of different views within ECON about the link between levels 1 and 2 and about the MA. When the vote was further postponed until 23 January 2012, it became clear that it would no longer be possible to adopt all legislative measures in time for the start of Solvency II on either 1 November 2012 (the date set in the Solvency II FD) or on 1 January 2013 (the new date suggested in the Omnibus II proposal). When the EC communicated this to the Rapporteur, Burkhard Balz replied that this was a matter for the EC and that the EP could not be blamed for the fact that the EC had introduced the Omnibus II proposal a year later than initially planned (10 January 2011 instead of early 2010).

In a letter of 31 January 2012 from the Chairman of EIOPA, Gabriel Bernardino, to Commissioner Michel Barnier,[100] the former stressed the importance of having a vote on Omnibus II in ECON as soon as possible and he urged the EP, the EC and the Council "to agree within the context of the trilogue on a clear timeline, which would ensure the entry into force in 2014 with sufficient assurance for a due process to prepare the Solvency II implementation. This timeline should be appropriately communicated to all stakeholders in order to eliminate the current uncertainties".

This action from EIOPA should be seen in the context of the complete uncertainty about the future of the Solvency II reform. Neither from the EC, nor from the EP or the Council, was a clear and consistent message passed on to the outside world as to when this reform would actually take effect.[101] The EP (ECON) was busy with the discussion of a number of other legislative proposals, particularly relating to banking, and the Council was paralysed because it could not agree to the proposals made by ECON. In the absence of clear indications from the EU institutions on the timing and the urgency of this reform, many undertakings started to reduce their budgets for the implementation of Solvency II because they did not believe that this project would ever see the light of the day. For EIOPA, the delays in the final adoption of the level 1 text created problems for the delivery of the level 3 measures. As stated in its letter to the EC of 31 January 2012, without a final level 1 text and

99 The EC eventually submitted the draft implementing measures to the EP, without recitals, making clear that this was not a text that had already been officially adopted by the EC. Some MEPs criticised the lack of transparency. See the discussion paper circulated by the Greens, *Solvency II Implementing Measures. Legislation through the back door*, 2012, 13 p.

100 https://eiopa.europa.eu/Publications/Other%20Documents/2012-01-31_EIOPA_12_036_Implementation_on_Solvency_II_-_Letter_to_Commissioner_Barnier.pdf.

101 The Commissioner responsible for financial services, Michel Barnier, was frustrated with the criticism that was voiced against Solvency II by industry representatives. This frustration was shown in some of his speeches when he indicated that Solvency II was not his responsibility as he had not started the project (the Solvency II FD had indeed been proposed and adopted under his predecessor, Charlie McCreevy).

a level 2 text, it was impossible for EIOPA to consult "on the standards and guidelines which will complement the new regulatory framework".

ECON finally voted on 21 March 2012, but its position was very different from that adopted by the Council in September 2011, although it moved closer to the LTG package agreed in the Council. In his Report,[102] Burkhard Balz proposed a limited MA as a transitional measure, an extended MA as an MS option, a counter-cyclical premium for long-term liabilities (over seven years) involving the ESRB, and a solution to the extrapolation with the time for the extrapolation set in the text instead of in a recital.[103]

Insurance Europe expressed disappointment with the package proposed by ECON: "We recognise that the current text contains the package of measures that could, in principle, ensure that risks are correctly measured and avoid artificial balance sheet volatility but regret that it currently includes inappropriate restrictions that would prevent these measures from working as intended."[104]

A different voice could be heard from Sven Giegold (Greens, Germany), fiscal and economic policy spokesman of the Greens in the EP and Shadow Rapporteur, who called the Omnibus II negotiations "a lobby festival". In his view, the matching premium was tailor-made for UK and Spanish insurers. The counter-cyclical premium was there to please French and Italian companies, and the new extrapolation was particularly welcomed by German life insurers. He was particularly critical of the absence of an impact assessment. In his view, "this legislative process was a case study of the dominance of vested interests of financial lobbies over general interests of consumer protection, financial stability and tax payers".[105]

4.2.3. *"Quick-Fix Directive"*

On 16 May 2012, the EC introduced a proposal for a so-called "quick-fix" Directive, suggesting a postponement of the date for the transposition of the Solvency II FD from 31 October 2012 to 30 June 2013 and of the date for the application of Solvency II from 1 November 2012 to 1 January 2014. Because all parties concerned were worried that the date for the first application of Solvency II would lapse before the adoption of Omnibus II and

102 BALZ, B., Report on the proposal for a Directive of the EP and of the Council amending Directives 2003/71/EC and 2009/138/EC in respect of the powers of EIOPA and ESMA, ECON, A7-0077/2012, 28 March 2012, 89 p.

103 The inclusion of the time for the extrapolation in a recital had been a specific request from Germany in the Council.

104 Insurance Europe, *Insurers seek further improvements to Omnibus II text*, Press Release, 21 March 2012.

105 GIEGOLD, S., *Solvency II/Omnibus II: Lobby Festival in the European Parliament*, 21 March 2012, https://sven-giegold.de/solvency-ii-omnibus-ii-lobby-festival-in-the-european-parliament/.

the level 2 implementing measures, the co-legislators quickly agreed to the postponement[106] by adopting the "quick-fix" Directive on 12 September 2012.

In its Preamble, the "quick-fix" Directive justifies the postponement of the date of first application with the following reasons:

- the risk that Omnibus II would not have entered into force before the date of transposition and the date of application of the Solvency II FD. Leaving these dates unchanged would result in the Solvency II FD being implemented before the entry into force of the transitional rules and relevant adaptations in Omnibus II;
- avoidance of overly burdensome obligations for Member States (double transposition);
- the need for sufficient time for NSAs and (re)insurance undertakings to prepare for the application of the new supervisory regime;
- the need to postpone the repeal of Solvency I for reasons of legal certainty.

4.2.4. Trilogue Negotiations

Trilogue negotiations started in April 2012. The parliamentary delegation was composed of Sharon Bowles (ALDE, UK), Chair of ECON; Burkhard Balz (EPP, Germany), Rapporteur; and five Shadow Rapporteurs (Peter Skinner (S&D, UK), Sylvie Goulard (ALDE, France), Sven Giegold (Greens, Germany), Ashley Fox (ECR, UK) and Marisa Matias (GUE-NGL, Portugal)). The Council delegation was led by Denmark, which held the Presidency of the EU in the first semester of 2012. Initially, the atmosphere was good: the plenary vote in the EP was scheduled for April 2012. However, the trilogue parties found it difficult to meet because the EP delegation was busy with the negotiations on the banking package, which was considered a higher priority. The plenary vote was postponed until July 2012, but still most people believed that this would not upset the newly agreed timeline, i.e. application of Solvency II on 1 January 2014.

Although a number of other issues – such as a capital charge for sovereign bonds, third-country equivalence, mediation powers for EIOPA and correlation tables – were on the table for the trilogue, most of the time was spent on two crucial issues: the LTG package and the procedure for the implementing measures.

On the LTG package, it became clear very quickly that the EP was unlikely to agree with the package that had been agreed between Member States, as evidenced from the Balz Report. This created anxiety between Member States

[106] See Directive 2012/23/EU of the EP and of the Council of 12 September 2012 amending Directive 2009/138/EC as regards the date for its transposition and the date of its application, and the date of repeal of certain Directives, *OJ* L 249, 14.9.2012, p. 1.

because they feared that the solution that had been worked out for them would no longer appear in the final compromise text. Lobby by the insurance industry intensified. The parliamentary delegation was divided and the trilogue negotiations, which were now carried out under the Presidency of Cyprus, broke down in July 2012 when the EP delegation refused to accept the extended MA, requested by a number of Member States. These Member States felt that it was unfair to provide for a MA just for annuity business as conducted in the UK and Spain, where no lapses are permitted. They believed that it should also be possible to provide for an extension of this concept in those cases where policyholders have a limited ability to surrender.

The discussion became more complex when some Member States wanted to prohibit a cross-border application of certain LTG measures, such as the MA, because they did not want domestic insurers to apply such an "imprudent" measure. This was clearly not in line with the objective of furthering an internal market for insurance.

Because of the highly technical nature of the debate, some people in the EP delegation suggested carrying out an impact assessment of the various LTG measures that were being discussed. Sven Giegold (Greens, Germany) in particular supported this idea. As he commented in a press release:[107] "This is intended to avoid distortion of competition within the internal market, to guarantee financial market stability and to ensure the protection of policyholders". Commenting on the negotiations, he added:

> "For the moment, the European Parliament has stopped all the lobbying hustle by the industry. The delay caused by all the nationally driven requests for special rules is regrettable. But the responsibility lies solely with the Council of Member States and the lobbying activities of the insurance industry, which have finally gone too far."

Although the Rapporteur, the Presidency of the Council and the EC were in favour of an impact assessment, they were not enthusiastic about the idea of carrying out such an assessment before the adoption of Omnibus II, as this would further delay the Solvency II project. The delays caused by the prolonged negotiation were already creating major difficulties in practice: neither the EC nor EIOPA could officially work on the level 2 and level 3 measures as long as there was no agreement on the level 1 text and until the text was published in the Official Journal. The Council and the EC were therefore reluctant to further

[107] GIEGOLD, S., *Solvency II: Durchmarsch der Versicherungslobby aufgehalten*, 12 July 2012, https://sven-giegold.de/solvency-ii-durchmarsch-der-versicherungslobby-aufgehalten/. See also, Solvency II Wire, Solvency II News: Omnibus II trialogue calls for impact assessment on long-term guarantee measures, 13 July 2012, http://www.solvencyiiwire.com/solvency-ii-news-omnibus-ii-triologue-agreement-calls-for-impact-assessment-on-long-term-guarantee-measures/34108.

postpone the negotiations pending an impact assessment. Their preference was clearly in favour of an impact study carried out after adoption of Omnibus II, during the preparation of the level 2 measures. This was also the position of the Rapporteur and of most members of the parliamentary delegation.

Whilst the discussion on the LTG package was dragging on, a compromise was reached in the trilogue on another hot topic, i.e. the procedure for the implementing measures ("Lisbonisation"). Under the Solvency II FD, the implementing measures had to be adopted by the EC under the so-called comitology procedure. Under this procedure, the EC would ask CEIOPS to provide advice on the matter to be dealt with in the implementing measure. The measure itself would be drafted by the EC in close cooperation with MS experts in the Solvency Working Group of the EIOPC. The EP would have a right of scrutiny.

This procedure was changed by the Treaty of Lisbon (2007), which strengthened the powers of the EP, which had always resented the fact that the EC worked more closely with Member States than with the EP in the development of basic EU legislation.

The Treaty of Lisbon distinguishes between delegated acts (Art. 290 TFEU) and implementing acts (Art. 291 TFEU).[108] When it receives the power to adopt a delegated act under Art. 290 TFEU, the EC is authorised to supplement or amend the work of the legislator on non-essential elements of a legislative act. Such a delegation is always discretionary: the legislator delegates its powers to the EC in the interests of efficiency. When it receives the power to adopt an implementing act under Art. 291 TFEU, the EC is not exercising "quasi-legislative" powers but purely executive powers for areas that require uniform implementation across the EU.

The co-legislators retain a certain level of control over the empowerment: implementing acts include a right of scrutiny for the EP and for the Council, whereas with delegated acts the EP or the Council can object to an individual act or revoke the delegation altogether.

In Omnibus II, the EC had proposed to replace the existing empowerment with the new procedure introduced by the Lisbon Treaty. A distinction was made between delegated acts and implementing acts. Delegated acts would be adopted by the EC in areas such as governance, valuation, supervisory reporting and public disclosure, determination and classification of own funds, the standard formula for the calculation of the SCR, and the choice of methods and assumptions for the calculation of technical provisions. In areas where the

---

108 See EC, Communication to the EP and the Council on Implementation of Art. 290 of the TFEU, COM (2009) 673 final, 9 December 2009, 14 p. The procedure introduced by the Lisbon Treaty for delegating powers to the executive replaces the comitology system that was set up by the Treaty establishing the European Community.

EC had considered there to be a need for uniform rules, such as the combination of the single and the group SFCR or internal models, the EC had proposed the adoption of an implementing act, based upon draft implementing technical standards prepared by EIOPA. The EC had indicated that the development of regulatory technical standards (RTS) by EIOPA – a special form of delegated acts introduced by Art. 10 EIOPA Regulation – would have to await the adoption of the level 2 measures as foreseen under the Lamfalussy approach. The EC also included in its proposal a time period of two months during which the EP or the Council could object to a delegated act.

The Rapporteur was unhappy with this proposal and wanted to introduce in the Solvency II FD a number of cases where EIOPA would draft regulatory technical standards (RTS) that could then be adopted by the EC as delegated acts. In doing so, the EP wanted to give recognition to the technical expertise of EIOPA. In its view, all essential ("political") issues should be dealt with in the basic legislative act, i.e. the Solvency II FD. Technical issues should be further implemented by EIOPA, rather than by the EC, as ITS (implementing technical standards) or RTS, following the procedure set out in Arts. 10–14 EIOPA Regulation (see further Chapter 11, section 2.1.1). This was problematic for two reasons: because the EP approach departed from the Lamfalussy approach, which had been agreed on by the co-legislators as the legislative approach for Solvency II, and because the implementing measures had already been drafted by the EC.

Furthermore, as the LTG measures were considered "political", the EP insisted on including them in the FD, rather than leaving this for implementation by the EC, thereby transforming a principles-based directive into a directive that – in areas such as the LTG measures – would go into considerable detail. This would have the surprising consequence that there would only be one article dealing with the valuation of all assets and liabilities in the solvency balance sheet (Art. 75 FD), but nine dealing with the valuation of technical provisions (Arts. 76, 77, 77a–77f and 78 FD).

Although perfectly understandable, this is a regrettable development: Baron Lamfalussy had pointed out in his report the disadvantages of detailed primary legislation at EU level, particularly in the financial services area, where the economic reality changes very quickly. However, the insurance industry wanted to have detailed rules on the LTG measures in the FD, as there was fear that the EC or EIOPA might not take their concerns sufficiently into account. The Rapporteur, Burkhard Balz, admitted that as a result of the financial crisis, a more comprehensive adaptation of the FD became unavoidable:

> "Every legislative act has its history and its lessons to be drawn. One outcome of the Solvency II and Omnibus II process is a clear shift from a principles-based to a rules-based approach. This approach helps to enhance the democratic accountability and it provides a clearer guidance to the Commission for the work on the

> technical specifications. A more precise legislation that at the same time reflects the difficult market conditions underlines the responsibilities of the legislators themselves."[109]

In the approach followed by the EP, Omnibus II should empower EIOPA to draft the RTS for the implementation of the Solvency II FD and thus redraft the implementing measures (about 300 pages) that the EC had already prepared in the period 2009–2011 based upon advice from CEIOPS/EIOPA and after extensive consultation with Member States and stakeholders. Neither EIOPA, nor the EC, nor Member States, nor stakeholders were in favour of such an approach, which would have delayed the final adoption of Solvency II even further and would have included the risk of renegotiation of a large number of issues, for which compromise solutions had already been agreed.

In the end, a magic solution was found: the introduction of a sunrise clause. For the first implementation of the Solvency II FD, all implementing measures (including those that are considered RTS) would be adopted by the EC following the procedure for the adoption of delegated acts (rather than the procedure for the adoption of RTS as foreseen in the EIOPA Regulation), subject to a sunrise clause. In that solution, the measures should be adopted before 24 May 2016. After that date, the powers of the EC to proceed with a delegated act rather than with RTS would no longer exist and any amendments of the delegated act after that date would also have to take place through RTS (Art. 301b FD). In other words, the sun will rise again and things will return to normal after 24 May 2016.

Although this debate might seem somewhat legalistic, it is not without importance: it clearly showed that the EP considers EIOPA as its principal technical adviser for the implementation of the new solvency regime. The question of who should prepare and propose the implementing measures might appear to have little technical significance, as the process for approving the text seems quite similar. However, the change clearly has political implications. Nobody knows this better than the EC, which – in the past – was the only institution that could table legislative proposals. In the future, it is EIOPA that will be in the drafting seat. The EC will still have to endorse and the Council and the EP will still have the right to object, but the change in procedure is important. At the insistence of the EP, the period for the Council and the EP to object to a draft implementing measure was extended from two months to three months, with a possible further extension by another three months.

Meanwhile, not much progress was made on the LTG package. Whilst all trilogue parties agreed that Solvency II should include regulatory measures to deal with the issues associated with insurance products with long-term

---

109 BALZ, B., Lessons learnt from Solvency II: more rules than principles, *Eurofi Newsletter*, 31 March 2014, p. 20, https://www.eurofi.net/wp-content/uploads/2014/03/2014_NEWSLETTER_Athens.pdf.

guarantees that may be affected by "artificial volatility",[110] it was unclear which measures were really needed. A number of difficult questions were raised: should account be taken of the value of the assets in measuring the corresponding liabilities? Which discount rate should replace the government bond rate as the risk-free rate? How to calculate the illiquidity premium that is attached to long-term liabilities that remain firm whilst the corresponding assets go up and down like a yo-yo as a result of market turbulence? Should a distinction be made in the spread of government bonds between market risk and default risk?

At the trilogue meeting on 12 July 2012, the Presidency (Cyprus) was for the first time able to present a position backed by a qualified majority of Member States (excluding Germany). However, the Rapporteur rejected the proposed text as a basis for negotiation because of the reservations expressed in ECON against an extended MA. In order to make progress, the trilogue parties and EIOPA agreed at an informal meeting on 19 July 2012 to have the LTG package tested by EIOPA. The usefulness of such an assessment was supported by the ESRB, which had been examining the impact of the financial crisis on the insurance sector and in particular the systemic risk of a possible double hit – a combination of low asset prices and low interest rates – and had indicated in a letter to the trilogue parties that it was particularly interested in the results of an assessment of the LTG package.

The question was now whether an assessment by EIOPA should be carried out before or after the adoption of Omnibus II. In both cases, the deadline for the application of Solvency II, which had just been agreed (1 January 2014), would no longer be realistic. The Rapporteur, the EP delegation, the EC and most Member States favoured an ex-post assessment of the LTG measures. Such an assessment could provide further clarity for the development of the delegated act that would underpin the framework agreed as part of Omnibus II. That exercise could not be carried out efficiently and effectively in the absence of an agreed Omnibus II Directive. Only France and Germany preferred an ex-ante assessment.[111]

4.2.5. *Impact Assessment Carried Out by EIOPA*

When the trilogue parties reconvened on 18 September 2012, the EC – this time represented by Commissioner Michel Barnier – suddenly announced that the

---

110 "Artificial volatility" can be defined as volatility of technical provisions, own funds or capital requirements that can reasonably be considered to be due to short-term inefficiency of market pricing and does not reflect changes in the long-term financial position or risk exposure of (re)insurance undertakings carrying out insurance business of a long-term nature.

111 For a good description of the atmosphere in the trilogue at that time, see Solvency II Wire, *Solvency II News: Omnibus II trilogue in disarray*, 9 October 2012, http://www.solvencyiiwire.com/solvency-ii-news-omnibus-ii-trilogue-in-disarray/56934.

EC would prefer an impact assessment to be carried out before the adoption of Omnibus II. The Council, the Rapporteur and the EP delegation were caught by surprise. The EC justified its position with the following arguments. An ex-ante assessment:

- would allow for a broader examination of the LTG package to be tested, without being constrained by the political compromises that were on the table;
- would ultimately ensure that the co-legislators would take informed decisions when agreeing the final LTG package;
- would allow the co-legislators to communicate more clearly with the market about the intended way forward;
- would be more likely to result in an outcome that would be consistent with the single market objective, as nervousness about the potential impact of the measures had led many parties to call for MS options in relation to the LTG measures. Such MS options would be rendered redundant if the results of the assessment showed that the LTG package was prudentially sound and workable.[112]

After a break, which allowed the Council and the EP delegation to agree their positions internally, the trilogue parties agreed to ask EIOPA to carry out the assessment and to do so before the adoption of Omnibus II. It was however unclear whether EIOPA or the EC would report back to the trilogue about the results of the assessment.

Insurance Europe was pleased with the agreement to carry out an impact assessment on the measures dealing with long-term guarantee issues: "It is regrettable that this may lead to a delay in the Solvency II process, but it is vital that the results of the tests can be reflected in Omnibus II in order to ensure that the new regulatory regime is both appropriate and workable".[113]

Although EIOPA was willing to carry out the assessment, it feared further delays and wrote again to Commissioner Barnier, outlining the reasons why Solvency II was urgently needed. In his letter of 4 October 2012,[114] the EIOPA Chairman (Gabriel Bernardino) wrote:

> "The lack of certainty about the implementation is undermining EU credibility in international discussions as Solvency II is meant as a reference framework for risk

---

112 These arguments were further developed in a "non-paper" circulated by the EC to the trialogue parties on 24 September 2012.

113 Insurance Europe, *Impact assessment results should be reflected in Omnibus II*, Press Release, 20 September 2012, https://www.insuranceeurope.eu/sites/default/files/attachments/Impact%20assessment%20results%20should%20be%20reflected%20in%20Omnibus%20II.pdf.

114 https://eiopa.europa.eu/Publications/Other%20Documents/EIOPA-12-348_Letter_to_Commissioner_Barnier.pdf.

> insurance based supervision at the international level. In order to keep the momentum and to be consistent with all the financial and human resources already dedicated to this project both by supervisors and the industry, we urge the political parties involved to come up with a sound and reliable timetable for the implementation of Solvency II as soon as possible. The timetable should consider a realistic assessment of the expected time needed to deliver the different milestones and it should be appropriately communicated to all stakeholders in order to eliminate the current uncertainty. To secure the credibility of the project it is clearly preferable to set operationally achievable timings. Once a credible overall timeline is agreed, a reflection should be made on the possibility of earlier implementation of some Solvency II elements ..."

In his letter, Gabriel Bernardino also suggested bringing forward the application of some aspects of Solvency II in order to keep up momentum. Some people had indeed suggested that the introduction of the Pillar 1 requirements should be delayed until an agreement had been reached on the LTG package, but that the Pillar 2 and possibly Pillar 3 requirements should already enter into force.

In his response, dated 8 November 2012, Commissioner Barnier stressed the importance of a technical assessment of the LTG package and thanked EIOPA in advance for its valuable work in this respect. He indicated that the trilogue parties were still discussing the date of application of Solvency II. Once a decision had been made, the trilogue parties would publish a joint statement, outlining a clear, realistic timeline for the implementation of Solvency II. On the issue of an early application of some aspects of Solvency II, the Commissioner observed that this would require a new legislative proposal and that the discussion of such a proposal would take time. He suggested that EIOPA should come forward with a list of best practices, in the form of an opinion, to ensure a common level of preparedness amongst supervisors, which could also include what national supervisory authorities would expect of their undertakings. He proposed that EIOPA act to ensure that there was convergence towards a Solvency II approach within the limits of what was possible under the existing framework and suggested focusing on the speedy implementation of Pillar 2 (governance and risk management) and Pillar 3 (common reporting formats and templates).

Commissioner Barnier also indicated in his letter that he was not in favour of starting Solvency II with Pillars 2 and 3, as had been suggested by a number of people. This would have required an amendment of the FD. Furthermore, if this approach were taken, it would create a risk that the whole reform would need to be postponed for a number of years.[115]

---

115 The issue was raised at the Second Annual Conference of EIOPA on 21 November 2012 in Frankfurt. Following a question from the audience, the EC's representative made it quite clear that the EC was opposed to an introduction of Solvency II in stages, i.e. starting with Pillar 2 or with Pillars 2 and 3.

Following the Commissioner's letter, EIOPA published an Opinion on Interim Measures regarding Solvency II on 20 December 2012.[116] In this opinion, NSAs were asked to put in place from 1 January 2014 certain important aspects of a prospective and risk-based supervisory approach, such as an effective system of governance and an effective risk management system, including a forward-looking assessment of the undertaking's own risks (based on the ORSA principles). The NSAs should put in place a pre-application process for internal model approval and were encouraged to request all the information necessary for applying a prospective and risk-based supervisory approach.[117]

In terms of the assessment of the LTG package, the request made by the trilogue parties to EIOPA, which was formally transmitted to EIOPA by a letter from the EC dated 19 December 2012, was very extensive and was only agreed between them with great difficulty (the negotiation of the terms of reference took two months). The timing imposed upon EIOPA (14 June 2013) for completing the assessment was very tight, as the LTG package assessment could only start at the beginning of 2013. The assessment is sometimes (incorrectly) referred to as QIS 6.

EIOPA was asked to examine the impact of six measures and to test them in different combinations through a series of 13 quantitative scenarios and tailored qualitative questions based upon 2011 year-end data. The following measures were included in the assessment:

- *counter-cyclical premium*: crisis measure to be activated by EIOPA to complement market observations when these are determined to be temporarily unreliable or unfit for prudential purposes, due to spread-related crisis situations in financial markets;
- *extrapolation*: properties of modelling used to value liabilities in order to supplement market observations when reliable market information is no longer available (because of the length of the duration of the liabilities);
- *classical MA*: permanent measure providing an adjusted risk-free rate for (re)insurance annuities managed under a strict asset–liability matching regime which results in an immaterial exposure to short-term market volatility;

116 EIOPA, Opinion on Interim Measures regarding Solvency II, EIOPA-12-338, 20 December 2012, 4 p.

117 See also the preparatory guidelines published by EIOPA on 31 October 2013 on a forward-looking assessment of own risks (based on the ORSA principles), on the pre-application of internal models, on the submission of information to NSAs and on the system of governance. This was in fact an early start of parts of Solvency II. Although rather unusual, EIOPA no doubt felt strengthened to proceed in this way because it was supported in this initiative by the EC.

- *extended MA*: extension of the classical MA to cover business of a long-term nature, but with a lower degree of certainty and predictability of cash flows (because of the existence of a surrender option for the policyholder);
- *transitional measure*: measure smoothing the transition from Solvency I to Solvency II for long-term guarantee business underwritten under different economic and prudential conditions (Solvency I);
- *extension of the recovery period*: possibility of extending the recovery period if there is a breach of the SCR in the case of an exceptional fall in financial markets.

Insurance Europe was very supportive of the impact assessment:

> "It is of the utmost importance that alternatives are tested to enable the European Parliament, Council and Commission discussions to come to suitable solutions when they resume after the impact assessment. The final Solvency II measures must be designed and calibrated in a way that allows them to work in all European markets and not to be artificially limited or unnecessarily conservative."[118]

In its report on the LTG assessment,[119] EIOPA confirmed the importance of LTG measures for many Member States in periods of financial stress, such as those experienced in 2011, and agreed that a package of different measures was needed to cater for the different insurance products offered in Member States. A number of proposals were made:

- there should be no extended MA because this would introduce false risk management incentives, particularly in terms of credit quality of assets and with regards to the management of liquidity risk. The measure – because of its complexity – would also be difficult to supervise;
- it would be preferable to have no counter-cyclical premium, as this would significantly increase the capital requirements in a number of Member States and the triggering process (EIOPA decision) might result in possible severe implications for financial market stability. The counter-cyclical premium

---

118 Insurance Europe, *Testing of Solvency II measures welcomed*, Press Release, 28 January 2013, https://www.insuranceeurope.eu/testing-solvency-ii-measures-welcomed. Two documents were published on the website of Insurance Europe to inform interested parties about the measures that would be tested: Insurance Europe, *The package of measures to avoid artificial volatility and pro-cyclicality*, 8 February 2013, 23 p., https://www.insuranceeurope.eu/sites/default/files/attachments/The%20package%20of%20measures%20to%20avoid%20artificial%20volatility%20and%20pro-cyclicality.pdf and Insurance Europe, *The matching adjustment – Theory and practice*, 8 February 2013, 49 p., https://www.insuranceeurope.eu/sites/default/files/attachments/The%20matching%20adjustment%20-%20Theory%20and%20practice.pdf.

119 EIOPA, Technical findings on the Long-Term Guarantee Assessment, EIOPA/13/286, 14 June 2013, 166 p.

should therefore be replaced with a predictable volatility adjustment mechanism, called a volatility balancer, which might turn negative under certain conditions and would adjust own funds rather than technical provisions;
- the conditions for the MA should be defined very carefully (the composition of the portfolio must guarantee regular cash flows);
- there should be a transitional regime in order to smooth the transition between different regulatory regimes, which would ultimately lead to more stability in the insurance sector;
- extending the recovery period for a restoration of the SCR could be a powerful tool in crisis periods, but should not be seen as an excuse to postpone action by undertakings in order to restore the situation; the extension should not exceed seven years. The triggering event should also cover other crisis situations than a steep fall in financial markets, such as a situation of low interest rates or a combination of major insurance risk events;
- the extrapolation approach would benefit from an extension of the convergence period significantly beyond 10 years, for example to 40 years; it should also be combined with dedicated Pillar 2 measures such as a sensitivity analysis;
- the LTG measures should not be linked to MS options and cross-border business should not be excluded from any measure;
- the impact of all LTG measures should be publicly disclosed.

The LTG Assessment Report covered 427 undertakings and all EEA Member States (except for the Czech Republic, Latvia and Iceland). It showed clearly that a scenario without LTG measures would result in a significant number of participating undertakings (40%) not being able to meet the SCR requirements. As indicated in EIOPA's Report, most of the quantitative analysis was based on 2011 year-end data, which in itself constituted an "adverse scenario", as financial market conditions at the end of 2011 were particularly difficult for insurers, especially in the Eurozone, with the combination of very high spreads in some markets (Portugal, Spain and Italy) and a low risk-free rate.

Because of the criticism that had been voiced against Solvency II, EIOPA set out in its report some of the conclusions that it had drawn from the financial crisis:[120]

- the crisis underlined the urgent need for Solvency II and its robust design, acknowledged by external parties such as the IMF;

[120] EIOPA, Technical findings on the Long-Term Guarantee Assessment, EIOPA/13/286, 14 June 2013, p. 21.

- the crisis highlighted the need to address volatility and its consequences: volatility is a fact, which is shown by market-consistent valuation, and should be an integral part of the risk management of companies, both as a risk and as a potential business opportunity;
- the interaction of the three pillars of Solvency II is of crucial importance: market-consistent valuation puts a price on all options and guarantees embedded in (re)insurance products and provides management with information on the economic costs embedded in the product.

Following the submission of the EIOPA Report, the trilogue negotiations were resumed on 10 July 2013 and a compromise proposal was presented by the Lithuanian Presidency, very much inspired by the EIOPA proposals and by a draft prepared by the EC services:

- MA with strict criteria (no combination with volatility adjustment (VA) or the risk-free interest rate transitional measure and subject to prior approval by the supervisory authority);
- extrapolation;
- VA (Member States may require prior approval);
- extension of the recovery period for breaches of the SCR in stressed circumstances (up to seven years);
- transitional measure on risk-free interest rate (16 years, particularly important for Germany);
- transitional measure on technical provisions (16 years, particularly important for the UK);
- possibility to further develop the LTG package by delegated act or by RTS and ITS;
- annual reporting by EIOPA on the application of the LTG package;
- reporting by the EC after five years, with possible review;
- new risk management and reporting obligations for undertakings using one of the measures in the LTG package.

4.2.6. Second "Quick-Fix" Directive

Whilst the discussion between the trilogue parties continued, on 2 October 2013 the EC presented a new proposal[121] for a second "quick-fix" Directive extending the dates of transposition and application of the Solvency II FD from

121 EC, Proposal for an amendment of Directive 2009/138/EC (Solvency II) as regards the date of its transposition and the date of its application, and the date of repeal of certain Directives (Solvency I), COM (2013) 680 final, 2 October 2013.

30 June 2013 and 1 January 2014 to 31 January 2015 and 1 January 2016 respectively.

In the explanatory memorandum to its proposal, the EC noted that "the parties to the on-going legislative negotiations have agreed that there should be no further changes to either the transposition or application dates during the Omnibus II negotiations in order to ensure legal clarity for insurance and reinsurance undertakings and supervisory authorities during their preparations".

The fact that the EC introduced this proposal after the then-recently (in 2012) agreed date for the transposition of the FD (30 June 2013) had already lapsed showed the total confusion in the negotiations. It was difficult for any party to predict the outcome of the negotiations and nobody was willing to put a new proposal with new dates on the table until it was certain that the negotiations would succeed and that a reasonable date could be set, considering the extensive work that still needed to be undertaken at level 2 (EC) and level 3 (EIOPA) before Solvency II could become applicable.

The second "quick-fix" Directive was adopted on 11 December 2013.[122] In the meantime, EIOPA had adopted its preliminary guidelines and had de facto put parts of Solvency II in motion.

4.2.7. Political Agreement

A political agreement between the trilogue parties was reached on 13 November 2013.[123] There is no doubt that all parties concerned were happy that a deal had finally emerged. Until the very end, a lot of issues remained on the table: the details of the LTG measures, equivalence and deemed equivalence for third countries (see further Chapter 10), the treatment of sovereign debt, and last but not least a number of inter-institutional issues such as correlation tables (should Member States be required to produce tables showing how the various articles of the Directive have been implemented in national law?) and the right of inquiry for the EP.

The EC welcomed the agreement as follows:

> "This agreement is a very important step towards the introduction of a modern and risk-based solvency regime for the insurance industry in Europe as of 1 January 2016,

---

122 Directive 2013/58/EU of the EP and of the Council of 11 December 2013 amending Directive 2009/138/EC (Solvency II) as regards the date of its transposition and the date of its application, and the date of repeal of certain Directives (Solvency I), *OJ* L 341, 18.12.2013, p. 1.

123 For a lively description of the negotiations, see COELHO, H., The twists and turns of Solvency II negotiations, *Insurance ERM*, 22 December 2015, 5 p., https://www.insuranceerm.com/analysis/the-twists-and-turns-of-solvency-ii-negotiations.htmlt.

> making it both safer and more competitive. In practice it makes the implementation of Solvency II possible. Notably Omnibus II contains important provisions that should allow the insurance industry to continue offering long term guaranteed products (typically life insurance policies being paid out in a lump sum when the policy holder reaches a certain age or in the form of annuities). This kind of policy is an essential part of retirement planning for citizens in many Member States. Moreover, it will ensure that insurance companies in general and life assurance companies in particular can match these long-term liabilities with investments in long-term assets such as infrastructure projects."[124]

In a press statement on 14 November 2013, the Lithuanian Presidency of the Council indicated:

> "This is a very important legislative dossier aiming at financial stability in the insurance sector and beyond. The agreement comes in time for the revised directive to enter into force. The agreement should create a momentum for the final adoption by the EU Council and the European Parliament."

At a press conference held on 14 November 2013 by the Rapporteur, Burkhard Balz, and the Chair of ECON, Sharon Bowles, both noted that the Omnibus II text presented an "efficient and practical solution" under Solvency II for (re)insurance undertakings offering LTG products and ensured that these undertakings could continue to operate in difficult market conditions and in low interest rate environments. Balz specified that the solutions set out in the Omnibus II Directive would allow (re)insurance undertakings to continue to offer these products and to maintain their role as long-term investors.

Whilst the package of measures deviated from that set out by EIOPA following the long-term guarantees assessment carried out earlier in 2013, in particular with less onerous calibrations on a number of the measures, Sharon Bowles and Burkhard Balz pointed out that this was balanced by the introduction of important qualitative requirements relating to the governance and disclosure of these measures. The emphasis was also put on the need for (re)insurance undertakings to set up a liquidity plan when applying the MA or the VA, on the importance for proper supervision of the LTG measures, and on the requirement for these measures to be applied in a transparent way.

Whilst Balz acknowledged that the new rules introduced under Solvency II were ambitious, he highlighted the importance of respecting the principle of

[124] EC, *Commissioner Barnier welcomes trilogue agreement by Council and Parliament on the "Omnibus II" Directive*, Press Release, 14 November 2013, http://europa.eu/rapid/press-release_MEMO-13-992_en.htm.

proportionality when applying them. Supervisory reporting included quarterly reporting on an asset-by-asset basis, but exemptions from this requirement were available for smaller undertakings.

In particular for European (re)insurance groups, Balz underlined that the approved text included an extended provision for transitional equivalence for third-country solvency regimes. This would allow the EC to grant provisional equivalence to third countries for a period of 10 years, at which point it would be reviewed, with the option to extend the regime for a further 10 years (and potentially indefinitely). This solution would allow the USA to be considered an equivalent regulatory regime, allowing European groups with US subsidiaries to use local regulatory requirements when calculating the group SCR. While this solution had been designed as a specific response to the (complex) regulatory situation in the USA, it was stressed that the solution adopted would provide flexibility to develop pragmatic solutions for regulatory regimes in other third countries, so as to ensure that European groups were not disadvantaged when operating in these countries.

A different voice could be heard from Sven Giegold MEP, fiscal and economic policy spokesman of the Greens in the EP and Shadow Rapporteur:

> "The EU has missed an opportunity to truly reduce risk in the insurance sector and protect policyholders. Intense lobbying by big insurance companies and their backers in their national governments and the EP has paid off, as they succeeded in lowering prudential capital requirements. While this will clearly increase profits for long term insurance products, it flies in the face of the recommendations of the ESRB and EIOPA."

And he continued:

> "One silver lining is a provision, insisted on by the Greens, to ensure that insurance companies using any of the long-term guarantee measures must report the quantitative effect to the public. We will make sure that all companies making use of these privileges are named and shamed on a website including their brands and the billions of missing capital."[125]

Although industry did not obtain from the negotiations everything it wanted, Insurance Europe nevertheless welcomed the agreement on Omnibus II:

> "While the compromise reached between the institutions on Omnibus II is not the ideal solution the insurance industry would have wished for in terms of correctly reflecting

125 GIEGOLD, S., *EU insurance rules (Solvency II): Industry lobby pays off, as EU fails to protect policyholders*, Press Release, 14 November 2013.

> insurers' long-term business and low exposure to market volatility, we do believe it is a workable base from which to develop the technical details of the new regulatory regime."[126]

The agreement was endorsed by the EP at its plenary session on 11 March 2014, with 560 votes in favour against 130 and four abstentions. The Council confirmed the agreement at the Agriculture and Fisheries Council in Luxembourg on 14 April 2014. Omnibus II was formally adopted by the co-legislators on 16 April 2014.[127]

It is regrettable that it took so long to negotiate Omnibus II. As indicated before, important reasons for the delay were a lack of leadership on the file, the technical and legal complexity of the issues, the further development of the financial crisis, the priority given to the banking agenda, and very strong lobbying from Member States and from the (re)insurance industry. At times, it felt as if nobody wanted an agreement. The enthusiasm for this reform that was clearly present in 2007 when the negotiations on Solvency II started seemed to have evaporated. Much credit should be given to EIOPA, which kept reminding the co-legislators and the EC that Solvency II was both necessary and urgent, and that it was not in the interest of the insurance industry and policyholders to keep this file pending. Although it would probably have been possible to deal with the problem of market volatility through level 2 measures (supervisory action) under the existing FD, there was clearly a lack of trust between the (re)insurance industry and the supervisory community (both NSAs and EIOPA) and between Member States, which did not want to give each other a competitive advantage.

Notwithstanding the difficulties with Omnibus II, Solvency II continued to influence regulatory reforms in many parts of the world[128] and within the IAIS.[129]

---

[126] Insurance Europe, *Insurance Europe welcomes EU agreement on Omnibus II*, Press Release, 14 November 2013, https://www.insuranceeurope.eu/sites/default/files/attachments/EU%20agreement%20on%20Omnibus%20II%20welcomed.pdf.

[127] Directive 2014/51/EU of the EP and of the Council of 16 April 2014 amending Directives 2003/71/EC and 2009/138/EC and Regulations (EC) No 1060/2009, (EU) No 1094/2010 and (EU) No 1095/2010 in respect of the European Supervisory Authority (European Insurance and Occupational Pensions Authority) and the European Supervisory Authority (European Securities and Markets Authority), *OJ* L 153, 22.5.2014, p. 1.

[128] For instance, in Argentina, Bermuda, Brazil, Chile, China, Israel, Japan, Jordan, Mexico, Morocco, Singapore, South Africa, Switzerland, Turkey, and the USA.

[129] See QUAGLIA, L., The European Union, the USA and International Standard Setting by Regulatory For a in Finance, *New Political Economy*, 2014, No 3, pp. 427–441. The author refers to Solvency II as one of the most influential projects in the financial services area.

4.3. CHANGES BROUGHT ABOUT BY OMNIBUS II

Omnibus II brings important changes to the FD adopted in 2009. The most important changes are summarised below.

4.3.1. Long-Term Guarantee Measures

The Solvency II regulatory framework does not include a legal definition of "long-term guarantee measures".[130] The common use of the term is mainly linked to the type of guarantee offered or the duration of the contract. The following types of products including a long-term guarantee can be observed in national markets in the EEA:[131]

- traditional life insurance, such as with profit contracts, saving products, endowments policies and annuities;
- unit-linked policies with guaranteed investment yield or capital protection;
- variable annuities;
- some types of health insurance, such as annuities stemming from protection contracts that offer the policyholder the maintenance of its wages in case of severe illness;
- non-life annuities, for instance stemming from third-party liability insurance;
- specific non-life insurance products, such as construction risk and borrowers' insurance.

The most common types of guarantees included in these long-term products are: a guaranteed interest rate which is explicitly set in the contract, a guaranteed sum assured and paid on death, a guaranteed sum assured and paid on any cause other than death, a guaranteed surrender value, a guaranteed annuity benefit, or a guaranteed return of the premium.

The proportion of products with guarantees differs by country. In 16 EEA countries, products with at least one guarantee make up over 95% of the market. In other countries, the proportion of products with guarantees is much lower. In general the countries with a low proportion of products with guarantees have significant volumes of unit-linked life insurance, whereby the investment risk is born by the policyholder. Overall, the availability of LTG products is stable or decreasing across the EEA, because of the low yield environment and incentives given by undertakings for policyholders to switch to unit-linked products.

---

130 For a summary of these measures, see also EIOPA, *Solvency II tools with macro-prudential impact*, Publications Office of the EU, Luxembourg, 2018, 50 p.

131 EIOPA, Report on long-term guarantee measures and measures on equity risk 2016, EIOPA-BoS-16/279, 16 December 2016, pp. 33–34.

Overall, there is a decrease in the size of guarantees, in particular interest rate guarantees.[132]

Under Solvency II, insurers are incentivised to match cash flows with the long-term guarantees they offer using long-term assets available in the market. This long-term cash flow-based investment strategy means that insurers are less reliant on short-term price movements in their assets, where these are unrelated to default. The LTG measures aim at mitigating the "artificial" volatility stemming from a valuation of assets and liabilities in the balance sheet on a market-consistent basis. By incorporating the long-term investment strategies of insurers into the market-consistent valuation framework, the long-term ability of insurers to meet their cash flow needs is more accurately captured, enabling them to continue offering guarantees at affordable prices.

The LTG measures include the extrapolation, the MA, the VA, the extension of the recovery period, the transitional measure on the risk-free rate and the transitional measure on technical provisions.[133] Whilst the MA, the VA and the transitional measures on the risk-free rate and on technical provisions are optional for undertakings, the extrapolation is applicable to all undertakings for the calculation of their technical provisions.

1. *Extrapolation of the relevant risk-free interest rate term structure (Art. 77a FD)*

   Extrapolation of the relevant risk-free interest rate term structure deals with the issue whereby liabilities have significantly longer durations than the last liquid point for risk-free assets. This could cause practical matching problems as it means that long-dated assets cannot be matched with long-term liabilities of the same duration. The relevant risk-free interest rate term structure should avoid artificial volatility of technical provisions and eligible own funds and provide an incentive for good risk management.

   Therefore, the risk-free rate of longer maturities needs to be extrapolated towards a level of interest rate that is stable over time. The extrapolation of the risk-free interest rate term structure is not an optional measure. It is applicable to all (re)insurance undertakings for the calculation of their technical provisions.

   For further details on the extrapolation of the risk-free interest rate term structure, see Chapter 6, section 2.3.2.

---

132 For more details, see EIOPA, Report on long-term guarantee measures and measures on equity risk 2018, EIOPA-BoS-18/471, 18 December 2018, pp. 63–75.

133 The measures on equity risk, such as the symmetric adjustment mechanism to the equity risk capital charge and the duration-based equity risk sub-module, were already available under the FD adopted in 2009.

2. *MA to the relevant risk-free interest rate term structure (Arts. 77b and 77c FD)*
The matching premium discussed between the Council and the EP became the MA. Where a (re)insurance undertaking holds bonds or other assets with similar cash flow characteristics to maturity, it is not exposed to the risk of changing spreads (spread risk) on those assets, but only to credit risk (counterparty default risk). In order to prevent changes in asset spreads from impacting the amount of own funds of the undertaking, the undertaking should be allowed to adjust the relevant risk-free interest rate term structure for the calculation of technical provisions in line with the spread movements of its assets.
The MA was designed to dampen the volatility in the case of a fully matched portfolio of insurance liabilities which are completely illiquid (no surrender option for the policyholder or surrender option where the surrender value does not exceed the value of the assets covering the insurance obligations), such as is the case for annuity business in the UK and in Spain.
For further details on the MA, see Chapter 6, section 2.3.3.
3. *Volatility adjustment to the relevant risk-free interest rate term structure (Art. 77d FD)*
The counter-cyclical premium discussed during the negotiations between the Council and the EP became the VA, a measure for which Member States may require prior approval and which aims at preventing pro-cyclical investment behaviour.
Undertakings have to cover their technical provisions with assets. Where in a situation of stressed financial markets some of these assets lose value (for example, bond prices decrease because markets become illiquid or credit spreads widen), there might be a strong incentive for the undertakings to sell the deteriorating assets. Selling the assets avoids the undertaking's regulatory balance sheet being exposed to the volatility of the assets' market values and the undertaking incurring further market value losses. Where this reaction is widespread in the insurance market, it has a pro-cyclical effect: undertakings sell into a falling market, thereby accelerating the deterioration of market prices. Such a downward spiral is a serious threat to financial stability.
The VA is an adjustment to the relevant risk-free interest rate term structure, which is set in order to counteract short-term artificial volatility due to spreads exaggeration in bond markets. As a measure against pro-cyclical investment behaviour, the VA was strongly supported by a number of Member States, including Belgium, France, Italy and Portugal, all countries that had experienced credit risk exaggerations for government bonds in the aftermath of the financial crisis.
For further details on the VA, see Chapter 6, section 2.3.4.
4. *Extension of the recovery period*
If a (re)insurance undertaking no longer complies with the SCR or when there is a risk of non-compliance with the SCR in the following three months,

the situation needs to be redressed as soon as possible in the interest of policyholders. Action must be taken (submission of a realistic recovery plan) in close cooperation with the supervisory authority (Art. 138 (2) and (3) FD).

If a number of (re)insurance undertakings find themselves in a similar situation, the problem becomes more complex. This point was raised during the negotiations of Omnibus II. The insurance industry was afraid that problems might arise as a result of the low interest rate environment and that supervisory authorities might not show sufficient understanding if the insurance industry were to find itself in a situation of severe distress. Omnibus II therefore introduced a provision into the FD (Art. 138 (4) FD) setting out a specific procedure that would apply in the event of exceptional adverse situations affecting (re)insurance undertakings representing a significant share of the market or of the affected lines of business. This could be the result of a fall in financial markets that is unforeseen, sharp and steep, a persistent low interest rate environment or a high-impact catastrophic event.

In order to ensure a level playing field, only EIOPA can declare the existence of an exceptional adverse situation. Once EIOPA has officially declared the existence of an exceptional adverse situation, NSAs may extend, for affected undertakings, the recovery period for a restoration of the SCR by a maximum of seven years.

For the details of the procedure, see Chapter 6, section 4.2.1.3.

5. *Transitional measure on the risk-free rate (Art. 308c FD)*

Because of the low interest rate environment, using the prevailing risk-free interest rate on 1 January 2016 would likely put a number of (re)insurance undertakings in difficulty. Subject to supervisory approval, (re)insurance undertakings can therefore gradually introduce the impact of moving from their current discount rate to a Solvency II discount rate over a period of 16 years.

If approved, an adjustment of the risk-free interest rate may be applied to (re)insurance obligations concluded before 1 January 2016. The adjustment is equal to the difference between the interest rate as determined under Solvency I at the last date at which Solvency I is in force, and the annual effective rate as determined under Solvency II.

Those undertakings that apply the VA have to account for the VA before performing the described adjustment. The adjustment will be fully taken into account at year-end 2016, i.e. when (re)insurance undertakings disclose their solvency position for the first time after Solvency II comes into force. In the following years, the adjustment will decrease in a linear manner until the benefit disappears at year-end 2032.

In order to promote transparency and allow for comparability, public disclosure must be made of the solvency position with and without the application of the transitional measure on the risk-free interest rate (see Chapter 6, section 2.3.6).

This measure may not be combined either with the MA (Arts. 77b and 77c FD) or with the transitional measure on technical provisions (Art. 308d FD). It only applies for business in force on the date of implementation of Solvency II and cannot be applied to new business (Art. 308c (3) FD).

Where the undertaking would not comply with the SCR without using the transitional measure, it must inform the supervisory authority immediately and take the necessary measures to ensure compliance with the SCR at the end of the transitional period, submit a phasing-in plan within two months and report progress annually. If the report shows that it is unrealistic for the undertaking to comply with the SCR at the end of the period, the transitional measure may be revoked (Art. 308e FD).

6. *Transitional measure on technical provisions (Art. 308d FD)*
As an alternative to the transitional measure on the risk-free interest rate, undertakings may seek supervisory approval for a transitional deduction to technical provisions, which has to be applied at the level of homogeneous risk groups (Art. 80 FD). The two transitional measures cannot be combined. The objective of this measure is to smooth the transition to Solvency II, to limit interference with existing products and to ensure the availability of insurance products.

The transitional deduction is equal to the difference between technical provisions net of recoverable from reinsurance and SPVs as prescribed under Solvency II and technical provisions net of recoverable from reinsurance as prescribed under Solvency I.

The deduction applies in full in 2016 and is reduced in a linear manner to 0% in 2032. It may be combined with the VA, but not with the MA. In order to promote transparency and allow for comparability, public disclosure must be made of the solvency position with and without the application of the deduction (see Chapter 6, section 2.3.6).

Where the undertaking would not comply with the SCR without using the transitional measure, it must inform the supervisory authority immediately and take the necessary measures to ensure compliance with the SCR at the end of the transitional period, submit a phasing-in plan within two months and report progress annually. If the report shows it is unrealistic that the undertaking will comply with the SCR at the end of the period, the transitional measure may be revoked (Art. 308e FD).

In cases where the application of this transitional measure would result in a solvency position that would be lower than that prescribed by Solvency I, the supervisory authority may reduce the deduction.

4.3.2. Transposition and Application Dates of Solvency II

The FD, as amended by Omnibus II, had to be transposed by Member States by 31 March 2015 (Art. 7 (1) Omnibus II). Contrary to what had initially been agreed between the co-legislators in the trilogue (see above section 4.2), the date for transposition by Member States was moved from 1 January 2015 (as stated in the second "quick-fix" Directive) to 31 March 2015. Whilst the EC and the EP wanted implementation before 1 January 2015, many Member States were in favour of a later transposition date as parliamentary procedures take time. Some Member States had stopped the preparatory work for the transposition of the FD after the introduction of the Omnibus II proposal. To restart the process was not an easy matter. It was therefore considered safer to go for a later transposition date.

The date of first application was already set by the second "quick-fix" Directive at 1 January 2016 (Art. 7 (2) Omnibus II), subject to the phasing-in provisions discussed below.

4.3.3. *Phasing-In of Solvency II*

Although it had been agreed that the new solvency regime should become applicable from 1 January 2016 onwards, all parties concerned agreed that there was a need to provide for a phasing-in of Solvency II. This was particularly important as some parts of the new solvency regime required supervisory approval (for instance, the possibility of using an internal model). Sufficient time had to be provided to NSAs for the examination of applications by (re)insurance undertakings so as to ensure that the new solvency regime could effectively start on 1 January 2016. This required a transposition date well ahead of 1 January 2016 and an early application of some provisions in the FD.

The phasing-in provisions are included in Art. 308a FD, which received an early application date of 1 April 2015 (Art. 311, second paragraph FD).

Art. 2 (25), (43) and (82) Omnibus II – relating respectively to the supervisory approval of ancillary own funds (Art. 92 FD), the information from Member States to the EC and to EIOPA (Art. 176 FD) and the report by EIOPA on staffing and resource needs (Art. 310a FD) – apply from 31 March 2015 (Art. 8 Omnibus II).

The other articles relevant to Solvency II apply from 1 January 2016 (Art. 7 (2) Omnibus II).

In accordance with Art. 308a (1) FD, Member States had to ensure that NSAs had the power to decide from 1 April 2015 on the approval of:

- ancillary own funds (Art. 90 FD);
- the classification of own funds items (Art. 95, third paragraph FD);
- USPs (Art. 104 (7) FD);
- a full or partial internal model (Arts. 112 and 113 FD);
- SPVs to be established in their territory (Art. 211 FD);
- ancillary own funds of an intermediate insurance holding company (Art. 226 (2) FD);
- a group internal model (Arts. 230, 231 and 233 (5) FD);

- the use of the duration-based equity risk sub-module (Art. 304 FD);
- the use of the MA (Arts. 77b and 77c FD);
- the use of the VA (Art. 77d FD);
- the use of the transitional measure on the risk-free interest rate (Art. 308c FD);
- the use of the transitional measure on technical provisions (Art. 308d FD).

Furthermore, in accordance with Art. 308a (2) FD, Member States had to ensure that NSAs had the power from 1 April 2015 to:

- determine the level and scope of group supervision in accordance with Title III, Chapter I, sections 2 and 3 FD;
- identify the group supervisor in accordance with Art. 247 FD;
- establish a college of supervisors in accordance with Art. 248 FD.

Finally, in accordance with Art. 308a (3) FD, Member States had to ensure that supervisory authorities had the power from 1 July 2015 to:

- decide on the deduction of any participation in a credit institution, investment firm or financial institution from the own funds eligible for the group solvency of a (re)insurance undertaking (Art. 228 FD);
- determine the choice of the method for the group solvency calculation (consolidation or deduction and aggregation) (Art. 220 FD);
- make the determination on equivalence in accordance with Art. 227 FD (subsidiary undertaking in a third country) or Art. 260 FD (group supervision in the case of a parent undertaking situated outside the EEA);
- permit (re)insurance undertakings to be subject to Arts. 238 and 239 FD (groups with centralised risk management) (Art. 236 FD);
- make the determinations referred to in Art. 262 FD (measures to be applied for group supervision in the case of absence of equivalence with a parent undertaking situated outside the EEA) and in Art. 263 FD (verification of equivalence of group supervision at the ultimate parent undertaking level, in the case of a parent undertaking situated outside the EEA which is an intermediate holding company);
- determine, where appropriate, the application of transitional measures in accordance with Art. 308b FD.

4.3.4. Proportionality

The FD already gave specific recognition to the principle of proportionality. However, it was difficult to find specific cases where the principle should apply, and the Rapporteur, Burkhard Balz, made it very clear that he wanted to use Omnibus II to further reduce the burden on small and medium-sized (re)insurance undertakings. This was done in two ways:

- clarification in the FD that the principle of proportionality must be respected in all legally binding and non-legally binding measures adopted in the context of Solvency II;
- introduction of a specific provision in the FD that allows NSAs to reduce the requirements concerning supervisory reporting.

Art. 29 (4) FD, which was reformulated by Omnibus II, clarifies that all implementing measures of the FD (delegated acts, regulatory and implementing technical standards) must take into account the principle of proportionality, particularly in relation to small (re)insurance undertakings. The principle is also extended to the work of EIOPA. All draft RTS and ITS submitted to the EC, as well as all guidelines and recommendations, must respect the principle of proportionality.

In relation to supervisory reporting, there was fear that the requirements that had to be further developed at levels 2 and 3 would be particularly burdensome for small and medium-sized (re)insurance undertakings. As indicated in recital 24 (Omnibus II), only such information should be provided to NSAs as is relevant for the purposes of supervision, taking into account the objectives of supervision as laid down in Arts. 27 and 28 FD. Information on a full list of assets to be provided on an item-by-item basis and other information to be provided more frequently than annually (for instance, quarterly information) should be required only where the additional knowledge obtained by the NSAs for the purpose of monitoring the financial health of (re)insurance undertakings, or taking into account the potential impacts of their decisions on financial stability, outweighs the burden associated with the calculation and submission of that information.

Art. 35 (6) and (7) FD, introduced by Omnibus II, allow NSAs, under certain conditions, to limit regular supervisory reporting (in particular quarterly reporting) by (re)insurance undertakings or to exempt (re)insurance undertakings from reporting on an item-by-item basis, when the submission of the information would be overly burdensome in relation to the nature, scale and complexity of the risks inherent in the business of the undertaking, on the condition that the information is reported at least annually. This limitation of supervisory reporting, also applicable when the undertaking is part of a group, was not particularly popular with EIOPA, which feared that this exemption could seriously damage the new supervisory reporting regime. In a letter dated 16 December 2011 from the Chairman of EIOPA (Gabriel Bernardino) to the

Rapporteur (Burkhard Balz),[134] it was pointed out that the removal of quarterly reporting would actually not be in the interest of SMEs, as it would mean that supervisors would have to carry out more on-site inspections, thereby increasing the burden, particularly for SMEs.

As a compromise, Art. 35 (6), third subparagraph and (7), third subparagraph FD include a threshold: the limitation on reporting does not apply if the undertaking represents more than 20% of a MS's life and non-life insurance and reinsurance market respectively, expressed in gross written premium for non-life and gross technical provisions for life. Member States need to give priority to the smallest undertakings when determining the eligibility of the undertakings under the exemptions.

Art. 35 (8) FD lists a number of criteria that NSAs should consider in their assessment of whether the submission of information would be overly burdensome in relation to the nature, scale and complexity of the risks of the undertaking. For instance, an exemption could be justified for a captive (re)insurance undertaking that only covers risks associated with the industrial or commercial group to which it belongs.

Also inspired by the wish not to overburden small and medium-sized (re)insurance undertakings, Omnibus II added a new subparagraph to Art. 129 (4) FD that states that the requirement for (re)insurance undertakings to check on a quarterly basis that the MCR neither falls below 25% nor exceeds 45% of the SCR does not mean that the SCR must also be calculated on a quarterly basis.

4.3.5. *Transparency*

As the former EU insurance regulatory regime was outdated, it did not follow new developments in terms of transparency in the interest of public authorities and market operators. The FD deals with this issue by introducing detailed supervisory reporting and public disclosure requirements. Omnibus II adds further transparency requirements that are applicable to (re)insurance undertakings, to NSAs, to Member States and to EIOPA.

The new reporting requirements should allow:
- better insight into the functioning of the EU insurance and reinsurance market (disclosures under points 1, 3, 10, 16 and 19 listed below);
- better insight into the relationship with third countries (disclosures under points 11, 12, 13, 14 and 18 listed below);
- better insight into the way the new supervisory regime is applied in practice (disclosures under points 2, 4, 5, 6, 7, 8, 9, 15 and 17 listed below).

---

[134] https://eiopa.europa.eu/Publications/Other%20Documents/EIOPA_11_237_Burkhard_Balz.pdf.

Omnibus II introduces the following new reporting requirements:

1. notification of every authorisation or withdrawal of authorisation of a (re)insurance undertaking to EIOPA, which must keep an up-to-date list on its website of the name of each (re)insurance undertaking to which authorisation has been granted (Art. 25a FD);
2. annual submission of information to NSAs concerning the impact of the application of the LTG measures relating to extrapolation, the MA and the VA (Art. 44 (2a) FD);
3. description in the SFCR of the application of the MA or the VA, as well as a quantification of the impact of a change to zero of the MA or the VA on the undertaking's financial position (Art. 51 (1a) FD);
4. annual submission of information by NSAs to EIOPA, concerning capital add-ons imposed by them and the number of (re)insurance undertakings or groups benefiting from a limitation from regular supervisory reporting and from an exemption of reporting on an item-by-item basis (Art. 52 (1) FD);
5. public disclosure on an annual basis by EIOPA concerning the total distribution of capital add-ons for the various categories of (re)insurance undertakings and the total number of (re)insurance undertakings or groups for all Member States collectively benefiting from a limitation from regular supervisory reporting and from an exemption of reporting on an item-by-item basis (Art. 52 (2) FD);
6. information to be provided by EIOPA to the EP, the Council and the EC on capital add-ons as well as on limitations from regular reporting and exemptions of reporting on an item-by-item basis, together with a report outlining the degree of supervisory convergence in the use of capital add-ons between NSAs (Art. 52 (3) FD);
7. quarterly publication by EIOPA, for each relevant currency, of the following technical information: a relevant risk-free interest rate term structure to calculate the best estimate without any MA or VA; for each relevant duration, credit quality and asset class, a fundamental spread for the calculation of the MA; and for each relevant national insurance market, a VA to the relevant risk-free interest rate term structure (Art. 77e FD);
8. annual reporting by EIOPA to the EP, the Council and the EC until 1 January 2021 on the impact of the LTG package (Art. 77f (1), first subparagraph FD);[135]

[135] See EIOPA, Report on long-term guarantee measures and measures on equity risk 2016, EIOPA-BoS-16/279, 16 December 2016, 145 p.; EIOPA, Report on long-term guarantee measures and measures on equity risk 2017, EIOPA-BoS-17/334, 20 December 2017, 171 p.; and EIOPA, Report on long-term guarantee measures and measures on equity risk 2018, EIOPA-BoS-18/471, 18 December 2018, 215 p.

9. quarterly publication by EIOPA concerning the symmetric adjustment mechanism in the equity risk sub-module (Art. 109a FD);
10. submission by every insurance undertaking of information to the NSA of its home MS in respect of transactions carried out under the right of establishment or under the freedom to provide services; this information must be communicated in aggregate from and in reasonable time by the NSA of the home MS to the NSAs of each of the Member States concerned, upon their request (Art. 159 FD);
11. publication by EIOPA of the list of all third countries whose solvency regime for reinsurance undertakings has been determined by the EC to be equivalent (Art. 172 (2) FD) or temporarily equivalent (Art. 172 (4) FD);
12. information to be provided by NSAs to the EC, EIOPA and the NSAs of the other Member States of any authorisation of a direct or indirect subsidiary, one or more of whose parent undertakings are governed by the law of a third country. The information must also contain an indication of the structure of the group concerned. Where a third-country undertaking acquires a holding in an EU (re)insurance undertaking that would turn that undertaking into a subsidiary of the third-country undertaking, the NSA of the home MS must inform the EC, EIOPA and the NSAs of the other Member States (Art. 176 FD);
13. information to be provided by Member States to the EC and EIOPA of any general difficulties encountered by their (re)insurance undertakings in establishing themselves and operating or pursuing activities in a third country (Art. 177 (1) FD);
14. publication by EIOPA of the list of all third countries whose solvency regime for (re)insurance undertakings has been determined by the EC to be equivalent (Art. 227 (4) FD) or provisionally equivalent (Art. 227 (5) FD);
15. information at least on an annual basis by EIOPA to the EP, the Council and the EC of any major difficulties with the application of the provisions concerning the appointment of a group supervisor (Art. 247 (7) FD);
16. public disclosure – in a manner to be decided by Member States – by (re)insurance undertakings, insurance holding companies and mixed financial holding companies, at the level of the group and on an annual basis, of the legal structure and the governance and organisational structure, including a description of all subsidiaries, material related undertakings and significant branches belonging to the group (Art. 256a FD);
17. annual reporting by EIOPA to the EP (in accordance with Art. 50 EIOPA Regulation), inter alia, on all relevant and significant experiences concerning group supervision and the cooperation between the group supervisor and the other supervisors in the supervisory college (Art. 259 FD);

18. publication by EIOPA of the list of all third countries whose group supervision regime for (re)insurance undertakings has been determined by the EC to be equivalent (Art. 260 (3) FD) or temporarily equivalent (Art. 260 (5) FD);
19. communication by Member States to all other Member States of the list of (re)insurance undertakings that are in run-off on 1 January 2016 (Art. 308b (4) FD).

4.3.6. *Specific Tasks for EIOPA*

4.3.6.1. Power to Draft RTS and ITS

Omnibus II clearly expresses the view that all policy issues should be decided by the co-legislators and that follow-up technical work should be handled by EIOPA. As indicated in recital 10 Omnibus II, the identification of areas in which technical standards should be adopted should strike an appropriate balance between building a single set of harmonised rules and avoiding unduly complicated regulation and enforcement. The areas selected should be only those in which consistent technical rules will contribute significantly and effectively to the achievement of the objectives of the relevant legislative acts, while ensuring that policy decisions are taken by the EP, the Council and the EC in accordance with their usual procedures (co-decision).

The FD, as amended by Omnibus II, transformed most of the implementing measures into RTS or ITS. RTS and ITS are both technical standards. RTS supplement or amend non-essential elements of a legislative act, such as the FD. ITS aim at a uniform application of the rules (single rulebook) and do not leave any policy choices. Examples of ITS under Omnibus II are uniform reporting templates, harmonised technical input to the standard formula, harmonised procedures and templates for cooperation between NSAs and exchange of information between NSAs.

The draft text of an RTS or ITS has to be submitted by EIOPA to the EC, which needs to endorse the standards in order to make them legally binding. After endorsement by the EC, the draft takes the form of a Commission regulation. Submission is only possible after consultation with interested parties. Omnibus II contains a number of deadlines for submission, which aimed at ensuring a timely adoption of measures that were considered necessary for the application of Solvency II on 1 January 2016. The workload for EIOPA resulting from this was considerable. EIOPA decided to develop the ITS (as well as its own initiative Guidelines) in two stages. The first stage comprised those ITS that covered all the supervisory approval procedures that were crucial for the Solvency II phasing-in period that started on 1 April 2015. These texts were submitted to the EC in October 2014. After endorsement by the EC, six Implementing Regulations were published in March 2015. The second stage contained a series of ITS that were submitted in draft to the EC in June 2015. After endorsement by the EC, seven Implementing Regulations were published in November 2015 and three Implementing Regulations, including the reporting templates, were published in December 2015. Two further Implementing Regulations were published in 2016.

4.3.6.1.1. Regulatory Technical Standards (RTS)

In a number of areas, EIOPA received the task of drafting RTS.[136] However, with application of the sunrise clause in Art. 301b (1) FD, these RTS were drafted by the EC upon the advice of EIOPA and were incorporated in the Delegated Act (DA). This was possible until 24 May 2016. Since that date, all amendments to these RTS or any new RTS must follow the procedure laid down in Arts. 10–14 EIOPA Regulation. The following areas relating to Solvency II[137] are mentioned for further development by way of RTS:

- specification of the fit and proper requirements for persons who effectively run the undertaking or have other key functions[138] and of the conditions for outsourcing, in particular to service providers located in third countries[139] (Art. 50 (2) FD);
- specification of the elements of the ORSA (Art. 50 (3) FD);[140]
- specification of the extent to which IAS/IFRS are consistent with a market-consistent valuation of assets and liabilities, of the methods and assumptions to be used where quoted market prices are either not available or where the IAS/IFRS adopted by the EC are either temporarily or permanently inconsistent with a market-consistent valuation of assets and liabilities, and of the methods and assumptions to be used in the valuation of assets and liabilities where it is possible to use an alternative valuation method (Art. 75 (3) FD);[141]
- specification of the methodologies to be used when calculating the counterparty default adjustment designed to capture expected losses due to default of the counterparty[142] and, where necessary, specification of the methods and techniques to calculate technical provisions, in order to ensure

136 See further, Chapter 11, section 2.1.1.
137 The RTS referred to in Art. 58 (8) FD concerning the notification of the acquisition of a qualifying holding is not directly related to Solvency II.
138 See Art. 273 DA.
139 See Art. 274 DA.
140 See EIOPA, Guidelines on own risk and solvency assessment, EIOPA-BoS-14/259, 14 September 2015.
141 See, Arts. 7–16 DA.
142 See Art. 211 DA.

that the actuarial and statistical methods are proportionate to the nature, scale and complexity of the risks supported by (re)insurance undertakings, including captives[143] (Art. 86 (2) FD);

- specification of the criteria for granting supervisory approval of ancillary own funds (Art. 92 (1) FD);[144]
- specification of the methods to be used by supervisory authorities when approving the assessment and classification of own-fund items (Art. 97 (2) FD);[145]
- specification of the quantitative limits and asset eligibility criteria where risks are not adequately covered by a sub-module in the standard formula (Art. 111 (4) FD);
- specification of the methodologies for the calculation of a proportionate additional capital charge that may be imposed when the requirements for investment in loans repackaged into tradable securities and other financial instruments (securitisations) have been breached (Art. 135 (3) FD);[146]
- specification of the recovery plan in the case of non-compliance with the SCR, the finance scheme in the case of non-compliance with the MCR and the supervisory powers in deteriorating financial conditions (Art. 143 (2) FD);
- identification of a significant risk concentration at group level and determination of appropriate thresholds (Art. 244 (5) FD);[147]
- identification of significant intra-group transactions (Art. 245 (5) FD);[148]
- operational functioning of colleges of supervisors (Art. 248 (6) FD);[149]
- coordination between supervisory authorities in the context of group supervision (Art. 248 (7) FD);[150]
- items which are, on a systematic basis, to be gathered by the group supervisor and disseminated to other supervisory authorities concerned or to be transmitted to the group supervisor by the other supervisory authorities concerned and on the items essential or relevant for supervision at group level with a view to enhancing convergence of supervisory reporting (Art. 249 (3) FD);[151]

---

143 See Arts. 56–61 DA.

144 See Arts. 62–67 DA and EIOPA, Guidelines on ancillary own funds, EIOPA-BoS-14/167, 2 February 2015.

145 See Art. 79 DA and EIOPA, Guidelines on classification of own funds, EIOPA-BoS-14/168, 2 February 2015.

146 See Art. 257 DA.

147 See Art. 376 DA.

148 See Art. 377 DA.

149 See Arts. 354–357 DA and EIOPA, Guidelines on the operational functioning of colleges, EIOPA-BoS-14/146, 2 February 2015.

150 Art. 355 DA.

151 Art. 357 DA.

- adjustment to the delegated acts adopted by the EC to technical developments on the financial markets (Art. 301b (3) FD).[152]

4.3.6.1.2. Implementing Technical Standards (ITS)

The following areas relating to Solvency II[153] are mentioned for further development by way of ITS:[154]

- templates and structure for the collection of statistical data (Art. 31 (5) FD);
- templates for the submission of information to the supervisory authorities (Arts. 35 (10), 244 (6) and 245 (6) FD);
- procedures for decisions to set, calculate and remove capital add-ons (Art. 37 (8) FD);
- procedures for assessing external credit assessments (Art. 44 (4a) FD);
- procedures, formats and templates for the SFCR (Arts. 56 and 256 (5) FD);
- procedures for the approval of the application of the MA (Art. 86 (3) FD);
- procedures for granting supervisory approval for the use of ancillary own funds (Art. 92 (3) FD);
- allocation of credit assessments of external credit assessment institutions (ECAIs) to an objective scale of credit quality steps (Art. 109a (1) FD);
- lists of regional governments and local authorities, exposures to whom are to be treated as exposures to the central government of the jurisdiction in which they are established (Art. 109a (2) (a) FD);
- equity index for the symmetric adjustment mechanism in the equity risk sub-module (Art. 109a (2) (b) FD);
- adjustments to be made for currencies pegged to the euro in the currency risk sub-module (Art. 109a (2) (c) FD);
- health underwriting risk module (Art. 109a (4) FD);
- procedures for supervisory approval of USPs (Art. 111 (2) FD);
- procedures for the approval of an internal model (Art. 114 FD);
- procedures for granting supervisory approval to establish SPVs and on the formats and templates to be used for the reporting requirements (Art. 211 (2a) FD);
- procedures for the cooperation and exchange of information between supervisory authorities, where the SPV which assumes risk from a

---

[152] These technical standards had to be submitted at the latest by 24 May 2016. It was not a requirement but a possibility in order to take account of potential important developments in financial markets. No adjustment based on this provision has been necessary.

[153] The ITS referred to in Art. 58 (9) FD concerning the procedures, forms and templates for the consultation process in relation with the acquisition of a qualifying holding is not directly related to Solvency II.

[154] For the list of the relevant Commission implementing regulations, see further, Chapter 11, section 2.1.1.

(re)insurance undertaking is established in a MS which is not the MS in which the (re)insurance undertaking is authorised (Art. 211 (2b) FD);[155]
- conditions for the joint decision process for the approval of a group internal model (Art. 231 (4) FD);
- conditions for the joint decision process for the permission to apply the regime for groups with centralised risk management (Art. 237 (4) FD);[156]
- forms and templates for reporting on risk concentrations (Art. 244 (6) FD);
- procedures, forms and templates for reporting on intra-group transactions (Art. 245 (6) FD);
- procedures and templates for the submission of information to the group supervisor and for the cooperation and the exchange of information between supervisory authorities (Art. 249 (4) FD);
- procedures, templates and means of disclosure of the single and group SFCR (Art. 256 (5) FD);
- standard perimeters to be used for equities purchased on or before 1 January 2016 when calculating the equity risk sub-module in accordance with the standard formula (Art. 308b (13) FD).

4.3.6.2. Guidelines

Art. 16 EIOPA Regulation specifically allows EIOPA to issue guidelines and recommendations addressed to NSAs or financial institutions, in order to establish consistent and effective supervisory practices and to ensure the common, uniform and consistent application of EU law. Although these guidelines and recommendations are strictly speaking not legally binding, their application in practice is almost guaranteed once an NSA has indicated that it intends to comply with the guideline or the recommendation adopted by EIOPA.[157]

Besides EIOPA's own initiative guidelines, Omnibus II lists a number of areas where it believes that the adoption by EIOPA of a guideline is necessary ("shall") or could be particularly useful ("may"). These guidelines should be distinguished from the preparatory guidelines issued by EIOPA in 2013 in order to help NSAs and (re)insurance undertakings prepare themselves for the application of Solvency II.

Omnibus II specifically foresees the following mandatory guidelines:
- Guideline on methods to determine the market share for the purpose of exemptions from supervisory reporting (Art. 35 (11) FD);

155 No requirement for EIOPA to submit a draft and no draft submitted.
156 No requirement for EIOPA to submit a draft and no draft submitted.
157 See also Art. 71 (2) FD, which requires NSAs to cooperate with EIOPA.

- Guideline of the Joint Committee concerning the information by the group supervisor of cases of application of sectorial rules in the case of group supervision (Art. 213 (6) FD).

It also includes one optional Guideline on the imposition of a capital add-on where any of the supervisory authorities concerned in the context of group supervision considers that the risk profile of an insurance undertaking under its supervision significantly deviates from the assumptions underlying the internal model approved at group level (Art. 231 (7) FD).

4.3.6.3. Binding Mediation

Art. 19 EIOPA Regulation sets out a procedure for the settlement of disagreements between NSAs in cross-border situations. The financial crisis, which was at the origin of the 2010 reform of the EU supervisory architecture, had shown very clearly that there was a need to deal with disagreements between NSAs. It was decided to allow the ESAs to take a binding decision at the request of one or more of the NSAs concerned or on their own initiative in cases specified in EU law.

EIOPA will in the event of disagreement between NSAs set a time limit for conciliation between the NSAs, during which EIOPA will act as a mediator.

Omnibus II specifies the cases where EIOPA may be asked to intervene "where supervisory authorities refer the matter to EIOPA and request its intervention", so as to settle a disagreement between NSAs:

- on-site verifications in the case of supervision of branches (Art. 33 FD);
- supervision of outsourced functions and activities (Art. 38 FD);
- insurance undertakings not complying with the law of the host MS (Art. 155 FD);
- reinsurance undertakings not complying with the law of the host MS (Art. 158 FD);
- decision by the group supervisor concerning the equivalence of a third-country solvency regime in the case of an EEA group with a subsidiary in that third country (Art. 227 (2) FD);
- decision by the group supervisor on the use of a group internal model (Art. 231 (3) FD);
- decision by the group supervisor on the application to a subsidiary of the regime for groups with centralised risk management (Art. 237 (3) FD);
- calculation of the SCR of a subsidiary belonging to a group with centralised risk management (Art. 238 (5) FD);
- non-compliance with the SCR in the case of a subsidiary belonging to a group with centralised risk management (Art. 239 (4) FD);
- designation of the group supervisor (Art. 247 (4) FD);

- operational functioning of the college of supervisors (Art. 248 (2) and (4) FD);
- failure of a supervisory authority to communicate relevant information or rejection by a supervisory authority of a request for cooperation (Art. 249 (1a) FD);
- failure to honour a request made to another supervisory authority to have an on-site verification carried out (Art. 255 (2) FD);
- decision by the acting group supervisor concerning the equivalence of a third-country supervisory regime in the case of a (re)insurance undertaking with a parent undertaking outside the EEA (Art. 260 (1) FD).

4.3.6.4. Further Strengthening of the Powers of EIOPA

Although EIOPA is not recognised as a supervisory authority (see Art. 13 (10) FD), it has nevertheless received a number of powers that fall within the competence of a supervisory authority, such as the right to participate in the activities of colleges of supervisors, the right to take part in on-site examinations carried out jointly by two or more NSAs (Art. 21 (1) EIOPA Regulation),[158] or the right to take individual supervisory decisions directly applicable to (re)insurance undertakings in the case of a breach of EU law (Art. 17 (6) EIOPA Regulation) or in the case of a settlement of a disagreement between NSAs in cross-border situations (Art. 19 (4) EIOPA Regulation).

The supervisory powers of EIOPA are further increased by Omnibus II, which also strengthens the position of EIOPA with regards to NSAs.

Although the right of EIOPA to participate in *on-site examinations* carried out jointly by two or more supervisory authorities is already recognised in Art. 21 (1) EIOPA Regulation, Omnibus II specifically refers to this right in relation to branches established in another MS (Art. 33, fourth subparagraph FD), supervision of outsourced functions and activities (Art. 38 (2), fourth subparagraph FD), and group supervision (Art. 255 (2), fifth subparagraph FD).

A new Art. 65a FD specifies that Member States must ensure that their supervisory authorities *cooperate with EIOPA* and that they provide EIOPA, without delay, with all the information necessary for it to carry out its duties in conformity with the EIOPA Regulation.

This is further specified in Art. 71 (2) FD, which requires Member States to ensure that:

- their supervisory authorities participate in the activities of EIOPA;

---

158 EIOPA is specifically considered as a supervisory authority for that purpose. See Art. 21 (2), second subparagraph EIOPA Regulation.

- their supervisory authorities make every effort to comply with the guidelines and recommendations issued by EIOPA in accordance with the EIOPA Regulation and state the reasons if they do not do so;
- national mandates conferred on their supervisory authorities do not inhibit the performance of their duties as members of EIOPA.

4.3.6.5. Technical Input to be Provided by EIOPA

The difficult discussions relating to the LTG package could only successfully conclude with further powers being given to EIOPA. It was important to find an independent outside party with technical expertise to make the complex rules that had been agreed work in practice. Further powers were therefore given to EIOPA in the context of the application of the LTG measures, the extension of the recovery period for the SCR in the event of exceptional adverse situations, and the examination of the equivalence of a third country's solvency regime.

Considering the amount of new tasks allocated to EIOPA under Omnibus II, Art. 310a FD asked EIOPA to assess the staffing and resources needs arising from the assumption of its powers and duties in accordance with the FD and to submit a report to the EP, the Council and the EC in relation thereto. This Report was presented by EIOPA on 7 May 2015.[159] In its Report, EIOPA concluded that its existing funding did not allow it to carry out the additional tasks assigned to it under Omnibus II and called for urgent action from the European institutions to provide it with the necessary resources.[160]

4.3.6.5.1. Application of the LTG Measures

Art. 77e (1) FD requires EIOPA to lay down and publish for each relevant currency the following technical information at least on a quarterly basis:

- a relevant risk-free interest rate term structure to determine the best estimate for the calculation of technical provisions, without any MA or VA;
- for each relevant duration, credit quality and asset class, a fundamental spread for the calculation of the MA;

---

159 See EIOPA, Report on staffing and resource needs for accomplishing the tasks under Directive 2009/138/EC, EIOPA-BoS-15/078, 7 May 2015, 24 p.

160 The financing of the ESAs was one of the points dealt with in the ESFS reform. See EC, Communication on Reinforcing integrated supervision to strengthen Capital Markets Union and financial integration in a changing environment, COM (2017) 542 final, 20 September 2017, pp. 6–7. See also BALZ, B., Report on stocktaking and challenges of the EU Financial Services Regulation: impact and the way forward towards a more effective EU framework for Financial Regulation and a Capital Markets Union, A8-0360/2015, 9 December 2015. It was agreed on 21 March 2019 between the Council and the EP not to change the funding structure of the ESAs.

- for each relevant national insurance market, a VA to the relevant risk-free interest rate term structure in the calculation of technical provisions.

As indicated in recital 29 Omnibus II, in order to allow for the consistent calculation of technical provisions, it is necessary for a central body to derive, publish and update certain technical information relating to the relevant risk-free interest rate term structure on a regular basis, taking account of observations in the financial market. The manner in which the relevant risk-free interest rate term structure is derived should be transparent. Given the technical and insurance related-nature of those tasks, they should be carried out by EIOPA.

Art. 77f (1) FD requires EIOPA to report, on an annual basis and until 1 January 2021, to the EP, the Council and the EC about the impact of the application of the LTG measures (Arts. 77a–77e, 106, 138 (4), 308c and 308d FD) and about the impact of the application of the measure on equity risk (Art. 304 FD), including the delegated or implementing acts adopted pursuant thereto.

Furthermore, before 1 January 2021,[161] EIOPA must, where appropriate after consulting the ESRB and conducting a public consultation, submit to the EC an opinion on the assessment of the application of the LTG measures, including the delegated or implementing acts adopted pursuant thereto. This assessment must in particular look at the availability of long-term guarantees in insurance products, the behaviour of (re)insurance undertakings as long-term investors and, more generally, financial stability (Art. 77 (2) FD).[162]

EIOPA must also publish technical information concerning the symmetric adjustment mechanism for equity risk (Art. 106 FD), on at least a quarterly basis (Art. 109a (3) FD).

4.3.6.5.2. Recovery of the SCR in the Event of Exceptional Adverse Situations

Art. 138 (4) FD requires EIOPA to declare, following a request by the supervisory authority concerned, the existence of exceptional adverse situations affecting (re)insurance undertakings representing a significant share of the market or of the affected lines of business, under which the recovery period for these undertakings to restore their financial situation in case of non-compliance with the SCR may be extended up to seven years. Granting this power to EIOPA

[161] No specific date is set, but as the EC must submit a report based upon EIOPA's opinion to the EP and to the Council by 1 January 2021, EIOPA's report will have to be submitted some time in 2020.

[162] Important preparatory work has already been undertaken through the LTG reports published on an annual basis by EIOPA.

should help ensuring a level playing field between (re)insurance undertakings established in different Member States.

The Directive defines three factors to be considered by EIOPA when assessing the existence of an exceptional adverse situation: a fall in financial markets that is unforeseen, sharp and steep, a persistent low interest rate environment, or a high-impact catastrophic event.

Furthermore, EIOPA must, in cooperation with the supervisory authority concerned, assess on a regular basis whether the conditions leading to the declaration of an exceptional adverse situation still exist and must, in cooperation with the supervisory authority concerned, declare when that situation has ceased to exist.

Arts. 288 and 289 DA add supplementary bottom-up factors to be taken into account in declaring the existence of adverse situations (such as the availability of an active market for assets held by (re)insurance undertakings and the liquidity of that market or the capacity of the reinsurance market to provide reinsurance or retrocession cover) or in determining the extension of the recovery period (such as the impact of an extension on policyholders and beneficiaries or the extent to which the (re)insurance undertaking is affected by the exceptional adverse situation).

4.3.6.5.3. Equivalence Assessment of Third-Country Solvency Regimes

EIOPA must assist the EC in its decision-making process concerning the equivalence, provisional equivalence or temporary equivalence of a third country's solvency regime (Arts. 227 (4) and (5) and 260 (3) and (5) FD) and must assist the group supervisor, in the absence of a decision by the EC, in the assessment of the equivalence of a third country's solvency regime (Arts. 227 (2) and 260 (1) FD).

4.3.7. Overreliance on External Credit Ratings

Heavy reliance on external credit ratings as well as a lack of independence of CRAs contributed to the financial crisis. The EU has addressed this issue by regulating CRAs and submitting them to EU supervision through ESMA[163] and by amending existing EU legislation in banking and insurance, stressing the importance of a direct assessment by financial institutions as part of their risk management.

163 See Regulation (EC) No 1060/2009 of the EP and of the Council of 16 September 2009 on credit rating agencies, *OJ* L 302, 17.11.2009, p. 1, as amended by Regulation (EU) No 513/2011 of the EP and of the Council of 11 May 2011, *OJ* L 145, 31.5.2011, p. 30 and Regulation (EU) No 462/2013 of the EP and of the Council of 21 May 2013, *OJ* L 146, 31.5.2013, p. 1.

A new paragraph 4a was therefore added by Omnibus II to Art. 44 FD, clarifying that when (re)insurance undertakings use external credit ratings in the calculation of technical provisions or the SCR, they must assess the appropriateness of those external credit ratings as part of their risk management by using additional assessments wherever practicably possible in order to avoid any automatic dependence on external credit ratings. Further guidance is provided in a Commission Implementing Regulation.[164]

In order to ensure that certain technical inputs to the SCR using the standard formula are provided on a harmonised basis, for instance to allow for harmonised approaches to the use of ratings, specific tasks are assigned to EIOPA (Art. 109a (1) FD). The objective is to ensure consistency between the approach followed by the three ESAs. A similar approach must be followed in insurance and banking and optimal use must be made of the experience of ESMA. The Joint Committee of the ESAs was tasked with developing draft ITS on the allocation of credit assessments of ECAIs to an objective scale of credit quality steps, consistent with the use of external credit assessments from ECAIs in the calculation of the capital requirements for credit institutions and financial institutions.[165] These implementing technical standards were issued in October 2016 and were amended in April 2018.[166]

4.3.8. *Transmission of Information to Central Banks, Monetary Authorities, Payment Systems Overseers and the ESRB*

The creation of new European authorities since the financial crisis made it necessary to clarify the question of to what extent NSAs can transmit information to these new authorities. This matter is now dealt with in Art. 70 (1) FD, which allows NSAs to transmit information intended for the performance of their tasks to:

- central banks of the European System of Central Banks (ESCB), including the ECB[167] and other bodies with a similar function in their capacity as monetary

164 Commission Implementing Regulation (EU) 2015/2015 of 11 November 2015 laying down implementing technical standards on the procedures for assessing external credit assessments in accordance with Directive 2009/138/EC of the EP and of the Council, *OJ* L 295, 12.11.2015, p. 16.

165 As defined, respectively, in Arts. 4 (1) (1) and 4 (1) (26) CRR.

166 See Commission Implementing Regulation (EU) 2016/1800 of 11 October 2016 laying down implementing technical standards with regard to the allocation of credit assessments of external credit assessment institutions to an objective scale of credit quality steps in accordance with Directive 2009/138/EC of the EP and of the Council, *OJ* L 275, 12.10.2016, p. 19, as amended by Commission Implementing Regulation (EU) 2018/633 of 24 April 2018, *OJ* L 105, 25.4.2018, p. 6.

167 See further, Chapter 8, section 3.7.

authorities, where this information is relevant to their respective tasks, including the conduct of monetary policy and related liquidity provision, oversight of payments, clearing and securities settlement systems, and safeguarding the stability of the financial system;
- where appropriate, other national public authorities responsible for overseeing payment systems;
- the ESRB, where that information is relevant to carrying out its tasks.

In emergency situations, such as those described in Art. 18 EIOPA Regulation, communication without delay is specifically allowed to the central banks of the ESCB, including the ECB and to the ESRB (Art. 70 (2) FD).

4.3.9. Review of the Standard Formula for the SCR

Since the adoption of the FD in 2009, a number of questions have been raised by stakeholders concerning the calibration[168] adopted in the standard formula. This calibration, which is included in the DA, is based upon advice delivered by EIOPA after extensive consultation. EIOPA's proposals were justified in a document that was published in 2014.[169] It was clear from the outset that the calibration in the standard formula should not be set in stone and that the EC should at any time have the possibility of reviewing these calibrations, indeed like other aspects of the standard formula. This was considered the logical application of the Lamfalussy approach.

The questions that Omnibus II raised related primarily to market risk calibration and especially to the treatment of long-term investments, including securitisations in the standard formula and the differences between the treatment of certain investments in banking under the CRD IV and the Capital Requirements Regulation (CRR) and under Solvency II.

These questions were already before the co-legislators when they negotiated Omnibus II. Because it was difficult to provide an immediate answer to all the questions raised, Art. 111 (3) FD, introduced by Omnibus II, requires the EC to make an assessment of the appropriateness of the methods, assumptions and standard parameters used when calculating the SCR standard formula by 31 December 2020. This review is justified as follows in recital 60 Omnibus II:

> "In order to ensure that the Union's objective of long-term sustainable growth and the objectives of Directive 2009/138/EC of primarily protecting policyholders and

168 For the establishment of the SCR, capital requirements are calculated for individual component risks. The process for the determination of the capital requirements is commonly referred to as "calibration".

169 See EIOPA, The underlying assumptions in the standard formula for the SCR calculation, EIOPA-14-322, 25 July 2014, 74 p. See also, CEIOPS, Solvency II – Calibration paper, CEIOPS-SEC-40-10, 15 April 2010, 384 p.

also ensuring financial stability, continue to be met, the Commission should review the appropriateness of the methods, assumptions and standard parameters used when calculating the standard formula for the SCR within five years of the application of Directive 2009/138/EC. The review should, in particular, be based on the overall experience of insurance and reinsurance undertakings using the standard formula for the SCR during the transitional period. The review should also take into account the performance of any asset class and financial instruments, the behaviour of investors in those assets and financial instruments as well as developments in international standard setting in financial services. The review of the standard parameters for certain asset classes, such as fixed-income securities and long-term infrastructure, may need to be prioritised."

The DA (18 January 2015) already took into account some of these concerns by introducing a specific calibration in the standard formula for high-quality securitisations, which was in line with the treatment in the banking sector.[170]

The EC made it clear[171] that it intended to review the calibration in the standard formula as quickly as possible so as to facilitate long-term investments in infrastructure. This resulted in the adoption of two delegated regulations amending the DA, in 2016[172] and in 2017[173] respectively, leading to an adaptation of the standard formula for long-term investments in qualifying infrastructure and for qualifying infrastructure corporate investments. (See below, section 5.6).

Although an early revision of important elements of the standard formula might appear premature, it should be recognised that the calibration in the standard formula had already been agreed on in the period 2009–2011 and that some experience had been gained since then. The delayed application of Solvency II made it impossible to "officialise" this experience. On the other hand,

---

170 The DA was further amended in June 2018 following the EC's 2015 securitisation initiative in order to align the prudential treatment of simple, transparent and standardised securitisations (STS) held by (re)insurance undertakings with the treatment of investments in STS securitisations by credit institutions and investment firms. See further, Chapter 6, section 4.2.2.2.4.

171 See Call for advice to EIOPA on the identification and calibration of infrastructure investment risk categories, February 2015. This call resulted in a proposal from EIOPA. See EIOPA, Final Report on Consultation Paper No 15/004 on Call for Advice from the EC on the identification and calibration of infrastructure investment risk categories, EIOPA-BoS-15-223, 29 September 2015, 194 p.

172 Commission Delegated Regulation (EU) 2016/467 of 30 September 2015 amending Commission Delegated Regulation (EU) 2015/35 concerning the calculation of regulatory capital requirements for several categories of assets held by insurance and reinsurance undertakings, *OJ* L 85, 1.4.2016, p. 6.

173 Commission Delegated Regulation (EU) 2017/1542 of 8 June 2017 amending Delegated Regulation (EU) 2015/35 concerning the calculation of regulatory capital requirements for certain categories of assets held by insurance and reinsurance undertakings, *OJ* L 236, 14.9.2017, p. 14.

political pressure exercised by some Member States, which wanted to stimulate infrastructure investments as one of the remedies to fuel their economy, and by the insurance industry,[174] which looked at Solvency II as an impediment to offering long-term guarantees and to continuing their role as institutional investors, "forced" the EC to act quickly. Although EIOPA agreed to help out, it was clear that there was some reluctance from insurance supervisors[175] to promote an approach that was seen as a form of "regulatory capture", not necessarily contributing to the consistency of the regime.[176]

4.3.10. Increase of the Absolute Floor for the Calculation of the MCR

Because of the delayed application of Solvency II, it was necessary to review the absolute floor for the MCR, which was as a result slightly increased:

- from €2,200,000 to €2,500,000 for non-life insurance undertakings, including captive insurance undertakings, and from €3,200,000 to €3,700,000 where all or some of the risks included in one of classes 10–15 listed in Part A of Annex I FD are covered;
- from €3,200,000 to €3,700,000 for life insurance undertakings, including captive insurance undertakings;
- from €3,200,000 to €3,600,000 for reinsurance undertakings, except for captive reinsurance undertakings, for which the amount was increased from €1,000,000 to €1,200,000.

The revision of the initial amounts was a logical implementation of Art. 300, first paragraph FD, which provides for a revision every five years based upon movements in the consumer price index.

4.3.11. Equivalence

It was obvious from the outset that, in developing Solvency II, account had to be taken of the fact that not all countries in the world were equally advanced in terms of the stage of development of their solvency regime on the way towards a risk-based solvency regime. It was important to prevent this situation being to the disadvantage of EEA (re)insurance undertakings (faced with possibly stricter EEA requirements). On the other hand, third countries had to be

174 See, for instance, Insurance Europe, *How insurance stimulates growth*, 2014, 12 p. and Insurance Europe, *The benefits of insurance*, 2015, p. 24.

175 See, for instance, BERNARDINO, G., Infrastructure projects – Improved data is needed to support the reassessment of risk, *Eurofi Newsletter*, 31 March–1 April 2014, p. 13 and MONTALVO, C., The (re)calibration dilemma, *Eurofi Newsletter*, 31 March–1 April 2014, p. 21.

176 See also below, section 5.6.

encouraged to move their solvency regime in the direction of Solvency II. The FD dealt with this issue by introducing the concept of "equivalence": the EC could decide by delegated decision and technical assistance from EIOPA that the solvency/prudential regime of a third country was considered equivalent to Solvency II.[177]

Equivalence could apply in three cases:

- reinsurance contracts concluded with a (re)insurance undertaking having its head office in a third country (Art. 172 FD): if the solvency regime of the third country is deemed equivalent under Art. 172 FD, its reinsurers must be treated by EEA supervisors in the same way as EEA reinsurers and cannot be subject to a requirement to post collateral in the EEA (Art. 172 (3) FD);
- calculation of the group SCR in the case of a third-country subsidiary (re)insurance undertaking of an EEA (re)insurance group (Art. 227 FD): if the solvency regime of the third country is deemed equivalent under Art. 227 FD, EEA (re)insurance groups can use the local (third-country) solvency data instead of recalculating them on the basis of Solvency II, if deduction and aggregation is allowed by the group supervisor as the consolidation method (Art. 227 (1) FD);
- group supervision in the case of an EEA (re)insurance undertaking that is the subsidiary of a third-country (re)insurance group (Art. 260 FD): if the group supervision regime of the third country is deemed equivalent under Art. 260 FD, the supervisory authorities of the EEA (re)insurance undertaking can rely on the group supervision exercised by the supervisory authority of the third-country (re)insurance group (Art. 261 (1) FD).

Three additional questions relating to equivalence played an important role during the negotiation of Omnibus II:

- Should the EP have the right to intervene in decisions to be made by the EC concerning the equivalence of a third-country solvency regime?
- How could the burden be mitigated for EEA (re)insurance groups operating in third countries (such as the USA) whose solvency regime cannot yet be considered as equivalent with Solvency II?
- How could EEA supervisors be prevented from exercising sub-group supervision in their national jurisdiction, in the case of an EEA sub-group of a third-country (re)insurance group?

The first two questions are dealt with in Omnibus II. The last question was not specifically addressed because it was difficult to justify a restriction on

[177] For further details, see Chapter 10.

EEA supervisors exercising sub-group supervision in the case of an EEA sub-group of a third-country group (for instance, an EEA sub-group of the US insurer MetLife) when EEA supervisors have the right to do so at national level (MS option) in the case of a sub-group of an EEA group (for instance, a sub-group of the German insurer Allianz in Spain).

The first question was basically a political question: should the EC take a decision (in which case neither the Council nor the EP would have a specific right of scrutiny) or should the EC adopt a delegated act (in which case both the Council and the EP would have a right of scrutiny). The question was not unimportant. For the EC, allowing the EP in particular to intervene in this process would set a precedent.[178] The insurance industry was afraid that the EP might add some political considerations to the process: for instance, in the case of Switzerland by linking the issue with other discussions such as tax or the treatment of EU citizens in Switzerland, or in the case of Bermuda by linking the issue with its perceived status as a "tax haven".

In Arts. 172, 227 and 260 DA, it is now made clear that if the EC wants to take an equivalence decision, the decision must take the form of a delegated act. The EC is assisted by EIOPA in making the assessment. Although this was already clear from Art. 33 (2) EIOPA Regulation, this was specifically added to the FD by Omnibus II. The criteria for assessing the equivalence of the third-country solvency/prudential regime are set out in Arts. 378, 379 and 380 DA.

Equivalence decisions in principle apply for an unlimited period of time, but must be regularly reviewed taking into account new developments in the supervisory regime, both within the EU and in the third country concerned. EIOPA must keep an up-to-date list of all third countries whose supervisory regime has been considered equivalent.

The second question was particularly relevant for EU (re)insurance groups with subsidiaries in third countries (particularly the USA). On the one hand, it was unrealistic to presume that all third countries would be equally eager to introduce a supervisory regime that was very similar to Solvency II. On the other hand, many countries in the world were in the process of upgrading their supervisory regime and it would have appeared politically unwise not to officially recognise these efforts, whilst at the same time providing EU (re)insurance groups with a less burdensome regime for the calculation of their group SCR. From an EU perspective, the equivalence regime dealt with under Art. 227 FD was the most important issue. For third countries, the other provisions dealing with equivalence, i.e. Arts. 172 FD (reinsurance) and 260 FD (group supervision), were of course equally (or indeed more) relevant.

[178] A Commission decision would have been sufficient under the 2009 Solvency II Directive.

After much debate, a solution was put forward and strongly defended by Peter Skinner (S&D, UK), who was the Rapporteur for the implementing measures of Solvency II. The solution would allow the EC to grant third countries a limited equivalence status, awaiting further development of their supervisory regime in the direction of Solvency II. In terms of Art. 227 (5) FD, this would exempt the EU parent undertaking from having to recalculate the data for its third-country subsidiary undertakings in line with the Solvency II requirements.

Omnibus II thus introduced the concepts of temporary (Arts. 172 (4) and 260 (5) FD) and provisional (Art. 227 (5) FD) equivalence. Under both temporary and provisional equivalence, the decision to be taken by the EC under the same conditions as a full equivalence decision can only apply for a limited period of time:

- for Art. 172 (4) and 260 (5) FD, until 31 December 2020 at the latest, with the possibility of a one-year extension to allow EIOPA and the EC to carry out a full equivalence assessment;
- for Art. 227 (5) FD, for a period of 10 years with a possible renewal for further periods of 10 years.

The hurdle for a third country to clear is higher under Arts. 172 (4) and 260 (5) FD.

For *temporary equivalence*, the third country must have complied with at least the following criteria:

- it must have given a commitment to the EU to adopt and apply a solvency/supervisory regime that is capable of being assessed equivalent to Solvency II before the end of the limited period and to engage in the equivalence assessment process;
- it must have established a work programme to fulfil that commitment;
- it must have allocated sufficient resources to fulfil that commitment;
- it must have a solvency/prudential regime that is risk-based and establishes quantitative and qualitative solvency requirements and requirements relating to supervisory reporting and transparency;
- it must have entered into written arrangements to cooperate and exchange confidential information with EIOPA and supervisory authorities;
- it must have established obligations on professional secrecy for all persons acting on behalf of its supervisory authorities, in particular on the exchange of information with EIOPA and supervisory authorities.

In making its decision, the EC must take into account the treatment reserved for EU undertakings in the third country concerned (Art. 177 (2) FD). The decision itself must be regularly reviewed on the basis of progress reports by the relevant third country, which are to be presented to and assessed by the EC,[179] assisted in this by EIOPA, which must also keep an up-to-date list of the decisions.

For *provisional equivalence*, the situation is different. The word "provisional" already indicates that the situation can be a lasting one, i.e. awaiting the introduction in the third country of a solvency regime that can be considered in all material respects to be equivalent. Furthermore, the situation can be prolonged. There is no specific end-date. A decision granted for 10 years can be extended by subsequent periods of 10 years (Art. 227 (6) FD). Meanwhile, the EEA (re)insurance group continues to benefit from the less stringent requirements for the calculation of its group SCR.

A provisional equivalence decision can be taken by the EC, where:
- it can be shown that a solvency regime capable of being assessed equivalent to Solvency II is currently in place or may be adopted and applied by the third country (no commitment is required from the third country to introduce an equivalent solvency regime);
- the third country has a solvency regime that is risk-based and establishes quantitative and qualitative solvency requirements and requirements relating to supervisory reporting and transparency;
- the third country's law in principle allows cooperation and exchange of confidential supervisory information with EIOPA and supervisory authorities (there is no requirement for a written agreement on cooperation or exchange of confidential information);
- the third country has an independent system of supervision;
- the third country has established obligations on professional secrecy for all persons acting on behalf of its supervisory authorities (there is no specific mention of exchange of information with EIOPA and other EU supervisors).

It is obvious that it was the intention to make decisions on provisional equivalence not too difficult. As Sharon Bowles, Chair of ECON, admitted during the press conference following the result of the trialogue, the co-legislators had specifically the USA in mind when developing the regime for provisional equivalence. EU policymakers were conscious of the damage the absence of equivalence would cause to EU operations in the US market if such undertakings were to be required to hold additional regulatory capital or collateral compared to their domestic peers in the USA.

4.3.12. Lisbonisation

Under the Lamfalussy approach, which was followed in the FD, the EC would discuss the implementing measures, which had been delegated to it under

[179] Annually in the case of reinsurance. See Art. 172 (4), second subparagraph FD.

the FD, with MS experts in the EIOPC, after receiving the advice of CEIOPS. Under this procedure, Member States (the Council) were thus closely associated with the development of the implementing measures. This was not the case for the EP, which would not participate in the discussions but would be kept informed and would receive all drafts that were discussed in the EIOPC. In order to more closely connect the EP with the development of Solvency II, the EC decided to invite a member of the secretariat of ECON, Ivo van Es, to attend all technical meetings held with MS experts as an observer. The EP also had the option to object if an implementing measure was not in line with the delegation provided for in the FD.

Following the entry into force of the Treaty of Lisbon, the EP acquired new powers. The EP (and the Council) received an official right of scrutiny of the draft measures prepared by the EC. This right of scrutiny puts the EP on an equal footing with the Council. All political decisions are now to be taken jointly by the co-legislators. Implementing measures only deal with matters that are genuinely technical. They are developed by supervisory experts (EIOPA) and take the form of delegated acts, introducing regulatory technical standards or implementing technical standards.

Regulatory technical standards (RTS) adopted as delegated acts in the form of a Commission delegated regulation, pursuant to Art. 290 TFEU, further develop, specify and determine the conditions for consistent harmonisation of the rules included in the legislative acts adopted by the EP and the Council, supplementing or amending certain non-essential elements thereof.

Implementing technical standards (ITS) adopted as implementing acts in the form of a Commission implementing regulation, pursuant to Art. 291 TFEU, establish conditions for the uniform application of legislative acts and may not involve policy choices.

The procedure for the adoption of RTS or ITS is set out in Arts. 10 and 15 EIOPA Regulation. The drafts prepared by EIOPA become legally binding after endorsement by the EC.

The Omnibus II proposal took account of the changes introduced by the Lisbon Treaty. However, the EP wanted to go a step further. It wanted a number of implementing measures included in the FD to be directly drafted by EIOPA as RTS or ITS. After the adoption of the FD in 2009, the EC, on the basis of advice delivered by CEIOPS, had developed several hundred pages of implementing measures, which had been consulted upon and discussed extensively with interested parties. Following the approach proposed by the EP, much of the work carried out by the EC in cooperation with Member States since the adoption of the FD would have had to be redone on the basis of drafts to be prepared by EIOPA. That was clearly a bridge too far.

In order to accommodate the EP, the draft implementing measures (version of 31 October 2011) had been made available to the EP, at its specific request. This had created an un-level playing field in the market as – following the release of the text to the EP – some people had obtained the text through their contacts with MEPs, while others did not have the text. The EC could not make the text officially available to everybody as it had not yet been officially adopted by the EC. In order to re-establish a level playing field, it was decided to put the draft implementing measures on the EC's website as a staff working document.

After difficult negotiations, the EP agreed to recognise the work already carried out on the implementing measures and, in the interest of the early finalisation of these measures, the EP accepted that the EC could, during a transitional period, adopt the RTS provided for in the FD, in accordance with the procedure for the adoption of delegated acts. Any amendments to these delegated acts or, after the transitional period expired, any RTS implementing the FD, would have to be adopted in accordance with the normal procedure provided for in Arts. 10–14 EIOPA Regulation.[180]

The result of this compromise is found in Arts. 301a and 301b FD.

4.3.12.1. Procedure for the Adoption of Delegated Acts

Art. 301a FD (Exercise of the delegation) grants to the EC the power to adopt delegated acts in the cases provided for in the FD[181] for a period of four years from 23 May 2014.[182] The delegation of power is tacitly extended unless the EP or the Council oppose such an extension. Neither the EP nor the Council opposed the extension in 2018.[183] The delegation of power may be revoked at any time by the EP or by the Council.

A delegated act enters into force only if no objection has been expressed either by the EP or the Council within three months of the notification of the act or if, before that period elapses, the EP and the Council have both informed the EC that they will not object. The objection period can be extended by three months on the initiative of the EP or of the Council.[184]

---

180 Recital 16 Omnibus II.

181 Arts. 17, 31, 35, 37, 50, 56, 75, 86, 92, 97, 99, 109a, 111, 114, 127, 130, 135, 143, 172, 210, 211, 216, 217, 227, 234, 241, 244, 245, 247, 248, 256, 258, 260 and 308b.

182 Date of entry into force of Omnibus II.

183 See EC, Report to the EP and to the Council on the exercise of the power to adopt delegated acts conferred on the Commission pursuant to the FD, COM (2017) 740 final, 7 December 2017, 12 p.

184 This is not a theoretical hypothesis. For the DA, the Chair of ECON agreed, in the interest of having Solvency II go live as of 1 January 2016, not to ask for an extension of the scrutiny period on the condition that the EC would respond to a number of concerns of the EP before 31 January 2015. In the case of the first amendment of the DA, the Chair of ECON, Roberto Gualtieri (S&D, Italy), informed the EC and the Council in a letter dated 30 November 2015 that the EP wanted an extension of the scrutiny period by three months until 30 March 2016. See: http://www.europarl.europa.eu/cmsdata/94221/D56680%20-%20Hill%20-%20Solvency%20II%20-%20Extending%20the%20scrutiny%20period%20by%20three%20months.pdf.

4.3.12.2. Sunrise Clause

Art. 301b FD (Sunrise provision for RTS) allowed the EC, until 24 May 2016, to follow the procedure for the adoption of delegated acts (Art. 301a FD) for the first-time adoption of the RTS provided for in Arts. 50, 58, 75, 86, 92, 97, 111, 135, 143, 244, 245, 248 and 249 FD, i.e. these RTS could be adopted as delegated acts without following the procedure provided for in Arts. 10–14 EIOPA Regulation. However, EIOPA regained its powers (sunrise) for any amendments to these acts or for any new RTS adopted after the expiry of the transitional period (24 May 2016).

This meant that, by 24 May 2016, EIOPA could have proposed updates to the delegated acts adopted by the EC taking into account technical developments in the financial markets. These updates had to be limited to technical aspects of the relevant delegated acts and could not have involved strategic decisions or policy choices. No such update was proposed.

The delegation of power to the EC could have been revoked at any time by the EP or the Council in accordance with Art. 12 EIOPA Regulation. This did not happen.

4.3.13. Date Changes

Omnibus II also changed a number of dates in the Solvency II FD, which was necessary because of the delays incurred:

- Member States can provide that the capital add-on or the impact of USPs that must be used because of significant deviations from the assumptions underlying the standard formula calibration need not be separately disclosed in the SFCR until 31 December 2020 (instead of 31 October 2017) (Art. 51 (2), third subparagraph FD);
- supervisory authorities may require (re)insurance undertakings to apply the percentages setting out the relationship between the SCR and the MCR exclusively to the SCR calculated in accordance with the standard formula until 31 December 2017 (instead of 31 October 2014) (Art. 129 (3), second subparagraph FD);
- submission by the EC to the EP and to the Council of a report on Member States' rules and supervisory authorities' practices concerning the calculation of the MCR by 31 December 2020 (instead of 31 October 2017) (Art. 129 (5) FD);
- transitional arrangement concerning compliance with the MCR until 31 December 2016 (instead of 31 October 2013) (Art. 131 FD);
- SPVs authorised prior to 31 December 2015 (instead of 31 October 2012) remain subject to the law of the MS that has authorised them (Art. 211 (3) FD);

- review by the EC of the group supervision regime by 31 December 2017 (instead of 31 October 2014) (Art. 242 (1) FD);
- review by the EC of the possible reintroduction of a group support regime by 31 December 2018 (instead of 31 October 2015) (Art. 242 (2) FD);
- revision of amounts expressed in euros based upon the harmonised indices of consumer prices of all Member States published by Eurostat starting from 31 December 2015 (instead of 31 October 2012) (Art. 300, first paragraph FD);
- transposition date for Member States of the FD: 31 March 2015 (instead of 31 October 2012) (Art. 309 (1) FD);
- repeal of the old Directives from 1 January 2016 (instead of 1 November 2012) (Art. 310 FD);
- date of entry into force of the Solvency II FD as amended by Omnibus II: 23 May 2014 (instead of 6 January 2010) (Art. 311 FD);
- application date for the other articles relevant to Solvency II on 1 January 2016 (instead of 1 November 2012) (Art. 311, third paragraph FD).

4.3.14. Transitional Measures

As the date of application of Solvency II became closer and more experience had been gathered as a result notably of QIS 5, it became clear that a smooth transition from Solvency I to Solvency II would require a number of targeted transitional measures. The EC decided to include in its Omnibus II proposal a large number of empowerments for the EC to develop these transitional measures by way of delegated acts. This approach was necessary as the EC did not know exactly what transitional measures were needed and it did not want to further delay the presentation of the Omnibus II proposal, as the start date of Solvency II, i.e. 1 November 2012, was approaching quickly. Because the empowerments were formulated in general terms, the EC's proposal led to much confusion in the market as many people believed that the EC was planning to postpone large parts of Solvency II.

The co-legislators decided to change this approach and the transitional measures are now explicitly set out in Arts. 308b–308e of the Solvency II FD. As indicated in recital 61 (Omnibus II):

> "The transitional measures should aim to avoid market disruption and limiting interferences with existing products as well as ensuring the availability of insurance products. The transitional measures should encourage undertakings to move towards compliance with the particular requirements of the new regime as soon as possible."

Some people have criticised the transitional measures because they would not be in line with the objective of Solvency II, i.e. to protect policyholders. This criticism was in particular raised concerning the transitional measures on risk-free interest rates and technical provisions because of the length of the transitional period (16 years). However, both of these transitional measures impose a cap on the amount of transitional benefit a (re)insurance undertaking may derive, i.e. to maintain financial resources equal to the amount under the existing regime. Furthermore, these measures provide undertakings with more time to meet any incremental capital costs that result from Solvency II. This avoids the need to take short-term capital raising and/or other management actions, such as asset allocation decisions or winding-down of existing business, that may not be optimal for long-term policyholder protection. Another benefit is that undertakings can remain in the market and are free to compete, whilst existing policyholders are protected appropriately.[185]

The FD includes the following transitional measures.

4.3.14.1. Insurers in Run-Off (Art. 308b (1)–(4) FD)

Insurers in run-off at 1 January 2016 are not subject to the Solvency II requirements (except for Title IV in respect of reorganisation and winding-up) provided they have satisfied their supervisory authority that activities will be terminated before 1 January 2019. If still in existence then, these insurers will become subject to the requirements of Solvency II after three years (or earlier where the supervisory authority is not satisfied with progress that has been made towards terminating the insurer's activities).

Insurers in run-off that are subject to reorganisation measures and where an administrator has been appointed are not subject to the Solvency II requirements (except for Title IV in respect of reorganisation and winding-up) for five years, i.e. until 1 January 2021 (or earlier where the supervisory authority is not satisfied with the progress that has been made towards terminating the insurer's activities).

The undertakings concerned may not be part of a group unless all group undertakings are in run-off. They must provide the supervisory authority with an annual report setting out their progress towards terminating their activity and they must notify the supervisory authority that they intend to apply the transitional regime.

Member States must draw up a list of the undertakings concerned and communicate this to all other Member States. This last requirement is the result of some uneasiness between Member States about the number of undertakings that can benefit from the transition. In most Member States, except for the UK and Ireland, it is rather unusual for insurance undertakings to be in run-off for a lengthy period of time. Undertakings in run-off can always decide to apply the Solvency II rules.

---

185 See Bank of England, Prudential Regulation Authority, Solvency II: transitional measures and the treatment of participations, Consultation Paper CP3/15, January 2015, p. 7.

4.3.14.2. Deadline for Submitting Information (Art. 308b (5)–(8) FD)

It was generally agreed that reporting would be the most costly part of Solvency II, as it required significant changes in most (re)insurance undertakings, introducing for the first time extensive reporting requirements both to supervisory authorities (annual and quarterly reporting) and to the public at large (SFCR).

In order to smooth the transition, the timing for submitting the *annual* information is shortened by two weeks each financial year over a period of four years, starting from 1 January 2016, from 20 weeks after the end of the financial year ending on or after 30 June 2016 but before 1 January 2017 to 14 weeks after the end of the financial year for financial years ending on or after 30 June 2019 but before 1 January 2020, and the timing for submitting the *quarterly* information (quantitative reporting templates, QRTs) is shortened by one week over a period of four years, from eight weeks after the end of each quarter to five weeks.

For group reporting, these deadlines are extended by another six weeks.

4.3.14.3. Grandfathering for Tier 1 and Tier 2 Capital (Art. 308b (9) and (10) FD)

As there was no harmonised definition of own funds under Solvency I, it was necessary to smooth the introduction of the new own-fund requirements under Solvency II for basic own-fund items included in both Tier 1 and Tier 2. This was particularly important for outstanding hybrid capital,[186] and was done through the introduction of a system of grandfathering over a transitional period of 10 years (until 1 January 2026).[187]

Basic own-fund items that met the requirements of Solvency I on 31 December 2015 could be included in Tier 1 or Tier 2 basic own funds, depending on their treatment under Solvency I. The own-fund item had to have been issued prior to 18 January 2015. The lack of harmonisation of own-fund requirements under Solvency I[188] makes it technically possible that, during the transitional period, instruments that qualify as transitional Tier 1 capital might be of a lower quality in terms of loss absorbency than Solvency II-compliant Tier 2 capital.

These provisions also apply at group level (Art. 308b (17) FD).

---

186 In 2007, CEIOPS noted that the use of hybrid instruments was increasing, although it did not represent a significant portion of regulatory capital in insurance companies or was not dealt with differently from subordinated loans in most Member States. The amount of outstanding hybrid capital held by (re)insurance undertakings at the time of adoption of Omnibus II was estimated at €80 billion.

187 This is in line with the grandfathering regime in banking. See Art. 484 (2) CRD IV.

188 See CEIOPS, Report on the implementation of the current insurance Directives with regard to the eligible elements to meet the solvency margin, CEIOPS- P1-14/07, August 2007, 32 p.

4.3.14.4. Investments in Securitisations (Art. 308b (11) FD)

This provision, which introduced a transitional regime for investments in tradable securities or other financial instruments based on repackaged loans that were issued before 1 January 2011, was deleted by Art. 39 (2) STS Regulation of 12 December 2017.[189]

4.3.14.5. Exposure to Member States' Central Governments or Central Banks Denominated and Funded in the Domestic Currency of Another MS (Art. 308b (12) FD)

Until 31 December 2017, for the purpose of the concentration risk sub-module and the spread risk sub-module of the SCR standard formula, exposures to Member States' central governments or central banks denominated and funded in the currency of any MS were treated in the same way as exposures funded in the domestic currency (and were therefore not subject to a capital charge).

In 2018 and 2019, the standard parameter to be used when calculating the concentration risk sub-module and the spread risk sub-module of the SCR standard formula is reduced by 80% and 50% respectively. From 2020 onwards, there will be no further reduction.

This provision also applies at group level (Art. 308b (17) FD).

4.3.14.6. Calculation of the Equity Risk Sub-Module (Art. 308b (13) and (17) FD)

Within the SCR standard formula, the capital charge that applies to equities (purchased on or before 1 January 2016) not otherwise subject to the duration-based approach (Art. 304 FD) moves on a straight-line basis over seven years from initially being the charge that would apply under the duration-based approach (22%) to the charge that would otherwise apply (either 39% or 49% plus or minus the up to 10% effect of the equity dampener).

This provision also applies at group level (Art. 308b (17) FD).

4.3.14.7. Relief for SCR Non-Compliance for an Initial Period of Two Years (Art. 308b (14) FD)

Because of the financial crisis, and particularly the low interest rate environment, it was expected that a number of insurance undertakings that

189 Regulation (EU) 2017/2402 of the EP Parliament and of the Council of 12 December 2017 laying down a general framework for securitisation and creating a specific framework for simple, transparent and standardised securitisation, and amending Directives 2009/65/EC, 2009/138/EC and 2011/61/EU and Regulations (EC) No 1060/2009 and (EU) No 648/2012, *OJ* L 347, 28.12.2017, p. 35.

perfectly met the solvency requirements under Solvency I (which were less risk-sensitive) would not meet the SCR in 2016. In order to smooth the transition to Solvency II and to allow the undertakings concerned to adapt themselves to the new solvency requirements, supervisory authorities could depart from the procedure foreseen in Art. 138 FD for non-compliance with the SCR and allow the undertakings concerned to take the necessary measures (increase in capital or reduction of their risk profile) in order to ensure compliance by 31 December 2017.

The undertaking concerned had to submit a progress report to its supervisory authority every three months. The extension of the recovery period had to be withdrawn when the progress report showed no progress between the date of the observation of non-compliance and the date of submission of the progress report.

This provision also applied at group level where a group that did not comply with the group SCR on 1 January 2016 complied on that date with the adjusted solo solvency under the Insurance Groups Directive (IGD)[190] (Art. 308b (17) FD).

4.3.14.8. Occupational Pension Business (Art. 308b (15) FD)

Occupational pension funds (IORPs) offering defined benefit products (similar to life insurance) were required by the IORP I Directive[191] to calculate a solvency margin following the rules applicable to life insurance undertakings (Solvency I). Art. 4 of the IORP I Directive allowed Member States to permit (life) insurance undertakings carrying out occupational pension business and offering defined benefit products not to apply the solvency rules concerning the calculation of a solvency margin applicable to life insurance undertakings[192] to their occupational pension business. The (life) insurance undertakings concerned could therefore apply the same solvency rules to their occupational pension business as occupational pension funds, thereby establishing a level playing field between both sectors. This optional exemption from the solvency rules applicable to life insurance undertakings (Solvency II) still applies (Art. 4 of the IORP II Directive).[193]

---

190 Directive 98/78/EC of the EP and of the Council of 27 October 1998 on the supplementary supervision of insurance undertakings in an insurance group, *OJ* L 330, 5.12.1998, p. 1.

191 Directive 2003/41/EC of the EP and of the Council of 3 June 2003 on the activities and supervision of institutions for occupational retirement provision, *OJ* L 235, 23.9.2003, p. 10.

192 Art. 28 of Directive 2002/83/EC of the EP and of the Council of 5 November 2002 concerning life assurance, *OJ* L 345, 19.12.2002, p. 1.

193 Directive (EU)2016/2341 of the EP and of the Council of 14 December 2016 on the activities and supervision of institutions for occupational retirement provision (IORPs) (recast), *OJ* L 354, 23.12.2016, p. 37.

In order to avoid distortions of competition in those Member States that had made use of the option in Art. 4 of the IORP I Directive, a transitional provision (Art. 308b (15) FD) was inserted by Omnibus II into the FD allowing Member States to permit life insurance undertakings carrying out occupational pension business and offering defined benefit products to continue applying the solvency regime for life insurance undertakings (Solvency I) to their occupational pension business until 31 December 2019. This article was amended by Art. 63 (2) of the IORP II Directive, which extends this period until 31 December 2022. The EC had to report to the Council and to the EP before 31 December 2017 (Art. 308b (15), third subparagraph FD) on the operation of this transitional period. In its report, dated 5 April 2018,[194] the EC commented that it was too soon to decide whether a further extension of the transitional period would be desirable and that a decision might be taken nearer to the end of 2022.

Life insurance undertakings benefiting from this regime must calculate their SCR as the sum of a notional SCR that covers their insurance activity (excluding the occupational retirement business), calculated on the basis of the new Solvency II regime, and the solvency margin that covers their occupational retirement business, calculated on the basis of the old Solvency I regime (Art. 308b (15), second subparagraph FD).

This provision also applies at group level (Art. 308b (17) FD).

4.3.14.9. Application for the Approval of an Internal Group Model (Art. 308b (16) FD)

Groups often have complicated structures. This transitional provision allows the ultimate parent of a group (until 31 March 2022) to apply for an internal group model that will only be applicable to a part of the group. Both the ultimate parent of the group and the undertaking must be situated in the same MS and the part of the group covered by the internal model must form a distinct part of the group and have a significantly different risk profile from the rest of the group.

4.3.14.10. Transitional Measure on the Risk-Free Interest Rate (Art. 308c FD)

Because of the low interest rate environment, using the prevailing risk-free interest rate on 1 January 2016 would have likely put a number of (re)insurance

194 EC, Report to the EP and the Council on the application of Title III of Directive 2009/138/EC of the EP and the Council of 25 November 2009 on the taking-up and pursuit of the business of Insurance and Reinsurance (Solvency II) as regards the supervision of insurance and reinsurance undertakings in a group, and the assessment of the transitional period for the occupational retirement provision business of life insurance undertakings, COM (2018) 169 final, 5 April 2018, 5 p.

undertakings in difficulty. Subject to supervisory approval, (re)insurance undertakings can therefore gradually introduce the impact of moving from their current discount rate to a Solvency II discount rate over a period of 16 years, until 1 January 2032. See above, section 4.3.1.

4.3.14.11. Transitional Measure on Technical Provisions (Art. 308d FD)

As an alternative to the transitional measure on the risk-free interest rate, undertakings may seek supervisory approval for a transitional deduction from technical provisions, which has to be applied at the level of homogeneous risk groups as defined in Art. 80 FD. This measure cannot be combined with the transitional measure in Art. 308c FD. See above, section 4.3.1.

4.3.15. Review Clause on LTG Measures and Measures on Equity Risk

Omnibus II added one review clause, relating to the application of the LTG measures and the measures on equity risk (Art. 77f FD). This review clause reflects the compromise reached between the co-legislators on the LTG package. The review of the LTG measures and the measures on equity risk should be carried out by 1 January 2021 and comprises the following steps:

- *An assessment of the application of the measures by EIOPA*, where appropriate after consulting the ESRB and conducting a public consultation. The assessment should focus on the availability of long-term guarantees in insurance products, the behaviour of (re)insurance undertakings as long-term investors and, more generally, on financial stability. This assessment can take into account the annual reports that EIOPA is required to submit on the LTG measures and the measures on equity risk;
- *A report submitted by the EC* on the basis of the assessment by EIOPA by 1 January 2021, or, where appropriate, earlier, to the EP and to the Council. This report must take into account supervisory experience and must focus in particular on the effects of the measures on:
  - policyholder protection;
  - the functioning and stability of European insurance markets;
  - the internal market and in particular the competition and level playing field in European insurance markets;
  - the extent to which (re)insurance undertakings continue to operate as long-term investors;
  - the availability and pricing of annuity products;
  - the availability and pricing of competing products;
  - the long-term investment strategies by insurance undertakings in relation to the products to which the MA and the VA apply relative to those in relation to other LTG products;

- consumer choice and consumer awareness of risk;
- the degree of diversification in the insurance business and asset portfolio of (re)insurance undertakings;
- financial stability.

– *Possible legislative proposals submitted by the EC.*

4.3.16. Powers of Investigation of the European Parliament

Art. 226 TFEU, introduced by the Treaty of Lisbon, allows the EP to set up a temporary Committee of Inquiry "to investigate, without prejudice to the powers conferred by the Treaties on other institutions and bodies, alleged contraventions or maladministration in the implementation of Union law, except where the alleged facts are examined before a court and while the case is still subject to legal proceedings".

The EP insisted on the inclusion of a new Art. 67a in the FD to indicate that the rules on professional secrecy (Art. 64 FD) and on the use of confidential information (Art. 67 FD) cannot be invoked in the context of an investigation launched by the EP on the basis of Art. 226 TFEU. Agreement on the inclusion of this article was difficult and was a significant cause of the delay in the adoption of Omnibus II.[195]

5. COMMISSION DELEGATED REGULATION OF 10 OCTOBER 2014

5.1. A LONG GESTATION

On 10 October 2014, the EC adopted the Delegated Regulation[196] implementing the Solvency II FD and presented the text to the EP and to the Council. In order to ensure that Solvency II could "go live" on 1 January 2016 and to give as early as possible certainty to all stakeholders, the co-legislators gave their consent within the three-month deadline foreseen in Art. 301a (5) FD. The Council did so in an official statement. The EP gave its consent through a letter from the Chair of ECON (Roberto Gualtieri, S&D, Italy) dated 19 December 2014 and addressed to Commissioner Jonathan Hill. The EP raised a number of issues to which the Commissioner replied in a letter dated 27 January 2015.

---

[195] This was inspired by the experience of MEPs with the Committee of Inquiry set up by the EP to look into the crisis of the Equitable Life Assurance Society. See Report by Diana Wallis on the crisis of the Equitable Life Assurance Society, A6-0203/2007, 4 June 2007.

[196] Hereafter referred to as the Delegated Act (DA). See EC, *Solvency II Delegated Act – Frequently asked questions*, 10 October 2014.

The DA was published on 17 January 2015[197] and entered into force on 18 January 2015. It is an impressive document comprising 797 pages, including 571 pages of Annexes. As the FD was conceived as a principles-based document, many provisions of the FD are further developed in the DA, which is based upon a total of 76 empowerments in the FD. The list of these empowerments is included in the Preamble to the DA.[198]

As indicated before, some of the empowerments refer to EIOPA but fall within the scope of Art. 301b FD, which provides for a sunrise clause whereby RTS are first adopted in the form of delegated acts, derogating from Arts. 10–14 EIOPA Regulation.

As indicated in the Explanatory Memorandum to the DA, the DA is based on more than 4,000 pages of technical advice provided by EIOPA in 2009 and 2010. A formal call for advice was sent by the EC to EIOPA in March 2009. EIOPA's advice, which was subject to public consultation, was provided to the EC between November 2009 and January 2010. After receiving EIOPA's advice, the EC organised a public hearing on the draft DA on 4 May 2010 and carried out its own public consultation between November 2010 and January 2011.

The EC held more than 20 meetings of the Solvency Expert Group (an expert group within the EIOPC),[199] during which the draft was discussed among experts from the finance ministries and supervisory authorities of Member States, involving observers from the EP and from EIOPA. Numerous meetings were also held with representatives from the various stakeholder organisations, including Insurance Europe, the AMICE, the CRO Forum, the CFO Forum and the AAE.

The most important issues dealt with in the DA are the following:
- external credit assessments;
- market-consistent valuation of assets and liabilities, including technical provisions;
- the eligibility of insurers' own-fund items, covering capital requirements to improve the risk sensitivity of the regime and to allow timely supervisory intervention;
- the methodology and calibration of the MCR and of the standard formula for the calculation of the SCR;

197 Commission Delegated Regulation (EU) 2015/35 of 10 October 2014 supplementing Directive 2009/138/EC of the European Parliament and of the Council on the taking-up and pursuit of the business of insurance and reinsurance (Solvency II), *OJ* L 12, 17.1.2015, p. 1.

198 For a more detailed overview of the empowerments per article, see LOWET, L., *European Solvency II Law*, Knops Publishing, Antwerp, 2016, pp. 494–504.

199 Following the Treaty of Lisbon, the EIOPC has been replaced by a new committee, called the Expert Group on Banking, Payments and Insurance, whose composition changes depending on the topics on the agenda. If the committee discusses insurance matters, it will be composed of insurance experts from Member States, with the EP and EIOPA as observers.

- use and approval of internal models;
- governance and the role of the key governance functions;
- capital add-ons;
- the supervisory review process and the elements to consider in deciding on an extension of the recovery period for undertakings that are in breach of the SCR;
- supervisory reporting and public disclosure;
- criteria for the supervisory approval of SPVs taking on reinsurance risk and requirements related to their operation;
- group supervision, the calculation of the group SCR, group internal model, the operation of branches and the coordination between supervisory authorities;
- the criteria for assessing whether the solvency or prudential regime of a third country is equivalent.

5.2. PROPORTIONALITY

Much importance was attached to respecting the principle of proportionality. A number of provisions were therefore included in the DA that reflect the application of the principle:

- simplified methods for the calculation of technical provisions (Arts. 56–61 DA);
- simplified methods for the calculation of the SCR, including for captive (re)insurance undertakings (Arts. 88–112 DA);
- exemption from the use of IFRS in the valuation of assets and liabilities for undertakings that do not already use IFRS in their financial statements (Art. 9 (4) DA);
- possibility to combine key governance functions, including the internal audit function, under certain conditions (Art. 271 (2) DA);
- specific provisions for reporting by smaller insurers: quarterly reporting is of core data only (Art. 304 (1) (d) and (3) DA); supervisors can waive quarterly reporting partly or entirely and some of the annual reporting (Art. 304 DA);
- supervisors can decide to require narrative reporting only every three years instead of annually (Art. 312 (3) DA).

5.3. LONG-TERM INVESTMENTS AND SECURITISATIONS

The EC very much wanted to use the DA to contribute to stimulating long-term investments by the insurance industry, a subject that had already been raised in the context of Omnibus II. It was therefore decided to lower the capital charges for certain long-term investments based upon advice received from EIOPA[200] and from EBA. A similar amendment was made for the banking sector.[201]

Of particular importance is the treatment of securitisations where a distinction is made in the DA between type 1 and type 2 securitisations, whereby type 1 securitisations receive a very favourable capital treatment (Arts. 177 and 178 DA). As stated in the explanatory memorandum to the DA, a more granular treatment of securitisations has the added advantage of increasing the risk sensitivity of the capital requirements, thereby promoting good risk management incentives and supporting the prudential robustness of the overall regime.

Other changes which are also relevant in the context of promoting long-term investments:

- favourable treatment of equities held in certain types of investment funds created by EU legislation (European social entrepreneurship funds[202] and European venture capital funds[203]) (Art. 168 (6) (a) and (b) DA); the recently created European long-term investment fund (ELTIF)[204] was added to this list later,[205] as it did not yet exist when the DA was adopted;
- favourable treatment of investments in closed-ended, unleveraged alternative investment funds, which captures in particular other private equity funds and infrastructure funds that do not take the form of one of the European funds (Art. 168 (6) (c) DA);
- investment in infrastructure project bonds are treated as corporate bonds, even when credit risk is split in tranches (Art. 180 (8) DA), instead of being treated as securitisations; this is in line with their treatment in banking under the CRR;[206]

---

200 EIOPA, Technical Report on Standard Formula Design and Calibration for certain Long-Term Investments, EIOPA/13/513, 19 December 2013, 190 p.

201 See Art. 10 of the Commission Delegated Regulation (EU) 2015/61 of 10 October 2014 supplementing Regulation (EU) No 575/2013 with regard to liquidity coverage requirement for Credit Institutions, *OJ* L 11, 17.1.2015, p. 1.

202 Regulation (EU) No 346/2013 of the EP and of the Council of 17 April 2013 on European social entrepreneurship funds, *OJ* L 115, 25.4.2013, p. 18.

203 Regulation (EU) No 345/2013 of the EP and of the Council of 17 April 2013 on European venture capital funds, *OJ* L 115, 25.4.2013, p. 1.

204 Regulation (EU) 2015/760 of the EP and of the Council of 29 April 2015 on European long-term investment funds (ELTIFs), *OJ* L 123, 19.5.2015, p. 98.

205 See Commission Delegated Regulation (EU) 2016/467 of 30 September 2015 amending Commission Delegated Regulation (EU) 2015/35 concerning the calculation of regulatory capital requirements for several categories of assets held by insurance and reinsurance undertakings, *OJ* L 85, 1.4.2016, p. 6

206 See recital 50 (CRR): "An exposure that creates a direct payment obligation for a transaction or scheme used to finance or operate physical assets should not be considered an exposure to a securitisation, even if the transaction or scheme has payment obligations of different seniority".

- insurers investing in unrated bonds and loans can use proxy ratings (for example using the rating of the issuer or of other debt instruments that are part of the same or similar issuing programmes (Art. 5 DA)); this is in line with their treatment in banking[207] and helps to reduce overreliance on ratings by avoiding a punitive capital treatment for unrated instruments;
- where unrated debt instruments are guaranteed by collateral, the risk-mitigating effect of the collateral on spread risk is recognised (Art. 176 (5) DA);
- where debt instruments are fully guaranteed by multilateral development banks, such as the EIB or the EIF, they are exempted from any capital requirement for spread and concentration risk (Art. 180 (10) DA).[208]

5.4. ELIGIBILITY OF OWN FUNDS AND LIMITS APPLIED TO TIERS 1, 2 AND 3

Art. 82 DA amends the quantitative limits set out for the eligibility of own-fund items in Art. 98 FD. The issue relates to the classification of own-fund items in three tiers depending on their quality. This classification had been taken over from a similar classification in banking under Basel II. After the financial crisis, the classification of capital in tiers was changed under Basel III and the implementing EU legislation (CRR), as experience had shown that credit institutions need the highest level of capital. Tier 3 has therefore disappeared in banking.

During the Solvency II negotiations, the possibility for the EC to further subdivide own-fund items into sub-tiers in an implementing measure was deleted, as the co-legislators were afraid that this would needlessly complicate the solvency rules. On the other hand, the three-tier classification was kept, thereby creating a difference with the banking sector, justified by the fact that capital in insurance does not necessarily play the same role as in banking.

Art. 82 DA in fact amends Art. 98 FD by including stricter requirements:

- the percentage of SCR capital to be covered by Tier 1 items is increased from one third to one half (Art. 82 (1) (a) DA);
- the percentage of SCR capital to be covered by Tier 3 items is decreased from one third to 15% (Art. 82 (1) (b) DA);
- the sum of the eligible amounts of Tier 2 and Tier 3 items may not exceed 50% of the SCR (Art. 82 (1) (c) DA);
- the percentage of MCR capital to be covered by Tier 1 capital is increased from 50% to 80% (Art. 82 (2) (a) DA);

---

207 See Art. 139 CRR.

208 This is in line with Arts. 117 and 235 CRR.

- the percentage of MCR capital to be covered by Tier 2 items may not exceed 20% (Art. 82 (2) (b) DA);
- within Tier 1, a further restriction is introduced to 20% for the sum of paid-in subordinated mutual member accounts, paid-in preference shares and the related premium account, paid-in subordinated liabilities and basic own funds considered as Tier 1 capital under the transitional rules of Art. 308b (9) FD (Art. 82 (3) DA).

The last amendment (Art. 82 (3) DA), which goes back to advice delivered by CEIOPS to the EC in 2009, is not justified by the empowerment given to the EC in Art. 99 FD, which required the EC to "lay down the quantitative limits referred to in Art. 98 (1) and (2)" and does not allow the EC to reopen the question of sub-tiers.

In its above-mentioned letter of 19 December 2014 to the EC, the EP showed its concern about Art. 82 (3) DA, which it considered "a clear infringement of the political will of the co-legislators", and called upon the EC "to remove this paragraph as soon as possible". It further indicates that this amendment "could in particular penalise mutual insurers who do not have access to the equity markets, and therefore depend more on subordinated debt".

In its response, the EC stated that:

> "[B]y virtue of Art. 97 FD, the Commission is empowered to adopt Delegated Acts specifying the features of own funds items that determine classification in three tiers. This mandate is not restricted to qualitative features, hence the 20% limit within Tier 1 set out in Article 82(3) of the Delegated Act for certain own funds items, e.g. subordinated liabilities. This quantitative limit merely has a classification purpose, it does not per se limit the eligibility of these items which can be eligible as Tier 2 too. In practice, quantitative impact studies revealed that this limit was far from binding on average, as less than 1% of total available own funds were actually subordinated liabilities in solo undertakings (5% in groups). Therefore, the provisions of the Delegated Act regarding the classification of subordinated debt seem both legally robust and proportionate for the EU insurance sector."

This argument is not convincing. Art. 82 (3) DA is not in conformity with the empowerment given to the EC in Art. 99 FD and should therefore be deleted as long as the co-legislators have not decided otherwise.

The question whether to retain the 20% limit was raised again in the context of the 2018 review of the DA. Most respondents from the insurance industry were in favour of retaining the limit from a level playing field point of view: removing the limit would give a competitive advantage to those undertakings that have a large stock of hybrid capital. A further reason was that EIOPA had proposed, as an alternative, further strengthening the criteria for the recognition of Tier 1 capital in the event that the 20% limit was removed. This was seen by the insurance industry as the worst-case scenario.[209] In its final advice to the EC, EIOPA advised that the 20% limit should be retained, because EIOPA

> "cannot support any regime in which hybrid instruments could represent all or the most significant part of Tier 1. It therefore reconfirms the view that any inclusion of high quality hybrids should be restricted. If the 20% limit is removed, undertakings would be able to comply with the requirement for at least 50% of the SCR to be represented by Tier 1 own funds by holding more hybrid capital and equity-like capital than at present. This would weaken the ability of Solvency II to deliver protection to policy holders and beneficiaries at the 1 in 200 level of risk."[210]

The EC has followed this advice in its draft regulation amending the DA. The illegality therefore continues, although its impact will progressively diminish. It resulted in any case in making the transitional measure introduced by the co-legislators in Omnibus II (Art. 308b (9 FD) largely useless.

5.5. REMUNERATION POLICY

The financial crisis showed the importance of a good remuneration policy that promotes sound and effective risk management and that does not encourage excessive risk-taking. The EC adopted a recommendation on remuneration policies in 2009.[211] Elaborating on this, specific provisions on remuneration were included in the CRD (Arts. 92–95), in the Implementing Regulation of 4 March 2014,[212] and in Art. 13 of the Directive of 8 June 2011 on Alternative Investment Fund Managers.[213] As the FD was developed before the financial crisis broke out, it did not include anything specific on remuneration.

Art. 158 (1) (l) DA requires (re)insurance undertakings to adopt a written remuneration policy, which is further detailed in Art. 275 DA. Although (re)insurance undertakings might be expected to adopt a policy on

---

209 See Insurance Europe, *Comments on amendments to Solvency II Delegated Regulation*, Position Paper, 6 December 2018, p. 17.

210 EIOPA, Second set of advice to the EC on specific items in the Solvency II Delegated Regulation, EIOPA-BoS-18/075, 28 February 2018, p. 396.

211 For instance, Commission Recommendation 2009/384/EC of 30 April 2009 on remuneration policies in the financial services sector, *OJ* L 120, 15.5.2009, p. 22, which also applies to insurance.

212 Commission Delegated Regulation (EU) No 604/2014 of 4 March 2014 supplementing Directive 2013/36/EU of the European Parliament and of the Council with regard to regulatory technical standards with respect to qualitative and appropriate quantitative criteria to identify categories of staff whose professional activities have a material impact on an institution's risk profile, *OJ* L 167 of 6.6.2014, p. 30.

213 Directive 2011/61/EU of the European Parliament and of the Council of 8 June 2011 on Alternative Investment Fund Managers, *OJ* L 174, 1.7.2011, p. 1.

remuneration as part of their risk management policy, the question can be raised whether the EC is able to introduce specific requirements on remuneration policy by way of a delegated act without a specific empowerment in this respect. It is particularly doubtful whether the principles on remuneration set out in Art. 275 (2) DA, which are still less stringent than those in Art. 94 CRD, could be introduced without a specific empowerment in the FD (see further, Chapter 7, section 3.8).

5.6. AMENDMENTS TO THE DELEGATED REGULATION

The three amendments to the DA carried out so far relate primarily to changes in the standard formula for the capital treatment of certain types of investments. These changes were the result of extensive research carried out by EIOPA at the request of the EC. The objective is to allow (re)insurers to diversify their investments and to promote long-term investments as part of the Investment Plan for Europe.

A more substantive review of the standard formula was announced in recital 50 DA. This review took place during the course of 2018 and has led to the presentation by the EC of a draft regulation, which was adopted on 8 March 2019.

5.6.1. Capital Requirements for Several Categories of Assets

A first amendment of the DA took place in 2016[214] as part of the EC's review of the calibration of infrastructure investments (see further Chapter 6, section 4.2.2.2.4). The amendment provides a more favourable capital treatment for investments in qualifying infrastructure assets subject to adequate due diligence carried out prior to making the investment (Art. 261a DA).

A more favourable capital treatment was also included in the DA for investments by (re)insurers in ELTIFs,[215] in line with the treatment already provided in Art. 168 DA for investments in European venture capital funds[216] and in European social entrepreneurship funds.[217]

---

214 Commission Delegated Regulation (EU) 2016/467 of 30 September 2015 amending Commission Delegated Regulation (EU) 2015/35 concerning the calculation of regulatory capital requirements for several categories of assets held by insurance and reinsurance undertakings, *OJ* L 85, 1.4.2016, p. 6.

215 Regulation (EU) 2015/760 of the EP and of the Council of 29 April 2015 on European long-term investment funds (ELTIFs), *OJ* L 123, 19.5.2015, p. 98.

216 Regulation (EU) No 345/2013 of the EP and of the Council of 17 April 2013 on European venture capital funds, *OJ* L 115, 25.4.2013, p. 1.

217 Regulation (EU) No 346/2013 of the EP and of the Council of 17 April 2013 on European social entrepreneurship funds, *OJ* L 115, 25.4.2013, p. 18.

Other changes relate to equities traded on multilateral trading facilities, which now benefit from the same capital treatment as equities traded on regulated markets (Art. 168 (2) DA). Transitional provisions for equity investments, phasing in Solvency II capital charges over seven years, are extended to unlisted equities (Art. 173 DA). Furthermore, some minor drafting errors in the DA were corrected.

5.6.2. *Qualifying Infrastructure Corporate Investments*

The favourable treatment of infrastructure investments was extended in 2017[218] to investments in infrastructure through corporate structures, subject to adequate due diligence carried out prior to making the investment (Art. 261a DA) (see further Chapter 6, section 4.2.2.2.4).

5.6.3. *Securitisations and Simple, Transparent and Standardised Securitisations*

In line with Regulation (EU) 2017/2402 of 12 December 2017,[219] which laid down the substantive elements of an overarching securitisation framework, with criteria to identify simple, transparent and standardised (STS) securitisations and a system of supervision to monitor the correct application of those criteria by originators, sponsors, issuers and institutional investors, the DA was amended in 2018[220] so as to provide a similar capital treatment for securitisations and for STS securitisations as already introduced for credit institutions with effect from 1 January 2019 (Arts. 178, 178a, 180 and 257 DA) (see further Chapter 6, section 4.2.2.2.4).

5.6.4. *Review of the Standard Formula*

During the discussions preceding the adoption of the DA, the question of a possible revision of the standard formula played a prominent role. It was agreed between the co-legislators that the revision of the standard formula should

218 Commission Delegated Regulation (EU) 2017/1542 of 8 June 2017 amending Delegated Regulation (EU) 2015/35 concerning the calculation of regulatory capital requirements for certain categories of assets held by insurance and reinsurance undertakings (infrastructure corporates), *OJ* L 236, 14.9.2017, p. 14.

219 Regulation (EU) 2017/2402 of the EP and of the Council of 12 December 2017 laying down a general framework for securitisation and creating a specific framework for simple, transparent and standardised securitisation, and amending Directives 2009/65/EC, 2009/138/EC and 2011/61/EU and Regulations (EC) No 1060/2009 and (EU) No 648/2012, *OJ* L 347, 28.12.2017, p. 15.

220 Commission Delegated Regulation (EU) 2018/1221 of 1 June 2018 amending Delegated Regulation (EU) 2015/35 as regards the calculation of regulatory capital requirements for securitisations and simple, transparent and standardised securitisations held by insurance and reinsurance undertakings, *OJ* L 227, 10.9.2018, p. 1.

be further accelerated and not await the deadline foreseen in Art. 111 (3) FD, i.e. 31 December 2020. Recital 150 (DA) therefore stated that before December 2018 the EC would review the methods, assumptions and standard parameters used when calculating the SCR with the standard formula. The review should make use of the experience gained by (re)insurance undertakings during the transitional period and the first years of application of the DA.

On 30 September 2015, the EC launched a call for evidence on the EU regulatory framework for financial services. Fifty respondents from the insurance sector participated in that exercise, comprising industry representatives, public authorities and non-governmental organisations. The call for evidence provided further insights into the functioning of the Solvency II framework, highlighting issues regarding its proportionality and technical consistency (both within the Solvency II framework and with other regulations applicable to the financial sector), as well as emphasising concerns about unjustified constraints on financing in asset classes like private equity and privately placed debt.

Building on the feedback collected in the call for evidence, the EC issued two consecutive calls for technical advice to EIOPA, on 18 July 2016[221] and 21 February 2017[222] respectively, on the review of 20 specific areas in the DA. Whilst the first call for technical advice focused on questions relating to the proportionate and simplified application of the requirements and the removal of unintended technical inconsistencies, the second call for technical advice dealt more specifically with the removal of unjustified constraints to financing.

EIOPA's technical advice was received in two parts, on 30 October 2017[223] and 28 February 2018.[224] On 27 March 2018, the EC organised a public hearing on the 2018 review of the delegated regulation. As indicated by the EC in the Explanatory Memorandum to the draft[225] Commission Delegated Regulation, EIOPA's advice was generally welcomed but

> "speakers from the industry expressed concerns following EIOPA's own-initiative advice on a strengthened capital requirement for interest rate risk in order to reflect

221 EC, Request to EIOPA for technical advice on the review of specific items in the Solvency II Delegated Regulation, 18 July 2016, 8 p.

222 EC, Request to EIOPA for technical advice on the review of specific items in the Solvency II Delegated Regulation as regards unjustified constraints to financing, 21 February 2017, 5 p.

223 EIOPA, First set of advice to the EC on specific items in the Solvency II Delegated Regulation, EIOPA-BoS-17/280, 30 October 2017, 137 p.

224 EIOPA, Second set of advice to the EC on specific items in the Solvency II Delegated Regulation, EIOPA-BoS-18/075, 28 February 2018, 612 p.

225 The Delegated Regulation was published on 8 March 2019 and will enter into force after the three month scrutiny period will have expired, i.e. on 8 June 2019. See, EC, Commission Delegated Regulation of 8 March 2019 amending Delegated Regulation (EU) 2015/35 supplementing Directive 2009/138/EC of the EP and of the Council on the taking-up and pursuit of the business of Insurance and Reinsurance (Solvency II), C(2019) 1900 final, 8 March 2019.

the potential of negative interest rates. ... Some stakeholders were also critical about EIOPA's own-initiative advice to provide more harmonized guidance on the calculation of the loss-absorbing capacity of deferred taxes, claiming that divergences might be justified by different national tax regimes. With regard to EIOPA's proposals to further simplify the standard formula calculations, stakeholders highlighted [at the public hearing] that the effective application of the proportionality principle is highly dependent on national supervisors' implementations of the Solvency II provisions. Finally, whilst EIOPA's proposals on improved treatments for unlisted equity and unrated debt were positively welcomed, a few stakeholders suggested considering more ambitious actions stimulating long-term investments in equity".[226]

Based upon EIOPA's technical advice and comments received from stakeholders, the EC developed a draft regulation amending the DA,[227] which was published on its Better Regulation website[228] on 9 November 2018, allowing for feedback until 7 December 2018. The draft regulation proposes amendments to the DA in the following areas:

- removal of unjustified constraints on the financing of the economy by the introduction of prudential criteria that allow reducing the capital charges in the standard formula for (re)insurers' unrated debt and unlisted equity investments. The shock factor is lowered by up to 56% for the spread risk, and by 20% for the equity risk. A new category of ring-fenced long-term investments in equity is introduced that will benefit from the same capital charge (22%) as strategic participations, provided that some criteria related to asset–liability and investment management of the (re)insurer are met;
- introduction, with application of the proportionality principle, of further simplifications, including a carve-out from the mandatory application of the look-through in investment funds, exceptions to the use of external ratings, simplified calculations of the risk-mitigating effect on underwriting risk, of the loss-given default for reinsurance and of the capital requirement for counterparty default risk on type 1 exposures and simplifications of a number of sub-modules, such as the non-life lapse risk sub-module, the natural catastrophe risk sub-modules, the man-made catastrophe risk sub-module, the life lapse risk sub-module, the similar to life techniques (SLT) health lapse risk

226 EC, Explanatory Memorandum to the Commission Delegated Regulation amending Delegated Regulation (EU) 2015/35 supplementing Directive 2009/138/EC of the EP and of the Council on the taking-up and pursuit of the business of Insurance and Reinsurance (Solvency II), C(2019) 1900 final, 8 March 2019, p. 4.

227 EC, Draft Commission Delegated Regulation amending Delegated Regulation (EU) 2015/35 supplementing Directive 2009/138/EC of the EP and of the Council on the taking-up and pursuit of the business of Insurance and Reinsurance (Solvency II), Ares (2018) 5720906, 8 November 2018.

228 https://ec.europa.eu/info/law/better-regulation/initiatives/ares-2018-5720906_en.

sub-module, the spread risk sub-module, and the market risk concentration sub-module;
- removal of unjustified inconsistencies between insurance and banking regulation by aligning some of the requirements in the DA with those applicable in the banking sector, in areas such as the classification of own funds, exposures to central counterparties and the treatment of exposures to regional governments and local authorities;
- adjustment of the treatment of derivatives following the adoption of the European Market Infrastructure Regulation (EMIR);[229]
- improvement of the level playing field between Member States in the recognition of the loss-absorbing capacity of deferred taxes by introducing a number of guiding principles;
- update of a number of standard parameters, including risk calibrations for non-life premium and reserve risk and for health and non-life catastrophe risk;
- refinement of the recognition of risk-mitigation techniques, the group solvency calculation and the volume measure for non-life premium risk;
- introduction of a more rigorous framework for amendments to the methodologies, principles and techniques for laying down the technical information on the relevant risk-free interest rate term structure;
- correction of a number of drafting errors.

In a letter of 7 December 2018 to the EC,[230] the Chairman of EIOPA, Gabriel Bernardino, welcomed the fact that the EC has taken on board most of the advice presented by EIOPA, which was widely consulted upon with stakeholders. Critical comments were made about the postponement of EIOPA's own initiative proposal with regard to a modification of the current design of the interest rate risk sub-module, "which underestimates the real risk, since it does not cater for negative interest rates and is less effective at very low rates". EIOPA had estimated that its proposal would have led to a decrease in solvency ratios by 14 percentage points, though up to 75 percentage points in one MS. The industry had estimated that EIOPA's proposal would represent a €200 billion increase in capital requirements for the EU as a whole. EIOPA is also critical of the introduction of a calibration of 22% for a portfolio of long-term equity investments, because the change is not evidence-based. Finally, EIOPA is also unhappy with the amendments made with regard to the definition of the relevant risk-free interest rate term structure, which it considers "difficult to apply in practice and influenced by short-term political considerations".

229 Regulation (EU) No 648/2012 of the EP and of the Council of 4 July 2012 on OTC derivatives, central counterparties and trade repositories, *OJ* L 201, 27.7.2012, p. 1.

230 https://eiopa.europa.eu/Publications/Other%20Documents/EIOPA-18-879%20Letter%20COM%20Mr%20Olivier%20Guersent%20%28GBE%29.pdf.

In a letter of 18 September 2018[231] from the Chair of ECON (Roberto Gualtieri, S&D, Italy) to the EC, the Chair expressed his support for the introduction of a new category of long-term equity investments with a lower capital charge. There is also an agreement with the EC to postpone the review of the interest rate risk sub-module until the first review of the FD in 2020. The EC has been urged to provide some short-term relief in terms of the cost of capital rate (6%) for the calculation of the risk margin (a strong request from industry). In its response letter of 27 November 2018, the Vice-President of the EC (Valdis Dombrovskis) replied that the EC preferred to postpone the discussion about the risk margin to the 2020 review of the FD, following the advice of EIOPA, which had indicated that the cost of capital rate of 6% should be increased rather than lowered.

In its position paper of 6 December 2018,[232] Insurance Europe provided detailed comments on the proposed amendment of the DA. The main concerns relate to the absence of a review of the cost of capital rate in the risk margin, the "arbitrary limits" on the loss-absorbing capacity of deferred taxes, the restrictive approach concerning long-term equity investments and the absence of a short-term improvement in the calculation of the national market component of the VA.[233]

In a press release dated 22 January 2019, the Chair of ECON, Roberto Gualtieri, S&D, Italy, reiterated the position of ECON with regard to the draft DA:[234]

- support for a reduction of the current risk margin in order to boost the financing of the real economy and to encourage insurers to invest in long-term projects;
- support for the introduction of a new equity class for long-term investments but concern with the design of the criteria, particularly the 12-year duration and the ring-fencing;
- need to find a short-term solution to address the shortcomings of the current functioning of the VA;
- careful consideration of the start date for the application of the new requirements in order to unnecessary complications for (re)insurance undertakings.

---

231 http://www.europarl.europa.eu/cmsdata/153463/D(35975)%20-%20Dombrovskis%20-%20Solvency%20II%20Review.pdf.

232 Insurance Europe, *Insurance Europe comments on amendments to Solvency II Delegated Regulation*, Position Paper, 6 December 2018, pp. 15–17 (https://www.insuranceeurope.eu/sites/default/files/attachments/Comments%20on%20amendments%20to%20Solvency%20II%20Delegated%20Regulation_0.pdf).

233 This is an issue that is of particular importance for a number of Member States, such as Italy.

234 EP, *Solvency II: Economic Committee MEPs concerned about preparation of SCR review*, Press release, 22 January 2019 (http://www.europarl.europa.eu/news/en/press-room/20190122IPR24026/solvency-ii-economic-committee-meps-concerned-about-preparation-of-scr-review).

The EC adopted the amending regulation on 8 March 2019. The text takes account of some of the criticism that was voiced since the publication of the draft on the Better Regulation Portal on 8 November 2018. As indicated in the Explanatory Memorandum to the draft Delegated Regulation,[235] the following comments made during the public feedback period until 8 December 2018 were taken into account:

- the required average holding period for long-term equity investments was reduced from 12 years to five years and the undertaking should demonstrate the ability to hold the investment under stressed conditions for another 10 years. The ring-fencing requirement was removed. Further explanation on how to apply the new provisions on unrated debt and on long-term equity investments is given in a Commission Staff working document that will be published together with the draft Regulation;
- for the credit assessment of unrated bonds or loans based on an approved internal model, where a (re)insurance undertaking has concluded an agreement to invest in these bonds or loans jointly with another insurer or bank, the investment threshold which the co-investor must retain in the bond or loan is reduced from 50% to 20%;
- the application date of the provisions on the calculation of LAC-DT was moved to 1 January 2020 in order to allow undertakings to prepare for the changes.

Following legal advice that the proposals on the VA put forward by ECON were incompatible with the FD, the EC has asked EIOPA, for the review of the methodology for the activation of the "country component" of the VA, to explore the possibility of improving the functioning and efficiency of the country component within the present requirements of the FD. The country component is meant to provide additional capital relief during times of severe market volatility in a particular country. Under the current interpretation of the rules, it only provides partial relief. Further changes to the functioning of the VA will be part of the review of the FD in 2020.[236] Similarly, the review of the risk margin and the calibration for the interest rate module are postponed until the 2020 review of the FD.[237]

---

235 EC, Explanatory Memorandum to the Commission Delegated Regulation amending Delegated Regulation (EU) 2015/35 supplementing Directive 2009/138/EC of the EP and of the Council on the taking-up and pursuit of the business of Insurance and Reinsurance (Solvency II), C(2019) 1900 final, 8 March 2019, pp. 4–5.

236 See the letter from 7 February 2019 of Olivier Guersent, Director-General of DG FISMA, to Gabriel Bernardino, https://eiopa.europa.eu/Publications/Requests%20for%20advice/signed_letter_08_02_19.pdf.

237 See the letter from 1 February 2019 of Olivier Guersent, Director-General of DG FISMA to Gabriel Bernardino, https://eiopa.europa.eu/Publications/Other%20Documents/I-2019-030%20COM%20letter%20on%20review%20of%20SII%20implementing%20measures%20%28GBE%29.pdf.

Overall, the increased simplifications in the DA should be welcomed. The creation of a new category of long-term equity investments with a lower capital charge is a step in the right direction, but there is a need for a more fundamental reconsideration of long-term investments linked with long-term liabilities. A better recognition of the long-term business model of insurance within the Solvency II framework is needed. This will be an important aspect of the review of the FD in 2020.[238]

The amendment of the DA is now before the EP and the Council, for a three month scrutiny period, after its adoption by the EC on 8 March 2019. It should enter into force on 8 June 2019, with some changes only becoming applicable from 1 January 2020 onwards.

In a meeting between ECON and the EC on 2 April 2019, Pervenche Berès (SLD, France) indicated that the EP would not raise any objections against the draft amendment. During the trilogue negotiations on the ESFS review, it was agreed – following strong lobbying from Italy – to amend Art. 77 d, fourth paragraph FD so as to facilitate the functioning of the "country component" of the VA as negotiated by ECON.[239]

---

238 See further, Chapter 12.

239 Council, Proposal for a Directive of the EP and of the Council amending Directive 2014/65/EU on markets in financial instruments and Directive 2009/138/EC on the taking-up and pursuit of the business of Insurance and Reinsurance (Solvency II), 7940/19, ADD 2, 29 March 2019.

PART II

SOLVENCY II: REGULATORY FRAMEWORK

CHAPTER 4
SCOPE OF APPLICATION

1. GENERAL PRINCIPLE

The Solvency II FD applies to all direct life and non-life insurance undertakings and to all reinsurance undertakings that are established in the territory of a MS of the EEA or that wish to become established there (Art. 2 (1) FD).

Some undertakings that provide insurance services are not covered by the FD because of their legal status, their nature – as being closely linked to public insurance (social security) systems – or the specific services they offer. A similar exemption applies to certain institutions in Member States whose activities cover only a very limited sector and are restricted by law to a specific territory[1] or to specified persons (recital 4 FD). These exclusions can be found in Arts. 5–8 (non-life) and 9–10 (life) FD. They were taken over from the old Insurance Directives and were not rewritten nor renegotiated.[2]

What is new is that all very small insurance undertakings are excluded from the scope of the FD (Art. 4 FD).

Based upon information provided by EIOPA, as of 31 December 2017 2,912 (re)insurance undertakings and 363 groups in the EEA were applying Solvency II.[3]

---

1 See, for instance, Germany, where 567 insurance undertakings are supervised by the federal supervisory authority, BaFin, while just under 900 undertakings, most of them relatively small, regional mutual insurance associations are supervised by individual supervisory authorities of the federal states.

2 The EC followed the advice of CEIOPS regarding the exemption of small undertakings. See CEIOPS, Answers to the EC on the third wave of Calls for Advice in the framework of the Solvency II project, CEIOPS-DOC-03/06, 3 May 2006, para. 23.35; the EC did not ask CEIOPS for advice on any of the other exemptions.

3 EIOPA, Report on long-term guarantee measures and measures on equity risk 2018, EIOPA-BoS-18/471, 18 December 2018, p. 12.

Figure 2a. Number of undertakings

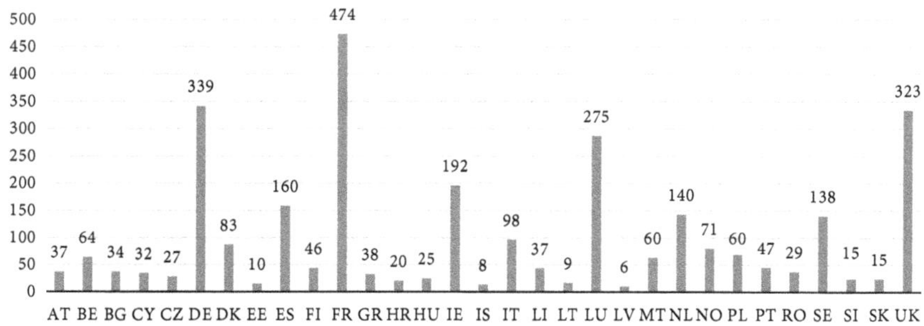

Source: EIOPA, Report on long-term guarantee measures and measures on equity risk 2018, EIOPA-BoS-18/471, 18 December 2018, p. 208.

Figure 2b. EEA market share in technical provisions and gross written premiums per country

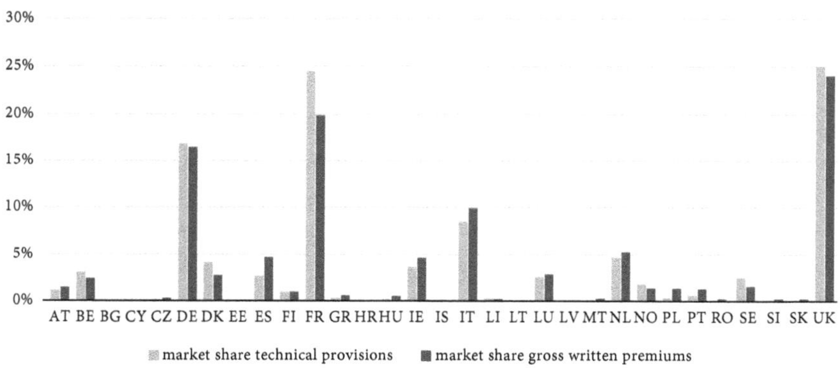

Source: EIOPA, Report on long-term guarantee measures and measures on equity risk 2018, EIOPA-BoS-18/471, 18 December 2018, p. 208.

2. EXCLUSION OF VERY SMALL INSURANCE UNDERTAKINGS

During the negotiations, there was a lot of debate on whether very small insurance undertakings should be exempted from the new solvency regime and whether all or some of these exempted undertakings should be subject to a different solvency regime, for instance Solvency I.[4]

In the end, it was decided to automatically exclude very small insurance undertakings from the scope of the FD but to give these undertakings the option

[4] For more details, see LOWET, L., De minimis not curat praetor: how the Solvency II Directive exempts the very small insurers, *Tijdschrift voor Bank- en Financiewezen*, 2010, No 5, pp. 294–299.

of seeking authorisation (i.e. to become subject to the FD) and thus applying Solvency II (Art. 4 (5) FD). An important reason for this was that nobody – including very small insurance undertakings – wanted to create two insurance markets: one for small, medium-sized and large insurance undertakings and one for very small insurance undertakings. This would confuse policyholders and would not be in the interest of smaller players in the market, which might be considered "second class".

It was also decided not to retain Solvency I as an alternative regime for exempted undertakings, as Solvency I was after all no longer considered fit for purpose. This means that Member States are entirely free to introduce such rules for these very small insurance undertakings as they see fit. The exempted undertakings fall outside the scope of EU insurance regulation. As undertakings established in the EU they obviously continue to benefit from freedom of establishment (one of the four freedoms established under the TFEU, i.e. free movement of goods, people, capital and labour) but they do not enjoy the advantages of the European passport, i.e. the possibility of offering their services cross-border without specific authorisation in the host MS, unless they seek authorisation and become subject to the FD.

The exclusion from the scope of the FD and thus from Solvency II applies to an insurance undertaking that meets all the following conditions (Art. 4 (1) FD):

- the annual gross written premium income does not exceed €5 million;
- the total amount of technical provisions, gross of the amount recoverable from reinsurance contracts and SPVs, does not exceed €25 million;
- where the undertaking belongs to a group, the total amount of technical provisions of the group, gross of the amount recoverable from reinsurance contracts and SPVs, does not exceed €25 million;
- the business of the undertaking does not include (re)reinsurance activities covering liability, credit and suretyship insurance risks;
- the business of the undertaking does not include reinsurance operations exceeding €0.5 million of its gross written premium income or €2.5 million of its technical provisions gross of the amounts recoverable from reinsurance contracts and SPVs, or more than 10% of its gross written premium income or more than 10% of its technical provisions gross of the amounts recoverable from reinsurance contracts and SPVs.

Exceeding one of the amounts stated above for three consecutive years means that the FD will be applicable from the fourth year (Art. 4 (2) FD).

If an undertaking seeks authorisation and it is expected that its annual gross written premium income or its technical provisions will exceed the amounts stated above within the following five years, the FD applies (Art. 4 (3) FD).

The FD no longer applies to insurance undertakings that existed at the time of the entry into force of the FD if the supervisory authority has verified that none of the thresholds stated above has been exceeded for the previous three consecutive years and that none of these thresholds is expected to be exceeded in the following five years (Art. 4 (4) FD).

The exclusion thus applies to very small insurance undertakings operating at local level, which are sometimes referred to as "non-directive insurers". Once these undertakings set up a branch in another MS or offer cross-border services, they have to seek authorisation and will then be subject to Solvency II (Art. 4 (4), second paragraph FD).

It is difficult to know how many insurance undertakings benefit from this exemption. Member States may require them[5] to register (recital 6 FD). There is however no mechanism to collect information at a European level on these "non-directive insurers", as is the case with insurance undertakings authorised under the FD.[6]

3. MUTUAL INSURANCE UNDERTAKINGS

Mutual insurance undertakings[7] are also subject to the FD, except for the specific case mentioned in Art. 7, whereby all risks contracted by non-life mutual insurance undertakings are fully reinsured by other mutual insurance undertakings. In that case, only the accepting mutual insurance undertaking, which bears the risks, is subject to Solvency II (Art. 7 FD).[8]

Mutual insurance undertakings have the specific characteristic that they are collectively and indivisibly owned by their members–policyholders.[9] Mutual insurers cover a significant proportion of the EU insurance market. The FD recognises the specific nature of these insurers, which have to look for capital to their members–policyholders and which have a legal structure that is different from insurers that are limited liability companies. An example of the FD's recognition of these insurers' specific nature is Art. 96 FD, which classifies future claims that certain mutual insurance undertakings may have against their members by way of a call for supplementary contributions (members' calls), within the following 12 months, as Tier 2 capital.[10]

---

5 And also all other undertakings excluded from the scope of the FD.

6 Art. 8 (2) (j) EIOPA Regulation specifically empowers EIOPA to set up a centrally accessible database of registered undertakings.

7 Mutual insurers are sometimes referred to in the FD as "mutual or mutual-type associations". For a full list of the various legal forms of undertakings, see Annex III FD.

8 This exemption was not questioned during the negotiation of the FD, although it can be argued that 100% reinsurance is from a risk-based perspective the same whether it is ceded to a mutual undertaking, a limited liability company or a cooperative undertaking.

9 See also, IAIS, *Application paper on the regulation and supervision of mutuals, cooperatives and community-based organisations in increasing access to insurance markets*, September 2017, 51 p.

10 For an overview of the use of supplementary members' calls before the entry into force of Solvency II, see CEIOPS, Report on the use of innovative instruments & supplementary members' calls as eligible elements of capital, CEIOPS-P1-15/07, pp. 7–13.

4. REINSURANCE UNDERTAKINGS

Reinsurance undertakings are subject to the FD. However, if the reinsurance activity is conducted or fully guaranteed by the government of a MS, and thus the government is acting as a reinsurer of last resort, the undertaking falls outside the scope of the FD (Art. 11 FD).

Reinsurance undertakings that had ceased to conduct new reinsurance contracts by 10 December 2007 and are only administering their existing portfolio in order to terminate their activity are not subject to the FD (Art. 12 FD).

Reinsurance is a type of risk mitigation on the basis of an insurance contract between an insurer or pure reinsurer (the reinsurer) and another insurer or pure reinsurer (the cedant) to indemnify against losses, partially or fully, on one or more contracts issued by the cedant in exchange for a consideration (the premium).[11] From a supervisory point of view, it is irrelevant whether the provider of reinsurance is categorised as a primary insurer or as a reinsurer.

Reinsurance is defined in Art. 13, point (7) FD as one of the following:

- the activity consisting in accepting risks ceded by an insurance undertaking or third-country insurance undertaking, or by another reinsurance undertaking or third-country reinsurance undertaking;
- in the case of the association of underwriters known as Lloyd's, the activity consisting in accepting risks, ceded by any member of Lloyd's, by an insurance or reinsurance undertaking other than the association of underwriters known as Lloyd's; or
- the provision of cover by a reinsurance undertaking to an IORP.[12]

5. CAPTIVE (RE)INSURANCE UNDERTAKINGS

A captive (re)insurer[13] is a (re)insurance undertaking, owned either by a non-insurance financial undertaking or group or by a non-financial undertaking, the purpose of which is to provide (re)insurance cover exclusively for the risks of the undertaking or undertakings to which it belongs or of an undertaking or undertakings of the group of which it is member (Art. 13 (2) and (5) FD).

---

11 CEA and Groupe Consultatif, *Solvency II Glossary*, March 2007, p. 48.

12 This last point was added by Art. 63 (1) IORP II in order to clarify that the transfer of risk by an IORP to a reinsurance undertaking is also considered as reinsurance, although an IORP is strictly speaking not an insurance undertaking.

13 For more information, see IAIS, *Application paper on the regulation and supervision of captive insurers*, November 2015, 23 p.

Captive (re)insurers are subject to the FD. The FD does however recognise the unique nature of captive business, which only covers risks associated with the industrial or commercial group to which the captive belongs. An example of the FD's recognition of this is Art. 129 (1) (d) (iii) FD, which sets the absolute floor for the MCR of captive reinsurance undertakings at a lower amount (€1,200,000 instead of €3,600,000).[14]

It has been argued that captives should not be subject to Solvency II because they are different from other insurance undertakings in that their business is primarily supplied by and controlled by their owners. This argument is difficult to accept as it cannot be denied that captives carry out an insurance activity. Excluding them from the FD would create an un-level playing field with other undertakings carrying out commercial lines' insurance business.[15]

The application of the FD to captive (re)insurers was not uncontroversial and it was generally agreed that the proportionality principle would have to play an important role for them.[16] This was particularly stressed by the EP, which added a specific recital in the preamble to the FD that appropriate approaches should be provided for captives in line with the proportionality principle (recital 21 FD).

6. (RE)INSURANCE UNDERTAKINGS IN RUN-OFF

Without prejudice to Art. 12 FD, (re)insurance undertakings that had ceased to conduct new (re)insurance contracts by 1 January 2016 and are only administering their existing portfolio in order to terminate their activity (insurers and reinsurers in run-off) are not subject to the FD (except for the provisions on reorganisation and winding-up), provided they have satisfied their supervisor that activities will be terminated before 1 January 2019 (Art. 308b (1)–(4) FD).

---

14 See also, Arts. 89 and 90 DA.

15 For an overview of the captive insurance market and the challenges concerning supervision, see NEVILLE, P., Growth and Diversification of the Captive Insurance Market, in KEMPLER, C., FLAMEE, M., YANG, C.H. and WINDELS, P. (Eds.), *Global Perspectives on Insurance Today*, Palgrave Macmillan, New York, 2013.

16 See for instance, the report (p. 18) produced by L. NIHOUL on the occasion of the "Luxembourg Rendez-vous", an annual gathering of the captive industry, in 2012: "In the beginning, the new regulatory constraints coming from the Solvency II Directive were presented as the scariest threat captives' owners would ever have to face. The captive world seemed to be going towards a total collapse and European domiciles were predicted to lose almost all their captive undertakings", https://www.aon.com/luxembourg/attachments/SolvencyII_and_Captives.pdf. This has not been the case. The ICPs apply equally to captives as to commercial insurers.

If still in existence then, these undertakings will become subject to the requirements of Solvency II after three years (or earlier where the supervisory authority is not satisfied with the progress made towards terminating their activities).[17]

7. OCCUPATIONAL PENSION FUNDS

Occupational pension funds are not subject to the FD (Art. 9 (2) FD). Before the EC tabled its original proposal in July 2017, it was agreed at a meeting of the EIOPC that occupational pension funds would be excluded from the scope of the FD. However, during the negotiations of the FD, the issue came up again and amendments were tabled in the EP asking for full application of the Solvency II regime to occupational pension funds. These amendments were supported by the insurance industry which was of the view that there was no reason for insurance undertakings carrying out pension business to be treated differently from occupational pension funds ("same risk, same rules, same capital") and that Solvency II should serve as a benchmark for the regulatory treatment of all financial institutions offering occupational pension products, including occupational pension funds.

The EC opposed application of Solvency II to occupational pension funds for the following reasons:

- occupational pension business is different from insurance as the pension promise can be changed by the social partners that set up the occupational pension fund;
- as the pension promise can be changed, the capital buffer needed to ensure the solvency of the occupational pension fund may have to be lower;
- as better regulation was one of the key principles underlying the FD, it would not be acceptable to apply the FD to occupational pension funds without prior impact assessment.

In order to facilitate the discussions in the context of the negotiation of the FD, the EC asked CEIOPS to identify some of the key issues that needed to be examined if one were to develop a proper solvency regime for occupational pension funds,[18] as the basis for a broad consultation that was launched on 3 September 2008.[19] This was followed by a public hearing on 27 May 2009.

---

17 See also above Chapter 3, section 4.3.14.

18 CEIOPS, Key issues on solvency for the European occupational pension sector, CEIOPS-OPSSC-11/08, 30 May 2008.

19 EC, Consultation on the harmonization of solvency rules applicable to IORPs covered by Article 17 of the IORP Directive and IORPs operating on a cross-border basis, Ares (08) 14717, 3 September 2008.

Following a call for advice from the EC on 7 April 2011, EIOPA[20] submitted specific proposals to the EC on how to apply a regime, such as Solvency II, to occupational pension funds.[21] The EC initially hinted at the possibility of applying a risk-based solvency regime to occupational pension funds.[22] However, it changed its mind because of political pressure from a number of Member States (in particular Belgium, Germany, Ireland, the Netherlands and the UK) and from the social partners.[23] As a result, the amendment of IORP I[24] – the first EU initiative aimed at creating an internal market for occupational pension funds – which followed the consultation, only includes a limited number of quantitative requirements (more akin to a Solvency I regime) and deals mainly with the further liberalisation of the internal market for IORPs, improved governance and risk management for IORPs and more extensive disclosure, particularly to the members of IORPs (pension statement). This proposal, commonly referred to as IORP II, was adopted by the co-legislators on 14 December 2016.[25]

It states in recital 77:

> "The further development at Union level of solvency models, such as the holistic balance sheet (HBS), is not realistic in practical terms and not effective in terms of costs and benefits, particularly given the diversity of IORPs within and across Member States. No quantitative capital requirements, such as Solvency II or HBS models derived therefrom, should therefore be developed at Union level with regard to IORPs, as they could potentially decrease the willingness of employers to provide occupational pension schemes."

The question of whether and to what extent IORPs should come under the scope of the FD was complicated by the fact that in some Member States (such as Sweden) life insurance undertakings carry out occupational pension

---

20 Meanwhile, CEIOPS had been transformed into EIOPA. See Chapter 11, section 1.

21 EIOPA, Advice to the EC on the review of the IORP Directive 2003/41/EC, EIOPA-BOS-12/015, 15 February 2012, 515 p., following a call for advice from the EC in April 2011.

22 See EC, Green Paper on adequate, sustainable and safe European pension systems, COM (2010) 365 final, 7 July 2010, 36 p. and EC, White Paper on adequate, sustainable and safe European pension systems, COM (2012) 55 final, 16 February 2012, 40 p. In both documents, the EC announced a review of the IORP I Directive in order to make occupational pensions safer.

23 See, for instance, the letter sent by the Secretary-General of the European Trade Union Confederation and the Director General of BusinessEurope to José Manuel Barroso, President of the EC, on 14 February 2012.

24 Directive 2003/41/EC of the EP and of the Council of 3 June 2003 on the activities and supervision of institutions for occupational retirement provision, *OJ* L 235, 23.9.2003, p. 10.

25 Directive (EU) 2016/2341 of the EP and of the Council of 14 December 2016 on the activities and supervision of institutions for occupational retirement provision (IORPs), *OJ* L 354, 23.12.2016, p. 37.

business, i.e. provide retirement benefits in the context of an occupational activity as opposed to the management of group pension funds, which is considered life insurance under Art. 2 (3) (b) (iii) and (iv) FD. If IORPs were to be excluded from the scope of the FD, there would be a risk that a number of insurance companies would transform themselves into occupational pension funds in order to escape the new solvency regime for insurance undertakings. It was clear that care had to be taken to establish a level playing field between insurance undertakings and IORPs in order to avoid distortions of competition.

Another problem was that Art. 17 (2) IORP I required the Solvency I regime applicable to life insurance undertakings to also apply to IORPs offering defined benefit contracts by reference to the relevant articles in the consolidated Life Insurance Directive.[26] The FD however repeals this Directive. In order to maintain the status quo, it was necessary to retain the references to the relevant articles of the Solvency I regime in the FD until such time as the EC developed a "proper system of solvency rules concerning occupational pension funds, whilst fully reflecting the essential distinctiveness of insurance" (recital 138 FD). The old Solvency I articles of the consolidated Life Insurance Directive were therefore copied into Art. 303 FD.

IORP I already recognised that a number of life insurance undertakings were carrying out occupational pension business. In order to establish a level playing field between these undertakings and IORPs carrying out the same business, Art. 4 IORP I allowed Member States to exempt insurance undertakings carrying out occupational pension business from the application of the Solvency I regime applicable to life insurance undertakings and to opt for the application of the specific regime for occupational pension funds instead.

This option is still available under Art. 4 IORP II. Life insurance undertakings applying the option are specifically exempted from the FD for their occupational pension business. The assets and liabilities relating to that business must be ring-fenced, managed and organised separately from the other activities of the life insurance undertaking, without any possibility of transfer. NSAs must see to it that this strict separation is maintained.

In order to avoid distortions of competition in those Member States that had made use of the option in Art. 4 IORP I, a transitional provision (Art. 308b (15)) was inserted by Omnibus II into the FD, allowing life insurance undertakings that offer defined benefit contracts (similar to life insurance) as part of their occupational pension business to continue applying the Solvency I regime until 31 December 2019. This article was amended by Art. 63 (2) IORP II, which extends this period until 31 December 2022. The EC had to

26 Directive 2002/83/EC of the EP and of the Council of 5 November 2002 concerning life assurance, *OJ* L 345, 19.12.2002, p. 1.

report to the Council and to the EP before 31 December 2017 (Art. 308b (15), third subparagraph FD) on the operation of this transitional regime. In its report, dated 5 April 2018,[27] the EC argues that it is too soon to decide on whether a further extension of the transitional period (beyond 2022) is desirable. The EC announced that it might take a decision nearer to the end of 2022.

Life insurance undertakings benefiting from this regime must calculate their SCR as the sum of a notional SCR that covers their insurance activity (excluding the occupational retirement business), calculated on the basis of the new Solvency II regime, and the solvency margin that covers their occupational retirement business, calculated on the basis of the old Solvency I regime (Art. 308b (15), second subparagraph FD).

8. FINANCIAL CONGLOMERATES

The European framework for financial services regulation assumes that sector-specific risks incurred by authorised financial undertakings are sufficiently addressed in the sector-specific regulation, i.e. Solvency II for (re)insurance undertakings and the CRD/CRR for credit institutions and investment firms. When a group includes both banking (credit institutions or investment firms) and (re)insurance operations and has been qualified as a financial conglomerate, a system of supplementary supervision applies on the basis of the FICOD. This supplementary supervision should ensure that the group-specific risks of the financial conglomerate are properly captured.

In order to qualify as a financial conglomerate, the group must meet the requirements listed in Arts. 2 and 3 FICOD.[28] At least one of the entities in the group must belong to the insurance sector and at least one entity must belong to the banking or investment services sector. The activities within each financial sector must be significant and the activities of the group must exceed a certain threshold (the balance sheet total of the smallest financial sector

---

27 EC, Report to the EP and the Council on the application of Title III of Directive 2009/138/EC of the EP and the Council of 25 November 2009 on the taking-up and pursuit of the business of Insurance and Reinsurance (Solvency II) as regards the supervision of insurance and reinsurance undertakings in a group, and the assessment of the transitional period for the occupational retirement provision business of life insurance undertakings, COM (2018) 169 final, 5 April 2018, 5 p.

28 Directive 2002/87/EC of the EP and of the Council of 16 December 2002 on the supplementary supervision of credit institutions, insurance undertakings and investment firms in a financial conglomerate and amending Council Directives 73/239/EEC, 79/267/EEC, 92/49/EEC, 92/96/EEC, 93/6/EEC and 93/22/EEC and Directives 98/78/EC and 2001/12/EC of the EP and of the Council, *OJ* L 35, 11.2.2003, p. 1, as amended by Directive 2011/89/EU of the EP and of the Council of 16 November 2011, *OJ* L 326, 8.12.2011, p. 113.

in the group must exceed €6 billion). Where the head of the group is not a regulated entity, the group's activities must mainly occur in the financial sector (more than 40% of the total balance sheet of the group).[29]

The financial conglomerate has its own capital adequacy rules,[30] rules on internal control and risk management and rules on supplementary supervision of risk concentrations and intra-group transactions.[31]

The multiple use of elements eligible for the calculation of own funds (double gearing) at the level of the financial conglomerate, as well as any inappropriate intra-group creation of own funds, are eliminated in order to accurately reflect the availability of the conglomerate's own funds to absorb losses and to ensure supplementary capital adequacy at the level of the financial conglomerate. Own funds in excess of sectorial solvency requirements (Solvency II or CRD/CRR) are only included at conglomerate level if there are no impediments to the transfer of assets or repayment of liabilities across different conglomerate entities, including across sectors.

The own funds of the financial conglomerate only include funds that exceed sectorial solvency requirements and that are transferable across entities within the financial conglomerate. Sector-specific own-fund requirements should only cover risks related to that sector and are not intended to cover risks outside that sector.

If the most important part of a financial conglomerate is in insurance, the financial conglomerate is characterised as an *insurance-led financial conglomerate*. Its solvency capital is the SCR calculated on the basis of Art. 100 FD (solo SCR) and Art. 218 FD (group SCR). For non-regulated financial sector entities, notional own funds and notional solvency requirements are calculated.

An insurance group can also be a financial conglomerate at the same time, and if there is a holding company at the top of the group, that holding would qualify as a mixed financial holding company, i.e. a parent undertaking, other than a regulated entity, which, together with its subsidiaries – at least one

---

29 The list of financial conglomerates is published annually by the Joint Committee of the ESAs. The 2018 list contains 78 financial conglomerates and three financial conglomerates with the head of the group outside the EEA, i.e. in CH, USA and BDA. See Joint Committee, List of Financial Conglomerates 2018, JC 2018 68, 30 October 2018, 7 p. (available on the website of EIOPA).

30 Commission Delegated Regulation (EU) No 342/2014 of 21 January 2014 supplementing Directive 2002/87/EC of the EP and of the Council and Regulation (EU) No 575/2013 of the EP and of the Council with regard to regulatory technical standards for the application of the calculation methods of capital adequacy requirements for financial conglomerates, *OJ* L 100, 3.4.2014, p. 1.

31 Commission Delegated Regulation (EU) 2015/2303 of 28 July 2015 supplementing Directive 2002/87/EC of the EP and of the Council with regard to regulatory technical standards specifying the definitions and coordinating the supplementary supervision of risk concentration and intra-group transactions, *OJ* L 326, 11.12.2015, p. 34.

of which is a regulated entity that has its registered office in the EU - and other entities, constitutes a financial conglomerate (Art. 212 (1) (h) FD and Art. 2 (15) FICOD). In that case, the insurance group is by default subject to two supervisory regimes: group supervision under Solvency II (see further, Chapter 9) and supplementary supervision as a financial conglomerate under the FICOD.[32]

32 See also, CEBS and CEIOPS, Recommendations on the supplementary requirements of the FICOD for supervisory colleges of financial conglomerates, 21 December 2010, 10 p. (https://eiopa.europa.eu/CEIOPS-Archive/Documents/Standards/Recommendations.pdf).

CHAPTER 5
PROPORTIONALITY

Following CEIOPS' advice, the EC decided not to create a special regime for small and medium-sized insurers: "policyholders should not expect a lower degree of protection simply because their cover is provided by a smaller undertaking".[1] On the other hand, it was clear that account had to be taken of the fact that the large majority of insurance undertakings that would apply Solvency II would be small and medium-sized undertakings and that insurance markets in the EEA are very different and complex. It was immediately agreed that a one-size-fits-all approach would not be appropriate.[2]

The proportionality principle was chosen as a means to ensure that the FD would not be too burdensome for small and medium-sized insurance undertakings (recital 19 FD) and that all insurance undertakings covered by the FD would be able to apply the new solvency regime.

1. ELEMENTS OF THE PRINCIPLE OF PROPORTIONALITY

The inclusion of the proportionality principle in the FD was not obvious. As this principle is explicitly referred to in Art. 5 (4) TFEU and is therefore one of the core principles of EU law, it could be argued that a specific reference to this principle in the case of Solvency II was not necessary. The principle was nevertheless included in the EC's initial proposal in order to remind all parties concerned that they have to give due consideration to this principle. This was all the more necessary because Solvency II is a principles-based regulatory regime, leaving much scope for interpretation.[3]

---

1 CEIOPS, Answers to the EC on the third wave of Calls for Advice in the framework of the Solvency II project, CEIOPS-DOC-03/06, 3 May 2006, para. 23.40.

2 See, for instance, ECIROA, *Position Paper on Solvency II – the Principle of Proportionality and its Application*, 2010, 16 p.

3 WANDT, M., *Prinzipienbasiertes Recht und Verhältnismässigkeitsgrundsatz im Rahmen von Solvency II*, Mannheimer Vorträge zur Versicherungswissenschaft Vol. 91, VVW, Karlsruhe, 2012, p. 25.

The principle covers all actions undertaken by the co-legislators (Council and EP) in developing EU legislation (Art. 5 (4) TFEU), by Member States in applying the requirements of the FD (Art. 29 (3) FD), by the EC in developing delegated acts and regulatory and implementing technical standards (Art. 29 (4), first subparagraph FD), by EIOPA in preparing technical standards, guidelines and recommendations (Art. 29 (4), second subparagraph FD) and by supervisory authorities[4] in applying their supervisory powers (Art. 34 (6) FD).

The principle applies to all requirements of Solvency II, i.e. to the three pillars, to group supervision and to all implementing measures and guidelines. The reference to the principle in specific articles should not lead to the conclusion that the principle does not apply or applies less stringently where it is not explicitly mentioned.

Proportionality does not entail the introduction of automatic and systematic simplifications for certain undertakings, although simplifications might be a proportionate solution. The principle applies where the application of a requirement without relief would be disproportionate to the nature, scale and complexity of the business of an undertaking. This means that there is always a need to show that a particular requirement would be too burdensome. This requires judgement. The message to all parties concerned is that this judgement should be exercised in a positive manner, i.e. proportionality should apply as a matter of principle and not as a matter of exception. This means, for instance, that a supervisory authority may not adopt an attitude of always requiring the strictest interpretation, putting the burden of proof on undertakings to show that such strict interpretation is in their case disproportionate.

As Solvency II is a risk-based solvency regime, the individual risk profile of the undertaking will be the guiding principle in deciding whether or not proportionality applies. This means that in the case of low risk (for instance, a small insurer with a simple risk profile), simplifications or less burdensome requirements are justified. It also means that in the case of high risk (for instance, a small insurer with a complex insurance portfolio), more sophisticated methods and techniques may have to be applied. Size alone is therefore not sufficient to justify the application of the proportionality principle.[5]

Proportionality can never lead to the non-application of a requirement. For instance, the possibility for a small insurer to outsource the actuarial function can never lead to the conclusion that this key governance function can be left out, for instance for financial reasons.

---

4 See, for instance, Central Bank of Ireland, *Corporate Governance Requirements for Captive Insurance and Captive Reinsurance Undertakings*, 2015, 34 p.

5 See also SHARMA, P. and CADONI, P., Solvency II: A New Regulatory Frontier, in KEMPLER, C., FLAMEE, M., YANG, C.H. and WINDELS, P. (Eds.), *Global Perspectives on Insurance Today*, Palgrave Macmillan, New York, 2013, p. 59.

There is no specific definition of proportionality in the FD. However, Art. 29 (3) FD which deals with Member States' application of the requirements of the FD states clearly what is meant by proportionality:[6] "The requirements of the Directive must be applied in a manner which is proportionate to the nature, scale and complexity of the risks inherent in the business of an insurance or reinsurance undertaking".

This is further explained in recital 1 DA: "Account should be taken of the nature, scale and complexity of the risks inherent in the business of an insurance or reinsurance undertaking. The burden and the complexity imposed on insurance undertakings should be proportionate to their risk profile."

In a letter dated 19 July 2007, the EC asked CEIOPS to deliver advice on the application of the proportionality principle. This advice was considered necessary because it turned out that everybody around the negotiation table agreed that the proportionality principle was very important, but that it was virtually impossible to find clear examples that could be inserted into the FD.

In its advice to the EC,[7] CEIOPS elaborated on how the three elements of the proportionality principle are interlinked and how they must be seen in the context of a risk-based solvency regime. This advice also contains a number of examples and indicates how CEIOPS sees the application of the principle in practice.

1.1. NATURE OF THE BUSINESS

The reference to the nature of the business means that consideration has to be given to the underlying risk profiles of the classes of business an undertaking is writing, for instance whether it is long- or short-tail business, or whether it is a low-frequency/high-severity business or one of high-frequency/low-severity risks. Particular attention needs to be paid to the activity carried out by the undertaking.

Recital 20 FD thus indicates that:

> "the Directive should not be too burdensome for insurance undertakings that specialise in providing specific types of insurance or services to specific customer segments and that it should recognise that specialising in this way can be a valuable tool for efficiently and effectively managing risk. Undertakings should therefore be allowed to use their own data to calibrate the parameters in the underwriting risk modules of the SCR in the standard formula."[8]

6 See also recital 19 FD.

7 CEIOPS, Advice to the EC on the Principle of Proportionality in the Solvency II Framework Directive Proposal, CEIOPS-DOC-24/08, May 2008, 26 p.

8 On USPs, see Art. 104 (7) FD.

More specifically, reference is made in recital 21 FD to the "specific nature of captive insurance and reinsurance undertakings: as those undertakings only cover risks associated with the industrial or commercial group to which they belong, appropriate approaches should thus be provided in line with the principle of proportionality to reflect the nature, scale and complexity of their business".[9]

Another example is given in recital 22 FD: "the supervision of reinsurance activity should take account of the special characteristics of reinsurance business, notably its global nature and the fact that the policy holders are themselves insurance or reinsurance undertakings".

By recognising supplementary members' calls as Tier 2 capital, for example in the case of mutual or mutual-type associations of ship-owners with variable contributions, the FD recognises the specific nature (or legal form) of certain types of insurers (Art. 96 FD).

1.2. COMPLEXITY

The concept of complexity is closely linked to the nature of the business, but has an implicit broader application, looking at other risks than the insurance risk, such as market risk or operational risk. The complexity of business may dictate the use of more demanding methods or a more sophisticated system of risk management. Examples given by CEIOPS include unlimited motor liability insurance, investment in a complex option, annuities (instead of a lump sum), non-proportional reinsurance[10] (as opposed to straightforward direct insurance business) or proportional reinsurance.[11] Another example could be the way in which a group is structured. A complex structure might require more sophisticated rules and supervision; on the other hand, a business involving less risk or a structure that is more straightforward calls for less onerous requirements under a risk-based regime.

---

9 For an example in the case of captive (re)insurance undertakings, see Art. 35 (8) (j) FD, which lists the particular situation of a captive as one of the criteria to be considered by supervisory authorities in deciding whether or not to grant an exemption in the area of supervisory reporting.

10 Under non-proportional reinsurance, the reinsurer has a concrete obligation towards the insurer only if the individual losses or aggregate loss amounts exceed the amount set forth in the reinsurance contract (retention). The reinsurer is then obliged to indemnify the insurer for the loss exceeding this amount (excess loss) on a non-proportional basis (International Credit Insurance & Surety Association FAQ).

11 Under proportional reinsurance, the insurer and the reinsurer share in an agreed ratio all premiums, losses and loss expenses arising out of the original business covered under the reinsurance agreement (IAIS Glossary).

1.3. SCALE

The concept of scale refers to the size of the risk or business and is closely linked to the concept of materiality, which is used in financial reporting and allows undertakings not to report information which is considered insignificant. Even if a business is small, a simplified approach might still be problematic.

For instance, the approximation error caused by the simplified calculation of technical provisions must not be expected to be material: "a simplified calculation shall not be proportionate where the approximation error leads to a misstatement of the SCR that could influence the decision-making or the judgement of the user of the information relating to the SCR" (Art. 88 DA).

A similar reference to the concept of materiality can be found in recital 1 DA: "The burden and the complexity imposed on insurance undertakings should be proportionate to their risk profile. In applying the requirements set out in this Regulation, information should be considered as material if that information could influence the decision-making or judgement of the intended users of the information."[12]

As stated before, a small undertaking can carry out complex business. Size in itself may not be an adequate proxy for the risk to which an undertaking is exposed.

2. EXAMPLES

The FD, the implementing measures[13] and the EIOPA Guidelines provide many references to the application of the proportionality principle. There are, however, few examples of the Solvency II regulatory regime providing for specific treatment because of the principle of proportionality.

Obvious candidates for the application of proportionality are the complex calculations under Pillar 1, the governance requirements under Pillar 2 and the disclosure and reporting requirements under Pillar 3.

Allowing simplified calculations under Pillar 1 entails the risk that the result might be misleading. However, it should be possible to apply simplifications if they are immaterial to the calculation of the SCR.

The governance requirements (Pillar 2) can be very burdensome if not applied in a proportionate manner. This was recognised by CEIOPS in its 2008 advice to the EC, where it is stated that in some undertakings full segregation

12 A similar definition of materiality can be found in Art. 2 (16) Accounting Directive.

13 The number of simplified calculations applying the proportionality principle increased with the last amendment of the DA in 2018/2019.

of duties may be considered unreasonable and disproportionate.[14] By applying the proportionality principle, Solvency II therefore allows governance functions to be combined or outsourced. In the case of a combination of functions, care must be taken to avoid conflicts of interest, for instance by ensuring that a person with operation and controlling duties does not assess his/her own operational work, or by introducing compensating actions such as additional checks/reviews for potential cases of conflicts of interest.[15]

A good example of proportionality under Pillar 3 is the exemption from regular reporting applicable to small insurance undertakings, which may or may not be part of a group (Art. 35 (6) and (7) FD). This was introduced by Omnibus II. NSAs are encouraged to exempt small (re)insurance undertakings from quarterly reporting or from reporting on an item-by-item basis because there is a presumption that such reporting might be too burdensome for them. As indicated in recital 24 Omnibus II:

> "After assessing the nature, scale and complexity of the risks inherent in the business of the undertaking, national supervisory authorities should have the power to allow limitations on the frequency and the scope of information to be reported or to exempt from reporting on an item-by-item basis only where that undertaking does not exceed specific thresholds. It should be ensured that the smallest undertakings are eligible for limitations and exemption and that those undertakings do not represent more than 20% of a Member State's life and non-life insurance or of its reinsurance market."

In its second report[16] on the use of limitations and exemptions from reporting, looking at reporting in 2017 and in the first quarter of 2018, EIOPA indicated that only 13 NSAs (Belgium, Denmark, France, Germany, Italy, Liechtenstein, Luxembourg, Malta, Norway, the Netherlands, Portugal, Sweden and the UK) used the possibility of exempting undertakings from quarterly and/or annual reporting. EIOPA provided the following picture:

- as at year-end 2017, 133 solo undertakings from five Member States and seven groups from three Member States were exempted from reporting item-by-item templates for the *annual reporting* of 2017;
- in the first quarter 2018, 791 solo undertakings from 13 Member States and 33 groups from three Member States were exempted from *quarterly reporting.*

---

14 CEIOPS, Advice to the EC on the Principle of Proportionality in the Solvency II Framework Directive Proposal, CEIOPS-DOC-24/08, May 2008, p. 14.

15 For examples, see EIOPA, *Peer review of key functions: supervisory practices and application in assessing key functions*, Publications Office of the EU, Luxembourg, 2018, 11 p.

16 EIOPA, *Report on the use of limitations and exemptions from reporting during 2017 and Q1 2018*, Publications Office of the EU, Luxembourg, 2018; EIOPA, Report on the use of limitations and exemptions from reporting 2017, EIOPA-BoS/17-340 rev2, 21 December 2017, p. 3.

At country level, the top three Member States allowing exemptions by number of undertakings are Luxembourg, France and Norway. In terms of total assets, the top three Member States are Liechtenstein, Malta and France.

The number of NSAs granting exemptions has slightly increased (from 10 in 2017 to 13 in 2018), in line with EIOPA's expectations, as expressed in its first report in 2017. The numbers must also be read in the context of the additional proportionate and risk-based approaches in reporting, whereby reporting only has to take place if a certain threshold is reached, for instance in the case of derivatives or for the application of the look-through approach for investments.

However, this picture is not good at all and is in stark contrast with the clear wish of the co-legislators during the negotiations of Omnibus II to see the principle of proportionality being applied not only in theory but also in practice. Following critical comments, particularly from representatives of the financial services sector, on its 2015 call for evidence on possible improvements to the regulatory regime in financial services, in 2017 the EC published an action plan also containing suggestions on supervisory reporting.[17] This was immediately followed by a consultation launched on 1 December 2017[18] on ways and means to streamline supervisory reporting.

In its response to the EC,[19] EIOPA pointed out that there is a common misunderstanding regarding the origins of the costs relating to reporting. In a risk-based solvency regime, undertakings have to hold adequate data to properly identify, assess, manage, mitigate and report the risks they face. The need for data availability and data quality is therefore not mainly driven by reporting obligations, but rather by the sound prudential requirements on risk management, technical provisions and capital requirements. EIOPA points out that it has been working extensively on ways and means to reduce the costs and burden of supervisory reporting by facilitating data collection and through standardisation.

On the occasion of the review of the standard formula in 2018, a number of further simplifications and simplified calculations were included in the draft DA following the advice of EIOPA and at the specific request of the EC.[20]

---

17 EC, Report to the EP, the Council, the EESC and the CoR: Follow-up to the Call for evidence – EU regulatory framework for financial services, COM (2017) 736 final, 1 December 2017, pp. 14–19.

18 EC, *Consultation Document – Fitness check on supervisory reporting*, 1 December 2017, 19 p.

19 Letter from Gabriel Bernardino to the Director-General of DG FISMA Olivier Guersent, dated 5 March 2018, https://eiopa.europa.eu/Publications/Letters/EIOPA-18-072%20Letter%20to%20Olivier%20Guersent%20on%20Fitness%20Check%20on%20Supervisory%20reporting.pdf.

20 See Chapter 3, section 5.6.4.

2.1. EXAMPLES OF PROPORTIONALITY IN PILLAR 1

The following examples of the application of the proportionality principle are found under Pillar 1:

- Recognition of future claims of mutual insurers as Tier 2 capital (Art. 89 (1), second subparagraph and Art. 96 FD);
- Use of USPs (Art. 104 (7) FD);
- Use of a simplified calculation for a specific sub-module or risk module of the standard formula where the nature, scale and complexity of the risks faced justifies this and where it would be disproportionate to require all insurance and reinsurance undertakings to apply the standardised calculation (Art. 109 FD);
- Increase of the absolute floor for the calculation of the MCR for captives that engage in third-party business (Art. 129 (1)(d) FD);
- (Re)insurance undertakings should only be required to have own credit assessments on their larger or more complex exposures (recital 2 DA);
- (Re)insurance undertakings shall, taking due account of the principle of proportionality, ensure that internal users of the relevant assumptions about rules relating to the valuation of assets and liabilities, own funds, the SCR, the MCR and investment rules, and service providers to whom internal functions have been outsourced, are informed about their relevant content, their degree of reliability and their limitations (Art. 2 (2) DA);
- Possibility, by respecting the principle of proportionality, to depart from a valuation on the basis of IAS/IFRS and to recognise and value an asset or a liability based on the valuation method used for preparing the annual or consolidated financial statements (Art. 9 (4) DA);
- Calculation of technical provisions using methods that are proportionate to the nature, scale and complexity of the risks underlying (re)insurance obligations (Art. 56 DA);[21]
- Simplified calculation of recoverables from reinsurance contracts and SPVs (Art. 57 DA);
- Simplified calculation of the risk margin (Art. 58 DA);
- Possibility to derive the risk margin for calculations that need to be performed quarterly from the result of an earlier calculation of the risk margin (Art. 59 DA);
- Simplified calculation of the best estimate for insurance obligations with premium adjustment mechanism (Art. 60 DA);

21 See also, EIOPA, Guidelines for the valuation of technical provisions, EIOPA-BoS-14/166, 2 February 2014, Guidelines 44–49.

- Simplified calculation of the counterparty default adjustment (Art. 61 DA);
- Where the look-through approach cannot be applied to a collective investment undertaking or investment packaged as funds, a simplified approach can be used based on the last reported asset allocation of the collective investment undertaking or fund, provided that this simplified approach is proportionate to the nature, scale and complexity of the risks concerned (Art. 84 (3) and recital 11 DA);
- Simplified calculations of a specific sub-module or risk module of the standard formula if the simplified calculation can be considered proportionate to the nature, scale and complexity of the risks (Art. 88 DA):
  - general provisions for simplifications for captives (Art. 89 DA);
  - simplified calculation for captive insurance and reinsurance undertakings of the capital requirement for non-life premium and reserve risk (Art. 90 DA);
  - simplified calculation for discontinuance of insurance policies in the non-life lapse risk sub-module (Art. 90a DA);
  - simplified calculation of the sum insured for natural catastrophe risks (Art. 90b DA);
  - simplified calculation of the capital requirement for fire risk (Art. 90c DA);
  - simplified calculation of the capital requirement for life mortality risk (Art. 91 DA);
  - simplified calculation of the capital requirement for life longevity risk (Art. 92 DA);
  - simplified calculation of the capital requirement for life disability–morbidity risk (Art. 93 DA);
  - simplified calculation of the capital requirement for life-expense risk (Art. 94 DA);
  - simplified calculation of the capital requirement for permanent changes in lapse rates (Art. 95 DA);
  - simplified calculation of the capital requirement for risks in the life lapse risk sub-module (Art. 95a DA);
  - simplified calculation of the capital requirement for life-catastrophe risk (Art. 96 DA);
  - simplified calculation for discontinuance of insurance policies in the not similar to life techniques (NSLT) health lapse risk sub-module (Art. 96a DA);
  - simplified calculation of the capital requirement for health mortality risk (Art. 97 DA);
  - simplified calculation of the capital requirement for health longevity risk (Art. 98 DA);
  - simplified calculation of the capital requirement for medical-expense disability–morbidity risk (Art. 99 DA);

- simplified calculation of the capital requirement for income protection disability–morbidity (Art. 100 DA);
- simplified calculation of the capital requirement for health-expense risk (Art. 101 DA);
- simplified calculation of the capital requirement for SLT health lapse risk (Art. 102 DA);
- simplified calculation of the capital requirement for risks in the SLT health lapse risk sub-module (Art. 102a DA);
- simplified calculation of the capital requirement for interest rate risk for captive insurance or reinsurance undertakings (Art. 103 DA);
- simplified calculation for spread risk on bonds and loans (Art. 104 DA);
- simplified calculation for captive insurance or reinsurance undertakings of the capital requirement for spread risk on bonds and loans (Art. 105 DA);
- simplified calculation for the risk factor in the spread risk sub-module and the market risk concentration sub-module (Art. 105a DA);
- simplified calculation of the capital requirement for market risk concentration for captive (re)insurance undertakings (Art. 106 DA);
- simplified calculation of the risk-mitigating effect for reinsurance arrangements or securitisation (Art. 107 DA);
- simplified calculation of the risk-mitigating effect for proportional reinsurance arrangements (Art. 108 DA);
- simplified calculations for pooling arrangements (Art. 109 DA);
- simplified calculation for grouping of single-name exposures (Art. 110 DA);
- simplified calculation of the risk-mitigating effect (Art. 111 DA);
- simplified calculation of the risk-mitigating effect on underwriting risk (Art. 111a DA);
- simplified calculation of the risk-adjusted value of collateral to take into account the economic effect of the collateral (Art. 112 DA);
- simplified calculation of the loss-given default for reinsurance (Art. 112a DA);
- simplified calculation of the capital requirement for counterparty default risk on type 1 exposures (Art. 112b DA);

- The cost of acquiring ratings for the calculation of the SCR using the standard formula should be proportionate to the nature, scale and complexity of the associated asset risk. (Re)insurance undertakings that have nominated an ECAI should therefore be able to use a simplified calculation for those parts of the debt portfolio for which external ratings have not been acquired (Arts. 176a and 176b and recital 16 DA);
- USPs (Arts. 218–220 DA);
- For the design of the internal model, the modelling approaches should reflect the nature, scale and complexity of the risks inherent in the activities of the undertaking that are within the scope of the internal model (Art. 224 (a) DA);

- In deciding whether to apply the default method for the calculation of the group SCR, the group supervisor needs to assess whether the nature, scale and complexity of the risks of the group are such that the use of method 2[22] in relation to a related undertaking does not materially affect the results of the group solvency calculation (Art. 328 (1) (d) DA);
- When including the procedural aspects of additional assessments of the appropriateness of external credit assessments into their policy on risk management and documenting the results of the additional assessments and the way in which those assessments are carried out, (re)insurance undertakings should take into account the nature, scale and complexity of their business;[23]
- The proportionality assessment outlined in the guidelines on the validation of technical provisions is not only relevant for selecting the methodologies to calculate technical provisions. It should also help to deal with other aspects relating to the calculation of technical provisions, such as data quality, segmentation, assumptions-setting and validation.[24]

2.2. EXAMPLES OF PROPORTIONALITY IN PILLAR 2

The following examples of the application of the proportionality principle are found under Pillar 2:

- The system of governance shall be proportionate to the nature, scale and complexity of the operations of the (re)insurance undertaking (Art. 41 (2) and recital 31 FD);[25]
- The ORSA process must be proportionate to the nature, scale and complexity of the risks inherent in the business (Art. 45 (2) FD);
- The undertaking should decide for itself how to perform the own risk and solvency assessment given the nature, scale and complexity of the risks inherent in its business;[26]

---

22 See Chapter 9, section 7.2.2.

23 Commission Implementing Regulation 2015/2015 of 11 November 2015 laying down implementing technical standards on the procedures for assessing external credit assessments in accordance with Directive 2009/138/EC of the EP and of the Council, *OJ* L 295, 12.11.2015, p. 16, recital 3.

24 EIOPA, Guidelines for the valuation of technical provisions, EIOPA-BoS-14/166, 2 February 2014, para. 1.10.

25 Recital 31 specifically refers to the possibility of relying on advice from outside experts or outsourcing functions, and recital 32 states that it should be possible, in smaller and less complex undertakings, for more than one function to be carried out by a single person or organisational unit.

26 EIOPA, Guidelines on own risk and solvency assessment, EIOPA-BoS-14/259, 14 September 2015, para. 1.4.

- The actuarial function must be carried out by persons who have knowledge of actuarial and financial mathematics, commensurate with the nature, scale and complexity of the risks inherent in the business of the (re)insurance undertaking (Art. 48 (2) FD);
- Measures taken by supervisory authorities to safeguard the interests of policyholders in the event of deteriorating financial conditions must be proportionate and thus reflect the level and duration of the deterioration of the solvency position of the (re)insurance undertaking concerned (Art. 141 FD);
- In the design of the internal model, the modelling approaches must reflect the nature, scale and complexity of the risks inherent in the activities of the undertaking that fall within the scope of the internal model (Art. 224 (a) DA);
- (Re)insurance undertakings shall establish, implement and maintain effective decision-making procedures and an organisational structure that clearly specifies reporting lines, allocates functions and responsibilities, and takes into account the nature, scale and complexity of the risks inherent in their business (Art. 258 (1) (b) DA);
- The stress tests which (re)insurance undertakings with a qualifying infrastructure investment must regularly monitor and perform on the cash flows and collateral values supporting the infrastructure project entity must be commensurate with the nature, scale and complexity of the risk inherent in the infrastructure project (Art. 261 (2) DA);
- The persons carrying out the internal audit function may also carry out other key functions where this is appropriate with respect to the nature, scale and complexity of the risks inherent in the undertaking's business (Art. 271 (2) (a) DA);
- The remuneration policy shall be designed in such a way as to take into account the internal organisation of the insurance or reinsurance undertaking, and the nature, scale and complexity of the risks inherent in its business (Art. 275 (3) DA);
- In concluding that the system of governance of an insurance undertaking deviates significantly from the governance standards laid down in the FD, for the imposition of a capital add-on, supervisory authorities must take into account the different ways of organising an effective system of governance that is proportionate to the nature, scale and complexity of the risks inherent in the business of the undertaking (Art. 277 (c) DA);
- The system of governance of SPVs must be appropriate to the nature, scale and complexity of the risks it assumes and the uses for which it is authorised (Art. 324 (1) DA);
- The administrative, management or supervisory body (AMSB) of the undertaking should determine the scope and frequency of the internal

reviews of the system of governance, taking into account the nature, scale and complexity of the business, both at individual and at group level, as well as the structure of the group;[27]
- The NSA should ensure that the principle of proportionality is observed throughout all the stages of the supervisory review process.[28]

2.3. EXAMPLES OF PROPORTIONALITY IN PILLAR 3

The following examples of the application of the proportionality principle are found under Pillar 3:

- Supervisory information must reflect the nature, scale and complexity of the business of the undertaking concerned and in particular the risks inherent in that business (Art. 35 (4) (a) FD);
- Limitation of regular reporting where the submission of that information would be overly burdensome in relation to the nature, scale and complexity of the risks inherent in the business of the undertaking (Art. 35 (6) (a) FD);
- Limitation of regular reporting in the case of (re)insurance undertakings that are part of a group (Art. 35 (6), second subparagraph FD);
- Limitation of regular reporting or exemption from reporting on an item-by-item basis where the submission of that information would be overly burdensome in relation to the nature, scale and complexity of the risks inherent in the business of the undertaking (Art. 35 (7) (a) FD);
- Limitation of the exemption from reporting on an item-by-item basis in the case of (re)insurance undertakings that are part of a group (Art. 35 (7), second subparagraph FD);
- Criteria for assessing of whether the submission of information would be overly burdensome in relation to the nature, scale and complexity of the risks of the undertaking (Art. 35 (8) FD);
- Establishment by supervisory authorities of the minimum frequency and the scope of the supervisory review process having regard to the nature, scale and complexity of the activities of the (re)insurance undertaking concerned (Art. 36 (6), second subparagraph FD);
- Public disclosure should not result in (re)insurance undertakings being required to disclose any information that would not be relevant to their business or would not be material (recital 107 DA);

---

27 EIOPA, Guidelines on system of governance, EIOPA-BoS-14/253, 14 September 2015, Guideline 6.

28 EIOPA, Guidelines on supervisory review process, EIOPA-BoS-14/179, 2 February 2015, Guideline 3.

- Supervisory reporting should not result in (re)insurance undertakings or branches established within the EU being required to submit any information that would not be relevant to their business or would not be material (recital 115 DA);
- Inclusion of an assessment in the SFCR of the adequacy of the system of governance of the (re)insurance undertaking in relation to the nature, scale and complexity of the risks inherent in its business (Art. 294 (9) DA);
- NSAs must inform (re)insurance undertakings that are part of a group about the process, including the timeframe, for demonstrating that quarterly reporting or reporting on an item-by-item basis is inappropriate, given the nature, scale and complexity of the risks inherent in the business of the group;[29]
- A third-country insurance undertaking that has established a branch in an EEA MS may be exempted by the host supervisory authority of the country in which the branch is established from submitting certain information where the submission of that information would be unduly burdensome in relation to the nature, scale and complexity of the risks inherent in the business of the branch.[30]

3. PROPORTIONALITY: AN UNFINISHED DEBATE

The question still remains as to whether or not the Solvency II regime is too burdensome and whether the right balance has been struck between the risk sensitivity of the requirements and their usefulness and practicability from a cost–benefit perspective. Principles can be applied in different ways to achieve an equivalent standard of policyholder protection. EIOPA and NSAs have an important responsibility in this regard.

Solvency II is a principles-based regime that should be applied looking at the risks involved. (Re)insurance undertakings should not be forced to apply a checklist approach to ensure that each and every single provision of the otherwise rather complex regulatory regime is complied with. Unless supervisory authorities are prepared to more readily accept the application of the proportionality principle in practice, the co-legislators may have to revisit the regulatory requirements in order to restore the balance and to exempt small and medium-sized undertakings from those requirements that are considered too burdensome. In the end, more proportionate rules will help promote

29 EIOPA, Guidelines on methods for determining the market shares for reporting, EIOPA-BoS-15/106, 14 September 2015, Guideline 8.

30 EIOPA, Guidelines on the supervision of branches of third-country insurance undertakings, EIOPA-BoS-15/110, 23 October 2015, Guideline 48.

competition and increase the resilience of the financial system by safeguarding its diversity while also preserving policyholder protection, financial stability and overall resilience.

Fifty respondents from the insurance sector, comprising people from industry, from public authorities and from non-governmental organisations,[31] participated in the EC's 2015 call for evidence on the EU regulatory framework for financial services,[32] referred to above. The call for evidence provided further insights into the functioning of Solvency II. Some respondents felt that the reporting and governance requirements under Solvency II are too burdensome for small and medium-sized (re)insurers and that the framework does not sufficiently take account of the particular nature of mutual/cooperative insurers.[33]

In its request to EIOPA for technical advice on the review of specific items in the Solvency II DA, dated 22 February 2017, the EC asked EIOPA to look specifically into some areas where it believed that more could be done to achieve a better balance between the legal requirements and the risks that they are supposed to address. EIOPA was asked to suggest improvements to the existing simplifications in order to ensure that simple and easy-to-apply methodologies are provided for all standard formula calculations, bearing in mind the need to strengthen the proportionate application of the requirements.

In its response to the EC,[34] EIOPA pointed out that it did not believe that there was a need to modify the requirements of Art. 88 (1) DA, which set out the conditions that must be satisfied if a (re)insurance undertaking wants to apply a simplified calculation for a specific sub-module or risk module in the standard formula on the basis of the proportionality principle. Art. 88 (1) DA requires an assessment of the nature, scale and complexity of the risks of the undertaking that fall within the relevant module or sub-module for which a simplified calculation is envisaged, and an evaluation in qualitative or quantitative terms of the error that will result from the simplified calculation.

In accordance with Art. 88 (2) DA, a simplified calculation is not considered proportionate to the nature, scale and complexity of the risks where the error would lead to a misstatement of the SCR that could influence the decision-making or the judgement of the user of the information relating to the SCR.

---

31 EC, Report to the EP, the Council, the EESC and the CoR – Follow-up to the Call for evidence – EU regulatory framework for financial services, COM (2017) 736 final, 1 December 2017, 22 p.

32 EC, Communication to the EP, the Council, the EESC and the CoR – Call for evidence – EU regulatory framework for financial services, COM (2016) 855 final, 23 November 2016, 15 p.

33 EC, Summary of contributions to the "Call for Evidence", 2016, http://ec.europa.eu/finance/consultations/2015/financial-regulatory-framework-review/docs/summary-of-responses_en.pdf, pp. 12–13.

34 EIOPA, First set of advice to the EC on specific items in the Solvency II Delegated Regulation, EIOPA-BoS-17/280, 30 October 2017, pp. 6–13.

Based upon an analysis of the information provided by undertakings applying the FD, EIOPA concluded that the proportionality principle had been applied appropriately by (re)insurance undertakings and by NSAs. Where a qualitative evaluation indicates that the error resulting from the simplified calculation is immaterial, the error does not need to be evaluated in quantitative terms, nor is it necessary for (re)insurance undertakings to demonstrate that the model error is immaterial by calculating it with the standard method.

Rather than broadening Art. 88 DA, for instance by adding a threshold of materiality, EIOPA suggested adding some further simplifications of the standard formula (for instance, for the lapse risk sub-module). A number of further proposals for simplification were made in its second set of advice to the EC on specific aspects in the DA.[35] These simplifications were taken up by the EC and were included in the amendment of the DA as a result of the 2018 review of the standard formula.

These changes are welcome, but the question can still be raised as to whether it is not disproportionate to require all (re)insurance undertakings to apply a standardised calculation when non-specifically authorised simplifications that are immaterial would in fact be justified and would contribute to reducing the regulatory burden.[36]

Experience with the application of Solvency II shows that it would be better to state more clearly in the FD where proportionality applies, particularly in those areas where simplicity should override risk sensitivity. Similarly, it might not be the best solution to always make the application of a simplified procedure or calculation subject to specific authorisation from the supervisory authority, because there is a natural tendency to prefer the rule over the exception.

Proportionality should lead to simpler, but not necessarily less stringent rules.[37]

---

35 EIOPA, Second set of advice to the EC on specific items in the Solvency II Delegated Regulation, EIOPA-BoS-18/075, 28 February 2018, 612 p.

36 See the opinion of the IRSG on the Consultation Paper on EIOPA's first set of advice to the EC on specific items in the Solvency II Delegated Regulation, EIOPA-IRSG-17-14, 31 August 2017, p. 2. See also, EIOPA, Application of the proportionality principle in the supervision of the SCR, Supervisory Statement, EIOPA-BoS-19-033, 11 March 2019, 9 p.

37 See also for the banking sector, CASTRO CARVALHO, A.P., HOLL, S., RASKOPF, R. and RUHNAU, S., Proportionality in banking regulation: a cross-country comparison, *FSI Insights on Policy Implementation*, No 1, August 2017, 27 p.; EBA, *Proportionality in bank regulation: Report by the EBA Banking Stakeholder Group*, 30 June 2014, 58 p; DOMBRECHT, A., *On the road to greater regulatory proportionality?*, speech delivered on 29 April 2017 at the strategy conference of the Rhineland Savings Banks and Giro Association, https://www.bundesbank.de/en/press/speeches/on-the-road-to-greater-regulatory-proportionality--711552.

CHAPTER 6

PILLAR 1

Quantitative Requirements

Solvency II is a risk-based solvency capital regime. It follows a three-pillar approach. The first pillar deals with quantitative requirements. As indicated before, the Pillar 1 requirements are closely linked to the requirements in Pillars 2 and 3. They should therefore not be considered in isolation. When a (re)insurance undertaking is adopting a high-quality risk management (Pillar 2), it will normally have a sufficient amount of capital (Pillar 1). Market discipline following from the supervisory reporting and disclosure requirements (Pillar 3) will encourage undertakings to operate with the right amount of capital (Pillar 1).

The quantitative requirements under Pillar 1 deal with the solvency balance sheet, valuation of assets and liabilities in the solvency balance sheet, own funds, calculation of the capital requirements and investment rules.

The quantitative requirements logically start with the solvency balance sheet, which is the basis for establishing the capital requirements. The solvency balance sheet comprises all assets and liabilities, including own funds, valued on a market-consistent (fair-value)[1] basis.

Own funds are further defined to ensure that the undertaking possesses capital that is sufficiently solid. The capital buffer (capital requirements) for the protection of policyholders is defined taking into account all (quantifiable) risks to which the (re)insurance undertaking is exposed.

Solvency II establishes two capital requirements: the solvency capital requirement (SCR) and the minimum capital requirement (MCR).

The SCR is risk-based and prospective and includes all important risks that can be quantified (including underwriting risk, market risk, credit risk, operational risk).

The SCR serves to calculate the solvency ratio (own funds/SCR%). The solvency ratio must be at least 100%. A solvency ratio of 100% does not mean that an insurer cannot fail. Solvency II is not a zero-failure regime. It ensures

[1] The FD does not define "market consistent" or "fair value". However, the definition contained in Art. 75 FD corresponds with the definition of "fair value" under IAS/IFRS.

that an insurer with a solvency ratio of 100% can withstand the worst annual loss over the next 200 years.

The MCR represents the minimum level of security. It is calculated in a simpler manner and will usually be between 25% and 45% of the SCR.

1. SOLVENCY BALANCE SHEET

The insurance business is different from other types of activities. It is characterised by an inverted production cycle. Insurers first receive premiums from policyholders. They then invest the money received. It is only after claims have been reported, managed and settled that insurers will know whether they have made a profit on their underwriting (and investments).

The balance sheet of an insurer reflects this reality. The asset side comprises investments and reinsurance recoverables. The liabilities side includes capital (own funds), technical provisions and other debts.

Figure 3. The solvency balance sheet

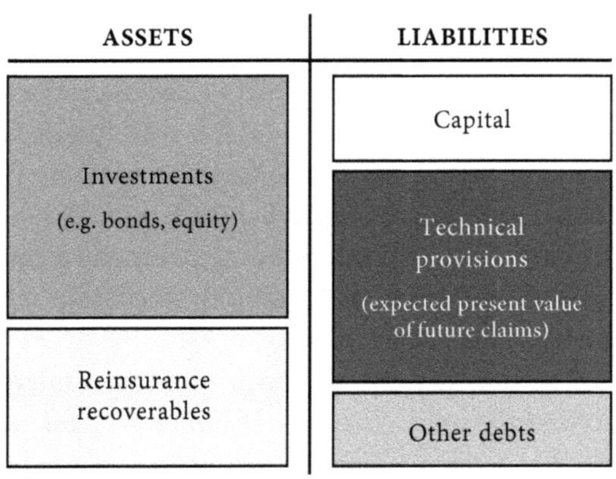

Source: Produced by the author.

On the *assets side* of the balance sheet, the investments are mainly composed of bonds, equities and real estate, held directly or through investment funds. Reinsurance recoverables represent the claims of the insurer against one or more reinsurers to whom insurance risks have been transferred.

On the *liabilities side* of the balance sheet, the own funds represent assets minus unsubordinated liabilities. The own funds consist of capital brought in by shareholders (or members in the case of a mutual), various types of reserves (retained profits) and subordinated liabilities (liabilities that are only repaid after all other liabilities have been settled).

The most important item on the liabilities side is technical provisions. They reflect the expected present value of future claims. As soon as a (re)insurer has underwritten a risk, a technical provision has to be set up for the expected loss that might result from that underwriting. The statistics published by EIOPA show that for EEA insurers (end 2017) technical provisions accounted for 89.8% of total liabilities.[2] Technical provisions are often referred to as "reserves". From an accounting perspective, this is incorrect as reserves are part of own funds, whilst technical provisions are liabilities. The DA is not wholly consistent in this regard. An example is the reference in Arts. 115–117 to "reserve risk", which refers to the risk of existing claims being greater than expected because of a difference in the timing of claims payments from expected payments and in claims frequency from those expected.[3] It would therefore be technically more correct to refer to "provision risk".

Insurers usually have very little other debt.[4] As they regularly receive premiums, their cash position is usually very good. There is very little need to obtain further money from banks.

Insurers can suffer different kinds of shock which affect their financial position. Claims might increase as compared to expectations (for instance, as a result of a storm that is more severe than expected). Administrative costs might go up. These costs are generally still quite high as new technologies (InsurTech) have not yet had as much of an impact on the insurance sector as on the banking sector. Investments might decrease in value or have lower yields, for instance as a result of interest rate changes or a drop in financial markets. Reinsurers might default, meaning that the amount of recoverables becomes uncertain.

From a prudential point of view, much attention is paid to ensuring that insurers invest prudently (prudent person principle) and that technical provisions are calculated prudently (not over-optimistically) and with due care (using proper actuarial techniques). The value of technical provisions will never be "correct", as it is based upon assumptions and estimates that require judgement.

In accordance with Art. 9 (1) DA, the solvency balance sheet is drawn up on the basis of international accounting standards adopted by the EC in accordance with the IAS Regulation,[5] to the extent that they are consistent with the

2 EIOPA, *Accompanying note to the statistics*, https://eiopa.europa.eu/Publications/Insurance%20Statistics/SA_Accompanying_note.pdf, p. 4.

3 CEA and Groupe Consultatif, *Solvency II Glossary*, March 2007. See also EIOPA, Calibration of the Premium and Reserve Risk Factors in the Standard Formula of Solvency II: Report of the Joint Working Group on Non-Life and Health NSLT Calibration, EIOPA 11/163, 12 December 2011, 77 p.

4 Non-insurance liabilities might include amounts payable, tax liabilities, employee benefits or wholesale funding obligations, including senior and subordinated debt securities or other loan arrangements. See SHARMA, P. and CADONI, P., Solvency II: A New Regulatory Frontier, in KEMPLER, C., FLAMEE, M., YANG, C.H. and WINDELS, P. (Eds.), *Global Perspectives on Insurance Today*, Palgrave Macmillan, New York, 2013, p. 61.

5 Regulation (EC) No 1606/2002 of the EP and of the Council of 19 July 2002 on the application of international accounting standards, *OJ* L 243, 11.9.2002, p. 1. See VAN HULLE, K.,

valuation approach set out in Art. 75 FD. IAS/IFRS make a distinction between recognition and measurement in the balance sheet. Solvency II incorporates this distinction. Assets and liabilities can only be recognised in the solvency balance sheet to the extent that this is allowed under IAS/IFRS.[6]

Technical provisions for (re)insurance obligations may only be recognised in the balance sheet at the date the undertaking becomes a party to the contract that gives rise to the obligation or at the date the (re)insurance cover begins, whichever date is the earlier. Only the obligations within the boundary of the contract may be recognised in the balance sheet. De-recognition of technical provisions for (re)insurance obligations may only take place when the (re)insurance obligation is extinguished, discharged, cancelled or expires (Art. 17 DA).

Much debate occurred on the definition of contract boundaries. The insurance industry wanted a definition that was similar to that included in the international accounting standard dealing with insurance contracts. However, that standard (IFRS 17)[7] was not yet complete when Solvency II was developed. A definition of the boundary of a (re)insurance contract is included in Art. 18 DA. The principle is that all obligations relating to the contract, including obligations relating to unilateral rights of the (re)insurance undertaking to renew or extend the scope of the contract and obligations that relate to paid premiums, belong to the contract, unless otherwise stated in Art. 18 DA.[8] The objective of the principle is to determine when an existing contract ends and a new contract begins. Once that boundary has been determined, the expected value of all the cash flows falling within the contract must be included in the measurement of the liability. Cash flows that are not in the boundary of the contract relate to future insurance contracts.

Normally, cash flows are considered to be within the boundary of a contract if they arise from rights and obligations that exist during the period in which the policyholder is obliged to pay premiums or, if the insurer has a substantive obligation, to provide the policyholder with insurance coverage or other services. The contract boundary determines in particular how much expected profit from future premiums is recognised in the own funds. The wider the contract boundary, the more profit will be recognised, thereby increasing the own funds.

From Accounting Directives to International Accounting Standards, in LEUTZ, C., PFAFF, D. and HOPWOOD, A. (Eds.), *The Economics and Politics of Accounting*, Oxford University Press, New York, 2004.

6 IASB, *IFRS Conceptual Framework for Financial Reporting*, March 2018, 86 p.

7 Meanwhile, the IASB adopted IFRS 17 – Insurance Contracts on 18 May 2017. EIOPA has reservations with parts of the new standard, such as the determination of the applicable discount rate. See EIOPA, Analysis of IFRS 17 Insurance Contracts, EIOPA-BoS-18-717, 18 October 2018, 34 p.

8 See also EIOPA, Guidelines on contract boundaries, EIOPA-BoS-14/165, 2 February 2014.

This is particularly important as the expected profit in future premiums (EPIFP) is part of Tier 1 capital. The definition of contract boundary is also important for calibrations of the SCR lapse risk and of non-life premium and reserve risk.

The solvency balance sheet drawn up under Solvency II may be different from the balance sheet produced for general purpose financial reporting. In many Member States of the EU, the financial statements (balance sheet, income statement, notes and sometimes cash flow statement) prepared by (re)insurance undertakings for general purpose financial reporting both on a solo and group level are drawn up under national accounting rules (national GAAP), which are usually heavily influenced by tax considerations.

The national accounting rules for preparing (general purpose) financial statements of (re)insurance undertakings are based upon the Insurance Accounts Directive (IAD) of 19 December 1991.[9] After discussion with MS experts and with CEIOPS, the EC decided not to amend the IAD in the context of Solvency II. It would indeed have been very difficult to agree on a uniform accounting regime for (re)insurance undertakings both on a solo (annual accounts) and on a group (consolidated accounts) basis.[10] On the other hand, it was considered premature to introduce new accounting rules in the EU when the IASB was still working on a new international standard for insurance contracts.[11] The EC therefore decided to deal directly with the applicable accounting rules in the Solvency II FD and its implementing measures.

All listed (re)insurance undertakings must prepare and publish their consolidated financial statements in accordance with IAS/IFRS as adopted by the EC.[12] Each individual (re)insurance undertaking must however also

---

9 Council Directive 91/674/EEC of 19 December 1991 on the annual accounts and consolidated accounts of insurance undertakings, *OJ* L 374, 31.12.1991, p. 7.

10 See, CEIOPS, Recommendations regarding the implications of the IAS/IFRS introduction for the prudential supervision of insurance undertakings, CEIOPS-DOC-05/05, September 2005, 19 p. with annexes (https://eiopa.europa.eu/CEIOPS-Archive/Documents/Standards/recommendations_DOC0505.pdf).

11 Meanwhile, the IASB adopted IFRS 17 – Insurance Contracts on 18 May 2017 after nearly 20 years of discussion. IFRS 17 supersedes IFRS 4 – Insurance Contracts and related interpretations and is effective for financial years beginning on or after 1 January 2021. It is however contested and the insurance industry is asking for a two-year delay in its application in order to allow for an improvement of the standard. See Insurance Europe, *Position on IFRS 17*, 3 October 2018. See also the letter written on 3 September 2018 by EFRAG to Hans Hoogervorst, Chairman of the IASB, in which the EFRAG Board asks to review a number of concerns raised during outreach with constituents, https://www.efrag.org/Assets/Download?assetUrl=%2Fsites%2Fwebpublishing%2FSiteAssets%2FMr.%2520Hans%2520Hoogervorst%2520letter%2520signed%2520-%2520IFRS%252017%2520Insurance%2520Contracts.pdf. The IASB decided in November 2018 to delay the implementation of IFRS 17 and the related (for the insurance industry) standard IFRS 9 – *Financial instruments* by one year, until 1 January 2022.

12 Art. 4 of Regulation (EC) No 1606/2002 of the EP and of the Council of 19 July 2002 on the application of international accounting standards, *OJ* L 24, 11.9.2002, p. 1 (IAS Regulation).

prepare and publish annual financial statements.[13] It is for Member States to decide whether these annual financial statements or the consolidated financial statements in the case of a (re)insurance group that is not listed are prepared on the basis of IAS/IFRS or on the basis of national GAAP.[14]

The solvency rules relating to the recognition and valuation of assets and liabilities may therefore be different from the rules for the preparation of the financial statements for general purpose financial reporting.[15] They could be similar if the undertaking is preparing its annual financial statements on the basis of IAS/IFRS. In most Member States, this is at present the exception.

Although the eventual aim is a convergence between solvency rules and general purpose financial reporting standards,[16] it is not illogical that these rules diverge. The solvency balance sheet has an objective that is different from that of a balance sheet prepared for general purpose financial reporting. For the solvency balance sheet, prudential considerations play an important role. The balance sheet must provide supervisors with relevant (economic risk-based) information that makes it possible for them to carry out their supervisory task. In the context of general purpose financial reporting, financial statements are prepared from an investor point of view, i.e. with a view to defining the profit available for distribution. The income statement (or profit and loss account) reflects the income and expenditure relating to the activities carried out during the financial year. Solvency II is interested in the solvency position of the undertaking and not so much in the amount of profit available for distribution.

Although everybody agreed that there had to be as much consistency as possible between prudential rules and accounting rules, the insurance industry, which at the time of developing Solvency II was very much in favour of a market-consistent (fair-value) valuation of assets and liabilities in the solvency balance sheet,[17] made it very clear that accounting rules should not affect the calculation for solvency purposes. This was particularly true for the calculation of technical provisions. While it was considered important that the calculation of insurance

---

13 On 21 March 2018, the EC launched a consultation in order to assess whether the requirements for public reporting by companies, including insurance undertakings, are still fit for purpose. The results of this consultation, which closed on 21 July 2018, will feed into a Staff Working Document on the fitness of the EU framework for public reporting by companies, to be published in 2019. https://ec.europa.eu/info/consultations/finance-2018-companies-public-reporting_en.

14 Art. 5 IAS Regulation.

15 This is, for instance, the case in Belgium, where assets and liabilities are valued mainly at depreciated, amortised or historical cost under Belgian GAAP.

16 During the negotiations of Solvency II, the EC proposed amending the IAD by introducing an option for Member States allowing (re)insurance undertakings to make use in their financial statements of the rules on the calculation of technical provisions and valuation of admissible assets to be contained in the Solvency II FD. Most Member States had a clear preference for not touching the IAD at that stage.

17 See, for instance, AIGRAIN, J., How do we square the circle between accounting and solvency?, *The Geneva Papers*, 2009, No 34, pp. 42–46.

liabilities for accounting and solvency purposes was consistent and reconcilable, it was recognised that the value might not be the same. On the other hand, because of market-consistent valuation of technical provisions in the solvency balance sheet, there were strong voices within the insurance industry pleading in favour of keeping some prudence in the calculation of technical provisions for general purpose financial reporting in order to limit volatility in own funds. However, for solvency purposes, financial liabilities should not contain prudence on top of the market-consistent (fair-value) valuation.[18]

The distinction between prudential rules and accounting rules is an important change from the earlier regime. Under Solvency I, financial statements prepared for general purpose financial reporting served as a basis for prudential supervision. This was particularly relevant for the calculation of technical provisions and of admissible assets.

The balance sheet under Solvency II is an *economic balance sheet*, i.e. a balance sheet based on an accounting approach using market-consistent values for all current assets and current liabilities relating to in-force business, including off-balance sheet items.[19] In addition, Solvency II follows a total balance sheet approach, which recognises the interdependence between assets, liabilities, regulatory capital requirements and capital resources and ensures that risks are appropriately taken into account. A total balance sheet approach requires that the impact of relevant material risks on an insurer's overall financial position be appropriately and adequately recognised.[20] All risks relating to assets and (unsubordinated) liabilities, including off-balance sheet items and the correlations between these risks, are taken into account in calculating the capital requirements. In this way, Solvency II is more risk-sensitive than the Basel framework for banks, which primarily looks at the risks relating to the asset side of the balance sheet.

This economic approach has several advantages:[21]

- it can be calibrated to provide a better balance between the protection of policyholders and the encouragement of efficient operations of companies;
- it is more transparent and limits arbitrage opportunities;
- it leads to a closer alignment of regulatory capital requirements with good-practice internal risk management processes;
- it can better cope with changing market circumstances and practices;
- it is likely to limit double counting of risks and capital requirements.

---

18 Presentation by CEA and CRO Forum at the EIOPC meeting of 16 February 2006.

19 CEA and Groupe Consultatif, *Solvency II Glossary*, March 2007, p. 24.

20 IAIS, ICP 17 – Capital Adequacy, para. 17.1.1.

21 See SHARMA, P. and CADONI, P., Solvency II: A New Regulatory Frontier, in KEMPLER, C., FLAMEE, M., YANG, C.H. and WINDELS, P. (Eds.), *Global Perspectives on Insurance Today*, Palgrave Macmillan, New York, 2013, p. 60.

2. VALUATION RULES

2.1. VALUATION PRINCIPLES

In accordance with Art. 75 FD, the solvency balance sheet is prepared on the assumption that the undertaking will pursue its business as a going concern and not on a "stress scenario" assumption.

The going-concern principle assumes that an entity will remain in business for the foreseeable future. Conversely, this means that the entity will not be forced to halt operations and liquidate its assets in the near term at what may be very low fire-sale prices.

Assets and liabilities in the solvency balance sheet are valued in accordance with IAS/IFRS adopted by the EC in accordance with the IAS Regulation, provided that those standards include valuation methods that are consistent with the valuation method approach set out in Art. 75 FD, i.e. that they are valued on a market-consistent (fair-value) basis. Where those standards allow for the use of more than one valuation method (for instance, historic cost), (re)insurance undertakings may only use those valuation methods that are in line with a market-consistent approach (Art. 9 (2) DA). Similarly, where the valuation methods under IAS/IFRS are not in line, either temporarily or permanently, with a market-consistent approach, (re)insurance undertakings must use other valuation methods that are deemed to be in conformity with a market-consistent approach (Art. 9 (3) DA). The FD thus specifically prohibits certain valuation methods, such as historic cost, depreciated cost or amortised cost.

Art. 16 DA includes a number of examples of where (re)insurance undertakings must depart from one of the methods allowed under IAS/IFRS because that method does not provide a market-consistent value:

- financial assets or liabilities may not be valued at cost or amortised cost (IFRS 9 – *Financial Instruments*);
- valuation models may not result in a value that is the lower of the carrying amount and fair value less cost to sell (IFRS 9 – *Financial Instruments*);
- property, investment property, plant and equipment may not be valued with cost models where the asset value is determined at cost less depreciation and impairment (IAS 16 – *Property, Plant and Equipment*);
- in the case of a financial lease, lease assets must be valued at fair value. For the determination of the minimum lease payments market-consistent inputs must be used and no subsequent adjustments can be made to take account of the own credit standing of the undertaking; valuation at depreciated cost may not be applied (IFRS 16 – *Leases*);
- the net realisable value for inventories must be adjusted by the estimated cost of completion and the estimated cost necessary to make the sale where

those costs are material. Those costs are considered material where their non-inclusion could influence the decision-making or the judgement of the users of the balance sheet, including the supervisory authorities; valuation at cost may not be applied (IAS 2 – *Inventories*);
- non-monetary grants may not be valued at a nominal amount (IAS 20 – *Accounting for Grants and Disclosure of Government Assistance*);
- when valuing biological assets, the value shall be adjusted by adding the estimated costs to sell if the estimated costs to sell are material (IAS 41 – *Agriculture*).

Market-consistent valuation, i.e. valuation on the basis of market values or in the absence of market values on the basis of a market-based valuation model (fair value), is the logical consequence of the adoption of an economic risk-based approach. This approach reduces or eliminates, where possible, accounting mismatches where no underlying economic mismatches exist, thereby providing a more accurate picture of an entity's solvency position and enhancing overall protection for policyholders.[22]

In order to reduce the administrative burden on undertakings because of the difference between accounting and prudential standards, Art. 9 (4) DA allows for some flexibility on the basis of the principle of proportionality.

A (re)insurance undertaking may recognise and value an asset or a liability based on the valuation method it uses for preparing its annual or consolidated financial statements provided that:

- the valuation method is consistent with Art. 75 FD;[23]
- the valuation method is proportionate with respect to the nature, scale and complexity of the risks inherent in the business of the undertaking;
- the undertaking does not value that asset or liability using IAS/IFRS in its financial statements.

It is doubtful that many undertakings will be able to use this simplification in their annual or consolidated financial statements. The complexity results more from the application of a market-consistent valuation than from a different valuation in the financial statements and in the solvency balance sheet. However, Art. 9 (4) DA does not allow a valuation that is not market-consistent.

22 Bermuda Monetary Authority, *Consultation Paper – Economic Balance Sheet Framework for General Business Insurers*, August 2012, p. 6.

23 For guidance, see EIOPA, Guidelines on the recognition and valuation of assets and liabilities other than technical provisions, EIOPA-BoS-15, 14 September 2015, Guideline 12 and Technical Annex 1. EIOPA has not assessed which national GAAP rules used in annual or consolidated financial statements are consistent with Art. 75 FD.

Undertakings that are within the scope of the consolidation of a group preparing consolidated financial statements in accordance with IAS/IFRS may not apply the derogation in Art. 9 (4) DA.[24] This is a logical consequence of the consolidation process: for consolidation purposes, all assets and liabilities in the consolidated balance sheet must be valued on a uniform basis.[25]

(Re)insurance undertakings are required to provide detailed information in their SFCR on the valuation of assets and liabilities in the solvency balance sheet and on any material differences between the bases, the methods and main assumptions used for the valuation for solvency purposes and those used for the valuation in the financial statements (Art. 296 (1) (a)–(b) and (2) (a)–(c) DA).[26]

Individual assets and liabilities must be valued separately (Art. 9 (5) and (6) DA). This makes it impossible to take account of the value of assets in the valuation of the liabilities and vice versa. This was one of the issues raised in the context of developing the LTG package. It was argued that there was no need to change the value of the assets, i.e. to value them on a market-consistent basis if they were held to maturity and were covering long-term (illiquid) liabilities of the same duration. This would avoid volatility in own funds. Even without the specific provision in Art. 9 (5) and (6) DA, such an approach would not have been possible as it would have been contrary to IAS/IFRS.[27]

When valuing assets and liabilities, undertakings should consider the materiality principle.[28] Information is considered material if that information could influence the decision-making or judgement of the intended users of that information.[29]

Undertakings should also apply valuation methods consistently. It may be necessary to change a valuation method if there is a change in circumstances, for instance new market developments that change market conditions.[30]

The requirement to use market values for the valuation of all assets and liabilities in the balance sheet was not controversial during the negotiation of Solvency II. It was considered a major improvement of the situation compared

---

24 EIOPA, Guidelines on the recognition and valuation of assets and liabilities other than technical provisions, EIOPA-BoS-15, 14 September 2015, Guideline 12.

25 See IFRS 10 – Consolidated Financial Statements and Art. 24 (10) Accounting Directive.

26 For an interesting example, see the 2017 group SFCR of Allianz, pp. 73–74, https://www.allianz.com/content/dam/onemarketing/azcom/Allianz_com/investor-relations/en/results-reports/sfcr/2018/en-Allianz-Gruppe-SFCR-2017.pdf.

27 The High-Level Expert Group on Sustainable Finance suggests examining whether the IAS Regulation of 2002 can be amended so as to allow for accounting methods that depart from international accounting standards in cases where this would further sustainability.

28 EIOPA, Guidelines on recognition and valuation of assets and liabilities other than technical provisions, EIOPA-BoS-15, 14 September 2015, Guideline 1.

29 Recital 1 DA. See also, Art. 2 (16) Accounting Directive.

30 EIOPA, Guidelines on recognition and valuation of assets and liabilities other than technical provisions, EIOPA-BoS-15, 14 September 2015, Guideline 2.

with Solvency I, where assets were usually valued on a market-consistent basis, whilst liabilities (particularly technical provisions) were valued at historic cost. This led to mismatches in the balance sheet between assets and liabilities. This made no economic sense as the assets in the balance sheet are held to cover the liabilities.

The insurance industry (CEA) broadly supported this economic approach. This was also the position of most members of CEIOPS, of the CRO Forum and of the EC. There was a strong desire for the Solvency II valuation approach and IAS/IFRS (particularly IFRS 4 Phase 2[31]) to develop consistently. This was underlined by supervisors, who were concerned about the auditability of the solvency balance sheet if there were not a clear link with the accounting rules.

It was recognised that the application of a market-consistent valuation increases the volatility in the value of assets and liabilities, leading to volatility in the own funds held by the insurer. This was said not to adequately reflect the long-term perspective of life insurance business in particular.[32]

Nevertheless, as indicated in the Impact Assessment Report accompanying the proposed Solvency II FD, the economic risk-based approach was considered a key element of Solvency II by the insurance industry. If Solvency II had not required insurers to hold capital in line with the economic cost of the risks they run, this could have undermined its effectiveness and efficiency. In particular, it could increase the likelihood and severity of some of the potential short-term side effects, such as the difficulty of insuring certain risks or market consolidation. CEA reported that "if the final implementation of Solvency II is not in line with sound economic principles, this could more than double the implementation costs".[33]

Since the financial crisis and the low interest rate environment, criticism has been voiced by the insurance industry that an approach that is entirely based on market values may lead to the mistaken assumption that insurers trade all their assets and liabilities at all times.[34] This would limit the ability of insurers to invest in long-term assets that support economic growth. It is also argued that the approach followed under Solvency II does not sufficiently take into account the business model of insurance. Insurers invest in the long term to match their

---

31 Now IFRS 17 – Insurance Contracts.

32 CEIOPS, Report on the fourth Quantitative Impact Study (QIS 4) for Solvency II, CEIOPS-SEC-82/08, p. 7.

33 See EC, Commission Staff Working Document: Accompanying document to the Proposal for a Directive of the EP and of the Council on the taking-up and pursuit of the business of Insurance and Reinsurance. Solvency II: Impact Assessment Report, SEC (2007) 871, 10 July 2007, Industry Reports – Annex C.8c.

34 JONES, O., Solvency II: sophisticated but excessive, in Insurance Europe, *Annual Report 2016–2017*, pp. 34–38. See also Insurance Europe and Oliver Wyman, *Funding the future – Insurers' role as institutional investors*, June 2013, 49 p.

long-term insurance liabilities. Insurers are therefore ideally situated to support a sustainable economy.[35]

As a result of the low interest rate environment, insurers are suffering a double hit: when their investments (particularly in bonds) arrive at maturity, they will have to reinvest in assets with a lower yield; at the same time, the value of their embedded guarantees will increase when interest rates go down. Attempts have been made to deal with this issue under the LTG measures that were included in the FD by Omnibus II. The insurance industry would however prefer a regime that better recognises the long-term nature of insurance. This issue will have to be looked at again when the FD is revised based upon a report from the EC to be presented by 31 December 2020 (Art. 111 (3) FD).

2.2. VALUATION OF ASSETS AND LIABILITIES OTHER THAN TECHNICAL PROVISIONS

As a principle, all assets and liabilities in the solvency balance sheet are valued at market value.

For assets, the market value is the amount for which they could be exchanged between knowledgeable willing parties in an arm's-length transaction (Art. 75 (1) (a) FD).

For liabilities, the market value is the amount for which they could be transferred, or settled, between knowledgeable willing parties in an arm's-length transaction (Art. 75 (1) (b) FD).

When valuing insurance liabilities using market values, no adjustment may be made to take account of the undertaking's own credit standing (Art. 75 (1), second subparagraph FD). This prudential filter was added to avoid a situation whereby a (re)insurance undertaking experiencing difficulties would be able to record a profit because the market value of its liabilities would have decreased.

Art. 10 DA recognises that market prices may not be readily available for all assets and liabilities. It therefore establishes the so-called fair-value hierarchy.[36] This hierarchy, which results in a market-based rather than entity-specific measurement, gives the highest priority to (unadjusted) quoted prices

---

35 EC, *Financing a sustainable European economy: Final Report 2018 by the High-Level Expert Group on Sustainable Finance*, January 2018, pp. 70–73.

36 See also, IFRS 13 – Fair Value Measurement. Not all supervisory authorities in the EU were so happy with the adoption of the fair value hierarchy. See, for instance, FLAMEE, M., IFRS and Solvency II: Global exposure and interaction – The work of the IAIS, *The Geneva Papers*, 2008, No 33, pp. 54–59. The author (Chair of the IAIS) refers (p. 59) to the problem of auditability when fair value is based on inputs that are not directly extracted or straightforwardly stemming from deep and liquid markets.

in active markets for identical assets or liabilities and the lowest priority to unobservable inputs. The hierarchy takes into account the characteristics of the asset or liability where market participants would take those characteristics into account when pricing the asset or liability at the valuation date, including the condition and location of the asset or liability and restrictions, if any, on the sale or use of the asset (Art. 10 (1) DA).

In establishing fair value of an asset or a liability, three levels are recognised:

- use of quoted market prices in active markets for the *same* assets or liabilities (default valuation method) (Art. 10 (2) DA);
- in the absence of such prices, use of quoted market prices in active markets for *similar* assets and liabilities, with adjustments to reflect differences (Art. 10 (3) DA);
- in the absence of such prices, use of alternative valuation methods (Art. 10 (5) DA).

When using alternative valuation methods, (re)insurance undertakings must rely as little as possible on undertaking-specific inputs and make maximum use of relevant market inputs,[37] including the following (Art. 10 (6) DA):

- quoted prices for identical or similar assets or liabilities in markets that are not active;
- inputs other than quoted prices that are observable for the asset or liability, including interest rates and yield curves observable at commonly quoted intervals, implied volatilities and credit spreads;
- market-corroborated inputs, which may not be directly observable, but are based on or supported by observable market data.

The alternative valuation methods must be consistent with one or more of the following approaches (Art. 10 (7) DA):

- a *market approach* using prices and other relevant information generated by market transactions involving identical or similar assets, liabilities or groups of assets and liabilities;
- an *income approach*, which converts future amounts, such as cash flows or income or expenses, into a single current amount;
- a *cost approach* or *current replacement cost approach*, which reflects the amount that would be required currently to replace the service capacity of an asset.

[37] See also EIOPA, Guidelines on recognition and valuation of assets and liabilities other than technical provisions, EIOPA-BoS-15, 14 September 2015, Guidelines 3 and 4, dealing with investment property and other properties.

Particularly in Central and Eastern Europe or in the Baltic countries, it may not always be possible for undertakings to use quoted market prices based on the criteria of active markets, as defined under IAS/IFRS, because markets may not be as active as in other parts of the EEA. Alternative valuation methods will then have to be used. In practice, (re)insurance undertakings will apply as an alternative valuation method a discounted cash flow method for debt securities, loans, financial liabilities, payables by insurers or intermediaries, etc. if there is no active market. For property, values determined by licensed valuers are often used.[38]

Information on the use of alternative valuation methods can be found in section D.4 of the SFCR (Art. 296 DA and Annex XX to the DA).

As the solvency balance sheet serves prudential purposes, intangible assets are looked at very critically because of the uncertainty in their valuation. Goodwill must therefore be valued at zero. The rationale is that goodwill is an item that cannot be separately identified and transferred in the marketplace and as a result it does not have an 'economic' value that can be separately sold or transferred if necessary to a third party.

The same applies to other intangibles, unless the intangible asset can be sold separately and the (re)insurance undertaking can demonstrate that there is a value for the same or similar assets that has been derived on the basis of IAS/IFRS (Art. 12 DA). As (re)insurers are investing increasingly in digital assets in the context of digitalisation, there is a need to have another look at this prudential requirement, as well as in the context of the debate on sustainability.

A valuation hierarchy is introduced in Art. 13 DA for the valuation of holdings in related undertakings, i.e. undertakings that qualify as a subsidiary undertaking, an undertaking in which a participation is held or an undertaking that is part of a horizontal group.[39] The hierarchy starts with quoted market prices in active markets for the same holdings as a start and ends with the use of an alternative valuation method.

In two situations, holdings in related undertakings are valued at zero:

- the related undertaking is excluded from the scope of group supervision (for instance, because it is of negligible interest);
- the related undertaking is deducted from the own funds eligible for the group solvency (because the necessary information is not available).

Deferred tax assets and liabilities must be recognised and valued in the balance sheet in relation to all items that are recognised for solvency purposes or in

---

[38] For interesting examples, see the 2017 group SFCR of Aviva plc (pp. 59–60), https://www.aviva.com/content/dam/aviva-corporate/Solvency-FCR-2017 and the 2017 group SFCR of PZU (pp. 73–74), https://www.pzu.pl/_fileserver/item/1512907.

[39] For the definitions, see further, Chapter 9, section 3.

the tax balance sheet in order to ensure that all amounts which could give rise to future tax cash flows are captured (recital 8 DA).

Deferred taxes arise for two reasons in the solvency balance sheet:[40]

- where the valuation principles for the solvency balance sheet differ from the fiscal valuation principles and the profits and losses have not yet been fiscally recognised, temporary differences may occur between the fiscal and solvency valuations;
- where fiscal losses from previous years can be carried forward to reduce tax payments in future years, when future fiscal profits are available, a deferred tax asset arises.

Deferred tax assets occur when the valuation of an asset (liability) is lower (higher) in the solvency balance sheet than in the fiscal balance sheet and fewer taxes will be paid on that asset (liability) than if that asset (liability) were to be bought (sold) today.

Deferred tax assets may only receive a positive value where it is probable that future taxable profit will be available against which the deferred tax asset can be used, taking into account any legal or regulatory requirements on the time limits relating to the carry-forward of unused tax losses or the carry-forward of unused tax credits (Art. 15 (3) DA). Deferred taxes in relation to all assets and liabilities, including technical provisions, that are recognised for solvency or tax purposes must be included in the solvency balance sheet and valued in accordance with IAS/IFRS.[41]

Deferred tax liabilities occur when the valuation of an asset (liability) is higher (lower) in the solvency balance sheet than in the fiscal balance sheet and more taxes will be paid on that asset (liability) than if that asset (liability) were to be bought (sold) today.

Deferred tax assets and liabilities may not be discounted. Deferred tax assets and deferred tax liabilities may only be offset if the undertaking has a legally enforceable right to set off current tax assets against current tax liabilities and if the deferred tax assets and the deferred tax liabilities relate to taxes levied by the same tax authority on the same taxable undertaking.[42]

Contingent liabilities must be recognised in the balance sheet as normal liabilities if they are material (Art. 11 (1) DA). A contingent liability is a possible

40 EIOPA, Consultation Paper on EIOPA's first set of advice to the EC on specific items in the Solvency II Delegated Regulation, EIOPA-CP-17/004, 4 July 2017, p. 94.

41 IAS 12 – Income Taxes. Valuation in accordance with IAS/IFRS does not apply when the undertaking uses the derogation in Art. 9 (4) DA (use of the same valuation methods as in the financial statements).

42 EIOPA, Guidelines on the recognition and valuation of assets and liabilities other than technical provisions, EIOPA-BoS-15, 14 September 2015, Guideline 9.

obligation depending on whether some uncertain future event occurs, or a present obligation where payment is not probable or the amount cannot be measured reliably. Such liabilities would not be recognised in the balance sheet as normal liabilities under IAS/IFRS.[43] However, this is a solvency balance sheet, where prudential concerns are given priority.

Contingent liabilities are material where information about the current or potential size or nature of the liability can influence the decision-making or judgement of the intended user of that information, including the supervisory authorities (Art. 11 (2) DA). The value of contingent liabilities is equal to the expected present value of future cash flows required to settle the contingent liability over the lifetime of that contingent liability, using the basic risk-free interest rate term structure (Art. 14 (2) DA).

When entering into an arrangement that represents an ancillary own-fund item (for instance, a letter of credit or a guarantee) for the counterparty, undertakings should carefully assess whether to recognise the corresponding contingent liability as a liability in compliance with Art. 11 DA. Undertakings should be able to provide a justification to the supervisory authority where they have not recognised a contingent liability as a liability in the balance sheet in circumstances where they have entered into an arrangement with another undertaking, including any other undertakings belonging to the group, and that arrangement has received approval as an ancillary own funds item.[44]

2.3. VALUATION OF TECHNICAL PROVISIONS

In order to meet their commitments towards policyholders and beneficiaries, (re)insurance undertakings must establish adequate technical provisions. The harmonisation in the EU of the principles and actuarial and statistical methodologies underlying the calculation of technical provisions has been a major challenge. The FD introduces for the first time a uniform regime for the calculation of technical provisions. As technical provisions constitute the main item on a (re)insurance undertaking's balance sheet, the progress achieved in this area cannot be sufficiently underlined.

The basic principle is that the calculation of technical provisions should be consistent with the valuation of assets and liabilities, i.e. it should follow the same market-consistent approach.[45] Whilst there are observable market values

---

43 See IAS 17 – Provisions, Contingent Liabilities and Contingent Assets.

44 EIOPA, Guidelines on the recognition and valuation assets and liabilities other than technical provisions, EIOPA-BoS-15, 14 September 2015, Guideline 8.

45 See DHAENE, J., STASSEN, B., BARIGOU, K., LINDERS, D. and CHEN, Z., Fair valuation of insurance liabilities: merging actuarial judgement and market-consistency, *Insurance Mathematics and Economics*, 2017, No 76, pp. 14–27. The authors define fair valuation of insurance liabilities as a valuation which is both market-consistent (mark-to-market for any

for most assets,[46] this is not the case with insurance liabilities for which no ready market is available in most situations.

Technical provisions are therefore marked to model, but the model is prescribed by the legislator. An economic approach was developed for valuing insurance liabilities (technical provisions) using consistent economic valuation methodologies without adding additional prudence, as was often the case under Solvency I. Under the FD, there is no prudence included on top of the market value of technical provisions to cover the risk of the actual values varying over time from the current market value estimates. The SCR should cover that risk. The MCR automatically provides a prudence level above the market value of technical provisions.[47]

Liability values for solvency purposes should reflect the cost to sell or hedge them. Within that logic, the value of technical provisions corresponds to the amount a (re)insurance undertaking would have to pay if it transferred its contractual rights and obligations immediately to another undertaking. It is the amount which another (re)insurance undertaking (the reference undertaking) would be expected to require to take over and fulfil the underlying (re)insurance obligations. The amount of technical provisions must reflect the characteristics of the underlying insurance portfolio. Undertaking-specific information, such as that regarding claims management and expenses, should therefore be used in the calculation only in so far as that information enables (re)insurance undertakings to better reflect the characteristics of the underlying insurance portfolio (recital 55 FD).

For the valuation of technical provisions, the FD adopts a transfer value or current exit value approach.[48] Other approaches would have been possible, such as a fulfilment/production cost value (the value of the liabilities is determined with reference to the insurer itself, i.e. entity-specific) or a distress valuation (the value of the liabilities is defined with reference to the entity in the event of run-off in a financial distress).[49] They were not retained.

Technical provisions must be calculated in a prudent, reliable and objective manner (Art. 76 (4) DA). Expert judgement is a key component of the calculation of technical provisions. The calculation of technical provisions will normally be carried out by actuaries or by other professionals with similar qualifications.

---

hedgeable part of a claim) and actuarial (mark-to-model for any claim that is independent of financial market evolutions).

46 This may not be the case in Member States where markets are not equally sophisticated, such as Bulgaria or Romania.

47 SINGH, R. and JONES, O., *Solutions to major issues for Solvency II, Joint Submission by the CRO Forum and CEA*, CEIOPS Consultative Panel, Frankfurt, 11 January 2006.

48 The transfer value of a (re)insurance obligation may be lower than the surrender value of the underlying contracts. The calculation of technical provisions should not be subject to surrender value floors (recital 12 DA).

49 SANDSTRÖM, A., *Handbook of Solvency for Actuaries and Risk Managers. Theory and Practice*, Chapman & Hall/CRC, Boca Raton, 2011, p. 75.

The calculation of technical provisions must be based upon internal processes and procedures that ensure the appropriateness, completeness and accuracy of the data used (Art. 82 FD).[50] The actuarial function should deliver recommendations to the AMSB on the procedures to be performed in order to improve the quality and the quantity of available data. It should identify the sources of material limitations and propose possible solutions, taking into account their effectiveness and the time necessary to implement them.[51]

(Re)insurance undertakings must be able to demonstrate to the supervisory authority the appropriateness of the level of their technical provisions, as well as the applicability and relevance of the methods applied and the adequacy of the underlying statistical data used (Art. 84 FD). The supervisory authority may require an increase in the amount of technical provisions, if it believes that technical provisions have not been calculated in accordance with the legal requirements (Art. 85 FD).

When calculating technical provisions, (re)insurance obligations are segmented into homogeneous risk groups, as a minimum by lines of business (Art. 80 FD).[52] The lines of business are listed in Annex I to the DA, divided into non-life insurance obligations,[53] proportional non-life reinsurance obligations, non-proportional non-life reinsurance obligations,[54] life insurance obligations[55] and life reinsurance obligations.[56] The segmentation must reflect the nature of the risks underlying the obligation. This may justify a departure from the allocation of insurance activities to life insurance activities and non-life insurance activities and from the classes of non-life insurance and life insurance set out in Annexes I and II FD.[57]

---

50 See also Arts. 19–21 DA and EIOPA, Guidelines on the valuation of technical provisions, EIOPA-BoS-14/166, 2 February 2015, Guidelines 1–16. For an example, in the case of long-term, non-life cross-border business, see EIOPA, Opinion on non-life cross-border insurance business of a long-term nature and its supervision, EIOPA-BoS-18/527, 21 December 2018, 25 p.

51 EIOPA, Guidelines on the valuation of technical provisions, EIOPA-BoS-14/166, 2 February 2015, Guideline 12.

52 See also Art. 55 DA and EIOPA, Guidelines on the valuation of technical provisions, EIOPA-BoS-14/166, 2 February 2015, Guidelines 17–23.

53 Medical expense insurance; income protection insurance; workers' compensation insurance; motor vehicle liability insurance; other motor insurance; marine, aviation and transport insurance; fire and other damage to property insurance; general liability insurance; credit and suretyship insurance; legal expenses insurance; assistance; and miscellaneous financial loss.

54 Non-proportional health reinsurance; non-proportional casualty reinsurance; non-proportional marine, aviation and transport reinsurance; and non-proportional property reinsurance.

55 Health insurance; insurance with profit participation; index-linked and unit-linked insurance; other life insurance; annuities stemming from non-life insurance contracts and relating to health insurance obligations; and annuities stemming from non-life insurance contracts and relating to insurance obligations other than health insurance obligations.

56 Health reinsurance and life reinsurance.

57 Recital 24 DA.

The value of technical provisions for which there is no ready market, i.e. those that cannot be hedged or easily transferred to a third party, is equal to the sum of a best estimate and a risk margin (Art. 77 FD).

The best estimate corresponds to the probability-weighted average of future cash flows,[58] taking account of the time value of money (expected present value of future cash flows), using the relevant risk-free interest rate term structure.[59] The calculation of the best estimate must be based upon up-to-date information and realistic assumptions[60] and be performed using adequate, applicable and relevant actuarial and statistical methods (Art. 77 (2) FD).[61] The best estimate must take account of future developments, such as demographic, legal, medical, technological, social, environmental and economic developments that will impact the cash in- and outflows required to settle the obligation (recital 13 DA).

The best estimate also includes EPIFP, i.e. profits resulting from the inclusion in technical provisions of premiums on existing (in force) business that will be received in the future, but that have not yet been received (Art. 260 (2) and (3) DA).[62] The treatment of EPIFP has been the subject of a lot of debate.[63] It can be an important element of the reconciliation reserve (Art. 70 DA).

It is important to stress that the best estimate is not an absolute truth and that the calculation of the best estimate is a challenge in practice. It is expected that, at some stage, actuarial standards will be developed to guide actuaries in the calculation of the best estimate. These standards may initially be developed by EIOPA in cooperation with the AAE. Ultimately, a process will have to be agreed that involves all relevant stakeholders, as is the case with the development of IAS/IFRS and international standards on auditing (ISAs).[64]

Technical provisions must be discounted in order to arrive at their present value. This was not a general practice for non-life insurance under Solvency I.

---

58 For the calculation of the cash flow projections for calculating the best estimate, see Arts. 28–36 DA.

59 See Arts. 43–48 DA.

60 See Arts. 22–26 DA and EIOPA, Guidelines on the valuation of technical provisions, EIOPA-BoS-14/166, 2 February 2015, Guidelines 24–43.

61 See also EIOPA, Guidelines on the valuation of technical provisions, EIOPA-BoS-14/166, 2 February 2015, Guidelines 44–88.

62 In the case of Brexit, the value of technical provisions of existing contracts concluded by EEA insurance undertakings in the UK by way of FoE or FoS may have to be changed because the expected profit from these contracts cannot be earned anymore or only with delay.

63 See EIOPA, Report of the Task Force on Expected Profits arising from Future Premiums, EIOPA-TFEPIFP-11/003, 20 June 2011, 35 p.

64 See the ongoing debate about making audit standard setting more independent from the accounting profession: *Monitoring Group Consultation: Strengthening the governance and oversight of the international audit-related standard-setting boards in the public interest*, 2017, 28 p. and Accountancy Europe, *Standard setting in the 21st century*, Cogito, Brussels, June 2017, 46 p.

Discounting has a significant impact on the size of technical provisions: the higher the discount rate, the lower the technical provisions. For example, the present value of a payment of €100 due in 20 years is €55 (assuming a discount rate of 3%). A change of the discount rate by one percentage point would change the present value of the payment by about 20%.

The debate on the appropriate discount rate to use has excited the actuarial profession and others, for instance the accounting profession, for decades and will continue to do so for many more years.[65] Finding the appropriate discount rate is not straightforward. An inappropriately high discount rate exposes policyholders to unacceptable risk since the (re)insurer would then be holding insufficient capital to cover liabilities. Similarly, a discount rate that is too low requires (re)insurers to hold excessive amounts of capital, pushing up the prices for insurance products, thus possibly harming the economy, growth and jobs by increasing the cost of insurance products for households and businesses. In defining the discount rate, the FD refers to the relevant risk-free interest rate, i.e. the theoretical rate of return of an investment with zero risk.[66] The EC initially suggested using the government bond rate as the risk-free rate, as the likelihood of a government defaulting is very low (at least for countries with a strong economy). The insurance industry preferred the swap rate. This was in the end retained.

In order to allow for a consistent calculation of technical provisions and to ensure uniform conditions for the choice of discount rates by (re)insurance undertakings, EIOPA publishes every month on its website technical information relating to the relevant risk-free interest rate term structures for the different currencies, taking account of observations in financial markets (Art. 77e (1) FD). In order to ensure legal certainty about the proper discount rate to be applied by undertakings, the EC publishes every three months, on the basis of information provided by EIOPA, the relevant risk-free interest rate term structures to calculate the best estimate by way of an implementing act (Art. 77e (2) and (3) FD).[67]

The risk margin[68] corresponds to the additional amount above the best estimate that a (re)insurance undertaking would be expected to require in order

---

65 See, for instance, PATEL, C. and DAYKIN, C.D., *Actuaries and Discount Rates – A Discussion Paper*, Institute of Actuaries and Faculty of Actuaries, London, May 2010, 130 p.

66 For instance, an investment in the same currency as the liability.

67 See, for instance, the first implementing act: Commission Implementing Regulation (EU) 2016/1376 of 8 August 2016 laying down technical information for the calculation of technical provisions and basic own funds for reporting with reference dates from 30 June until 29 September 2016 in accordance with Directive 2009/138/EC of the EP and of the Council on the taking-up and pursuit of the business of Insurance and Reinsurance, *OJ* L 224, 18.8.2016, p. 1. These implementing acts are also published on the EC's website.

68 For the calculation of the risk margin, see Arts. 37–39 DA and EIOPA, Guidelines for the valuation of technical provisions, EIOPA-BoS-14/166, 2 February 2015, Guidelines 62 and 63.

to take over and meet the whole portfolio of (re)insurance obligations, taking into account the diversification of the whole portfolio. The risk margin was initially referred to by the CRO Forum as the market value margin (MVM), i.e. the additional amount that the market demands above the best estimate because of the risk and uncertainty involved. It is the explicit cost for a non-hedgeable risk and is in fact introducing prudence into the valuation of technical provisions.[69]

The risk margin is defined in the FD as the cost of providing an amount of eligible own funds equal to the solvency capital (SCR) necessary to support the insurance liabilities over their lifetime, i.e. the present value of the cost of future capital requirements for non-hedgeable risk. The rate used in the determination of the cost of providing that amount of eligible own funds (cost of capital rate) is the same for all (re)insurance undertakings. It was set at 6%[70] in the DA, i.e. the same percentage as in the Swiss Solvency Test, where it had proved to work.[71] The cost of capital approach for the definition of the risk margin was considered preferable to the originally proposed percentile approach, which had proved problematic in Australia.[72]

In its second set of advice to the EC on the 2018 review of the DA, EIOPA proposed not changing the cost of capital rate of 6% but instead reviewing the methodology for the calculation of the risk margin on the occasion of the review of the FD in 2020.[73] The EC has followed this advice and did not include any change to the cost of capital rate nor to the methodology for calculating the risk margin in its 2019 amendment of the DA.

The best estimate and the risk margin must be calculated separately. However, where future cash flows associated with technical provisions can be replicated reliably using financial instruments for which a reliable market value is observable, i.e. that can be transferred to a willing, rational, diversified counterparty in an arm's-length transaction under normal business conditions (hedgeable risk), the value of those technical provisions is determined on the basis of the market value of those financial instruments. In this case, separate calculation of the best estimate and the risk margin is not required, because

---

69 See also IAIS, ICP 14 – Valuation, which uses the term "margin over current estimate (MOCE)", which reflects the inherent uncertainty related to all relevant future cash flows that arise in fulfilling insurance obligations over the full time horizon thereof (para. 14.9).

70 Art. 39 DA.

71 KELLER, P., *Risk based supervision and the Swiss Solvency Test*, Federal Office of Private Insurance, 1 December 2006, and Federal Office of Private Insurance, *Technical Document on the Swiss Solvency Test*, 2 October 2006, 115 p.

72 For more details, see CRO Forum, *A market cost of capital approach to market value margins – Discussion Paper*, 17 March 2006.

73 EIOPA, Second set of advice to the EC on specific items in the Solvency II Delegated Regulation, EIOPA-BoS-18/075, 28 February 2018, pp. 341–370. The level of the risk margin at the end of 2016 was €161 billion.

in that case the observed market value already includes the risk margin (Art. 77 (4), second subparagraph FD).

The expected present value of (re)insurance liabilities must be calculated on the basis of current and credible information[74] and realistic assumptions[75] (for instance with respect to the likelihood that policyholders will exercise contractual options, including lapses and surrenders), taking account of financial guarantees and options in (re)insurance contracts in order to deliver an economic valuation (Art. 79 FD). Account must also be taken of all expenses that will be incurred in servicing (re)insurance obligations, inflation (including expenses and claims inflation) and all payments to policyholders and beneficiaries, including future discretionary bonuses[76] (Art. 78 FD). Future discretionary benefits are benefits that are paid in addition to guaranteed benefits and that result from profit participation by the policyholder. They do not include index-linked or unit-linked benefits.[77]

Where (re)insurance contracts include financial guarantees and options, the present value of cash flows arising from those contracts may depend on the expected outcome of future events and developments, as well as on how the actual outcome in certain scenarios could deviate from the expected outcome. The methods used to calculate the best estimate must take such dependencies into account.[78]

When calculating amounts recoverable from reinsurance contracts and SPVs,[79] account must be taken of the time difference between recoveries and direct payments. The result of that calculation must be adjusted to take account of expected losses due to default of the counterparty. That adjustment must be based on an assessment of the probability of default of the counterparty and the average loss resulting therefrom (loss-given-default (LGD)) (Art. 81 DA). This shows clearly that through reinsurance, the insurance risk transferred to a reinsurance undertaking or the reinsurance risk retroceded to another reinsurer becomes a credit risk, i.e. a risk that the reinsurer is incapable of paying.

(Re)insurance undertakings must have processes and procedures in place to ensure that best estimates and the assumptions underlying their calculation are regularly compared against experience (reality check). Where the comparison identifies a systematic deviation between experience and the best estimate calculation, the undertaking concerned must make appropriate adjustments

74 See Art. 27 DA.
75 See Arts. 28–36 DA.
76 See Arts. 24 and 25 DA.
77 Recital 17 DA.
78 Recital 16 DA.
79 See also Arts. 41 and 42 DA.

to the actuarial methods applied and the adequacy of the underlying statistical data used (Art. 83 DA).[80] This is an important task for the actuarial function. See further, Chapter 7, section 3.7.

Figure 4. Overview of Pillar 1

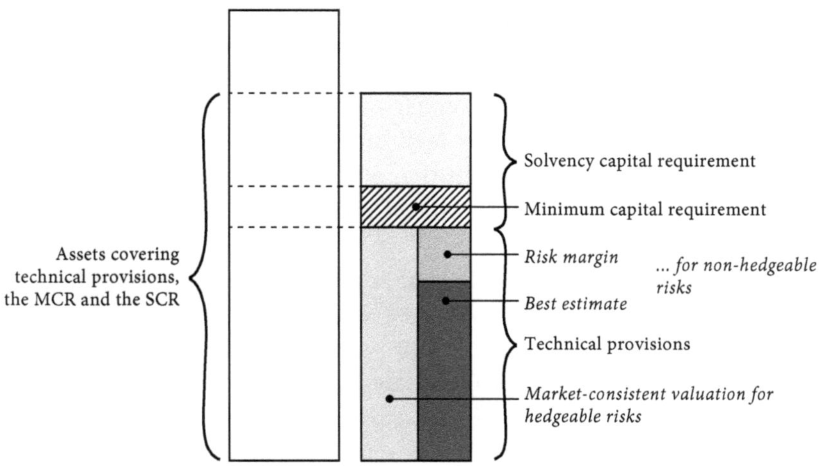

Source: Produced by the author.

2.3.1. Insurance Products with Long-Term Guarantees

Insurance products with long-term guarantees are common throughout the EU. They are highly relevant from a social perspective as they contribute to addressing demographic and healthcare challenges. Several types of insurance products include long-term guarantees. Such guarantees can be found for example in savings and retirement products where the insurer guarantees a minimum payment to the beneficiary, or in healthcare products, such as health insurance, which in some countries provides life-long cover for medical expenses. In addition, specific non-life insurance products, like liability insurance (e.g. construction liability, medical professional liability) may provide long-term guarantees. The duration of a long-term guarantee product may be as long as 70 years.[81]

---

80 See EIOPA, Guidelines for the valuation of technical provisions, EIOPA-BoS-14/166, 2 February 2015, Guidelines 87 and 88.

81 Because of the risk involved in providing long-term guarantees and the capital required for such guarantees, there has been a clear trend to reduce the duration of guarantees. For instance, in Belgium, the duration has been reduced from 40 years to about eight years or even lower now. See IMF, *Belgium FSAP. Technical Note: Banking, Insurance and Financial Conglomerate Supervision*, March 2018, p. 48.

Insurance products with long-term guarantees have been strongly affected by the volatility in financial markets present since 2008. Small fluctuations in interest rates cause significant changes in technical provisions, which has a corresponding impact on capital and also on the capital requirements under Solvency II. The fact that these amounts are not static and can change in the short as well as the long term is not of itself problematic. Any risk-based and economic supervisory system includes a certain degree of volatility. It is clear that when either the financial position of a (re)insurer or its risk exposure changes, then its capital or its capital requirements should change. These features of Solvency II enable the (re)insurer and the supervisory authority to properly assess the solvency situation of the undertaking, so that both can take the appropriate measures to protect policyholders and beneficiaries and ensure financial stability.

Notwithstanding this, particularly after QIS 5, it was noted that insurance products with long-term guarantees were also affected by "artificial" volatility. Although some people considered any volatility to be artificial (a classic debate in a fair-value context), there was clearly an issue that needed to be addressed in order to make the new solvency regime workable.

Artificial volatility can be defined as a volatility of technical provisions, capital or capital requirements that does not reflect changes in the financial position or risk exposure of the (re)insurer, but which is caused by regulatory requirements that do not capture the long-term nature of the business. The objective of the LTG measures introduced by Omnibus II was to remove these imperfections.[82] With the exception of group supervision (including group support), no issue relating to Solvency II was so heavily debated and discussed. The compromise solution that was eventually arrived at includes a review by 1 January 2021 of the LTG package, as well as annual reporting by EIOPA on the use and the impact of the LTG measures (Art. 77f FD).

Not all LTG measures relate to technical provisions.[83] Some of the LTG measures are applied by (re)insurance undertakings on an optional basis, while the use of other measures is mandatory. The MA, the VA and the transitional measures on the risk-free interest rate and on technical provisions are optional measures, as opposed to the extrapolation, which is an integral part of the Solvency II framework and is applicable to all undertakings for the calculation of their technical provisions.

EIOPA provided its first LTG measures report on 16 December 2016. The second report was delivered on 20 December 2017 and the third report was

82 See also EIOPA, Guidelines on the implementation of the long-term guarantee measures, EIOPA-BoS-15/112, 14 September 2015.

83 The other measures are the symmetric adjustment mechanism to the equity capital charge, the extension of the recovery period in the case of a breach of the SCR, and the duration-based equity risk sub-module.

produced on 18 December 2018.[84] In its reports, EIOPA provides detailed information about the use and the impact of the LTG measures and the measures on equity risk on the financial position of undertakings, on policyholder protection, on the investments of undertakings, on consumers and products, on competition and the level playing field in the EU insurance market, and on financial stability.

On 31 December 2017, 737 (re)insurance undertakings in 23 EEA countries were using at least one of the optional LTG measures, i.e. the MA, the VA, the transitional measure on the risk-free rate, the transitional measure on technical provisions or the duration-based equity risk sub-module.[85] The measures are used differently by different types of undertaking, although they are primarily used by life insurers. The aggregated amount of technical provisions for the undertakings using at least one of the optional LTG-measures represents 74% of the technical provisions in the EEA (re)insurance market. Out of a total of 2,912 undertakings applying Solvency II, 2,175 undertakings – nearly three out of four – are not using any of the LTG measures. The undertakings not using any measures represent 26% of the technical provisions in the EEA (re)insurance market. There are eight countries where none of these measures are applied by any undertaking (Croatia, Estonia, Iceland, Lithuania, Latvia, Malta, Poland and Slovenia).

Figure 5. Number of EEA undertakings using the LTG measures

Type of undertaking	Total number of undertakings	VA	TTP	MA	TRFR	DBER	No measure
Life	596	273	110	20	4	0	293
Non-life	1,620	220	11	0	0	1	1,398
Both life and non-life	402	179	40	13	2	0	213
Reinsurance	294	24	1	1	1	0	271
Total	**2,912**	**696**	**162**	34	7	1	**2,175**

Source: EIOPA, Report on long-term guarantee measures and measures on equity risk 2018, EIOPA-BoS-18/471, 18 December 2018, p. 15.

84 See EIOPA, Report on long-term guarantee measures and measures on equity risk 2016, EIOPA-BoS-16/279, 16 December 2016, 145 p.; EIOPA, Report on long-term guarantee measures and measures on equity risk 2017, EIOPA-BoS-17/334, 20 December 2017, 171 p.; and EIOPA, Report on long-term guarantee measures and measures on equity risk 2018, EIOPA-BoS-18/471, 18 December 2018, 215 p.

85 EIOPA, Report on long-term guarantees measures and measures on equity risk 2018, EIOPA-BoS-18/471, 18 December 2018, p. 13. The overall picture is very similar to the situation on 31 December 2016.

Of the 363 EEA insurance groups subject to Solvency II, 138 groups use the VA, 77 groups use the transitional measure on technical provisions and 21 groups use the MA. The transitional measure on the risk-free rate is used by three insurance groups. Within a group, use can of course be made of more than one of the measures.

Figure 6. Number of EEA groups using the LTG measures

	Total number of EEA groups	VA	TTP	MA	TRFR	DBER	No measure
EEA Groups	363	138	77	21	3	1	207

Source: EIOPA, Report on long-term guarantee measures and measures on equity risk 2018, EIOPA-BoS-18/471, 18 December 2018, p. 18.

2.3.2. Extrapolation of the Relevant Risk-Free Interest Rate Term Structure

The risk-free interest rate for the discounting of technical provisions is derived on the basis of observed market data. These data cannot be observed for all maturities because financial markets are not deep and liquid enough for instruments with long maturities to provide reliable information. Therefore, the risk-free rate of longer maturities (past a certain future date – "the starting point") needs to be extrapolated towards a level of interest rate that is stable over time. This can be done in different ways. The FD uses the ultimate forward rate (UFR) for that purpose. See also above, Chapter 3, section 4.3.1.

Information derived from relevant financial instruments (such as interest rate swaps or government bonds) of those maturities where the markets are deep, liquid and transparent must be used for determining the relevant risk-free interest rate term structure. For maturities where the markets are not deep, liquid and transparent, i.e. in the case of long-term liabilities, the relevant risk-free interest rate term structure must be extrapolated. The extrapolated part of the relevant risk-free interest rate term structure is based on forward rates converging smoothly from one or a set of forward rates in relation to the longest maturities for which the relevant financial instrument and the bonds can be observed in a deep, liquid and transparent market to a UFR (Art. 77a FD).

The principles applied when extrapolating the relevant risk-free interest rate term structure are the same for all currencies. This also applies to the determination of the longest maturities for which interest rates can be observed in a deep, liquid and transparent market and the mechanism to ensure a smooth convergence to the UFR (Art. 46 (1) DA). Under market conditions similar to those on 23 May 2014,[86] when determining the last maturity for which

[86] The date of entry into force of Omnibus II.

markets for bonds are no longer deep, liquid and transparent, the markets for bonds denominated in euros should not be regarded as deep and liquid where the cumulative volume of bonds with maturities larger than or equal to the last maturity is less than 6% of the volume of all bonds in that market (recital 21 DA).

The rationale for the extrapolation is included in recital 30 Omnibus II. The relevant risk-free interest rate term structure should avoid artificial volatility of technical provisions and eligible own funds, and provide an incentive for good risk management. The choice of the starting point for the extrapolation of risk-free interest rates should allow undertakings to match with bonds the cash flows that are discounted with non-extrapolated interest rates in the calculation of the best estimate.

For the euro, the starting point for the extrapolation is set at a maturity of 20 years. Under market conditions similar to those prevalent on 23 May 2014, the extrapolated part of the relevant risk-free interest rate term structure, in particular for the euro, should converge in such a way to the UFR that for maturities 40 years past the starting point of the extrapolation, the extrapolated forward rates do not differ more than three basis points from the UFR. For currencies other than the euro, the characteristics of the local bond and swap markets should be taken into account when determining the starting point for the extrapolation of risk-free interest rates and the appropriate convergence period to the UFR.[87]

Where an undertaking applies the VA, the extrapolation is applied to the risk-free interest rates, including the VA (Art. 46 (2) DA). Where an undertaking applies the MA, the extrapolation is based on the risk-free interest rates without an MA. The MA is applied to the extrapolated risk-free interest rates (Art. 46 (3) DA). For the UFR, see Art. 47 DA and the technical information published by EIOPA on a monthly basis on its website.[88]

Specific risk management measures must be applied with respect to extrapolation, such as a sensitivity analysis of technical provisions and own funds to the assumptions underlying the extrapolation of the relevant risk-free interest rate term structure (Art. 44 (2a) FD). The results of these

---

[87] Recital 30 Omnibus II. It is remarkable that this recital contains technical information that should normally be included in an implementing measures. However, in order to provide "political" certainty, particularly to Germany, which was the main addressee of this LTG measure because of the large number of very long-term life insurance contracts, this technical information was included in a recital to Omnibus II.

[88] EIOPA has calculated the UFR for 2019. See, EIOPA, Risk-free interest rate term structure. Report on the calculation of the UFR for 2019, EIOPA-BoS-18/141, 21 March 2018, 10 p. (https://eiopa.europa.eu/Publications/Reports/Calculation%20of%20the%20UFR%20for%202019.pdf).

assessments must be communicated to the supervisory authority (Art. 44 (2a), second subparagraph FD).[89]

As indicated before, the extrapolation of risk-free interest rates is not an optional LTG measure but is applicable to all undertakings for the calculation of their technical provisions.

2.3.3. *Matching Adjustment to the Relevant Risk-Free Interest Rate Term Structure*

The MA[90] is an adjustment to the risk-free interest rate to discount technical provisions of products with the highest predictability on the amount and timing of the payments to policyholders backed by assets with yields that reproduce these payments: every time a payment to policyholders and beneficiaries is due, the undertaking receives a payment of the same amount on its bonds (cash-flow matching). The bonds used for cash-flow matching are held to maturity.

Where the cash flows are matched in this way, the undertaking is not exposed to the risk of spreads widening because of changing risk appetite or risk perception in the financial markets. This risk only materialises when the bonds have to be sold before maturity. The undertaking is still exposed to default risk, i.e. the risk of the issuer of the bond not being willing or able to make the payment that is due. This must be considered in the calculation of the adjustment.

Since the FD is based on a market-consistent (fair-value) valuation of assets, a widening of bond spreads automatically leads to a decrease in the bond's value and a loss in capital. Undertakings that match their insurance business in the way described above would also incur these losses in their balance sheet. However, this does not reflect the economic situation of the undertaking, because to the extent that the spread widening exceeds the default risk, these losses are only temporary and will be recovered before the bond matures. At the same time, if bond spreads decrease, the MA decreases and the gains of the assets are not reflected in the solvency position. The MA seeks to remove this artificial volatility.

The MA reflects the level of spreads of the undertaking's bonds. If the spreads widen, the MA increases. A deterioration of bond value due to the spread widening is therefore counterbalanced by a corresponding decrease in technical provisions. The MA effectively stabilises the capital of the insurer, in particular in crisis situations where spreads increase severely.

---

89 See EIOPA, Report on long-term guarantees measures and measures on equity risk 2018, EIOPA-BoS-18/471, 18 December 2018, pp. 193–194.

90 For more information on the functioning of the MA and its impact, see EIOPA, *Solvency II tools with macro-prudential impact*, Publications Office of the EU, Luxembourg, 2018, pp. 22–24.

The MA can only be applied under strict conditions[91] to a portfolio of life (re)insurance obligations, including annuities stemming from non-life (re)insurance contracts and is subject to prior approval from the supervisory authority. The conditions are listed in Art. 77b FD. The MA can only be applied where technical provisions are covered by bonds or other assets with similar cash flow characteristics. Equity and property are not allowed as cover because they do not generate predictable cash flows that can match the payments due under the insurance contracts.

Once the MA has been applied to a portfolio of obligations, that portfolio cannot revert back to an approach that does not include the MA (no cherry-picking). Specific supervisory action is foreseen in the event that the undertaking can no longer comply with the conditions for the MA (Art. 77b (2) FD).

Undertakings that use the MA must identify, organise and manage the portfolio of assets and obligations separately from other parts of the business. The assets cannot be used to cover losses arising from other activities of the undertaking. This does however not imply that Member States must require the undertaking to ring-fence the portfolio to which the MA is applied.[92]

For details on the calculation of the MA, see Art. 77c FD and Arts. 52 and 53 DA. Every three months, the EC publishes, by way of an implementing act,[93] based upon information provided by EIOPA, the fundamental spreads for the calculation of the MA.

Specific risk management measures must be complied with in the case of applying the MA, such as setting up a liquidity plan, carrying out a sensitivity analysis of technical provisions and own funds, and measuring the impact of a reduction of the MA to zero (Arts. 44 (2), second subparagraph and 44 (2a) FD).[94] The results of these assessments must be communicated to the supervisory authority (Art. 44 (2a), second subparagraph FD).[95]

The MA cannot be combined with the VA with respect to the same (re)insurance obligations nor with the interest rate transitional measure under Art. 308c FD. A combination is however possible with the transitional

---

91 See in particular Art. 77b (2) FD.

92 Undertakings must, however, calculate a notional SCR for each MA portfolio under the standard formula. See Art. 217 DA.

93 See, for instance, Commission Implementing Regulation (EU) 2018/1699 of 9 November 2018 laying down technical information for the calculation of technical provisions and basic own funds for reporting with reference dates from 30 September until 30 December 2017 in accordance with Directive 2009/138/EC of the EP and of the Council on the taking-up and pursuit of the business of insurance and reinsurance, *OJ* L 285, 13.11.2018, p. 1.

94 EIOPA reported that 13 undertakings would not comply with the SCR if the MA were reduced to zero. See EIOPA, Report on long-term guarantees measures and measures on equity risk 2018, EIOPA-BoS-18/471, 18 December 2018, p. 195.

95 For an overview of the risk management aspects when using the MA, see EIOPA, Report on long-term guarantees measures and measures on equity risk 2018, EIOPA-BoS-18/471, 18 December 2018, pp. 189–208.

measure on technical provisions (Art. 308d FD).[96] Its application is subject to additional supervisory reporting (Art. 44 (2a), second subparagraph FD and Art. 311 (4) DA) and public disclosure. In particular, the SFCR must contain, under the heading "Valuation for solvency purposes", a description of the MA and of the portfolio of obligations and assigned assets to which the MA is applied, as well as a quantification of the impact on the undertaking's financial position of a change to zero of the MA, including on the amount of technical provisions, the SCR, the MCR, the basic own funds and the amounts of own funds eligible to cover the MCR and the SCR (Art. 296 (2) (d) DA).

As could have been expected, the MA is applied only in Spain (15 undertakings) and in the UK (19 undertakings).[97]

Figure 7. Number of undertakings using the MA

Country	Life	Non-life	Both life and non-life	Reinsurance	Total
ES	4	0	11	0	15
UK	16	0	2	1	19
EEA	**20**	**0**	**13**	**1**	**34**

Source: EIOPA, Report on long-term guarantee measures and measures on equity risk 2018, EIOPA-BoS-18/471, 18 December 2018, p. 104.

2.3.4. *Volatility Adjustment to the Relevant Risk-Free Interest Rate Term Structure*

The VA aims to prevent pro-cyclical investment behaviour by mitigating the effect of an extreme widening of bond spreads in stressed market conditions. Pro-cyclical behaviour could consist of forced sales but also of a switch from long-term to short-term investments. This would reduce the traditional role of insurers as long-term investors and would create a serious threat to financial stability.[98]

The VA (Art. 77d FD) is an adjustment to the relevant risk-free interest rate term structure by addition of a constant spread. This spread is derived from the difference between the interest rate that can be earned from a reference portfolio and the basic risk-free rate for each currency. Additionally, if market

---

96 28 undertakings were using this possibility in 2017. See EIOPA, Report on long-term guarantees measures and measures on equity risk 2018, EIOPA-BoS-18/471, 18 December 2018, p. 19.

97 EIOPA, Report on Long-term guarantee measures and measures on equity risk 2018, EIOPA-BoS-18/471, 18 December 2018, p. 104.

98 For more information on the functioning of the VA and its impact, see EIOPA, *Solvency II tools with macro-prudential impact*, Publications Office of the EU, Luxembourg, 2018, pp. 16–21. As the MA reduces the amount of technical provisions, it may affect the amount of profit available for distribution. See FORD, J., Investors should beware the insurance magic money tree, *Financial Times*, 15 April 2019, p. 6.

spreads are very wide in a country, a conditional country spread can be added to the currency spread.

The reference portfolio for each currency and each country is defined by EIOPA, and includes different assets typically held by (re)insurers to cover the best estimate for (re)insurance obligations, i.e. bonds, securitisations and loans, including mortgage loans, equity and property (Art. 49 DA).

For the calculation of the spread, the portfolio is divided into two classes: government bonds and non-government bonds, including loans and securitisations. The portfolio spread can be calculated by using the portfolio weights and the average spreads of the two components. The spread must be corrected in order to remove the portion of the spread that is attributable to a realistic assessment of expected losses, unexpected credit risk or any other risks of the assets.

The VA consists of two components: the risk-corrected currency spread plus a conditional risk-corrected country spread. The VA will normally be 65% of the risk-corrected currency spread. A calibrated risk-corrected country spread can be added only in exceptional circumstances, when the spreads in a particular country are very wide. When the risk-corrected country spread is higher than 85 basis points, the difference between the risk-corrected country spread and twice the risk-corrected currency spread can be added (Art. 77d (3) and (4) FD). Every three months, the EC publishes, by way of an implementing act,[99] based upon information provided by EIOPA, the VA for each relevant national insurance market. EIOPA has been asked by the EC to re-examine the methodology to derive the "country component" of the VA as it does not seem to work as intended. The new methodology should enter into force at the same time as the 2019 amendment of the DA.[100]

Member States may require prior approval from NSAs for the application of the VA (Art. 77d (1) FD). Ten Member States impose such an approval process.[101] The VA is used by 696 undertakings in 23 Member States.[102]

---

99 See, for instance, Commission Implementing Regulation (EU) 2018/1699 of 9 November 2018 laying down technical information for the calculation of technical provisions and basic own funds for reporting with reference dates from 30 September until 30 December 2017 in accordance with Directive 2009/138/EC of the EP and of the Council on the taking-up and pursuit of the business of insurance and reinsurance, *OJ* L 285, 13.11.2018, p. 1.

100 See the letter from 7 February 2019 of Olivier Guersent, Director-General of DG FISMA, to Gabriel Bernardino, https://eiopa.europa.eu/Publications/Requests%20for%20advice/signed_letter_08_02_19.pdf. Meanwhile, as part of the ESFS review, Art. 77 d (4) FD has been amended so as to allow the country spread to kick in more quickly by reducing the basis points from 100 to 85.

101 Croatia, Denmark, Estonia, Germany, Ireland, Poland, Portugal, Romania, Slovenia and the UK.

102 Austria, Belgium, Bulgaria, Cyprus, Czech Republic, Denmark, Finland, France, Germany, Greece, Hungary, Ireland, Italy, Liechtenstein, Luxembourg, the Netherlands, Norway, Portugal, Romania, Spain, Sweden, Slovakia and the UK. EIOPA, Report on long-term guarantee measures and measures on equity risk 2018, EIOPA-BoS-18/471, 18 December 2018, p. 124.

For all EEA Member States concerned, the VA, calculated on a common reference portfolio for all of these Member States, raised the average solvency ratio of (re)insurance undertakings from 199% to 223%.[103]

Figure 8. Number of undertakings using the VA

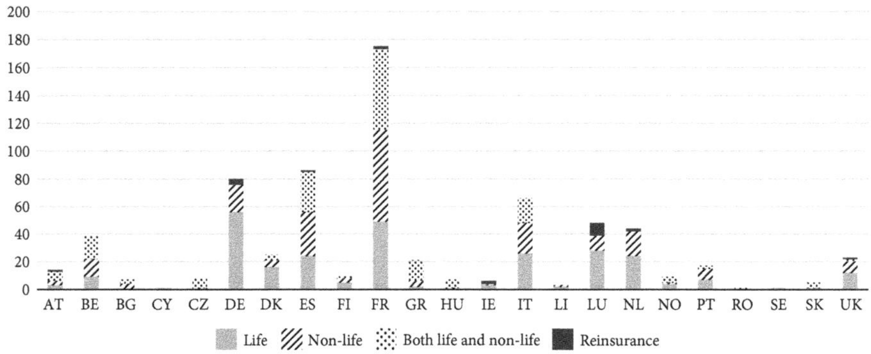

Source: EIOPA, Report on long-term guarantee measures and measures on equity risk 2018, EIOPA-BoS-18/471, 18 December 2018, p. 124.

The VA cannot be combined with the MA (Art. 77d (5) FD). It can however be combined with the transitional measure on technical provisions (Art. 308d FD).[104] Specific risk management measures[105] must be complied with in the case of applying the VA, such as setting up a liquidity plan projecting the incoming and outgoing cash flows in relation to the assets and liabilities subject to the adjustment, carrying out a sensitivity analysis of technical provisions and own funds, and measuring the impact of a reduction of the VA to zero (Art. 44 (2a) FD). The results of these assessments must be communicated annually to the supervisory authority (Art. 44 (2a), second subparagraph FD). The written policy on risk management must include a policy on the criteria for the application of the VA.

Where the reduction of the VA to zero would result in non-compliance with the SCR,[106] the undertaking must submit an analysis of the measures it could apply in such a situation to re-establish the level of eligible own funds covering the SCR or to reduce its risk profile to restore compliance with the SCR (Art. 44 (2a) FD).

---

[103] EIOPA, *Solvency II tools with macro-prudential impact*, Publications Office of the EU, Luxembourg, 2018, p. 21.

[104] 124 undertakings were using this possibility in 2018. See EIOPA, Report on long-term guarantee measures and measures on equity risk 2018, EIOPA-BoS-18/471, 18 December 2018, pp. 127–128.

[105] For an overview of the risk management aspects when using the VA, see EIOPA, Report on long-term guarantees measures and measures on equity risk 2018, EIOPA-BoS-18/471, 18 December 2018, pp. 189–208.

[106] In 2017, this was the case for three undertakings. See EIOPA, Report on long-term guarantees measures and measures on equity risk 2018, EIOPA-BoS-18/471, 18 December 2018, p. 195.

Application of the VA is subject to additional supervisory reporting (Art. 44 (2a), second subparagraph FD) and public disclosure. In particular, the SFCR must contain, under the heading "Valuation for solvency purposes", a statement on whether the VA is used by the undertaking and a quantification of the impact of a change to zero of the VA on the undertaking's financial position, including on the amount of technical provisions, the SCR, the MCR, the basic own funds and the amounts of own funds eligible to cover the MCR and the SCR (Art. 296 (2) (e) DA).

2.3.5. *Proportionality and Simplifications*

Calculation of technical provisions is complex. It was obvious that simplified methodologies had to be included for small and medium-sized (re)insurance undertakings. In the logic of Solvency II, these simplifications are linked to the riskiness of the business.

The principle is that undertakings must use methods to calculate technical provisions that are proportionate to the nature, scale and complexity of the risks underlying their (re)insurance obligations (Art. 56 DA).[107]

In determining whether a method is proportionate, an assessment must be carried out of the nature, scale and complexity of the risks underlying the obligations and of the model error of the method, without having to calculate the precise amount of the error (Art. 56 (2) DA and recital 25 DA).

A method is considered to be disproportionate to the nature, scale and complexity of the risks if the model error leads to a misstatement of technical provisions or their components that could influence the decision-making or judgement of the intended user of the information (Art. 56 (4) DA).[108]

The actuarial function must ensure that the process of validating technical provisions is proportionate, considering the significance of the impact, both in isolation and in combination, of assumptions, approximations and methodologies on the value of technical provisions.[109]

2.3.6. *Transitional Measures*

The transitional measures introduced by Omnibus II into the FD are a legitimate part of the Solvency II regime. They do not distort the solvency reality.[110]

[107] See also recital 15 DA.

[108] See also for specific examples of simplified calculations, Arts. 57–61 DA and EIOPA, Guidelines on the valuation of technical provisions, EIOPA-BoS- 14/166, 2 February 2015, Guidelines 79–81 and the Technical Annexes I–VI.

[109] EIOPA, Guidelines on the valuation of technical provisions, EIOPA-BoS-14/166, 2 February 2015, Guideline 83.

[110] BERNARDINO, G., *Milestones of preparation of Solvency II*, European Insurance Conference, London, 2 June 2015, p. 5, https://eiopa.europa.eu/Publications/Speeches%20and%20presentations/2015-06-02%20European%20Insurance%20Conference.pdf.

The purpose of these measures, which are subject to supervisory approval, is to smooth the transition to the new solvency regime, to avoid market disruption and to limit interference with existing products. The transitional measures should encourage undertakings to move towards compliance with the new requirements as soon as possible, allowing them a certain period to fully recognise the impact on old books of contracts that have been underwritten in a different regulatory framework.

The transitional measure relating to the relevant risk-free interest rate term structure is an adjustment to the risk-free interest rate term structure that is based on the difference between the discount rates of Solvency I and the Solvency II relevant risk-free interest rates term structure. At the beginning of Solvency II, the transitional adjustment is 100% of that difference. Over the transitional period of 16 years, the transitional adjustment is linearly reduced to zero. The transitional measure only applies to (re)insurance obligations arising from contracts concluded before 1 January 2016 (Art. 308c FD).[111] It cannot be combined with the transitional measure on technical provisions, but can be combined with the VA for the same liabilities.[112]

On 31 December 2017, the transitional measure on the risk-free interest rate term structure was being applied by seven undertakings in five countries (France, Germany, Greece, Ireland and the UK) and by three groups.[113]

Figure 9. Number of undertakings using the transitional measure on the risk-free interest rate term structure

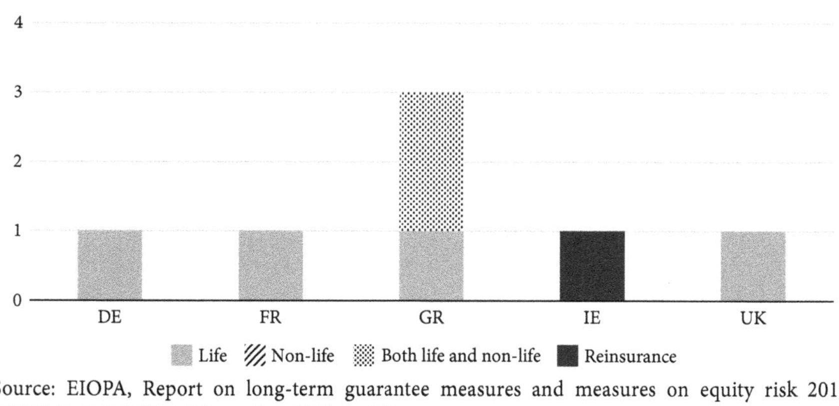

Source: EIOPA, Report on long-term guarantee measures and measures on equity risk 2018, EIOPA-BoS-18/471, 18 December 2018, p. 153.

111 For more details, see above, Chapter 3, section 4.3.1

112 This was the case for six undertakings in 2017. See EIOPA, Report on long-term guarantees measures and measures on equity risk 2018, EIOPA-BoS-18/471, 18 December 2018, p. 153.

113 EIOPA, Report on long-term guarantees measures and measures on equity risk 2018, EIOPA-BoS-18/471, 18 December 2018, p. 153.

The transitional measure relating to technical provisions[114] is based on the difference between the technical provisions for (re)insurance obligations arising from contracts concluded before 1 January 2016 calculated under Solvency I and the technical provisions calculated under Solvency II. That amount is deducted from the technical provisions required under Solvency II, decreasing every year by one sixteenth until 1 January 2032 when no further deduction can be made and the (re)insurance undertaking is expected to meet the Solvency II requirements in full (Art. 308d FD).[115]

The transitional measure on technical provisions cannot be combined with the transitional measure on the risk-free interest rate term structure but can be combined with the VA and the MA.[116]

On 31 December 2017, the transitional measure on technical provisions was being applied by 162 undertakings in 11 Member States[117] and by 77 groups in 12 Member States.[118]

Figure 10. Number of undertakings using the transitional measure on technical provisions

Country	Life	Non-life	Both life and non-life	Reinsurance	Total	Last year	Variation from last year
AT	1	0	4	0	5	4	1
BE	1	0	0	0	1	1	0
DE	56	2	0	0	58	63	–5
ES	9	1	13	0	23	22	1
FI	3	2	2	0	7	7	0
FR	8	0	9	0	17	13	4
GR	0	0	1	0	1	1	0
LI	1	0	0	0	1	1	0
NO	2	0	4	0	6	6	0
PT	7	5	4	0	16	16	0
UK	22	1	3	1	27	29	–2
EEA	**110**	**11**	**40**	**1**	**162**	**163**	**–1**

Source: EIOPA, Report on long-term guarantee measures and measures on equity risk 2018, EIOPA-BoS-18/471, 18 December 2018, p. 163.

---

114 For more information on the functioning of the transitional measure relating to technical provisions, see EIOPA, *Solvency II tools with macro-prudential impact*, Publications Office of the EU, Luxembourg, 2018, pp. 22–24.

115 For more details, see above, Chapter 3, section 4.3.1.

116 In 2017, 124 undertakings were using the combination with the VA and 25 undertakings the combination with the MA. See EIOPA, Report on long-term guarantees measures and measures on equity risk 2018, EIOPA-BoS-18/471, 18 December 2018, p. 165.

117 Austria, Belgium, Germany, Finland, France, Greece, Liechtenstein, Norway, Portugal, Spain and UK.

118 Austria, Belgium, Finland, France, Germany, Greece, the Netherlands, Norway, Portugal, Spain, Sweden and the UK.

Figure 11. Number of groups using the transitional measure on technical provisions

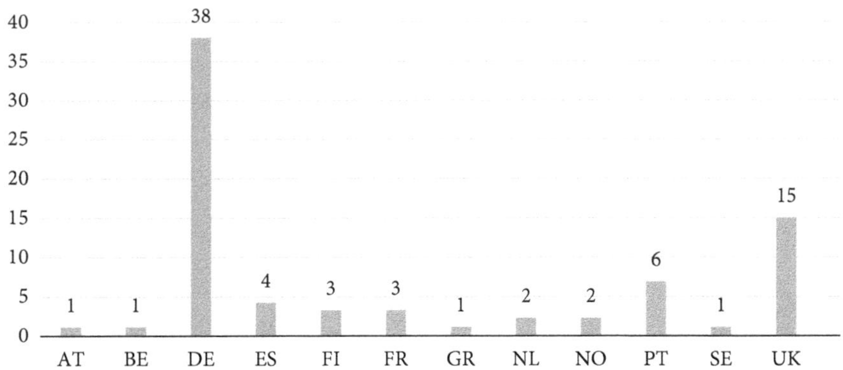

Source: EIOPA, Report on long-term guarantee measures and measures on equity risk 2018, EIOPA-BoS-18/471, 18 December 2018, p. 166.

The SFCR must include, under the heading "Valuation for solvency purposes", a statement on whether a transitional measure has been applied, as well as a quantification of the impact of not applying the transitional measure on the undertaking's financial position, including on the amount of technical provisions, the SCR, the MCR, the basic own funds and the amounts of own funds eligible to cover the MCR and the SCR (Art. 296 (2) (f) and (g) DA).[119]

3. OWN FUNDS

Once assets and (unsubordinated) liabilities have been valued on a market-consistent basis under Art. 75 FD, the net arithmetical result constitutes own funds, which are shown as a separate item on the balance sheet.

Not all own-fund items on the balance sheet automatically qualify as solvency capital. The primary purpose of solvency capital is to act as a safeguard for policyholders and as a cushion against unexpected losses. The amount of capital a (re)insurance undertaking holds should therefore enable the undertaking to absorb significant unforeseen losses over a specified time horizon and to a defined confidence level, and should give reasonable assurance to policyholders that payments will be made as they fall due. This means that it is not enough to have the right amount of capital. It is also important that the capital is available when needed. This is the reason why the possibility for an

119 For an example, see the 2017 SFCR of Union Mutualité Retraite (UMR), p. 67, https://umr-retraite.fr/sites/default/files/2018-04/Rapport_SFCR-2018_exercice-2017.pdf.

own-fund item to absorb losses on a going-concern basis plays an important role in its classification into different tiers of capital.

The solvency capital must be covered by eligible own funds. The solution adopted under Solvency II to define eligible own funds is complex.[120] It excludes certain items from inclusion under own funds (for instance, significant participations in financial and credit institutions) and it distinguishes within own-fund items between different tiers of capital, following the approach adopted for banks under Basel II. In addition, it recognises as capital different forms of contingent capital, taking into account the specific nature of insurance and the important role played by mutual insurance undertakings.

Although there was a clear intention to align the treatment of own funds under Solvency II with the treatment of own funds in the banking sector,[121] it was recognised that the role of capital is not the same in insurance and in banking. In the banking sector a greater emphasis is placed on immediate availability of capital to protect against potential runs on deposits, which rules out most forms of contingent capital. For (re)insurers, the longer-term nature of their liabilities means that contingent capital can be a valuable resource as long as reliance can be placed on the counterparty's willingness and ability to pay.[122]

In order to establish a level playing field between banking and insurance, it was decided to give proper recognition to innovative capital, i.e. hybrid capital instruments with characteristics of both debt and equity, which provide cheaper funding than share capital. Although hybrid capital was more widely used in the banking sector, it was considered important to provide a more favourable treatment of hybrid capital in the insurance sector too, in order to allow easier access to capital markets.

The determination of the amount of own funds eligible to cover the two capital requirements (MCR and SCR) is based on a three-step process.

3.1. FIRST STEP: IDENTIFICATION OF AVAILABLE OWN FUNDS

In the first step, the amounts of available own funds must be identified. Under Solvency II, the available own funds for the calculation of the capital requirements

120 See Arts. 98 and 99 FD and Arts. 80–82 DA. This is also the case in banking under the CRD IV and the CRR.

121 See EIOPA, Report on Comparison of the calculation of own funds in Insurance and Banking sectors and issues to address the undesirable differences, EIOPA-CRDIVSII-11/001, 12 January 2011, 71 p. See also the analysis in EIOPA's second advice to the EC in the context of the 2018 review of the Delegated Regulation, EIOPA-BoS-18/075, 28 February 2018, pp. 371–392.

122 CEIOPS, Further advice on Pillar I issues in the Framework of the Solvency II project, CEIOPS-CP-04/06, 26 October 2006, p. 60.

comprise both on-the-balance-sheet items, called basic own funds, and off-the-balance-sheet items, called ancillary own funds (Art. 87 FD).[123]

3.1.1. *Basic Own Funds*

Basic own funds are defined as the excess of assets over liabilities valued on a market-consistent basis, with the addition of subordinated liabilities, which, from an economic perspective, can be considered as a form of capital (Art. 88 FD).[124]

3.1.2. *Ancillary Own Funds*

Ancillary own funds are defined as items other than basic own funds that can be called upon to absorb losses. Examples of ancillary own funds are listed in Art. 89 FD and are expanded on further in Art. 74 DA:

- unpaid and uncalled ordinary share capital, callable on demand;
- unpaid and uncalled initial funds, members' contributions or the equivalent basic own-fund item for mutual and mutual-type undertakings, callable on demand;
- unpaid and uncalled preference shares, callable on demand;
- a legally binding commitment to subscribe and pay for subordinated liabilities on demand;
- letters of credit and guarantees which are held in trust for the benefit of insurance creditors by an independent trustee and provided by credit institutions authorised in accordance with Art. 8 CRD;[125]
- letters of credit and guarantees provided that the items can be called up on demand and are clear of encumbrances;
- any future claims which mutual or mutual-type associations of ship-owners, with variable contributions and solely insuring maritime risks, may have against their members by way of a call for supplementary contributions, within the following 12 months;
- any future claims which mutual or mutual-type associations may have against their members by way of a call for supplementary contributions, within the following 12 months, provided that a call can be made on demand and is clear of encumbrances;

---

123 Own shares are deducted from the amount of basic own funds (Art. 88 FD).

124 See also EIOPA, Guidelines on classification of own funds, EIOPA-BoS-14/168, 2 February 2014, Guidelines 12–19.

125 Letters of credit and guarantees provided by a UK credit institution may no longer fall under this category after the withdrawal date for Brexit and may lose their characteristic as ancillary own funds.

- other legally binding commitments received by a (re)insurance undertaking, provided that the item can be called up on demand and is clear of encumbrances.

Ancillary own funds are contingent assets as they have not been paid in. They are therefore not recognised on the balance sheet. If, at some undetermined point in the future, the ancillary own-fund items are called up,[126] then they cease to be contingent and become basic own-fund items represented by assets on the balance sheet.

The amount at which an ancillary own-fund item can be taken into account when determining own funds is subject to supervisory approval.[127] The amount has to reflect the loss absorbency of the item and must be based on prudent and realistic assumptions. Supervisory approval can result in the approval of a monetary amount (Art. 66 DA) or of a method by which the amount of each ancillary own-fund item is determined (Art. 67 DA). Supervisory approval is based on an assessment of the status of the counterparties (ability and willingness to pay), the recoverability of the funds and any information on the outcome of past calls to the extent that such information can be reliably used to assess the expected outcome of future calls (Art. 90 FD). These assessment criteria are further specified in Arts. 62–65 DA.[128]

Supplementary members' calls may represent a significant source of funding for mutual and mutual-type associations, particularly when those associations are confronted with adverse business fluctuations. In order to establish a level playing field between insurance undertakings established as limited liability companies or cooperative societies and mutual insurance undertakings, it was decided to give special recognition to supplementary members' calls which these undertakings can make to their members and to treat these calls as ancillary own-fund items. In the case of mutual or mutual-type associations of ship-owners with variable contributions solely insuring maritime risks,[129] the recourse to supplementary members' calls is a long-established practice

---

126 Except in the case of members calls, as they must already have been called for payment within 12 months and can only become basic own funds when paid.

127 For the approval process, see Commission Implementing Regulation (EU) 2015/499 of 24 March 2015 laying down implementing technical standards with regard to the procedures to be used for granting supervisory approval for the use of ancillary own-fund items in accordance with Directive 2009/138/EC of the EP and of the Council, *OJ* L 79, 25.3.2015, p. 12.

128 See also EIOPA, Guidelines on ancillary own funds, EIOPA-BoS-14/167, 2 February 2014, 6 p.

129 This refers to the so-called "P&I clubs" in the London and international reinsurance market. These are mutual insurance companies established, for example in Luxembourg or Sweden, to provide cover (protection and indemnity insurance) to their ship-owner and charterer members against third-party liabilities arising from the use and operation of ships. The members of a P&I Club are large commercial enterprises, which do not offer insurance to other parties. In preparing for Brexit, all six UK-regulated groups have taken steps to set up EU-regulated entities in various EU Member States. See International Group of P&I Clubs, *Annual Review 2017/2018*, p. 5, https://www.igpandi.org/annual-reviews.

and the approved amount of these members' calls is therefore treated as good-quality capital, i.e. ancillary own funds (recital 52 FD).

3.1.3. *Surplus Funds*

In several Member States (Denmark, Germany,[130] Slovenia and Sweden), collective bonus "provisions" are set up as part of the statutory provisions backing traditional participating life insurance business. Although primarily reserved for policyholders' future surplus participation, these funds are also used to cover future losses. As long as these funds are not allocated yet to individual policyholders, they can serve as a risk buffer. The funds belong to the insurance undertaking that has generated them.

In line with the economic risk-based approach of Solvency II, these surplus funds are treated under Solvency II as own funds and not as technical provisions, regardless of their treatment in the annual accounts for general purpose financial reporting. Although the treatment of these surplus funds as capital was a continuation of the regulatory regime under Solvency I,[131] this treatment was heavily opposed, particularly by France and the UK, which argued that such treatment was not in conformity with the principles of Solvency II. They believed that it was creating a competitive advantage for certain undertakings and that it was not logical to treat surplus funds as own funds because policyholders were being asked to subsidise shareholders.

Although multiple interventions were made at the highest level[132] to amend the draft Solvency II proposal in its final version and to turn these surplus funds into technical provisions, the Commission Services stuck to the advice provided by CEIOPS (and shared by CEA) because they believed that surplus funds met the conditions of own funds, i.e. subordination, loss absorbency, permanence and absence of mandatory servicing costs.[133]

---

130 Referred to in Germany as "*Rückstellung für Beitragsrückerstattung*", which is confusing as the name suggests that these funds are a "provision" (liability) rather than a "reserve" (own fund). For further discussion, see BURKHART, T., REUSS, A. and ZWIESLER, H.-J., *Allowance for surplus funds under Solvency II: Adequate reflection of risk sharing between policyholders and shareholders in a risk-based Solvency framework?*, Institute for Finance and Actuarial Science, University of Ulm, 26 June 2016, 35 p.

131 Art. 27 of Directive 2002/83/EC of the EP and of the Council of 5 November 2002 concerning life assurance, *OJ* L 345, 19.12.2002, p. 1.

132 France and the UK wanted concessions from Germany with regard to group supervision and the treatment of equity before they would allow surplus funds to be treated as own funds.

133 See also the paper presented by the German insurance association (GDV), which shows that many German life insurers would not fulfil the capital requirements under Solvency II if surplus funds were not treated as own funds: GDV, *Key Positions on Own Funds under Solvency II*, September 2007, 44 p. Surplus funds are called "the consolidation fund" in mutually operated life insurance companies in Sweden: see http://nft.nu/en/swedish-life-insurance-model-facing-major-challenges.

The discussion continued until the co-legislators agreed to include in the final text via a parliamentary amendment (in line with the Council's text) a definition of surplus funds that clarifies the nature of these funds. Surplus funds are defined in Art. 91 (1) FD as accumulated profits that have not been made available for distribution to policyholders and beneficiaries. In order to avoid any misunderstanding about their treatment, Art. 91 (2) FD states that surplus funds cannot be considered technical provisions to the extent that they fulfil the criteria defined in Art. 94 (1) FD (see further, section 2).

3.1.4. Participations

In order to avoid double counting of own funds between the insurance and banking sectors, (re)insurance undertakings must deduct from the amount of basic own funds any participation in a financial or credit institution[134] in excess of 10% of certain Tier 1 own-fund items (paid-in ordinary share capital and the related share premium account, paid-in initial funds or members' contributions, surplus funds and the reconciliation reserve).[135]

Participations in financial and credit institutions that in aggregate exceed this threshold must be partially deducted on a proportional basis. The deduction is not necessary where the participations are strategic and where the undertakings are consolidated for the group solvency calculation (Art. 68 DA).

Figure 12. Visualising own funds

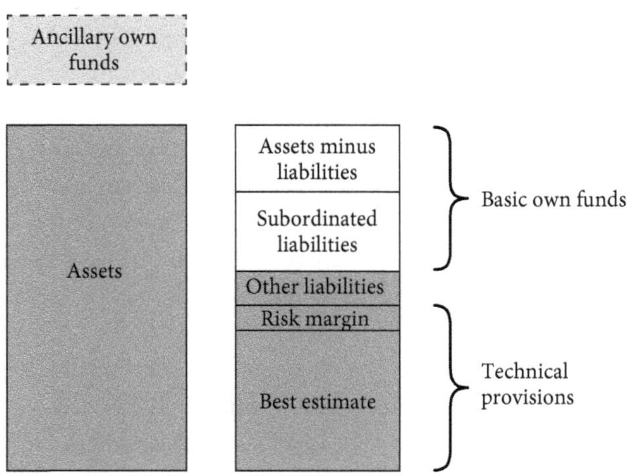

Source: Produced by the author.

---

134 This specific treatment applies to all participations in financial or credit institutions and is therefore not affected by Brexit. See EIOPA, Opinion on the solvency position of insurance and reinsurance undertakings in light of the withdrawal of the UK from the EU, EIOPA-BoS-18/201, 18 May 2018, p. 5.

135 For credit institutions holding participations in insurance undertakings, the treatment is different. See Art. 46 CRR. This is presently being discussed between the Council and

3.2. SECOND STEP: CLASSIFICATION OF OWN FUNDS INTO TIERS

As own-fund items possess different qualities and provide for different levels of absorption of losses, own funds items are classified into three tiers, depending on their nature and the extent to which they meet a number of key criteria, with Tier 1 representing the strongest level of capital.

Figure 13. Classification of own funds into tiers

Quality \ Nature	On the balance-sheet (basic own funds)	Off the balance-sheet (ancillary own funds)
High	Tier 1	Tier 2
Medium	Tier 2	Tier 3
Low	Tier 3	–

Source: Produced by the author.

The classification of own-fund items into three tiers depends on whether they are basic or ancillary own-fund items and the extent to which they possess the characteristics of permanent availability and subordination.

The own-fund item must be permanently available or callable on demand to absorb losses on a going-concern basis and in the case of winding-up. In the case of winding-up, the total amount of the own-fund item must be available to absorb losses and the repayment of the item cannot be made to its holder until all other obligations, including obligations towards policyholders and beneficiaries, have been met (Art. 93 (1) (a) and (b) FD).

When assessing the extent to which own-fund items possess these two characteristics, due consideration must be given to the duration of the item, in particular whether the item is dated or not. Where an own-fund item is dated, the relative duration of the item as compared to the duration of the (re)insurance obligations of the undertaking must be considered (sufficient duration) (Art. 93 (2), first subparagraph FD).

Due consideration must also be given to whether the item is free from requirements or incentives to redeem the nominal sum (absence of incentive to redeem), whether the item is free from mandatory fixed charges (absence

the EP. See SIMON, P., Report on the proposal for a regulation of the EP and of the Council amending Regulation (EU) No 575/2013 as regards the leverage ratio, the net stable funding ratio, requirements for own funds and eligible liabilities, counterparty credit risk, market risk, exposures to central counterparties, exposures to collective investment undertakings, large exposures, reporting and disclosure requirements and amending Regulation (EU) No 648/2012, A8-0242/2018, 28 June 2018.

of mandatory servicing costs) and whether the item is clear of encumbrances (absence of encumbrances)[136] (Art. 93 (2), second subparagraph FD).

On the basis of these characteristics and features, Art. 94 FD classifies own-fund items as follows:

- Tier 1: basic own-fund items that substantially possess all the above-mentioned characteristics (permanent availability and subordination), as well as the above-mentioned features of sufficient duration, absence of incentives to redeem, absence of mandatory servicing costs and absence of encumbrances;
- Tier 2: basic own funds that substantially possess the above-mentioned characteristic of subordination, as well as the above-mentioned features of sufficient duration, absence of incentives to redeem, absence of mandatory servicing costs and absence of encumbrances;
- Tier 3: all other basic or ancillary own-fund items that do not possess the characteristics of Tier 1 or Tier 2 items.

Surplus funds are automatically classified as Tier 1 capital, while letters of credit and guarantees and members' calls are classified as Tier 2 capital (Art. 96 FD).

A list of *Tier 1 basic own-fund items* can be found in Art. 69 DA. These basic own-fund items are deemed to substantially possess the characteristics referred to in Art. 93 (1) (a) and (b) FD, as well as the features referred to in Art. 93 (2) FD:

- part of excess of assets over liabilities valued on a market-consistent basis, comprising the following items:
  - paid-in ordinary share capital and the related share premium account;[137]
  - paid-in initial funds, members' contributions or the equivalent basic own-fund item for mutual or mutual-type undertakings;
  - paid-in subordinated mutual member accounts;
  - surplus funds;
  - paid-in preference shares and the related share premium account;
  - reconciliation reserve;
- paid-in subordinated liabilities valued on a market-consistent basis.[138]

---

136 An encumbrance may be a contingent liability, contract, purchase order, payroll commitment, tax payable or legal penalty that is chargeable to an account. It ceases to be an encumbrance when paid out or when the actual liability amount is determined and recorded as an expense. See http://www.businessdictionary.com/definition/encumbrance.html.

137 A separate account or reserve to which the share premium, i.e. the difference between the value received and the nominal value of the share at issuance or the value received at issuance and the value recognised in share capital is transferred in accordance with national law (EIOPA, Guidelines on classification of own funds, EIOPA-BoS-14/167, 2 February 2015, p. 2).

138 Only in the case of sensitivity to interest rate changes, as there is no adjustment for own credit standing.

These items are only considered Tier 1 capital if they also display all the features referred to in Art. 71 DA,[139] which further stresses their quality as "strong" capital.[140] For instance, ordinary share capital can only qualify as Tier 1 capital if the legal or contractual arrangements governing the terms of the ordinary shares or national legislation allow for the cancellation of distributions (dividends) where there is non-compliance with the SCR or where the distribution would lead to such non-compliance (Art. 71 (1) (l) (i) DA).[141]

Paid-in ordinary share capital, including its related share premium account, and paid-in initial funds, members' contributions or the equivalent basic own-fund item for mutual and mutual-type undertakings, form the highest-quality own funds that can be relied on to absorb losses on a going-concern basis.

The reconciliation reserve represents the total excess of assets over liabilities reduced by the amount of own shares held by the undertaking, foreseeable dividends, distributions and charges, the basic own-fund items classified under Tier 1 and Tier 2, the restricted own-fund items and the amount of participations held in financial and credit institutions (Art. 70 DA).[142] The reconciliation reserve includes EPIFP, defined in Art. 1 (46) DA as:

> "the expected present value of future cash flows (future premiums) which result from the inclusion in technical provisions of premiums relating to existing (re)insurance contracts that are expected to be received in the future, but that may not be received for any reason, other than because the insured event has occurred, regardless of the legal or contractual rights of the policyholder to discontinue the policy."

The inclusion of EPIFP was controversial, as EIOPA[143] initially wanted to include EPIFP in Tier 3, arguing that this amount does not represent own funds of the highest quality. The compromise was to include EPIFP in Tier 1, but to require undertakings to explicitly monitor these future cash flows as part of liquidity risk management (Art. 260) (1) (d) DA) and to disclose the amount of the EPIFP in the SFCR (Art. 295 (5) DA) in the part dealing with liquidity risk under the heading "risk profile". The amount of EPIFP depends very much on the definition of the boundary of the (re)insurance contract: the wider the

139 As amended by Art. 1 (4) of Commission Delegated Regulation (EU) of 8 March 2019.

140 See also EIOPA, Guidelines on classification of own funds, EIOPA-BoS-14/167, 2 February 2015, Guidelines 1–8.

141 As a dividend validly adopted by the general meeting is considered a debt of the company, the company can only refrain from distributing the dividend if it is prohibited from doing so by action of the supervisory authority.

142 EIOPA, Guidelines on classification of own funds, EIOPA-BoS-14/167, 2 February 2015, Guideline 2.

143 See EIOPA, Report of the Task Force on Expected Profits arising from Future Premiums, EIOPA-TFEPIFP-11/003, 20 June 2011, 35 p.

contract boundary, the larger the amount of EPIFP, as the amount refers to existing business, also called "in-force" business.

The stress test carried out by EIOPA in 2016 shows that for a representative sample of (re)insurance undertakings from 30 EEA countries, the Tier 1 unrestricted eligible own funds represented 90% of total own funds. The quality of own funds of (re)insurance undertakings can therefore be regarded as generally very high.[144]

A list of *Tier 2 basic own-fund items* can be found in Art. 72 DA. These basic own-fund items are deemed to substantially possess the characteristic referred to in Art. 93 (1) (b) FD, as well as the features referred to in Art. 93 (2) FD:

- part of excess of assets over liabilities valued on a market-consistent basis:
  - ordinary share capital and the related share premium account;
  - initial funds, members' contributions or the equivalent basic own-fund item for mutual and mutual-type undertakings;
  - subordinated mutual member accounts;
  - preference shares and the related share premium account;
- subordinated liabilities valued on a market-consistent basis.

These items are only considered Tier 2 capital if they satisfy the conditions referred to in Art. 73 DA.[145]

A list of *Tier 2 ancillary own-fund items* can be found in Art. 74 DA, with further specification in Art. 75 DA:

- unpaid and uncalled ordinary share capital, callable on demand;
- unpaid and uncalled initial funds, members' contributions or the equivalent basic own-fund item for mutual and mutual-type undertakings, callable on demand;
- unpaid and uncalled preference shares, callable on demand;
- a legally binding commitment to subscribe and pay for subordinated liabilities on demand;
- letters of credit and guarantees which are held in trust for the benefit of insurance creditors by an independent trustee and provided by an authorised credit institution;
- letters of credit and guarantees provided that the items can be called up on demand and are clear of encumbrances;

---

144 EIOPA, 2016 EIOPA Insurance Stress Test Report, EIOPA 16/302, 15 December 2016, p. 20. This is confirmed in the 2017 year-end statistics, which show that for the majority (26/31) of EEA countries, Tier 1 unrestricted eligible own funds represent 90% or more of total own funds. See EIOPA, *European Insurance Overview 2018. Solo undertakings. Year-end 2017*, Publications Office of the EU, Luxembourg, 2018, p. 15.

145 See also EIOPA, Guidelines on classification of own funds, EIOPA-BoS-14/167, 2 February 2015, Guidelines 9 and 10.

- any calls for supplementary contributions within the following 12 months of mutual or mutual-type associations of ship-owners against their members;
- any calls for supplementary contributions within the following 12 months of mutual or mutual-type associations against their members, provided that a call can be made on demand and is clear of encumbrances;
- other legally binding commitments received by (re)insurance undertakings, provided the item can be called up on demand and is clear of encumbrances.

A list of *Tier 3 basic own-fund items* can be found in Art. 76 DA. These basic own-fund items are deemed to not substantially possess the characteristic referred to in Art. 93 (1) (b) FD, nor the features referred to in Art. 93 (2) FD:

- part of excess of assets over liabilities valued on a market-consistent basis:
  - subordinated mutual member accounts;
  - preference shares and the related share premium account;
  - an amount equal to the value of net deferred taxes;
- subordinated liabilities valued on a market-consistent basis.

These items are only considered Tier 3 capital if they display all the features set out in Art. 77 DA:[146]

Ancillary own-fund items that have been approved by supervisory authorities in accordance with Art. 90 FD and which do not display all of the features applicable to Tier 2 ancillary own-fund items are classified as Tier 3 ancillary own funds (Art. 48 DA).

Where an own-fund item is not included in the preceding lists of own-fund items, (re)insurance undertakings can only consider that item to be own funds where an approval of the item's assessment and classification has been received from the supervisory authority (Art. 79 (1) DA).[147] The assessment criteria are laid down in Art. 79 (2) DA.

The FD does not require (re)insurance undertakings to have a capital management plan. Art. 71 (1) (g) DA does however refer to "the undertaking's medium-term capital management plan" in the context of the repayment or redemption of subordinated liabilities counted as Tier 1 own funds.[148] This is picked up by EIOPA in its Guidelines on the system of governance, where Guideline 36 requires (re)insurance undertakings to have a capital management

146 See also EIOPA, Guidelines on classification of own funds, EIOPA-BoS-14/167, 2 February 2015, Guideline 11.

147 See also EIOPA, Guidelines on classification of own funds, EIOPA-BoS-14/167, 2 February 2015, Guidelines 21–26.

148 This issue was raised by the Chair of ECON in a letter of 19 December 2014 to the EC, concerning the DA. The EC responded in its letter of 27 January 2015 that capital management is a cornerstone of the sound management of an insurance undertaking.

policy and Guideline 37 requires undertakings to develop a medium-term capital management plan, which is monitored by the AMSB.[149] The undertaking's capital management policy must be disclosed in the SFCR under the heading "Capital management" (see further, Chapter 8, section 2.2).

3.2.1. *Ring-Fenced Funds*

Ring-fenced funds are arrangements where an identified set of assets and liabilities are managed as though they were a separate undertaking. The reduced transferability of the assets of a ring-fenced fund must be reflected in the calculation of the excess of assets over liabilities, as this reduces the capacity of the undertaking to fully absorb losses on a going-concern basis. The own-fund items within a ring-fenced fund are therefore deducted from the reconciliation reserve (Arts. 80 and 81 DA).

(Re)insurance undertakings must calculate a notional SCR for each ring-fenced fund and for the remaining part of the undertaking as if those ring-fenced funds and the remaining part of the undertaking were separate undertakings. In the case of ring-fenced funds, the SCR is the sum of the notional SCRs for each ring-fenced fund and for the remaining part of the undertaking (Art. 217 DA).

The requirement to calculate a notional SCR in respect of a ring-fenced fund does not require undertakings to maintain an amount of own funds within a ring-fenced fund that is equal to or greater than the notional SCR. However, where the amount of own funds within a ring-fenced fund is less than the notional SCR, the undertaking will not be in compliance with its SCR unless the total of the own funds within the ring-fenced fund and within the remaining part of the undertaking combined are sufficient to cover that SCR, taking account of the quantitative limits in Art. 82 DA.[150]

3.2.2. *Transitional Measures*

Existing basic own-fund items (for instance, hybrid capital issued under Solvency I) may be included in basic own funds as Tier 1 or Tier 2 for up to ten years after 1 January 2016 as long as they were used to meet existing solvency margin requirements at 31 December 2015 and were issued before 18 January 2015 (date of entry into force of the DA), even though these items do not meet the own funds criteria specified in Arts. 93 and 94 FD.[151]

---

149 One could argue that the requirement to develop a capital management plan goes beyond the mandate given by the FD. However, there can be no doubt that a capital management policy is an essential feature of Solvency II, which links capital with risk.

150 EIOPA, Guidelines on ring-fenced funds, EIOPA-BoS-14/169, 2 February 2015, para. 1.5.

151 Art. 308b (9) and (10) FD, and EIOPA Guidelines on classification of own funds, EIOPA-BoS-14/167, 2 February 2015, Guideline 27.

(Re)insurance undertakings need to be aware of the fact that these grandfathering provisions will eventually cease to apply and that they must provide for new financing in time.

3.3. THIRD STEP: QUANTITATIVE LIMITS

As Tier 2 and Tier 3 items do not provide for full absorption of losses in all circumstances, it is necessary to take this into account for supervisory purposes. Art. 82 DA therefore introduces two sets of limits on available own funds, in order to determine the amounts eligible for supervisory purposes:

- with respect to the *SCR*, the eligible amount of Tier 1 items must be at least 50% of the SCR, the proportion of Tier 3 items may not be higher than 15% and the sum of the eligible amounts of Tier 2 and Tier 3 items may not exceed 50% of the SCR;
- with respect to the *MCR*, the eligible amount of Tier 1 items must be at least 80% of the MCR and the eligible amount of Tier 2 items may not exceed 20% of the MCR.

Art. 82 (3) FD further restricts the amount of certain basic own-fund items that can qualify as Tier 1 items with respect to the SCR and the MCR by introducing a limit of 20%. As indicated before (see above, Chapter 3, section 5.4), this additional restriction was introduced by the DA but is not supported by any empowerment for the EC.[152] It is interesting to see that EIOPA, in its second set of advice to the EC on the 2018 review of the DA, advised the EC to retain the 20% limit,[153] although there can be no question about the lack of legal basis for this additional quantitative limit.[154]

In its advice, EIOPA supported the retention of the additional limit of 20% in order to protect the prudential quality of Tier 1 own funds. It feared that the

152 The EC seems to disagree. See EC, Report to the EP and the Council on the exercise of the power to adopt delegated acts conferred on the Commission pursuant to Directive 2009/138/EC of the EP and the Council of 25 November 2009 on the taking-up and pursuit of the business of insurance and reinsurance (Solvency II), COM (2017) 740 final, 7 December 2017, pp. 5–6.

153 EIOPA, Consultation Paper on EIOPA's second set of advice to the EC on specific items in the Solvency II Delegated Regulation, EIOPA-CP-17-006, 6 November 2017, p. 317, and EIOPA, Second set of advice to the EC on specific items in the Solvency II Delegated Regulation, EIOPA-BoS-18/075, 28 February 2018, p. 400.

154 The EC hides behind the opinion of EIOPA, as pointed out in the letter written by Commissioner Hill to the Chair of ECON on 11 May 2015: "On your point on the sub-tiers, I understand your concerns, but our view – which is in line with EIOPA's advice – is that the limit is conceptually consistent with the own funds requirements set out for banks in the CRD".

removal of the 20% limit would lead to the inclusion of too high a proportion of hybrid capital in Tier 1. EIOPA could not support any regime in which hybrid instruments would represent all or the most significant part of Tier 1 own funds.

The IRSG, in its opinion on EIOPA's advice to the EC,[155] asked for the removal of the 20% limit because the introduction of this additional limit is not supported by the empowerment of the EC in the FD. Introducing this limit would require an amendment of the FD. This could only be done on the basis of a new proposal by the EC, supported by the Council and the EP.

The introduction of the 20% limit reduces the impact of the grandfathering provision in Art. 308b (9) FD. As the threshold is the result of an action by the EC, EIOPA found itself on comfortable ground. Most stakeholders were supportive of EIOPA's view, as they feared that a removal of the threshold would disadvantage those (re)insurance undertakings that hold less hybrid capital instruments in Tier 1. The 20% limit is retained in the 2019 amendment of the DA.

4. CAPITAL REQUIREMENTS

One could argue that imposing capital requirements on (re)insurers is not necessary because the risks underwritten by (re)insurance undertakings are dealt with in technical provisions. To the extent that technical provisions are calculated on a historical-cost basis, i.e. without discounting, thus including additional prudence, (re)insurers might not need an additional capital buffer, because a lot of prudence is already built into technical provisions. This was to some extent the case under Solvency I. The amount of technical provisions held by (re)insurance undertakings by far exceeded, in most cases, the present value of these provisions. This is of course very different under Solvency II, where technical provisions are valued on a market-consistent basis. This explains why most (re)insurance undertakings managed the transition from Solvency I to Solvency II without needing to obtain additional capital. Because of the market-consistent valuation of technical provisions and the removal of in-built prudence, the excess amount in technical provisions was transferred into own funds.

Although their ultimate objective is to protect policyholders, it is important to make a clear distinction between technical provisions and capital requirements, as they each serve a different purpose.[156] Under Solvency II, technical provisions reflect the expected losses faced by (re)insurance undertakings as a

155 EIOPA, Opinion of the IRSG on the Consultation Paper of EIOPA's second set of advice to the EC on the Solvency II review, EIOPA-IRSG-17-19, 3 January 2018, p. 7.

156 See the Geneva Association, *The nature and role of capital in insurance*, November 2016, 18 p.

result of their underwriting activity. These technical provisions are calculated on a market-consistent basis and must be matched by assets that are invested in the best interest of policyholders and beneficiaries. For unexpected losses (for instance, changes in the interest rate, unforeseen demographic changes or severe natural catastrophes caused by climate change) a capital buffer must be set up in order to protect policyholders against risks which are not taken into account in technical provisions. Much of Solvency II has to do with the question of how high this additional capital buffer should be and how it should be calculated.

The capital buffer that (re)insurance undertakings must hold over and above technical provisions is referred to under Solvency II as the solvency capital requirement (SCR). The philosophy behind the SCR is stated in recital 64 FD:

> "In order to promote good risk management and align regulatory capital with industry practices, the SCR should be determined as the economic capital to be held by insurers in order to ensure that ruin occurs no more often than once in every 200 cases or, alternatively, that an insurer will still be in a position, with a probability of at least 99,5%, to meet its obligations over the following 12 months. That economic capital should be calculated on the basis of the true risk profile of those undertakings, taking account of the impact of possible risk-mitigation techniques, as well as diversification effects."

In its advice to the EC, CEIOPS points out that the concept of the SCR shares many features with economic capital in value-based risk management. An undertaking will define its risk appetite and, where applicable, the public rating it wishes to obtain. It then determines the economic capital that will be necessary to limit its probability of insolvency to a defined level.[157]

This defined level is the confidence level. The confidence level of the SCR under Solvency II is set at 99.5% of the value at risk (VaR) over a one-year time horizon (the period over which the impact of changes to risks is tested). This was already the case in the EC's Framework for Consultation. It was inspired by the insurance reform in Australia, where a similar confidence level had been introduced.[158] Solvency II is therefore *not* a zero-failure regime. This is not always sufficiently recognised. In many Member States, insurance supervisors still carry out their supervision with the objective of preventing all insurance failures. Although this objective is very laudable, it often involves the introduction of

---

157 CEIOPS, Answers to the EC on the second wave of Calls for Advice in the framework of the Solvency II project, CEIOPS-DOC-07/05, October 2005, p. 81.

158 A major reform of insurance regulation took place in Australia after the collapse of the second-largest insurance company in Australia, HIH, which was put into liquidation on 15 March 2001 with total losses amounting to AU$5.3 billion. See TROWBRIDGE, J., The Architecture of Group Supervision, in KEMPLER, C., FLAMEE, M., YANG, C.H. and WINDELS, P. (Eds.), *Global Perspectives on Insurance Today*, Palgrave Macmillan, New York, 2013, p. 138.

additional prudence into the system, for instance by requiring a solvency ratio that is well above 100% (see below, section 4.1). This is not necessarily in the interest of policyholders and beneficiaries because it makes insurance more expensive.

It would be good for the law to state clearly that supervisory authorities cannot guarantee that (re)insurance undertakings under their supervision can never fail and that it is not the objective of insurance supervision to ensure this. This is the reason why, from a conceptual point of view, it makes a lot of sense to combine a risk-based solvency capital regime with the additional protection provided by an insurance guarantee scheme.[159] As long as there is no insurance guarantee scheme in all Member States, there is a risk that the cost of carrying out insurance in the EU is hampered by unintentionally high solvency requirements. In addition, from an internal market perspective, there is no level playing field between Member States, as some Member States provide the additional protection of an insurance guarantee scheme while others do not.[160] Policyholders who buy their insurance from an insurance undertaking in another MS offering cross-border services may not know whether or not they are protected by an insurance guarantee scheme in that MS.[161]

Solvency II has been designed to ensure that the amount of economic capital held by (re)insurers is at a level that ruin only occurs in exceptional circumstances. This would be the case if assets no longer exceed technical provisions (valued for solvency purposes) and (unsubordinated) liabilities. The level of the SCR must be such that if a (re)insurance undertaking were to start the year with a capital base equal to the level of the SCR, and losses occurred during the year at the 99.5% confidence level, the assets remaining would be at a level sufficient to provide for payment of the insurance liabilities and

---

159 See EC, White Paper on Insurance Guarantee Schemes, COM (2010) 370 final, 12 July 2010, 14 p. and CEIOPS, Comments on the EC's White Paper on Insurance Guarantee Schemes, CEIOPS-DOC-96/10, 2010, 10 p. See also EIOPA, Report on the Role of Insurance Guarantee Schemes in the Winding-Up Procedure of Insolvent Insurance Undertakings in the EU/EEA, EIOPA-TFIGS-12/007, 25 May 2012, 12 p. and EIOPA, Report on the cross-border cooperation mechanisms between Insurance Guarantee Schemes in the EU, EIOPA-TFIGS-11/007, June 2011, 13 p.

160 Insurance guarantee schemes exist in various degrees in 20 Member States of the EEA. CEIOPS (first) and EIOPA (later) have been advocating the introduction of a harmonised regime for insurance guarantee schemes. See the latest document: EIOPA, Discussion paper on resolution funding and national insurance guarantee schemes, EIOPA-CP-18-003, 30 July 2018, 61 p. In 2010, the EC launched a consultation about the possible introduction of a regime for insurance guarantee schemes, but did not take action afterwards. See EC, White Paper on Insurance Guarantee Schemes, COM (2010) 370 final, 12 July 2010, 14 p.

161 For a recent case, see the bankruptcy of Qudos Insurance A/S in Denmark, which operated in Denmark, France, Germany, Greece, Ireland, Italy, Malta, Norway, Sweden and the UK. The claims of all European policyholders were partly covered by the Danish Guarantee Fund for non-life insurance undertakings. See EIOPA, *Bankruptcy of Qudos Insurance A/S – Equal treatment of European policyholders*, 20 December 2018.

other liabilities[162] at the end of the year. The 99.5% confidence level does not mean that a ruin event will occur once in every 200 years, or that one in every 200 undertakings will fail annually. It should ensure that if such an event occurs, the undertaking will have sufficient capital to cover that unexpected situation for the next 12 months.[163] This corresponds to a BBB rating,[164] which was assigned by Standard & Poor's to insurance undertakings with "good" capital adequacy, i.e. the actual capital at the disposal of the undertaking is 100–125% of the minimum economic capital considered necessary.[165]

If we consider that almost 3,000 (re)insurance undertakings within the EEA apply Solvency II, the definition of ruin under Solvency II means that 15 undertakings could still fail in a given year. However, that has not happened since the introduction of Solvency II on 1 January 2016. When preparing the Solvency II FD, some people – including from the insurance industry – considered this confidence level too low. A higher confidence level was tested in the context of QIS 2, but it was rejected based upon numbers obtained via that QIS. It would have increased costs for EU (re)insurers and would have undermined their international competitiveness. Since the financial crisis and the low interest rate environment, views have changed and the agreed confidence level is no longer called into question.

The solvency position of an undertaking is looked at from a time horizon of one year. This is not obvious, as a one-year time horizon does not reflect the long-term nature of many insurance products (for instance, life or health insurance). The one-year time horizon approach has been criticised, particularly in France.[166] The argument is made that a one-year time horizon combined with a market-consistent valuation of assets and liabilities brings a short-term perspective into a sector that is by nature long-term. This could have

---

162 Except for those liabilities that are part of own funds.

163 MONTALVO, C., Risk management under Solvency II: Solvency capital requirements, in DREHER, M. and WANDT, M. (Eds.), *Solvency in der Rechtsanwendung*, Verlag Versicherungswirtschaft, Karlsruhe, 2009, p. 45.

164 The same confidence level had already been introduced in the UK as part of the individual capital adequacy standard (ICAS) regime. See HUMPHRY, D., Solvency II in the UK: Evolution rather than Revolution, in MARANO, P. and SIRI, M. (Eds.), *Insurance Regulation in the European Union*, Palgrave Macmillan, Cham, 2017, p. 115.

165 See EC, Commission Staff Working Document: Accompanying document to the Proposal for a Directive of the EP and of the Council on the taking-up and pursuit of the business of Insurance and Reinsurance. Solvency II: Impact Assessment Report, SEC (2007) 871, 10 July 2007, p. 31, and EC, *Study into the methodologies to assess the overall financial position of an insurance undertaking from the perspective of prudential supervision*, May 2002, p. 153 (the KPMG Report).

166 See also, MITTNIK, S., *Solvency II Calibrations: Where Curiosity Meets Spuriosity*, Center for Quantiative Risk Analysis, University of Munich, Working Paper 2011, No 4, 44 p. (https://www.cequra.uni-muenchen.de/download/solvency.pdf). The author particularly criticises the calibration of the equity risk sub-module in the standard formula because of the one-year time horizon.

a negative impact on the traditional role of insurers as long-term investors.[167] This criticism has some validity. However, it is not obvious that another timeline would be better, as the duration of liabilities differs from one undertaking to another.[168] It is however possible for an insurer to adopt a different time horizon in its (partial) internal model.

The one-year time horizon was chosen because it aligns with the normal financial reporting cycle and allows for a maximum of convergence between solvency calculations and calculations in the financial statements produced for general-purpose financial reporting. It would also be difficult for insurers to have a different time horizon from that set in banking: that would make supervision and reporting extremely complex (and confusing), particularly in the case of financial conglomerates.[169]

The risk measure chosen under Solvency II is VaR. VaR assesses the probability of ruin at a specified quantile (e.g. 99.5%). By contrast, tail VaR considers both the probability and the severity of losses in the event that a specified quantile is breached. Tail VaR encourages supervisors, undertakings and policyholders to consider the consequences of a potential default, rather than focusing simply on the probability of insolvency. While recognising the advantages of tail VaR, CEIOPS pointed in its advice to the EC[170] to one of the disadvantages of tail VaR, i.e. the scarcity of data, which could lead to increased modelling error. A formula based on tail VaR might be difficult to generalise in such a way as to provide a good fit for the majority of (re)insurance undertakings (i.e. the standard formula would over- or underestimate capital requirements in many cases because it would be calibrated using tail data that may not be representative).

The EC opted for the VaR approach in its initial proposal for a number of reasons:[171] the higher cost of tail VaR for the industry and particularly for

---

167 It has been argued that Solvency II fails to take account of the fact that undertakings with different liabilities have different capacities for absorbing different risks and that it is the exploitation of these differences that creates systemic resilience. This is in particular an issue for life insurers because the riskiness of the assets of a life insurer with liabilities that will not materialise in 10 or sometimes 20 years is not well measured by the amount by which prices may fall during the next year. See PERSAUD, A., *How not to regulate insurance markets: the risks and dangers of Solvency II*, Peterson Institute for International Economics Policy Brief PB15-5, April 2015, p. 2.

168 See above, section 2.1.

169 Only one in five European insurance groups is a bancassurance group. See LOWET, L., De grootste Europese verzekeringsgroepen (the largest European insurance groups), *Tijdschrift voor Bank- en Financiewezen*, 2010, No 6, pp. 373–377.

170 CEIOPS, Answers to the EC on the second wave of Calls for Advice in the framework of the Solvency II project, CEIOPS-DOC-07/05, October 2005, pp. 82–83.

171 EC, Commission Staff Working Document: Accompanying document to the Proposal for a Directive of the EP and of the Council on the taking-up and pursuit of the business of Insurance and Reinsurance. Solvency II: Impact Assessment Report, SEC (2007) 871, 10 July 2007, p. 35.

small and medium-sized insurers, the lack of cross-sectoral consistency, as the VaR approach is also applied in the banking sector, and difficulties with the implementation of tail VaR as outlined by CEIOPS. However, it was agreed to allow (re)insurers to apply tail VaR in their internal model, as tail VaR is a coherent risk measure that might appeal to (re)insurers using an internal model, and it was also believed to be a better approach from a supervisory point of view.[172]

4.1. TWO CAPITAL REQUIREMENTS: SCR AND MCR

The FD introduces two capital requirements: the SCR and the MCR. The SCR and the MCR are the two extremes of the so-called "ladder of supervisory intervention" (see further, Chapter 7, section 2.3). If available capital falls below the SCR, supervisors must take proportionate corrective measures. In the event that available capital falls further, the severity of measures applied is increased, and in the event that the MCR is breached, ultimate supervisory action is triggered.

The SCR ratio is the ratio of eligible own funds and the SCR. If the SCR ratio is 100% or higher, the SCR is complied with, otherwise not. The MCR ratio is the ratio of eligible own funds and the MCR. If the MCR ratio is 100% or higher, the MCR is complied with, otherwise not.

The logic of having two capital requirements, whereby the SCR is higher than the MCR, and the existence of a supervisory ladder of intervention is often overlooked today. People (including supervisory authorities) look at the SCR as an absolute number: the SCR ratio should always be higher than 100%, ideally 200% or even more. This is not in line with the philosophy of Solvency II, which introduces the SCR as a target level of capital that must be looked at in relation to the MCR. If the SCR were to be an absolute number, there would be no reason to have an MCR. In practice, the SCR is often looked at as the MCR and a (re)insurance undertaking is considered virtually insolvent when it breaches the SCR.[173] The SCR ratio should therefore always be above 100%. This misconception leads to actions aiming at preventing a breach of the SCR at all costs, such as prohibiting an acquisition unless the acquired (re)insurer has an SCR that is at least 150% or introducing an additional (early) intervention level before the SCR is breached.[174]

172 The Swiss Solvency Test adopts the tail VaR approach with a confidence level of 99%. See FINMA, *Circular 2017/3: Swiss Solvency Test*, 7 December 2016, 27 p.

173 See, for instance, the interesting report released by EIOPA on failures and near misses in insurance, which cites a breach or imminent breach of the SCR as "a real financial threat". See EIOPA, *Failures and near misses in insurance. Overview of the causes and early identification*, Publications Office of the EU, Luxembourg, 2018, 47 p.

174 This seemed to be the direction in which EIOPA was moving, although – after consultation – EIOPA has refrained from introducing a new intervention level in the context of its proposal

Such actions and interpretations are disturbing. They ignore the fact that an important objective of Solvency II is the more efficient allocation of capital, which is made possible by the introduction of two capital requirements. One of these capital requirements, the SCR, is by definition volatile, as it is the result of a market-consistent valuation in the balance sheet. This volatility should not be a problem and needs to be properly explained.[175] To see the SCR as an absolute number is misleading. Not only is it important to know what influences the SCR, the SCR must also be looked at over time and as part of a (re)insurer's capital management. A (re)insurer with a solvency ratio of 250% might have a different risk appetite from a (re)insurer with a solvency ratio of 120%. A (re)insurer might also want to have a higher solvency ratio in order to be more attractive in the (capital) market. A high solvency ratio, without any link to a corresponding underlying capital management, is not in the interest of policyholders, nor is it in the interest of the economy as a whole. Capital requirements are not there to serve the ego of (re)insurance undertakings ("I have the highest SCR!") nor that of insurance supervisors ("All companies under my supervision have a solvency ratio of at least 150%!").

The stress test carried out by EIOPA in 2016[176] showed that for a representative sample of 236 (re)insurance undertakings from 30 EEA countries, the overall SCR ratio was 196%, compared with an MCR ratio of 533%. Only two companies reported an SCR ratio below 100%. The overall SCR ratio falls to 136% if all LTG and transitional measures are excluded. In this case, the proportion of entities with an SCR cover below the 100% threshold increases to 14% of the sample.

The latest statistics disclosed by EIOPA for the third quarter of 2018 show, at an aggregated EEA level, an SCR ratio of 243%,[177] with the lowest SCR ratio for Latvia (124%) and the highest for Germany (343%).[178]

The level of the SCR should reflect a (re)insurer's capital management. One of the important innovations of Solvency II is the introduction of a supervisory dialogue,[179] which requires the management of the undertaking to discuss the financial position and strategy of the undertaking with the supervisory authority

on recovery and resolution. See EIOPA, Opinion to the Institutions of the European Union on the harmonisation of recovery and resolution frameworks for (re)insurers across the Member States, EIOPA-BoS/17-148, 5 July 2017, p. 25.

175 See for supervisory reporting Art. 297 DA, and for public disclosure Art. 311 DA.

176 EIOPA, 2016 EIOPA Insurance Stress Test Report, EIOPA16/302, 15 December 2016, pp. 21–22.

177 For year-end 2017, the ratio was 239% with application of the LTG measures and 201% without application of the LTG measures. See EIOPA, Report on long-term guarantees measures and measures on equity risk 2018, EIOPA-BoS-18/471, p. 24.

178 EIOPA, Insurance Statistics, Own funds, solo entities, Q 3 2018, Accompanying note, 5 February 2019, p. 9, https://eiopa.europa.eu/Publications/Insurance%20Statistics/SQ_Accompanying%20note.pdf, 2018, p. 15.

179 This is part of the SRP referred to in Art. 36 FD. See further, Chapter 7, section 2.

at regular intervals. Capital management plays a central role in this debate, as it is the reflection of the undertaking's risk appetite and risk tolerance.

The SCR is a target level of capital. This distinguishes the SCR from the solvency margin under Solvency I. This concept of a target level of capital, which was clearly present during the discussions preceding the development of Solvency II,[180] is not specifically stated in the legal text, which does not provide a definition of the SCR. It is however very clearly expressed in Art. 41 of the Swiss Ordinance on the supervision of private insurance undertakings in the context of the Swiss Solvency Test (SST): "An insurance company meets the solvency condition under the SST at a given point in time if, at that point in time, the risk-bearing capital is at least equal to the target capital."[181]

That the SCR is a target level of capital was implicitly recognised by the EC when it examined the equivalence of the SST with Solvency II. Because the SST was inspired by the same considerations as Solvency II, it should come as no surprise that the EC considers the treatment of the target capital under the SST to be equally strong as the treatment of the SCR under Solvency II:

> "The main capital requirement, known as the *target capital* under the SST, is calculated to cover unexpected losses arising from the existing business. In addition, the absolute minimum capital requirement (minimum capital) for insurers varies under the SST depending on the insurance business line. Both requirements are at least as strong as the corresponding Directive 2009/138/EC requirements for all current Swiss insurers' combinations of business lines."[182]

The SCR is also an early-warning signal that allows supervisory authorities to intervene at an early stage. Temporary breaches of the SCR are therefore tolerated and will not prevent the undertaking from continuing as a going concern, but they will lead to supervisory action. This is part of the supervisory review process (SRP) (see further, Chapter 7, section 2). Under Solvency II, it is of the utmost importance that there is an ongoing dialogue between the supervisory authority and the supervised undertakings. Supervisory authorities should know the undertaking and understand when a breach of the SCR is a sign of financial distress that goes beyond the normal volatility of the SCR. Upon breaching the SCR, the management of the undertaking should meet with the supervisory authority in order to discuss the causes of the breach and the measures needed to restore the target capital as soon as possible. Depending on

---

180 It was even referred to as "desired capital" in the early stages; See also, ELING, M., SCHMEISER, H. and SCHMIT, J.T., The Solvency II Process: Overview and Critical Analysis, *Risk Management and Insurance Review*, 2007, No 1, p. 75.

181 Verordnung vom 9. November 2005 über die Beaufsichtigung von privaten Versicherungsunternehmen, Amtliche Sammlung, 2005, p. 5305.

182 Recital 11 Commission Delegated Decision 2015/1602/EU of 5 June 2015 on the equivalence of the solvency and prudential regime for insurance and reinsurance undertakings in force in Switzerland based on Articles 172 (2), 227 (4) and 260 (3) of Directive 2009/138/EC of the EP and of the Council, *OJ* L 248, 24.9.2015, p. 95.

the level of the breach, the supervisory ladder of intervention will determine the action to be taken (see further, Chapter 7, section 2.3).[183]

Initially, the SCR was seen as a soft threshold.[184] This changed during the negotiations of the FD, in order to ensure that all supervisory authorities would deal with the SCR in the same way. Although the SCR under Solvency II is a target level of capital, it is not a "mere" target, i.e. a threshold that requires no action when breached.[185] Undertakings must immediately inform the supervisory authority of a breach or expected breach of the SCR and action must be undertaken (Art. 138 FD). The SCR should not however be understood as a hard measure that can never be breached, requiring the solvency capital to always be well above 100%. That is the role of the MCR. The SCR should therefore always be higher than the MCR. Because of the design of the MCR, this is not always the case. Situations may occur where the MCR exceeds the SCR. This is not the intention and will be rather unusual. One of the reasons why such situations might occur is the absolute floor that was introduced for the MCR and which might be too high in certain cases, for instance in the case of a small insurer that has bought reinsurance for 100%, which would result in a low SCR amount.

4.2. SOLVENCY CAPITAL REQUIREMENT

4.2.1. General Principles

The body of the FD does not contain a definition of the SCR. A definition is however included in recital 62 FD:

> "The SCR reflects a level of eligible own funds that enables insurers to absorb significant losses and that gives reasonable assurance to policyholders and beneficiaries that payments will be made as they fall due."

Member States must require (re)insurance undertakings to hold eligible own funds covering the SCR (Art. 100 FD).[186] This basically means that the

---

183 As stated by Standard & Poor's: "It is important that the SCR functions as a target rather than a minimum. The perception of some market participants, and even some insurance supervisors, is that the SCR is a minimum requirement and insurers may therefore take action (possibly including forced asset sales) to avoid breaching it": Standard & Poor's, Basel III and Solvency II could have unintended cross-sectoral consequences, Global Credit Portal, RatingsDirect, 28 February 2012, p. 6.

184 See SANDSTRÖM, A., *Handbook of Solvency for Actuaries and Risk Managers. Theory and Practice*, Chapman & Hall/CRC, Boca Raton, 2011, p. 579.

185 See also SCHUERMANS, P., Solvency II: A Balancing Act, in KEMPLER, C., FLAMEE, M., YANG, C.H. and WINDELS, P. (Eds.), *Global Perspectives on Insurance Today*, Palgrave Macmillan, New York, 2013, p. 39.

186 For the definition of eligible own funds, see above, section 3.

solvency ratio (eligible own funds/SCR%) must be 100%. In implementing the FD, some Member States have added the requirement that (re)insurance undertakings must ensure, on a permanent basis, that the SCR will always be at the level required by law.[187] As indicated before, too narrow an interpretation of this requirement should be avoided, as this would ignore the by definition volatile nature of the SCR because of the market-consistent valuation of assets and liabilities and would indirectly introduce a new requirement, i.e. a requirement to have a solvency ratio that is always well above 100%.

The SCR is calculated on the presumption that the undertaking will pursue its business as a going concern. It covers existing business, as well as the new business expected to be written over the following 12 months. With respect to existing business, it covers only unexpected losses, as expected losses are covered by technical provisions and asset valuations are based on market expectations. It corresponds to the VaR of the basic own funds of the undertaking to a confidence level of 99.5% over a one-year period (Art. 101 FD).

The SCR covers (at least) the following *quantifiable risks* (Art. 101 (4) FD):
- non-life underwriting risk, i.e. the risk (due to inadequate pricing and provisioning assumptions) arising from non-life (re)insurance obligations in relation to the perils covered and the processes used in the conduct of business;[188]
- life underwriting risk, i.e. the risk (due to inadequate pricing and provisioning assumptions) arising from life (re)insurance obligations, in relation to the perils covered and the processes used in the conduct of business;[189]
- health underwriting risk, i.e. the risk (due to inadequate pricing and provisioning assumptions) arising from the underwriting of health (re)insurance obligations, whether it is pursued on a similar technical basis to that of life insurance or not, following from both perils covered and the processes used in the conduct of business;[190]
- market risk, i.e. the risk arising from the level or volatility of market prices of financial instruments that have an impact upon the value of the assets and liabilities of the undertaking and the structural mismatch between assets and liabilities (duration gap);[191]
- credit risk or counterparty default risk, i.e. the risk of possible losses due to unexpected default or deterioration in the credit standing of counterparties and debtors over the following 12 months;[192]

---

187 See, for instance, Art. 74 of the Belgian Law of 13 March 2016 on the supervision of insurance and reinsurance undertakings. A coordinated version of this law is available on the website of the National Bank of Belgium.

188 Arts. 13 (30) and 105 (2) FD.

189 Arts. 13 (30) and 105 (3) FD.

190 Arts. 13 (30) and 105 (4) FD.

191 Art. 105 (5) FD.

192 Art. 105 (6) FD.

- operational risk, i.e. the risk of loss arising from inadequate or failed internal processes, personnel or systems, or from external events, including risks arising from strategic decisions but excluding reputation risks.[193]

Particularly after the financial crisis, the question was raised whether liquidity risk – i.e. the risk of (re)insurance undertakings not being able to realise investments and other assets in order to settle their financial obligations when they fall due because of a lack of sufficient cash or other liquid assets – should also be part of the SCR. CEIOPS[194] advised not including it because it was considered less important and because it is difficult to calculate.[195] However, it was agreed that liquidity risk should be taken into account as part of risk assessment under Pillar 2, both through the ORSA (see further, Chapter 7, section 3.4.2) and the SRP (see further, Chapter 7, section 2).[196] A good example can be found in Art. 44 (2), third subparagraph FD, which requires (re)insurance undertakings applying the MA or the VA to set up a liquidity plan projecting the incoming and outgoing cash flows in relation to the assets and liabilities subject to these adjustments.

Besides liquidity risk, the SCR does not include other types of known or emerging risks,[197] such as systemic risk – i.e. the risk of disruption to the financial system that is caused by an impairment of all or parts of the financial system and that has the potential to have serious negative consequences for the real economy[198] – that may be relevant depending on the activity exercised by the undertaking. The question of whether certain activities of (re)insurance undertakings, certain (re)insurance undertakings or more broadly the (re)insurance sector may be systemically risky is controversial.[199]

---

193 Arts. 13 (33) and 101 (4), second subparagraph FD.

194 CEIOPS, Lessons learned from the crisis (Solvency II and beyond), CEIOPS-SEC-107/08, 19 March 2009, p. 9

195 This was also the view of the CRO Forum, which argued that requiring capital to provide for liquidity risk was an ineffective means of managing that risk. Liquidity is a risk to be managed at all times and no amount of capital can replace comprehensive liquidity risk management. See CRO Forum, *Liquidity Risk Management. Best Risk Management Practices*, October 2008, p. 6.

196 Liquidity risk is becoming more important, as many insurers are moving from traditional insurance products to asset management-type products, which reduces their exposure to interest rate risk but renders them more vulnerable to liquidity risk.

197 For a further analysis of the various risks, see EC, *Study into the methodologies to assess the overall financial position of an insurance undertaking from the perspective of prudential supervision*, May 2002, pp. 19–29 (the KPMG Report).

198 This is the definition that was developed by the Financial Stability Board. See FSB, IMF and BIS, *Report to the G20 Finance Ministers and Governors. Guidance to Assess the Systemic Importance of Financial Institutions, Markets and Instruments: Initial Considerations*, October 2009, p. 5.

199 See IAIS, *Systemic Risk and the Insurance Sector; Insurance and Financial Stability; Global Systemically Important Insurers; Initial Assessment Methodology; Global Systemically Important Insurers: Policy Measures; Systemic risk from insurance product features (previously referred to as Non-traditional Non-insurance activities*, 16 June 2016, 26 p. See also ESRB, *Report on systemic risks in the EU insurance sector*, December 2015, 93 p.; the Geneva Association,

Any material risks that the undertaking has identified and that are not fully covered in the calculation of the SCR must be communicated to the supervisory authority in the regular supervisory report (RSR) (Art. 308 (3) (c) DA). These risks must be taken into account under Pillar 2.

4.2.1.1. Frequency of Calculation

The SCR must be calculated at least once every year. The result of that calculation must be reported to the supervisory authority. Undertakings must hold eligible own funds that cover the last reported SCR (Art. 102 FD).

Because of the complexity of calculating it,[200] undertakings do not have to calculate the SCR as frequently as the MCR, which must be calculated on a quarterly basis.[201] They must however monitor the amount of eligible own funds and the SCR on an ongoing basis. If the risk profile deviates significantly from the assumptions underlying the last reported SCR, the undertaking concerned must recalculate the SCR without delay and report it to the supervisory authority. Where there is evidence to suggest that the risk profile of the undertaking has altered significantly since the date on which the SCR was last reported, the supervisory authority may require the undertaking concerned to recalculate the SCR (Art. 102 FD). In exceptional circumstances, the supervisory authority may, following the SRP, impose a capital add-on (Art. 37 FD).

4.2.1.2. Supervisory Reporting and Public Disclosure

Information about the SCR must be provided to the supervisory authority in the RSR (Arts. 35 (1) (a) FD and 311 DA). This includes information about the expected developments of the undertaking's anticipated SCR over its

Systemic Risk in Insurance: An analysis of insurance and financial stability, March 2010, 118 p. There is an abundant literature on the subject. See, for instance, ACHARYA, V., PHILIPPON, T. and RICHARDSON, M., Measuring Systemic Risk for Insurance Companies, in HUFELD, F., KOIJEN, R.S.J. and THIMANN, C. (Eds.), *The Economics, Regulation and Systemic Risk of Insurance Markets*, Oxford University Press, New York, 2017; BALUCH, F., MUTENGA, S. and PARSONS, C., Insurance, Systemic Risk and the Financial Crisis, *The Geneva Papers on Risk and Insurance – Issues and Practice*, Vol. 36, No 1, January 2011, pp. 4–49; GUINE, C., Global Systemically Important Insurers, in EIOPA, *Financial Stability Report 2014*, EIOPA-FS-14, 14 May 2014, pp. 54–63; HUFELD, F., A Regulatory Framework for Systemic Risk in the Insurance industry, in HUFELD, F., KOIJEN, R.S.J. and THIMANN, C. (Eds.), *The Economics, Regulation and Systemic Risk of Insurance Markets*, Oxford University Press, New York, 2017. The issue of systemic risk is also raised in the context of the debate on macroprudential policy. See, EIOPA, Discussion Paper on Systemic Risk and Macroprudential Policy in Insurance, EIOPA-BoS-19-131, 29 March 2019, 46 p.

200 Depending on the size and the complexity of the undertaking, the calculation of the SCR might take several days.

201 Art. 129 (4) FD.

business planning time period given the undertaking's business strategy, as well as information on any reasonably foreseeable risk of non-compliance with the undertaking's SCR and the undertaking's plans for ensuring that compliance is maintained.

The amount of the SCR, as well as further information regarding the SCR (such as the undertaking's capital management policy), must be included in the "Capital management" section of the SFCR. That section must also include information about any significant non-compliance with the SCR during the reporting period, and in particular the duration and maximum amount of each significant non-compliance, an explanation of its origin and the consequences, as well as any remedial measures taken and an explanation of the effects of such remedial measures. Where a significant non-compliance with the SCR has not subsequently been resolved, the amount of the non-compliance at the reporting date must be disclosed (Arts. 51 (1) (ii) FD and 297 (5) (c) and (d) DA).

The disclosure of the SCR must show separately the amount calculated on the basis of the standard formula or on the basis of an internal model. It must also include any capital add-on imposed by the supervisory authority, as well as the impact of the use of USPs, together with concise information on its justification by the supervisory authority (Art. 51 (2) FD). Member States may provide that the information concerning capital add-ons and the use of USPs need not be separately disclosed during a transitional period ending no later than 31 December 2020. This option does not prevent disclosure that might be required by other legal or regulatory requirements, such as capital market requirements. The information may indeed be price sensitive from a capital market perspective. The disclosure must, where applicable, be accompanied by an indication that its final amount is still subject to supervisory assessment.

4.2.1.3. Non-Compliance with the SCR

As stated above (section 4.1), a breach of the SCR does not mean that the undertaking is insolvent.[202] It is designed to provide the supervisory authority with a so-called "supervisory ladder of intervention" (see further, Chapter 7, section 2.3). This ensures that the supervisory response is tailored to the specific situation of the undertaking.[203]

In order to prevent a breach of the SCR and because of the volatility of own funds resulting from a market-consistent valuation of assets and liabilities,

---

202 For the transitional measure for undertakings that complied with Solvency I capital requirements at the end of 2015 but did not comply with the SCR in the first year of application of Solvency II, see above, Chapter 3, section 4.3.14.

203 MONTALVO, C., *Understanding a breach of the SCR*, 29 January 2012, https://www.solvencyiiwire.com/understanding-a-breach-of-the-scr/7928.

it is sometimes argued that (re)insurance undertakings must hold a volatility capital buffer, which ensures that the undertaking meets the SCR on a continuous basis.[204]

As indicated above, a breach of the SCR as a result of market volatility should in principle not be a major cause for concern. Establishing a volatility capital buffer might provide the undertaking with more comfort and seems to be widespread, as most (re)insurance undertakings hold levels of capital that are well above that required by law.

A number of measures may automatically kick in upon a breach of the SCR, such as the cancellation or deferral of dividends and distributions. Whether it is a cancellation or deferral depends on the nature and tiering of the own-fund item (Arts. 71 (1) (l), 73 (1) (g) and 77 (1) (f) DA.

A (re)insurer must immediately inform its supervisory authority as soon as it observes that it no longer complies with the SCR or where there is a risk of non-compliance in the following three months (Art. 138 FD). The following procedure applies:

- submission of a realistic recovery plan for approval by the supervisory authority within two months of the observation of non-compliance;
- adoption of the necessary measures to re-establish the level of eligible own funds or to reduce the risk profile in order to ensure compliance with the SCR within six months of the observation of non-compliance;
- extension by the supervisory authority of the recovery period by three months, where appropriate.

There are no formalities required for the recovery plan. It can however be presumed that the plan must be submitted in writing because it must be officially approved by the supervisory authority. The recovery plan must be realistic (as opposed to "wishful thinking") and must at least include particulars or evidence of the following:

- estimates of management expenses, in particular current general expenses and commissions;
- estimates of income and expenditure in respect of direct business, reinsurance acceptances and reinsurance cessions;
- a forecast balance sheet;
- estimates of the financial resources intended to cover technical provisions and the SCR and the MCR;
- the overall reinsurance policy.

---

204 ZUBOR, Z., Volatility capital buffer to prevent the breach of the Solvency II capital requirements, *Financial and Economic Review*, 2016, Vol. 15, No 1, pp. 91–123.

Where a (re)insurance undertaking has agreed to take over a portfolio of insurance contracts from another (re)insurance undertaking established in another MS, the supervisory authority of the accepting undertaking that has requested a recovery plan from that undertaking because of non-compliance with the SCR may not issue the certificate referred to in Art. 39 FD indicating that the undertaking possesses the necessary capital to cover the SCR so long as the authority considers that the rights of the policyholders or the contractual obligations of the undertaking are threatened (Art. 142 (2) FD). This means in practice that the transfer of portfolio cannot be executed before the accepting undertaking has re-established its eligible own funds at a level that is at least that of the SCR.

It may well be that the financial situation of the undertaking deteriorates and that further measures are necessary. In exceptional circumstances, the supervisory authority may restrict or prohibit the free disposal of the assets of the undertaking. If the undertaking is carrying out cross-border activities, the home supervisory authority needs to inform the supervisory authorities of the host MS in which the undertaking carries out its activities of any measures taken. These authorities may take the same measures (restriction or prohibition of the free disposal of assets) in cooperation with the supervisory authority of the home MS (Art. 138 (5) FD). Further measures may be taken by supervisory authorities to safeguard the interests of policyholders (Art. 141 FD).

The statutory auditor must report promptly to the supervisory authority any non-compliance with the SCR (Art. 72 (1) (d) FD).

If an individual undertaking does not comply with the SCR, it is clear that this is a problem, as compliance with the SCR is in the interest of policyholders. The situation must be redressed as soon as possible. This can be done by finding new capital, by moving out of areas or activities that are too risky or by taking other strategic actions. Action must be taken in close cooperation with the supervisory authority, which may already have received advance warning when examining and discussing the ORSA report with the undertaking concerned.

If a number of undertakings find themselves in a similar situation, the problem becomes slightly different. It may well be that for a variety of reasons, for instance the low interest rate environment, a number of (re)insurance undertakings experience serious difficulties. In that case, it has to be possible for the supervisory authority to agree with the undertakings concerned appropriate measures to deal with the adverse situation, including a progress report every three months.

Because the insurance industry was afraid that supervisory authorities might not show sufficient understanding in situations of severe distress, Omnibus II introduced a new provision in the FD that deals with this type of situation and allows the supervisory authority to extend the additional recovery period of three months by a further period of a maximum of seven years,[205] with a progress report every three months.

The procedure involves intervention by EIOPA and possibly by the ESRB. Through the required intervention by EIOPA, the FD ensures a level playing field between Member States. Supervisory authorities cannot use this measure to favour (re)insurance undertakings in their own national markets.

The procedure can be summarised as follows (Art. 138 (4) FD):
- a supervisory authority requests EIOPA to declare the existence of an exceptional adverse situation;
- EIOPA may consult the ESRB before declaring the existence of an exceptional adverse situation;
- once EIOPA has declared the existence of an exceptional adverse situation, the supervisory authority may decide on an extension of the recovery period and determine its length for individual insurance and reinsurance undertakings;
- EIOPA, in cooperation with the supervisory authority concerned, assesses on a regular basis whether the exceptional adverse situation persists and declares when the exceptional adverse situation has ceased to exist.

The supervisory authority may only request action by EIOPA if (re)undertakings representing a significant share of the market or of the affected lines of business are unlikely to recover from their situation of non-compliance with the SCR following the normal procedure (Art. 138 (4), second subparagraph FD).

Exceptional adverse situations exist where the financial situation of (re)insurance undertakings representing a significant share of the market or of the affected lines of business are seriously or adversely affected by one or more of the following conditions:

- a fall in financial markets which is unforeseen, sharp and steep;
- a persistent low interest rate environment;
- a high-impact catastrophic event.

Although, initially, the concern related specifically to possible adverse situations resulting from the financial crisis, the extension of the recovery period was also made applicable to high-impact catastrophic events, which includes natural catastrophes. EIOPA has not yet received a request to declare an exceptional adverse situation.

---

205 Before amendment by Omnibus II, Art. 138 (4) FD did allow supervisory authorities to extend the recovery period in the case of an exceptional fall in financial markets by an appropriate period of time, taking into account all relevant factors.

In assessing whether an exceptional adverse situation exists, EIOPA must take account of the factors and criteria listed in Art. 288 DA. These include, for instance, possible pro-cyclical effects of re-establishing compliance with the SCR, including distressed sales of assets on financial markets. In deciding on an extension and on the length of the extension of the recovery period, the supervisory authority must take account of the factors and criteria listed in Art. 289 DA. To ensure a consistent approach to the extension of the recovery period, on 14 September 2015 EIOPA issued its Guidelines on the extension of the recovery period in exceptional adverse situations.[206] The Guidelines relate in particular to the decision to grant an extension, the duration of the extension and the withdrawal and revocation of the extension.

The (re)insurance undertakings concerned must submit a progress report to the supervisory authority every three months, setting out the measures taken and the progress made to re-establish the level of eligible own funds or to reduce the risk profile. The extension of the recovery period is withdrawn where the progress report shows that no significant progress has been made between the date of the observation of non-compliance and the date of submission of the progress report (Art. 138 (4), fourth and fifth subparagraphs FD).

The following table shows the number of undertakings that were in breach of the SCR (taking into account all LTG measures and equity measures applied) on 31 December 2017. For EEA countries not listed in the table, all undertakings met the SCR.

Figure 14. Number of undertakings in breach of the SCR

Country	Undertakings breaching the SCR	Market share in non-life gross written premiums	Market share in life technical provisions
BU	1	5.86%	0.00%
CY	1	6.15%	0.00%
CZ	1	1.27%	0.00%
GR	1	2.89%	1.77%
IE	1	0.94%	0.00%
LU	6	1.83%	0.04%
NL	1	0.00%	0.00%
NO	1	1.17%	0.00%
PT	2	5.25%	0.34%
UK	10	0.32%	0.00%
Total EEA	**25**	**0.39%**	**0.01%**

Source: EIOPA, Report on long-term guarantee measures and measures on equity risk 2018, EIOPA-BoS-18/471, 18 December 2018, p. 188.

[206] EIOPA, Guidelines on the extension of the recovery period in exceptional adverse situations, EIOPA-BoS-15/108, 14 September 2015.

4.2.2. *Standard Formula*

4.2.2.1. General Principles and Structure

4.2.2.1.1. General Principles

The SCR can be calculated either in accordance with the standard formula or using an internal model approved by the supervisory authority (Art. 100, second subparagraph FD).[207]

In a risk-based solvency capital regime, it would be logical for all undertakings to calculate the SCR on the basis of an internal model, as only an internal model can fully capture the specific risk situation of an individual undertaking. Considering the importance of the reform and the fact that the large majority of the market is made up of small and medium-sized undertakings, it would have been unreasonable to require all undertakings to calculate their SCR on the basis of an internal model. Although risk modelling has existed in insurance for a long time, it is fair to say that only a relatively small number of mostly large (re)insurance groups had experience with developing a full internal model when the FD was drafted. Furthermore, supervisory authorities did not have much experience with the approval of internal models and lacked the necessary resources to deal with them.

A standard formula is generally viewed as advantageous because it provides a benchmark against which the individual situation of different undertakings can be assessed. Developing a standard formula for the large majority of (re)insurance undertakings in the EEA proved quite a challenge. It was developed by a working group within CEIOPS/EIOPA and extensively tested through various QIS.[208] The standard formula changed considerably during the testing phase. Initially considered too simple (to the disadvantage of small and medium-sized undertakings), it was expanded and again reduced in size at the request of large (re)insurance undertakings, which feared that too detailed a standard formula would take away the incentive for undertakings to develop their own internal model.[209]

The final standard formula is therefore a compromise and it was agreed from the outset that it would be adapted regularly based upon the experience gathered

---

207 For more information, see EIOPA, The underlying assumptions in the standard formula for the Solvency Capital Requirement calculation, EIOPA-14-322, 25 July 2014, 76 p.

208 A number of standard models already existed prior to the development of Solvency II and served as examples. For an overview, see CEA and Mercer Oliver Wyman, *Solvency Assessment Models Compared. Essential Groundwork for the Solvency II Project*, 2005, 50 p. See also EC, *Study into the methodologies to assess the overall financial position of an insurance undertaking from the perspective of prudential supervision*, May 2002, Appendix, pp. 18–68 (the KPMG Report).

209 Rating agencies still use their own capital adequacy model, which is different from the standard formula. See, for instance, Standard & Poor's, Standard & Poor's highlights differences in capital adequacy between its methodology and Europe's solvency II framework, Global Credit Portal, RatingsDirect, February 2010, 16 p. and The impact of solvency II capital adequacy on our rating analysis for European insurers, Standard & Poor's Rating Services, 19 May 2015, 5 p.

in its application. This is the reason why only the structure of the standard formula is included in an Annex to the FD, while the details of the formula itself were moved to the implementing measures and can be found in the Annexes to the DA. Since its adoption, the standard formula has been changed three times.[210] A fourth amendment was carried out in 2019 as part of the 2018 review of the DA. The proposed amendment has been adopted by the EC[211] but has not yet been officially published. The key objectives of this first major review were to make greater use of the proportionality principle and to simplify the standard formula.[212] Indeed, it cannot be denied that the standard formula is very complex.

The following diagram sets out the modular architecture of the standard formula.

Figure 15. Standard formula for the SCR

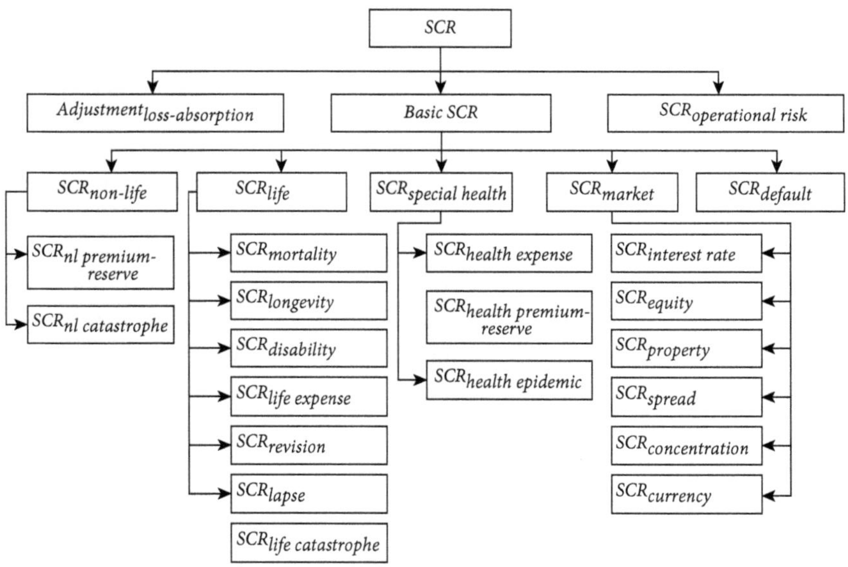

---

210 Commission Delegated Regulation (EU) 2016/467 of 30 September 2015 amending Commission Delegated Regulation (EU) 2015/35 concerning the calculation of regulatory capital requirements for several categories of assets held by insurance and reinsurance undertakings, *OJ* L 85, 1.4.2016, p. 6; Commission Delegated Regulation (EU) 2017/1542 of 8 June 2017 amending Delegated Regulation (EU) 2015/35 concerning the calculation of regulatory capital requirements for certain categories of assets held by insurance and reinsurance undertakings (infrastructure corporates), *OJ* L *236*, 14.09.2017, p. 14; Commission Delegated Regulation (EU) 2018/1221 of 1 June 2018 amending Delegated Regulation (EU) 2015/35 as regards the calculation of regulatory capital requirements for securitisations and simple, transparent and standardised securitisations held by insurance and reinsurance undertakings, *OJ* L 227, 10.9.2018, p. 1.

211 The document was published on the EC's Better Regulation website on 9 November 2018 and was formally adopted by the EC on 8 March 2019. See, Commission Delegated Regulation (EU) of 8 March 2019 amending Delegated Regulation (EU) 2015/35 supplementing the Solvency II Directive.

212 See the EC's request for advice from EIOPA on the review of specific items in the Solvency II Delegated Regulation, dated 18 July 2016, and the advice delivered by EIOPA on 30 October 2017, EIOPA-BoS-17/280, 137 p. and on 28 February 2018, EIOPA-BoS-18/075, 612 p.

The standard formula aims to capture the material quantifiable risks to which most undertakings are exposed. The standard formula might however not cover all material risks to which a specific undertaking is exposed (see above, section 4.2.1). A standard formula is, by its very nature and design, a standardised calculation method and is therefore not tailored to the individual risk profile of a specific undertaking. For this reason, in some cases the standard formula might not reflect the risk profile of a specific undertaking and consequently the level of own funds it needs. This might become apparent as a result of the ORSA or the SRP.

(Re)insurance undertakings can adapt the standard formula to better reflect their own specific risks by using USPs. Alternatively, they can develop a partial internal model for specific risks or completely depart from the standard formula by developing their own internal model.

As indicated in the EC's impact assessment for the FD,[213] a number of possible approaches exist to calculate capital requirements using a standard formula. These range from simple factor-based approaches to more complex scenario-based approaches.

A factor-based approach involves multiplying a specified factor by a risk exposure measure, often an item from the insurer's balance sheet or profit and loss account. This factor is calibrated in line with a specified confidence level and time horizon and/or the volatility or uncertainty that it is trying to capture. For example, a fixed proportion of provisions for outstanding claims is a natural proxy for measuring provisioning risk in non-life insurance.

A factor-based approach has the advantage of being simple to describe and to calculate. Its main drawbacks are that it is often not that risk-sensitive as it does not capture the specificities of an individual insurer's risk profile. Indeed, it is generally recognised that for certain types of risk, a factor-based approach will not work, because of the uniqueness of risks covered by each insurer, the difficulty in defining a loss distribution or the importance of infrequent yet catastrophic losses. Factor-based approaches also struggle with the interaction between assets and liabilities, for instance in the case of insurance liabilities with loss-absorbing capacity (participating business). In addition, risk mitigation and tax are not easy to capture.

Under a scenario-based approach, insurers are required to test their solvency position against a range of adverse conditions by assessing the impact of a number of defined scenarios on their overall financial standing. For example, for the purpose of calculating the capital charge for interest rate risk, insurance undertakings could be required to assess the change in net asset value of all their interest-rate-sensitive instruments (fixed-income investments, insurance

---

[213] EC, Commission Staff Working Document: Accompanying document to the Proposal for a Directive of the European Parliament and of the Council on the taking-up and pursuit of the business of Insurance and Reinsurance. Solvency II: Impact Assessment Report, SEC (2007) 871, 10 July 2007, pp. 123–127.

liabilities, loans and derivatives) following an upward and a downward shock in interest rates.

A scenario-based approach is more risk-sensitive than a simple factor-based approach and can be dynamic (i.e. can take account of how management would react to the event underlying the scenario during a specified time horizon). Its main drawbacks are that it can be difficult to find scenarios that can be tested using available data and that represent a worst-case event for the vast majority of insurers, given the uniqueness of the risks covered by individual insurers. In addition, compliance costs can be high, as testing usually requires a substantial amount of IT and modelling work to be conducted.

The standard formula was first tested in QIS 2. It was based on a modular approach whereby individual risk exposures are assessed and then aggregated. In line with the economic risk-based approach of Solvency II and after testing in further quantitative impact studies (QIS 3, QIS 4 and QIS 5), the EC decided to adopt a mixed approach in the standard formula, whereby a factor-based approach is followed for some risk modules and a scenario-based approach for other risk modules. Where a scenario-based approach is chosen, a simplified factor-based approach can be used as a proxy by (re)insurance undertakings with simple risk profiles.

The SCR standard formula uses a building-block approach to compute the overall SCR. First, capital requirements are calculated for individual component risks, such as non-life underwriting risk, life underwriting risk, health underwriting risk, market risk, credit risk and operational risk. These amounts are then combined using correlation factors to obtain the overall capital requirement (SCR). In some cases, the individual component risks are themselves composed of sub-risks, as is the case with market risk, life risk, non-life risk and health risk. In these cases, the capital requirements for the sub-risks are combined (using specified correlation factors) to determine the capital requirement for the relevant individual component risk.

To understand the calibration in the standard formula, it is important to know the component risks and sub-risks that are used, how these risks or sub-risks are individually calibrated, how the correlation factors are determined and how the results are combined to produce the SCR.[214]

To ensure that the overall SCR is calibrated using the VaR of the basic own funds of an undertaking subject to a confidence level of 99.5% over a one-year time horizon, this calibration is applied to each individual risk module in a consistent manner.

The outcome of a risk module is usually determined by calculating how a prescribed scenario would affect the balance sheet of a (re)insurance undertaking. For instance, in the case of equity risk, i.e. the risk an undertaking runs by

214 See, HERZOG, Th., *Summary of CEIOPS calibration work on standard formula*, 5 January 2011, pp. 2–3, https://www.naic.org/documents/index_smi_solvency_ii_calibration.pdf.

investing in equities, the scenario would be a sharp fall in the stock market. The outcome of the module is the decline in the own funds of the undertaking as a result of the scenario.

The SCR covers all quantifiable risks for existing business as well as new business expected to be written in the following 12 months. However, in the scenario-based calculations under the standard formula, the changes in the value of assets and liabilities over the 12 months following the scenario stress are not taken into account, given the instantaneous nature of the stresses. Therefore, in such cases, the capital requirements do not take into account the profit or loss of the business expected to be written in the following months.

Factor-based calculations are used for sub-modules where a scenario-based approach was not considered to be most appropriate (for example, the operational risk module). Factor-based calculations make it possible to capture risks associated with new business expected to be written in the following 12 months. However, the effects of risk-mitigation techniques are more difficult to take into account when using a formula-based calculation.

The outcomes of all risk modules are aggregated step by step. For this purpose, use is made of correlations that show the connection between different risk modules. Basically, these correlations provide an estimate of the probability of different risks occurring at the same time. In cases where risks always occur simultaneously, the outcomes of the modules must be aggregated to determine the capital requirement. If the likelihood of risks occurring simultaneously is low, the risks are considered to be diversified and the capital requirement is therefore lower than the sum of the modules.

The selection of the correlation parameters has a significant influence on the final SCR, since the choice of correlation parameters has an impact on the level of diversification recognised within the standard formula. The aggregation in the standard formula is based on the assumption that the dependence between the distributions can be fully captured by linear correlations. For risks that are unrelated, a low correlation parameter is chosen.

The scenario-based calculations of the SCR standard formula are based on the impact of instantaneous stresses on the basic own funds of insurance undertakings. All of the following assumptions are made in that calculation:

- the scenario does not change the size of the risk margin included in technical provisions;
- the scenario does not change the value of deferred tax assets and liabilities;
- the scenario does not change the value of future discretionary benefits included in technical provisions;[215]
- no management actions are taken by the undertaking during the scenario.[216]

---

215 This is captured in the adjustment for LAC-DT. See further, section 4.2.2.4.

216 Art. 83 (1) DA.

Some quantifiable risks are not specifically covered by the standard formula (see above, section 4.2.1), for instance because the data is very scarce or because the exposure is not always material enough to justify a separate and more granular SCR quantification within the context of the standard formula (for instance, a further subdivision of property risk). Other risks have not been included on purpose, because they are expected to be covered through Pillar 2 requirements, i.e. through risk management requirements for the appropriate monitoring and disclosure of the risk profile of the undertaking.

Besides systemic risk and liquidity risk (see above, section 4.2.1), other risks that are not included in the standard formula include: inflation risk (sensitivity to changes in the term structure of inflation rates); reputation risk (risk related to the trustworthiness of the undertaking); contagion risk (risk that an adverse event or situation will spread from one undertaking to another); legal environment risk[217] (risk resulting from a sudden or unexpected change in the legal environment); and the risk resulting from equity and interest rate volatility.

The underlying assumptions in the standard formula for the SCR calculation were published by EIOPA.[218] Further details on the standard formula itself (the various risk modules, the calibration factors, the correlation factors and the various formulas) are included in the DA and in annexes to the FD and to the DA. Useful information can also be found in the advice delivered by CEIOPS/EIOPA during the course of developing the standard formula and in the technical specifications given by CEIOPS/EIOPA in the context of the QIS. The material is extensive and only the main elements are reflected in this book.

a. Undertaking-Specific Parameters

The FD recognises the inherent weakness of a standardised approach by allowing undertakings to adapt the standard formula using undertaking-specific parameters (USPs), i.e. by replacing a subset of parameters within the standard formula (standard parameters) by parameters specific to the undertaking (USPs), if the standard formula does not provide an appropriate representation of the underlying risks.[219] Undertakings can do so when

217 Legal environment risk must be distinguished from legal risk, which refers to the possibility of lawsuits, adverse judgments from courts or contracts turning out to be unenforceable or disrupting or adversely affecting the operations or condition of a (re)insurer. See CEA and Groupe Consultatif, *Solvency II Glossary*, March 2007, p. 36. Legal risk is included in operational risk (Art. 101 (4), second subparagraph FD).

218 EIOPA, The underlying assumptions in the standard formula for the SCR calculation, *EIOPA-14-322*, 25 July 2014, 74 p. This is also important for the ORSA. See Art. 45 (1) (c) FD.

219 The subset of standard parameters that may be replaced by USPs are listed in Art. 218 DA.

calculating the life, non-life and health underwriting risk modules. The use of USPs must be approved by the supervisory authority. The details of the approval procedure are laid down in a Commission Implementing Regulation of 24 March 2015.[220] Further guidance can be found in the EIOPA Guidelines.[221]

USPs must be calibrated on the basis of the internal data of the undertaking concerned or of data that is directly relevant for the operations of the undertaking. These data must be complete, accurate and appropriate, as explained in Art. 219 DA. When granting supervisory approval, supervisory authorities must verify the completeness, accuracy and appropriateness of the data used (Art. 104 (7) FD). For the calculation of USPs, undertakings can select a method from a number of standardised methods prescribed in Art. 220 DA and Annex XVII to the DA.

The possibility of using USPs should promote sound risk management. The decision to apply for the use of USPs is a strategic decision to be taken by the AMSB and should not be dictated only by a desire to lower capital requirements. The use of USPs should not however prevent an undertaking from reverting to the standard parameters if the USPs no longer reflect the risk profile of the undertaking. In that case, the undertaking should inform the supervisory authority of the reasons why the USPs are no longer appropriate.

When it is inappropriate to calculate the SCR in accordance with the standard formula because the risk profile of the undertaking concerned deviates significantly from the assumptions underlying the standard formula calculation, the supervisory authority might require the undertaking to use USPs (Art. 110 FD).

b. Look-Through Approach

The SCR must be calculated so as to ensure that all quantifiable risks to which a (re)insurance undertaking is exposed are taken into account. In order to ensure that (re)insurance undertakings understand the underlying risk of their investments in collective investment funds, Art. 84 (1) DA requires them to calculate their SCR on the basis of each of the underlying assets held by the fund. This is what is referred to as the "look-through approach". Art. 84 (2) DA extends this approach to indirect exposures to market risk (other than collective

---

220 Commission Implementing Regulation (EU) 2015/498 of 24 March 2015 laying down implementing technical standards with regard to the supervisory approval procedure to use undertaking-specific parameters in accordance with Directive 2009/138/EC of the European Parliament and of the Council, *OJ* L 79, 25.3.2015, p. 8. For the first year of application of Solvency II, 83 USPs were approved by NSAs and only two applications were rejected because of insufficient data. See EIOPA, First set of advice to the EC on specific items in the Solvency II Delegated Regulation, EIOPA-BoS-17/280, 30 October 2017, pp. 59–60.

221 EIOPA, Guidelines on undertaking-specific parameters, EIOPA-BoS-14/178, 2 February 2015, 7 p.

investment undertakings and investments packaged as funds), to underwriting risk and to counterparty default risk.

The look-through approach under the standard formula does not apply to investments in related undertakings (Art. 84 (4) DA). Following EIOPA's first set of advice to the EC in the context of the 2018 review of the DA, Art. 84 (4) DA was amended in 2019 so as to extend the application of the look-through approach to "investment-related undertakings", i.e. related undertakings that are substantially investment funds. Although this might lead to a lower SCR, as the SCR resulting from the underlying assets (for instance, 25% for property) might be lower than the SCR obtained from applying the equity risk capital charge (for instance, 49% for unlisted equity), applying the look-through approach is considered more risk-sensitive.[222]

Where the look-through approach cannot be applied to collective investment undertakings or investments packaged as funds, Art. 84 (3) DA allows for a simplified approach. The SCR may be calculated on the basis of the target underlying asset allocation of the collective investment undertaking or fund or, if the target underlying asset allocation is not available, on the basis of the last reported asset allocation of the collective investment undertaking or fund, provided that, in either case, the underlying assets are managed according to that target allocation or last reported allocation and that exposures and risks are not expected to vary materially over a short period of time. For the purposes of that calculation, data groupings may be used, provided they enable all relevant sub-modules and scenarios of the standard formula to be calculated in a prudent manner, and that they do not apply to more than 20% of the total value of the assets of the (re)insurance undertaking. Underlying assets backing unit-linked or index-linked obligations for which the market risk is borne by the policyholders must be excluded from this calculation.[223]

c. *Risk Mitigation*

In calculating the SCR, full account is taken of risk-mitigating techniques, such as reinsurance, securitisation[224] and derivatives,[225] provided that credit risk and other risks arising from the use of such techniques are properly reflected in the SCR.[226] This is an important departure from Solvency I and is perfectly

---

222 EIOPA, First set of advice to the EC on specific items in the Solvency II Delegated Regulation, EIOPA-BoS-17/280, 30 October 2017, p. 55.

223 Art. 84 (3) and (3a) DA as introduced by the EC after the 2018 review of the standard formula (forthcoming).

224 For instance, insurance-linked securities (ILS), such as catastrophe bonds. See also section 4.2.2.3.4.d. Spread Risk.

225 For instance, insurance derivatives that have their values related to loss events, such as catastrophe swaps or derivatives that reduce investment risk in the portfolio.

226 Art. 101 (5) FD.

logical in a risk-based solvency capital regime. Risk-mitigating techniques are part of risk management. To the extent that risks are appropriately captured (and possibly transferred), (re)insurance undertakings should be able to benefit from this.

Risk-mitigating techniques are defined in Art. 13 (36) FD as all techniques that enable a (re)insurance undertaking to transfer part or all of its risks to another party. To the extent that risk is effectively transferred, capital requirements will take this into account. Solvency II actively promotes good risk management by giving full[227] recognition to risk-mitigating measures. These measures can be deployed in each risk area (for instance investment) and are not limited to underwriting risk.

Chapter V, section 10 DA lays down the requirements for risk mitigation through reinsurance,[228] finite reinsurance and other financial risk-mitigation techniques, including the use of collateral arrangements and guarantees.

Risk-mitigation techniques can only be taken into account when a number of qualitative criteria are met:[229]

(a) the contractual arrangements and transfer of risk are legally effective and enforceable in all relevant jurisdictions;[230]
(b) the (re)insurance undertaking has taken all appropriate steps to ensure the effectiveness of the arrangement and to address the risks related to that arrangement;
(c) the (re)insurance undertaking is able to monitor the effectiveness of the arrangement and the related risks on an ongoing basis;
(d) the (re)insurance undertaking has, in the event of a default, insolvency or bankruptcy of a counterparty or other credit event set out in the transaction documentation for the arrangement, a direct claim on that counterparty;
(e) there is no double counting of risk-mitigation effects in own funds and in the calculation of the SCR or within the calculation of the SCR.

Only risk-mitigation techniques that are in force for at least the next 12 months are fully taken into account in the basic SCR (BSCR). In all other cases, the

227 This has not been the case for non-proportional reinsurance and adverse development covers. There is a need to adapt the regulatory framework to recognise reinsurance more fully in all its operations, as an application of the proportionality principle.

228 See also EIOPA, Guidelines on application of outwards reinsurance arrangements to the non-life underwriting risk sub-module, EIOPA-BoS-14/173, 2 February 2015, 16 p. For new developments in reinsurance, see Swiss Re, Strategic reinsurance and insurance: the increasing trend of customised solutions, *Sigma*, 2016, No 5, 39 p.

229 Art. 209 (1) DA.

230 Important considerations are whether the contractual arrangement is subject to any condition that could undermine the effective transfer of risk, the fulfilment of which is outside the direct control of the undertaking, and whether there are any connected transactions that could undermine the effective transfer of risk (Art. 210 (4) DA).

risk-mitigation effect of risk-mitigation techniques that are in force for a period shorter than 12 months and that meet the qualitative criteria are taken into account in the BSCR in proportion to the length of time involved for the shorter of the full term of the risk exposure or the period that the risk-mitigation technique is in force.[231]

Where contractual arrangements governing the risk-mitigation techniques will be in force for a period shorter than the next 12 months and the (re)insurance undertaking intends to replace that risk-mitigation technique at the time of its expiry with a similar arrangement, the risk-mitigation technique is only fully taken into account in the BSCR when all of the following qualitative criteria are met:

(a) the (re)insurance undertaking has a written policy on the replacement of that risk-mitigation technique;
(b) the replacement of the risk-mitigation technique will not take place more often than every three months;
(c) the replacement of the risk-mitigation technique is not conditional on any future event that is outside of the control of the (re)insurance undertaking; where the replacement of the risk-mitigation technique is conditional on any future event that is within the control of the (re)insurance undertaking, then the conditions must be clearly documented in the written policy;
(d) the replacement of the risk-mitigation technique must be realistic based on replacements undertaken previously by the undertaking and consistent with its current business practice and business strategy;
(e) the risk that the risk-mitigation technique cannot be replaced due to an absence of liquidity in the market is not material;
(f) the risk that the cost of replacing the risk-mitigation technique increases during the following 12 months is reflected in the SCR;
(g) the replacement of the risk-mitigation technique is not contrary to the requirements that apply to future management actions.[232]

In order to qualify as a risk-mitigation technique, there must be an effective transfer of risk. The contractual arrangements governing the risk-mitigation technique must ensure that the extent of the cover provided by the risk-mitigation technique and the transfer of risk is clearly defined and incontrovertible. The contractual arrangement may not result in material basis risk or in the creation of other risks, unless this is reflected in the calculation of the SCR. Basis risk is material if it leads to a misstatement of the risk-mitigating effect on the (re)insurance undertaking's BSCR that could

[231] Art. 209 (2) DA.
[232] Art. 209 (3) DA.

influence the decision-making or judgement of the intended user of that information, including the supervisory authority.[233]

The most well-known risk-mitigation technique in insurance is *reinsurance*, which is the main mechanism for non-life insurance undertakings to mitigate their exposures.[234] Reinsurance is insurance purchased by an insurer (the ceding insurer) to provide protection against certain risks, primarily underwriting risks of the insurance policies issued by the insurer. Reinsurers assume these risks in exchange for a premium. Reinsurers may also retro-cede risks to other reinsurers. Other forms of risk transfer include alternative reinsurance arrangements, such as risk transfer to the capital markets.[235] After transferring insurance risk to a reinsurance undertaking, the risk becomes a credit risk, which must be taken into account under the counterparty default risk module (see Art. 196 DA).

Reinsurance is defined in Art. 13, point (7) FD as "the activity consisting in accepting risks ceded by an insurance undertaking or third-country insurance undertaking, or by another reinsurance undertaking or third-country reinsurance undertaking".[236] In order to have reinsurance recognised as a risk-mitigating technique for the calculation of the SCR, there must be an effective risk transfer.[237] In addition, the counterparty must be either a (re)insurance undertaking that complies with the SCR, a third-country (re)insurance undertaking situated in a country whose solvency regime is deemed equivalent or temporarily equivalent to Solvency II[238] and which complies with the solvency requirements of that third country, or a third-country (re)insurance undertaking which is not situated in a country whose solvency regime is deemed equivalent or temporarily equivalent to Solvency II but which has a CQS of 3 or better (Art. 211 (2) DA).[239]

---

233 Art. 210 (1), (2) and (3) DA.

234 Reinsurance also exists in life insurance. For an overview of different types of reinsurance, see IAIS, *Guidance Paper No 11 on Risk Transfer, Disclosure and Analysis of Finite Reinsurance*, October 2006, Appendix II, pp. 23–28. Reinsurance is particularly attractive for small undertakings with capital-intensive lines of business. See HALL, D.J. and BERSET, J., Toward Global Reinsurance Regulation, in KEMPLER, C., FLAMEE, M., YANG, C.H. and WINDELS, P. (Eds.), *Global Perspectives on Insurance Today*, Palgrave Macmillan, New York, 2013, pp. 100–101.

235 IAIS, ICP 13 – Reinsurance and Other Forms of Risk Transfer, para. 13.0.1.

236 There is a special definition of reinsurance in the context of Lloyd's (Art. 13, point (7) (b)). Providing cover to an occupational pension fund is now also considered reinsurance. See Art. 13, point (7) (c), introduced by Art. 63 of the IORP II Directive.

237 See also IAIS, ICP 13 – Reinsurance and Other Forms of Risk Transfer.

238 See Art. 172 FD and further, under Chapter 10.4.

239 In the context of Brexit, reinsurance cover provided by UK (re)insurance undertakings may fall under the last scenario, i.e. the risk-mitigating effect of the reinsurance contract can only be recognised if the undertaking has a rating of CQS 3 or better. Where (re)insurance undertakings currently account for reinsurance recoverables from a UK (re)insurance undertaking and that UK undertaking would no longer be authorised

The FD replaces the former collateral requirements that were sometimes imposed on reinsurance undertakings with risk-based capital charges on the primary insurer's balance sheet, capturing the risk of counterparty default by combining the probability of default and the LGD as a measure of the exposure. Insurance undertakings that are looking to cede business must now focus more on the financial strength of the counterparty and on its stability over the longer term. By diversifying their reinsurance coverage across several reinsurers, concentration risk can be avoided. On the other hand, this increases operational complexity, particularly for smaller insurance undertakings that are used to working with a single counterparty.

Where the counterparty to a reinsurance contract is a (re)insurance undertaking that ceases to comply with the SCR after the reinsurance contract has been entered into, the protection offered by the reinsurance contract may be partially recognised for a period no longer than six months after the counterparty ceases to comply with the SCR, unless it becomes clear before the end of that period that it is unlikely that the counterparty will be able to restore compliance with the SCR. The effect of the risk-mitigation technique is in that case reduced by the percentage by which the SCR is breached (Art. 211 (3) DA). This partial recognition of reinsurance avoids pro-cyclicality. No recognition of the risk-mitigating effect would result in a "spike" in the SCR for the insurer taking out reinsurance. Where the counterparty fails to restore compliance with the SCR within the six-month period or where the counterparty ceases to comply with the MCR, the effect of the risk-mitigation technique is no longer recognised (Art. 211 (3a) DA).[240]

If an insurance undertaking is using finite reinsurance for the transfer of an underwriting risk, the contractual arrangement is only recognised in a scenario-based calculation in the standard formula to the extent that underwriting risk is transferred to the counterparty of the contract (Art. 208 (2) DA). Finite reinsurance is a broad term used to describe an entire spectrum of limited risk transfer reinsurance contracts, from relatively simple transactions to sophisticated individually designed structures.

Art. 210 FD defines finite reinsurance as reinsurance under which the explicit maximum loss potential, expressed as the maximum economic risk transferred, arising both from a significant underwriting risk and timing risk transfer, exceeds the premium over the lifetime of the contract by a limited but significant amount. "Underwriting risk" is the possibility that losses and expenses

---

for reinsurance activities after the withdrawal date, these undertakings may need to reduce the amount of recoverables because the payments expected from the UK undertaking may not be made anymore or only with a delay. See EIOPA, Opinion on the solvency position of insurance and reinsurance undertakings in light of the withdrawal of the UK from the EU, EIOPA-BoS-18/201, 18 May 2018, p. 4.

240 See also EIOPA, First set of advice to the EC on specific items in the Solvency II Delegated Regulation, EIOPA-BoS-17/280, 30 October 2017, pp. 46–49.

recoverable by the ceding undertaking from the reinsurance undertaking will exceed the consideration received by the reinsurance undertaking, thus resulting in an underwriting loss for the reinsurance undertaking. "Timing risk" is the risk arising from uncertainties about the timing of the receipt and payment of losses and expenses recoverable by the ceding undertaking and the consideration received by the reinsurance undertaking.[241]

Although recognising that there is no universally accepted definition of finite reinsurance,[242] the IAIS defines finite reinsurance as "a spectrum of reinsurance arrangements that transfer limited risk relative to aggregate premiums that could be charged under the contract".[243] What is important is that sufficient insurance risk is transferred in order to qualify the arrangement as reinsurance.

Risks can also be transferred to an SPV, in which case the amounts recoverable from the SPV are usually treated like reinsurance recoverables. An SPV is defined in Art. 13, point (26) FD as "any undertaking, whether incorporated or not, other than an existing insurance or reinsurance undertaking, which assumes risks from insurance or reinsurance undertakings and which fully funds its exposure to such risks through the proceeds of a debt issuance or any other financing mechanism where the repayment rights of the providers of such debt or financing mechanism are subordinated to the reinsurance obligations of such an undertaking."

SPVs or special-purpose entities (SPEs) are used in liability-based securitisations, also called insurance securitisations, whereby a (re)insurance undertaking transfers underwriting risk out of the undertaking to capital market investors. This is done by ceding risk to an SPV that will issue securities and will use the proceeds from the sale to pay out any claims emerging from the risk transferred. Securities issued and marketed in this manner are referred to as insurance-linked securities (ILSs).[244]

In order to ensure that the use of an SPV effectively results in a risk transfer, strict conditions must be satisfied.[245] Prior to assuming risks from (re)insurance undertakings, SPVs must receive supervisory approval from the supervisory authority of the MS in whose territory the SPV is establishing its head office under the conditions set out in Art. 218 DA. If the SPV was authorised

241 Central Bank of Ireland, *Additional requirements for non-life finite reinsurance*, 2012, p. 6.

242 See IAIS, *Guidance Paper No 11 on Risk Transfer, Disclosure and Analysis of Finite Reinsurance*, October 2006, 64 p. This paper contains a number of commonly used definitions of finite reinsurance in Appendix III, pp. 29–30.

243 IAIS, ICP 13 – Reinsurance and Other Forms of Risk Transfer, para. 13.3.5.

244 See RAMELLA, M., Securitization and Insurance, in KEMPLER, C., FLAMEE, M., YANG, C.H. and WINDELS, P. (Eds.), *Global Perspectives on Insurance Today*, Palgrave Macmillan, New York, 2013, p. 321.

245 See also CEIOPS, Consultation Paper No 36. Draft Advice for Level 2 Implementing Measures on Solvency II: Special Purpose Vehicles, CEIOPS-CP-36/09, 26 March 2009, 34 p.

before 31 December 2015, it is subject to the law of the MS that authorised the SPV. However, any new activity commenced by the SPV is subject to the same strict conditions as those applying to newly established SPVs (Art. 211 (3) FD). Art. 211 (5) DA also requires that the risk-mitigating technique resulting from the use of an SPV can only be taken into account in the BSCR if the solvency regime of the SPV is at least equivalent to that specified in Art. 211 (2) DA, i.e. Solvency II,[246] and that it is also effectively complied with by the SPV.

Where the SPV is established in a different MS from that in which the (re)insurance undertaking that transfers the risk is established, there is a need for cooperation between the supervisory authorities concerned. This is particularly important during the process of supervisory approval, but also if there are material changes that may affect the SPV's compliance with the authorisation and/or solvency requirements and when the authorisation is withdrawn or lapses. This cooperation is set out in a Commission Implementing Regulation of 19 March 2015.[247]

The following conditions apply in the case of risk transfers to an SPV:
(a) the SPV must be fully funded at all times (as defined in Art. 326 DA);
(b) the transfer of risk must be effective, clearly defined and incontrovertible (Art. 320 DA);
(c) the claims of the providers of debt or financing mechanisms must at all times be subordinated to the reinsurance obligations of the SPV to the (re)undertaking (Art. 321 DA);
(d) the persons who effectively run an SPV, as well as the shareholders or members with a direct or indirect holding of 10% or more of the capital or the voting rights or who have the possibility of exercising a significant influence over the management of the SPV (qualifying holding within the meaning of Art. 13, point (21) FD), must be fit and proper (Arts. 322 and 323 DA);
(e) the SPV must have an effective system of governance that provides for sound and prudent management and that is appropriate to the nature, scale and complexity of the risks it assumes and the uses for which it is authorised (Art. 324 DA);
(f) the investments of the SPV must be made in line with the prudent person principle (Art. 327 DA);
(g) the SPV must report detailed information to the supervisory authority of the MS in which it is established (Art. 325 DA).

---

246 This may be a problem for UK SPVs after the withdrawal date in the case of Brexit.

247 Commission Implementing Regulation (EU) 2015/462 of 19 March 2015 laying down implementing technical standards with regard to the procedures for supervisory approval to establish special purpose vehicles, for the cooperation and exchange of information between supervisory authorities regarding special purpose vehicles as well as to set out formats and templates for information to be reported by special purpose vehicles in accordance with Directive 2009/138/EC of the European Parliament and of the Council, *OJ* L 76, 20.3.2015, p. 23.

The requirement for an SPV to be fully funded requires the SPV to satisfy the following solvency requirements (Art. 326 (1) DA):

(a) the assets of the SPV must be valued on a market-consistent (fair-value) basis;
(b) the SPV must at all times have assets the value of which is equal to or exceeds the aggregate maximum risk exposure;
(c) the SPV must be able to pay the amounts it is liable for as they fall due;[248]
(d) the proceeds of the debt issuance or other financing mechanism are fully paid in.

In assessing whether the SPV at all times has assets the value of which is equal to or exceeds the aggregate maximum risk exposure and whether the SPV is able to pay the amounts it is liable for as they fall due, supervisory authorities must consider in particular the liquidity risk of the SPV, the quantifiable risks of the SPV and the arrangements for holding assets in the SPV (Art. 326 (2) DA).

Payments relating to existing (re)insurance contracts that the SPV expects to receive in the future from the (re)insurance undertaking that has transferred risk to it may be included in the assets of the SPV, provided that all of the following requirements are satisfied (Art. 326 (4) DA):

(a) the future liabilities of the SPV to the providers of debt or finance only arise subject to the receipt of the payments from the (re)insurance undertaking that has transferred risk to the SPV;
(b) there is no scenario under which the basic own funds of the (re)insurance undertaking that has transferred risks to the SPV would be negatively affected by the payment not being received by the SPV;
(c) the SPV remains solvent in the event that the payments from the (re)insurance undertaking that has transferred risk to the SPV are not received;
(d) the payments do not relate to expenses that are excluded from the aggregate maximum risk exposure of the SPV.[249]

If the SPV is situated in a third country whose solvency regime is deemed equivalent or temporarily equivalent[250] to Solvency II, it must comply with the solvency requirements of that third country. If the SPV is situated in a third country whose solvency regime is not deemed equivalent or temporarily

248 This must be assessed by the supervisory authority when granting supervisory approval, considering each individual contractual arrangement and transfer.
249 As defined in Art. 1 (44) DA.
250 Art. 172 FD. See further, Chapter 10, section 4.

equivalent to Solvency II, it must have a credit quality of step 3 or better (Art. 211 (2) DA).

Where the SPV ceases to be fully funded after the arrangement has been entered into, the effect of the risk-mitigation technique is reduced by the percentage of the aggregated maximum risk exposure of the SPV that is not covered by the assets of the SPV (Art. 211 (4) DA).

In terms of supervisory reporting, the supervisory authority in the MS in which the SPV is established may request such information from the SPV as is necessary for supervisory purposes (Art. 325 (1) DA).

SPVs must submit an annual report to the supervisory authority of the MS in which they are established. This report must be submitted within 14 weeks of the financial year-end date, subject to a transitional period during which the date for submission is progressively reduced from 20 weeks to 14 weeks in 2019 (Art. 325 (4) DA). The report must include the following (Art. 325 (2) DA):[251]

(a) the value of the assets of the SPV valued on a fair-value basis;
(b) the aggregate maximum risk exposure of the SPV;
(c) conflicts of interest between the SPV, the insurance or reinsurance undertakings and the providers of debt or finance;
(d) significant transactions entered into by the SPV during the last reporting period;
(e) demonstration that the SPV fully satisfies the solvency requirements.

SPVs must immediately inform the supervisory authority in the MS in which they are established of any changes that could affect their compliance with the authorisation (Arts. 318–324 DA) or solvency (Art. 326 DA) requirements.

Other forms of risk transfer (financial risk-mitigation techniques) and situations where the qualitative requirements are not met are dealt with in Arts. 212 and 213 DA respectively. The risk-mitigating effect of derivatives may be affected by Brexit because one of the conditions is that the transfer of risk is legally effective and enforceable in all relevant jurisdictions (Art. 209 (1) (a) DA). After the withdrawal date, UK banks and investment firms will lose their MiFID passport to provide derivative services in the EU. This could have an impact on the ability of derivatives provided by UK banks and investment firms to transfer risk after the withdrawal date.[252]

---

251 See also the templates annexed to Commission Implementing Regulation (EU) 2015/462 of 19 March 2015.

252 EIOPA, Opinion on the solvency position of insurance and reinsurance undertakings in light of the withdrawal of the UK from the EU, EIOPA-BoS-18/201, 18 May 2018, p. 3. In order to safeguard financial stability in the EU, the EC has adopted a number of measures that will apply from the withdrawal date if the withdrawal agreement is not ratified: a temporary and conditional equivalence decision for 12 months to ensure that there will be no disruption

Collateral arrangements and guarantees only qualify for risk mitigation under the conditions set out in Arts. 214 and 215 DA. Collateral arrangements are arrangements under which collateral providers either transfer full ownership of the collateral to the collateral taker for the purpose of securing or otherwise covering the performance of a relevant obligation, or provide collateral by way of security in favour of, or to, a collateral taker, and the legal ownership of the collateral remains with the collateral provider or a custodian when the security right is established (Art. 1 (26) DA).

Collateral arrangements are only recognised as a risk-mitigation technique if the qualitative criteria are met and if there is an effective transfer of risk. In order to be eligible, a number of conditions must be met:

(a) the (re)insurance undertaking transferring the risk must have the right to liquidate or retain, in a timely manner, the collateral in the event of a default, insolvency or bankruptcy or other credit event of the counterparty;
(b) there must be sufficient certainty as to the protection achieved by the collateral because of either of the following:
  (i) it is of sufficient credit quality, of sufficient liquidity and sufficiently stable in value;
  (ii) it is guaranteed by a counterparty other than one that has been assigned a risk factor for concentration risk of 0%;
(c) there is no material positive correlation between the credit quality of the counterparty and the value of the collateral;
(d) the collateral is not securities issued by the counterparty or a related undertaking of that counterparty.[253]

Guarantees are only recognised in the calculation of the BSCR where (in addition to the qualitative criteria in Arts. 209 and 210 DA) all the following conditions are met (Art. 215 DA):

- the credit protection provided by the guarantee is direct;
- the extent of the credit protection is clearly defined and incontrovertible;
- the guarantee does not contain any clause the fulfilment of which is outside the direct control of the lender;

in the central clearing of derivatives; a temporary and conditional equivalence decision for 24 months to ensure that there will be no disruption in services provided by UK central securities depositories; and two delegated regulations facilitating novation, for a fixed period, of certain over-the-counter derivative contracts with a counterparty established in the UK. See EC, Communication to the EP, the European Council, the Council the ECB, the EESC, the CoR and the EIB: Preparing for the withdrawal of the UK from the EU on 30 March 2019: Implementing the Commission's Contingency Action Plan, COM (2018) 890 final, 19 December 2018, p. 6.

253 Art. 214 (1) DA. For collateral held by a custodian, see Art. 214 (2) DA.

- if a credit event occurs (such as default or insolvency), the (re)insurance undertaking has the right to pursue, in a timely manner, the guarantor for any monies due under the claim in respect of which the protection is provided and the payment by the guarantor is not subject to the (re)insurance undertaking first having to pursue the obligor;
- the guarantee is an explicitly documented obligation assumed by the guarantor;
- the guarantee fully covers all types of regular payment the obligor is expected to make in respect of the claim.

For guarantees by Member States' central governments and regional governments and local authorities, see below, section 4.2.2.2.4, d (on spread risk).

d. Risk Diversification

(Re)insurance undertakings can improve their capital position by maximising diversification. Diversification effects are defined in Art. 13 (37) FD as the reduction in the risk exposure of a (re)insurance undertaking or a group following from a diversification of business resulting from the fact that the adverse outcome from one risk can be offset by a more favourable outcome from another risk, where those risks are not fully correlated.

Diversification helps to reduce the risks among assets and/or liabilities by accumulating risks that are not fully correlated in an aggregated risk position. Diversification is based on the principle that not all risks will crystallise at the same amount and at the same time, provided that the underlying sources of risk, i.e. risk drivers or triggers, are not fully dependent. As it can be assumed that not all risks captured in the SCR will occur at the same time, a simple addition of the risks would overstate the appropriate amount of capital.[254]

Diversification with respect to insurance obligations is typically achieved through writing a large portfolio of independent contracts, by writing insurance across a number of different lines, or by spreading the risk geographically or directly through capital markets. Asset diversification is typically achieved through spreading investments, in order to avoid excessive concentration of assets or exposure to a single counterparty (i.e. avoiding concentration risk).[255]

Diversification benefits can therefore arise as a result of different product lines (see below for the list of different lines of business), different perils (fire, flood), different portfolios (personal lines, commercial lines), or as a result of different risk types (credit, market, underwriting), geographical differences (a windstorm

254 SCHUERMANS, P., Solvency II: A Balancing Act, in KEMPLER, C., FLAMEE, M., YANG, C.H. and WINDELS, P. (Eds.), *Global Perspectives on Insurance Today*, Palgrave Macmillan, New York, 2013, p. 44.

255 CEA and Groupe Consultatif, *Solvency II Glossary*, March 2007, p. 23.

in Germany and in Spain are usually not related) or different entities in a group (motor insurance in France and in Finland). Diversification is an important element of risk management. It limits the economic impact of any single event, brings about a balanced risk profile and avoids any disproportionately large risk concentration and accumulation.

Undertakings that specialise in a certain type of insurance, such as professional liability insurance or credit insurance may not be able to benefit from diversification because they are less diversified in terms of lines of business. This is particularly relevant for mutual insurers, which often specialise in long-tail risks, such as workers' compensation, medical malpractice liability or decennial liability in construction.[256] The lack of diversification may be partly compensated for if there is geographic diversity. For these undertakings, the standard formula may be quite punitive, creating an incentive – or even an absolute need – to use USPs or to put in place a partial or full internal model. The use of USPs might however not provide the same capital reduction as diversification. In addition, it requires supervisory approval, which is time-consuming and creates additional cost. An unintended consequence has been that specialised insurers have therefore sought to acquire additional geographical or lines of business portfolios in order to be able to make use of diversification benefits. Diversification is clearly more supported under Solvency II than specialisation.

It is obvious that under a risk-sensitive capital regime such as Solvency II, (re)insurance undertakings must be able to benefit from the economic effects of diversification. Diversification is therefore an important element of capital management, because it can help to reduce capital requirements both at solo level and at group level.

Diversification effects already impact the balance sheet where the risk margin in the calculation of the technical provisions is allocated to the different lines of business listed in Annex I to the DA (Art. 80 FD and Art. 55 DA):

Non-life insurance obligations:

1. *Medical expense insurance*: medical expense insurance obligations, where the underlying business is not pursued on a similar technical basis to that of life insurance, other than obligations resulting from workers' compensation insurance;
2. *Income protection insurance*: income protection insurance obligations where the underlying business is not pursued on a similar technical basis to that of life insurance, other than obligations resulting from workers' compensation insurance;

---

256 See AISAM and ACME, *The European mutual insurance sector and Solvency II: an overview*, 10 July 2007, p. 3, presented to the Dutch Parliament. See https://www.eerstekamer.nl/eu/behandeling/20070710/notitie_the_european_mutual/info.

3. *Workers' compensation insurance*: health insurance obligations which relate to accidents at work, industrial injury and occupational diseases where the underlying business is not pursued on a similar technical basis to that of life insurance;
4. *Motor vehicle liability insurance*: insurance obligations which cover all liabilities arising out of the use of motor vehicles operating on land (including carrier's liability);
5. *Other motor insurance*: insurance obligations which cover all damage or loss of land vehicles (including railway rolling stock);
6. *Marine, aviation and transport insurance*: insurance obligations which cover all damage or loss to sea, lake, river and canal vessels, aircraft, and damage or loss of goods in transit or baggage irrespective of the form of transport, and insurance obligations which cover liabilities arising out of the use of aircraft, ships, vessels or boats on the sea, lakes, rivers or canals (including carrier's liability);
7. *Fire and other damage to property insurance*: insurance obligations which cover all damage to or loss of property other than those included in other motor insurance or marine, aviation and transport insurance due to fire, explosion, natural forces, including storm, hail or frost, nuclear energy, land subsidence and any event such as theft;
8. *General liability insurance*: insurance obligations which cover all liabilities other than those in motor vehicle liability insurance and marine, aviation and transport insurance;
9. *Credit and suretyship insurance*: insurance obligations which cover insolvency, export credit, instalment credit, mortgages, agricultural credit and direct and indirect suretyship;
10. *Legal expenses insurance*: insurance obligations which cover legal expenses and cost of litigation;
11. *Assistance*: insurance obligations which cover assistance for persons who get into difficulties while travelling, while away from home or while away from their habitual residence;
12. *Miscellaneous financial loss*: insurance obligations which cover employment risk, insufficiency of income, bad weather, loss of benefit, continuing general expenses, unforeseen trading expenses, loss of market value, loss or rent or revenue, indirect trading losses other than those mentioned above, other financial loss (non-trading) as well as any other risk of non-life insurance not covered by the lines of business (1)–(11).

Proportional non-life reinsurance obligations:
The lines of business (13)–(24) include proportional reinsurance obligations relating to the obligations included in the lines of business (1)–(12) respectively.

Non-proportional non-life reinsurance obligations:

25. *Non-proportional health reinsurance*: non-proportional reinsurance obligations relating to obligations included in lines of business (1)–(3);
26. *Non-proportional casualty reinsurance*: non-proportional reinsurance obligations relating to obligations included in lines of business (4) and (8);
27. *Non-proportional marine, aviation and transport reinsurance*: non-proportional reinsurance relating to obligations included in line of business (6);
28. *Non-proportional property reinsurance:* non-proportional reinsurance relating to obligations included in lines of business (5), (7) and (9)–(12).

Life insurance obligations:

29. *Health insurance*: health insurance obligations where the underlying business is pursued on a similar technical basis to that of life insurance, other than those include in line of business (33);
30. *Insurance with profit participation*: insurance obligations with profit participation other than obligations included in line of business (33) and (34);
31. *Index-linked and unit-linked insurance*: insurance obligations with index-linked and unit-linked benefits other than those included in lines of business (33) and (34);
32. *Other life insurance*: other life insurance obligations other than obligations included in lines of business (29)–(31), (33) and (34);
33. *Annuities stemming from non-life insurance contracts and relating to health insurance obligations;*
34. *Annuities stemming from non-life insurance contracts and relating to insurance obligations other than health insurance obligations.*

Life reinsurance obligations:

35. *Health reinsurance*: reinsurance obligations which relate to the obligations included in lines of business (29) and (33);
36. *Life reinsurance*: reinsurance obligations which relate to the obligations included in lines of business (30)–(32) and (34).

The assignment of a (re)insurance obligation to a line of business must reflect the nature of the risks relating to the obligation. The legal form of the obligation is not necessarily determinative of the nature of the risk. Where a (re)insurance contract covers risks across life and non-life insurance, the insurance obligations must be unbundled into their life and non-life parts. Where the same contract covers risks across different lines of business, the obligations must, where possible be unbundled into the appropriate lines of business. Where a contract includes health (re)insurance obligations and other (re)insurance obligations, those obligations must, where possible, be unbundled (Art. 55 DA).

Diversification effects are taken into account in the design of each risk module (Art. 104 (4) FD). They are also taken into account when capital requirements are aggregated in the standard formula by using correlation matrices.[257] For aggregating the individual risk sub-modules and modules to obtain the overall SCR, linear correlation techniques are applied. This acknowledges the fact that the individual risks are not all expected to materialise at the same time. For instance, a shock on financial markets and a loss on underwriting risks would not necessarily happen at the same time. The setting of the correlation coefficients is intended to reflect potential dependencies in the tail of the distributions, as well as the stability of any correlation assumption under stress conditions.

The selection of the correlation parameters has a significant influence on the result of the SCR calculation. For example, if five capital requirements of equal size are aggregated, the result is 55% lower if the correlation parameter 0 is used instead of parameter 1 to describe the relation between each pair of risks. Hence, the choice of correlation parameters has an impact on the level of diversification to be obtained within the SCR standard formula.[258]

In QIS 5, the sum of the individual risks modelled totalled €1.328 billion. Diversification benefits amounted to a €466 billion reduction (–35.1%) in the total risk charge at solo level.[259]

The standard formula is composed of several modules, the results of which are aggregated via an aggregation matrix to reflect the correlation between risks and to allow for diversification benefits. Most of the modules are also composed of sub-modules, and aggregation matrices are applied at that sub-level too. The BSCR is therefore not a simple addition of the capital requirements of each module, since diversification benefits are taken into account. In order to simplify the calculation, EIOPA proposed in its first set of advice to the EC in the context of the 2018 review of the DA allowing undertakings to calculate their BSCR or their SCR for a given sub-module without taking into account diversification benefits, i.e. not applying correlation matrices, where this would lead to a more conservative outcome.[260]

4.2.2.1.2. Structure of the SCR

The calculation of the SCR follows a dynamic approach looking at the current balance sheet pre-stress and the balance sheet post-stress. The capital charge

257 These correlation matrices are included in annexes to the DA.

258 CEIOPS, Advice for Level 2 Implementing Measures on Solvency II: SCR Standard Formula – Art. 111 (d) Correlations, CEIOPS-DOC-70/10, 29 January 2010, p. 8.

259 EIOPA, Report on the fifth Quantitative Impact Study (QIS 5) for Solvency II, EIOPA-TFQIS5-11/001, 14 March 2011, p. 31.

260 EIOPA, First set of advice to the EC on specific items in the Solvency II Delegated Regulation, EIOPA-BoS-17/280, 30 October 2017, p. 12.

for each individual risk is determined as the difference between the net asset value in the unstressed balance sheet and the net asset value in the stressed balance sheet for a particular risk. The overall BSCR is then calculated by combining these separate risk charges, allowing for diversification by means of correlation matrices, other methodologies or explicitly modelling the structural dependencies.[261]

The SCR calculated on the basis of the standard formula consists of:
- the basic SCR (BSCR);
- the capital requirement for operational risk;
- the adjustment for the loss-absorbing capacity of technical provisions and deferred taxes (LAC-DT).[262]

4.2.2.2. Basic SCR

The BSCR is calculated by aggregating the different risk modules and risk sub-modules of the standard formula with due regard to correlation effects.

The BSCR (Art. 104 FD[263]) comprises the following individual risk modules, which are aggregated:

- non-life underwriting risk;
- life underwriting risk;
- health underwriting risk;
- market risk;
- counterparty default risk.

These modules themselves consist of sub-modules. Insurance operations are allocated to the underwriting risk module that best reflects the technical nature of the underlying risks.

The correlation coefficients for the aggregation of the risk modules, as well as the calibration of the capital requirements for each risk module, must result in an overall SCR that complies with the basic principles underlying the SCR (for instance, the going-concern principle). Each of the risk modules is calibrated using a VaR measure with a 99.5% confidence level over a one-year period (Art. 104 (2), (3) and (4) FD).

The same design and specifications for the risk modules are used for all (re)insurance undertakings, with respect to both the BSCR and any simplified

261 CADONI, P. and KERFRIDEN, C., Internal Models and Solvency II, in DOFF, R. (Ed.), *The Solvency II Handbook. Practical Approaches to Implementation*, Incisive Media, London, 2014, p. 43.

262 Art. 103 FD.

263 See also Annex IV FD.

calculations (Art. 104 (5) FD). No distinct models were developed for life insurance, non-life insurance and reinsurance.[264]

4.2.2.2.1. Non-Life Underwriting Risk Module

For non-life business, the key risk drivers are the number of claims and potential errors in the estimation of technical provisions, which are captured in the premium and reserve risk sub-modules. In the case of short-tail business, premium risk is more relevant; in the case of long tail business, reserve risk is more relevant. Lapse risk is a residual risk.

The non-life underwriting risk module (Art. 105 (2) FD and Arts. 114–135 DA) reflects the risk arising from non-life insurance obligations. It takes account of the uncertainty related to existing (re)insurance obligations, as well as to new business expected to be written over the following 12 months. It consists of the following sub-modules:[265]

- *non-life premium and reserve risk*: the risk of loss, or of adverse change in the value of insurance liabilities, resulting from fluctuations in the timing, frequency and severity of insured events and in the timing and amount of claim settlements (Arts. 115–117 and Annexes II, III and IV DA);
- *non-life catastrophe risk*: the risk of loss, or of adverse change in the value of insurance liabilities, resulting from significant uncertainty of pricing and provisioning assumptions related to extreme or exceptional events. It consists of the following sub-modules (Art. 119 DA):
  - the *natural catastrophe risk* sub-module (Art. 120 DA), divided into the windstorm risk sub-module (Art. 121 and Annex V DA), the earthquake risk sub-module (Art. 122 and Annex VI DA), the flood risk sub-module (Art. 123 and Annex VII DA), the hail risk sub-module (Art. 124 and Annex VIII DA) and the subsidence[266] risk sub-module (Art. 125 DA);
  - the sub-module for *catastrophe risk of non-proportional property reinsurance* (Art. 127 DA);
  - the *man-made catastrophe risk* sub-module (Art. 128 DA), divided into the motor vehicle liability risk sub-module (Art. 129 DA), the marine risk sub-module (Art. 130 DA), the aviation risk sub-module

264 This was the subject of a lot of debate. It has been argued that it would be better to develop separate standard formulas for life and non-life insurance. This is not straightforward. For instance, in some Member States, health insurance is dealt with as non-life insurance, while in other Member States it is treated as life insurance.

265 For the design of this sub-module, see CEIOPS, Advice for Level 2 Implementing Measures on Solvency II: SCR Standard Formula - Art. 111, Non-Life Underwriting Risk, CEIOPS-DOC-41-09, October 2009, 53 p. For the calibration of this sub-module, see CEIOPS, Advice for Level 2 Implementing Measures on Solvency II: SCR Standard Formula – Calibration of Non-Life Underwriting Risk, CEIOPS-DOC-67/10, 8 April 2010, 198 p.

266 The sinking or downward movement of a building.

(Art. 131 DA), the fire risk sub-module (Art. 132 DA), the liability risk sub-module (Art. 133 and Annex XI DA) and the credit and suretyship risk sub-module (Art. 134 DA);
  - the sub-module for *other non-life catastrophe risk* (Art. 135 and Annex XII DA)
- *non-life lapse risk*: the risk of loss, or of adverse change in the value of insurance liabilities, resulting from changes in the level or volatility of the rates of policy lapses, terminations, renewals and surrenders (Art. 118 DA).

The capital charge for non-life underwriting risk is derived by combining the capital charges for the non-life sub-risks using a correlation matrix (Art. 114 (3) DA).

a. Non-Life Premium and Reserve Risk Sub-Module (Arts. 115–117 and Annexes II–IV DA)

Premium risk is the risk of loss that arises through an increase in damage in the next year, for instance as a result of a higher damage frequency or a higher level of average damage than expected. Premium risk relates to future claims arising during and after the period for the solvency assessment. The risk is that the expenses, plus the amount of (covered but not incurred) losses for these claims (comprising both amounts paid during the period and (incurred but not settled) claim provisions made at its end) are higher than the premiums received. Premium risk is present at the time the policy is issued, before any events occur. Premium risk also arises because of uncertainties prior to the issue of policies during the time horizon.

Reserve risk is the risk of loss resulting from an adverse development in claims settlement. Reserve risk stems from two sources. On the one hand, the absolute level of the claims provisions could be underestimated. On the other hand, the actual claims will fluctuate around their statistical mean value because of the stochastic nature of future claims pay-outs.

The premium and reserve risk sub-module only takes into account losses that occur at a regular frequency. Extreme events, which occur very rarely, have not been taken into account when calibrating the premium and reserve risk factors. Such extreme events are taken into account in the catastrophe risk sub-module.

The underlying assumptions for the non-life premium and reserve sub-module can be summarised as follows:[267]

- the risk of an accumulation of a large number of similar claims that are covered by third-party liability insurance obligations is not material;
- the underlying risk follows a lognormal distribution;

[267] EIOPA, The underlying assumptions in the standard formula for the SCR calculation, EIOPA-14-322, 25 July 2014, pp. 40–41.

- complex relationships between different risks that could give rise to dependencies in the risk profile are implicitly taken into account in the correlation parameters between the segments, lines of business[268] and between premium and reserve risk for each line of business;
- the final factors are reflective of the average size and performance of the portfolios of insurers in the European market;
- net earned premium can be used as a proxy for premium risk exposure;
- net provisions for claims outstanding can be used as a proxy for reserve risk exposure;
- expenses do not evolve independently from or inversely to the underlying risk over time;
- non-proportional reinsurance reduces the premium risk volatility by 20% in segments 1 (motor vehicle liability insurance and proportional insurance), 4 (fire and other damage to property insurance and proportional insurance) and 5 (general liability insurance and proportional insurance) listed in Annex II DA. No reduction is allowed for other segments if USPs are not used;
- for the use of a simplified calculation (see below, section 4.2.2.5) of the capital requirement for non-life premium and reserve risk for captives it is assumed that the segmentation of insurance obligations by captives can be considered materially less diversified in terms of lines of business compared to the portfolio used in the calibration of the standard formula;
- in the design of the geographical diversification coefficient adjusting the volume measure for non-life premium and reserve risk, it is assumed that geographically diversified portfolios are diversified in respect of the size and timing of losses that a (re)insurance undertaking faces.

b. Non-Life Catastrophe Risk Sub-Module (Arts. 119–135 and Annexes V–XII DA)

The non-life catastrophe risk sub-module is essentially split into three separate and independent sub-sub-modules that cover catastrophe risk related to natural perils, risk related to man-made events and other catastrophe events.[269]

The underlying assumptions for the natural catastrophe risk sub-module can be summarised as follows:[270]

- the calibration of the natural catastrophe risk sub-module is based on "average" conditions for any given country–peril combination. It is assumed that the

268 See the lines of business in Annex I DA.

269 Swiss Re publishes annually an overview of natural catastrophes and man-made disasters. See Swiss Re, Natural catastrophes and man-made disasters in 2017: a year of record-breaking losses, *Sigma*, 2018, No 1, 58 p.

270 EIOPA, The underlying assumptions in the standard formula for the SCR calculation, EIOPA-14-322, 25 July 2014, p. 49.

undertaking's non-life insurance portfolio is not focused on residential, commercial, industrial or agricultural risks;
- there is an underlying assumption of an average vulnerability per peril–country combination, as well as an average deductible and an insured-to-value relationship;
- the scenario-based approach for the natural catastrophe risk sub-module assumes that the portfolio of the financial statement date is representative of the whole year. In the design of the geographical diversification coefficient adjusting the volume measure for non-life premium and reserve risk, it is assumed that geographically diversified portfolios are diversified in respect of the type and timing of losses that an insurance undertaking faces;
- in the design of the geographical diversification coefficient adjusting the volume measure for natural catastrophe risk (windstorm, earthquake, flood, hail and non-proportional property reinsurance), it is assumed that geographically diversified portfolios are diversified in respect of the type and timing of losses that an insurance undertaking faces;
- in the design of the geographical diversification coefficient adjusting the volume measures for natural catastrophe risk (windstorm, earthquake, flood, hail and non-proportional property reinsurance), it is also assumed that the regions represent an appropriate geographical division of the undertaking's insurance portfolio in each line of business, i.e. it is assumed that an insurance portfolio of an undertaking with contracts in different regions does not contain sub-portfolios split per region that in fact generate positively correlated losses. This situation can occur where the portfolios are located in a few similar (in respect of type and timing of losses) countries but assigned to different regions or where the portfolios are locally concentrated on both sides of the border between two regions.

For *man-made catastrophe risk*, a factor-based approach was chosen. A factor is applied to premiums that represents the additional loss from a 1-in-200 liability catastrophe. An event scenario-based approach was assumed to be less appropriate for a number of reasons:

- to cover the range of insurances falling into the liability category, a lengthy set of scenarios would need to be specified;
- liability scenarios are more varied and less predictable in their nature than natural catastrophe losses, so specifying a list of scenarios that represent current and potential concerns at a particular moment in time runs the risk of missing out the scenario behind the next actual major event;
- an undertaking with material potential liability catastrophe risk, but not in an area picked up by any of the listed scenarios would not be subject to a capital charge.

The underlying assumptions for the man-made catastrophe risk sub-module can be summarised as follows:[271]

- the calibration factors for man-made catastrophe risk are likely to be understated, compared to the risk for an individual undertaking. Countering this, the market represented by the data is likely to have a mix of business that is likely to be higher risk (larger-sized risks and risks that are inherently more exposed to risk of loss) than the typical EU undertaking. Hence the factors calculated could overstate the 1-in-200 loss for undertakings writing only small limits and/or risks with low inherent exposure to liability losses. It is assumed that the overestimation/underestimation of the factors cancel each other out;
- for motor vehicle third-party liability, the fundamental assumption is that the number of vehicles insured is the best measure of exposure. The resulting loss is extrapolated down to a 1-in-200-year level using a Pareto assumption and allowance is made for policy limits common in some countries. The main implicit assumption is that the number of vehicles insured is a good measure of frequency of extreme loss, i.e. all vehicles are equally likely to cause a major loss, or all undertakings have a similar mix of vehicle types;
- for fire risk (fire, explosion and acts of terror), although explosion or acts of terrorism can trigger general liability insurance coverage losses, the general liability line of business is assumed not to be considered in the fire sub-module;
- it is assumed that for third-party liability insurance, the risk of an accumulation of a large number of similar claims is not material.

The capital requirements for natural catastrophe risk are set out in the DA: Art. 121 and Annexes V and XXII (windstorm risk); Art. 122 and Annexes VI and XXIII (earthquake risk); Art. 123 and Annexes VII and XXIV (flood risk); Art. 124 and Annexes VIII and XXV (hail risk); and Art. 125 and Annex XXVI (subsidence risk).

The capital requirements for man-made catastrophe risk are also set out in the DA: Art. 129 (motor vehicle liability risk); Art. 130 (marine risk); Art. 131 (aviation risk); Art. 132 (fire risk); Art. 133 (liability risk); and Art. 134 (credit and suretyship risk). The capital requirement for other non-life catastrophe risk is set out in Art. 135 DA.

The various scenarios for the calibration of natural catastrophe risk and man-made catastrophe risk were developed by a task force within CEIOPS/EIOPA. It was already recognised in the final set of advice to the EC that these scenarios might not always be fully reflective of the real risks.[272] In its second set

---

[271] EIOPA, The underlying assumptions in the standard formula for the SCR calculation, EIOPA-14-322, 25 July 2014, p. 51.

[272] CEIOPS, Advice for Level 2 Implementing Measures on Solvency II: SCR Standard Formula – Art. 111, Non-Life Underwriting Risk, CEIOPS-DOC-41-09, October 2009, p. 19.

of advice to the EC on the 2018 review of the DA, EIOPA proposed a number of simplifications (mass accident risk, accident concentration risk, pandemic risk, fire risk) and recalibrations (country factors, more granular parameters, risk zone weights, aggregation matrices).[273] These proposals were developed by a new catastrophe risk work-stream within EIOPA including external stakeholders and are incorporated in the 2019 amendment of the DA. They only focus on a limited set of man-made catastrophic risks: marine, aviation, motor and fire risks, excluding liability risk and credit and suretyship risk.

c. *Non-Life Lapse Risk Sub-Module (Art. 118 DA)*

Lapse risk is the risk of a change in value caused by deviations from the actual rate of policy lapses from their expected rates.[274] Lapses occur when the policy is cancelled, for instance because the policyholder fails to pay the premium.

For non-life lapse risk it is assumed either that relevant option exercise rates are not used in the calculation of technical provisions for non-life obligations or that, where they are used, changes of the relevant option exercise rates would not have a material impact on the value of technical provisions.

The design of this module is therefore different from the design for life lapse risk. The module does not cover a change of lapse rates used in the calculation of technical provisions like the lapse-up and lapse-down scenario in life underwriting risk. The capital charge for non-life lapse risk is instead calculated in such a way that it would cover a loss in basic own funds that would result from a discontinuance of 40% of the policies where the discontinuance would result in an increase in technical provisions, without the risk margin. Undertakings that write reinsurance must calculate a capital charge for policies that cover business to be written in the future in a way that the capital charge would cover a loss in basic own funds that would result from a decrease of 40% in the number of those future contracts used in the calculation of technical provisions.[275]

The capital requirement for the non-life lapse risk sub-module is set out in Art. 118 DA. It is equal to the loss in basic own funds of the insurance undertaking resulting from a combination of the following instantaneous events:

- the discontinuance of 40% of the insurance policies for which discontinuance would result in an increase in technical provisions, without the risk margin;
- where reinsurance contracts cover (re)insurance or contracts that will be written in the future, the decrease of 40% of the number of those future contracts used in the calculation of technical provisions.

---

273 EIOPA, EIOPA's second set of advice to the European Commission on specific items in the Solvency II Delegated Regulation, EIOPA-BoS-18/075, 28 February 2018, pp. 84–100.

274 CEA and Groupe Consultatif, *Solvency II Glossary*, March 2007, p. 35.

275 EIOPA, The underlying assumptions in the standard formula for the SCR calculation, EIOPA-14-322, 25 July 2014, p. 48.

4.2.2.2.2. Life Underwriting Risk Module

The main risk drivers of the life underwriting risk module are lapse risk[276] and longevity risk. This module (Art. 105 (3) FD and Arts. 136–143 DA)[277] reflects the risk arising from life insurance obligations. It consists of the following sub-modules:

- *mortality risk*: the risk of loss, or of adverse change in the value of insurance liabilities, resulting from changes in the level, trend or volatility of mortality rates, where an increase in the mortality rate leads to an increase in the value of insurance liabilities (Art. 137 DA);
- *longevity risk*: the risk of loss, or of adverse change in the value of insurance liabilities, resulting from changes in the level, trend or volatility of mortality rates, where a decrease in the mortality rate leads to an increase in the value of insurance liabilities (Art. 138 DA);
- *disability–morbidity*[278] *risk*: the risk of loss, or of adverse change in the value of insurance liabilities, resulting from changes in the level, trend or volatility of disability, sickness and morbidity rates (Art. 139 DA);
- *life-expense risk*: the risk of loss, or of adverse change in the value of insurance liabilities, resulting from changes in the level, trend or volatility of the expenses incurred in servicing insurance or reinsurance contracts (Art. 140 DA);
- *revision risk*: the risk of loss, or of adverse change in the value of insurance liabilities, resulting from fluctuations in the level, trend or volatility of the revision rates applied to annuities, due to changes in the legal environment or in the state of health of the person insured (Art. 141 DA);
- *lapse risk*: the risk of loss, or of adverse change in the value of insurance liabilities, resulting from changes in the level or volatility of the rates of policy lapses, terminations, renewals and surrenders (Art. 142 DA);
- *life-catastrophe risk*: the risk of loss, or of adverse change in the value of insurance liabilities, resulting from the significant uncertainty of pricing and provisioning assumptions related to extreme or irregular events (Art. 143 DA).

An underlying assumption in the life underwriting risk module is the diversification of insurance portfolios. The reference population underlying all calibration work is an insured population that is well diversified with respect

---

276 In a low interest rate environment, there is a risk that policyholders will surrender their policies when interest rates rise again. This risk might affect the financial stability of life insurers. See BERDIN, E., GRÜNDL, H. and KUBITZA, C.H., *Rising Interest Rates, Lapse Risk and the Stability of Life Insurers*, ICIR Working Paper Series No 29/17, July 2017, 59 p.

277 See also EIOPA, Guidelines on application of the life underwriting risk module, EIOPA BoS-14/175, 2 February 2015, 2 p.

278 Change of value caused by the actual disability and illness rates of the persons insured deviating from the ones expected: CEA and Groupe Consultatif, *Solvency II Glossary*, March 2007, p. 61.

to age, gender, smoking status, socio-economic class, level of life insurance cover, type of insurance cover, degree of underwriting applied at the inception of the cover and geographic location. An example of a deviation from the assumptions underlying the standard formula calculation would be an insurance portfolio with a higher-than-average level of concentration in one or more risk factors. Equally, a niche player is likely to have a materially different risk exposure from that reflected in the calibration of the standard formula.

a. *Mortality Risk Sub-Module (Art. 137 DA)*

The capital requirement for mortality risk[279] is equal to the loss in basic own funds resulting from an instantaneous permanent increase of 15% in the mortality rates used for the calculation of technical provisions.[280]

The stress factor for mortality risk reflects the uncertainty in mortality parameters as a result of an error in the estimation and/or changes in the level, trend and volatility of mortality rates and captures the risk of more policyholders than anticipated dying during the policy term.

The underlying assumptions for the mortality risk sub-module can be summarised as follows:[281]

- the undertaking has established a system to restrict adverse selection;
- the probability distribution for mortality is skewed, with a current trend towards improving mortality;
- for the simplified calculation of the capital requirement for mortality risk (see below, section 4.2.2.5), it is assumed that there is no material decrease in the respective sum of capital at risk in the next n years, where n is the modified duration (in years) of payments payable on death included in the best estimate projection. It is furthermore assumed that the average mortality rate of the insured persons (weighted by sum insured) will not increase materially over the next n years.

b. *Longevity Risk Sub-Module (Art. 138 DA)*

The capital requirement for longevity risk is equal to the loss in basic own funds resulting from an instantaneous permanent decrease of 20% in the mortality rates used for the calculation of technical provisions.

The stress factor for longevity risk is intended to reflect the uncertainty in mortality parameters as a result of an error in the estimation and/or changes

279 A recent study reports a slow-down in mortality improvement. See Swiss Re, Mortality improvement: understanding the past and framing the future, *Sigma*, 2018, No 6, 40 p.

280 For the calibration, EIOPA used the Human Mortality Database.

281 EIOPA, The underlying assumptions in the standard formula for the SCR calculation, EIOPA-14-322, 25 July 2014, p. 31.

in the level, trend and volatility of mortality rates and captures the risk of policyholders living longer than anticipated.

The underlying assumptions for the longevity risk sub-module can be summarised as follows:[282]

- the annual mortality improvements follow a normal distribution;
- for the simplified calculation of the capital requirement for longevity risk, the average age of policyholders within the portfolio is 60 or over;
- the average mortality rate of the insured persons does not increase by more than 10% each year.

c. *Disability–Morbidity Risk Sub-Module (Art. 139 DA)*

The capital requirement for the disability–morbidity risk[283] sub-module is equal to the loss in basic own funds resulting from the combination of the following instantaneous permanent changes:

- an increase of 35% in the disability and morbidity rates that are used in the calculation of technical provisions to reflect the disability and morbidity experience in the following 12 months;
- an increase of 25% in the disability and morbidity rates that are used in the calculation of technical provisions to reflect the disability and morbidity experience for all months after the following 12 months;
- a decrease of 20% in the disability and morbidity recovery rates used in the calculation of technical provisions in respect of the following 12 months and for all years thereafter.

The stress factors for disability–morbidity risk reflect the risk of more policyholders than anticipated becoming disabled or sick during the policy term (inception risk), and of disabled people recovering less than expected (recovery risk).

The underlying assumptions for the disability–morbidity risk sub-module can be summarised as follows:[284]

- the insurance portfolio is well diversified in terms of likelihood of disability or sickness (inception rates) or change in the severity of disability or sickness (recovery rate);

[282] EIOPA, The underlying assumptions in the standard formula for the SCR calculation, EIOPA-14-322, 25 July 2014, p. 32.

[283] Disability risk relates to cover against loss of income, as opposed to morbidity risk, which relates to cover other than loss of income, for instance medical expenses. CEA and Groupe Consultatif, *Solvency II Glossary*, March 2007, p. 22.

[284] EIOPA, The underlying assumptions in the standard formula for the SCR calculation, EIOPA-14-322, 25 July 2014, p. 33.

- for the simplified calculation of the capital requirement for disability–morbidity risk (see below, section 4.2.2.5), it is assumed that there is no material decrease in the respective sum of capital at risk in the next n–1 years after the following year, where n is the modified duration (in years) of payments payable on disability–morbidity included in the best estimate projection. It is furthermore assumed that the expected average disability–morbidity rate of insured persons (weighted by the sum insured) will not increase materially during that period. Finally, it is also assumed that the expected average disability–morbidity rate and the expected termination rates do not increase by more than 10% each year.

d. Life-Expense Risk Sub-Module (Art. 140 DA)

The capital requirement for life-expense risk is equal to the loss in basic own funds resulting from the combination of the following instantaneous permanent changes:

- an increase of 10% in the amount of expenses taken into account in the calculation of technical provisions;
- an increase by 1 percentage point of the expense inflation rate (expressed as a percentage) used for the calculation of technical provisions.

The underlying assumptions for the expense risk sub-module can be summarised as follows:[285]

- undertakings are exposed to the risk of a change of expenses arising predominantly from staff costs, cost of commissions to sales intermediaries (on the basis of the contractual terms of the arrangements), cost of IT infrastructure, and cost of land and buildings occupied;
- the undertaking operates in a macro-economic environment where inflation, though subject to fluctuations, is broadly under control (i.e. inflation targeting);
- for the simplified calculation of the capital requirement for expense risk (see below, 4.2.2.5), it is assumed that there is no material increase due to other sources than inflation in the expenses incurred in servicing life insurance obligations, and where the projected cash flows follow a certain pattern.

e. Revision Risk Sub-Module (Art. 141 DA)

Revision risk is intended to capture the risk of adverse variation of an annuity's amount, as a result of an unanticipated revision of the claims process.

285 EIOPA, The underlying assumptions in the standard formula for the SCR calculation, EIOPA-14-322, 25 July 2014, pp. 34–35.

This risk is only applied to annuities and to those benefits that can be approximated by a life annuity arising from non-life claims, including accident insurance but excluding workers' compensation, that are allocated to the life underwriting risk module.

The capital requirement for revision risk is equal to the loss in basic own funds resulting from an instantaneous permanent increase of 3% in the amount of annuity benefits only on annuity (re)insurance obligations where the benefits payable under the underlying insurance policies could increase as a result of changes in the legal environment or in the state of health of the person insured.

f. Lapse Risk Sub-Module (Art. 142 DA)

The lapse risk sub-module captures the adverse change in the value of insurance liabilities resulting from changes in the level or volatility of the rates of policy lapses, terminations, renewals and surrenders. The capital requirement for lapse risk is the maximum capital requirement in one of the following scenarios: a permanent increase of lapse rates, a permanent decrease of lapse rates or a mass lapse event.

The underlying assumptions for the lapse risk sub-module can be summarised as follows:[286]

- the increase and decrease of lapse rates is a symmetrical stress for the scenarios of increase and decrease of lapse rates (not a mass lapse event);
- the risk relating to the options that a ceding (re)insurance undertaking of a reinsurance contract can exercise is not material;
- a distinction between insurance policies falling or not falling within the scope of management of group pension funds in the mass lapse event shock is assumed appropriate. This is due to the fact that for management of group pension funds, the risk of a mass lapse is deemed to be substantially greater because there are generally no surrender penalties, and institutional investors tend to be better informed and therefore would be quick to withdraw funds if there were any question about the solvency of an insurance undertaking;
- for the simplified calculation of the capital requirement for life lapse risk (see below, section 4.2.2.5), the following is assumed: the simplified calculation is done at an appropriate granularity, such that the group of policies to which the method is applied is homogeneous in terms of lapse rate; the lapse rates are not significantly sensitive to trends in economic variables; the lapse rates do not vary significantly with the age of the policyholder; and the capital requirement for life lapse risk determined with the simplification is not material compared to the overall capital requirement.

---

[286] EIOPA, The underlying assumptions in the standard formula for the SCR calculation, EIOPA-14-322, 25 July 2014, pp. 36–38.

g. Life Catastrophe Risk Sub-Module (Art. 143 DA)

The life catastrophe risk sub-module captures the risk stemming from extreme death events that are not sufficiently captured by the mortality risk sub-module.

Life catastrophe risks are one-time shocks from the extreme, adverse tail of the probability distribution that are not adequately represented by extrapolation from more common events and for which it is usually difficult to specify a loss value, and thus an amount of capital to hold. For example, a contagious disease process or a pandemic can affect many persons simultaneously, nullifying the usual assumption of independence among persons.

The capital requirement for the life catastrophe risk sub-module is calculated as an absolute increase in the rate of policyholders dying over the following year. The life catastrophe risk stress factor is restricted to obligations that are contingent on mortality, i.e. where an increase in mortality leads to an increase in technical provisions.

The underlying assumptions for the life catastrophe risk sub-module can be summarised as follows:[287]

- life catastrophe risk is restricted to obligations that are contingent on mortality, i.e. where an increase in mortality leads to an increase in technical provisions;
- the sub-module is assumed not to be applicable to obligations, such as annuities, where the increase in mortality leads to a reduction in technical provisions. Although this seems to reflect the economic substance of insurance – allowing for the diversification between different lines of business – enough evidence suggests that this diversification benefit might not exist in reality. For instance, historic data indicates that it is primarily young and healthy people that die as a result of influenza pandemics;
- for the simplified calculation of the capital requirement for catastrophe risk (see below, section 4.2.2.5), it is assumed that the capital at risk is an appropriate proxy for the instantaneous loss caused by the death of the person insured by the contract.

4.2.2.2.3. Health Underwriting Risk Module

Health underwriting risk[288] is the risk of loss, or of adverse change in the value of insurance liabilities, resulting from:

- changes in the level, trend or volatility of the medical expenses incurred in servicing insurance contracts (NSLT health);

[287] EIOPA, The underlying assumptions in the standard formula for the SCR calculation, EIOPA-14-322, 25 July 2014, pp. 38–39.

[288] See also Annexes XIV, XV and XVI DA.

- fluctuations in the timing, frequency and severity of insured events, and in the timing and amount of claim settlements (NSLT health);
- changes in the level, trend or volatility of the underlying risk drivers (longevity, incidence, lapse, expense, recovery and revision percentages) for disability insurance (SLT health);[289]
- significant uncertainty of pricing and provisioning assumptions related to outbreaks of major epidemics, as well as the unusual accumulation of risks under such extreme circumstances (health catastrophe).

The health underwriting risk module (Art. 105 (4) FD and Arts. 144–163 DA) reflects the risk arising from the underwriting of health insurance obligations, whether it is pursued on a similar technical basis to that of life insurance (SLT health) or not (NSLT health), following from both the perils covered and the processes used in the conduct of business. It is split into the following sub-modules:

- *NSLT health underwriting risk*, covering health (re)insurance obligations pursued on a similar technical basis to that of non-life insurance and further subdivided into the following sub-modules: NSLT health premium and reserve risk (Arts. 146–148 DA) and NSLT health lapse risk (Art. 150 DA);
- *SLT health underwriting risk*, covering health (re)insurance obligations pursued on a similar technical basis to that of life insurance and further subdivided into the sub-modules: SLT health mortality risk (Art. 152 DA); SLT health longevity risk (Art. 153 DA); SLT health disability–morbidity risk (Art. 154–156 DA); SLT health expense risk (Art. 157 DA); SLT health revision risk (Art. 158 DA); and SLT health lapse risk (Art. 159 DA);
- *health catastrophe risk*, covering (re)insurance obligations exposed to catastrophe risk and further subdivided into the following sub-modules: mass accident (Art. 161 DA); accident concentration (Art. 162); and pandemic risk (Art. 163 DA).

a. NSLT Health Underwriting Risk Sub-Module (Arts. 145–150 DA)

All underlying assumptions for the non-life underwriting risk module, with the exception of the non-life natural catastrophe risk sub-module, are assumed to be valid for the NSLT health underwriting risk sub-module.

b. Health Equalisation Systems (Art. 109a (4) and (5) FD and Art. 149 DA)

Member States may adopt a national health insurance system that permits the sharing of claims payments in respect of health risk between

289 This involves the use of life actuarial techniques.

insurance undertakings. Such a system is called a health risk equalisation system (HRES). If the system corresponds to the criteria set out in Art. 109a (5) FD, the standard parameters to be used for the determination of the NSLT health premium and reserve risk are adjusted by a reduced parameter determined by EIOPA.

The system used in the Netherlands for mandatory basic health insurance is the only system in the EEA that complies with all the requirements of Art. 109a (5) FD. EIOPA has determined the appropriate standard deviations for NSLT health insurance premium risk and NSLT health insurance reserve risk in cooperation with the supervisory authority in the Netherlands (de Nederlandsche Bank (DNB)). These standard deviations were included in a Commission Implementing Regulation of 11 November 2015.[290]

c. *SLT Health Underwriting Risk Sub-Module (Arts. 151–159 DA)*

The underlying assumptions for the SLT health underwriting risk module are assumed to be the same as for the life underwriting risk module, with the exception of disability risk for medical expense insurance, SLT health lapse risk, SLT health revision risk and health catastrophe risk.

A simplified calculation (see below, section 4.2.2.5) for the health underwriting risk sub-modules (mortality risk, longevity risk, disability–morbidity risk, expense risk and lapse risk) is available for undertakings where that simplified calculation is proportionate to the nature, scale and complexity of the risks faced and where the standard calculation would lead to an undue burden on the undertaking. The underlying assumptions for the simplified calculation are the same as for the life underwriting risk sub-modules, except for medical expense disability–morbidity risk.

The capital requirement for health mortality risk is equal to the loss in basic own funds resulting from an instantaneous permanent increase of 15% in the mortality rates used for the calculation of technical provisions (Art. 152 DA).

The capital requirement for health longevity risk is equal to the loss in basic own funds resulting from an instantaneous permanent decrease of 20% in the mortality rates used for the calculation of technical provisions (Art. 153 DA).

The capital requirement for health disability–morbidity risk is equal to the sum of the capital requirement for medical expense disability–morbidity risk and the capital requirement for income protection disability–morbidity risk (Art. 154 DA).

290 Commission Implementing Regulation (EU) 2015/2013 of 11 November 2015 laying down implementing technical standards with regard to standard deviations in relation to health risk equalisation systems in accordance with Directive 2009/138/EC of the European Parliament and of the Council, *OJ* L *295*, 12.11.2015, p. 9.

The capital requirement for medical expense disability–morbidity risk is equal to the larger of the capital requirement for the increase of medical payments (an increase of 5% in the amount of medical payments combined with an increase by 1 percentage point of the inflation rate of medical payments) and the capital requirement for the decrease of medical payments (a decrease of 5% in the amount of medical payments combined with a decrease by 1 percentage point of the inflation rate of medical payments) (Art. 155 DA).

The capital requirement for income protection disability–morbidity risk is equal to the loss in basic own funds resulting from:

- an increase of 35% in the disability and morbidity rates reflecting the disability and morbidity in the following 12 months;
- an increase of 25% in the disability and morbidity rates reflecting the disability and morbidity in the years after the following 12 months;
- where the disability and morbidity recovery rates are lower than 50%, a decrease of 20% in those rates;
- where the disability and morbidity persistency rates are equal or lower than 50%, an increase of 20% in those rates (Art. 156 DA).

The capital requirement for health expense risk is equal to the loss in basic own funds resulting from the combination of an increase of 10% in the amount of expenses and an increase by 1 percentage point of the expense inflation rate (Art. 157 DA).

The capital requirement for health revision risk is equal to the loss in basic own funds resulting from an instantaneous permanent increase of 4% in the amount of annuity benefits relating to annuity insurance and reinsurance obligations where the benefits payable under the underlying insurance policies could increase as a result of changes in inflation, the legal environment or the state of health of the person insured (Art. 158 DA).

The capital requirement for SLT health lapse risk is equal to the largest of the following capital requirements:

- capital requirement for the risk of a permanent increase in SLT health lapse rates (Art. 159 (2) DA);
- capital requirement for the risk of a permanent decrease in SLT health lapse rates (Art. 159 (3) DA);
- capital requirement for SLT health mass lapse risk (Art. 159 (6) DA).

d. Health Catastrophe Risk Sub-Module (Arts. 160–163 DA)

The health catastrophe risk sub-module is further subdivided into sub-modules for mass accident risk, accident concentration risk, and pandemic risk.

The following underlying assumptions apply to the health catastrophe risk sub-module:[291]

- the three health catastrophe risk scenarios (mass accident, accident concentration and pandemic) are assumed to be independent events;
- the scenario-based approach for the health catastrophe risk sub-module assumes that the portfolio on the financial statement date is representative of the whole year.

The health catastrophe risk module is based on standardised scenarios as a method for estimating the catastrophe risk charge to apply across all countries for medical expense plus accident and sickness products. The final calibration aims to provide a catastrophe risk charge at 99.5% of the VaR for undertakings that are exposed to extreme or exceptional events relevant for health insurance obligations. It is assumed that all events are independent (arena scenario for mass accident risk for health insurance obligations other than workers' compensation, concentration scenario for accident concentration risk for workers' compensation and group income protection insurance obligations, pandemic scenario for pandemic risk for health insurance obligations other than workers' compensation).

The three health catastrophe risk scenarios (mass accident, accident concentration and pandemic) are based on standardised scenarios, as these risks are unlikely to be appropriately captured by a formula-based approach. These standardised scenarios are a trade-off between accuracy and ease of use. It is perfectly possible for these standardised scenarios to be inadequate because the risk profile of the (re)insurance undertaking deviates from the assumptions underlying the standard formula calculations.

EIOPA therefore recommends that (re)insurance undertakings consider alternative measures, in particular partial internal models,[292] before choosing to use the standardised scenarios. This particularly applies to undertakings with significant exposure to health catastrophe events where close proximity to the source of the event requires a more sophisticated approach in order to resolve the geographical distribution of the risk, or those with a need to distinguish between the vulnerability of different lines of business, rather than the aggregate approach provided by the scenarios.

---

291 EIOPA, The underlying assumptions in the standard formula for the SCR calculation, EIOPA-14-322, 25 July 2014, pp. 63–67.

292 As USPs cannot be used here. It is almost impossible for a single insurer to have sufficient claims experience to estimate a one-in-200-year event.

4.2.2.2.4. Market Risk Module

Market risk is a very important risk module, accounting for between 25% and 80% of the BSCR for all EEA countries.[293] The main components within the market risk module are equity, spread and interest rate risks.

The market risk module (Art. 105 (5) FD and Arts. 164–188 DA), reflects the risk arising from the level of volatility of market prices of financial instruments that have an impact upon the value of the assets and liabilities of the undertaking, as well as the structural mismatch in duration between assets and liabilities. It consists of the following sub-modules:

- *interest rate risk*: the sensitivity of the values of assets, liabilities and financial instruments to changes in the term structure of interest rates, or in the volatility of interest rates (Arts. 165–167 DA);
- *equity risk*: the sensitivity of the values of assets, liabilities and financial instruments to changes in the level or in the volatility of market prices of equity (Arts. 168–173 DA);
- *property risk*: the sensitivity of the values of assets, liabilities and financial instruments to changes in the level or in the volatility of market prices of real estate (Art. 174 DA);
- *spread risk*: the sensitivity of the values of assets, liabilities and financial instruments to changes in the level or in the volatility of credit spreads over the risk-free interest rate term structure (Arts. 175–181 DA);
- *currency risk*: the sensitivity of the values of assets, liabilities and financial instruments to changes in the level or in the volatility of currency exchange rates (Art. 188 DA);
- *market risk concentrations*: additional risks to the undertaking stemming either from lack of diversification in the asset portfolio or from large exposure to default risk by a single issuer of securities or a group of related issuers (Arts. 182–187 DA).

a. Interest Rate Sub-Module

Interest rate risk exists for all assets and liabilities for which the net asset value is sensitive to changes in the term structure of interest rates or interest rate volatility. Assets sensitive to interest rate movements include fixed-income investments, financing instruments (for example loan capital), policy loans,

---

[293] EIOPA, *European Insurance Overview 2018. Solo undertakings. Year-end 2017*, Publications Office of the EU, Luxembourg, 2018, p. 15.

interest rate derivatives and any insurance assets. The discounted value of future liability cash flows is sensitive to a change in the rate at which those cash flows are discounted.[294]

The capital requirement for interest rate risk is equal to the larger of the following (Art. 165 DA (1)):

- the sum, over all currencies, of the capital requirements for the risk of an increase in the term structure of interest rates as set out in Art. 166 DA;
- the sum, over all currencies, of the capital requirements for the risk of a decrease in the term structure of interest rates as set out in Art. 167 DA.

b. Equity Risk Sub-Module

The equity risk sub-module (Arts. 168–173 DA) has been the subject of a lot of debate.[295] It includes a risk sub-module for type 1 equities (equities listed in regulated markets in EEA or OECD countries or traded on multilateral trading facilities),[296] a risk sub-module for type 2 equities (other than type 1), and two further risk sub-modules, for qualifying infrastructure equities and for qualifying infrastructure corporate equities, which were added in 2016 and in 2017 respectively in order to stimulate investment in infrastructure.[297]

In order to qualify for special treatment as an investment in infrastructure, the investment must take place in an infrastructure entity. An infrastructure entity is defined as an entity or corporate group which, during the most recent financial year of that entity or group for which figures are available or in a financing proposal, derives the substantial majority of its revenues from owning, financing, developing or operating infrastructure assets (Art. 1 (55b) DA).

294 CEIOPS, Advice for Level 2 Implementing Measures on Solvency II: SCR Standard Formula – Art. 109, Structure and Design of Market Risk Module, CEIOPS-DOC-40/09, October 2009, p. 13

295 See, for instance, CEIOPS, Advice for Level 2 Implementing Measures on Solvency II – Art. 111 and 304, Equity Risk Sub-module, CEIOPS-DOC-65/10, 29 January 2010, 50 p.

296 Other equities considered to be type 1 equities include equities held within collective investment undertakings which are qualifying social entrepreneurship funds under Regulation (EU) No 346/2013 of the EP and of the Council of 17 April 2013 on European social entrepreneurship funds, *OJ* L 115, 25.4.2013, p. 18, or undertakings which are qualifying venture capital funds under Regulation (EU) No 345/2013 of the EP and of the Council of 17 April 2013 on European venture capital funds, *OJ* L 115, 25.4.2013, p. 1. See Art. 168 (6) DA.

297 Commission Delegated Regulation (EU) 2016/467 of 30 September 2015 amending Commission Delegated Regulation (EU) 2015/35 concerning the calculation of regulatory capital requirements for several categories of assets held by insurance and reinsurance undertakings, *OJ* L 85, 1.4.2016, p. 6; Commission Delegated Regulation (EU) 2017/1542 of 8 June 2017 amending Delegated Regulation (EU) 2015/35 concerning the calculation of regulatory capital requirements for certain categories of assets held by insurance and reinsurance undertakings (infrastructure corporates), *OJ* L 236, 8.6.2017, p. 14.

An infrastructure asset is a physical asset, structure or facility, a system or a network that provides or supports essential public services (Art. 1 (55a) DA).[298]

Qualifying infrastructure investments are essentially investments in infrastructure projects where a SPV is used, i.e. a legal entity that is established for a specific purpose, such as the building of a bridge or a hospital. In order to qualify, the project must meet certain conditions, for example a predictable cash flow and robust contractual framework. These conditions are listed in Art. 146a DA.

Qualifying infrastructure corporate investments are investments in an entity or corporate group that carries out infrastructure activities. Unlike qualifying infrastructure investments, the investment here is in a regular company, which does not normally have a fixed lifetime, as is the case with project finance through an SPV. The corporate investment must meet certain conditions listed in Art. 164b DA. For instance, the substantial majority of the infrastructure entity's revenues must be derived from owning, financing, developing or operating infrastructure assets located in the EEA or the OECD.

Even prior to the adoption of the FD, many (re)insurance undertakings had already considerably reduced their investments in equity[299] following the capital market crisis at the beginning of the 21st century, but also in preparation for Solvency II, which favours investment in bonds, as the value of such investments is less volatile and the investment offers a better match for long-term liabilities and delivers in addition regular cash flows.[300] Most experts agree that an investment in equity is risky in the context of a one-year time horizon and that the capital charge should reflect this. The equity risk sub-module is based on risk scenarios that envisage a fall in equity market prices of 39% or 49%, depending on the type of equity, not taking into account diversification.

The equity risk sub-module does not have a fixed shock, contrary to all the other sub-modules of the market risk module. The base shock level is 39% for type 1 equity investments and 49% for type 2 equity investments.

---

298 Infrastructure assets can be of an economic nature, such as transport (roads, rails, bridges, tunnels, parking lots, airports, canals or ports), utilities (energy supply such as windmills or power plants, generation, transmission, distribution of oil and gas or water), telecommunication (cable networks, transmission, satellites, radio towers) or of a social nature, such as hospitals, retirement homes, schools, nursery homes, sports structures, recreation or administrative buildings. See, GATZERT, N. and KOSUB, Th., *Insurers' Investment in Infrastructure: Overview and Treatment under Solvency II*, The Geneva Papers, 2014, No 39, p. 353.

299 For instance, Allianz decreased its equity allocation from 35% in 2000 to 7% in 2009, and AXA from 22% in 2000 to 4% in 2009. Source: Natixis Securities.

300 See ECB, *Potential impact of Solvency II on financial stability*, July 2007, 59 p. The econometric analysis carried out by the ECB as part of the impact assessment of the Solvency II proposal indicates that, despite the strong performance of the European stock and real estate markets, anticipation of the introduction of Solvency II led to portfolio reallocations that have tended to reduce market risk in insurers' balance sheet by increasing the share of fixed-income investments at the expense of equity.

It is then modulated by plus or minus 10 points, according to the status of the equity markets over a three-year cycle. In simple terms, this means that in a bull market the SCR for equities goes up, while in a bear market the SCR goes down. This is the so-called symmetric adjustment of the equity capital charge, which was introduced in the Solvency II FD (Art. 106) as a result of the financial crisis in 2008/2009 with the aim of mitigating pro-cyclical market effects, for instance fire sales as a result of short-term market price movements.[301] It is sometimes referred to as the equity dampener or Pillar 1 dampener and is further detailed in Art. 172 DA. EIOPA publishes the symmetric adjustment of the equity capital charge on its website on a monthly basis. For instance, on 30 April 2019, the symmetric adjustment published by EIOPA was −0.34%.

The symmetric adjustment mechanism makes investment in equity more capital-expensive in an upward market and less expensive in times of falling equity indices. The objective is to avoid (re)insurance undertakings being unduly forced to raise additional capital or sell their investments as a result of adverse movements in financial markets and to discourage or avoid fire sales that would further negatively impact the equity prices, i.e. prevent a pro-cyclical effect of the capital requirements that would in times of stress lead to an increase in the capital requirements and hence have a potential destabilising effect on the economy. Taking the symmetric adjustment into account, the shock for type 1 equities lies between a minimum of 29% and a maximum of 49% and for type 2 equities between a minimum of 39% and a maximum of 59%.

Art. 169 DA sets the capital charges for investments in equity as follows:

- investments in type 1 equities:
  - 39% (without application of the symmetric adjustment);
  - 22% in the case of a strategic investment in related undertakings;
  - 22% in the case of a long-term investment;[302]
- investments in type 2 equities:
  - 49% (without application of the symmetric adjustment);
  - 22% in the case of a strategic investment in related undertakings;
  - 22% in the case of a long-term investment;
- investments in qualifying infrastructure equities:
  - 30% and application of 77% of the symmetric adjustment;
  - 22% in the case of a strategic investment in related undertakings;
  - 22% in the case of a long-term investment;

301 See recital 61 FD. It obviously does not apply to strategic investments, long-term investments or to qualifying infrastructure investments and investments in infrastructure corporates, as these investments are held for a long time and are therefore not as subject to market volatility as normal investments in equity.

302 See for all new capital charges for long-term investments, the new Art. 171a DA, introduced as part of the EC's 2019 amendment of the DA.

- investments in qualifying infrastructure corporate equities:
  - 36% and application of 92% of the symmetric adjustment;
  - 22% in the case of a strategic investment in related undertakings;
  - 22% in the case of a long-term investment.

Strategic investments are defined in Art. 171 DA as equity investments of a strategic nature for which the participating (re)insurance undertaking can show:

- that the value of the investment is likely to be materially less volatile for the following 12 months than the value of other equities over the same period, as a result of both the nature of the investment and the influence exercised by the participating undertaking in the related undertaking;
- that the nature of the investment is strategic, taking into account all relevant factors, such as the existence of a clear decisive strategy to continue holding the participation for a long period, the consistency of that strategy with the main policies of the undertaking or the group, the ability of the undertaking to continue holding the participation and the existence of a durable link.

The actual capital charges for equity investments will be much lower as the equity portfolio of (re)insurance undertakings will not only consist of the same type of investment. Through the diversification of their investment portfolio, (re)insurance undertakings can lower the actual capital charge, as long as the investments are not correlated.

The capital charge for strategic investments in related undertakings reflects the likely reduction in the volatility of their value arising from their strategic nature and the influence exercised by the participating undertaking on those related undertakings (recital 57 DA).

In order to promote investment in infrastructure, the symmetric adjustment in the case of an investment in other qualifying infrastructure equities or other qualifying infrastructure corporate equities has been reduced to 77% and 92% respectively.

During the negotiation of the FD, the capital charge for investment in equity was one of the most hotly debated issues. While the UK wanted a capital charge for listed equity between 40% and 42%, as it was not unusual for market stress to be even higher, France insisted on having a capital charge not higher than 32%.[303] In addition, France wanted a special regime for equity investment in the context of retirement provision. The argument was made that the typical

303 Although Henri de Castries, former CEO of the largest French insurance group, AXA, admitted at the Eurofi conference in Nice (September 2008) that AXA was applying a capital charge of 42% for equity investment in its internal model. Equity investments by insurers were at that time on average greater in France than in any other MS of the EEA (14% compared to 6%).

holding period for equity investments in the context of retirement business was consistent with the average duration of the liabilities and that this was at least 12 years. As these equity investments were used to back liabilities beyond 12 years, the short-term volatility in market values could be disregarded and a lower capital requirement for such investments in equity was therefore justified.

After an intense debate, as part of which France supported a coalition of 12 Member States opposing group support (see further, Chapter 9, section 2) in order to have them support the French position on equity risk, a compromise was reached whereby a capital charge for type 1 equity of 39% was agreed, combined with the introduction of a duration-based equity risk sub-module (Art. 304 FD) which is, in relation to certain equity investments, based on a risk scenario that envisages a fall in equity market prices of 22%. The duration-based equity risk sub-module can only be applied by life insurance undertakings that provide certain occupational retirement provision business or retirement benefits and meet further requirements, in particular that the average duration of the undertaking's liabilities exceeds an average of 12 years and that the undertaking is able to hold the equity investments for at least 12 years. In addition, the assets and liabilities corresponding to the business must be ring-fenced and the undertaking cannot extend its (retirement provision) activities cross-border.

The possibility of applying the duration-based equity risk sub-module is an MS option (Art. 304 (1) FD). Its application is subject to supervisory approval. In its 2018 report on LTG measures and measures on equity, EIOPA noted that only one undertaking in the EEA (based in France) was using this sub-module as of 31 December 2017.[304]

The lower capital charges for investments in the context of this "duration" approach are set as follows in Art. 170 DA:

- investments in type 1 equities:
  - 39% (without application of the symmetric adjustment);
  - 22% in the case of a strategic investment in related undertakings;
  - 22% where the assets and liabilities of the business are ring-fenced;
- investments in type 2 equities:
  - 49% (without application of the symmetric adjustment);
  - 22% in the case of a strategic investment in related undertakings;
  - 22% where the assets and liabilities of the business are ring-fenced;
- investments in qualifying infrastructure equities:
  - 30% and application of 77% of the symmetric adjustment;
  - 22% in the case of a strategic investment in related undertakings;
  - 22% where the assets and liabilities of the business are ring-fenced;

304 EIOPA, Report on LTG measures and measures on equity 2018, EIOPA-BoS-17/471, 18 December 2018, p.15.

- investments in qualifying infrastructure corporate equities:
  - 36% and application of 92% of the symmetric adjustment;
  - 22% in the case of a strategic investment in related undertakings;
  - 22% where the assets and liabilities of the business are ring-fenced.

The introduction of the duration-based equity risk sub-module was very controversial. In fact, it was the first time that the idea of linking insurance with long-term investments appeared in the Solvency II discussions. Since then, the debate has re-emerged in the context of the LTG discussions. It found its first concrete realisation with the introduction of the MA, under which long-term (illiquid) liabilities are fully matched with long-term investments in specific types of assets (mostly bonds). In the context of a review of the FD in 2021, it would be interesting to examine to what extent this concept of linking long-term liabilities with long-term investments might receive a prudential treatment that is more favourable than is presently the case, if it can be shown that these types of investments are less risky because of their link with illiquid liabilities.[305]

In order to smooth the transition from Solvency I to Solvency II and to prevent sudden or large-scale portfolio reallocations in the area of equities, Art. 308 (13) FD introduced a transitional measure for equities purchased on or before 1 January 2016 that are not subject to the duration-based approach (Art. 304 FD) by introducing the capital requirement for equities purchased before that date progressively over seven years (Art. 173 (1) DA). The same treatment was extended in 2016[306] to type 2 equities and to equities held within collective investment undertakings or investments packaged as funds (Art. 173 (2) DA).

The EC is continuing its push in favour of more long-term investment, particularly by (re)insurers.[307] This has resulted in two amendments of the DA, particularly for investments in infrastructure and infrastructure corporates, and continued with a second call for advice to EIOPA to examine the possibility of changing the prudential treatment of private equity, strategic equity investments and privately placed corporate debt as part of the

305 This is presently being looked at by EIOPA at the request of the EC. See EIOPA, Request for feedback on methodological considerations regarding illiquid liabilities, EIOPA-PSC-18/093, 29 October 2018, 30 p.

306 Commission Delegated Regulation (EU) 2016/467 of 30 September 2015 amending Commission Delegated Regulation (EU) 2015/35 concerning the calculation of regulatory capital requirements for several categories of assets held by insurance and reinsurance undertakings, *OJ* L 85, 1.4.2016, p. 6.

307 The EC also launched on 19 December 2017 a study on the drivers of investments in equity by insurers and pension funds. The results of this study are not available yet. For the importance of the insurance industry as an institutional investor, see Insurance Europe and Oliver Wyman, *Funding the future. Insurers' role as institutional investors*, June 2013, 49 p.

2018 review of the DA.[308] This is also part of the EC's Action Plan to build stronger capital markets in the EU.[309]

In its second set of advice to the EC in the context of the 2018 review of the DA, EIOPA proposed a methodology that, when correctly applied, would allow the same prudential treatment for unlisted equity as for listed equity.[310] This proposal was included by the EC in its 2019 amendment of the DA, which introduces in Art. 168 (6) (e) DA a new category of type 1 equities, called qualifying unlisted equity portfolios and in Art. 171a DA a new category of long-term equity investments.[311]

Qualifying unlisted equity portfolios are defined in Art. 168a DA as a set of investments consisting solely of investments in ordinary shares of companies that are not listed in any regulated market. These investments receive the same treatment as investments in equities that are listed in regulated markets (type 1 equities). The investments must be of high quality.[312] The companies in which the investment is made must be medium-sized (the annual turnover and the balance sheet total must each exceed €10 million and the number of staff employed must exceed 50) and have their head office in an EEA country. The value of the investment in each company may not represent more than 10% of the total value of the set of investments.[313]

Art. 171a DA introduces a new category of long-term equity investments. A sub-set of equity investments may be treated as long-term equity investments if the (re)insurance undertaking demonstrates, to the satisfaction of the supervisory authority, that all of the following conditions are met (Art. 171a (1)DA):

- the sub-set of equity investments as well as the holding period of each equity investment within the sub-set are clearly identified;
- the sub-set of equity investments is included within a portfolio of assets which is assigned to cover the best estimate of a portfolio of (re)insurance

308 EC, *Request to EIOPA for technical advice on the review of specific items in the Solvency II Delegated Regulation as regards unjustified constraints to financing*, 21 February 2017.

309 EC, Communication on the Action Plan on Building a Capital Markets Union, COM (2015) 468 final, 28 p.; EC, Communication on Capital Markets Union – Accelerating Reform, COM (2016) 601 final, 14 September 2016, 28 p.; EC, Communication on the Mid-Term Review of the Capital Markets Union Action Plan, COM (2017) 292 final, 8 June 2017, 19 p.

310 EIOPA, Second set of advice to the EC on specific items in the Solvency II Delegated Regulation, *EIOPA*-BoS-18/075, 28 February 2018, pp. 184–213.

311 See also, the Commission Staff Working Document, Supporting insurers' investment in equity and unrated debt, 8 March 2019, which accompanies the Commission Delegated Regulation of 8 March 2019 amending the DA.

312 The beta of the set of investments may not exceed 0.796, i.e. the volatility must be lower than the market volatility. For the definition of the beta of a set of investments, see Art. 168a (2) DA.

313 For the other criteria, see Art. 168a (1) DA, introduced as part of the EC's 2019 amendment of the DA.

obligations corresponding to one or several clearly identified businesses, and the undertaking maintains that assignment over the lifetime of the obligations;
- the portfolio of (re)insurance obligations, and the assigned portfolio of assets are identified, managed and organised separately from the other activities of the undertaking, and the assigned portfolio of assets cannot be used to cover losses arising from other activities of the undertaking;
- the technical provisions within the portfolio of (re)insurance obligations only represent a part of the total technical provisions of the (re)insurance undertaking;
- the average holding period of equity investments in the sub-set exceeds five years, or where the average holding period of the sub-set is less than five years, the (re)insurance undertaking does not sell any equity investments within the sub-set until the average holding period exceeds five years;
- the sub-set of equity investments consists only of equities that are listed in the EEA or of unlisted equities of companies that have their head offices in countries that are members of the EEA;
- the solvency and liquidity position of the (re)insurance undertaking, as well as its strategies, processes and reporting procedures with respect to asset-liability management, are such as to ensure, on an ongoing basis and under stressed conditions, that it is able to avoid forced sales of each equity investment within the sub-set for at least 10 years;
- the risk management, asset-liability management and investment policies of the (re)insurance undertaking reflect the undertaking's intention to hold the sub-set of equity investments for a period that is compatible with the requirement to hold the investment for a long period.

Where the equities are held within collective investment undertakings or within alternative investment funds, the conditions defining the long-term nature of the investment may be assessed at the level of the funds and not of the underlying assets held within those funds (Art. 171a (2) DA).

(Re)insurance undertakings that treat a sub-set of equity investments as long-term equity investments may not revert back to an approach that does not include long-term equity investments. Where a (re)insurance undertaking that treats a sub-set of equity investments as long-term equity investments is no longer able to comply with the conditions set out in Art. 171a (1), it must immediately inform the supervisory authority and can no longer apply the reduced capital charge to any of its equity investments for a period of 36 months (Art. 171a (3) DA).

In its initial proposal that was published for public feedback on the Better Regulation Portal, the conditions for an equity investment to qualify as a long-term equity investment were stricter, i.e. a minimum average holding period of

12 years, a demonstration of the ability to hold the investment for 12 years and a ring-fencing of the corresponding portfolio of assets and liabilities. This was heavily criticised by the insurance industry, which argued that these conditions made the regime unworkable.[314] The criticism was shared by the EP.[315] The EC therefore decided to lower the requirements, particularly by reducing the holding period of the investment from 12 to five years. This was coupled with a prohibition for undertakings to turn a long-term equity investment into a short-term equity investment and with a sanction for undertakings that have treated an equity investment as a long-term equity investment and are no longer able to respect the conditions for treating that investment as such.

It is clear from these recent amendments to the DA that the intention of the EC is not only to encourage equity investments but to provide a favourable treatment for equity investments in EEA companies that have their main activity in the EEA.

Although these initiatives should be welcomed because they help (re)insurers to diversify their investments and to support the real economy, it is important to keep in mind that it cannot be the objective of a prudential regime to incentivise any asset class in particular. Investment decisions should be taken by company managers and not by regulators.[316] For infrastructure investments, there is the additional difficulty that there are insufficient investment opportunities. Opportunities should become available when transitioning the present economy to a more sustainable economy becomes a higher political priority.[317]

Developing a more sustainable economy will have further consequences for the prudential framework. Following its Action Plan on Financing Sustainable Growth,[318] the EC has invited EIOPA to provide an opinion on the impact of prudential rules on (re)insurers' sustainable investments, with a particular focus on climate change mitigation, and to collect good practices of (re)insurers concerning investments and asset–liability management with a view to gaining an insight into how insurers incorporate sustainability into their investment practice. EIOPA should also provide an opinion on the extent to which current

---

314 Insurance Europe, *Insurance Europe comments on amendments to Solvency II Delegated Regulation*, Position Paper, 11 December 2018, p. 21, https://www.insuranceeurope.eu/sites/default/files/attachments/Comments%20on%20amendments%20to%20Solvency%20II%20Delegated%20Regulation_0.pdf.

315 See the letter of 6 December 2018 by Roberto Gualtieri, Chair of ECON, to Vice-President Valdis Dombrovskis, http://www.europarl.europa.eu/cmsdata/158466/D(47737)%20-%20Dombrovskis%20-%20Solvency%20II%20Review%20follow-up%20-%20WdJ.pdf.

316 BERNARDINO, G., *Milestones of preparation for Solvency II*, European Insurance Conference, London, 2 June 2015, p. 6, https://eiopa.europa.eu/Publications/Speeches%20and%20presentations/2015-06-02%20European%20Insurance%20Conference.pdf.

317 It would have been a good idea to require, as another condition, that the long-term equity investment had to be an investment in sustainable assets.

318 EC, Communication to the EP, the European Council, the ECB, the EESC and the CoR – Action Plan: Financing Sustainable Growth, COM (2018) 97 final, 8 March 2018, p. 9.

practices in product design and in product pricing account for sustainability factors, with particular regard to the climate risk the insurance obligations are exposed to and the extent to which these practices are incentivised by Solvency II. The opinion should be provided by 30 September 2019 and is part of the preparation for the review of the FD in 2021.[319]

c. *Property Risk Sub-Module*

Property risk arises as a result of the sensitivity of assets, liabilities and financial investments to the level or volatility of market prices of property.

The following investments are treated as property and their risks considered accordingly in the property risk sub-module:[320]

- land, buildings and immovable property rights;
- direct or indirect participations in real estate companies that generate periodic income or that are otherwise intended for investment purposes;
- property investment for the insurance undertaking's own use.

The following investments are treated as equity and their risks considered accordingly in the equity risk sub-module:

- an investment in a company engaged in real estate management;
- an investment in a company engaged in real estate project development or similar activities;
- an investment in a company that took out loans from institutions outside the scope of the insurance group in order to leverage its investments in properties.

Collective real estate investment vehicles are treated like other collective investment vehicles, namely with a look-through approach.

The capital charge for a direct investment in property is 25% (Art. 174 DA). No distinction is made for different property classes. Even though the calibration is based on UK data, it was implicitly assumed that the UK property market could be used as a good proxy for the average European property market.[321]

---

319 See letter sent by Olivier Guersent, Director-General of DG FISMA to Gabriel Bernardino, Chairman of EIOPA, on 28 August 2018. See also the letter sent by Olivier Guersent to EIOPA and to ESMA on 24 July 2018, inviting them to provide an opinion by 30 April 2019 on possible amendments to, inter alia, the DA, with the aim of incorporating sustainable risks, i.e. environmental, social and governance risks, into the investment decisions of (re)insurers. See also EIOPA, *Financial Stability Report*, June 2018, pp. 8–22.

320 See also CEIOPS, Advice for Level 2 Implementing Measures on Solvency II: SCR Standard Formula – Art. 109, Structure and Design of Market Risk Module, CEIOPS-DOC-40/09, October 2009, pp. 23–24.

321 This has been criticised by a number of players in the real estate market. See, for instance, the study published by a number of real estate associations, *MSCI Real Estate Solvency II 2017 Update Report*, March 2017, which advocates a capital charge of 15%.

The risk profile of any exposures to property located in third countries is assumed not to be materially different from the risk profile of European property markets.[322]

It is questionable whether the UK property market can really be treated as being representative of European property markets.[323] Representative organisations from the real estate sector have argued that research they have carried out shows that the capital charge should be brought down to 15%.[324] An alternative solution would be to develop a more granular sub-module in the standard formula, further distinguishing between different types of property, or for (re)insurance undertakings that have an sizeable real estate portfolio to develop a partial internal model.[325]

d. *Spread Risk Sub-Module*

Spread risk is the risk of a change in value due to a deviation of the actual market price of credit risk from the expected price of credit risk.[326] The spread risk sub-module addresses changes in both the level and the volatility of spreads.[327]

The spread risk sub-module covers the risk of bonds and loans (Art. 176 DA), securitisation positions (Arts. 177 and 178 DA), and credit derivatives (Art. 179 DA). Art. 180 DA deals with specific exposures in the form of covered bonds, sovereign exposures, exposures in the form of bonds and loans to (re)insurance undertakings and exposures in the form of bonds and loans to credit institutions and financial institutions.

Essentially, the spread risk is made up of two elements: the credit quality, which is represented by a credit quality step (CQS), equivalent to an aggregated rating class (for instance a CQS of 0 is equal to a credit rating of AAA), and the sensitivity of the instrument to a shock on the credit spread.

---

322 EIOPA, The underlying assumptions in the standard formula for the SCR calculation, EIOPA-14-322, 25 July 2014, p. 21.

323 This will become even more so when the UK leaves the EU. In that case, a re-examination of the calibration of property risk should take place.

324 See, for instance, the position paper by INREV, *Real estate investment under Solvency II*, May 2017, 2 p. https://www.inrev.org/system/files/2017-05/SolvencyII_snapshot_ONLINE_MAY2017_v3.pdf.

325 This is, for instance, done by the Vienna Insurance Group, which distinguishes in its partial internal model for property between directly held real estate and holding companies, non-profit housing societies and real estate funds. See the 2017 SFCR of Vienna Insurance Group, p. 90, https://www.vig.com/fileadmin/web/Investor_Relations/Downloads/Solvency_II/180530_-_SFCR_Bericht_mit_Anhang_Englisch__final_.pdf.

326 CEA and Groupe Consultatif, *Solvency II Glossary*, March 2007, p. 50.

327 See also CEIOPS, Advice for Level 2 Implementing Measures on Solvency II: SCR Standard Formula – Art. 109, Structure and Design of Market Risk Module, CEIOPS-DOC-40/09, October 2009, pp. 18–21.

For bonds, loans and notes, this sensitivity is a function of the spread duration, which is defined for each CQS and depends on the nature of the instrument (government bond, corporate bond, covered bond, securitisation).

For credit derivatives, the sensitivity is a function of the variation of the present value under certain upward and downward shocks, the size of which depends on the CQS.

For the definition of the spread risk, a distinction is made between bonds or loans for which a credit assessment by a nominated ECAI is or is not available.

(Re)insurance undertakings may use an external credit assessment for the calculation of the SCR in accordance with the standard formula only where it has been issued or endorsed by an ECAI in accordance with the CRA I Regulation.[328]

If the exposure is in the form of bonds or loans to another (re)insurance undertaking and a credit assessment by a nominated ECAI is not available, the solvency ratio of that undertaking may be used instead of an external rating (Art. 180 (4) and (5) DA). This is perfectly logical as it takes account of the solvency reform in insurance.

(Re)insurance undertakings must nominate one or more ECAIs for their credit assessment. Credit assessments must be used consistently and not selectively (Art. 4 DA). In order to avoid the risk of biased estimations of credit risk, (re)insurance undertakings that do not use an approved internal model to calculate credit risk may not use their own credit assessment if that assessment would result in a lower capital requirement than that resulting from an external rating (recital 4 DA).

Arts. 4 and 5 DA further elaborate on how credit assessments issued by an ECAI should be used. This is further developed in a Commission Implementing Regulation, which allocates the credit assessments issued by a list of ECAIs to an objective scale of CQSs.[329]

---

328 Regulation (EC) No 1060/2009 of the EP and of the Council of 16 September 2009 on credit rating agencies, *OJ* L 302, 17.11.2009, p. 1, as amended by Regulation (EU) No 513/2011 of the EP and of the Council of 11 May 2011, *OJ* L 145, 31.5.2011, p. 30 and Regulation (EU) No 462/2013, of the EP and of the Council of 21 May 2013, *OJ* L 146, 31.5.2013, p. 1. As a result of Brexit, UK ECAIs will be deregistered after the withdrawal date and will no longer qualify as ECAIs. Assets of an EEA (re)insurance undertaking may therefore lose their ECAI ratings. See Art. 24 (4) CRA Regulation.

329 Commission Implementing Regulation (EU) 2015/2015 of 11 November 2015 laying down implementing technical standards on the procedures for assessing external credit assessments in accordance with Directive 2009/138/EC of the EP and of the Council, *OJ* L 295, 12.11.2015, p. 16 and Commission Implementing Regulation (EU) 2016/1800 of 11 October 2016 laying down implementing technical standards with regard to the allocation of credit assessments of external credit assessment institutions to an objective scale of credit quality steps in accordance with Directive 2009/138/EC of the EP and of the Council, *OJ* L 275, 12.10.2016, p. 19. The Joint Committee of the three ESAs launched on 23 October 2018 a public consultation to amend the Implementing Regulations on the mapping of credit

In accordance with Art. 111 (1) (n) FD, the allocation of credit assessments of ECAIs for the purposes of the calculation of the SCR must be consistent with the allocation of credit assessments of ECAIs for the purposes of the calculation of the capital requirements for credit institutions and financial institutions. The allocation provided for in the Commission Implementing Regulation of 11 October 2016 is therefore based on the mapping methodology for credit institutions and financial institutions.[330] The allocation arrangements apply to credit assessments of ECAIs or central banks issuing credit ratings, as well as to credit assessments endorsed by an ECAI in accordance with the CRA I Regulation.

In order to ensure a balance between a solid prudential approach and competition in the credit rating market, the EC amended the draft text of the Commission Implementing Regulation produced by the Joint Committee of the ESAs in order to avoid undue material disadvantage to smaller/newer ECAIs due to their more recent entrance into the market.[331] The list of ECAIs was therefore expanded in the final text. As five new ECAIs were registered and certified after the adoption of the Commission's Implementing Regulation of 11 October 2016, that Implementing Regulation was amended again in 2018.[332]

The CQS of an asset is based on the second-best rating from three (or more) ECAIs. The choice of ECAI cannot be changed over the life of an instrument and must be the same for similar debts. The scale of CQSs comprises steps 0–6 (Art. 3 DA).

If only one rating from an ECAI is available, this rating must be used. If only two ratings are available, the worst rating should be used (Art. 4 DA). Securitisation positions with only one rating from an ECAI are considered unrated (Art. 6 DA).

In most cases, (re)insurance undertakings need to nominate several ECAIs to cover their whole portfolio. The contracts usually provided by ECAIs are

---

assessments of ECAIs for credit risk to reflect the outcomes of a monitoring exercise on the adequacy of existing mappings. This would imply changes to the CQS allocation for two ECAIs and the introduction of new credit rating scales for 10 ECAIs.

330 Commission Implementing Regulation (EU) 2016/1799 of 7 October 2016 laying down implementing technical standards with regard to the mapping of credit assessments of external credit assessment institutions for credit risk in accordance with Art. 136 (1) and (3) of Regulation (EU) No 575/2013 of the EP and of the Council, *OJ* L 275, 12.10.2016, p. 3.

331 Recital 9 to Commission Implementing Regulation (EU) 2016/1800 of 11 October 2016 laying down implementing technical standards with regard to the allocation of credit assessments of external credit assessment institutions to an objective scale of credit quality steps in accordance with Directive 2009/138/EC of the EP and of the Council, *OJ* L 275, 12.10.2016, p. 19.

332 Commission Implementing Regulation (EU) 2018/633 of 24 April 2018 amending Implementing Regulation (EU) 2016/1800 laying down implementing technical standards with regard to the allocation of credit assessments of external credit assessment institutions to an objective scale of credit quality steps in accordance with Directive 2009/138/EC of the EP and of the Council, *OJ* L 105, 25.4.2018, p. 6.

standardised and cover a certain number of asset classes. EIOPA's research shows that, on average, (re)insurance undertakings nominate 2.5 ECAIs to cover their whole portfolio of investments.[333] This may lead to situations where specific asset classes are covered by multiple ECAIs. Where a specific asset class is not covered by an existing contract with an ECAI, the (re)insurance undertaking needs to sign a new contract with another ECAI to ensure that all of its investments are covered.

In a situation where a (re)insurance undertaking has already nominated an ECAI to cover almost all of its debt portfolio, the question arises whether the risks of the asset classes not already covered justify the nomination of another ECAI. This would lead to asset classes being covered by two ECAIs and to licensing fees that are not proportionate to the risks of the asset classes not covered.

In its first set of advice to the EC in the context of the 2018 review of the DA, EIOPA therefore proposed introducing a new simplified calculation for the spread risk sub-module and the market risk concentration sub-module as an application of the proportionality principle referred to in Art. 88 DA, allowing (re)insurance undertakings to nominate only one ECAI for their whole portfolio of investments under certain conditions.[334] Based on EIOPA's advice, a simplified calculation was introduced in Art. 105a DA that allows (re)insurance undertakings to assign a risk factor equivalent to CQS 3 to certain bonds for which a credit assessment by a nominated ECAI is not available, on the condition that credit assessments from a nominated ECAI are available for at least 80% of the total value of the bonds in that category, subject to the conditions listed in Art. 105a DA.

In order to reduce overreliance on external ratings, (re)insurance undertakings must try to develop their own credit assessment for all their exposures. They must assess the appropriateness of external credit assessments as part of their risk management by using additional assessments wherever practically possible. The requirements for an undertaking's own internal credit assessment of bonds and loans are now clearly defined in the new Arts. 176a and 176b DA, introduced by the EC in the context of the 2018 review of the DA. The articles are based upon advice provided by EIOPA.[335] In its RSR, the undertaking must show how it verifies the appropriateness of credit assessments from ECAIs, including how and the extent to which credit assessments of ECAIs

333 EIOPA, First set of advice to the EC on specific items in the Solvency II Delegated Regulation, EIOPA-BoS-17/280, 30 October 2017, p. 17.

334 EIOPA, First set of advice to the EC on specific items in the Solvency II Delegated Regulation, EIOPA-BoS-17/280, 30 October 2017, p. 20.

335 See Art. 44 (4a) FD and Commission Implementing Regulation (EU) 2015/2015 of 11 November 2015 laying down implementing technical standards on the procedures for assessing external credit assessments in accordance with Directive 2009/138/EC of the EP and of the Council, *OJ* L 295, 12.11.2015, p. 16.

are used (Art. 308 (3) (e) DA). However, in view of the proportionality principle, (re)insurance undertakings are only required to produce their own internal credit assessment for their larger or more complex exposures (Art. 4 (5) DA). This internal assessment can, however only lead to a higher capital requirement than that obtained from an ECAI.

The capital requirements for spread risk on bonds and loans are set out in Art. 176 DA. Based upon proposals submitted by EIOPA[336] in the context of the 2018 review of the DA, new provisions were introduced in 2019 allowing for a less cumbersome procedure for the assessment of investments in high-quality private placements (unrated debt). A bond or a loan for which a credit assessment by a nominated ECAI is not available and for which debtors have not posted collateral that meets the criteria for collateral arrangements in Art. 214 DA may be assigned to CQS 2 or 3 if the conditions in Art. 176a DA are satisfied. The undertaking must be able to demonstrate to the supervisory authority's satisfaction that its own internal credit assessment and the allocation of a CQS to the bond or loan on the basis of that assessment are reliable and properly reflect the spread risk of the bond or loan (Art. 176b DA).

Where the (re)insurance undertaking has concluded an agreement with a credit institution or an investment firm to co-invest in bonds and loans for which a credit assessment by a nominated ECAI is not available, the undertaking is allowed to use the results of the approved internal ratings-based approach of the credit institution or investment firm to calculate its SCR, provided that the credit institution or investment firm has its head office in the EEA. The same applies where the (re)insurance undertaking has concluded an agreement with another (re)insurance undertaking that uses an approved internal model (Art. 176c DA).

Covered bonds that are rated CQS 0 and 1 (AAA and AA) benefit from a favourable treatment (see Art. 180 (1) DA).[337] Covered bonds are defined in Art. 52 (4) of Directive 2009/65/EC[338] as bonds issued by a credit institution that has its registered office in a MS and is subject by law to special public supervision designed to protect bondholders. In particular, sums deriving from the issue of those bonds must be invested in accordance with the law on assets which, during the whole period of validity of the bonds, are capable of covering claims attached to the bonds and which, in the event of failure of the issuer, would be used on a priority basis for the reimbursement of the principal and payment

---

336 See EIOPA, Second set of advice to the EC on specific items in the Solvency II Delegated Regulation, EIOPA-BoS-18/075, 28 February 2018, pp. 207–213.

337 A similar favourable treatment of exposures in the form of covered bonds also applies in the banking sector. See Art. 129 CRR.

338 Directive 2009/65/EC of the EP and of the Council of 13 July 2009 on the coordination of laws, regulations and administrative provisions relating to undertakings for collective investment in transferable securities (UCITS) (recast), *OJ* L 302, 17.11.2009, p. 32.

of the accrued interest. In a new proposal tabled by the EC, covered bonds are defined as "a debt obligation issued by a credit institution and secured by a cover pool of assets which covered bond investors have direct recourse to as preferred creditors".[339]

Banks and (re)insurance undertakings are important investors in covered bonds, which are called *Pfandbriefe* in Germany, *obligations foncières* in France, and *cedulas* in Spain. They are an attractive investment opportunity for two main reasons:

- dual recourse: double protection offered to bondholders: if the credit institution issuing the bond does not pay them, bondholders have a claim against the institution's assets, and – in event that the institution goes bankrupt – they have a claim against a separate "cover pool" of financial assets which has priority over unsecured creditors;
- asset segregation and dynamic cover pool: the credit institution that issues the bond is obliged to "ring-fence" the cover pool and to ensure that the value of the assets making up the cover pool is equal to, or even higher than, the value of the covered bonds at all times (also called over-collateralisation).

Infrastructure debt benefits from reduced shocks if the underlying infrastructure project and the debt instruments (bonds or loans) meet the criteria listed in Arts. 164a[340] and 180 (12) DA.

In relation to credit derivatives, only the credit risk that is transferred by the derivative is covered in the spread risk sub-module. Investments for the benefit of life-insurance policyholders who bear the investment risk are included only to the extent that the undertaking assumes spread risk.

Credit derivatives include, for example, credit default swaps, total return swaps and credit linked notes that are not held as part of a recognised risk-mitigation policy. They also include all tranches of structured credit products like collateralised debt obligations. In addition, this risk sub-module also includes traditional forms of asset-backed securities, such as commercial and residential mortgage-backed securities, home equity loans, credit card receivables, auto loans and student loans, as well as whole-business securitisations, infrastructure finance notes and other covered bonds.

Instruments sensitive to changes in credit spreads may also give rise to other risks, which must be treated accordingly in the appropriate risk modules. For instance, the counterparty default risk associated with the counterparty of a

[339] EC, Proposal for a Directive of the EP and of the Council on the issue of covered bonds and covered bond public supervision and amending Directive 2009/65/EC and Directive 2014/59/EU, COM (2018) 94 final, 12 March 2018.

[340] These reduced shocks do not apply to investments in infrastructure corporate debt.

risk-mitigating transaction must be addressed in the counterparty default risk module, rather than in the spread risk sub-module.

(i) Securitisations

Securitisations involve transactions that enable a lender or a creditor – typically a credit institution or a company – to refinance illiquid and non-tradable assets – a set of loans, exposures or receivables, such as mortgages, auto loans or leases, consumer loans, credit cards or trade receivables – by transforming them into tradable securities. The lender pools a portfolio of a homogeneous set of loans into a vehicle issuing a set of securities tailored to different investors, thus giving investors access to investments in loans and other exposures to which they normally would not have direct access. Returns to investors are generated from the cash flows of the underlying repackaged loans.[341]

Since the beginning of the financial crisis, European securitisation markets have remained subdued for various reasons: the stigma attached to this asset class, macro-economic conditions (for example limited growth prospects), the availability of cheaper financing sources and regulatory uncertainties.

Securitisation of subprime mortgages created in the USA contributed greatly to the financial crisis of 2008. Although losses resulting from EU securitisation products were much lower than those suffered in the USA,[342] regulators in the EU clamped down on securitisations, particularly by insisting that the originators of the securitisation should keep enough skin in the game, i.e. retain part of the risk on their own balance sheet. It was therefore required that the originator, sponsor or original lender would retain, on an ongoing basis, a material net economic interest that in any event should not be less than 5% (Art. 135 (2) FD).

During the negotiation of the FD, the co-legislators insisted that there should be a level playing field in regulation between credit institutions as originators of the securitisation and (re)insurance undertakings as investors. In accordance with the original text of Art. 135 (2) FD, the EC was empowered to adopt an implementing measure laying down:

- the requirements to be met by undertakings that repackage loans into tradable securities and other financial instruments (originators or sponsors) in order to allow (re)insurance undertakings to invest in these securities or instruments issued after 1 January 2011;

341 EC, *A European Framework for Simple and Transparent Securitisation: Fact Sheet*, 30 September 2015, p. 1.

342 As indicated by EBA, the worst-performing EU securitisation products rated AAA defaulted in only 0.1% of cases at the height of the crisis. In comparison, their US equivalents defaulted in 16% of cases. See EC, *A European Framework for Simple and Transparent Securitisation: Fact Sheet*, 30 September 2015, p. 3.

- the qualitative requirements that must be met by (re)insurance undertakings that invest in such securities or instruments;
- the specifications for the circumstances under which a proportionate additional capital charge may be imposed when the requirements have been breached.

Art. 135 (2) FD was implemented by Arts. 254–257 DA. Art. 254 (1) DA state as a principle that for the purposes of Art. 135 (2) FD, the originator, sponsor or original lender had to retain, on an ongoing basis, a material net economic interest that in any event could not be less than 5% and had to explicitly disclose that commitment to the (re)insurance undertaking in the documentation governing the investment. The retention of a material net economic interest of not less than 5% was further specified in Art. 254 (2)–(9) DA. The risk-retention requirement did not apply where the securitised exposures were exposures to sovereigns (Art. 255 (1) DA) or where the securitisation was based on a clear, transparent and accessible index (Art. 255 (2) DA).

In terms of the qualitative requirements, Art. 256 (2) DA required (re)insurance undertakings to conduct adequate due diligence prior to making a securitisation investment, including an assessment of the commitment of the originator, sponsor or original lender to respect the retention requirement and of the factors that could undermine that commitment. The (re)insurance undertaking had to ensure that the originator, sponsor or original lender was sufficiently solid (Art. 256 (3) DA) and complied with the risk management requirements stated in Art. 256 (4)–(7) DA.

If the investments in securitisation no longer complied with the risk-retention and qualitative requirements, the (re)insurance undertaking had to inform the supervisory authority immediately. The spread risk capital requirement was in that case increased (Art. 257 DA).

Based upon recommendations from EIOPA, the DA included a detailed list of criteria to identify high-quality (type 1) securitisations featuring a high degree of simplicity, transparency and credit quality (Art. 177 DA). The high-quality category included the most senior tranches of securitisations, backed by residential mortgages, auto loans and leases, SME loans or consumer loans and credit card receivables, but excluded re-securitisations and synthetic securitisations.

(Re)insurance undertakings investing in these securitisation positions had to hold less capital for market risk compared to other securitisation positions (Art. 178 DA). Their treatment under the standard formula followed the look-through approach, whereby capital requirements on those positions could not be higher than the capital requirements on the underlying securitised exposures if they were held directly by (re)insurance undertakings. The risk factor stress attached to type 1 securitisation positions was capped at 3%, as opposed to type 2 securitisation positions and re-securitisation positions, where the risk factor stress followed the CQSs, starting from 12.5% for type 2 securitisation positions and 33% for re-securitisation positions.

As part of its ambition to create a capital markets union,[343] the EC wanted to further revive the securitisation market in the EU, in order to offer new financing tools and ease credit provision, especially for SMEs. An increase in securitisation activity could help free up banks' balance sheets, which would also allow further lending to the real economy.

On 30 September 2015, the EC launched its "securitisation initiative", which included a Securitisation Regulation and an amendment to the CRR. Both regulations were adopted on 12 December 2017.[344] The main objectives are:[345]

- to revive markets on a more sustainable basis so that simple, standardised and transparent (STS) securitisation can act as an effective funding channel to the economy;
- to allow for efficient and effective risk transfers to a broad set of institutional investors;
- to allow securitisation to function as an effective funding mechanism for insurance undertakings as well as banks;
- to protect investors and to manage systemic risk.

The Securitisation Regulation creates, for the first time, a cross-sectorally applicable, common framework across the EU for the regulatory treatment of securitisations. In addition, it includes specific criteria for STS securitisations that receive preferential treatment in the area of capital requirements both for credit institutions and for (re)insurance undertakings. The concept of "simple, transparent and standardised" refers to the process by which the securitisation is structured. It does not mean that the securitisation is free of risks, but that the product meets a number of criteria and that a prudent and diligent investor will be able to analyse the risk involved.

"Simple" securitisation means that:

- assets packaged in the securitisation must be homogeneous loans/receivables in terms of underlying assets (e.g. car loans with car loans, residential mortgages with residential mortgages), maturity period and cash flow profile;

---

343 EC, Communication on the Action Plan on Building a Capital Markets Union, COM (2015) 468 final, 30 September 2015, 28 p.

344 Regulation (EU) 2017/2402 of the EP and of the Council of 12 December 2017 laying down a general framework for securitisation and creating a specific framework for simple, transparent and standardised securitisation, and amending Directives 2009/65/EC, 2009/138/EC and 2011/61/EU and Regulations (EC) No 1060/2009 and (EU) No 648/2012, *OJ* L 347, 28.12.2017, p. 35; Regulation (EU) 2017/2401 of the EP and of the Council of 12 December 2017 amending Regulation (EU) No 575/2013 on prudential requirements for credit institutions and investment firms, *OJ* L 347, 28.12.2017, p. 1.

345 EC, *A Framework for Simple and Transparent Securitisations: Fact Sheet*, 30 September 2015, pp. 2–3.

- no securitisation of securitisations is allowed;
- loans must have a credit history long enough to allow reliable estimates of default risk;
- the ownership of a loan must have been transferred to the securitisation issuer (i.e. they must be sold by the originator of the loans to the entity that will issue the securitisation).

"Transparent and standardised" securitisation means that:
- loans packaged in the securitisation must have been created using the same lending standards as any other loan, i.e. no cherry-picking is allowed;
- at least 5% of the loan portfolio must be retained by the originator;
- documents must provide details of the structure used and the payment cascade (i.e. the sequence and amount of payment to each tranche);
- data on packaged loans must be published on an ongoing basis;
- the contractual obligations, duties and responsibilities of all key parties to the securitisation must be clearly defined.

As pointed out by EBA in its report on qualifying securitisation,[346] empirical evidence on defaults and losses shows that STS securitisations exhibited better performance than other securitisations during the financial crisis, reflecting the use of simple and transparent structures and robust execution practices in STS securitisations, which deliver lower credit, operational and agency risks. The amendment of the CRR therefore provides for an appropriately risk-sensitive calibration for STS securitisations, provided that they also meet additional requirements to minimise risk, in the manner recommended by EBA. The most senior STS securitisation positions are therefore subject to a minimum risk weight of 10% instead of 15%.

The STS Regulation replaced Art. 135 (2) and (3) FD with a new empowerment for the EC to specify the circumstances under which a proportionate additional capital charge may be imposed when the requirements provided for in Arts. 5 or 6 STS Regulation have been breached.[347] On 1 June 2018, the EC adopted an amendment of the DA[348] that aligns the definitions in Art. 1 DA regarding securitisation with those in the STS Regulation and adapts the treatment of securitisations to that adopted for credit institutions and investment firms in December 2017 (Arts. 178 and 178a DA). The amendment

346 EBA, *Report on qualifying securitisation*, July 2015, 134 p. (https://eba.europa.eu/documents/10180/950548/EBA+report+on+qualifying+securitisation.pdf).

347 Art. 39 (1) STS Regulation.

348 Commission Delegated Regulation (EU) 2018/1221 of 1 June 2018 amending Delegated Regulation (EU) 2015/35 as regards the calculation of regulatory capital requirements for securitisations and simple, transparent and standardised securitisations held by insurance and reinsurance undertakings, *OJ* L 227, 10.9.2018, p. 1.

could not have been made earlier as a reference was needed to the STS Regulation, which was only adopted on 12 December 2017. The changes to the capital requirements for banks and (re)insurance undertakings apply from the same date, i.e. 1 January 2019 (Art. 2 Regulation (EU) 2018/1221 of 1 June 2018).

As stated in recital 6 of the amending Regulation of 1 June 2018:

> "The calibration of the SCR is risk based and is intended to provide the right incentives across the different forms of securitisation investments. In order to achieve that objective, the level of the calibration and the risk sensitivity across tranches should be commensurate with the features of STS securitisation, and consistent with the prudential requirements developed for credit institutions and investment firms. Therefore, the existing provisions in the Delegated Regulation on calibration of type 1 securitisation should be replaced by a more risk sensitive calibration for STS securitisation covering all possible tranches that also meet additional requirements in order to minimise risks."

Due to the direct applicability of the STS Regulation, the provisions in the DA concerning risk retention (Art. 254) and due diligence (Art. 256), noted above, were repealed in order to avoid (re)insurance undertakings being subject to different requirements under the STS Regulation and the DA. They are now covered by Arts. 6 and 5 STS Regulation, respectively. A more risk-sensitive spread risk capital charge on securitisation positions is included in the redrafted Art. 178 DA for non-senior tranches, along with some technical improvements for the calculation of the calibration for senior tranches.[349]

Transitional provisions for securitisations issued before 1 January 2019 are provided in the new Art. 178a DA. The principle in the redrafted Art. 157 DA remains that where a (re)insurance undertaking becomes aware that the originator, sponsor or original lender is failing to comply with the requirements of the STS Regulation or that the due diligence requirements of the STS Regulation are not being complied with by the (re)insurance undertaking, the undertaking must inform the supervisory authority immediately. In the case of negligence or omission by the (re)insurance undertaking, the supervisory authority must impose a proportionate increase to the SCR (Art. 257 (1) and (2) DA).

[349] In a press release dated 18 May 2018, Insurance Europe commented on the recent change that the capital requirements remain significantly high compared to the historical default experience of the assets and that this issue should be examined more broadly as part of the 2020 review of Solvency II. Similarly, a number of industry associations, including the Association for Financial Markets in Europe, published a letter on 6 June 2018 expressing the view that the capital charges are still too high (https://www.afme.eu/globalassets/downloads/letters/joint-trade-associations-sec-letter-4-june.pdf).

(ii) Sovereign Bonds

Government bonds made out 28.7% of investments by EEA (re)insurance undertakings in 2017.[350] This is in most Member States a very important investment class, and is treated very favourably under Solvency II. The underlying idea is that EEA governments do not fail and that an investment in government bonds of EEA Member States is therefore a safe investment.

Exposures in the form of bonds and loans issued or unconditionally and irrevocably guaranteed (under the conditions stated in Art. 215 DA) by the ECB, by the government of an EEA country or its central bank and funded in its domestic currency, by multilateral development banks referred to in Art. 117 (2) CRR or by international organisations referred to in Art. 118 CRR are exempt from capital requirements in the spread risk sub-module (Art. 180 (2) DA).[351]

Similar treatment is provided for exposures in the form of bonds and loans issued by regional governments and local authorities, which are treated as exposures to the central government of the jurisdiction in which they are established. The condition is (1) that there is no difference in risk between exposure to these regional governments and local authorities and exposures to the central government because of the specific revenue-raising power of the former, and (2) that specific institutional arrangements exist, the effect of which is to reduce the risk of default (Art. 85 DA). The list of the regional governments and local authorities is included in Art. 1 of Commission Implementing Regulation (EU) 2015/2011.[352] For instance, in France, an exposure to a region, department or commune is therefore considered an exposure to the central French government. Exposures in the form of bonds and loans to Member States' regional governments and local authorities not listed in Art. 1 are assigned a risk factor from the table in Art. 180 (3) DA corresponding to CQS 2 (Art. 180 (3a) DA).

Non-EEA sovereign bonds denominated and funded in the domestic currency (for instance, from the US or Japanese treasuries) or bonds issued by an EEA sovereign in a currency other than its own (for instance, government bonds issued by the Kingdom of Belgium in USD) are subject to capital requirements

---

350 See EIOPA, *European Insurance Overview 2018. Solo undertakings. Year-end 2017*, Publications Office of the EU, Luxembourg, 2018, p. 26.

351 For a discussion of the issue of sovereign exposure, see IVERSEN, A., Solvency II and sovereign bonds, in ADENAS, M., AVESANI, R., MANES, P., VELLA, F. and WOOD, P. (Eds.), *Solvency II: A dynamic challenge for the insurance market*, Il Mulino, Bologna, 2017.

352 Commission Implementing Regulation (EU) 2015/2011 of 11 November 2015 laying down implementing technical standards with regard to the lists of regional governments and local authorities, exposures to whom are to be treated as exposures to the central government in accordance with Directive 2009/138/EC of the EP and of the Council, *OJ* L 295, 12.11.2015, p. 3.

according to their ratings (Arts. 180 (3) and 187 (4) DA). The stress factor applied will depend on the CQS and the duration of the exposure. The shocks are much more favourable than those applicable to corporate bonds.

In order to align the treatment of guarantees that are issued by regional governments and local authorities with the rules for the recognition of guarantees issued by such bodies applicable to credit institutions and investment firms, Art. 180 DA was amended in 2019 so as to provide for the same treatment.[353] Bonds and loans that are fully, unconditionally and irrevocably guaranteed by regional governments and local authorities listed in Art. 1 of Commission Implementing Regulation (EU) 2015/2011 are treated as exposures to the central government when the guarantee meets the requirements in Art. 215 DA (Art. 180 (2), third subparagraph DA). If the exposure is to a Member States' regional government or local authority not listed in Art. 1, the exposure is assigned a risk factor from the table in Art. 180 (3) DA corresponding to CQS 2 (Art. 180 (3b) DA).

No capital requirement applies for spread risk on credit derivatives where the underlying financial instrument is a bond or a loan to one of the sovereign exposures listed in Art. 180 (2) DA.

Type 1 securitisations (see above under (i)) that are fully, unconditionally and irrevocably guaranteed (under the conditions stated in Art. 215 DA) by the EIF or the EIB are assigned a risk factor stress of 0% (Art. 180 (10) DA).

All government bonds are subject to interest rate risk and (re)insurers are required to hold capital for them in the interest rate risk module (like any other asset sensitive to interest rate fluctuations). In addition, a risk charge applies to investments that are denominated in a currency that is different from that of the undertaking's liabilities.

The absence of a capital charge for an investment in sovereign bonds was criticised during the negotiation of Solvency II. The EP in particular wanted the EC to propose a capital charge for investment in sovereign bonds. It was argued that even EU sovereign bonds were not immune to spread risk or even default risk and that this was a perpetuation of the undesirably high correlation between the fortunes of financial markets and sovereign finances.[354] The EC's response was that this issue needs to be addressed in a harmonised way in the whole financial sector and that it is not appropriate to come forward with a solution under Solvency II that would be different from the solution adopted under CRD/CRR IV. This would not establish a level playing field.

---

353 This amendment is based upon proposals made by EIOPA. See EIOPA, First set of advice to the EC on specific items in the Solvency II Delegated Regulation, EIOPA-BoS-17/280, 30 October 2017, pp. 22–43.

354 See the discussion paper of the Greens/European Free Alliance, *Solvency II Implementing Measures: Legislation by the back door*, February 2012, p.11.

Solvency II does however take account of the riskiness of an investment in sovereign bonds in different ways:

- if a (re)insurance undertaking holds sovereign bonds, these bonds are recorded in the solvency balance sheet at fair value. If the market value of these sovereign bonds decreases, that loss must be recorded in the balance sheet;
- NSAs will not approve an internal model in which no capital charge is assigned to a material investment in sovereign bonds.[355] If (re)insurance undertakings use a full internal model for the calculation of the SCR, they must give evidence to their supervisory authority that their risk assessment is more extensive than that in the standard formula;
- (re)insurance undertakings need to examine, within the framework of the ORSA, to what extent the undertaking is specifically at risk, for instance because of a high volume of investment in sovereign bonds;
- under the ORSA, (re)insurers must take account of risks that are covered inadequately or not at all by the standard formula. For instance, the German supervisory authority, BaFin, expects (re)insurance undertakings with a high level of sovereign exposure to attach particular importance to such exposure in their stress testing that is part of the ORSA and to simulate various scenarios, for instance the default of one or more countries' sovereign bonds;[356]
- like any other investment, an investment in sovereign bonds is subject to the requirements concerning risk management, which includes the prudent person principle.

The ESRB has examined the impact of investment by financial institutions in sovereign bonds and the possibility of attaching a risk weight to investment in this asset class. It has analysed various policy options.[357] For the insurance sector, the preliminary conclusion is that the impact of introducing a capital charge for investment in sovereign bonds will affect EU Member States differently. In three countries, the average SCR would increase by more than 150%. For more than half of the countries, the increase in SCR would be less than 20%. The aggregate additional capital charge needs would be between €35 billion and €80 billion. It would not be good from a financial stability perspective to change the present regime without at least a transitional period.[358]

---

355 See, for instance, PRA (UK), *Solvency II: treatment of sovereign debt in internal models*, Supervisory Statement SS30/15, 23 July 2015 (https://www.bankofengland.co.uk/prudential-regulation/publication/2015/solvency-2-treatment-of-sovereign-debt-in-internal-models).

356 See BaFin, *Government bonds: Treatment of risk under Solvency*, 1 August 2016 (https://www.bafin.de/SharedDocs/Veroeffentlichungen/EN/Fachartikel/2016/fa_bj_1607_staatsanleihen_en.html).

357 ESRB, *Report on the regulatory treatment of sovereign exposures*, March 2015, pp. 148–173.

358 A similar view was also expressed by Gabriel Bernardino, Chairman of EIOPA, in his introductory presentation at EIOPA's 5th Annual Conference in Frankfurt on 18 November 2015: *EIOPA and supervisory convergence – The beginning of a new journey*, p. 9.

e. *Currency Risk Sub-Module*

Currency risk arises from changes in the level or volatility of currency exchange rates. Undertakings may be exposed to currency risk arising from various sources, particularly from investments. Currency risk can be mitigated, for instance by matching liabilities in a foreign currency with assets denominated in the same foreign currency. The sub-module takes into account currency risk for a (re)insurance undertaking arising from all possible sources.[359]

The local currency is the currency in which the (re)insurance undertaking prepares its financial statements (Art. 188 (1), second subparagraph DA). All other currencies are referred to as foreign currencies. A foreign currency is relevant for the scenario calculations if the amount of basic own funds depends on the exchange rate between the foreign currency and the local currency.

The capital requirement for currency risk is equal to the sum of the capital requirements for currency risk for each foreign currency. For each foreign currency, the capital requirement for currency risk is equal to the larger of the capital requirement for the risk of an increase in the value of the foreign currency and the capital requirement for the risk of a decrease in the value of the foreign currency. The capital requirement for the risk of an *increase* in value of a foreign currency against the local currency is equal to the loss in the basic own funds that would result from an instantaneous increase of 25% in the value of the foreign currency against the local currency. The capital requirement for the risk of a *decrease* in the value of a foreign currency against the local currency is equal to the loss in the basic own funds that would result from an instantaneous decrease of 25% in the value of the foreign currency against the local currency (Art. 188 (2)–(4) DA).

f. *Market Risk Concentration Sub-Module*

Concentration risk is defined in Art. 13 (35) FD as all risk exposures with a loss potential that is large enough to threaten the solvency or financial position of the (re)insurance undertaking.

The market concentration risk sub-module covers assets considered in the equity, interest rate, spread risk and property risk sub-modules within the market risk module, to the extent that those assets are not covered by the counterparty default risk module, in order to avoid overlap.[360]

---

359 See also CEIOPS, Advice for Level 2 Implementing Measures on Solvency II: SCR Standard Formula – Art. 109, Structure and Design of Market Risk Module, CEIOPS-DOC-40/09, October 2009, pp. 15–17.

360 See also CEIOPS, Advice for Level 2 Implementing Measures on Solvency II: SCR Standard Formula – Art. 109, Structure and Design of Market Risk Module, CEIOPS-DOC-40/09, October 2009, pp. 25–30.

Assets that are allocated to policies where the policyholders bear the investment risk are excluded from this risk module. However, as these policies may have embedded options and guarantees, an adjustment (calculated using a scenario-based approach) is added to the formula to take into account the part of the risk effectively borne by the undertaking.

For the sake of simplicity and consistency, the definition of market risk concentration for financial investments is restricted to the risk arising from the accumulation of exposures with the same counterparty. It does not include other types of concentrations, such as geographical area or industry sector.

The capital requirement for market risk concentration is calculated on the basis of single name exposures. Exposures to undertakings that belong to the same corporate group are treated as a single name exposure. Similarly, immovable properties that are located in the same building are considered a single immovable property (Art. 182 (1) DA). Following the economic logic of Solvency II, exposures to a counterparty that belongs to the same group as the (re)insurance undertaking are not treated as independent exposures, under the conditions set out in Art. 184 (2) DA.

Exposures in the form of bonds and loans issued or unconditionally and irrevocably guaranteed (under the conditions stated in Art. 215 DA) by the ECB, by the government of an EEA country or its central bank and funded in its domestic currency, by multilateral development banks referred to in Art. 117 (2) CRR or by international organisations referred to in Art. 118 CRR are exempt from capital requirements in the risk concentration sub-module (Art. 187 (2) DA). Similar treatment is provided for exposures in the form of bonds and loans issued or guarantees extended by regional governments and local authorities listed in Art. 1 of Commission Implementing Regulation (EU) 2015/2011,[361] which are treated as exposures to the central government of the jurisdiction in which they are established (Art. 187 (3), third subparagraph DA).

Risks derived from concentration in cash held at a bank are captured in the counterparty default risk module, while risks corresponding to concentration in other bank assets are reflected in the concentration risk sub-module. Bank deposits considered in the concentration risk sub-module can be exempted to the extent that their value is covered by a deposit guarantee scheme in the EEA area, the guarantee is applicable unconditionally to the undertaking and provided there is no double counting of that guarantee with any other element of the SCR calculation (Art. 187 (5) DA).

For exposures in the form of covered bonds or exposures to a single immovable property, see Art. 187 (1) and (2) DA.

---

361 Commission Implementing Regulation (EU) 2015/2011 of 11 November 2015 laying down implementing technical standards with regard to the lists of regional governments and local authorities, exposures to whom are to be treated as exposures to the central government in accordance with Directive 2009/138/EC of the EP and of the Council, *OJ* L 295, 12.11. 2015, p. 3.

4.2.2.2.5. Counterparty Default Risk Module

This module (Art. 105 (6) FD and Arts. 189–202 DA) reflects possible losses due to unexpected default or deterioration in the credit standing of the counterparties and debtors of the undertaking over the following 12 months. It covers risk-mitigating contracts, such as reinsurance arrangements, securitisations and derivatives (excluding credit derivatives, which are already dealt with under the spread risk module), and receivables from intermediaries, as well as any other credit exposures not covered in the spread risk sub-module.[362]

The module takes appropriate account of the economic effect of collateral or other security held by or for the account of the (re)insurance undertaking and the risks associated therewith (Art. 197 DA).

For each counterparty, the risk module takes account of the overall counterparty risk exposure of the (re)insurance undertaking concerned to that counterparty, irrespective of the legal form of its contractual obligations to the (re)insurance undertaking.

In the calculation of the capital requirement for counterparty default risk, a distinction is made between type 1 exposures, which are assumed not to be diversified but likely to be rated, and type 2 exposures, which are assumed to be well diversified but unlikely to be rated. Retail loans secured by mortgages on residential property (mortgage loans) are treated as type 2 exposures, provided the requirements of Art. 191 DA are met.

Type 1 exposures (Art. 189 (2) DA) are exposures in relation to:
- risk-mitigation contracts including reinsurance, SPVs and insurance securitisations;
- cash at bank;
- deposits with ceding undertakings, where the number of single name exposures does not exceed 15;
- commitments received by a (re)insurance undertaking that have been called up but are unpaid;
- legally binding commitments provided or arranged by the undertaking and which may create payment obligations depending on the credit standing or default of a counterparty, including guarantees, letters of credit, letters of comfort provided by the undertaking;
- derivatives other than credit derivatives covered in the spread risk sub-module.[363]

---

362 See also CEIOPS, Advice for Level 2 Implementing Measures on Solvency II: SCR Standard Formula – Counterparty Default Risk Module, CEIOPS-DOC-23/09, October 2009, 62 p. and EIOPA, The underlying assumptions in the standard formula for the SCR calculation, EIOPA-14-322, 25 July 2014, pp. 70–74.

363 Based upon EIOPA's advice in the context of the 2018 review of the DA, Art. 189 (2) DA was amended so as to ensure that all derivatives are treated as type 1 exposures in the counterparty

Type 2 exposures (Art. 189 (3) DA) are all credit exposures that are not covered in the spread risk sub-module and that are not type 1 exposures, including:

- receivables from intermediaries;
- policyholder debtors;
- mortgage loans that meet the requirements in Art. 191 DA;
- deposits with ceding undertakings, where the number of single name exposures exceeds 15;
- commitments received by a (re)insurance undertaking that have been called up but are unpaid, where the number of single name exposures exceeds 15.

The capital requirement for counterparty default risk is calculated on the basis of single name exposures, whereby exposures to undertakings that belong to the same corporate group are treated as a single name exposure.

The module is based on the assumption that, for exposures that may be diversified and where the counterparty is likely to be rated (type 1 exposures), LGD on counterparties that do not belong to the same group are independent and LGD on counterparties that do belong to the same group are not independent. All exposures that are captured neither in the spread risk sub-module nor in the counterparty default risk module as type 1 exposures must be captured in this module as type 2 exposures (recitals 63 and 64 DA).

The capital requirement for type 1 and type 2 exposures is determined based on the LGD.[364] Any liability towards the counterparty can be used to reduce the LGD in the event of a default. No offsetting is allowed for if the liabilities are expected to be met before the credit exposure is cleared (Art. 192 (1) DA).

For type 1 exposures, the design of the counterparty default risk is not only driven by the LGD, but also by the probability of default (PD)[365] for a given single name counterparty. The PD is driven by the rating of the counterparty (for rated exposures). For single name exposures to unrated (re)insurance undertakings, subject to Solvency II, the PD is determined on the basis of the solvency ratio (Art. 199 DA). Because derivatives expose a (re)insurance undertaking to counterparty default risk, irrespective of whether those derivatives are held for hedging or for speculative purposes, all derivatives are treated as type 1 exposures.

---

default risk module, irrespective of whether they are held for hedging or speculation. See also the new Art. 192a DA introduced in 2018 for exposures to clearing members.

364 Loss-given-default is defined in Art. 4 (55) CRR as "the ratio of the loss on an exposure due to the default of a counterparty to the amount outstanding at default".

365 Loss-given-default is defined in Art. 4 (55) CRR as "the ratio of the loss on an exposure due to the default of a counterparty to the amount outstanding at default" and probability of default is defined in Art. 4 (54) CRR as "the probability of default of a counterparty over a one year period".

For type 2 exposures, the capital charge is based on the scenario of a 15% fall in the market value of the exposure, assuming a well-diversified portfolio and a credit quality rating between BBB and BB. For exposures to three-month past-due receivables from intermediaries, a higher fall of 90% of the value is assumed, given the higher probability of default and the limited recovery rate in the event of default (Art. 202 DA).

In its first set of advice to the EC in the context of the 2018 review of the DA, EIOPA proposed aligning the treatment of type 2 mortgage loan exposures in the counterparty default risk module with the treatment in banking (CRR) by recognising the risk-mitigating effect of a partial guarantee by Member States' central government or by regional governments and local authorities. This proposal was incorporated by the EC in its 2019 amendment of the DA.[366] In its second set of advice to the EC in the context of the 2018 review of the DA, EIOPA proposed a number of clarifications and further simplifications of the counterparty default risk module, which is generally considered to be complex. These proposals were also taken over by the EC into its 2019 amendment of the DA.[367] For instance, Art. 192 (1), second subparagraph DA now states that where contractual netting agreements covering several derivatives that represent credit exposure to the same counterparty have been concluded, the LGD on those derivatives may be calculated on the basis of the combined economic effect of all those derivatives that are covered by the same contractual netting agreement.

The relative significance of counterparty default risk is higher for smaller undertakings. Nevertheless, 14% of all undertakings use one or more of the simplifications for the counterparty default risk module, irrespective of the size of the undertaking.[368]

As Solvency II follows a risk-based approach, (re)insurance undertakings can take account of the use of risk-mitigating techniques, such as reinsurance arrangements, securitisation or derivatives, in the calculation of the SCR. See above, section 4.2.2.1.1.

4.2.2.2.6. Intangible Asset Risk Module

As indicated above (section 2.2), intangible assets will not normally appear in the solvency balance sheet. An intangible asset (other than goodwill) can only be recorded and valued on the solvency balance sheet when it can be sold separately

---

366 EIOPA, First set of advice to the EC on specific items in the Solvency II Delegated Regulation, EIOPA-BoS-17/280, 30 October 2017, p. 42. See the new paragraph 4 in Art. 192 DA.

367 See the amendments to Art. 192 (1) and (3) DA and the new paragraphs 3a and 3b in Art 192 DA. See also the addition of a new Art. 192a dealing with exposures to clearing members.

368 EIOPA, Second set of advice to the EC on specific items in the Solvency II Delegated Regulation, EIOPA-BoS-18/075, 28 February 2018, pp. 248–270.

and the (re)insurance undertaking can demonstrate that there is a (market) value for the same or similar asset (Art. 12 DA).

If an intangible asset appears on the balance sheet, the capital charge related to the risk concerning that asset will be recorded under the intangible asset risk module. The capital charge is calculated in accordance with the formula contained in Art. 203 DA.

4.2.2.3. Capital Requirement for Operational Risk

Operational risk is defined as the risk of loss arising from inadequate or failed internal processes, personnel or systems or from external events (Art. 13 (33) FD). Operational risk includes legal risk but excludes risk arising from strategic decisions, as well as reputational risk (Art. 101 (4) (f) FD).

Most insurance failures or near-failures in the EU are directly or indirectly attributable to operational risk.[369] Examples of operational risks are: business process risks (including data quality), risks associated with the outsourcing of functions (including distribution channels), fraud risk, personnel risks, information/IT security risks,[370] business interruption risk, and compliance risk (breaches of legal requirements or standards). Particularly important today are market conduct risk (behaviour of the undertaking in the market) and cybersecurity risk.[371]

The capital requirement for operational risk reflects operational risks to the extent that they are not already reflected in other risk modules (Art. 107 (1) FD). By unbundling operational risk from underwriting risk, Solvency II seeks to provide (re)insurers with the tools to identify weaknesses in their operations and to mitigate these risks in a more targeted manner.

In contrast to underwriting risk, which is entered into in a deliberate and controlled manner in the context of the regular business activity of a (re)insurance undertaking, operational risks are an indivisible part of business activity. It is therefore important for (re)insurance undertakings to focus on the avoidance and minimisation of operational risk. (Re)insurance undertakings can lower operational risk through better governance and risk management (Pillar 2). They can, for instance, decide to exit a certain line of business because

369 See Conference of Insurance Supervisory Services of the Member States of the EU, *Prudential Supervision of Insurance Undertakings*, December 2002, 112 p. (the so-called Sharma Report). A recent, more detailed analysis can be found in EIOPA, *Failures and near misses in insurance. Overview of the causes and early identification*, Publications Office of the EU, Luxembourg, 2018, 48 p. The study identifies "management and staff competence risk" as the first cause of failures and near misses in life insurance and as the third cause in non-life insurance.

370 Supervisory authorities attach increasing importance to IT risk in financial institutions. See, for instance, the Circular on Supervisory Requirements for IT in financial institutions (*Bankaufsichtliche Anforderungen an die IT – BAIT*) published by BaFin in Germany in November 2017.

371 See further, Chapter 7, section 3.4.1.6.

the operational risk exceeds the profitability of that line of business. They can also transfer the risk by purchasing insurance, thereby mitigating the risk.

Outsourcing of important operational functions or activities must be undertaken in such a way as to not unduly increasing operational risk (Art. 49 (2) (b) FD).

The calibration of operational risk has been quite challenging.[372] Operational risk increases with the size of the activity, unless the undertaking is well diversified and managed. The capital charge for operational risk under the standard formula may be too high for individual (re)insurance undertakings. This can be dealt with by developing a partial internal model for operational risk, although experience shows that this is not easy to do.

The overall assumption in the operational risk module is that a standardised level of management is present. The operational risk module is based on a linear formula and is therefore not risk-sensitive. The capital requirement is determined using a factor-based approach as a function of premiums, technical provisions and the BSCR.

With respect to (re)insurance operations, the calculation of the capital requirement for operational risk takes account of the volume of those operations in terms of earned premiums and technical provisions held in respect of those (re)insurance obligations. The capital requirement for operational risk, which is set at 25%, is capped at 30% of the BSCR relating to these (re)insurance obligations (Art. 107 FD and Art. 204 DA). With respect to unit-linked business, i.e. life insurance contracts where the investment risk is borne by the policyholders, the calculation of the capital requirement for operational risk takes account of the amount of annual expenses in respect of those insurance obligations (Art. 107 (2) FD). In this case, the insurance undertaking must take account of the operational risk that may be incurred in administrating the investment portfolio of policyholders.

4.2.2.4. Adjustment for the Loss-Absorbing Capacity of Technical Provisions and Deferred Taxes

The economic loss that results from shocks (capital charges) under Solvency II leads to fiscal losses, which might be recuperated if fiscal profits are available to utilise/offset these fiscal losses.

The loss-absorbing capacity of technical provisions and deferred taxes (LAC-DT) reflects the potential compensation of unexpected losses through a simultaneous decrease in technical provisions or deferred taxes or a combination of the two (Art. 108 FD). LAC-DT is the sum of the adjustment for the

372 See the analysis following QIS 4, CEIOPS, Advice for Level 2 Implementing Measures on Solvency II: SCR Standard Formula – Art. 111 (f), Operational Risk, CEIOPS-DOC-45/09, October 2009, 24 p.

loss-absorbing capacity of technical provisions (Art. 206 DA) and the adjustment for the loss-absorbing capacity of deferred taxes (Art. 207 DA). It ensures that there is no double counting of the risk-mitigating effect provided by future discretionary benefits or deferred taxes.

There is always a risk of (re)insurance undertakings using overly optimistic assumptions in the projection of future taxable profits after an exceptional loss scenario. When calculating the LAC-DT, undertakings must therefore take into account their financial and solvency position after the instantaneous loss, and the uncertainty regarding the projection of future taxable profits. The assumptions for projecting future taxable profits following the instantaneous loss, including the assumed rates of return on the undertaking's investments, may not be more favourable than the assumptions applied to the valuation of deferred taxes on the balance sheet and the projected total amount of new business may not exceed that of the business planning (Art. 207 DA).

The impact of LAC-DT is extremely important, with the potential to decrease the BSCR of (re)insurance undertakings by more than a third.[373]

Future discretionary benefits are usually a feature associated with life and SLT health insurance contracts. Therefore, the adjustment for the loss-absorbing capacity of technical provisions takes account of the mitigating effect provided by future discretionary benefits in relation to life underwriting risk, SLT health underwriting risk, health catastrophe risk, market risk and counterparty default risk. In order to limit the complexity of the standard formula and the calculation burden for (re)insurance undertakings, the adjustment does not apply to the non-life insurance risk and NSLT health insurance risk. As losses arising from inadequate or failed internal processes, personnel or systems, or from external events, might not be effectively absorbed by future discretionary benefits, the adjustment does not apply to operational risk (recital 69 DA).

The risk-mitigating effect provided by future discretionary benefits may not be greater than the sum of the technical provisions and deferred taxes relating to those discretionary benefits (Art. 108 FD).

The LAC-DT module in the SCR recognises that if risks were to materialise, part of their cost might be transferred to policyholders (for example, through a reduction in the bonuses attributed to policies with profit participation), and part of the remaining cost might result in a reduction in the future taxes expected to be paid to tax authorities.

Because of the importance of LAC-DT, EIOPA examined in its second set of advice to the EC on the 2018 review of the DA[374] ways and means to increase

---

[373] EIOPA, Report on the fifth Quantitative Impact Study (QIS 5) for Solvency II, EIOPA-TFQIS5-11/001, 14 March 2011, p. 13.

[374] EIOPA, Second set of advice to the EC on specific items in the Solvency II Delegated Regulation, EIOPA-BoS-18/075, 28 February 2018, pp. 333–340. By 31 December 2017,

convergence in the application of this adjustment and proposed a number of amendments to several articles in the DA. These amendments relate to Art. 207 (adjustment for the loss-absorbing capacity of deferred taxes), Art. 260 (risk management areas), Art. 272 (actuarial function), Art. 297 (SFCR – capital management) and Art. 311 (RSR – capital management). These proposals[375] were incorporated in the 2019 amendment of the DA. As these changes are burdensome, the application date for these new provisions has been moved to 1 January 2020.[376]

4.2.2.5. Simplifications in the Standard Formula

(Re)insurance undertakings may use a simplified calculation for a specific sub-module or risk module where the nature, scale and complexity of the risks they face justifies this and where it would be disproportionate to require them to apply the standardised calculation (Art. 109 FD). The application of the proportionality principle in this case is however linked to specific conditions included in the DA (Art. 111 (1) (l) FD).

In determining whether a simplified calculation is justified on the basis of the proportionality principle, the undertaking must first carry out a materiality assessment of the nature, scale and complexity of the risks of the undertaking falling within the relevant module or sub-module. It must then evaluate in qualitative and quantitative terms, as appropriate, the model error implied by the change of method and whether that error can be considered material (Art. 88 (1) DA).

A simplified calculation is not considered proportionate where the model error is material, i.e. when it leads to a misstatement of the SCR that could influence the decision-making or the judgement of the user of the information relating to the SCR, unless the SCR resulting from the simplified calculation exceeds the SCR resulting from the standard calculation (Art. 88 (2) DA).

---

the amount of LAC-DT for (re)insurance undertakings in all EEA countries amounted to €100 billion. There are large differences by country. The percentage of LAC-DT in own funds was the highest in Malta and the Czech Republic (almost 16%). See EIOPA, *European Insurance Overview 2018. Solo undertakings. Year-end 2017*, Publications Office of the EU, Luxembourg, 2018, p. 20.

375 With the exception of the proposed change to Art. 272 DA. The assumptions underlying the projection of future taxable profits can be examined by either the risk management or the actuarial function. See Art. 260 (1) (h) (iii) DA.

376 See Art. 2, second subparagraph of Commission Delegated Regulation (EU) of 8 March 2019 amending the DA. Industry did not favour these changes. See, Insurance Europe, *Insurance Europe comments on amendments to Solvency II Delegated Regulation*, Position Paper, 11 December 2018, pp. 5–7 (https://www.insuranceeurope.eu/sites/default/files/attachments/Comments%20on%20amendments%20to%20Solvency%20II%20Delegated%20Regulation_0.pdf).

As pointed out by EIOPA,[377] the responsibility for choosing an adequate and reliable calculation of the SCR ultimately lies with the AMSB of the undertaking. An assessment of the proportionality of the chosen methodology with regard to the nature, scale and complexity of the underlying risks should be part of the ORSA process.

As for the evaluation of the model error, EIOPA admits that this is not easy. Undertakings should not be required to quantify the degree of model error in precise quantitative terms or to re-calculate the value of the capital charge using the non-simplified (standard) method in order to demonstrate that the error is immaterial. Instead, it is sufficient to demonstrate that there is reasonable certainty that the model error is immaterial. It is enough that a qualitative evaluation indicates that the error is immaterial.

The following simplified calculations are provided for in the DA for all (re)insurance undertakings:[378]

- simplified calculation for discontinuance of insurance policies in the non-life lapse risk sub-module (Art. 90a DA);
- simplified calculation of the sum insured for natural catastrophe risk (Art. 90b DA);
- simplified calculation of the capital requirement for fire risk (Art. 90c DA);
- simplified calculation of the capital requirement for life mortality risk (Art. 91 DA);
- simplified calculation of the capital requirement for life longevity risk (Art. 92 DA);
- simplified calculation of the capital requirement for life disability–morbidity risk (Art. 93 DA);
- simplified calculation of the capital requirement for life-expense risk (Art. 94 DA);
- simplified calculation of the capital requirement for permanent changes in lapse rates (Art. 95 DA);
- simplified calculation of the capital requirement for risks in the life lapse risk sub-module (Art. 95a DA);
- simplified calculation of the capital requirement for life-catastrophe risk (Art. 96 DA);
- simplified calculation for discontinuance of insurance policies in the NSLT health lapse risk sub-module (Art. 96a DA);

377 EIOPA, First set of advice to the EC on specific items in the SII Delegated Regulation, EIOPA-BoS-17/280, 30 October 2017, p. 7.

378 Following EIOPA's advice, additional simplified calculations were introduced in 2019 for the lapse risk, natural catastrophe risk and fire risk sub-modules. See, Commission Delegated Regulation (EU) of 8 March 2019, amending the DA.

- simplified calculation of the capital requirement for health mortality risk (Art. 97 DA);
- simplified calculation of the capital requirement for health longevity risk (Art. 98 DA);
- simplified calculation of the capital requirement for medical expense disability–morbidity risk (Art. 99 DA);
- simplified calculation of the capital requirement for income protection disability–morbidity risk (Art. 100 DA);
- simplified calculation of the capital requirement for health expense risk (Art. 101 DA);
- simplified calculation of the capital requirement for SLT health lapse risk (Art. 102 DA);
- simplified calculation of the capital requirement for risks in the SLT health lapse risk sub-module (Art. 102a DA);
- simplified calculation for spread risk on bonds and loans (Art. 104 DA);
- simplified calculation for the risk factor in the spread risk sub-module and the market risk concentration sub-module (Art. 105a DA);
- simplified calculation of the risk-mitigating effect for reinsurance arrangements or securitisation (Art. 107 DA);
- simplified calculation of the risk-mitigating effect for proportional reinsurance arrangements (Art. 108 DA);
- simplified calculations for pooling arrangements (Art. 109 DA);
- simplified calculation – grouping of single name exposures (Art. 110 DA);
- simplified calculation of the risk-mitigating effect (Art. 111 DA);
- simplified calculation of the risk-mitigating effect on underwriting risk (Art. 111a DA);
- simplified calculation of the risk-adjusted value of collateral to take into account the economic effect of the collateral (Art. 112 DA);
- simplified calculation of the LGD for reinsurance (Art. 112a DA);
- simplified calculation of the capital requirement for counterparty default risk on type 1 exposures (Art. 112b DA).

Specific simplifications apply to the obligations of captives under the condition that all insured persons and beneficiaries are legal entities of the group to which the captive (re)insurance undertaking belongs and the obligations do not relate to any compulsory third-party liability insurance (Art. 98 DA):

- simplified calculation of the capital requirement for non-life premium and reserve risk (Art. 90 DA);
- simplified calculation of the capital requirement for interest rate risk (Art. 103 DA);
- simplified calculation of the capital requirement for spread risk on bonds and loans (Art. 105 DA);

- simplified calculation of the capital requirement for market risk concentration (Art. 106 DA).

This list includes the simplified calculations that EIOPA proposed in its first[379] and second[380] sets of advice to the EC in the context of the 2018 review of the DA and which were included in the DA after its amendment by the EC in 2019. EIOPA had indicated in its first set of advice that it was overall satisfied with the use of the simplified calculations in the standard formula. Concerns that the proportionality assessment was too burdensome and was unduly preventing (re)insurance undertakings from applying simplified calculations were not considered justified by EIOPA. Rather than amending the current requirements in Art. 88 DA, which establishes the conditions for the use of the simplified calculations, EIOPA proposed providing further guidance to NSAs in its Supervisory Handbook.[381] EIOPA also proposed a number of further simplifications in its first and second sets of advice to the EC.

In its first set of advice, EIOPA gave an overview of the use of the simplified calculations as at year-end 2017. From this overview, it appears that 595 undertakings were using the simplified calculations. However, the real number is much higher, particularly if the simplified calculations for the counterparty default risk module are included.[382] The simplified calculations for captives were used by 35 captives (for non-life premium and reserve risk), by 15 captives for interest rate risk, by eight captives for spread risk on bonds and loans, and by 10 captives for the market risk concentration.

Further simplifications in the standard formula proposed by EIOPA in its advice to the EC in the context of the 2018 review of the DA deal with the look-through approach, the look-through approach at group level, currency risk at group level, the reduction of reliance on external credit ratings, the treatment of guarantees issued by regional governments and local authorities, risk-mitigation techniques, and USPs. The EC has included these proposals in its 2019 amendment of the DA.

379 EIOPA, First set of advice to the EC on specific items in the Solvency II Delegated Regulation, EIOPA-BoS-17/280, 30 October 2017, 137 p.

380 EIOPA, Second set of advice to the EC on specific items in the Solvency II Delegated Regulation, EIOPA-BoS-18/075, 28 February 2018, 612 p.

381 EIOPA, First set of advice to the EC on specific items in the Solvency II Delegated Regulation, EIOPA-BoS-17/280, 30 October 2017, p. 10. For a first initiative, see EIOPA, Solvency II: Application of the proportionality principle in the supervision of the SCR, Supervisory Statement, EIOPA-BoS-19-033, 11 March 2019, 9 p.

382 Complementing its first set of advice, EIOPA indicated in its second advice to the EC in the context of the 2018 review that 14% of all insurance undertakings use one or more of the simplifications for the counterparty default risk module.

Figure 16. Number of undertakings using simplified calculations

Risk where simplified calculation is used	Number of undertakings using the simplified calculation	Number of undertakings calculating the module
Counterparty default risk	316	2,270
Disability-morbidity risk	15	1,009
Health disability-morbidity risk-income protection	12	299
Health disability-morbidity risk-medical expenses	4	99
Health expense risk	11	497
Health longevity risk	7	374
Health mortality risk	5	179
Lapse risk	13	1,012
Life catastrophe risk	106	1,013
Life expense risk	22	1,015
Longevity risk	16	1,010
Mortality risk	30	1,012
SLT lapse risk	5	291
Spread risk – bonds and loans	33	2,099

Source: EIOPA, First set of advice to the EC on specific items in the Solvency II Delegated Regulation, EIOPA-BoS-17/280, 30 October 2017, p. 8.

4.2.3. *Internal Model*

Solvency II is one of the first insurance regulatory regimes in the world to allow for the use of internal models to calculate capital requirements for (re)insurance undertakings. Conceptually, internal models are more risk-sensitive, better capture individual risk profiles and provide a better alignment between the truly underlying economic risks and the capital requirements placed on (re)insurance undertakings by Solvency II.[383] In an ideal world, all undertakings would apply an internal model for the calculation of their capital requirements, as a standard formula is incapable of capturing the specific risk position of each undertaking.

The SCR can be calculated (at solo level or at group level) either in accordance with the standard formula or using an internal model (Art. 100, second subparagraph FD). The internal model can be a partial or a full internal model. In both cases, if the model is used to calculate the SCR, it must be approved by the supervisory authority (Art. 112 (1) FD).

[383] BERNARDINO, G., *Milestones of preparation for Solvency II*, European Insurance Conference, London, 2 June 2015 (https://eiopa.europa.eu/Publications/Speeches%20and%20presentations/2015-06-02%20European%20Insurance%20Conference.pdf).

The choice between a partial internal model and a full internal model will depend on the situation of each individual undertaking or group. During the preparatory phase of Solvency II, it became clear that only a minority of mostly medium or large (re)insurance undertakings were applying a full internal model and that the quality of these models was not always as good as could have been expected. An important weakness was the absence of documentation. Many (re)insurance undertakings or groups had developed internal models in the context of their risk management prior to Solvency II.[384] These models were often partial internal models and helped the undertakings to have better insight into specific risks, such as catastrophe risk.[385]

Figure 17. Undertakings using the standard formula or an internal model

	Standard formula	Partial internal model	Full internal model	Total
Life undertakings	546	29	21	596
Non-life undertakings	1,541	42	37	1,620
Undertakings pursuing both life and non-life activities	365	29	8	402
Reinsurance undertakings	274	5	15	294
Total	**2,726**	**105**	**81**	**2,912**

Source: EIOPA, Report on long-term guarantee measures and measures on equity risk 2018, EIOPA-BoS-18/471, 18 December 2018, p. 12.

At the end of 2017, for the first year of application of Solvency II, 186 (re)insurance undertakings were using a full (81 undertakings) or partial (105 undertakings) internal model for the calculation of the SCR, while 2,726 undertakings were applying the standard formula.[386] This is a slight increase from the preceding year, when 78 undertakings were using a full internal model and 98 undertakings were using a partial internal model.[387] The number of users of internal models might further increase as undertakings and supervisory authorities become more comfortable with the new risk-based solvency capital regime,[388] but also when undertakings feel that the

384 For an overview, see EC, *Study into the methodologies to assess the overall financial position of an insurance undertaking from the perspective of prudential supervision*, May 2002, pp. 32–54 (the KPMG Report).

385 For further information, see the various QIS reports published by CEIOPS/EIOPA.

386 EIOPA, Report on long-term guarantees measures and measures on equity risk 2018, EIOPA-BoS-18/471, 18 December 2018, p. 12.

387 EIOPA, Report on long-term guarantees measures and measures on equity risk 2017, EIOPA-BoS-17/334, 20 December 2017, p. 11.

388 This is confirmed by a review carried out by Solvency II Wire Data of close to 800 solo undertakings, which identified 13 undertakings that changed their capital model in 2017.

structure of the standard formula and the calibration of the risks no longer reflect their specific risk situation. Some undertakings might start the process by applying for the use of a partial internal model for certain risk modules or sub-modules.

If the number of undertakings applying to use an internal model increases substantially, supervisory authorities might face problems in dealing with the additional work. They will need to attract experts, who may be difficult to find. This is an area where cooperation between supervisory authorities can be helpful. Convergence between NSAs in the context of EIOPA and benchmarking, by identifying good practice, can assist a lot in this regard.[389] This would give NSAs some guidance on how to proceed in the approval process. Care must however be taken to ensure that this does not lead to another kind of standard formula or does not put unnecessary constraints on undertakings that are experimenting in this area.

4.2.3.1. Risk Management Approach

There is no definition of an internal model in the FD. In the Glossary of the CEA and the Groupe Consultatif, an internal model is defined as: "A risk management system developed by an insurer to analyse the overall risk position, to quantify risks and to determine the economic capital required to meet those risks".[390]

This definition puts the development of an internal model clearly in the context of an undertaking's risk management, which is fully in line with the philosophy of Solvency II. Developing an internal model with the sole objective of lowering capital requirements is not an acceptable policy. This would be contrary to the use test (see below, section 2.3.2.1). In the same way, fully relying on a model provided by an external party (vendor model) is not compatible with a risk-based solvency capital regime.

The absence of a definition of an internal model is an important advantage, as it allows for flexibility in the approach both for (re)insurance undertakings and for NSAs.

Of these, eight had a standard formula in 2016. Five undertakings using the standard formula converted to a partial internal model and three to a full internal model. The five partial internal model users all switched to a full internal model. See https://www.solvencyiiwire.com/category/articles 5 June 2018. See, for instance, the 2017 SFCR of Hannover Re Group (p. 75), in which the Group indicates that it is now using a full internal model as the supervisory authority (BaFin) had given permission to extend the internal model to operational risk (https://www.hannover-re.com/1265699/2017-solvency-and-financial-condition-report-hannover-ruck-se.pdf).

389 See EIOPA, *Supervisory Convergence Plan 2018–2019. How EIOPA is building supervisory convergence*, Publications Office of the EU, Luxembourg, 2018, p. 9.

390 CEA and Groupe Consultatif, *Solvency II Glossary*, March 2007, p. 35.

No matter how much effort and how many skilled resources are dedicated to the development and implementation of an internal model, the model may still suffer from limitations in the same way as a standard formula. It is important to recognise those limitations and to continuously improve the model.

When thinking about model limitations, a useful paradigm was provided by Phillip Keller[391] at a meeting of the CEIOPS Internal Model Working Group in January 2009.[392] He suggested that when developing, implementing, reviewing and monitoring an internal model, there are:

1. things that are known;
2. things that are known to be unknown;
3. things that are believed to be known but are actually unknown;
4. things that are preferred to stay unknown; and
5. things that are unknown to be unknown.

The main focus of risk management and supervision is often on things that are known (for instance, high-frequency/low-impact risk or low-frequency/high-impact risk) and things that are known to be unknown (for instance, the development of interest rates). However, in many cases (re)insurance undertakings become financially distressed by things that are believed to be known but are actually unknown (for instance, market conduct risk), things that are preferred to stay unknown (for instance, risks that would force a change to the undertaking's business model) and things that are unknown to be unknown (unknown by definition).

Most dangerous are the situations described under (3) and (4). The things that are believed to be known but are actually unknown may lead to over-confidence and a belief that risks are under control. Things that are preferred to stay unknown are a sign of an inappropriate risk culture and likely the cause of most financial problems.

Not knowing about risks leaves management free in its strategy setting. The chief risk officer (CRO) or the chief actuary might be pressured or replaced by a more malleable person who conforms to the wishes of management. The AMSB and supervisory authorities need to be able to identify instances when management behaves in such a way, so that remedial action can be taken. Actuaries and CROs also need to have the courage to confront senior management with unpalatable truths.

This is, of course, very much dependent on the culture within the undertaking. If the culture is wrong, then there may be a preference for risks

391 Phillip Keller was closely involved in the development of the Swiss Solvency Test.

392 Quoted by CADONI, P. and KERFRIDEN, C., Internal Models and Solvency II, in DOFF, R. (Ed.), *The Solvency II Handbook. Practical Approaches to Implementation*, Incisive Media, London, 2014, pp. 55–57.

to remain unknown. However in an undertaking with a good risk culture, there is a strong desire to understand risk and to actively manage it. That does not of course prevent there being unknown unknowns.

A challenge with internal models is the risk of overreliance on models by (re)insurance undertakings or groups. There are no correct models, as models seek to capture future events that are by definition uncertain. There is also the issue of model risk, i.e. the risk of a model being incorrectly specified or implemented to such an extent that a knowledgeable user of the results of the model makes the wrong decision.[393] Model risk can occur if the model contains fundamental errors (for instance, incorrect data or assumptions) or if the model is used incorrectly or inappropriately. Model risk increases with greater model complexity and higher uncertainty about inputs and assumptions.[394] It is sometimes said that all models are wrong, but that some models are useful. The key is to make sure that the model outputs are fit for the purposes for which they are being used.

Although the design and implementation of an internal model is the primary responsibility of the risk management function (Art. 44 (5) FD), close cooperation between the risk management function and the actuarial function is needed in order to provide detailed actuarial information on the internal model to the risk management function. Similarly, the risk management function needs to liaise closely with the users of the outputs of the internal model (Art. 269 (2) (a) and (b) DA).

Developing an internal model should not be seen exclusively in the context of the calculation of the SCR. Internal models can be useful for other purposes, such as portfolio management, reinsurance optimisation, pricing, asset–liability management, defining underwriting limits, product development, etc. Many (re)insurance undertakings and groups have developed such models, and Solvency II should not stop them from continuing their efforts to continuously improve their risk management, in the interest not only of the undertaking or group, but also of policyholders.

Sometimes a (re)insurance undertaking may be *required* to use an internal model. That would be the case where it is inappropriate to calculate the SCR in accordance with the standard formula because the risk profile of the undertaking deviates significantly from the assumptions underlying the standard formula calculation. This far-reaching measure can only be taken by a supervisory authority when the reasons for that decision are clearly stated. The model could be a full internal model or a partial model for specific risk modules (Art. 119 FD).[395]

---

393 DEGENAAR, T., Managing Model Risk, in DOFF, R. (Ed.), *The Solvency II Handbook. Practical Approaches to Implementation*, Incisive Media, London, 2014, p. 203.

394 CADONI, P. and KERFRIDEN, C., Internal Models and Solvency II, in DOFF, R. (Ed.), *The Solvency II Handbook. Practical Approaches to Implementation*, Incisive Media, London, 2014, p. 48. Model validation and model governance are key in this regard.

395 See also Art. 37 FD for capital add-ons. See further, Chapter 7, section 2.4.

The recitals to the DA contain a number of important messages that describe the context in which the co-legislators consider internal models in the context of Solvency II:

"[78] It is likely that many aspects of internal models will change over time as knowledge about risk modelling improves, and supervisory authorities should accordingly have regard to current information and practice in making their assessment of the internal model to ensure that it keeps pace with recent developments.

[79] An internal model can only play an important role in the system of governance of an insurance or reinsurance undertaking where it is adapted to the business of the undertaking and understood by the persons who base decisions on its outputs. The use test for internal models should therefore ensure that approved internal models are appropriate to the business of the undertaking and are understood by the persons who effectively run the undertaking.

[80] Insurance and reinsurance undertakings calculating the Solvency Capital Requirement on the basis of an internal model should use the internal model in their risk-management system and in their decision-making processes in a way that creates incentives to improve the quality of the internal model itself.

[81] The requirement that the internal model is widely used in and plays an important role in their system of governance set out in Article 120 of Directive 2009/138/EC should not lead insurance and reinsurance undertakings to rely blindly on the output of the internal model. The undertakings should not make decisions based on the output of the internal model without challenging the appropriateness of the model. They should be aware of the limitations of the internal model and take them into account in their decisions.

[82] As no particular method for the calculation of the probability distribution forecast for internal models is prescribed in accordance with Article 121(4) of Directive 2009/138/EC and as internal models should be adapted to the specific business of the insurance and reinsurance undertaking, internal models may vary significantly in their methodology, the information, assumptions and data used for the internal model and in their validation processes. The statistical quality standards and the validation standards should therefore remain principle-based and include only specific minimum requirements. For the same reason, the documentation standards should not include a complete list of documents, but only a minimum list of documents that should exist for each internal model. Undertakings' documentation should contain any additional information that is necessary to comply with the documentation standards for internal models.

[83] In order to ensure that the internal model is up to date and reflects their risk profile in the best possible manner, insurance and reinsurance undertakings should be aware of the relevant actuarial developments and the generally accepted market practice of risk modelling. However, this does not imply that insurance and reinsurance undertakings should always adapt their internal model to the generally accepted market practices. In many cases it might be necessary to depart from the generally accepted market practice in order to arrive at an appropriate internal model.

[84] Internal models are likely to be based on a large amount of data stemming from a variety of sources and of differing characteristics and quality. In order to ensure the appropriateness of the data used for the internal model, insurance and reinsurance undertakings should collect, process and apply data in a transparent and structured manner.

[85] Insurance and reinsurance undertakings should be free to decide the structure of the internal model that most appropriately reflects their risks. This should be done subject to approval by the supervisory authorities. In the case of partial internal models it might be more appropriate to calculate different components separately and integrate them directly into the standard formula without further aggregation in the internal model. In this case a probability distribution forecast should be calculated for each component.

[86] Any integration technique of a partial internal model into the standard formula to calculate the Solvency Capital Requirement is part of that internal model and should, together with the other components of the partial internal model, fulfil the relevant requirements of Directive 2009/138/EC."

4.2.3.2. Conditions to be Satisfied

Before an internal model can be used for the calculation of the SCR, it must satisfy a number of qualitative and quantitative characteristics. These relate in particular to the following:

- use test;
- statistical quality standards;
- calibration standards;
- profit and loss attribution;
- validation standards;
- documentation standards.

4.2.3.2.1. Use Test

The objective of developing an internal model should not be to satisfy regulatory requirements.[396] The model must be effectively used and be part of the risk management system. It must fit the business (Art. 224 DA), which means that:

(a) the modelling approach reflects the nature, scale and complexity of the risks inherent in the activities of the undertaking that are within the scope of the internal model;

[396] See also EIOPA, Guidelines on the use of internal models, EIOPA-BoS-14/180, 2 February 2015, Guidelines 11–15.

(b) the outputs of the internal model and the content of the internal and external reporting of the undertaking are consistent;
(c) the internal model is capable of producing outputs that are sufficiently granular as to play an important role in the relevant management decisions of the undertaking; at a minimum, the outputs of the internal model must differentiate between lines of business, between risk categories and between major business units;
(d) the policy for changing the internal model provides that the internal model must be adjusted for changes in the scope or nature of the activities of the undertaking.

As the AMSB of the undertaking is responsible for the governance of the undertaking, including its risk management system, it is also responsible for ensuring the ongoing appropriateness of the design and operation of the internal model and ensuring that the internal model continues to appropriately reflect the risk profile of the undertaking (Art. 120, third subparagraph FD). In order to be able to do so, it is important that the AMSB and the other persons who effectively run the undertaking (see further, Chapter 7, section 3) have an overall understanding of the internal model. This means (Art. 225 DA) that they must have sufficient knowledge about:

(a) the structure of the internal model and the way the model fits the business and is integrated into the risk management system of the undertaking;
(b) the scope and purposes of the internal model and the risks that are or are not covered by the internal model;
(c) the general methodology applied in the internal model calculations;
(d) the limitations of the internal model;
(e) the diversification effects taken into account in the internal model.

Although internal models need not be complex, not all members of the AMSB can be expected to be familiar with the detailed aspects of the model. They should however understand where the model is expected to work well, in what circumstances it is likely to break down, whether the overall output is credible, what the main drivers are in terms of key assumptions and judgements, and whether those assumptions and judgements are reasonable. From persons who effectively run the undertaking, more can be expected. Art. 225 (2) DA requires these persons to have a sufficiently detailed understanding of the parts of the internal model used in the area for which they are responsible.

An internal model is only considered to be widely used and to play an important role in the system of governance of an undertaking where it meets all of the following conditions (Art. 226 DA):

(a) the internal model supports the relevant decision-making processes in the undertaking, including the setting of the business strategy;

(b) the internal model and its results are regularly discussed and reviewed in the AMSB;
(c) all material quantifiable risks identified by the risk management system that are within the scope of the internal model are covered by the model;
(d) the undertaking uses the internal model to assess, where material, the impact on its risk profile of potential decisions, including the impact on expected profit or loss and the variability of the profit or loss resulting from those decisions;
(e) the outputs of the internal model, including the measurement of diversification effects, are taken into account in formulating risk strategies, including the development of risk-tolerance limits and risk-mitigation strategies;
(f) the relevant outputs of the internal model are covered by the internal reporting procedures of the risk management system;
(g) the quantifications of risks and the risk ranking produced by the internal model trigger risk management actions where relevant;
(h) the internal model is changed as soon as possible where the results of the model validation process show that the model no longer complies with the legal requirements;
(i) the policy for changing the internal model provides that the model is changed, where relevant, to reflect changes in the risk management system.

The SCR must be calculated at least once a year. When the SCR is calculated using an internal model, the frequency of calculating the SCR must be consistent with the frequency with which the undertaking calculates the internal model for other purposes in the context of its risk management. For that recalculation, a simplified procedure may be applied under certain conditions (Art. 227 (2) DA). However, a simplified calculation is not possible if the risk profile of the undertaking has changed significantly. In that case a full recalculation is required in the same way as if the undertaking were using the standard formula. The supervisory authority might require a full recalculation of the SCR where there is evidence to suggest that the risk profile of the undertaking has altered significantly since the date on which the SCR was last reported (Art. 227 (4) DA).

4.2.3.2.2. Statistical Quality Standards

The probability distribution forecast underlying the internal model, i.e. the mathematical function that assigns a probability to an exhaustive set of mutually exclusive future events,[397] must assign probabilities to changes in either

[397] Art. 13 (38) FD.

the amount of basic own funds of the (re)insurance undertaking or to other monetary amounts, such as profit and loss, provided that those monetary amounts can be used to determine the changes in basic own funds. The exhaustive set of mutually exclusive future events must contain a sufficient number of events to reflect the risk profile of the undertaking (Art. 228 (1) DA).[398]

In the case of a partial internal model, the probability distribution forecast must be calculated at the highest level of aggregation of the components of the partial internal model. If the partial internal model consists of different components that are calculated separately and not aggregated within the partial internal model, the probability distribution forecast must be calculated for each component (Art. 228 (2) DA).

The methods used to calculate the probability distribution forecast must be based on adequate, applicable and relevant actuarial and statistical techniques, which must be consistent with the methods used by the undertaking in the calculation of its technical provisions (Art. 121 (2), first subparagraph FD). This means (Art. 229 DA) that:

(a) the techniques are based on up-to-date information and progress in actuarial science and generally accepted market practice is taken into account in the choice of the techniques;
(b) the undertaking has a detailed understanding of the economic and actuarial theory and the underlying assumptions;
(c) the outputs of the internal model indicate relevant changes in the risk profile of the undertaking;
(d) the outputs of the internal model are stable in relation to changes in the input data that do not correspond to a relevant change of the risk profile of the undertaking;
(e) the internal model captures all the relevant characteristics of the risk profile of the undertaking;
(f) the techniques are adapted to the data used for the internal model;
(g) the outputs of the internal model do not include a material model error or estimation error; wherever possible, the probability distribution forecast must be adjusted to account for model and estimation errors;
(h) the calculation of the outputs of the internal model can be set out in a transparent manner.

The methods used to calculate the probability distribution forecast must be based on current and credible information and realistic assumptions (Art. 121 (2), second subparagraph FD).

398 See also EIOPA, Guidelines on the use of internal models, EIOPA-BoS-14/180, 2 February 2015, Guidelines 16–28.

The information is only considered *credible* when the undertaking can provide evidence of the consistency and objectivity of that information, the reliability of the source of information and the transparency of the method by which that information is generated and processed (Art. 230 (1) DA).

The assumptions are only considered *realistic* when the undertaking can explain and justify each of the assumptions, taking into account the significance of the assumption, the uncertainty involved in the assumption and why the relevant alternative assumptions are not used. It must also be possible to clearly identify the circumstances under which the assumptions would be considered false. The undertaking must establish and maintain a written explanation of the methodology used to set those assumptions (Art. 230 (2) DA).

Data used for the internal model must be accurate, complete and appropriate (Art. 121 (3), first subparagraph FD). Data quality is obviously a very important element in the construction of an internal model. What is not put into the model will not come out of the model. If incorrect data are put into the model, the model will be incorrect; this is often referred to by actuaries as "garbage in, garbage out".

The data sets used in the calculation of the probability distribution forecast must be updated at least annually (Art. 121 (3), second subparagraph FD).

Data used in the internal model are only considered *accurate* where they are free from material errors, where data from different time periods used for the same estimation are consistent and where the data are recorded in a timely manner and consistently over time (Art. 231 (1) DA).

Data used in the internal model are only considered *complete* when they include sufficient historical information to assess the characteristics of the underlying risk, and in particular to identify trends in the risks. These data must also be available for all relevant model parameters and no such relevant data may be excluded from the use in the internal model without justification (Art. 231 (2) DA).

Data used in the internal model are only considered *appropriate* (Art. 231 (3) DA), where:

(a) the data are consistent with the purposes for which it is to be used;
(b) the amount and nature of the data ensure that the estimations made in the internal model on the basis of the data do not include a material estimation error;
(c) the data are consistent with the assumptions underlying the actuarial and statistical techniques that are applied to them in the internal model;
(d) the data reflect the relevant risks to which the undertaking is exposed;
(e) the data are collected, processed and applied in a transparent and structured manner, based on a specification of the definition and assessment of the quality of data, including specific qualitative and quantitative standards for different data sets, the use and setting of assumptions made in the collection, processing and application of data, and the process for carrying out data

updates, including the frequency of regular updates and the circumstances that trigger additional updates.

No particular method for the calculation of the probability distribution forecast is prescribed. Regardless of the calculation method chosen, the ability of the internal model to rank risk must be sufficient to ensure that the model is widely used and plays an important role in the risk management system, in the decision-making processes of the undertaking, and in the economic and solvency capital assessment and allocation processes (Art. 121 (4), first and second subparagraphs FD).

The internal model must be able to rank all material risks covered by the model. The ability to rank risks must be consistent with the classification of risks used in the internal model and the classification of risks used in the risk management system. Similar risks must be ranked consistently throughout the undertaking and ranked consistently over time. The ranking of risks must be consistent with the capital allocation process (Art. 232 DA).

The internal model must cover all material risks to which the undertaking is exposed (Art. 121 (4), third subparagraph FD). In the case of a full internal model, this means that the model must include at least the following risks: non-life underwriting risk, life underwriting risk, health underwriting risk, market risk, credit risk and operational risk. The undertaking must assess, at least on a quarterly basis, whether the internal model covers all material quantifiable risks within its scope. This assessment must take into account an appropriate set of qualitative and quantitative indicators (Art. 233 (1) DA).

The *qualitative* indicators must include the identification in the ORSA of risks other than those that are covered by the internal model, as well as the existence of a dedicated risk management process and dedicated risk-mitigation techniques for these other risks (Art. 233 (2) DA).

The *quantitative* indicators must include the capital allocation, the amount of profits and losses that cannot be explained by the risks covered by the internal model, and the results of stress testing and scenario analysis and any tool used in the model validation process (Art. 233 (3) DA).

As regards diversification effects, the undertaking may take account in its internal model of dependencies within and across risk categories, provided that the supervisory authority is satisfied that the system used for measuring those diversification effects is adequate (Art. 121 (5) FD). This means that the system used for measuring diversification effects identifies the key variables driving dependencies and that it takes into account any non-linear dependence and any lack of diversification under extreme scenarios, any restrictions of diversification that arise from the existence of a ring-fenced fund or MA portfolio, and the characteristics of the risk measure used in the internal model. The assumptions underlying the system used for measuring diversification effects must be justified on an empirical basis (Art. 234 DA).

The internal model may also take full account of the effect of risk-mitigating techniques, as long as credit risk and other risks arising from the use of risk-mitigation techniques are properly reflected in the internal model (Art. 121 (6) FD).

In the context of risk-mitigating techniques, risks arising from the following situations cannot be considered to be risks that are properly reflected in the internal model (Art. 235 (1) DA):

(a) the contractual arrangements relating to the risk-mitigation technique are, in any relevant jurisdiction, not legally effective and enforceable or do not ensure that the transfer of risk is clearly defined and incontrovertible;
(b) the undertaking does not have a direct claim on the counterparty in the event of the default, insolvency or bankruptcy of the counterparty or other credit event set out in the transaction documentation to the arrangements relating to the risk-mitigation technique;
(c) the legal arrangements underlying the risk-mitigation technique do not contain an explicit reference to a specific risk exposure clearly defining the extent of the cover provided by the risk-mitigation technique.

Where the risk-mitigation technique does not cover the risk exposure of the undertaking in all cases, the internal model cannot be considered to properly reflect the risk arising from the risk-mitigation technique unless it takes into account the reduced effectiveness of the risk-mitigation technique resulting from this deviation of risk exposures (Art. 235 (2) DA).

Where the risk-mitigation technique is subject to a condition the fulfilment of which is outside the direct control of the undertaking and which could undermine the effective transfer of risk, the internal model cannot be considered to properly reflect the risk arising from the risk-mitigation technique unless it takes into account the effects of those conditions and any reduced effectiveness of that risk-mitigation technique (Art. 235 (3) DA).

The undertaking must accurately assess the particular risks associated with financial guarantees and any contractual options in its internal model, where material. It must also assess the risks associated with both policyholder options and contractual options for the undertaking. Account must be taken of the impact that future changes in financial and non-financial conditions may have on the exercise of those options (Art. 121 (7) FD).

Account may be taken in the internal model of future management actions that the undertaking would reasonably expect to carry out in specific circumstances and allowance may be made for the time necessary to implement such actions under the following conditions (Art. 236 DA):

(a) the assumptions on future management actions are determined in an objective manner;

(b) assumed future management actions are realistic and consistent with the undertaking's current business practice and business strategy, including the use of risk-mitigation techniques, and, where there is sufficient evidence that the undertaking will change its practices or strategy, the assumed management actions are consistent with the changed practices or strategy;
(c) assumed future management actions are consistent with each other;
(d) assumed future management actions are not contrary to any obligations towards policyholders and beneficiaries or to legal provisions;
(e) assumed future management actions take account of any public information or communication by the undertaking as to the actions that it would expect to take or not to take;
(f) the assumptions on future management actions are realistic and include a comparison of assumed future management actions with management actions taken previously by the undertaking, as well as a comparison of future management actions with management actions taken into account in the current and past calculations of the internal model. The undertaking must be able to explain any relevant deviation from these assumptions;
(g) a comprehensive future management actions plan is developed that has been approved by the AMSB and that includes the elements required under Art. 236 (3) DA.

Parts of the internal model obtained from a third party must be subject to all of the same tests and standards as the parts developed by the undertaking itself. In addition, for the parts obtained from a third party or the data obtained from a third party, the undertaking must be able to demonstrate a detailed understanding of those parts or those data, including their limitations (Art. 237 DA).

The undertaking remains responsible when it uses an external model or external data in its internal model. When it chooses not to operate the external model directly, it must put in place an outsourcing agreement with the service provider that complies with the requirements on outsourcing (Art. 49 FD and Art. 274 DA).[399]

4.2.3.2.3. Calibration Standards

The undertaking may use a different time period (for instance, a period exceeding[400] one year) or risk measure (for instance, tail VaR) for internal modelling purposes,

[399] See EIOPA, Guidelines on the use of internal models, EIOPA-BoS-14/180, 2 February 2015, Guidelines 56 and 57.

[400] See also EIOPA, Guidelines on the use of internal models, EIOPA-BoS-14/180, 2 February 2015, Guidelines 28–30.

as long as the result provides an equivalent level of protection for policyholders as that provided by the standard formula (Art. 122 (1) FD). This option applies both to the internal model as a whole and to different risk categories or major business units within the internal model (Art. 238 (1) DA). The undertaking may also adopt a stronger confidence level than 99.5%.[401]

Where practicable, the undertaking must derive the SCR directly from the probability distribution forecast generated by the internal model, using the 99.5% VaR over a one-year time horizon confidence level (Art. 122 (2) FD). Where this is not possible, the supervisory authority may allow the use of approximations, as long as the undertaking can demonstrate that policyholders are provided with an equivalent level of protection as that provided for in Art. 101 FD, i.e. the confidence level underlying the SCR (Art. 122 (3) FD). This includes evidence that the approximations do not introduce a material error in the SCR or do not lead to a lower SCR than that which is calculated in accordance with Art. 101 FD (Art. 238 (2), first subparagraph DA). Where the approximations are based on the rescaling of modelled risks, the undertaking must demonstrate that the rescaling does not impair the outcome of the approximations (Art. 238 (3), second subparagraph DA). The approximations are considered to be part of the internal model (Art. 238 (4) DA).

Where the time period of the risk measure used is different from the one provided under the standard formula (12 months) and the SCR cannot be derived directly from the probability distribution forecast generated by the internal model using the 99.5% VaR over a one-year time horizon, the undertaking must take into account all of the following (Art. 238 (3), third subparagraph):

(a) whether events are equally distributed over time and if not, how this is reflected in the approximations;
(b) whether all significant risks over a one-year period are properly managed;
(c) where the time period used is longer than 12 months, whether due consideration has been given to the solvency position during that time period;
(d) whether the time period used is appropriate, taking into account the average duration of the liabilities of the undertaking, the business of the undertaking and, where relevant, the uncertainties associated with long time periods;
(e) any assumptions made in the approximations about the dependencies between risks over consecutive periods of time.

---

401 See, for instance, the 2017 SFCR of Hannover Re Group, which indicates (pp. 75–76) that Hannover Re calculates the required risk capital in its internal model using the VaR at a confidence level of 99.97%, which is equivalent to a target ruin possibility of 0.03% (https://www.hannover-re.com/1265699/2017-solvency-and-financial-condition-report-hannover-ruck-se.pdf).

The undertaking must demonstrate the level of protection of policyholders once a year and each time the risk profile of the undertaking changes significantly (Art. 238 (3) DA).

4.2.3.2.4. Profit and Loss Attribution

The undertaking must review, at least annually, the causes and sources of profits and losses for each major business unit.[402] It must demonstrate how the categorisation of risk chosen in the internal model explains the causes and sources of profits and losses. The categorisation of risk and attribution of profits and losses must reflect the risk profile of the undertaking (Art. 123 FD).

For the purpose of profit and loss attribution, the undertaking must specify the profit and loss, the major business units, the categorisation of risks chosen in the internal model and the attribution of the overall profit or loss to the risk categories and major business units. The specification of profit and loss must be consistent with the increase and decrease of the monetary amount underlying the probability distribution forecast.

The categorisation of risks chosen in the internal model must be adequate, and sufficiently granular, for the purposes of risk management and decision-making. The categorisation of risk must distinguish between risks covered by the internal model and risks not covered by the internal model.

The attribution of profit and loss must be made in an objective and transparent manner and be consistent over time (Art. 240 DA).

4.2.3.2.5. Validation Standards

Proper governance of the internal model is necessary in order to ensure that the model remains fit for purpose over time.[403] This means that the undertaking must have a regular cycle of model validation that includes monitoring the performance of the model, reviewing the ongoing appropriateness of its specification and testing its results against experience (Art. 124, first subparagraph FD). This is the responsibility of the AMSB, which must put in place systems that ensure that the internal model operates properly on a continuous basis.

The model validation process must include an effective statistical process for validating the internal model that enables the undertaking to demonstrate to the supervisory authority that the resulting capital requirements are appropriate (Art. 124, second subparagraph FD). The process must apply to all parts of the internal model (Art. 241 (1) DA).

---

402 See also EIOPA, Guidelines on the use of internal models, EIOPA-BoS-14/180, 2 February 2015, Guideline 31.

403 See also EIOPA, Guidelines on the use of internal models, EIOPA-BoS-14/180, 2 February 2015, Guidelines 32–42.

For the model validation process, the undertaking must specify (Art. 241 (3) DA):

(a) the processes and methods used to validate the internal model and their purposes;
(b) for each part of the internal model, the frequency of regular validations and the circumstances that trigger additional validation;
(c) the persons who are responsible for each validation task;
(d) the procedure to be followed in the event that the model validation process identifies problems with the reliability of the internal model, and the decision-making process to address those problems.

In order to ensure independence of the model validation process from the development and operation of the internal model, the persons or organisational unit must, when carrying out the model validation process, be free from influence from those responsible for the development and operation of the internal model (Art. 241 (2) DA).

The undertaking must assess the quality and independence of the model validation process. In the case of an internal validation process, the undertaking must take account of the responsibilities and reporting structure of the persons involved in the process. In the case of an external validation process, the undertaking must take into account the remuneration structure of the persons, including, where applicable, their employees or other persons acting on their behalf, who are involved in the process and any other mandates these persons might have relating to the undertaking (Art. 241 (4) DA).

The undertaking must test the results and the key assumptions of the internal model at least annually against experience and other appropriate data to the extent that data are reasonably available. These tests must be applied at the level of single outputs, as well as at the level of aggregated results. The undertaking must identify the reason for any significant divergence between assumptions and data and between results and data (Art. 242 (1) DA).

As part of the testing of the internal model results against experience, the undertaking must compare the results of the profit and loss attribution referred to above with the risks modelled in the internal model (Art. 242 (2) DA). The statistical process for validating the internal model must be based on current information, taking into account, where it is relevant and appropriate, developments in actuarial techniques and the generally accepted market practice, and on a detailed understanding of the economic and actuarial theory and the assumptions underlying the methods of calculating the probability distribution forecast of the internal model (Art. 242 (3) DA).

The model validation process must include an analysis of the stability of the outputs of the internal model for different calculations of the internal model using the same input data, and in particular the testing of the sensitivity of the results of the internal model to changes in key underlying assumptions (including assumptions about future management actions) (Art. 124, fourth subparagraph FD and Art. 242 (5) DA). The validation process must also include an assessment of the accuracy, completeness and appropriateness of the data used by the internal model. Where the undertaking observes that changes in a key underlying assumption have a significant impact on the SCR, it must be able to explain the reasons for this sensitivity and how the sensitivity is taken into account in its decision-making process (Art. 242 (4) DA).

As part of the demonstration that the capital requirements resulting from the internal model are appropriate, the undertaking must compare the coverage and the scope of the internal model. For this purpose, the statistical process for validating the internal model must include a reverse stress test, identifying the most probable stresses that would threaten the viability of the undertaking (Art. 242 (6) DA).

4.2.3.2.6. Documentation Standards

As indicated before, the lack of appropriate documentation was an important issue that needed to be addressed. The FD and the DA deal extensively with this issue.[404]

The undertaking must document the design and operational details of its internal model (Art. 125 FD). This documentation must enable any independent, knowledgeable third party to understand the design and operational details of the internal model and form a sound judgement as to its compliance with the basic requirements of the SCR, the use test, the statistical quality standards, the calibration standards, the profit and loss attribution and the validation standards (Art. 243 (1) DA).

The documentation must be appropriately structured, detailed and complete, and must be kept up to date. Outputs of the internal model must be capable of being reproduced using the internal model documentation and all of the inputs into the internal model (Art. 243 (3) DA).

The documentation must provide a detailed outline of the theory, assumptions and mathematical and empirical bases underlying the internal model.[405] The documentation must also indicate any circumstances in which the internal model does not work effectively, with attention to be paid to (Art. 245 DA):

- risks that are not covered by the internal model;
- limitations in risk modelling used in the internal model;

---

404 See also EIOPA, Guidelines on the use of internal models, EIOPA-BoS-14/180, 2 February 2015, Guidelines 43–49.

405 For further details, see Art. 244 DA, which includes the minimum content of the documentation.

- the nature, degree and sources of uncertainty connected with the results of the internal model, including the sensitivity of the results to the key assumptions underlying the internal model;
- deficiencies in data used in the internal model and lack of data for the calculation of the internal model;
- risks arising out of the use of external models and external data in the internal model;
- limitations of information technology used in the internal model;
- limitations of internal model governance.

The documentation must also include a record of minor and major changes to the internal model.

4.2.3.3. Partial Internal Model

Not all (re)insurance undertakings are capable of developing a full internal model. In order to encourage undertakings to further improve their risk management, the FD allows them to use a partial internal model for one or more risk modules or sub-modules, for operational risk or for the adjustment for LAC-DT.[406] The partial internal model may be applied to the whole business or to one or more major business units (Art. 112 (2) FD).

The partial model must be integrated into the standard formula (Art. 239 DA). In order to do so, the undertaking must use as a default integration technique the correlation matrices and formulas of the standard formula.[407] Where this would not be appropriate, the undertaking must use the most appropriate integration technique set out in Annex XVIII to the DA or an alternative appropriate integration technique.

Where the undertaking is using a partial internal model, the requirements concerning the use test, the statistical quality standards, the calibration standards, the profit and loss attribution, the validation standards and the documentation standards[408] are adapted in order to take account of the limited scope of the model (Art. 243 (2 DA). This has an impact on the application for approval. In the case of a partial internal model, supervisory approval is only given where

406 It is not always clear what a partial model is. In its 2016 group SFCR (p.40), Allianz observes that "from a formalistic perspective, the German Supervisory Authority deems our model to be 'partial' because it does not cover all of our operations, some of our smaller operations report under the standard model and others under the deduction and aggregation approach" (https://www.allianz.com/content/dam/onemarketing/azcom/Allianz_com/investor-relations/en/results-reports/sfcr/en-Allianz-Group-SFCR.pdf).

407 As set out in Annex IV FD and Title I, Chapter V DA.

408 See also Art. 243 (2) DA.

the model fulfils the following additional conditions (Art. 113 (1) FD), which aim at avoiding cherry-picking:

(a) the reason for the limited scope of the model must be properly justified;
(b) the resulting SCR must reflect more appropriately the risk profile of the undertaking and must comply with the principles underlying the calculation of the SCR;
(c) the design of the model must be consistent with the principles underlying the calculation of the SCR so as to allow the partial internal model to be fully integrated into the SCR.

When assessing an application for the use of a partial internal model that only covers certain sub-modules of a specific risk module, or only some of the business units of the undertaking with respect to a specific risk module, or parts of both, the supervisory authority may require the undertaking to submit a realistic transitional plan to extend the scope of the model (Art. 113 (2), first subparagraph FD). Such a request must be justified and must set the minimum scope that the internal model must cover after the implementation of the transitional plan.

The transitional plan must set out the manner in which the undertaking plans to extend the scope of the model to other sub-modules or business units, in order to ensure that the model covers a predominant part of its insurance operations with respect to that specific risk module (Art. 113 (2), second subparagraph FD). If the undertaking fails to implement the transitional plan to extend the scope of the model, the supervisory authority may extend the period for implementing the plan, require the undertaking to use the standard formula or allow the use of a partial internal model with a more limited scope.

4.2.3.4. Policy for Changing a Full or Partial Internal Model

When a (re)insurance undertaking uses a full or partial internal model, it must develop a policy for changes to the model.[409] This is important for the undertaking, as its internal model must continuously reflect its specific risk profile. It is also important for the supervisory authority, which must approve the model.

As part of the initial approval process of an internal model, the supervisory authority must approve the policy for changing the model of the undertaking. The insurance undertaking may change its internal model in accordance with that policy.

---

409 See also EIOPA, Guidelines on the use of internal models, EIOPA-BoS-14/180, 2 February 2015, Guidelines 6–10.

The policy must include a specification of minor and major changes to the internal model. Major changes to the internal model, as well as changes to the policy, must always be subject to prior supervisory approval. Minor changes to the internal model are not subject to prior supervisory approval, in so far as they are developed in accordance with the policy (Art. 115 FD).

4.2.3.5. Approval of a Full or Partial Internal Model

A (re)insurance undertaking may only use a full or partial internal model for the calculation of the SCR when it has received approval from its supervisory authority (Art. 112 FD).[410] Such approval is obviously not required if the undertaking has developed an internal model for other purposes, such as portfolio management, reinsurance optimisation, pricing, asset–liability management, defining underwriting limits, product development, etc.

The application for approval of the internal model, as well as the application for approval of any subsequent major changes made to that model, must be approved by the AMSB.

Details about the procedure to be applied can be found in the Commission Implementing Regulation of 19 March 2015[411] and in the EIOPA Guidelines on the use of internal models.[412] In order to promote a common supervisory approach for the application for an internal model, EIOPA has developed a common application package to be used as a practical instrument for undertakings and NSAs. The package is composed of a template and an accompanying document made available to NSAs.[413]

The application must be filed in written form and must be accompanied by documentary evidence. During the approval process, the supervisory authority can request adjustments to the internal model or the submission of a transitional plan (to a full internal model) in the case of a partial internal model.

The supervisory authority must take a decision on the application within six months of the receipt of the complete application. It must determine within 30 days of the receipt of the application whether the application is complete. If the application is not complete, the undertaking must be informed immediately

---

410 For an interesting perspective on internal model approval, see CADONI, P. and KERFRIDEN, C., Internal Models and Solvency II, in DOFF, R. (Ed.), *The Solvency II Handbook. Practical Approaches to Implementation*, Incisive Media, London, 2014.

411 Commission Implementing Regulation (EU) 2015/460 of 19 March 2015 laying down implementing technical standards with regard to the procedure concerning the approval of an internal model in accordance with Directive 2009/138/EC of the EP and of the Council, *OJ* L 76, 20.3.2015, p. 13.

412 EIOPA, Guidelines on the use of internal models, EIOPA-BoS-14/180, 2 February 2015, Guidelines 1–5.

413 EIOPA, Opinion on the use of a Common Application Package for Internal Models, EIOPA-BoS-14/035, 27 March 2014, 2 p. and EIOPA, *Common Application Package for Internal Models: Explanatory Note*, November 2014, 9 p.

that the six-month approval period has not yet begun and why the application is not complete. Once the application is considered complete, the supervisory authority must inform the undertaking concerned and indicate the date from which the six-month period starts to run. This does not prevent the supervisory authority from requesting additional information during the assessment process.

A period of six months is clearly necessary for the examination of the application by a supervisory authority. Most supervisory authorities in the EU had very little experience with internal models, and they had to find experts in the market who had such experience. That was not easy, as (re)insurance undertakings were "fishing in the same pond", i.e. they were also looking for experts who could assist them in developing an internal model.

For EIOPA, it was important from the very beginning to aim at a convergence of supervisory practices with regard to the assessment of internal models. Several initiatives were taken in this area.[414] Convergence was also necessary to enable the approval of group internal models (see further, Chapter 9, section 7.3).

As early as in 2013, EIOPA published its Guidelines on Pre-Application of Internal Models.[415] These Guidelines were applicable from 1 January 2014 onwards and provided guidance on what (re)insurance undertakings engaged in a pre-application process needed to consider so that NSAs could form a view on how prepared the undertaking was to submit an application for the use of an internal model for the calculation of the SCR. EIOPA wanted to avoid NSAs developing national solutions. In the case of a pre-application for groups, there was the need for an appropriate level of communication between NSAs within the colleges of supervisors. The Guidelines also served as preparation for the introduction of Solvency II. NSAs were asked to send a progress report to EIOPA on the application of the Guidelines by the end of February following each relevant year.

On 14 April 2015, EIOPA published an Opinion on the preparation for Internal Model applications.[416] This opinion addressed three specific issues for which a convergent approach was considered important: the modelling of sovereign exposures, the practical preparation of the application for the use of an internal model in the absence of some related formal decisions, such as the risk-free interest rate term structure and the equivalence of third-country solvency regimes, and the use of comparative studies as a complementary tool

414 For instance, the publication of Guidelines on pre-application of internal models, which applied from 1 January 2014, and the Guidelines on the use of internal models, which applied from 1 April 2015, i.e. well before the start date of Solvency II (1 January 2016). See also EIOPA, Final Report on Public Consultation No 14/019 on the Guidelines on the use of internal models, EIOPA-BoS-14/180, 27 November 2014, 129 p.

415 EIOPA, Guidelines on Pre-Application of Internal Models, EIOPA-CP-13/011, 2013, 35 p.

416 EIOPA, Opinion on the preparation for Internal Model applications, EIOPA-BoS-15/083, 14 April 2015, 3 p.

in the analysis of internal models. EIOPA considers it good practice for NSAs to gain insights from the comparison of different internal models. To this end, NSAs are recommended to carry out comparative studies at national level and to contribute to and make use of corresponding studies at EU level, coordinated by EIOPA. EIOPA has carried out a number of internal model consistency projects and will continue to do so in the future.[417]

On 30 November 2017, EIOPA issued an Opinion on internal models including a dynamic VA. A number of internal models use dynamic VA approaches that take the VA into account in the SCR by allowing the VA to move in line with the modelled credit spreads during the one-year forecast of basic own funds. EIOPA has underlined that undertakings using a dynamic VA must demonstrate that the SCR is at least as high as that which would result from an application of the VA methodology applicable to undertakings applying the standard formula.[418]

In order to facilitate the application process, EIOPA recommends that supervisory authorities put in place a pre-application process in order to form a view on how prepared a (re)insurance undertaking is to submit an application for the use of an internal model and to meet the internal model requirements.[419] In order to promote more consistency in the application of internal models, EIOPA is also conducting a benchmarking exercise, which will be made available to NSAs and should facilitate the approval process.[420]

As part of its strategy to reinforce integrated supervision in the EU, the EC has proposed giving EIOPA a greater role in coordinating the approval of internal models, so as to avoid the risk of divergent supervisory standards and outcomes. As stated in the Explanatory Memorandum to the Proposal:

> "Divergence in the supervision and approval of internal models may lead to inconsistencies, and creates an un-level playing field. EIOPA will be able to obtain in a timely way all relevant information upon its request and issue opinions to the relevant competent authorities. Where there are disagreements between competent authorities with respect to group internal models, EIOPA will also be able to assist the authorities in reaching an agreement under Article 19 of the EIOPA Regulation, either at its own initiative, on the request of one or more of the competent authorities, or in certain circumstances on the request of the group concerned."[421]

---

417 EIOPA, Update on Internal Model Consistency Projects, EIOPA-BoS/17-269, 25 October 2017, 2 p. See also EIOPA, First comparative study on market and credit risk modelling, EIOPA-BoS/18-180, 22 May 2018, 13 p.

418 EIOPA, Opinion on the supervisory assessment of internal models including a dynamic volatility adjustment, EIOPA-BoS-17/366, 30 November 2017, 3 p.

419 See EIOPA, Guidelines on the use of internal models, EIOPA-BoS-14/180, 2 February 2015, Guideline 1.

420 See EIOPA, Revised Single Programming Document 2017–2019 (AWP 2018), EIOPA-BoS/18-019, 29 January 2018, p. 54.

421 Proposal for a Regulation of the EP and of the Council amending the ESA Regulations, COM (2017) 536 final, 20 September 2017, p. 22 and 81 and EC, Communication to the EP, the

An application to use an internal model can always be withdrawn by notifying the supervisory authority in writing at any time before the decision on the application is taken.

Approval will only be given if the supervisory authority is satisfied that the undertaking's procedures for identifying, measuring, monitoring, managing and reporting risk are adequate and that the internal model fulfils all the legal requirements. The decision must indicate the starting date from which the model can be used for the calculation of the SCR, as well as any terms and conditions related to the approval decision, together with the reasons for those terms and conditions. The supervisory authority may, by means of a reasoned decision, require the undertaking to provide an estimate of the SCR determined in accordance with the standard formula. This allows the supervisory authority to see the impact of the use of the internal model and makes it possible to compare the situation with that of other undertakings applying the standard formula.

Approval of the use of an internal model for the calculation of the SCR does not mean that the supervisory authority becomes responsible for the model. The ultimate responsibility for the use of the model and possible failures of the model rests with the AMSB of the undertaking or group.

If a supervisory authority rejects the application, its decision must state in writing the reasons for the rejection. This is a natural requirement in the EU for all administrative decisions.[422] Supervisory authorities may not disclose the fact that a particular (re)insurance undertaking has applied for the use of an internal model and that the application was rejected or withdrawn.

In order to allow undertakings to start the application process for the use of a full or partial internal model so that they could effectively apply the model from day one (1 January 2016), the date of application of the provisions in the FD relating to the approval process was set at 1 April 2015 (Arts. 308a (1) (d) and 311, second subparagraph FD).[423]

4.2.3.6. Reversion to the Standard Formula

After having received approval for using an internal model, the (re)insurance undertaking or group may not revert to calculating the whole or any part of

Council, the ECB, the EESC and the CoR on Reinforcing integrated supervision to strengthen Capital Markets Union and financial integration in a changing environment, COM (2017) 542 final, 20 September 2017, p. 6. As part of the ESFS review, a new paragraph 3a was added to Art. 112 FD, which requires NSAs to inform EIOPA of the applications to use or change an internal model. EIOPA may provide technical assistance if requested by NSA.

422 Art. 297 FD specifically provides for a right of appeal to the courts for any decision taken in respect of a (re)insurance undertaking under laws, regulations and administrative provisions. See also IAIS, ICP 2 – Supervisor, para. 2.8.

423 See also the very specific transitional provision in Art. 308b (16) FD, which allows an ultimate parent (re)insurance undertaking to apply for the approval of an internal group model applying to a part of a group under specific conditions until 31 March 2022.

the SCR in accordance with the standard formula, except in duly justified circumstances and subject to the approval of the supervisory authority (Art. 117 FD).

This requirement aims at avoiding cherry-picking and is fully in line with the philosophy underlying the use of an internal model, i.e. carrying out a more sophisticated management of the specific risk position of the undertaking or group.

4.2.3.7. Non-Compliance with the Internal Model

If, after having received approval for using an internal model, the undertaking or group ceases to comply with any of the legal requirements, it must, without delay, either present to the supervisory authority a plan to restore compliance within a reasonable period of time, or demonstrate that the effect of non-compliance is immaterial (Art. 118 (1) FD).

In the event that the undertaking or group fails to implement the plan to restore compliance, the supervisory authority may require the undertaking or group to revert to calculating the SCR in accordance with the standard formula (Art. 118 (2) FD).

4.2.3.8. Public Disclosure and Supervisory Reporting

Where an internal model is used to calculate the SCR, the SFCR must include in section E.4, under "Capital management", the following information (Art. 297 (4) DA):

(a) a description of the various purposes for which the undertaking is using its internal model;
(b) a description of the scope of the internal model in terms of business units and risk categories;
(c) where a partial internal model is used, a description of the technique that has been used to integrate the partial internal model into the standard formula including, where relevant, a description of alternative techniques used;
(d) a description of the methods used in the internal model for the calculation of the probability distribution forecast and the SCR;
(e) an explanation, by risk module, of the main differences in the methodologies and underlying assumptions used in the standard formula and in the internal model;
(f) the risk measure and time period used in the internal model and, where they are not the same as those applicable to the standard formula, an explanation of why the SCR calculated using the internal model provides policyholders and beneficiaries with an equivalent level of protection;
(g) a description of the nature and appropriateness of the data used in the internal model.

Where an internal model is used to calculate the SCR, the RSR must include the following information (Art. 311 (3) DA):

(a) the results of the review of the causes and sources of profits and losses, for each major business unit and how the categorisation of risk chosen in the internal model explains those causes and sources of profits and losses;
(b) information on whether, and if so to what extent, the risk profile of the undertaking deviates from the assumptions underlying the undertaking's internal model;
(c) information about future management actions used in the calculation of the SCR.

4.3. MINIMUM CAPITAL REQUIREMENT

4.3.1. General Approach

As indicated above (section 4.1), the FD introduces two capital requirements. Each of these requirements serves a different purpose. The SCR and the MCR are the two extremes of the so-called "ladder of intervention". If available capital falls below the SCR, supervisors take proportionate corrective measures. In the event that available capital falls further, the severity of the measures applied is increased, and in the event that the MCR is breached, ultimate supervisory action is triggered.

Whilst the SCR is a soft target that can be breached, leading to a dialogue with the supervisory authority about ways and means to restore the solvency capital as quickly as possible, the MCR is a hard limit that should not be breached. It ensures a minimum level below which the amount of financial resources (eligible basic own funds) should not fall.

Designing two capital requirements has not been easy. Several options were examined: MCR calculated as a percentage of the (Solvency I) solvency margin, MCR calculated as a percentage of the SCR, and MCR calculated using a simplified version of the SCR.

The final decision about the MCR was taken after QIS 3. It is a compromise. The MCR may not fall below 25% nor exceed 45% of the undertaking's SCR. In principle, the SCR should therefore be higher than the MCR. This is not always the case in practice, because two different formulas are used to calculate the capital requirement and because the FD sets an absolute floor for the MCR.[424]

---

424 CLUNE, D., *Topsy-turvy SCR ratios*, http://www.solvencyiiwire.com/topsy-turvy-scr-ratios/1587586, 4 July 2017.

It was agreed to set the absolute floor for the MCR at a level that was not too high, in order to ensure that most undertakings would meet that level. For the absolute floor, a level was chosen that was similar to that of the solvency margin under Solvency I.

Because the final decision was in the end a compromise, Art. 129 (5) FD requires the EC to submit a report to the EP and to the Council by 31 December 2020 setting out how Member States have implemented the MCR requirement and what difficulties may have arisen concerning the cap (45%) and floor (25%) for the MCR.

4.3.2. Calculation of the MCR

All (re)insurance undertakings must hold *eligible basic own funds* to cover the MCR (Art. 128 FD).

Basic own funds are defined in Art. 88 FD as the sum of the excess of assets over liabilities and subordinated liabilities (see above, section 3.1.1). These basic own funds must be *eligible* for supervisory purposes. That means that the MCR must be made up of at least 80% Tier 1 capital, and that Tier 2 capital items may not exceed 20% of the MCR. Furthermore, certain basic own-fund items referred to in Art. 82 (3) DA that can qualify as Tier 1 items may not exceed 20% of the Tier 1 capital (see above, section 3.3). This last restriction is questionable, but should further ensure that the MCR contains primarily "hard capital".

The MCR must be calculated in accordance with the following principles (Art. 129 FD):

(a) it must be calculated in a clear and simple manner and in such a way as to ensure that the calculation can be audited. Undertakings or groups cannot develop an internal model to calculate the MCR. Supervisory authorities must be able to see immediately – without extra calculations – whether the undertaking or group is sufficiently capitalised. The MCR must be easy to verify;

(b) the MCR must be calculated at least quarterly, and the result of the calculation must be communicated to the supervisory authority;

(c) the MCR corresponds to an amount of eligible basic own funds below which policyholders and beneficiaries are exposed to an unacceptable level of risk were the undertaking allowed to continue its operations;

(d) the MCR is calibrated at a confidence level of 85% VaR over a one-year time horizon;

(e) the MCR has an absolute floor of:

    (i) €2,500,000 for non-life insurance undertakings, including captive insurance undertakings, save in the case where all or some of the risks

included in one of classes 10–15 listed in Part A of Annex I to the FD are covered,[425] in which case the absolute floor is €3,700,000;
(ii) €3,700,000 for life insurance undertakings, including captive insurance undertakings;
(iii) €3,600,000 for reinsurance undertakings, except in the case of captive reinsurance undertakings, in which case the MCR is €1,200,000;
(iv) the sum of the amounts set out in points (i) and (ii) for undertakings that simultaneously pursue both life and non-life insurance[426] (composite insurers). The same sum of the amounts set out in points (i) and (ii) applies to composite insurers that have been authorised by Member States within the limits of Art. 73 (2) FD (see Art. 253 (1) FD);

Where – in the case of a composite insurer – the gross written premiums written for non-life business (accident and sickness) do not exceed 10% or the total gross written premiums of the undertaking as a whole, the absolute floor for the MCR is that applicable to life insurance undertakings, i.e. €3,700,000 (Art. 253 (2) DA).

Where – in the case of a composite insurer – the gross written premiums written for life insurance business do not exceed 10% of total gross written premiums of the undertaking as a whole, the absolute floor of the MCR is that applicable to life insurance undertakings, i.e. €3,700,000 (Art. 253 (3) DA).

On the one hand, the absolute floor should serve as a back stop to ensure a minimum level of capital. On the other hand, the amount of the absolute floor had to be situated at a level that was not too high, so as to facilitate the transition from Solvency I to Solvency II;

(f) the MCR is situated between 25% and 45% of the SCR calculated on the basis of the standard formula or using an internal model, including any capital add-on that might have been imposed following the SRP (see further, Chapter 7, section 2).[427] Although the MCR must be calculated on a quarterly basis, this requirement does not mean that the SCR must also be calculated on a quarterly basis.

The MCR is calculated as a linear function of a set or subset of the following variables: the undertaking's technical provisions, written premiums, capital-at-risk,

---

425 Motor vehicle liability, aircraft liability, liability for ships, general liability, credit and suretyship.

426 Subject to some grandfathering provisions, new insurance undertakings are in principle no longer allowed to pursue life and non-life insurance activities simultaneously. See Art. 73 FD.

427 For a period ending no later than 31 December 2017, Member States could allow supervisory authorities to require that the percentages of 25% and 45% were to be applied exclusively to a calculation of the SCR based on the standard formula (Art. 129 (3), second subparagraph FD).

deferred tax and administrative expenses. The variables used are measured net of reinsurance (Art. 129 (2) FD).

The formulas for the calculation of the MCR are set out in Arts. 248–252 DA. As opposed to the SCR, the calculation of the MCR does not make explicit allowance for diversification benefits. It is also retrospective (based on the prior year's measures), whereas the SCR is prospective.[428]

4.3.3. *Supervisory Reporting and Public Disclosure*

Information about the MCR must be provided to the supervisory authority in the RSR (Art. 35 (1) (a) FD and Art. 311 DA). This includes information about the expected developments of the undertaking's anticipated MCR over its business planning time period, given the undertaking's business strategy, as well as information on any reasonably foreseeable risk of non-compliance with the undertaking's MCR and the undertaking's plans for ensuring that compliance is maintained.

Together with the amount of the MCR, the following information regarding the MCR must be included in the "Capital management" section of the SFCR:

- information on the inputs used by the undertaking to calculate the MCR, any material change to the MCR over the reporting period and the reasons for any such change;
- information regarding any non-compliance with the MCR during the reporting period, and in particular the period and maximum amount of each significant non-compliance, an explanation of its origin and consequences, any remedial measures taken and an explanation of the effects of such remedial measures;
- where non-compliance with the MCR has not been subsequently resolved, the amount of the non-compliance at the reporting date (Art. 51 (1) (e) (v) FD and Art. 297 (5) (a) and (b) DA).

4.3.4. *Non-Compliance with the MCR*

The FD aims at ensuring that (re)insurance undertakings remain solvent. It cannot however be excluded that an undertaking might experience financial difficulties, which might ultimately lead to a breach of the MCR. Non-compliance with the MCR leads to ultimate supervisory action, i.e. the undertaking is no longer allowed to continue its business. The undertaking's authorisation, which

---

428 DRUMMOND, C., *MCR shock – testing the strength of the SCR coverage ratio*, http://www.solvencyiiwire.com/category/articles 30 October 2017.

is required for it to carry out direct insurance or reinsurance (Art. 14 FD), will be withdrawn.

The undertaking must inform the supervisory authority immediately where it observes that it is no longer complying with the MCR or where there is a risk of non-compliance in the following three months. Within one month of this observation, the undertaking must submit, for approval by the supervisory authority, a short-term realistic finance scheme to restore, within three months of the observation, the eligible basic own funds at least to the level of the MCR or to reduce its risk profile to ensure compliance with the MCR (Art. 139 (1) and (2) FD). In the case of an undertaking with cross-border business, the home MS supervisory authority that has approved the finance scheme must inform the host MS supervisory authority that the undertaking has submitted a short-term finance scheme.[429] Contrary to the situation of non-compliance with the SCR (Art. 138 (3) FD), the period of three months cannot be extended because of the urgency of the situation.[430]

There are no formalities required for the finance scheme.[431] It can however be presumed that the scheme must be submitted in writing because it must be officially approved by the supervisory authority. The finance scheme must be realistic (as opposed to "wishful thinking") and must at least include particulars or evidence of the following (Art. 142 (1) FD):

- estimates of management expenses, in particular current general expenses and commissions;
- estimates of income and expenditure in respect of direct business, reinsurance acceptances and reinsurance cessions;
- a forecast balance sheet;
- estimates of the financial resources intended to cover technical provisions and the SCR and the MCR;
- the overall reinsurance policy.

In order to avoid spill-over effects to other Member States, the supervisory authority of the home MS may restrict or prohibit the free disposal of the assets of the undertaking. It must inform the supervisory authorities of the host MS in which the undertaking operates by way of FoS or through a branch. At the request of the supervisory authority of the home MS, the authorities

[429] EIOPA, Decision on the collaboration of the insurance supervisory authorities, EIOPA-BoS-17/014, 30 January 2017, p. 48.

[430] This might be a problem in practice when there is a need to organise a general meeting of shareholders or to prepare a run-off.

[431] The finance scheme is different from a recovery plan. In the case of a breach of the MCR, the focus is more on finding appropriate short-term financing than on recovering the business.

of the host MS may take the same measures. The supervisory authority of the home MS designates the assets to be covered by these measures (Art. 139 (3) FD). Further measures may be taken by supervisory authorities to safeguard the interests of policyholders if the solvency position of the undertaking continues to deteriorate (Art. 141 FD).

When the amount of eligible basic own funds falls below the MCR *and* the supervisory authority considers that the finance scheme submitted is manifestly inadequate *or* the undertaking concerned fails to comply with the approved scheme within three months of the observance of non-compliance with the MCR, the supervisory authority of the home MS must withdraw the authorisation of the (re)insurance undertaking (Art. 144 (1), second subparagraph FD). The authorisation is withdrawn unless the undertaking is able to re-establish the amount of eligible basic own funds at the level of the MCR within a short period of time (recital 69 FD).

The consequences of a withdrawal of authorisation are covered by national law, subject to the provisions of Art. 144 (2) FD, which require the supervisory authority of the home MS to notify the supervisory authorities of the host MS in which the undertaking is conducting its business in order to allow for appropriate measures to be taken to protect policyholders.[432]

The undertaking might be put into run-off, i.e. it will further execute existing contracts but is no longer authorised to conclude new business.[433] It might also be subject to reorganisation measures[434] or winding-up proceedings.[435] The relevant provisions here are in Title IV (Arts. 267–296) FD, which deals with the reorganisation and winding-up of insurance undertakings. The provisions in this Title are taken over from the former Reorganisation and Winding-up Directive,[436] which was repealed by the FD. These provisions put the responsibility for the reorganisation and/or winding-up with the home MS.

---

432 See also EIOPA, Decision on the collaboration of the insurance supervisory authorities, EIOPA-BoS-17/014, 30 January 2017, p. 49.

433 See also Chapter 4, section 6 above and Chapter 7, section 1.3 below.

434 Reorganisation measures are defined as "measures involving any intervention by the competent authorities which are intended to preserve or restore the financial situation of an insurance undertaking and which affect the pre-existing rights of parties other than the insurance undertaking itself, including but not limited to measures involving the possibility of a suspension of payments, suspension of enforcement measures or reductions of claims" (Art. 268 (1) (c) FD).

435 Winding-up proceedings are defined as "collective proceedings involving the realisation of the assets of an insurance undertaking and the distribution of the proceeds among the creditors, shareholders or members as appropriate, which necessarily involve any intervention by the competent authorities, including where the collective proceedings are terminated by a composition or other analogous measure, whether or not they are founded on insolvency or are voluntary or compulsory" (Art. 268 (1) (d) FD).

436 Directive 2001/17/EC of the EP and of the Council of 19 March 2001 on the reorganisation and winding-up of insurance undertakings, *OJ* L 110, 20.4.2001, p. 28.

They also deal with the consequences of a reorganisation or winding-up in situations where the insurance undertaking[437] has operations (through a branch or by way of cross-border services) in other Member States.

The statutory auditor must report promptly to the supervisory authority any non-compliance with the MCR (Art. 72 (1) (e) FD).

The FD does not deal with recovery and resolution of (re)insurance undertakings. This is the subject of debate. EIOPA[438] and the ESRB[439] are in favour of the introduction of specific EU regulation dealing with recovery and resolution of (re)insurance undertakings, inspired by similar legislation adopted in the banking sector.[440] There is fear that the failure of a (re)insurance undertaking might cause financial instability. This could be the case if the (re)insurance undertaking is a systemically important financial institution (SIFI),[441] a large (re)insurance undertaking, or a (re)insurance undertaking that is part of a financial conglomerate. It is fair to say that the FD primarily deals with living undertakings and that there are only few provisions (leftovers from the past) that address undertakings in difficulty or which have become insolvent.

From a regulatory perspective, it is important not to embark too quickly on a new major regulatory exercise for recovery and resolution. The issues might be more complex than expected and one should not forget that the business model of insurance is different from that in banking.[442] At this stage, it would be preferable to ensure that the instruments that are already available under the FD are used to their full potential as preventive mechanisms of early intervention (risk management, stress tests, ORSA, supervisory review process, supervisory ladder of intervention). In the next revision of the FD in 2021, the addition of some resolution tools and competences that would

---

437 The situation of a reorganisation or a winding-up of a reinsurance undertaking is not dealt with as the Reorganisation and Winding-up Directive only deals with insurance undertakings and the Solvency II FD merely recasts the existing legal requirements. This is another area where it would be useful to amend the FD in its application to reinsurance undertakings, by application of the proportionality principle.

438 EIOPA, Opinion to Institutions of the EU on the harmonisation of recovery and resolution frameworks for (re)insurers across the Member States, EIOPA-BoS/17-148, 5 July 2017, 88 p. and EIOPA, Discussion Paper on Resolution Funding and National Insurance Guarantee Schemes, EIOPA-CP-18-003, 30 July 2018, 60 p.

439 ESRB, *Recovery & resolution for the EU insurance sector: a macro-prudential perspective*, August 2017, 68 p.

440 Directive 2014/59/EU of the EP and of the Council of 15 May 2014 establishing a framework for the recovery and resolution of credit institutions and investment firms (BRRD), *OJ* L 173, 12.6.2014, p. 190.

441 FSB, *Developing Effective Resolution Strategies and Plans for Systemically Important Insurers*, 6 June 2016, 24 p.

442 See also the Geneva Association, *Insurance and Resolution in Light of the Systemic Risk Debate*, February 2012, 44 p.

help to ease the effects of an insolvency might be considered, in the interest of protecting policyholders and financial stability.

5. INVESTMENT RULES

5.1. BACKGROUND

Under Solvency I, there was a requirement for (re)insurance undertakings to manage their investments in a "prudent manner".[443] From the perspective of protecting policyholders, investment rules are particularly important. Premiums received from policyholders must be invested in such a manner that the assets in which they are invested are safe, so that there is money available when the undertaking must pay out claims. The principle that investments must be managed prudently was supplemented by a series of detailed investment rules regarding the admissibility of assets covering technical provisions (as these assets will be called on first to pay out claims), as well as quantitative limits on investments (so as to avoid concentration risk). These rules were further developed at national level by additional, more stringent investment rules, further restricting the assets that could be used to cover technical provisions.

An advantage of this rules-based approach was that the requirements were relatively easy to enforce by NSAs, who could prohibit or deter (re)insurance undertakings from investing in assets that they believed not to be appropriate for them to hold. A disadvantage of this approach was that it stifled innovation and restrained (re)insurance undertakings from holding the assets that they believed to be most appropriate for meeting their financial objectives.

Solvency II introduces a principles-based approach, which provides more flexibility for (re)insurance undertakings in their choice of particular investments, so that they can follow an investment strategy that they believe is the most appropriate for their risk profile, risk tolerance and overall financial objectives. This is fully in line with the philosophy underlying Solvency II, which puts the responsibility for managing the business with the AMSB. This incentivises undertakings to improve their risk management and allows for more efficient allocation of capital resources.

Solvency II therefore abolishes the rules-based approach and replaces it with investment freedom, subject to the application of the prudent person principle. This principle was first introduced in 2003 for occupational pension funds.[444]

---

443 See also IAIS, ICP 15 – Investment.

444 See Art. 18 (1) of Directive 2003/41/EC of the EP and of the Council of 3 June 2003 on the activities and supervision of institutions for occupational retirement provision, *OJ* L 235, 23.9.2003, p. 10.

It is, however, a long-established legal principle governing the management of investments. The principle encapsulates the ideas of portfolio diversification and broad asset–liability matching, based on the premise that the manager of the investments should seek to manage them as if they were his own, with due diligence and skill, thus avoiding undue risks to the beneficiaries.[445]

Quantitative restrictions and asset admissibility rules[446] limit holdings of certain types of assets within the portfolio. Both the prudent person approach and an approach based on quantitative limits seek to ensure that there is no significant mismatch between assets and liabilities, and that assets are sufficiently well diversified and liquid.

The practical application of the prudent person principle will be influenced by the greater emphasis put on sustainability. The transition to a low-carbon economy could lead to new transition risks: the repricing of assets held in carbon-intensive industries and the rapid rise of green finance (green bonds), which carries the risk of a green bubble and greenwashing in the transition towards a low-carbon economy.[447] (Re)insurers will also be asked to reorient their investment policy towards investments that are respectful of environmental, social and governance issues.[448]

5.2. PRUDENT PERSON PRINCIPLE

Investment of the premiums collected from policyholders constitutes an important part of a (re)insurer's activity. The investment must be carried out in such a manner that the (re)insurance undertaking is capable of fulfilling its promise to policyholders and beneficiaries. Investment is of course risky. The main investment risks are credit risk (for instance, the risk of the issuer of a bond becoming insolvent), liquidity risk (for instance, the risk of the insurer having to accept a lower price if it has to sell a bond in a short period of time without waiting to find a more interesting buyer), and market risk (for instance, the risk of the price of a bond falling as a result of rising interest rates). Other risks, such as concentration risk (lack of diversification), should also be considered.

---

445 EC, Commission Staff Working Document: Accompanying document to the Proposal for a Directive of the European Parliament and of the Council on the taking-up and pursuit of the business of Insurance and Reinsurance. Solvency II: Impact Assessment Report, SEC (2007) 871, 10 July 2007, p. 39.

446 With a 100% deduction, admissibility rules are an extreme form of quantitative restriction.

447 EIOPA, *Financial Stability Report*, June 2018, pp. 8–19.

448 There is no need to await regulatory intervention in this area. Insurers can already deal with these emerging risks and take this into account in their investment decisions. See VAN HULLE, K., Do not wait until new regulation is introduced, *Insurance ERM*, 28 December 2018.

In accordance with Art. 132 FD, (re)insurance undertakings must invest all their assets in line with the prudent person principle,[449] which means that:

(a) investment can only be made in assets and instruments the risks related to which the undertaking can properly identify, measure, monitor, manage, control and report;[450]
(b) all assets, in particular those covering the MCR and the SCR, must be invested in such a manner as to ensure the security, quality, liquidity and profitability of the portfolio as a whole and must be localised in such a way as to ensure their availability;
(c) assets held to cover the technical provisions must be invested in a manner appropriate to the nature and the duration of the (re)insurance liabilities (matching) and must be invested in the best interest of all policyholders and beneficiaries (taking into account any disclosed policy objective);
(d) in the case of a conflict of interest, investment by the undertaking or by the entity that manages its assets portfolio (in the case of outsourcing) must be made in the interest of policyholders and beneficiaries;
(e) the use of derivative instruments is only possible in so far as they contribute to a reduction in risks or facilitate efficient portfolio management, i.e. they should be used as a risk management tool rather than for speculative investment;
(f) investments and assets that are not admitted to trading on a regulated financial market must be kept to prudent levels, as the assessment of their risks may be subjective;
(g) assets must be properly diversified in such a way as to avoid excessive reliance on any particular asset, issuer or group of undertakings, or geographical area and excessive accumulation of risk in the portfolio as a whole;
(h) investments in assets issued by the same issuer, or by issuers belonging to the same group, may not expose the undertaking to excessive risk concentration.

In its RSR, the undertaking must provide information on how it fulfils the obligation to invest all its assets in accordance with the prudent person principle (Art. 308 (3) (d) DA).

449 Initially, CEIOPS was considering the adoption of a "prudent person plus approach" for a safe transition from Solvency I (with a great number of quantitative investment limits) to Solvency II (with freedom of investment). This would have made it possible to retain some quantitative limits, possibly as an MS option during a transitional period. This approach was not followed by the EC.

450 The investment strategy must appropriately take into account the overall solvency needs of the undertaking, considering its specific risk profile, the approved risk tolerance limits and its business strategy.

In its Guidelines on governance, EIOPA identifies the following characteristics of the prudent person principle for managing investments:[451]

(a) *Due diligence and process*: the prudent person principle is as much a behavioural standard as an assessment of judgements and investment decisions. Prudence is to be found in the process by which investment strategies are developed, adopted, implemented, and monitored in light of the purposes for which funds are managed, as well as in the outcomes;
(b) *Care, skill and delegation*: the undertaking, while performing investment management, must have an adequate understanding of the risks associated with its investments, its investment risk management policy and the necessary level of "familiarity" with the liability and regulatory constraints to appropriately carry out its responsibilities. Similarly, the undertaking must have or acquire the care and skill sufficient to the tasks of investment management for which it is responsible.

    To obtain a sufficient level of skills satisfying the prudent person principle, the undertaking may obtain advice from relevant experts and delegate various activities to those with the requisite skill. When employing an expert:
    (i) the undertaking is responsible for assuring that the expert actually has the skills for which he or she is being employed, and therefore must adequately investigate the expert's qualifications and experience;
    (ii) the undertaking must also ensure that experts it employs acquire sufficient familiarity with the specific nature and needs of the managed portfolios by providing them with complete, accurate and sufficient information so that they can appropriately formulate requested advice or carry out delegated tasks;
    (iii) the undertaking must assess whether the hired parties have any conflicts of interest that could provide inappropriate incentives to act contrary to its interests.
(c) *Duty to monitor*: even when delegating tasks, the undertaking remains responsible for monitoring and reviewing the activities that it has delegated so as to ensure that they have been appropriately and prudently carried out. This includes the monitoring and reviewing of investment managers;
(d) *Duty to protect policyholders' and beneficiaries' interests*: the undertaking must protect the policyholders' and beneficiaries' interests, taking into consideration that risks such as legal risk, reputation risks, commercial risks, and operational risks resulting from a lack of care may also impair its solvency;

---

[451] EIOPA, Final Report on Public Consultation No 14/07 on Guidelines on system of governance, EIOPA-BoS-14/253, 28 January 2015, p. 71.

(e) *Principle of diversification*: the investments in portfolios managed by the undertaking must be suitably diversified, both among appropriate asset classes and within each asset classification, in order to avoid the unwarranted concentration of investment and the associated accumulation of risk in the portfolios.

In its investment strategy, the undertaking should not solely depend on the information provided by third parties, such as financial institutions, asset managers and rating agencies, but should develop its own set of key risk indicators in line with its investment risk management policy and business strategy.[452] In the case of non-routine investment activities (such as a large or complex investments), the undertaking should have procedures that require that, where such investment or investment activity entails a significant risk or change in the risk profile, the undertaking's risk management function communicate such a risk or change in the risk profile to the AMSB.[453] The security, quality, liquidity and profitability of the portfolio as a whole must be regularly reviewed and monitored.[454]

If the undertaking issues unit-linked or index-linked contracts, special care must be taken, because the investment risk of the assets held is borne by the policyholders:

- where the benefits provided by the contract are directly linked to the value of units in an undertakings for collective investment in transferable securities (UCITS) or to the value of assets contained in an internal fund held by the undertaking, usually divided into units, the technical provisions in respect of those benefits must be represented as closely as possible by those units or, in the case where units are not established, by those assets;
- where the benefits provided by the contract are directly linked to a share index or some other reference value, the technical provisions in respect of those benefits must be represented as closely as possible either by the units deemed to represent the reference value or, in the case where units are not established, by assets of appropriate security and marketability that correspond as far as possible to those on which the particular reference value is based;
- where the benefits include a guarantee of investment, performance or some other guaranteed benefit, the assets held to cover the corresponding additional technical provisions must be invested prudently, i.e. respecting the principles of diversification and avoidance of excessive risk concentration.

452 EIOPA, Guidelines on system of governance, EIOPA-BoS-14/253, 28 January 2015, Guideline 27.

453 EIOPA, Guidelines on system of governance, EIOPA-BoS-14/253, 28 January 2015, Guideline 28.

454 EIOPA, Guidelines on system of governance, EIOPA-BoS-14/253, 28 January 2015, Guideline 29.

The undertaking must ensure that its investments of unit-linked and index-linked contracts are selected in the best interests of policyholders and beneficiaries, taking into account any disclosed policy objectives.[455]

Particularly in the case of unit-linked policies, EIOPA has expressed concern about potential conflicts of interests. Insurance undertakings might be incentivised to choose underlying investment vehicles (underlying funds) on the basis of those that provide the highest level of monetary incentives and remuneration to the undertaking. EIOPA has identified five risks to the consumer's detriment that arise from market practices in this area:

(a) higher costs for policyholders, for example when the monetary incentives and remuneration received is not fully rebated to customers;
(b) information asymmetry or uninformed choices by policyholders, for example the impossibility for policyholders to assess whether the investment chosen achieves the best consumer outcome;
(c) unsuitable product offerings, for example where the selection of underlying funds is determined by levels of monetary incentives;
(d) unsuitable sales and biases in distribution, for example when the remuneration schemes provided for staff mirror the levels of incentives received from asset managers;
(e) poor investment outcomes for policyholders arising from inappropriate selection processes by insurance undertakings and poor governance systems and controls, for example when the undertaking fails to select the most relevant or competitive underlying funds in the structuring of unit-linked policies.

In order to mitigate these risks, EIOPA expects NSAs to take the necessary and proportionate supervisory actions to:

- remind insurance undertakings that they should take appropriate steps to prevent, identify, mitigate and manage conflicts of interest that might arise from monetary incentives received from asset managers;
- provide guidance to insurance undertakings on possible organisational or administrative arrangements to prevent conflicts of interest from adversely affecting the interests of policyholders;
- provide guidance on measures to manage assets of unit-linked policies in the best interests of policyholders.[456]

---

455 EIOPA, Guidelines on system of governance, EIOPA-BoS-14/253, 28 January 2015, Guideline 32.

456 EIOPA, Opinion on monetary incentives and remuneration between providers of asset management services and insurance undertakings, EIOPA-BoS-17/295, 11 December 2017, p. 7.

Member States may not require (re)insurance undertakings to invest in particular asset categories (for instance, sovereign bonds). Nor can they make investment decisions subject to any kind of prior approval or systematic notification. They may, however, restrict the types of assets or reference values to which policy benefits may be linked – in the case of unit-linked business, where the investment risk is borne by the policyholder, in the interest of policyholders (Art. 133 FD).

When investing in securitised instruments (securitisation), the undertaking must ensure that its interests and the interests of the originator or sponsor concerning the securitised assets are well understood and aligned.[457] For securitisations, see above, section 4.2.2.2.4 (on spread risk).

An overview provided by EIOPA of the investment behaviour of 87 large insurance groups and four solo undertakings across 16 European countries over the last five years shows that there were only marginal changes in all three main investment categories from 2011 to 2016. The three main investment categories are:

- bonds (sovereign, corporate, structured notes and collateralised securities);
- equity (listed and non-listed);
- other investments (commercial property, residential property, loans (excluding mortgages) and derivatives).

EIOPA's statistics from 31 December 2017 offer the following picture of investments by EEA (re)insurance undertakings:[458]

- government bonds: 28.7%;
- corporate bonds: 27.7%;
- equities:[459] 12.8%;
- investment funds and UCITS: 18.3%;
- structured notes: 1.3%;
- collateralised securities: 0.6%;

457 EIOPA, Guidelines on system of governance, EIOPA-BoS-14/253, 28 January 2015, Guideline 35.

458 EIOPA, *European Insurance Overview 2018. Solo undertakings. Year-end 2017*, Publications Office of the EU, Luxembourg, 2018, p. 26. This does not include investment in unit-linked or index-linked securities. The market for these securities has increased dramatically as a result of the low interest rate environment, thereby shifting market risk exposure from insurers to policyholders, which needs careful attention from a financial stability perspective.

459 There has been a slight shift in insurer investment from fixed-income assets towards equities. The main drivers of this change seem to be the macro-economic environment (low yield, inflation, economic growth and taxation) and company-specific reasons, such as undertakings with a high level of capital (so that they can support the higher capital requirement for investment in equity). See JAKUBIK, P. and TURTURESCU, E., Potential drivers of insurers' equity investments, in EIOPA, *Financial Stability Report*, June 2018, pp. 79–83.

- cash and deposits: 4.5%;
- mortgages and loans: 0.4%;
- property: 0.1%;
- other investments: 0.1%.

It is clear from this picture that the investment behaviour of EEA (re)insurance undertakings is still rather conservative. One must of course keep in mind that asset–liability matching is absolutely crucial for (re)insurance undertakings. That may make it difficult to further diversify the portfolio of investments. It remains to be seen whether the move towards a more sustainable economy will help (re)insurers to play a more important role as institutional investors in the real economy. This is not just a question of calibration, but also of availability of investment opportunities. At the same time, further diversification of investments should remain respectful of the prudent person principle and should not entail an unacceptable risk for policyholders and other beneficiaries.[460]

[460] As stated by Nikolaus von Bomhard, former Chairman of the Management Board of Munich Re, at the 2nd Annual Conference of EIOPA in Frankfurt on 21 November 2012: "I am not investing in infrastructure or equity because the government wants me to do so but because it is in the interest of policyholders."

CHAPTER 7

PILLAR 2

Qualitative Requirements

As indicated above, Solvency II follows a three-pillar approach. Each of these pillars is equally important. Pillar 2 deals with the qualitative requirements of the new solvency regime. These qualitative requirements comprise the supervisory regime (including supervisory powers), the supervisory review process and the governance regime (including key governance functions and the ORSA).

1. SUPERVISORY POWERS

The introduction of a risk-based solvency regime has important consequences for supervision,[1] if only because supervision under Solvency II is more intrusive, as Solvency II follows a principle-based approach and places the main responsibility for ensuring the solvency of the undertaking with its management (the AMSB). NSAs need to have the power to check how management has carried out this task and to what extent (re)insurance undertakings comply with the letter and the spirit of the legislation.

The possible impact of the introduction of Solvency II for insurance supervisors was examined as part of the impact assessment accompanying the EC's proposed FD (July 2017).[2] In their answers to a questionnaire developed by CEIOPS, 38% of NSAs indicated that Solvency II would require material changes to their supervisory system, tools and resources. It was agreed that Solvency II would help to realise more efficient and effective supervision, which would have "a preventative effect by enabling timely intervention".[3]

---

1 For an overview of new developments in financial supervision, see KELLERMANN, J., DE HAAN, J. and DE VRIES, F. (Eds.), *Financial Supervision in the 21st Century*, Springer, Heidelberg, 2013, 232 p.

2 CEIOPS, Report on the Impact of Solvency II on supervisory authorities: General Conclusion, CEIOPS-DOC-02/07, 21 February 2007, 12 p.

3 CEIOPS, Report on the Impact of Solvency II on supervisory authorities: General Conclusion, CEIOPS-DOC-02/07, 21 February 2007, p. 10.

A second examination of the preparedness of NSAs to implement Solvency II was carried out by CEIOPS in 2010,[4] again based upon a questionnaire sent to all NSAs. One of the conclusions was that fundamental changes were needed in the supervisory methodology, tools and procedures, in all the different areas of insurance supervision for nearly all NSAs. Internal models represented possibly the biggest challenge for supervisors.

The FD includes a number of provisions dealing with supervisory powers. These provisions must be seen in the context of the functioning of an internal market whereby (re)insurance undertakings operate cross-border by way of free provision of services or through the establishment of branches in other Member States. Cooperation between supervisory authorities is key to making the system work. This cooperation is institutionalised within EIOPA, which plays an essential role in the implementation in practice of the new solvency regime. The ultimate goal is the establishment of a common supervisory culture.[5]

1.1. OBJECTIVES OF SUPERVISION

The main objective of supervision[6] is the protection of policyholders and beneficiaries (Art. 27 FD).[7] To that generally agreed objective, another was added after the financial crisis, i.e. financial stability.

In the exercise of their general duties, supervisory authorities must duly consider the potential impact of their decisions on the stability of the financial systems concerned in the EU, in particular in emergency situations, taking into account the information available at the relevant time.[8] At times of exceptional fluctuations in financial markets, supervisory authorities must take into account the potential pro-cyclical effects of their actions (Art. 28 FD). Supervisory authorities should be aware that actions aimed at protecting policyholders from losses may also inadvertently encourage behaviour that worsens fluctuations in financial markets. The classic example is a fire sale of assets, as seen in the last financial crisis.[9]

---

4 CEIOPS, Report on the Preparedness of Insurance Supervisors to implement Solvency II, CEIOPS-DOC-83/10, June 2010, 20 p.

5 EIOPA, *A common supervisory culture: Key characteristics of high-quality and effective supervision*, Publications Office of the EU, Luxembourg, 2017, 16 p.

6 See also Chapter 1, section 3.1.

7 See also, IAIS, ICP 1 – Objectives, Powers and Responsibilities of the Supervisor, para. 1.3. (November 2017).

8 These words were added in order to clarify that supervisors should not be made responsible for situations that they could not have been aware of.

9 EC, *Report of the High-Level Group on financial supervision in the EU, chaired by Jacques de Larosière*, 25 February 2009, p. 12.

Although the protection of policyholders remains the main objective of insurance supervision, there may be situations in which it is difficult for supervisory authorities to ensure the stability of the financial system without infringing the rights of policyholders, particularly in emergency situations. This has been the case in several Member States after the financial crisis, when the low interest rate environment created problems, particularly for life insurance undertakings.

Member States must see to it that supervisory authorities have the necessary means – including the relevant expertise – capacity and mandate to achieve these objectives (Art. 27 FD). It is for Member States to decide how they organise and fund supervision. The funding and structure of insurance supervision is different from MS to MS.

In accordance with ICP 3 – Supervisory Authority, supervisory authorities must be operationally independent and accountable in the exercise of their functions and powers. This means that the staff must be free from undue political, governmental and industry interference in the performance of supervisory responsibilities and that the supervisory authority is financed in a manner that does not undermine its independence from political, governmental or industry bodies.

In terms of funding, supervisory authorities are often funded by contributions paid by the supervised entities. In other cases, the cost of supervision is part of the state budget. In both situations, there could be problems in the case of economic downturns (less turnover results in lower contributions) or budgetary difficulties (less money available for supervision). Mixed models may also exist.

In terms of the structure of supervision, there is a tendency to combine insurance supervision and banking supervision under one single authority, which may (for instance, in Belgium, France, Hungary, the Netherlands or the UK) or may not (for instance, in Austria, Estonia, Germany or Finland) be the central bank. In addition, some Member States have introduced a so-called "twin peaks" structure that divides supervision between two institutions, whereby one institution is responsible for prudential supervision and another authority is made responsible for market conduct supervision (for instance, in Belgium, the Netherlands and the UK).[10]

[10] The situation in the EEA is very diverse. For instance, in Bulgaria the Financial Supervision Commission supervises all public companies and other issuers of securities, investment firms, investment companies, management companies, regulated markets, central depositary, insurance companies, insurance intermediaries and pension companies. A similar situation exists in Croatia, where the Croatian Financial Services Supervisory Agency (Hanfa) has since 2005 combined three existing supervisory agencies, the Croatian Securities Commission, the Agency for Supervision of Pension Funds and Insurance, and the Insurance Companies Supervisory Authority.

1.2. GENERAL PRINCIPLES OF SUPERVISION

As part of its objective of establishing a common supervisory culture, EIOPA has identified the key characteristics of high-quality and effective supervision[11] – supervision needs to be:

- risk-based and proportionate;
- forward-looking, preventive and proactive;
- challenging, sceptical and engaged;
- comprehensive;
- conclusive.

1.2.1. Risk-Based and Proportionate Supervision

All (re)insurance undertakings are subject to a minimum level of supervision, but a risk-based system allows supervisory authorities to prioritise and use their own resources efficiently and effectively. Under a risk-based regime, the insurance market must be looked at as a whole and supervision should cover all activities, including distribution channels and products, which may be the cause of market conduct risk.[12]

Supervision must be carried out in a manner that is proportionate to the nature, scale and complexity of the risks inherent in the business of (re)insurance undertakings (Art. 29 (3) FD). See also Chapter 5.

1.2.2. Forward-Looking, Preventive and Proactive Supervision

Supervisors should assess not only current risks, but also those that could potentially arise in the future, including emerging risks.[13] They should consider the evolution of the market and focus on "what can go wrong?" rather than only on "what went wrong?". A forward-looking approach means that supervisors should intervene at an early stage in order to minimise disruption or loss on the part of policyholders. Attention should be paid to internal developments within (re)insurance undertakings. Regular discussions with management on important evolutions or key decisions should allow supervisors to appraise inherent and emerging risks.[14]

---

[11] EIOPA, *A common supervisory culture: Key characteristics of high-quality and effective supervision*, Publications Office of the EU, Luxembourg, 2017, 16 p.

[12] EIOPA, *A common supervisory culture: Key characteristics of high-quality and effective supervision*, Publications Office of the EU, Luxembourg, 2017, pp. 5–7.

[13] EIOPA, *A common supervisory culture: Key characteristics of high-quality and effective supervision*, Publications Office of the EU, Luxembourg, 2017, pp. 8–9.

[14] FLAMEE, M. and WINDELS, P., International Insurance Supervision, in KEMPLER, C., FLAMEE, M., YANG, C.H. and WINDELS, P. (Eds.), *Global Perspectives on Insurance Today*, Palgrave Macmillan, New York, 2013, p. 14.

Preventive supervision means that supervisors must adapt to emerging risks, such as new technologies, and their impact on business, risk management and internal controls. They must be able to act before any non-compliance with rules and regulations arises. A good example of preventive and proactive supervision is the work carried out by EIOPA on conduct risk.[15]

Proactive supervision means that supervisors need to plan ahead for their SRP and execute supervisory actions and measures well in time.

1.2.3. Challenging, Sceptical and Engaged Supervision

Supervisors need to question assessments by (re)insurance undertakings and challenge their conclusions and decision-making processes without interfering with entrepreneurial freedom.[16] Meeting such a challenge is only possible if the supervisory authority has an intimate knowledge of the market and the supervised entities. This knowledge is certainly served by the supervisory dialogue established under Solvency II, which requires supervisory authorities to regularly meet up with the leadership of the supervised undertakings. In this dialogue, both sides must apply the same approach in terms of openness, business knowledge, experience and transparency. A dialogue is not a combination of two monologues and is based on trust.

Trust should not prevent supervisors from applying a healthy dose of professional scepticism along with integrity and fairness. Professional scepticism is an attitude that includes a questioning mind. Integrity and fairness means that supervisors should approach their supervisory role in an objective manner, without prejudice against individual market players and independent of political interference.

Although (re)insurance undertakings and supervisors pursue objectives that may be seen as contradictory at first glance, the ongoing dialogue between them should demonstrate that supervisors really care and that they are committed to finding satisfactory solutions.

1.2.4. Comprehensive Supervision

A comprehensive view of the relevant markets, entities and products reduces the risk of supervisors not identifying significant risks, including emerging risks.[17] Supervisory authorities should ensure a similar level of protection

---

15 See EIOPA, Strategy towards a comprehensive risk-based and preventive framework for conduct of business supervision, EIOPA-16/015, 11 January 2016, 10 p.

16 EIOPA, *A common supervisory culture: Key characteristics of high-quality and effective supervision*, Publications Office of the EU, Luxembourg, 2017, p. 10.

17 EIOPA, *A common supervisory culture: Key characteristics of high-quality and effective supervision*, Publications Office of the EU, Luxembourg, 2017, pp. 11–12.

for policyholders across Member States, regardless of the location of the undertaking's head office. This is particularly important when a (re)insurance undertaking is conducting business in another MS. Supervisors of the home and host Member States should cooperate in order to ensure an adequate level of policyholder protection.[18]

1.2.5. Conclusive Supervision

Supervisors must draw conclusions and follow up on matters as soon as possible and in an appropriately timely manner, following due process through the SRP.[19] Issues that have been identified cannot be left without a proper conclusion and action plan.

Once supervisors have drawn their conclusions, these should be communicated appropriately and in a timely manner to the undertakings concerned.

1.3. SCOPE OF SUPERVISION

All (re)insurance undertakings subject to Solvency II may carry out cross-border business. This can be done either by providing cross-border services or through the establishment of a branch. The financial (prudential) supervision of the undertaking, including that of the cross-border business, is the sole responsibility of the supervisory authority of the home MS (Art. 30 (1) FD).

Financial supervision includes verification, with respect to the entire business of the undertaking, of its solvency, of the establishment of technical provisions, of its assets and of the eligible own funds, in accordance with the rules laid down or practices followed in the home MS under provisions adopted at EU level (Art. 30 (2) FD).

For instance, if an insurance undertaking established in Germany has set up a branch in France, the prudential supervision over the German undertaking and its branch in France is carried out exclusively by the German supervisory authority (BaFin). The German supervisory authority may, after having informed the French supervisory authority (ACPR), carry out at the branch in France on-site verifications of the information necessary for the prudential supervision of the German undertaking. The French supervisory authority and EIOPA may participate in these verifications (Art. 255 (2) FD). If the French supervisory authority were to prohibit the German supervisory authority from carrying out these verifications, or if the German supervisory authority were

[18] See EIOPA, Decision on the collaboration of the insurance supervisory authorities, EIOPA-BoS-17/014, 30 January 2017, 59 p.

[19] EIOPA, *A common supervisory culture: Key characteristics of high-quality and effective supervision*, Publications Office of the EU, Luxembourg, 2017, p. 13.

to prohibit the French supervisory authority from participating in these verifications, each supervisory authority could refer the matter to EIOPA, which can in such situations offer its services as a mediator (Art. 33 FD and Art. 19 EIOPA Regulation).

If the supervisory authority of a host MS has reason to believe that the activities of a (re)insurance undertaking might affect its financial soundness, it must inform the supervisory authority of the home MS of the undertaking, which will determine whether the undertaking is complying with the prudential requirements (Art. 30 (3) FD). For instance, if an insurance undertaking established in Belgium has sold a life policy to a policyholder living in the Netherlands and the Dutch supervisory authority (DNB) has doubts about the financial soundness of the Belgian insurance undertaking, it must inform the Belgian supervisory authority (National Bank of Belgium). It is then for the National Bank of Belgium to determine whether the Belgian insurance undertaking complies with the Belgian solvency requirements (based upon EU law).

The home MS of an insurance undertaking may not prohibit that undertaking from concluding a reinsurance contract with a reinsurance or insurance undertaking authorised in another MS on grounds directly related to the financial soundness of that reinsurance or insurance undertaking. Similarly, the home MS of a reinsurance undertaking may not prohibit that undertaking from concluding a retrocession contract with a reinsurance or insurance undertaking authorised in another MS on grounds directly related to the financial soundness of that reinsurance or insurance undertaking (Art. 32 FD).

1.4. TRANSPARENCY AND ACCOUNTABILITY

Supervisory authorities must conduct their tasks in a transparent and accountable manner[20] with respect for the protection of confidential information (Art. 31 (1) FD). Member States must provide for transparent procedures regarding the appointment and dismissal of the members of the governing bodies and managing bodies of their supervisory authorities (Art. 31 (3) FD).

In terms of transparency, supervisory authorities must disclose on their website information about their national insurance legislation, as well as on the way they apply Solvency II and carry out their supervisory activity. For the disclosure on their website, they must follow a common format set by EU law and do so in a manner that allows comparability between Member

[20] See also, IAIS, ICP 2 – Supervisor and CEIOPS, Recommendations on Independence and Accountability, CEIOPS-DOC-04/06, May 2006, 10 p.

States (Art. 31 (2) FD). The technical details can be found in the Commission Implementing Regulation of 2 December 2015.[21]

Care has to be taken not to disclose any confidential information. The disclosure must therefore take place in summary or aggregate form, such that individual undertakings or groups cannot be identified.

The aggregated statistical data to be disclosed on key aspects of Solvency II must include the information specified in Annex XXI to the DA. As can be seen from the topics that need to be disclosed, the website of each NSA now includes a wealth of information on how Solvency II is applied in practice in each MS. The information must be disclosed in the official language or languages of the MS concerned and in "a language customary in the sphere of international finance" (Art. 317 (1) DA). As all 24 official languages of the EU are of equal standing, this last reference is a diplomatic reference to the English language.[22] The information must be updated at least every year and within the deadlines set in Art. 317 (2) and (3) DA.

The following information must be disclosed on the website of each NSA on supervised undertakings and groups.

On (re)insurance undertakings supervised under Solvency II:[23]

1. the number of (re)insurance undertakings, the number of branches from EU (re)insurance undertakings (Art. 13 (11) FD) and the number of branches from third-country (re)insurance undertakings (Art. 162 (3) FD), established in the MS;
2. the number of branches of (re)insurance undertakings established in the MS carrying out relevant business in one or more other Member States;
3. the number of insurance undertakings established in the MS pursuing business in other Member States under the freedom to provide services;
4. the number of insurance undertakings established in other Member States which have notified their intention to pursue business in the MS of the supervisory authority under the freedom to provide services and those which actually pursue business;[24]
5. the number of (re)insurance undertakings to which Solvency II does not apply;

[21] See Commission Implementing Regulation (EU) 2015/2451 of 2 December 2015 laying down implementing technical standards with regard to the templates and structure of the disclosure of specific information by supervisory authorities in accordance with Directive 2009/138/EC of the EP and of the Council, *OJ* L 347, 31.12.2015, p. 1224.

[22] See, for instance, the website of the National Bank of Belgium which provides the information in Dutch, French and English or the website of BaFin, which provides the information in German and in English.

[23] As indicated in Chapter 4, section 1 above, a number of insurance undertakings fall outside the scope of Solvency II and are therefore supervised on the basis of national insurance law.

[24] Not all insurance undertakings that have notified their intention to offer cross-border services are actually carrying out this intention in practice.

6. the number of SPVs authorised (Art. 211 FD);
7. the number of (re)insurance undertakings subject to reorganisation measures or winding-up proceedings;[25]
8. the number of (re)insurance undertakings and the number of their portfolios to which the MA (Art. 77b FD) is applied;
9. the number of (re)insurance undertakings applying the VA (Art. 77d FD);
10. the number of (re)insurance undertakings applying the transitional risk-free interest rate term structure (Art. 308c FD);
11. the number of (re)insurance undertakings applying the transitional deduction to technical provisions (Art. 308d FD);
12. the total amount of assets of (re)insurance undertakings valued on a market-consistent basis (Art. 75 FD), by material asset classes;
13. the total amount of liabilities of (re)insurance undertakings valued in accordance with Arts. 75–86 FD, divided by technical provisions and other liabilities, with a separate indication of the subordinated liabilities that are not included in own funds;
14. the total amount of basic own funds, with separate indication of the subordinated liabilities that are included in own funds, and the total amount of ancillary own funds;
15. the total eligible amount of own funds to cover the SCR, classified by tiers;
16. the total eligible amount of basic own funds to cover the MCR, classified by tiers;
17. the total amount of the MCR;
18. the total amount of the SCR;
19. where the SCR is calculated using the standard formula, the total amount of the SCR by risk module and sub-module (at the level of aggregation available), expressed as percentage of the total amount of the SCR;
20. where the SCR for credit risk is calculated using the standard formula, the total amount of the SCR for the spread risk and market risk concentration sub-modules and for the counterparty default risk module for which a reassessment of the credit quality steps of the larger or more complex exposures has been conducted in accordance with Art. 4 (5) DA (at the level of aggregation available), expressed as percentage of the total amount of the respective sub-modules or module;
21. where the SCR is calculated using an approved partial internal model, the total amount of the SCR by risk module and sub-module (at the level of aggregation available), expressed as percentage of the total amount of the SCR, with separate disclosure of the data on internal models whose scope includes credit risk in both market risk and counterparty default risk;

[25] Although there is no EU regime for reorganisation or winding-up of reinsurance undertakings.

22. the number of (re)insurance undertakings using an approved full internal model and the number of (re)insurance undertakings using an approved partial internal model for the calculation of the SCR, with separate disclosure of the data on internal models whose scope includes credit risk in both market risk and counterparty default risk;
23. the number of capital add-ons, the average capital add-on per undertaking and the distribution of capital add-ons, measured as a percentage of the SCR, for all (re)insurance undertakings supervised under Solvency II.

The information set out under points (1)–(5) and (7)–(17) must be provided separately for all insurance and reinsurance undertakings, life insurance undertakings, non-life insurance undertakings, insurance undertakings that simultaneously pursue both life and non-life insurance activities, and reinsurance undertakings.

On insurance groups supervised under Solvency II:

24. the number of insurance groups of which the supervisory authority is the group supervisor, including the number of (re)insurance undertakings at national level, in other Member States and in third countries, further split by equivalent and non-equivalent third countries in accordance with Art. 260 FD;
25. the number of insurance groups of which the supervisory authority is the group supervisor, where the ultimate parent (re)insurance undertaking or insurance holding company or mixed financial holding company which has its head office in the EU is a subsidiary undertaking of a company which has its head office outside of the EU;
26. the number of ultimate parent (re)insurance undertakings or insurance holding companies or mixed financial holding companies subject to sub-group supervision at national level (Art. 216 FD), including for each such undertaking and holding company the number of its (re)insurance subsidiary undertakings at national level, in other Member States and third countries, further split by equivalent and non-equivalent third countries (Art. 260 FD);
27. the number of ultimate parent (re)insurance undertakings or insurance holding companies or mixed financial holding companies subject to sub-group supervision at national level (Art. 216 FD), where another related ultimate parent undertaking is present at national level (Art. 217 FD);
28. the number of cross-border insurance groups where the supervisory authority is the group supervisor;
29. the number of insurance groups that have been allowed to use the deduction and aggregation method or a combination of the consolidation method and the deduction and aggregation method (Art. 220 (2) FD) for the calculation of solvency at the level of the group;

30. the total amount of the group eligible own funds for the insurance groups of which the supervisory authority is the group supervisor, separately for group eligible own funds calculated in accordance with the consolidation method (Art. 230 (1) FD) and for group eligible own funds calculated in accordance with the deduction and aggregation method (Art. 233 FD);
31. the total amount of the group SCR for the insurance groups of which the supervisory authority is the group supervisor separately for the group SCR calculated in accordance with the consolidation method (Art. 230 (1) FD) and for the group SCR calculated in accordance with the deduction and aggregation method (Art. 233 FD);
32. the number of insurance groups of which the supervisory authority is the group supervisor using an approved full internal model for the calculation of the group SCR, and the number of insurance groups of which the supervisory authority is the group supervisor using an approved partial internal model for the calculation of the group SCR, with separate disclosure of approvals in accordance with Arts. 230 and 231 FD.

The information set out under points (1)–(32) must be provided in relation to the end of the last calendar year. For points (8)–(17), (25) and (26), the information must relate to the financial year-ends of (re)insurance undertakings and insurance groups that occurred in the last calendar year.

The following information must be disclosed on the website of each NSA in relation to the supervisory authority:[26]

1. the structure of the supervisory authority, including the number of staff at the end of the last calendar year;
2. the number of on-site inspections undertaken both at solo and group level, and the total number of man-days spent on them, also specifying the number of regular inspections and ad hoc inspections, inspections mandated to third parties and on-site inspections under group supervision which were undertaken jointly with other members of the group's college of supervisors, with separate disclosure of data on inspections conducted in order to review and evaluate the reliance of undertakings on external ratings;
3. the number of formal reviews both at solo and group level, of ongoing compliance of full or partial internal models with the requirements in relation to the number of internal models in use, with separate disclosure

---

[26] For examples, see Belgium: https://www.nbb.be/doc/cp/eng/2017/its_transparency_c.pdf; Slovenia: https://www.a-zn.si/en/agency/tasks-and-objectives/activities; and the UK: https://www.bankofengland.co.uk/-/media/boe/files/prudential-regulation/solvency-ii/template-c-august-2018.

of data on reviews conducted in order to review and evaluate the reliance of undertakings on external ratings;

4. the number of partial and of full internal models submitted for approval and how many of those applications were successful, divided into solo undertakings and groups, with separate disclosure of data on internal models whose scope includes credit risk in both market risk and counterparty default risk;
5. the number of corrective measures taken, as defined by Arts. 110, 117, 119, 137, 138 and 139 FD, by type of measure, and the number of corrective measures, as defined by Art. 119 FD, triggered by a deviation from the risk profile of the (re)insurance undertakings in terms of their credit risk;
6. the number of authorisations withdrawn;
7. the number of authorisations granted to (re)insurance undertakings;
8. the criteria used for the application of capital add-ons and the criteria for their calculation and removal;
9. the number of applications submitted to the supervisory authority to use the MA (Art. 77b FD) and how many were successful;
10. where Member States have chosen to require prior approval for the use of the VA (Art. 77d FD), the number of applications submitted to the supervisory authority to use this adjustment and how many were successful;
11. the number of extensions granted in accordance with Art. 138 (4) FD (non-compliance with the SCR in exceptional adverse situations), and their average duration;
12. the number of authorisations granted in accordance with Art. 304 FD (duration-based equity risk sub-module);
13. the number of applications submitted to the supervisory authority to use the transitional risk-free interest rate term structure (Art. 308c FD), how many were successful and the number of decisions to revoke the approval of this transitional measure pursuant to Art. 308e FD;
14. the number of applications submitted to the supervisory authority to use the transitional deduction to technical provisions (Art. 308d FD) and how many were successful;
15. the number of meetings of colleges of supervisors which the supervisory authority attended as a member and those chaired as group supervisor;
16. the number of applications submitted to the supervisory authority for the approval of ancillary own funds, how many of those applications were successful and the main feature of the items approved;
17. the number of applications submitted to the supervisory authority for approval of the assessment and classification of own-fund items not covered by the list of Arts. 69, 72, 74, 76 and 78 FD, how many of those applications were successful, the main features of the items and the method used to assess and classify them;

18. the number and scope of peer review analyses organised and conducted by EIOPA, in accordance with Art. 30 EIOPA Regulation, in which the supervisory authority participated.

The information set out under points (2)–(18) must be provided in relation to the last calendar year.

Transparency about the way supervision is carried out in practice reinforces accountability. Accountability is also reinforced by providing the possibility for an appeal to the courts against supervisory decisions. This right to apply to the courts against any decision taken on the basis of laws, regulations and administrative provisions implementing the FD is specifically foreseen in Art. 297 FD. If there is an alleged breach or non-application of EU law, there is the possibility for EIOPA to start an investigation upon the request of one or more competent authorities, the EP, the Council, the EC or the relevant stakeholder group (Art. 17 EIOPA Regulation).

Accountability means that the supervisory authority is accountable to the national parliament and/or government, the supervised undertakings and the public, although not to the same extent.[27] It also means that its decisions must be reasoned.[28] The supervisory authority must act in the public interest. Its staff should therefore be protected from personal and institutional liability for supervisory actions taken in good faith during the course of performing their supervisory duties.[29]

1.5. GENERAL SUPERVISORY POWERS

Supervisory authorities must have the power to take preventive and corrective measures that are timely, proportionate and necessary to ensure compliance with the laws, regulations and administrative provisions with which (re)insurance undertakings have to comply (Art. 34 (1) FD).[30] These measures may be of an administrative or financial nature and may be used against a (re)insurance undertaking or against members of the AMSB (Art. 34 (2) FD).

Supervisory authorities must have the power to require all information necessary for supervisory purposes (see further, Chapter 8) (Art. 34 (3) FD). They must have the power to carry out on-site investigations at the premises of

27 For instance, accountability to the government means that the authority must act within the limits of the law and that it must respect the rule of law and treat all supervised undertakings alike.

28 See also IAIS, ICP 4 – Licensing, para. 4.5.

29 See also IAIS, ICP 2 – Supervisor, para. 2.10.

30 See also, IAIS, ICP 10 – Preventive and Corrective Measures and ICP 11 – Enforcement.

(re)insurance undertakings (Art. 34 (5) FD). The powers must also be available with regard to outsourced activities (Art. 34 (7) FD).

Supervisory authorities should have the appropriate means, methods and powers to verify the system of governance of (re)insurance undertakings and to evaluate emerging risks identified by those undertakings that may affect their financial soundness. They must be able to require an improvement and strengthening of the system of governance if this is necessary (Art. 41 (5) FD).

Supervisory authorities must be able to enforce their decisions. They must be able to do so directly or by application to the competent judicial authorities (Art. 34 (8) FD).

They should as a minimum have the power to:[31]
- restrict business activities, for example prohibit the undertaking from issuing new policies or restrict the transfer of assets;
- require a reinforcement of the financial position, for example require a reduction or mitigation of risks or require an increase in capital;
- suspend or withdraw the authorisation;
- bar members of the AMSB or holders of key governance functions from such roles in the future;
- require the undertaking to replace members of the ASMB, key governance function holders or external auditors;
- require undertakings to use net profits to strengthen own funds;
- require undertakings to limit variable remuneration as a percentage of net revenues where it is inconsistent with the maintenance of a sound capital base;
- restrict or prohibit distributions or interest payments to shareholders or members.

The FD does not contain a specific section dealing with sanctions and administrative measures. An examination by the EC, after the financial crisis, of the level of sanctions imposed in the EU on financial institutions[32] showed that in some Member States sanctions were often too soft. In order to ensure a level playing field in this area, the EC announced in its 2010 Communication on sanctions, that it would include in all new proposals[33] a specific section dealing with sanctions. This has, for instance, been the case in CRD IV (Arts. 64–72) and in the IDD (Arts. 31–36). The principle is that administrative sanctions and other measures must be effective, proportionate and dissuasive. Sanctions can

[31] IAIS, ICP 11 – Enforcement.

[32] EC, Communication to the EP, the Council, the European Economic and Social Committee and the Committee of the Regions: Reinforcing sanctioning regimes in the financial services sector, COM (2010) 716 final, 8 December 2010, 17 p.

[33] As the FD was adopted before that decision was taken, it does not include a specific section dealing with sanctions.

be considered *effective* when they are capable of ensuring compliance with EU law, *proportionate* when they adequately reflect the gravity of the violation and do not go beyond what is necessary for the objectives pursued, and *dissuasive* when they are sufficiently serious to deter the perpetrators of violations from repeating the same offence, and other potential offenders from committing such violations.

Supervisory authorities must be able to issue a public statement identifying the natural person or undertaking that violated the law and the nature of the breach.[34]

1.6. SUPERVISION OF OUTSOURCED FUNCTIONS AND ACTIVITIES

Outsourcing is used increasingly as a means of both reducing costs and achieving strategic goals. In the age of digitalisation, it has become attractive to outsource certain activities to an outsourcing company, which may take over part of the activities of the undertaking, such as the sales and policy administration. When a (re)insurance undertaking outsources functions or activities, it remains fully responsible for the proper execution of these functions or activities (Art. 49 (1) FD). This means that somebody in the undertaking needs to remain responsible, must monitor the outsourced provider and be ultimately answerable to the supervisory authority.

Supervisory authorities have been worried about the increasing use of third parties to carry out activities that undertakings themselves would normally have undertaken themselves.[35] From a supervisory perspective, it is important to be able to check whether the undertaking has fulfilled its legal obligations. That may be difficult if activities have been off-shored. It is therefore important to ensure from the outset that the outsourcing undertaking remains in control of the outsourced function or activity and can exercise the necessary pressure on the outsourcing company.

In order to ensure effective supervision of outsourced functions or activities, it is essential that the supervisory authority of the outsourcing (re)insurance undertaking has access to all relevant data held by the outsourcing service

[34] For an example, see the sanction imposed on PartnerRe Ireland Insurance dac and Partner Reinsurance Europe SE by the Central Bank of Ireland for breaches of the requirements concerning the calculation of the SCR in respect of their solvency for 2016. See Central Bank of Ireland, *Enforcement Action: PartnerRe Ireland Insurance dac and Partner Reinsurance Europe SE fined 1.540.000 EUR*, Press Release, 21 August 2018.

[35] See the document of the Joint Forum, *Outsourcing in Financial Services*, published by the BIS in February 2005, which sets a number of guiding principles covering the responsibilities of regulated entities when they outsource their activities.

provider, regardless of whether the latter is a regulated or unregulated entity, as well as the right to conduct on-site inspections (recital 37 FD).

Art. 38 (1) FD sets out the conditions that must be satisfied when a function or activity is outsourced. (Re)insurance undertakings must take the necessary steps to ensure that the following conditions are satisfied:

- the service provider must cooperate with the supervisory authority in connection with the outsourced function or activity;
- the (re)insurance undertaking, its auditors and the supervisory authority must have effective access to data related to the outsourced functions or activities;
- the supervisory authority must have effective access to the business premises of the service provider and must be able to exercise those rights of access.

When critical or important functions or activities are outsourced, the outsourcing may not materially impair the quality of the system of governance of the undertaking, unduly increase operational risk, impair the ability of the supervisory authority to monitor compliance of the undertaking with its obligations, or undermine continuous and satisfactory service to policyholders. (Art. 49 (2) FD). The outsourcing must be based upon a written agreement between the (re)insurance undertaking and the service provider (Art. 274 DA) (see further, Chapter 7, section 3.9).

Critical or important functions would clearly be the key governance functions, such as the actuarial function or the internal audit function. Critical or important activities would include asset management, claims handling and settlement, provision of data storage, or the provision of day-to-day systems management or support.

When an insurance intermediary who is not an employee of the insurance undertaking is given authority to underwrite business or settle claims in the name and on account of the insurance undertaking, the insurance undertaking must ensure that the activity of that intermediary is subject to the outsourcing requirements.[36]

When a (re)insurance undertaking intends to outsource critical or important functions or activities, it must notify the supervisory authority in a timely manner. The same applies if there are subsequent material developments with respect to these outsourced functions or activities (Art. 49 (3) FD).

The MS where the service provider is located[37] must permit the supervisory authority of the outsourcing (re)insurance undertaking to carry out, directly

36 EIOPA, Guidelines on system of governance, EIOPA-BoS-14/253, 14 September 2015, Guideline 61. This is obviously not the case if the insurance intermediary is merely offering advice.

37 If the service provider is located outside the EEA, there is a need to conclude a cooperation agreement with the relevant third country in order to ensure that proper supervision of the

or through an intermediary, on-site inspections at the premises of the service provider. The supervisory authority of the outsourcing (re)insurance undertaking must inform the appropriate authority of the MS of the service provider prior to conducting the on-site inspection. If the service provider is a non-supervised entity, the appropriate authority is the supervisory authority of the MS of the service provider. If the supervisory authority of the MS of the service provider makes it difficult for the supervisory authority of the outsourcing undertaking to carry out the on-site inspection, the supervisory authority of the outsourcing undertaking may ask EIOPA for assistance. EIOPA can in that case mediate between both supervisory authorities (Art. 19 EIOPA Regulation) and take part in the on-site inspection (Art. 38 (2), third subparagraph FD).

1.7. PROFESSIONAL SECRECY, EXCHANGE OF INFORMATION AND PROMOTION OF SUPERVISORY CONVERGENCE

All persons who are working or who have worked for supervisory authorities, as well as external auditors and experts acting on behalf of those authorities (for instance, accountants or actuaries) are bound by the obligation of professional secrecy. Any confidential information received by such persons whilst performing their duties may not be divulged to any person or authority whatsoever, except in summary or aggregate form, such that individual (re)insurance undertakings cannot be identified (Art. 64 FD).[38]

Professional secrecy does not preclude an exchange of information between supervisory authorities of different Member States (Art. 65 FD). Furthermore, supervisory authorities are required to cooperate with EIOPA and to provide EIOPA, without delay, with all the information necessary for EIOPA to carry out its duty under the EIOPA Regulation (Art. 65a FD).

Supervisory authorities that receive confidential information may use this information only in the course of their duties and for the following purposes (Art. 67 FD):

- to check that the conditions governing the taking-up of the business of (re)insurance are met and to facilitate the monitoring of the conduct of such business, especially with regard to technical provisions, the SCR, the MCR and the system of governance;
- to impose sanctions;

outsourced function or activity is possible. The outsourcing may be made dependent on the existence of such an agreement. See also Art. 66 FD.

38 Art. 64 FD provides for an exception for criminal law cases and for bankruptcy and compulsory winding-up.

- in administrative appeals against decisions of the supervisory authority;
- in court proceedings under the Solvency II FD.

Conclusion of cooperation agreements providing for the exchange of information with supervisory authorities of third countries must include a guarantee of professional secrecy (Art. 66 FD). This was an important element in the conclusion of a bilateral cooperation agreement between the EU and the USA on insurance and reinsurance.[39] Art. 5 of that agreement states that:

> "The Parties shall encourage supervisory authorities in their respective jurisdictions to cooperate in exchanging information pursuant to the practices set forth in the Annex. The Parties understand that the use of such practices will enhance cooperation and information sharing, while respecting a high standard of confidentiality protection."

This is further elaborated in an annex, which includes a "Model Memorandum of Understanding with Provisions on Exchange of Information between Supervisory Authorities". That annex forms an integral part of the agreement.

Art. 68 FD contains a detailed list of authorities with whom and under which conditions information can be exchanged. This list includes supervisory authorities (for instance for credit institutions or for financial markets), bodies involved in bankruptcy procedures or the persons charged with carrying out statutory audits and authorities that are responsible for the detection and investigation of breaches of company law.

Art. 67a FD, which was added by Omnibus II, requires cooperation with the EP in the case of investigations under Art. 226 TFEU, which allows the EP, in the course of its duties, at the request of a quarter of its component members, to set up a temporary Committee of Inquiry to investigate, without prejudice to the powers conferred by the Treaties on other institutions or bodies, alleged contraventions or maladministration in the implementation of Union law, except where the alleged facts are being examined before a court and while the case is still subject to legal proceedings.

Art. 69 FD authorises the disclosure of certain information to other departments of the central government under certain conditions. Art. 70 FD allows the transmission of information to central banks, to the ECB and to the ESRB.

NSAs are required to cooperate with EIOPA. Their mandate must include a European dimension. They have to provide the information requested by EIOPA, must attend the meetings organised by EIOPA, participate in the activities

---

[39] Bilateral agreement between the EU and the USA on prudential measures regarding insurance and reinsurance, signed 22 September 2017, *OJ* L 258, 6.10.2017, pp. 4–21.

of EIOPA, make every effort to comply with the guidelines and recommendations issued by EIOPA and must perform their duties as members of EIOPA. In the exercise of their duties, they must have regard to convergence in respect of supervisory tools and practices (Art. 71 FD).

Supervisory convergence is a high priority for EIOPA. It is part of EIOPA's role to develop a European supervisory culture. In its recently released supervisory convergence plan 2018–2019,[40] EIOPA indicates how it intends to implement in practice the key characteristics of the common supervisory culture and the further development of supervisory tools, how it plans to deal with risks to the internal market and to the level playing field which result from a lack of convergence and which might lead to supervisory arbitrage, and how it intends to deal with the supervision of emerging risks (see further, Chapter 11).

2. SUPERVISORY REVIEW PROCESS

2.1. DEFINITION

The supervisory review process (SRP) can be defined as the overall process conducted by the supervisory authority in reviewing the situation of the undertakings subject to its supervision. It is used to evaluate individual undertakings' compliance with the laws, regulations and administrative provisions adopted pursuant to the FD (Art. 36 (1), first paragraph FD).

This review and evaluation comprises the assessment of the requirements relating to the system of governance, the technical provisions, the capital requirements, the investment rules, the quality and quantity of own funds and the ongoing compliance with the requirements for the use of a full or partial internal model (Art. 36 (2) FD). The review also comprises an assessment of the risks that the undertakings concerned face or may face (prospective supervision) and an assessment of the ability of undertakings to assess those risks, taking into account the environment in which they are operating (Art. 36 (1), second subparagraph FD). It is through the SRP that supervisors monitor all undertakings, and identify those with financial and/or organisational weaknesses susceptible to producing higher risks to policyholders (risk-based supervision).[41]

The SRP must be applied to all undertakings subject to Solvency II, to ensure that all policyholders receive an adequate level of protection. In accordance with

---

40 EIOPA, *Supervisory Convergence Plan 2018–2019*, Publications Office of the EU, Luxembourg, 2018, 12 p.

41 CEIOPS, Issues Paper: Supervisory Review Process and Undertakings' Reporting Requirements, CEIOPS-IGSRR-18/08, 15 August 2008, p. 3.

the principle of proportionality, the SRP must be adapted to the nature, scale and complexity of the risks of each undertaking. At the same time, it is the aim of supervision to determine the nature, scale and complexity of the risks facing each undertaking, and to prioritise and focus supervisory actions and efforts according to a risk-based approach.

The SRP brings together all the relevant information on an undertaking gathered in the course of supervisory activities.[42] Information may be received by supervisory authorities from different sources, for example:

- from the undertakings themselves: periodic information reported in the QRTs, the RSR, the SFCR or the ORSA report;
- from own sources: results of on-site inspections, historical information, early-warning indicators, thematic reviews or stress test results, or reports from external auditors;
- from other supervisory authorities, for instance within the context of a college of supervisors;
- from other competent authorities, for instance, competition authorities, market conduct authorities or securities supervisors;
- from external parties: market or sector information, information from consumer or industry bodies or associations, technical research papers, or press or media information.

There must be an appropriate level of communication between the supervisory authority and the supervised undertakings throughout the entire SRP. This is a crucial element of Solvency II, which establishes a permanent dialogue between the supervisory authority and the supervised undertakings. This dialogue should not be a combination of two monologues. It should be engaging and based upon trust. It should also be organised at the right level, both at the authority and at the (re)insurance undertaking. Senior personnel of the authority can be expected to have a face-to-face meeting with the chairman, the CEO and the key function holders of each important (re)insurance undertaking at least once a year. It would also be very helpful to have regular meetings with the chair of the audit committee and the external auditor.

Supervisors may use a variety of methods to undertake the supervisory review, which is likely to include their own supervisory judgement(s) informed by using supervisory techniques, such as on-site inspections and/or off-site analysis. The SRP does not mean that the same actions and/or resources should be used for all undertakings. Instead, in line with a risk-based approach and the

[42] EIOPA, Guidelines on supervisory review process, EIOPA-14/179, 2 February 2015, Guideline 11.

main objective of supervision, those undertakings that pose more of a perceived risk to policyholders should be subject to a more intensive supervisory review (and therefore actions) on a more frequent basis.

Although all policyholders should be afforded the same protection regardless of the undertaking with which they hold their policy, the frequency and intensity of supervisory actions must be based upon the risk profile of each undertaking.[43]

2.2. IMPLEMENTATION

The SRP is a process that starts well before any solvency or own funds requirement is breached. A useful exercise is the establishment of early-warning indicators. They will help to ensure that the supervisory authority becomes aware of a deteriorating financial position well before an undertaking breaches the SCR or is likely to do so within the next three months. These early-warning indicators should not be seen as a new solvency control level. They can be either quantitative or qualitative in nature, and do not necessarily indicate that the undertaking is in financial distress.[44]

Quantitative early-warning indicators could include:
- deteriorating capital strength;
- rapid growth;
- declining profitability;
- high expenses and low profitability;
- sudden increase in technical provisions;
- dramatic decrease in technical provisions;
- significant divergence from budgets and business plans;
- concentrated investments, particularly in related entities;
- number of consumer or intermediary complaints;
- inappropriate bonus and remuneration structure that could provide inadequate incentives from a supervisory perspective;
- increasing distribution of surplus funds, dividends or any other loss-absorbing buffers.

Qualitative early-warning indicators could include:
- change in strategy;
- new classes of business/sources of business being written;

43 CEIOPS, Issues Paper: Supervisory Review Process and Undertakings' Reporting Requirements, CEIOPS-IGSRR-18/08, 15 August 2008, p. 7.

44 CEIOPS, Issues Paper: Supervisory Review Process and Undertakings' Reporting Requirements, CEIOPS-IGSRR-18/08, 15 August 2008, pp. 16–17.

- a crude underwriting strategy (pricing and risk selection), for example little or no segmentation compared to peer group;
- changes to or delays in implementing an original business plan;
- frequent changes to the AMSB or key governance persons;
- failure to implement supervisory requirements;
- non-cooperation with the supervisor or delays in producing information;
- evidence of poor management (for example, poor quality internal information, not acting on supervisors' or auditors' recommendations or an unrealistic or incomplete business plan);
- vulnerability to legal or fiscal changes;
- pressure on management to achieve certain results or targets, for instance due to a stock market listing or imminent merger/acquisition;
- identification of types of reinsurance arrangements that appear inconsistent with normal commercial practice or for which the commercial rationale for either party is unclear;
- changes in investment strategy or concentration in innovative/unusual investment instruments or derivatives.

The Guidelines on the SRP[45] distinguish between the development of a risk assessment framework, detailed review activities and supervisory measures.[46]

NSAs must use a risk assessment framework to identify and assess current and future risks that (re)insurance undertakings face or may face, including the undertaking's capacity to identify, measure, monitor, manage and report on those risks. This framework should follow a risk-based and forward-looking approach and be carried out in the following stages:

- assessment of information;
- assessment of the potential impact on all (re)insurance undertakings and groups;
- assessment of the current and future risks that (re)insurance undertakings or groups face or may face;
- development of an impact and risk classification;
- development of a supervisory plan and determination of the intensity of supervision;
- inclusion of the group supervisory plan in the college work plan in the case of (re)insurance groups with a college of supervisors.

NSAs must undertake detailed review activities, whether off-site analysis or on-site inspections, based upon the supervisory plan, taking into account all

45 EIOPA, Guidelines on Supervisory Review Process, EIOPA-14/179, 2 February 2015, Guidelines 12–42.

46 See also the diagram attached to the Guidelines on Supervisory Review Process.

relevant information and focusing on the areas of risk as identified in the risk assessment framework.

Based upon the conclusions of the detailed review, NSAs must identify any weaknesses and actual or potential deficiencies or non-compliances with requirements that could lead them to imposing supervisory measures. These measures must vary according to the level of significance of the weaknesses and the actual or potential deficiencies or non-compliances faced by the (re)insurance undertaking concerned.

2.3. SUPERVISORY LADDER OF INTERVENTION

With the introduction of two capital requirements, Solvency II establishes a supervisory ladder of intervention whereby the degree of supervisory intervention intensifies when the capital level of the undertaking decreases and the financial situation of the undertaking deteriorates.

In its issues paper on the SRP,[47] CEIOPS provides an example of what this supervisory ladder of intervention could look like in the case of an individual (re)insurance undertaking:

Level A
Own funds ≥ SCR (SCR including any capital add-on)

In this situation, NSAs should use the normal monitoring tools provided for under the SRP to identify potential issues for discussion with the undertaking. These should be used in a flexible way. If capital levels move closer to the level of the SCR, NSAs might apply closer observations along with the use of early-warning indicators in order to identify possible "near misses". Where necessary, the supervisor may require the undertaking to remedy weaknesses or deficiencies identified in the SRP. There is no need to introduce an additional layer of intervention as long as the SCR ratio is above 100%. The normal monitoring tools, including early-warning indicators, are sufficient.

Level B
MCR < Own funds < SCR, or if the undertaking observes the risk of non-compliance with the SCR in the following three months (Art. 138 (1) FD)

---

47 CEIOPS, Issues Paper: Supervisory Review Process and Undertakings' Reporting Requirements, CEIOPS-IGSRR-18/08, 15 August 2008, pp. 18–19 (https://eiopa.europa.eu/CEIOPS-Archive/Documents/Issues%20papers/CEIOPS-IGSRR-18-08%20Issues%20Paper%20on%20SRP%20and%20Reporting-final.pdf#search=Issues%20paper%20on%20the%20supervisory%20review%20process).

In this situation, there may be a risk to the financial viability of the undertaking. If an undertaking does not meet the SCR, it should re-establish the amount of own funds covering the SCR or reduce its risk profile to reduce the SCR within six months, based on a realistic recovery plan submitted to the supervisory authority for approval within two months.

The intensity of supervisory intervention should vary depending on whether there has only just been a breach of the SCR or whether the undertaking's own funds are just above the MCR.

When the undertaking breaches the SCR:

1. The undertaking is obliged to notify the supervisory authority as soon as its own funds have fallen below the SCR level or if there is a risk of non-compliance in the following three months. The undertaking should submit a realistic recovery plan within two months of the observation of non-compliance and provide an explanation of how the situation has arisen;
2. Meetings should be organised with the AMSB and senior management of the undertaking to outline concerns and discuss remedial actions. External auditors would be expected to be kept informed of the situation by the undertaking;
3. The supervisory authority should ask the undertaking to take measures to rectify the situation by increasing own funds or adjusting the SCR. Measures that directly address the problem could include:
   (a) requiring the undertaking to raise additional own funds within six months of the observation – the supervisor may extend that period by three months;
   (b) limiting the redemption/repurchase of equity instruments or setting limitations on dividend payments if it is clear that the undertaking faces a deteriorating financial position;
   (c) requiring the undertaking to reduce its risk profile to comply with the SCR within six months (i.e. actions could be taken to adjust its investment portfolio or to purchase risk-mitigating instruments).

If the solvency of the undertaking deteriorates further towards the MCR, there should be an increase in the level of supervisory activity to enable the supervisor to better assess and control the situation. This could include:

(a) increased supervisory reporting and/or a requirement to appoint an independent party acceptable to the supervisor to provide a report prescribed by the supervisor;
(b) requiring the undertaking to extend the scope of internal or external auditors' or consultants' work (at the undertaking's expense), and for the

professionals concerned to report directly to the supervisory authority. Further actions could include additional stress-testing and scenario analysis, commissioning independent actuarial reviews, and applying prudential limits and restrictions more rigorously.

(c) measures to reduce risks, such as refusing, delaying or imposing conditions on requests or applications submitted for regulatory approval, for example in relation to acquisitions and redemptions or repurchases of equity, or setting restrictions on accepting new business or minimising the investment risks if the undertaking did not do so voluntarily.

Level C (ultimate supervisory action)
MCR > Own funds (including an absolute floor), or if the undertaking observes a risk of non-compliance with the MCR in the following three months (Art. 139 (1) FD)

In this situation, the undertaking's viability is in serious doubt and some restructuring/de-risking is needed. The following actions could be taken depending on the degree of the deterioration of the situation:

1. Within one month of the observation of non-compliance, the undertaking must submit to the supervisory authority a realistic finance scheme to restore own funds to at least the level of the MCR or to reduce its risk profile to ensure compliance with the MCR within three months of that observation (or future observation), or otherwise restructure or prepare for an orderly run-off of existing business. Failing to safeguard the interests of policyholders should lead to the winding-up of the undertaking;
2. During that period, the undertaking should explore options for rehabilitation, restructuring, or compromises with creditors. Supervisors should consider partially or wholly stopping the undertaking from writing new business, and may appoint an independent person to review the accuracy and adequacy of cash outflows other than to policyholders, unless the undertaking or its owners present a realistic finance scheme to the supervisory authority for restoring own funds to the level of the MCR within three months. However, restoring own funds to the level of the MCR does not extend the maximum period for restoring own funds to the level of the SCR in levels A or B above;
3. Supervisors should ensure that insolvency proceedings (for example for the withdrawal of the licence and dissolution of the undertaking) are commenced. This will depend on the national company or insolvency legislation, but will typically take place where assets are still sufficient to pay policyholders.

2.4. CAPITAL ADD-ON

2.4.1. General Context

The FD defines the capital requirements for (re)insurance undertakings. Undertakings can use the standard formula for the definition of the SCR, USPs or a partial or full internal model approved by the supervisory authority. The requirements in the FD would be superfluous if supervisory authorities were to have the option of imposing additional capital on (re)insurance undertakings whenever they feel that more capital is needed. Supervisory authorities should not second-guess the decisions taken by the co-legislators. In principle, undertakings that satisfy the capital requirements as defined in the FD should be allowed to operate without further capital add-ons imposed by the supervisory authority.

This was the view that came about after lengthy negotiations. Particularly in the UK, there was a tradition under the ICAS regime for the FSA to impose a capital add-on if the FSA believed that the internal capital assessment of the undertaking did not deliver the desired outcome. This was not the case in other Member States which were mostly still operating under the old Solvency I regime. The political agreement was that capital add-ons could only be imposed in exceptional circumstances. This is clear from the text of the Directive (Art. 37 FD) and from the requirement imposed upon EIOPA to report annually to the EP, the Council and the EC about the use of capital add-ons and the degree of supervisory convergence in the use of capital add-ons between supervisory authorities in the different Member States (Art. 52 (3) FD).

2.4.2. Circumstances for Imposing a Capital Add-On

Following the SRP, supervisory authorities may only impose a capital add-on in exceptional circumstances.[48] The possibility only exists in the following cases.

2.4.2.1. Significant Deviation from the Assumptions Underlying the SCR (Standard Formula) (Art. 37 (1) (a) FD)

Under the logic of Solvency II, a partial or full internal model must be used if the risk profile of the undertaking deviates significantly[49] from the assumptions underlying the standard formula. Supervisory authorities may impose the use of an internal model in this case (Art. 119 FD). A capital add-on can only be imposed if the imposition of an internal model under Art. 119 FD is inappropriate

48 For group capital add-ons, see Art. 232 FD.

49 See also Art. 279 DA for the determination of a significant deviation.

(for instance, because the estimated financial and other resources required to develop the model are disproportionate to the size of the deviation), or has been ineffective (for instance, because no internal model has been developed or the developed model fails to meet the conditions for approval), or while a partial or full internal model is being developed in accordance with Art. 119 FD.

In concluding that the risk profile of the undertaking significantly deviates from the assumptions underlying the standard formula, supervisory authorities must take into account all relevant factors, including those listed in Art. 276 DA, such as the nature, type and size of the deviation and the likelihood and severity of any adverse impact on policyholders and beneficiaries.

2.4.2.2. Significant Deviation from the Assumptions Underlying the SCR (Internal Model) (Art. 37 (1) (b) FD)

A capital add-on can only be imposed if the supervisory authority concludes that certain quantifiable risks are captured insufficiently in the model and the adaptation of the model to better reflect the given risk profile has failed within an appropriate timeframe, which may not exceed six months.

In concluding that the risk profile of the undertaking significantly[50] deviates from the assumptions underlying the standard formula, supervisory authorities must take into account all relevant factors, including those listed in Art. 276 DA, such as the nature, type and size of the deviation and the likelihood and severity of any adverse impact on policyholders and beneficiaries.

2.4.2.3. Significant Deviation from the Governance Standards (Art. 37 (1) (c) FD)

A capital add-on can only be imposed if the deviation prevents the undertaking from being able to properly identify, measure, monitor, manage and report the risks that the undertaking is or could be exposed to and the application of other measures is in itself unlikely to improve the deficiencies sufficiently within an appropriate timeframe, which may not exceed six months.

In concluding that the system of governance deviates significantly from the Solvency II standards, supervisory authorities must take into account all relevant factors, including those listed in Art. 277 DA, such as:

- the effect of the deviation on the sound and prudent management of the business and whether the deviation arises from an inadequate implementation of a requirement relating to the system of governance or a failure to implement such a requirement;

---

[50] See also Art. 279 DA for the determination of a significant deviation.

- the likelihood and severity of any adverse impact on policyholders and beneficiaries;
- the different ways of organising an effective system of governance that is proportionate to the nature, scale and complexity of the risks inherent in the business of the undertaking;
- the probable financial loss the undertaking could incur as a consequence of the deviation;
- the anticipated duration of the deviation.

It is obvious that a capital add-on is not a good measure to deal with a deficiency in the governance of an undertaking. The deficiency should be taken care of by making the necessary changes in the governance structure. However, there may be situations in which the management of the undertaking stubbornly refuses or needs (more) time for internal rearrangements or external hiring (than anticipated) to comply with the governance requirements imposed by law. If the non-compliance is serious, a capital add-on may be a means for the supervisory authority to force the undertaking to comply with the law. Such a capital add-on might be of short duration. The supervisory authority must ensure that the undertaking makes every effort to remedy the deficiencies that led to the imposition of the capital add-on (Art. 37 (3) FD). As a capital add-on for a failure in the standards of governance is considered rather unusual, Art. 37 (5), second subparagraph FD states that the SCR does not in this case include the capital add-on for the purposes of calculating the risk margin referred to in Art. 77 (5) FD.

2.4.2.4. Significant Deviation from the Assumptions Underlying the MA, VA or Transitional Measures (Art. 37 (1) (d) FD)

This option to impose a capital add-on applies to an undertaking that is applying one or more of the LTG measures, i.e. the MA (Art. 77b FD), the VA (Art. 77d FD), the transitional measure on the risk-free interest rate (Art. 308c FD) or the transitional measure on technical provisions (Art. 308d FD).

In concluding that the risk profile of the undertaking deviates significantly from the assumptions underlying these measures, supervisory authorities must take into account all relevant factors, including those listed in Art. 278 DA, such as the nature, type and size of the deviation and the likelihood and severity of any adverse impact on policyholders and beneficiaries.

The capital add-on may only be imposed in circumstances where the deviation from the assumptions is temporary in nature and does not justify revoking the supervisory approval[51] for the use of these measures (Art. 278 (2) DA).

---

[51] Prior supervisory approval is required for the use of the MA and the transitional measures on the risk-free interest rate and on technical provisions. Supervisory approval may also be imposed by Member States in the case of the VA (Art. 77d (1) FD).

2.4.3. Methods for Calculating a Capital Add-On

In the case of a deviation from the SCR assumptions, i.e. the situations referred to in sections 2.4.2.1 and 2.4.2.2 above, the capital add-on is calculated as the difference, at a given point in time, between (Art. 282 DA):[52]

- the modified SCR, i.e. the SCR of the (re)insurance undertaking, excluding any previous or simultaneous capital add-on, that would be calculated if the standard formula or the internal model were modified so as to reflect the actual risk profile of the undertaking and to ensure compliance with the characteristics of the SCR as stated in Art. 101 (3) FD), and
- the SCR of the (re)insurance undertaking, excluding any previous or simultaneous capital add-on.

In the case of a deviation from governance standards, i.e. the situation referred to in section 2.4.2.3 above, supervisory authorities must for the purpose of calculating the capital add-on take into account all relevant factors (Art. 286 DA), including, where appropriate, the factors referred to in Art. 277 DA (see section 2.4.2.3 above) and, where appropriate, capital add-ons set previously for comparable deviations of other (re)insurance undertakings with similar risk profiles provided that supervisory authorities ensure that the reasons for their decision to set a capital add-on are stated and that this statement complies with the professional secrecy requirements set in Art. 64 FD.

In the case of adjustments to the relevant risk-free rate or transitional measures, i.e. the situation referred to in section 2.4.2.4 above, the capital add-on is calculated as the sum, at a given point in time, of the following amounts (Art. 284 DA):[53]

(a) the negative of the amount of eligible own funds that would be calculated if the adjustment or transitional measure were modified in a manner that the assumptions underlying the adjustment or transitional measure would fit the actual assets, liabilities and risk profile of the (re)insurance undertaking;
(b) the amount of the SCR, excluding any previous or simultaneous capital add-on, that would be calculated if the adjustment or transitional measure were modified in a manner that the assumptions underlying the adjustment or transitional measure would fit the actual assets, liabilities and risk profile of the (re)insurance undertaking, and ensure compliance with the characteristics of the SCR as stated in Art. 101 (3) FD;
(c) the amount of eligible own funds;

---

52 For further details, see Art. 283 DA.

53 For further details, see Art. 285 DA.

(d) the negative of the amount of the SCR, excluding any previous or simultaneous capital add-on, of the (re)insurance undertaking.

Where an insurance undertaking simultaneously pursues life and non-life insurance activities, a notional capital add-on must be calculated for the life and the non-life business or the capital add-on must be objectively apportioned between the life and the non-life business (Art. 287 DA).

The SCR including the capital add-on replaces the inadequate SCR (Art. 37 (5), first subparagraph FD).

The procedures for decisions to set, calculate and remove capital add-ons are included in the Commission Implementing Regulation of 11 November 2015.[54] The supervisory authority must notify the (re)insurance undertaking concerned in writing of its decision to set a capital add-on. The decision must be sufficiently detailed to enable the undertaking to understand what measures it needs to take or what deficiencies it needs to remedy in order to have the capital add-on removed. The undertaking must inform the supervisory authority about the progress it has made in remedying the deficiencies. The supervisory authority must review the imposed capital add-on if there is a material change in the circumstances that led to the setting of the capital add-on.

2.4.4. Disclosure of a Capital Add-On

NSAs must, on an annual basis, provide EIOPA with detailed information about capital add-ons imposed. EIOPA must in turn publicly disclose, on an annual basis, information about capital add-ons imposed by NSAs, including the reasons why those capital add-ons have been imposed (Art. 52 (1) and (2) FD).

In its second report on the use of capital add-ons, published on 21 December 2018,[55] which relates to the situation as at year-end 2017, EIOPA indicated that six NSAs (as opposed to four in 2016) imposed a total of 23 capital add-ons (as opposed to 20 in 2016) at solo undertaking level (the UK 14, France 2, Ireland 2, the Netherlands 2, Norway 2 and Italy 1), and that two NSAs (as opposed to one in 2016) imposed a total of six capital add-ons (as opposed to four in 2016) at group level (the UK 4, the Netherlands 2). Most (19) of the 23 capital add-ons related to cases where the risk profile of the undertaking deviated significantly from the assumptions underlying the SCR calculated under the standard formula (Art. 37 (1) (a) FD). In two cases, the add-on was applied when the risk profile

---

54 Commission Implementing Regulation (EU) 2015/2012 of 11 November 2015 laying down implementing technical standards with regard to the procedures for decisions to set, calculate or remove capital add-ons in accordance with Directive 2009/138/EC of the EP and of the Council, *OJ* L 295, 12.11.2015, p. 5.

55 EIOPA, *Report on the use of capital add-ons during 2017*, Publications Office of the EU, Luxembourg, 2018, 15 p. The first report was published on 21 December 2017. See EIOPA, Report on the use of capital add-ons during 2016, EIOPA-BoS/17-336, 21 December 2017, 10 p.

of the undertaking deviated significantly from the assumptions underlying the SCR calculated under a full or partial internal model (Art. 37 (1) (b) FD). One capital add-on was imposed in a case where there was a significant deviation in the system of governance from the regulatory framework (Art. 37 (1) (c) FD). No capital add-on was set on the basis of a significant risk profile deviation following the application of the LTG measures (Art. 37 (1) (d) FD).

In the case of groups, four capital add-ons were imposed because the risk profile of the group deviated significantly from the assumptions underlying the SCR calculated under the standard formula, and two capital add-ons related to cases where the risk profile deviated significantly from the assumptions underlying the SCR calculated under a full or partial internal model.

In terms of amounts, the capital add-ons imposed varied from 1% to 83% of the total SCR. One capital add-on was over €1 billion, two capital add-ons were between €100 million and €700 million, and the rest were below €100 million.

Although it is clear from these figures that capital add-ons are very infrequent, the size of the capital add-ons is such that it has a material impact on the SCR of some undertakings.

According to Art. 51 (2) FD, Member States may provide that, even though the total SCR amount is disclosed in the SFCR, the capital add-on or the impact of the specific parameters the (re)insurance undertaking is required to use in accordance with Art. 110 FD need not be separately disclosed during a transitional period ending no later than 31 December 2020. In its report, EIOPA indicates that most EEA Member States have used this option, but that two Member States ended the transitional regime on 31 December 2017.

3. GOVERNANCE SYSTEM

3.1. GENERAL PRINCIPLES

The success of a business venture depends heavily on the quality of management. This is also true in insurance and was specifically recognised by insurance supervisors in the Sharma Report, which looked at the causes of insurance failures. As stated in the Report:[56]

> Although a well-managed firm can still fail, poor management makes a firm vulnerable and we believe that in practice it is the primary root cause of most problems

[56] Conference of Insurance Supervisory Services of the Member States of the EU, *Report on Prudential Supervision of Insurance Undertakings*, December 2002, p. 38. See also EIOPA, *Failures and near misses in insurance. Overview of the causes and early identification*, Publications Office of the EU, Luxembourg, 2018, 48 p., which lists "management and staff competence risk" as one of the top five causes of failures and near misses for EU life and non-life undertakings.

in insurance firms. We found that poor management can take one or more of the following forms:

(i) management are competent but have an excessive risk appetite or a lack of integrity or independence; or
(ii) they operate outside their field or level of competence;
(iii) they fail to put in place adequate decision-making processes or adequate internal controls.

Because of the importance of governance, detailed information about the way in which the undertaking organises its governance in practice must be provided in the RSR (Art. 308 DA) and in the SFCR (Art. 294 DA).

Corporate governance deals with the checks and balances within a company. It refers to the relationship between a company's senior management, its board of directors (and supervisory board), its shareholders and other stakeholders, and it determines the structure used to define a company's objectives, as well as the means to achieve them and monitor the results obtained.[57]

The governance system is covered by Arts. 41–50 FD and by Arts. 258–275 DA. It is further developed in the EIOPA Guidelines on the system of governance.[58] Useful guidance can also be found in ICP 7 – Corporate Governance, in the OECD Guidelines on Insurer Governance,[59] in Arts. 88–95 CRD IV, and in the EBA Guidelines on internal governance.[60]

It is important to underline that the system of governance must be proportionate to the nature, scale and complexity of the operations of the (re)insurance undertaking (Art. 41 (2) FD). The requirements described in this chapter must be read with this in mind. Not all requirements can apply in the same manner to all (re)insurance undertakings.[61] If the undertaking is small or medium-sized, or if its business is relatively simple and straightforward, a less-sophisticated governance system should be sufficient. If the undertaking is large and/or complex, the governance system should reflect this.

Although specifically asked by stakeholders to further expand on the application in practice of the proportionality principle in the context of the system of governance, EIOPA decided not to do so because it was of the opinion that the principle applies to the way undertakings implement the requirements,

---

57 G20/OECD, *Principles of Corporate Governance*, September 2015, p. 9.

58 EIOPA, Guidelines on system of governance, EIOPA-BoS-14/253, 14 September 2015, 25 p.

59 OECD, *OECD Guidelines on Insurer Governance*, 2017 edition, 90 p.

60 EBA, Final Report on Guidelines on internal governance under Directive 2013/36/EU, EBA/GL/2017/11, 26 September 2017, 104 p.

61 See also, SIRI, M., Corporate governance of insurance firms after Solvency II, in MARANO, P. and SIRI, M. (Eds.), *Insurance Regulation in the European Union: Solvency II and beyond*, Palgrave Macmillan, Cham, 2017, p. 141.

whereas the Guidelines aim to explain the expected outcome, rather than specific solutions. In EIOPA's view, the Guidelines cannot explain what proportionate "simplified" solutions might be. In addition, explaining the circumstances under which such simplified solutions could be applied is impossible as no comprehensive "list" of conditions that need to be in place for a solution to be considered appropriate can ever be given.[62] However, a peer review conducted by EIOPA in 2018 on the way NSAs apply the proportionality principle to the governance requirements for key function holders made it possible to identify some good practices.[63]

EBA adopts a similar approach but clarifies that the internal governance arrangements must be consistent with the individual risk profile and business model of the institution, in order that the objectives of the regulatory requirements are effectively achieved. Institutions should therefore take into account their size and internal organisation, and the nature, scale and complexity of their activities, when developing and implementing internal governance arrangements. Large institutions should have more sophisticated governance arrangements, while small and less complex institutions can implement simpler governance arrangements.

For the purpose of the application of the proportionality principle and in order to ensure the appropriate implementation of the requirements, EBA lists the following criteria that must be taken into account by supervisory authorities and institutions:

- the size in terms of the balance sheet total of the institution and its subsidiaries;
- the geographical presence of the institution and the size of its operations in each jurisdiction;
- the legal form of the institution, including whether the institution is part of a group and, if so, the proportionality assessment for the group;
- whether the institution is listed or not;
- whether the institution is authorised to use an internal model for the calculation of the capital requirements;
- the types of authorised activities and services performed by the institution;
- the underlying business model and strategy, the nature and complexity of the business activities, and the institution's organisational structure;
- the risk strategy, risk appetite and actual risk profile of the institution;
- the ownership and funding structure of the institution;
- the type of clients and the complexity of the products or contracts;

62 EIOPA, Final report on Guidelines on system of governance, EIOPA-BoS-14/253, 28 January 2015, p. 8.

63 EIOPA, *Peer review of key functions: supervisory practices and application in assessing key functions*, Publications Office of the EU, Luxembourg, 2018, 11 p.

- the outsourced activities and distribution channels;
- the existing information technology systems, including continuity systems and outsourcing activities in this area.[64]

The AMSB of the (re)insurance undertaking has ultimate responsibility for the undertaking's compliance with the laws, regulations and administrative provisions adopted pursuant to the FD. The fact that the AMSB has the ultimate responsibility for compliance with the Solvency II regulatory framework has important consequences. For instance, the AMSB must allow sufficient time to deal with the various requirements, for instance the various written policies that must be approved, the system of governance, the ORSA or the reporting requirements. That may not always be easy and should be kept in mind when new requirements are being considered.

The FD uses the term AMSB because there is no uniform corporate structure in the EU. In some Member States, there is a unitary (one-tier) board structure, whereby the board of directors includes executive (internal) and non-executive (external or independent) directors, whilst in other Member States, there is a dualistic (two-tier) board structure, whereby the administrative or management board (comprised of internal or executive directors) is supervised by a supervisory board comprised of external independent or non-executive directors. As the board structure is a matter of national law, reference is made in the FD to the term AMSB, which covers both structures.[65] Where a two-tier board system comprising a management body and a supervisory body exists under national law, the term AMSB means the management body or the supervisory body, or both of those bodies, as specified in national law. Where no specific body is specified in national law, the term AMSB means the management body (Art. 1 (43) DA).

The AMSB determines the general strategy of the undertaking, decides on the governance structure, monitors the risk management framework, decides on the undertaking's risk appetite, and approves the internal model as well as the results of the ORSA. It is also responsible for the culture and values within

---

64 EBA, Final Report on Guidelines on internal governance under Directive 2013/36/EU, EBA/GL/2017/11, 26 September 2017, pp. 17–18.

65 See also IAIS, ICP 7 – Corporate Governance, paras. 7.05 and 7.06. The use of the term "administrative" is a reference to the Belgian and French "conseil d'administration", which is not an administrative body but the body in charge of running the company. The CRD uses the term "management body", which is defined in Art. 3 (7) CRD as "the body or bodies which are appointed in accordance with national law, which are empowered to set the institution's strategy, objectives and overall direction, and which oversee and monitor management decision-making, and include the persons who effectively direct the business of the institution". It further distinguishes between the management function of the management body and the supervisory function of the management body, with the latter defined as "the management body acting in its role of overseeing and monitoring management decision-making".

the undertaking and must see to it that the undertaking treats its customers fairly by developing the right products and by overseeing that they are sold to the right people in the right manner.[66] The AMSB is usually assisted in its task by a number of committees, which may or may not be part of the board, and to which key function holders (such as the chief risk officer or the chief actuary) may be invited as guests. Depending on the corporate structure, these committees may be part of the management board, the supervisory board or the unitary board. The most common committees are the audit committee, the remuneration committee and the nomination committee. Other committees that are frequently found in (re)insurance undertakings are the IT committee and the investment or asset–liability management committee,

Good governance is the basis for effective and sound management, as well as being a key element of the regulatory framework. The system of governance of a (re)insurance undertaking must be based on the appropriate and transparent allocation of oversight and management responsibilities to provide for effective decision-making, to prevent conflicts of interest and to ensure effective management of the undertaking (recital 93 DA).

Each (re)insurance undertaking must have in place an effective system of governance that provides for sound and prudent management of the business (Art. 41 (1), first subparagraph FD). It must monitor and regularly evaluate the adequacy and effectiveness of its system of governance and take appropriate measures to address any deficiencies (Art. 258 (6) DA).

The system, carried out under the responsibility of the AMSB, must include at least an adequate, transparent organisational structure, with clear allocation and appropriate segregation of responsibilities and an effective system for ensuring the transmission of information (Art. 41 (1), second subparagraph FD). No specific system of governance is prescribed, because there is no perfect system of governance that works well for all undertakings.

If the undertaking is a mutual, its governance system might be different from that of a limited liability company,[67] because the undertaking is collectively owned (and/or controlled) by policyholders, thereby reducing the divergence of interests that arises in corporate structures between shareholders and policyholders.[68]

---

66 The AMSB is ultimately responsible for the design as well as for the oversight and governance of the sale of its products sold on the market. See EIOPA, Final Report on Public Consultation on Preparatory Guidelines on product oversight and governance arrangements by insurance undertakings and insurance distributors, EIOPA-BoS-16-071, 6 April 2016, 65 p.

67 See AISAM, *Governance of Mutual Insurance Companies: the current state of legislation*, Massoz, Liège, October 2006, 36 p. See also IAIS, ICP 7 – Corporate Governance, para. 7.0.7.

68 The concept of mutuality is becoming again more popular by the appearance of peer to peer insurance, whereby risks are shared by people with common interests, habits or behaviours. The sense of belonging to a group fosters responsible behaviour towards the other members of the group and benefits are redistributed between the members of the group. See, for instance, EIOPA, InsurTech Roundtable: How technology and data are reshaping the insurance landscape, EIOPA-BoS/17-165, 5 July 2017, pp. 12–13.

Mutual insurance undertakings have been sometimes reluctant to adapt their governance system in order to comply with the Solvency II requirements, arguing that their structure worked well in the past. They particularly opposed the tightening of fit and proper requirements, the requirement in the DA and in the EIOPA Guidelines of having two persons effectively running the undertaking, the lack of clarity in distinguishing between key function holders and those persons effectively running the company, the split of some AMSB competences between different bodies, and the introduction of the concept of independent directors, although this was not – strictly speaking – a Solvency II requirement.

Although the mutual structure has its advantages, as the business is owned by its customers, it has been admitted that these advantages were sometimes neutralised by a lack of independent control within the organisation.[69]

In the case of a branch established in an EEA MS by a third-country (re)insurance undertaking, the same governance requirements as those applicable to EU (re)insurance undertakings apply, but the governance system of the branch may have to be adapted to the particular situation of the branch.[70] For instance, the same key governance functions must be put in place regardless of whether these functions are specifically established for the branch operations or are applied by the undertaking's head office to the branch operations. This means, for instance, that the CRO of the third-country (re)insurance undertaking in charge of risk management for the undertaking as a whole can therefore also be put in charge of risk management for the branch operations.

Each (re)insurance undertaking must have written policies at least in relation to risk management, internal control, internal audit and, where relevant, outsourcing. These policies must be adopted by the AMSB, implemented in practice and reviewed at least annually (Art. 41 (3) FD). The policies must set out the relevant responsibilities, objectives and processes and reporting procedures to be applied, all of which must be consistent with the undertaking's overall business strategy (Art. 258 (2) DA). Although (re)insurance undertakings obviously had a system of governance in place prior to Solvency II, an important innovation is that undertakings are now required to turn their implicit system

69 Association of Financial Mutuals (AFM), *Corporate governance for mutual insurers*, Guidance published by AFM in response to the requirements contained in the Myners *Revue of the Governance of Life Mutuals*, January 2015, 31 p. (http://www.financialmutuals.org/files/files/ACGC%20guidelines,%20Jan%202015.pdf); HUBERT, S., *La gouvernance des sociétés d'assurance mutuelles et Solvabilité II: comment les sociétés d'assurance mutuelles adaptent-elles leurs mécanismes de gouvernance?* (https://www.strategie-aims.com/events/conferences/28-xxvieme-conference-de-l-aims/communications/4786-la-gouvernance-des-societes-d-assurance-mutuelles-et-solvabilite-ii-comment-les-societes-d-assurance-mutuelles-adaptent-elles-leurs-mecanismes-de-gouvernance/download).

70 EIOPA, Guidelines on the supervision of branches of third-country insurance undertakings, EIOPA-BoS-15/110, Guidelines 27–35.

of governance into an explicit system of governance, which clarifies who does what within the undertaking, to whom reporting takes place and what control mechanisms exist within the system of governance. This should ensure that all important duties are covered and that unnecessary overlaps are avoided. It also allows supervisory authorities to better understand how the business is organised and makes it possible for them to verify the system of governance.

Each undertaking must establish, implement and maintain a business continuity policy aimed at ensuring, in the case of an interruption to its systems and procedures (for example a cyberattack), the preservation of essential data and functions and the maintenance of its activities, or, where that is not possible, the timely recovery of such data and functions and the timely resumption of its activities. The contingency plan must be reviewed, updated and tested on a regular basis (Art. 258 (3) DA).

In terms of general governance requirements, each (re)insurance undertaking must (Art. 258 (1) DA):

(a) establish, implement and maintain effective cooperation, internal reporting and communication of information at all relevant levels;
(b) establish, implement and maintain effective decision-making procedures and an organisational structure that clearly specifies reporting lines, allocates functions and responsibilities, and takes into account the nature, scale and complexity of the risks inherent in its business;
(c) ensure that the members of the AMSB collectively possess the necessary qualifications, competency, skills and professional experience in the relevant areas of the business in order to effectively manage and oversee the undertaking in a professional manner;[71]
(d) ensure that each individual member of the AMSB has the necessary qualifications, competency, skills and professional experience to perform the tasks assigned;
(e) employ personnel with the skills, knowledge and expertise necessary to carry out the responsibilities allocated to them properly;
(f) ensure that all personnel are aware of the procedures for the proper carrying out of their responsibilities;

---

71 This is a requirement for the board "collectively". It would be unreasonable to require that each board member would have a perfect knowledge of all aspects of the business. Individual board members might be asked to bring to the board specific knowledge, for instance on underwriting, provisioning, modelling, accounting, etc. The AMSB may want to establish board committees, such as an audit committee, a risk committee or a remuneration committee. It may also request senior management and key function holders to provide relevant information and challenge that information, where necessary. For knowledge about internal models, see above, Chapter 6, section 4.2.3.2.1.

(g) ensure that the assignment of multiple tasks to individuals and organisational units does not or is not likely to prevent the persons concerned from carrying out any particular function in a sound, honest and objective manner;
(h) establish information systems that produce complete, reliable, clear, consistent, timely and relevant information concerning its business activities, the commitments assumed and the risks to which the undertaking is exposed;
(i) maintain adequate and orderly records of its business and internal organisation;
(j) safeguard the security, integrity and confidentiality of information, taking into account the nature of the information in question;
(k) introduce clear reporting lines that ensure the prompt transfer of information to all persons who need it in a way that enables them to recognise its importance as regards their respective responsibilities;
(l) adopt a written remuneration policy.

Each undertaking must ensure that at least two persons effectively run the undertaking (Art. 258 (4) DA). This is the application of the "four-eyes" principle, which is a basic principle of good governance: no individual should have power over decision-making without any form of control. Any significant decision concerning the undertaking should be reviewed by at least one other person who effectively runs the undertaking before the decision is implemented.[72]

The undertaking must ensure that effective processes and procedures are in place to prevent conflicts of interest and that potential sources of conflicts of interest are identified and procedures are established in order to ensure that those involved in the implementation of the undertaking's strategies and policies understand where conflicts of interest could arise and how such conflicts are to be addressed (Art. 258 (5) DA). An adequate segregation of responsibilities should ensure that nobody ends up monitoring or controlling his own work. If as a result of combining key governance functions, tasks performed by the same persons could give rise to conflicts of interest (for instance, risk management and internal audit being performed by the same person or persons), care must be taken to appropriately address such possible conflicts of interest.[73]

---

72 Recital 94 DA and EIOPA, Guidelines on system of governance, EIOPA-BoS-14/253, 14 September 2015, Guideline 3. A classical case was Equitable Life, where the CEO was at the same time the appointed actuary. See also SIRI, M., Corporate governance of insurance firms after Solvency II, in MARANO, P. and SIRI, M. (Eds.), *Insurance Regulation in the European Union: Solvency II and beyond*, Palgrave Macmillan, Cham, 2017, p. 136.

73 EIOPA, Final report on Guidelines on system of governance, EIOPA-BoS-14/253, 28 January 2015, p. 46.

3.2. THE FOUR KEY GOVERNANCE FUNCTIONS

Although the FD does not prescribe a specific governance structure, it introduces a requirement for all (re)insurance undertakings (including branches) to organise four key governance functions: risk management, internal control, internal audit and actuarial. Obviously, these functions do not encompass the whole governance system of a (re)insurance undertaking which – depending on its size and complexity – will often also include other key governance functions, such as the chief executive officer (CEO), the chief financial officer (CFO), the chief operating officer (COO), the chief investment officer (CIO), the chief information officer (CIO), etc.

The reason why four key governance functions are further developed under Solvency II relates to their importance as control functions. They are therefore sometimes referred to as the independent control functions.

The four key governance functions should be operationally independent, i.e. each function should retain responsibility for taking the decisions necessary for the proper performance of its duties without interference from others and must be able to report directly to the AMSB.[74] Each function must, where appropriate, cooperate with the other functions in carrying out its role. The function holders must be able to communicate on their own initiative with any staff member and must have the necessary authority, resources and expertise, as well as unrestricted access to all relevant information necessary to carry out their responsibilities. The function holders must promptly report any major problem in their area of responsibility to the AMSB (Art. 268 DA).

> "A function is an administrative capacity to undertake particular governance tasks. The identification of a particular function does not prevent the undertaking from freely deciding how to organise that function in practice save where otherwise specified in the FD. This should not lead to unduly burdensome requirements because account must be taken of the nature, scale and complexity of the operations of the undertaking. It is therefore possible for the four key functions to be staffed by own staff, to rely on advice from outside experts or to outsource key functions to experts within the limits set by the FD."[75]

Although it is possible to combine the key governance functions – with the exception of the internal audit function,[76] which must in principle exist as a separate control function – it is important to organise the governance system in a

[74] EIOPA, Final report on Guidelines on system of governance, EIOPA-BoS-14/253, 28 January 2015, pp. 46–47.
[75] Recital 31 FD.
[76] See, however, Art. 271 (2) DA.

manner that avoids conflicts of interest and ensures independence of judgement. Combinations of key functions in one holder must be justified by the principle of proportionality. Holding a key function should generally not be combined with membership of the AMSB or with operational tasks, as this would be contrary to the principle that the key functions are control functions. If such combinations occur, (re)insurance undertakings need to make the necessary arrangements to avoid potential conflicts of interest.[77]

Undertakings should be able to explain to the supervisory authority the logic behind their governance system, the role the various key function holders play and the reporting lines within the organisation. For instance, it would be difficult to explain a governance system in which the CFO is ultimately responsible for the risk management system. That would clearly run the risk of risk management being made dependent on the profitability of the undertaking. In a large undertaking, it would also be difficult to justify the CRO also being responsible for the actuarial function, as this might remove the specific role of the actuarial function as a separate control function.

Of course, in the case of smaller and less complex undertakings, common sense should apply, and it cannot be the intention to require them to introduce a complex governance structure. However, the four key governance functions – as control functions – must be present in one way or another. They may be outsourced, and it should be possible for a single person or organisational unit to carry out more than one function.[78] This does not mean that all undertakings must have four key governance functions as a starting point and that the supervisory authority must specifically permit these functions to be combined.

Solvency II does not specifically recognise the "three lines of defence" model that emerged from the work of COSO, which had developed a framework for evaluating internal controls in 1992.[79] The model was further developed by the Institute of Internal Auditors in 2013[80] and is commonly used in the banking sector.[81] The "three lines of defence" model distinguishes between the management of risk at the operating level (first line of defence), the monitoring of risk as part of risk management and internal control (second line of defence), and the independent review of the functioning of the two first lines of defence

---

77 EIOPA, *Peer review of key functions: supervisory practices and application in assessing key functions*, Publications Office of the EU, Luxembourg, 2018, p. 5.

78 Recital 32 FD.

79 ANDERSON, D. and EUBANKS, G., *Leveraging COSO across the three lines of defence*, COSO, July 2015, 25 p. (https://www.coso.org/Documents/COSO-2015-3LOD.pdf).

80 Institute of Internal Auditors, *The three lines of defence in effective risk management and control*, January 2013, 10 p. (https://na.theiia.org/standards-guidance/Public%20Documents/PP%20The%20Three%20Lines%20of%20Defense%20in%20Effective%20Risk%20Management%20and%20Control.pdf).

81 See EBA, Final Report on Guidelines on internal governance under Directive 2013/36/EU, EBA/GL/2017/11, 26 September 2017, pp. 9–10.

by the internal audit function (third line of defence). The FD follows the same logic by establishing risk management, internal control and internal audit as separate control functions, but the governance system is at the same time more sophisticated. Because of the specific nature of insurance, where the liabilities side of the balance sheet is more important, an additional line of defence, i.e. the actuarial function, was added. In practice, this function often forms part of the second line of defence.

As recognised by the Institute of Internal Auditors, the "three lines of defence" model must be looked at in a broader context. External auditors, regulators (supervisors) and other external bodies, when coordinated effectively, can be considered as additional lines of defence, providing assurance to stakeholders, including shareholders, the governing body of the undertaking and senior management.[82] The role of the supervisory authority is obviously well developed under Solvency II. One should however not ignore the important role that can be played by external auditors (see below, section 3.10).

3.3. FIT AND PROPER REQUIREMENTS

All persons who effectively run the undertaking or have other key functions must *at all times* be "fit and proper" (Art. 42 (1) FD). This requirement applies to the members of the AMSB and the holders of key governance functions, but also to the persons who are key decision-makers in the undertaking, including senior management.[83] The latter includes persons employed by the undertaking who are responsible for high level decision-making and for implementing the strategies devised and the policies approved by the AMSB. The requirement also applies to the "authorised agent" of a branch (Art. 146 (1) FD) and to all persons who effectively run an insurance holding company or mixed financial holding company (Art. 257 FD).

Persons having other key functions include all persons performing tasks related to a key function. Key function holders are the persons responsible for a key function, as opposed to persons having a key function or carrying out or performing a key function.[84]

---

82 Institute of Internal Auditors, *The three lines of defence in effective risk management and control*, January 2013, p. 6. (https://na.theiia.org/standards-guidance/Public%20Documents/PP%20The%20Three%20Lines%20of%20Defense%20in%20Effective%20Risk%20Management%20and%20Control.pdf).

83 IAIS, ICP 5 – Suitability of Persons, para. 5.2. This includes persons employed by the undertaking who are responsible for high level decision-making and for implementing the strategies devised and the policies approved by the AMSB.

84 EIOPA, Final report on the Guidelines on system of governance, EIOPA-BoS-14/253, 28 January 2015, p. 16. There is a lack of precision in the terminology, which is not helpful. This is clearly pointed out by DREHER, M., *Treatises on Solvency II*, Springer, Berlin/Heidelberg, 2015, pp. 217–241.

It is for the undertaking to decide which persons are covered by the fit and proper requirements and to include that in its policy on fit and proper requirements, which must be submitted to the supervisory authority (Art. 308 DA). The undertaking must include in its RSR information on how it ensures in practice that the fit and proper requirements are complied with (Art. 308 (2) DA).

The principle stated in Art. 42 (1) FD that the persons who effectively run the (re)insurance undertaking must be fit and proper is not new.[85] It was taken over from the earlier Insurance Directives.[86] This is also true for Art. 43 FD, which deals with proof of good repute.[87]

"Fit" means that the professional qualifications, knowledge and experience of the persons concerned are adequate to enable sound and prudent management. Indicators for an individual's assessment of fitness are the necessary qualities that will allow the individual to perform the duties and carry out the responsibilities required, competence in terms of professional or formal qualifications, and knowledge and/or pertinent experience, as well as the appropriate level of commitment to perform the role.

All members of the AMSB are to be considered as persons who effectively run the undertaking. In order to ensure that the undertaking is managed and overseen in a professional manner, the AMSB should *collectively* possess appropriate qualification, experience and knowledge about at least:

- insurance and financial markets, i.e. awareness and understanding of the wider business, economic and market environment in which the undertaking operates and an awareness of the level of knowledge of and needs of policyholders;
- the business strategy and business model, i.e. a detailed understanding of the undertaking's business strategy and model;
- the system of governance, i.e. awareness and understanding of the risks the undertaking is facing and the ability to manage them, including the ability to assess the effectiveness of the undertaking's arrangements to deliver effective governance, oversight and controls in the business and, if necessary, to oversee changes in these areas;
- financial and actuarial analysis, i.e. the ability to interpret the undertaking's financial and actuarial information, identify key issues, put in place appropriate controls and take necessary measures based on this information;

---

85 It is also a requirement in the banking sector. See Art. 91 (1) CRD.

86 See Art. 6 (1) (e) of Directive 2002/83/EC of the EP and of the Council of 5 November 2002 concerning life assurance, *OJ* L 345, 19.12.2002, p. 1, which states as a condition for authorisation that the persons who effectively run the undertaking are persons of good repute with appropriate professional qualifications or experience. See also IAIS, ICP 5 – Suitability of Persons.

87 See Art. 61 Directive 2002/83/EC concerning life assurance.

- the regulatory framework and requirements, i.e. awareness and understanding of the regulatory framework in which the undertaking operates, in terms of both the regulatory requirements and expectations, and the capacity to adapt to changes to the regulatory framework without delay.

Individual members of the AMSB must know the business of the undertaking and must have basic knowledge about accounting and financial reporting, capital investment, risk management and the legal framework applicable to insurance undertakings.[88]

"Proper" means that the persons concerned are of good repute[89] and integrity. Indicators for an individual's assessment of good repute may be criminal (criminal, administrative or disciplinary offences), financial (financial misconduct, bankruptcy, insolvency), supervisory (market conduct transgressions, prior refusal of regulatory approval) or other (non-compliance with internal policies or codes of conduct, being on a sanctions list or being an official of a country that has been put on an international sanctions list). Integrity is demonstrated through evidence of character and through business behaviour and business conduct.

In order to assess the reputation of the persons who effectively run the undertaking or have other key functions, the past conduct of those persons should be examined to see whether they may not be able to effectively discharge their duties in accordance with the applicable rules, regulations and guidelines. Information regarding past conduct may be sourced from criminal or financial records. A person's past business conduct could provide indications as to that person's integrity (recital 100 DA).[90]

"Proper" also means that the persons concerned must avoid, to the extent possible, activities that create conflicts of interest or the appearance of conflicts of interest.[91] Propriety is an ongoing requirement, which must be regularly reassessed. This reassessment can be part of the ongoing supervisory activity, be the subject of a themed review of a sample of (re)insurance undertakings or be carried out at the time of the renewal of the mandate or periodically, for instance, annually.[92]

The proportionality principle does not apply to the propriety requirement, i.e. there cannot be different standards for persons who effectively run the undertaking or have other key functions, since the good repute and integrity

---

88 DREHER, M., *Treatises on Solvency II*, Springer, Berlin/Heidelberg, 2015, p. 215.

89 For the proof of good repute, see Art. 43 FD.

90 For an overview on how the "proper" test is carried out in EEA Member States, see EIOPA, *Results of the peer review on propriety of AMSB members and qualifying shareholders*, Publications Office of the EU, Luxembourg, 2018, 44 p.

91 There are no specific requirements as to the number of directorships which may be held by a member of the AMSB contrary to what is the case in banking. See Art. 91 CRD.

92 See, EIOPA, *Results of the peer review on propriety of AMSB members and qualifying shareholders*, Publications Office of the EU, Luxembourg, 2018, p. 43.

of the person should always be at the same, adequate level, irrespective of the nature, size and complexity of the risks inherent in the business or of the undertaking.[93]

It is the (re)insurance undertaking that is responsible for ensuring that the persons who effectively run the undertaking or have other key functions are fit and proper. In order to carry out this responsibility, the undertaking must develop a policy on the fit and proper requirements, which must include at least:[94]

- a description of the procedure for identifying the positions for which notification is required and to the procedure for notifying the supervisory authority;
- a description of the procedure for assessing the fitness and propriety of the persons who effectively run the undertaking or have other key functions, both when being considered for the specific position and on an ongoing basis;
- a description of the situations that give rise to a re-assessment of the fit and proper requirements;
- a description of the procedure for assessing the skills, knowledge, expertise and personal integrity of other relevant personnel, both when being considered for the specific position and on an ongoing basis.

The assessment of whether a person is fit must include an assessment of the person's professional and formal qualifications, knowledge and relevant experience within the insurance sector, other financial sectors or other businesses, and must take into account the particular duties allocated to that person and, where relevant, the insurance, financial, accounting, actuarial and management skills of the person (Art. 273 (2) DA).

The assessment of whether members of the AMSB are fit must take account of the particular duties allocated to individual members. Appropriate diversity of qualifications, knowledge and relevant experience should ensure that the undertaking is managed and overseen in a professional manner (Art. 273 (3) DA).

The assessment of whether a person is proper must include an assessment of that person's honesty and financial soundness, based on evidence of that person's character, personal behaviour and business conduct, including any criminal, financial and supervisory concerns relevant for the purposes of the assessment (Art. 273 (4) DA).

The undertaking must notify the supervisory authority of any changes to the identity of the persons who effectively run the undertaking or who are

93 EIOPA, Final report on the Guidelines on system of governance, EIOPA-BoS-14/253, 28 January 2015, p. 55.

94 EIOPA, Guidelines on system of governance, EIOPA-BoS-14/253, 14 September 2015, Guideline 13.

responsible for other key functions, along with all information needed to assess whether any new persons appointed to manage the undertaking are fit and proper (Art. 42 (2) FD). The notification requirement applies to the persons who effectively run the undertaking and to the key function holders. EIOPA has developed a list of information that NSAs should ask for in order to carry out the fit and proper assessment.[95] Additional information might be requested if needed. The supervisory authority must assess the information provided and give feedback to the undertaking concerned within an appropriate timeframe from receipt of a complete notification.[96]

Notification is also required if any of the persons who effectively run the undertaking or who are responsible for other key functions has been replaced because the person no longer meets the fit and proper requirements (Art. 42 (3) FD).

The FD does not require notification prior to the person being nominated, nor does it require pre-approval of the nomination by the supervisory authority.[97] However, in most Member States,[98] prior notification is required. It might indeed be better to notify the supervisory authority and to carry out the fitness check before the person effectively starts the job in order to avoid difficulties afterwards. Although the supervisory authority does not have to approve the nomination, it can certainly – and at any time – object to a person holding a key function if that person lacks the necessary qualification(s). If the supervisory authority concludes, with adequate justification, that the person to be appointed or already appointed does not meet the relevant fit and proper requirements, the authority has the power to require the undertaking not to appoint the person or to replace the person. The authority may also decide to delay its decision, pending further professional training, if the person is considered not sufficiently qualified for the job.

3.4. RISK MANAGEMENT FUNCTION

The risk management function is one of the four key governance functions under Solvency II. The person in charge of this function must be fit and proper. In larger undertakings, the function is often carried out by the CRO. Experience has shown that it is important to place the CRO function at a level

[95] EIOPA, Guidelines on system of governance, EIOPA-BoS-14/253, 14 September 2015, Guideline 15 and Technical Annex.

[96] EIOPA, Guidelines on system of governance, EIOPA-BoS-14/253, 14 September 2015, Guideline 16.

[97] Recital 99 DA.

[98] See EIOPA, *Peer review of key functions: supervisory practices and application in assessing key functions*, Publications Office of the EU, Luxembourg, 2018, p. 7. For instance, in Belgium: see, National Bank of Belgium, Circular 17 June 2013 on "fit and proper".

that is sufficiently senior in the undertaking and independent from other key functions, such as the finance department. Sometimes, the CRO is a member of the AMSB. Although holders of a key governance function are generally not allowed to be members of the AMSB, membership of the AMSB offers the CRO the possibility to strengthen the AMSB's knowledge and expertise regarding risk management.[99] The person in charge of the risk management function must in any case report to the AMSB on risks that have been identified as potentially material, but also on other specific areas of risks, both on his or her own initiative or following a request from the AMSB.

In practice, the risk management function is often combined with the actuarial function or the compliance function. This is perfectly understandable in the case of small (re)insurance undertakings, in line with the proportionality principle, but less so in larger undertakings, as each key governance function has to play its role as an independent control function.[100]

The risk management function must be structured in such a way as to facilitate the implementation of the risk management system (Art. 44 (4) FD). The function includes all of the following tasks:

(a) assisting the AMSB and other functions in the effective operation of the risk management system;
(b) monitoring the risk management system;
(c) monitoring the general risk profile of the undertaking as a whole;
(d) detailed reporting on risk exposures and advising the AMSB on risk management matters, including in relation to strategic affairs such as corporate strategy, mergers and acquisitions and major projects and investments;
(e) identifying and assessing emerging risks.

The AMSB is ultimately responsible for ensuring the effectiveness of the risk management system, for setting the undertaking's risk appetite and overall risk-tolerance limits, and for approving the main risk management strategies and policies. EIOPA expects the AMSB to designate at least one member of the AMSB to oversee the risk management system on its behalf.[101] There is no requirement

---

99 See EIOPA, *Peer review of key functions: supervisory practices and application in assessing key functions*, Publications Office of the EU, Luxembourg, 2018, p. 7. It would in this case be advisable to ask a least one other member of the AMSB to take a specific interest in risk management so as to help the AMSB to carry out its oversight function.

100 See EIOPA, *Peer review of key functions: supervisory practices and application in assessing key functions*, Publications Office of the EU, Luxembourg, 2018, p. 7.

101 This may give rise to problems, particularly when the board member in charge of overseeing the risk management system is an executive director. See SIRI, M., Corporate governance of insurance firms after Solvency II, in MARANO, P. and SIRI, M. (Eds.), *Insurance Regulation in the European Union: Solvency II and beyond*, Palgrave Macmillan, Cham, 2017, p. 136.

to set up a risk committee within the AMSB, although some Member States do require this, following the practice in banking.[102]

Responsibility for the risk management system means ensuring that there is a coordinated and integrated approach to risk management and a common "risk language" with the right tone from the top. The AMSB must define the risk appetite of the undertaking and its risk tolerance. These must be included in a statement adopted by the AMSB which needs to be regularly reviewed.

The risk appetite set by the AMSB reflects the attitude of the AMSB toward the main categories of risks. It needs to be clear and detailed enough to express and reflect the strategic high-level objectives of the AMSB. Often stated in qualitative terms, the risk appetite statement defines how the undertaking weighs strategic decisions and communicates its strategy to key stakeholders with respect to risk taking. It is designed to enhance management's ability to make informed and effective business decisions while keeping risk exposures within acceptable boundaries.[103] It may include a quantitative assessment in terms of risk and capital.

The risk-tolerance limits reflect the restrictions the undertaking imposes on itself when taking risks. It takes into account the relevant constraints that effectively limit the capacity to take risks, the risk appetite and other relevant information (for example, the current risk profile of the undertaking and the interrelationship between risks). Qualitative risk tolerances are useful to describe the undertaking's preference for, or aversion to, particular types of risk, particularly for those risks that are difficult to measure. Quantitative risk tolerances are useful to set numerical limits for the amount of risk that the undertaking is willing to take.[104]

Although Solvency II assigns the primary responsibility for internal models to the risk management function, the latter must cooperate closely with the actuarial function in this area. It must also liaise closely with the users of the outputs of the internal model (Art. 269 (2) (a) and (b) DA).

The responsibilities of the risk management function with regard to internal models include (Art. 44 (5) FD):

- the design and implementation of the internal model;
- the testing and validation of the internal model;
- the documentation of the internal model and any subsequent changes to it;
- analysis of the performance of the internal model and the production of summary reports relating thereto;

102 See Art. 76 (3) CRD.

103 NAIC, ORSA Guidance Manual, July 2014, p. 13 (https://www.naic.org/store/free/ORSA_manual.pdf?73).

104 NAIC, ORSA Guidance Manual, July 2014, p. 13 (https://www.naic.org/store/free/ORSA_manual.pdf?73).

- informing the AMSB about the performance of the internal model, suggesting areas needing improvement, and updating the AMSB on the status of efforts to improve previously identified weaknesses.

3.4.1. Risk Management System

(Re)insurance undertakings must establish, implement and maintain an effective risk management system comprising strategies, processes and reporting procedures necessary to identify, measure, monitor, manage and report, on a continuous basis, the risks, at an individual and at an aggregated level, to which they are or could be exposed, and their interdependencies (Art. 44 (1), first subparagraph FD). Each of the verbs and adjectives in this sentence is important. The DA deals more specifically with what this means in practice and how undertakings are expected to organise their risk management system. In its RSR submitted to the supervisory authority, the undertaking must provide detailed information on how its risk management system is organised and what the significant risks to which the undertaking is exposed are (Art. 308 (3) DA).

The risk management system includes the following (Art. 259 (1) DA):

(a) a clearly defined risk management strategy that is consistent with the undertaking's overall business strategy. The objectives and key principles of the strategy, the approved risk-tolerance limits and the assignment of responsibilities across all the activities of the undertaking must be documented;
(b) a clearly defined procedure for the decision-making process;
(c) written policies that effectively ensure the definition and categorisation by type of the material risks to which the undertaking is exposed, and the approved risk-tolerance limits for each type of risk. Such policies must implement the undertaking's risk strategy, facilitate control mechanisms and take into account the nature, scope and time periods of the business and the associated risks;
(d) reporting procedures and processes that ensure that information on the material risks faced by the undertaking and the effectiveness of the risk management system are actively monitored and analysed and that appropriate modifications to the system are made where necessary.

The risk management system must be effective and well integrated into the organisational structure and decision-making processes of the undertaking. The undertaking must ensure that the persons who effectively run the undertaking or have other key functions take into account the information reported as part of the risk management system in their decision-making process (Art. 44 (1), second subparagraph FD and Art. 259 (2) DA).

The undertaking must establish a risk management policy. This written policy must at least include the following:[105]

(a) a definition of the risk categories and the methods to measure the risks;
(b) an outline of how the undertaking manages each relevant category, area of risks and any potential aggregation of risks;
(c) a description of the connection with the overall solvency needs assessment as identified in the ORSA, the regulatory capital requirements and the undertaking's risk-tolerance limits;
(d) a specification of the risk-tolerance limits within all relevant risk categories in line with the undertaking's risk appetite;
(e) a description of the frequency and content of regular stress tests and the situations that would warrant ad hoc stress tests;
(f) policies on at least the following areas that are covered by the risk management system:
    (i) underwriting and reserving;
    (ii) asset–liability management;
    (iii) investment, in particular derivatives and similar commitments;
    (iv) liquidity and concentration risk management;
    (v) operational risk management;
    (vi) reinsurance and other risk-mitigation techniques;
    (vii) deferred taxes;[106]
(g) where the VA is applied, a policy on the criteria for the application of that adjustment;
(h) a policy for the ORSA.

The risk management system must cover all material risks (including emerging risks) to which the undertaking is or might be exposed, i.e. all quantifiable risks and non-quantifiable risks, including reputational[107] and strategic risk[108] (Art. 44 (2), first subparagraph FD). Where appropriate, the risk management system must include the performance of stress tests and scenario analysis with regard to all relevant risks faced by the undertaking (Art. 259 (3) DA).

105 Art. 44 (2), third subparagraph FD and EIOPA, Guidelines on system of governance, EIOPA-BoS-14/253, 14 September 2015, Guideline 18.

106 This area was added in Art. 260 DA as part of the 2018 review of the DA.

107 In its 2017 SFCR (p. 58), Allianz SE defines reputational risk as "the risk of an unexpected drop in the value of the share price, the value of the in-force business or the value of future business caused by a decline in the reputation assessed by external stakeholders". The reputation can be influenced by the corporate behaviour in areas such as product quality, corporate governance, financial performance, customer service, employee relations, intellectual capital and corporate responsibility.

108 For strategic and reputational risk, see EIOPA, Guidelines on system of governance, EIOPA-BoS-14/253, 14 September 2015, Guideline 23.

In order to avoid overreliance on ECAIs, (re)insurance undertakings must, when using credit-rating assessment by ECAIs in the calculation of technical provisions and the SCR, assess the appropriateness of these external credit assessments as part of their risk management, by using additional assessments wherever practicably possible, in order to avoid any automatic dependence on external assessments (Art. 44 (4a) FD).[109]

3.4.1.1. Underwriting and Reserving Risk Management

This risk management area[110] is particularly important. The policy developed in this area must ensure that the undertaking sells the right products to the right persons in the right manner.[111] It presupposes that the undertaking knows the market in which it is selling its products. This may be an issue for long-term, non-life, cross-border business, when the undertaking has less knowledge of the local specificities.[112]

Managing underwriting and reserving risk includes (Art. 260 (1) (a) DA):

(a) actions to be taken by the undertaking to assess and manage the risk of loss or of adverse change in the values of (re)insurance liabilities, resulting from inadequate pricing and provisioning assumptions;
(b) the sufficiency and quality of relevant data to be considered in the underwriting process and in the calculation of technical provisions and their consistency with the standards of sufficiency and quality;
(c) the adequacy of claims management procedures, including the extent to which they cover the overall cycle of claims.

The risk management policy for underwriting and reserving risk must cover at least:[113]

(a) the types and characteristics of the insurance business, such as the type of insurance risk the undertaking is willing to accept;
(b) how the sufficiency of premium income to cover expected claims and expenses is to be ensured;

---

109 See also above, Chapter 6, section 4.2.2.2.4. "Spread risk".

110 The DA incorrectly uses the term "reserving" when what is meant is "provisioning".

111 The insurance undertaking is ultimately responsible for the design and the sale of its products. See EIOPA, Final Report on Public Consultation on Preparatory Guidelines on product oversight and governance arrangements by insurance undertakings and insurance distributors, EIOPA-BoS-16-071, 6 April 2016, 65 p.

112 See EIOPA, Opinion on non-life cross-border insurance business of a long-term nature and its supervision, EIOPA-BoS-18/527, 21 December 2018, p. 6.

113 EIOPA, Guidelines on system of governance, EIOPA-BoS-14/253, 14 September 2015, Guideline 20.

(c) identification of the risks arising from the undertaking's insurance obligations, including embedded options and guaranteed surrender values in its products;
(d) how, in the process of designing a new insurance product and the premium calculation, the undertaking takes account of the constraints related to investments and of reinsurance or other risk-mitigation techniques.

The undertaking must ensure that all policies and procedures established for underwriting are applied by all distribution channels of the undertaking. It also needs to take into account the constraints related to investments in the design of new products. For instance, if the undertaking is planning to sell a new life product with a minimum guaranteed rate, it has to take into account the return available on the market, or if the undertaking is planning to sell a new non-life contract, it has to take into account the liquidity constraints that could be linked to the contract.[114]

3.4.1.2. Asset–Liability Risk Management

Asset–liability management is the management of a business in such a way that decisions on assets and liabilities are coordinated in order to manage the exposure to the risk associated with the variation of their economic values. Along with the investment strategy, an asset–liability management strategy describes how financial and insurance risks will be managed in an asset–liability framework in the short, medium and long term. Where appropriate, the investment strategy and the asset–liability management strategy can be integrated into a combined investment/asset–liability management strategy. The written policies for investment risk management and asset-liability risk management should reflect the implementation of these strategies.[115]

Asset–liability management is very important in insurance. In particular for long-term liabilities in life insurance, it is difficult to match the duration of the liabilities with assets of the same duration. This duration mismatch must be carefully managed.

Managing asset–liability risk includes (Art. 260 (1) (b) DA):
(a) the structural mismatch between assets and liabilities and in particular the duration mismatch of those assets and liabilities;
(b) any dependency between risks of different asset and liability classes;

[114] EIOPA, Final report on guidelines on system of governance, EIOPA-BoS-14/253, 28 January 2015, p. 63.
[115] EIOPA, Final report on guidelines on system of governance, EIOPA-BoS-14/253, 28 January 2015, pp. 67–68.

(c) any dependency between the risks of different (re)insurance obligations;
(d) any off-balance sheet exposures of the undertaking;
(e) the effect of relevant risk-mitigating techniques on asset–liability management.

The risk management policy for asset–liability risk management must cover at least:[116]

(a) a description of the procedure for identification and assessment of different natures of mismatches between assets and liabilities, at least with regard to terms and currency;
(b) a description of risk-mitigating techniques to be used and the expected effect of relevant risk-mitigating techniques on asset–liability management;
(c) a description of deliberate mismatches permitted;
(d) a description of the underlying methodology and frequency of stress tests and scenario tests to be carried out.

As the application of the LTG measures has an impact on the level of technical provisions and eligible own funds, it is important for the undertaking to take account of the impact of those measures in its asset–liability risk management. Omnibus II therefore introduced a requirement for (re)insurance undertakings to regularly assess (Art. 44 (2a) FD):

(a) the sensitivity of their technical provisions and eligible own funds to the assumptions underlying the extrapolation of the relevant risk-free interest rate term structure;
(b) where the MA is applied:
    (i) the sensitivity of their technical provisions and eligible own funds to the assumptions underlying the calculation of the adjustment, including the calculation of the fundamental spread referred to in Art. 77c (1) (b) FD, and the possible effect of a forced sale of assets on their eligible own funds;
    (ii) the sensitivity of their technical provisions and eligible own funds to changes in the composition of the assigned portfolio of assets;
    (iii) the impact of a reduction of the MA to zero;
(c) where the VA is applied:
    (i) the sensitivity of their technical provisions and eligible own funds to the assumptions underlying the calculation of the adjustment and the possible effect of a forced sale of assets on their eligible own funds;
    (ii) the impact of a reduction of the VA to zero.

116 EIOPA, Guidelines on system of governance, EIOPA-BoS-14/253, 14 September 2015, Guideline 24.

In its RSR, the undertaking must include the results of these assessments (Art. 308 (3) (f) DA).

3.4.1.3. Investment Risk Management

Managing investment risk includes (Art. 260 (1) (c) DA):
(a) actions to be taken by the undertaking to ensure that its investments comply with the prudent person principle (for instance, by carrying out regular stress tests);
(b) actions to be taken by the undertaking to ensure that its investments take into account the nature of its business, its approved risk-tolerance limits, its solvency position and its long-term risk exposure (for instance, control procedures looking at the coordination between front and back office and compliance with authorisations and trading limits);
(c) the undertaking's own internal assessment of the credit risk of investment counterparties, including where the counterparties are central governments;
(d) where the undertaking uses derivatives or any other financial instrument with similar characteristics or effects, the objectives of and strategy underlying their use and the way in which they facilitate efficient portfolio management or contribute to a reduction of risks, as well as procedures to assess the risk of such instruments and the principles of risk management to be applied to them;
(e) where appropriate in order to ensure effective risk management, internal quantitative limits on assets and exposures, including off-balance sheet exposures. These quantitative limits may be fixed per counterparty, geographical area or industry, with the aim of managing risks in an appropriate manner and protecting the interests of policyholders.

The risk management policy with regard to investment risk must cover at least the following:[117]

(a) the level of security, quality, liquidity and profitability the undertaking is aiming for with regard to the whole portfolio of assets and how it plans to achieve this;
(b) its quantitative limits on assets and exposures, including off-balance sheet exposures, that are to be established to help to ensure the undertaking achieves its desired level of security, quality, liquidity, profitability and availability for the portfolio;

[117] EIOPA, Guidelines on system of governance, EIOPA-BoS-14/253, 14 September 2015, Guideline 25.

(c) the level of availability the undertaking is aiming for with regard to the whole portfolio of assets and how it plans to achieve this;
(d) consideration of the financial market environment;
(e) the conditions under which the undertaking can pledge or lend assets;
(f) the link between market risk and other risks in adverse scenarios;
(g) the procedure for appropriately valuing and verifying the investment assets;
(h) the procedures to monitor the performance of the investments and review the policy when necessary;
(i) how the assets are to be selected in the best interest of policyholders and beneficiaries.

3.4.1.4. Liquidity Risk Management

The purpose of liquidity risk management is to ensure that obligations to policyholders can be met whenever they fall due. The required degree of liquidity in the investment portfolio may differ between undertakings depending on the nature of the insurance business, especially the ability to predict the amount and timing of insurance payments.

While (re)insurance undertakings benefit from the inverted production cycle, i.e. they receive premiums upfront and pay claims later, upon the occurrence of an insured event, they are not immune to liquidity risk (for instance, when they invest in illiquid assets). They must therefore have appropriate risk management strategies and systems in place for managing their liquidity.[118]

Liquidity risk management includes (Art. 260 (1) (d) DA):
(a) actions to be taken by the (re)insurance undertaking regarding both short term and long-term liquidity risk;
(b) the appropriateness of the composition of the assets in terms of their nature, duration and liquidity in order to meet the undertaking's obligations as they fall due;
(c) a plan to deal with changes in expected cash inflows and outflows.

The risk management policy for liquidity risk must cover at least the following:[119]
(a) the procedure for determining the level of mismatch between the cash inflows and the cash outflows of both assets and liabilities, including

118 See, Bank of England, *Prudential Regulation Authority, Liquidity risk management for insurers*, Consultation Paper 4/19, March 2019, 28 p. (https://www.bankofengland.co.uk/-/media/boe/files/prudential-regulation/consultation-paper/2019/cp419.pdf?la=en&hash=603B1EE142951E9215EEF104554F63916B90E8C4).

119 EIOPA, Guidelines on system of governance, EIOPA-BoS-14/253, 14 September 2015, Guideline 26.

expected cash flows of direct (re)insurance such as claims, lapses or surrenders;
(b) consideration of total liquidity needs in the short and medium term, including an appropriate liquidity buffer (i.e. having enough liquid assets) to guard against a liquidity shortfall;
(c) consideration of the level and monitoring of liquid assets, including a quantification of potential costs or financial losses arising from an enforced realisation;
(d) identification and costs of alternative financing tools;
(e) consideration of the effect on the liquidity situation of expected new business.

Short-term liquidity, or cash management, includes the day-to-day cash requirements under normal business conditions. Liquidity considerations over the long term need to be assessed in a way that takes into consideration the possibility of various unexpected and potentially adverse business conditions where asset values may not be realised for current market values, including situations where accelerated sales of assets reduce expected returns. There are also liquidity considerations that arise from policyholder behaviour, such as unexpected or accelerated payments to policyholders as a result of surrenders (for instance, as a result of a decrease in consumer confidence with respect to a particular insurer or business model), large claims or the exercise of policy options.[120]

3.4.1.5. Concentration Risk Management

The concentration risk management policy must include actions to be taken by the (re)insurance undertaking (Art. 260 (1) (e) DA):

- to identify relevant sources of concentration risk to ensure that risk concentrations remain within established limits;
- to analyse possible risks of contagion between concentrated exposures.

3.4.1.6. Operational Risk Management

Operational risk is defined in Art. 13 (33) FD as the risk of loss arising from inadequate or failed internal processes, personnel or systems, or from external events.[121] As operational risk is typically harder to identify and assess than other

120 EIOPA, Final report on guidelines on system of governance, EIOPA-BoS-14/253, 28 January 2015, pp. 69–70.
121 For instance, Brexit, the imposition of sanctions or the introduction of trade barriers.

types of risks, it is even more important for the undertaking to have a conscious approach to it in its overall risk management. As some of the risk comes from the undertaking itself (for example, from inadequate or failed internal processes, personnel or systems), the undertaking plays a role in the occurrence and unfolding of operational risk.[122]

The operational risk management policy must include actions to be taken by the (re)insurance undertaking to assign clear responsibilities to regularly identify, document and monitor relevant operational risk exposures (Art. 260 (1) (f) DA).

In its risk management policy, the undertaking should cover at least the following with regard to operational risk:[123]

(a) identification of the operational risks it is or might be exposed to and assessment of the way to mitigate them;
(b) activities and internal processes for managing operational risks, including the IT system supporting them;
(c) risk-tolerance limits with respect to the undertaking's main operational risk areas.

The undertaking should have processes to identify, analyse and report on operational risk events. For this purpose, it should establish a process for collecting and monitoring operational risk events.

For its operational risk management, the undertaking should develop and analyse an appropriate set of operational risk scenarios based on at least the following approaches:

(a) the failure of a key process, personnel or system;
(b) the occurrence of external events.

Operational risk tends to interact with other risk types and therefore cannot be assessed in isolation. Operational risk may materialise through personnel execution errors, frauds and processing failures, as well as through the direct and indirect consequences of natural or man-made disasters, such as terrorist attacks, fire, flood, earthquake and pandemics. These natural or man-made disasters, which are low-frequency/high-impact events, are the type of operational risks that need to be considered when looking at scenario analysis. As their impact may be potentially catastrophic, the undertaking must pay particular attention

122 EIOPA, Final report on guidelines on system of governance, EIOPA-BoS-14/253, 28 January 2015, p. 64.

123 EIOPA, Guidelines on system of governance, EIOPA-BoS-14/253, 14 September 2015, Guideline 21.

to them and develop early-warning systems that allow for an effective and timely intervention.[124]

Very severe and unlikely, but not impossible, scenarios must also be considered. To perform this analysis, the undertaking can use pre-defined categories of operational risks and lists of its key processes. However, each undertaking is free to define a system of categorisation that better suits its individual circumstances.

The analysis of stress tests and scenarios for the operational risk framework might differ from other types of stress or scenario analysis (e.g. financial), as the definition of the different stages of the scenario (cause, failure of process, impacts) will be a key element of the analysis and monitoring of the risks. The main reason for this is that the controls and corrective measures that the undertaking puts in place will have an effect on the scenario itself.

In the case of operational risk, prevention and corrective actions take precedence over the precise measure. Identifying operational risks is very closely linked to prevention, mitigation and corrective measures.

The continuous monitoring and control of operational risks implies that all personnel are aware of the importance of this type of risk.

The controls and mitigation actions, such as insurance, automation of processes or the backing-up of data, need to be reviewed periodically, taking into account the developments in the operational risk and knowledge of those developments. The undertaking is also expected to put in place key risk indicators.

For the analysis of operational risk events, the undertaking may also consider how external data could supplement its collection of internal operational risk events data to produce more reliable estimates of operational risk events.

For each relevant event, at least the following information is needed:
(c) the cause of the event;
(d) the consequences of the event; and
(e) the actions taken or not taken on account of the event.

When defining the boundaries (for example, the materiality threshold) of the events that will be collected, the undertaking must keep in mind that operational risk can be related to both high-frequency/low-severity events and low-frequency/high-impact events, and that some events that have had no negative impact (like near misses) may be very useful to analyse to monitor more material operational risks.[125]

---

124 EIOPA, Final report on guidelines on system of governance, EIOPA-BoS-14/253, 28 January 2015, p. 64.

125 EIOPA, Final report on guidelines on system of governance, EIOPA-BoS-14/253, 28 January 2015, p. 65.

Although reputational risk is not included in the operational risk capital charge under the standard formula (see above, Chapter 6, section 4.2.2.3), it must of course be properly managed. A good example on how this can be done can be found in Aviva's 2017 group SFCR (p. 37):[126]

> We also assess operational risks in terms of their potential reputational impact which could adversely affect the Group's franchise value, being the value attributable to the Group's ability to sell profitable business in the future. In order to assess the level of risk to the Group's franchise value, we regularly analyse and review indicators of stakeholder perception of our reputation, threats to that reputation and any potential actions that we could take to maximise opportunities to build (or minimise threats to) our reputation. The stakeholders and indicators we assess are:
>
> - Investors: we track buy/hold/sell rating recommendations of equity analysts who track our shares
> - Rating agencies: We track the credit rating recommendations of credit rating agencies
> - People: We undertake a number of surveys of employee sentiments during the year, including an annual survey of all our staff
> - Customer: We track customer advocacy indicators
> - Regulators: We track qualitative indicators of the strength of our relationship with regulators
> - Opinion formers: We track qualitative indicators of the strength of our reputation in the media and with government and politicians (at a local, national and European Union level).

Cybersecurity risk, which is part of operational risk, is attracting increasing attention. (Re)insurance undertakings can face cyber risk from both internal and external sources. Insurers collect, process and store substantial volumes of data, including personally identifiable information. They are also connected to other financial institutions through multiple channels. Potential adverse consequences resulting from insurance cybersecurity incidents may include loss or corruption of confidential or sensitive business, consumer or third-party data, disruption of business, physical loss (for example, damage to hardware), financial loss and reputational damage. Because of the potential catastrophic consequences of a serious cybersecurity incident, operational risk management needs to deal with this issue. Cyber resilience, i.e. the ability to anticipate, withstand, contain and rapidly recover from a cyberattack should be an important objective of all (re)insurance undertakings, regardless of their size.[127]

---

126 https://www.aviva.com/content/dam/aviva-corporate/.../pdfs/.../solvency-FCR-2017Lpdf.

127 See IAIS, *Issues Paper on Cyber Risk to the Insurance Sector*, August 2016, 38 p. and EIOPA, *Understanding Cyber Insurance – A Structured Dialogue with Insurance Companies*, Publications Office of the EU, Luxembourg, 2018, 32 p. EIOPA intends to develop guidelines regarding Information & Communication Technologies (ICT), security and

Another risk that is attracting increasing interest is conduct of business risk. Insurers must implement proper processes to deal with product design, development and marketing and identify and manage consumer risks.[128] This is a key feature of ensuring that conduct risks are mitigated at inception. Any conflicts of interest in the design and distribution of insurance products need to be identified and managed. Otherwise, they might create vulnerabilities in the business model, possibly cause consumer detriment and ultimately damage the reputation of the insurer and the sector.[129] This has become a particular point of attention for EIOPA, which has developed a framework for conduct of business supervision based on Arts. 1, 8, 9, 29 and 35 EIOPA Regulation.[130]

3.4.1.7. Reinsurance and Other Risk-Mitigation Techniques

Reinsurance and similar risk-mitigation techniques can be used to keep the undertaking's risks within the scope of the approved risk-tolerance limits. In using these techniques, the undertaking has to consider the potential new risks they bear, such as the risk of counterparty default, as is the case with reinsurance, which transforms insurance risk into credit risk.[131]

This risk management area must include (Art. 260 (1) (g) DA):

(a) actions to be taken by the (re)insurance undertaking to ensure the selection of suitable reinsurance and other risk-mitigation techniques;

---

governance, including cyber resilience. See, BERNARDINO, G., Keynote speech at the 3rd Annual FinTech and Regulation Conference in Brussels, 26 February 2019, p. 5 (https://eiopa.europa.eu/Publications/Speeches%20and%20presentations/2019-02-26%20ThirdAnnualFinTechRegulationConferenceAforeConsultingSpeechGabrielBernardino.pdf).

128 See, EIOPA, *Framework for assessing conduct risk through the product lifecycle*, Publications Office of the EU, Luxembourg, 2019, 30 p.

129 BERNARDINO, G., *Implementation of Solvency II: The dos and the don'ts*, International Conference, Ljubljana, 2 September 2015, p. 7 (https://eiopa.europa.eu/Publications/Speeches%20and%20presentations/2015-09-02%20Solvency%20II%20Conference%20Slovenia.pdf). See also IAIS, *Issues Paper on conduct of business risk and its management*, November 2015, 47 p. This paper includes a number of examples of conduct of business risk and ways and means to identify and manage that risk which is defined (p. 6) as: "the risk to customers, insurers, the insurance sector or the insurance market that arises from insurers and/or intermediaries conducting their business in a way that does not ensure fair treatment of customers."

130 EIOPA, Strategy towards a comprehensive risk-based and preventive framework for conduct of business supervision, EIOPA-16/015, 11 January 2016, 10 p. See also Art. 25 IDD, Commission Delegated Regulation (EU) 2017/2358 of 21 September 2017 supplementing the IDD with regard to product oversight and governance requirements for insurance undertakings and insurance distributors, *OJ* L 341, 20.12.2017, p. 1, and Commission Delegated Regulation (EU) 2017/2359 of 21 September 2017 supplementing the IDD with regard to information requirements and conduct of business rules applicable to the distribution of insurance-based investment products, *OJ* L 341, 20.12.2017, p. 8.

131 EIOPA, Final report on guidelines on system of governance, EIOPA-BoS-14/253, 28 January 2015, p. 66.

(b) actions to be taken by the (re)insurance undertaking to assess which types of risk-mitigation techniques are appropriate in terms of the nature of the risks assumed and the capabilities of the undertaking to manage and control the risks associated with those techniques;
(c) the (re)insurance undertakings' own assessment of the credit risk of the risk-mitigation techniques.

In its risk management policy, the undertaking should cover at least the following with regard to reinsurance and other risk-mitigation techniques:[132]

(a) identification of the level of risk transfer appropriate to the undertaking's defined risk-tolerance limits and which kind of reinsurance arrangements are most appropriate considering the undertaking's risk profile;
(b) principles for selection of such risk-mitigation counterparties and procedures for assessing and monitoring the creditworthiness and diversification of reinsurance counterparties;
(c) procedures for assessing the effective risk transfer and consideration of basis risk;
(d) liquidity management procedures to deal with any timing mismatch between claim payments and reinsurance recoverables.

3.4.1.8. Loans and/or Mortgage (Re)insurance

Mortgage insurance is defined in Art. 1 (47) DA as credit insurance that provides cover to lenders in the event that their mortgage loans default. In their search for yield in a low-interest rate environment, providing loans may be an attractive alternative for (re)insurance undertakings. The problem is that (re)insurance undertakings may not have the same expertise concerning credit risk as their banking colleagues. Loans can be granted to business entities as well as to private individuals (for instance mortgages), and may be collateralised (by a financial security or by an insurance policy) or uncollateralised. Although there has been a slight increase in lending, the latest statistics published by EIOPA show that the total amount of investment in loans and mortgages by the (re)insurance industry in the EEA is only 0.4% of total investments.[133]

---

132 EIOPA, Guidelines on system of governance, EIOPA-BoS-14/253, 14 September 2015, Guideline 22.

133 EIOPA, *European Insurance Overview 2018. Solo Undertakings. Year-end 2017*, Publications Office of the EU, Luxembourg, 2018, p. 26.

In its written policy on loans and mortgages, the (re)insurance undertaking must ensure the following (Art. 261 (1) DA):

(a) that credit-granting is based on sound and well-defined criteria and that the process for approving, amending, renewing and refinancing credits is clearly established;
(b) that the undertaking has an internal methodology that enables it to assess the credit risk of exposures to individual obligors and at the portfolio level;
(c) that the ongoing administration and monitoring of the loan portfolio, including for identifying and managing problematic credits, and for making adequate value adjustments, is operated through an effective system;
(d) that the diversification of the loan portfolio is adequate given the target markets and overall investment strategy of the undertaking.

Where a (re)insurance undertaking engages in mortgage (re)insurance, it must base its underwriting on sound and well-defined criteria and comply with the requirements set out in points (b), (c) and (d) above with regard to the mortgage loans underlying its (re)insurance obligations (Art. 261 (2) DA).

3.4.1.9. Qualifying Infrastructure Investments or Qualifying Infrastructure Corporate Investments

The DA was amended in 2015 in order to provide specific capital requirements for qualifying infrastructure investments. Such investments may benefit from a lower capital charge in the case of equity investments and exposures in the form of loans and bonds (see above, Chapter 6, section 4.2.2.2.4). The DA was amended again in 2017 to extend the regime to qualifying infrastructure corporate investments (see above, Chapter 6, section 4.2.2.2.4).

In both cases, it is important that a (re)insurance undertaking which invests in infrastructure applies proper risk management techniques. In order to prevent it from underestimating the risk of the project,[134] the undertaking must conduct adequate due diligence prior to making a qualifying infrastructure investment or a qualifying infrastructure corporate investment (Art. 261a (1) DA). This due diligence must include:

(a) a documented assessment of how the infrastructure entity satisfies the criteria set out in Arts. 164a DA (qualifying infrastructure investment)

134 Many infrastructure projects are based upon a public/private partnership agreement. The political risk must be assessed.

or 164b DA (qualifying infrastructure corporate investment). This assessment must be subject to a validation process, carried out by persons who are free from influence from those responsible for the assessment of the criteria, and have no potential conflicts of interest with those persons;

(b) a confirmation that any financial model for the cash flows of the infrastructure entity has been subject to a validation process carried out by persons who are free from influence from those responsible for the development of the financial model, and have no potential conflicts of interest with those persons.

A (re)insurance undertaking with a qualifying infrastructure investment or a qualifying infrastructure corporate investment must regularly monitor and perform stress tests on the cash flows and collateral values supporting the infrastructure entity. These stress tests must be commensurate with the nature, scale and complexity of the risk inherent in the infrastructure project. The stress testing must consider risks arising from non-infrastructure activities, but the revenues generated by such activities may not be taken into account when determining whether the infrastructure entity is able to meet its financial obligations (Art. 261a (2) and (3) DA).

When the qualifying infrastructure investment or qualifying infrastructure corporate investment is material, the undertaking must include in its risk management policy provisions on active monitoring of these investments during the construction phase, and on maximising the amount covered from these investments in case of a work-out scenario (Art. 261a (4) DA).

If the qualifying infrastructure investment or the qualifying infrastructure corporate investment is in the form of bonds or loans, the undertaking must set up its asset–liability risk management in such a manner as to ensure that, on an ongoing basis, the undertaking is able to hold the investment to maturity (Art. 261a (5) DA).

3.4.1.10. Deferred Taxes

The LAC-DT has a significant impact on the solvency position of (re)insurance undertakings.[135] The risk management policy must therefore also include a policy related to deferred taxes, identifying the methods and assumptions for determining the amount and recoverability of the LAC-DT.

As (re)insurance undertakings can only ascribe a positive value to deferred taxes where it is probable that future taxable profit will be available against which the deferred tax asset can be utilised (Art. 15 (3) DA), the risk management policy must include an assessment of the underlying assumptions applied for

135 See above, Chapter 6, section 4.2.2.4.

the projection of future taxable profit and an explanation of any concerns about those assumptions.

The policy on deferred taxes must describe the involvement of the relevant key functions in the selection and assessment of methods and assumptions to demonstrate the amount and recoverability of the LAC-DT and how the outcome of that assessment is reported to the AMSB. The assessment must include an evaluation of the underlying assumptions applied for the projection of future taxable profit for the purposes of Articles 15 and 207 DA. Any concerns about these assumptions, which are carried out by either the actuarial function or the risk management function, must be explained (Art. 260 (1) (h) (ii) DA).

The policy must also look into the risks that the undertaking is or could be exposed to as a result of potential future changes in its risk profile due to its business strategy or the economic and financial environment (Art. 260 (1) (h) (iii) DA).[136]

3.4.2. *Own Risk and Solvency Assessment*

The own risk and solvency assessment (ORSA), introduced by Solvency II,[137] has become a key element of enterprise risk management in (re)insurance undertakings. The objective of the ORSA is to further good risk and capital management and to prevent undertakings from relying too much on the predefined capital requirements following from the standard formula or the internal model. The SCR, whether calculated on the basis of the standard formula or an internal model, is a regulatory requirement. It defines the level of capital which (re)insurance undertakings must hold for the protection of policyholders. However, from the perspective of the undertaking's overall risk management, it is important for the undertaking to regularly assess its own risk profile, independently of the assumptions underlying the calculation of the SCR, to compare that with available capital, to see to what extent there are divergences between the undertaking's own risk profile and the assumptions underlying the SCR and to decide on appropriate measures to be taken from a risk or capital perspective.

---

136 This point was added as a result of the 2018 review of the DA. See also EIOPA, Second set of advice to the EC on specific items in the Solvency II Delegated Regulation, EIOPA-BoS-18/075, 28 February 2018, pp. 304–340.

137 The ORSA was initially called IRCA (internal risk capital assessment) and was inspired by the internal capital adequacy assessment process (ICAAP) that had been introduced in the banking sector (initially Art. 123 CRD, now Art. 75 CRD) as part of the Basel II approach. It was however adapted to the Solvency II approach which is more sophisticated as it includes a scenario-based analysis of risk. There was also influence from the individual capital adequacy standard (ICAS) regime in the UK, which was developed as a Pillar 2 mechanism. See HUMPHRY, D., Solvency II in the UK: evolution rather than revolution, in MARANO, P. and SIRI, M. (Eds.), *Insurance Regulation in the European Union: Solvency II and beyond*, Palgrave Macmillan, Cham, 2017, p. 115. The IRCA became ORCA before it was then called ORSA.

There are two main reasons why there could be divergences between regulatory solvency capital and the result of the undertaking's own internal risk and solvency assessment:

- the undertaking may wish to hold additional capital for business purposes over and above the regulatory capital. For instance, it may choose to hold capital for rating purposes that represents a higher confidence level than that used to calibrate the SCR;
- the undertaking's risk profile may differ from the one implicit in the SCR. For instance, the insurer's assessment of the capital needed to back a particular risk might be different from the assessment in the standard formula, or the insurer's risk profile might include risks not covered by the SCR.[138]

The ORSA is an exercise that must be carried out by each (re)insurance undertaking. In order to ensure that this exercise is an "own assessment", the principles in Art. 45 FD are not expanded on further in implementing measures. This is intentional. The co-legislators did not want to prescribe a specific format for the ORSA report. It is for each undertaking to decide how to perform the ORSA, how to structure the ORSA report and how long the report should be, taking account of the nature, the scale and the complexity of the risks inherent in the business of the undertaking.[139]

The ORSA follows a similar approach to that adopted in the banking sector[140] and is also a requirement under ICP 16 – Enterprise Risk Management for Solvency Purposes. It was first introduced before the application date of Solvency II by EIOPA, by way of preparatory guidelines, in order to help (re)insurance undertakings prepare for Solvency II by adopting a forward-looking approach in their risk management.[141] Guidance on how to develop the ORSA can be found in the EIOPA Guidelines on own risk and solvency

---

[138] An example is NTNI (non-traditional, non-insurance business), i.e. the lending of securities such as stocks or derivatives to other institutions, outside the authorised insurance entities. This might expose the insurer to liquidity risk, and may potentially have systemic consequences. See, SWAIN, R. and SWALLOW, D., The prudential regulation of insurers under Solvency II, *Bank of England Quarterly Bulletin*, 2015, Q 2, p. 147.

[139] The ORSA can be considered as a reflection of the DNA of the undertaking. See BERNARDINO, G., *Implementation of Solvency II: The dos and the don'ts*, International Conference, Ljubljana, 2 September 2015, p. 6 (https://eiopa.europa.eu/Publications/Speeches%20and%20presentations/2015-09-02%20Solvency%20II%20Conference%20Slovenia.pdf).

[140] See Art. 73 CRD: Internal capital adequacy assessment process (ICAAP).

[141] EIOPA, Guidelines on forward looking assessment of own risks (based on the ORSA principles), EIOPA-CP-13/09, 2013, 12 p. The reference to FLAOR was necessary because at the time of adoption of the guidelines, there were no regulatory capital requirements as Solvency II did not yet apply. Although EIOPA did not have specific authorisation to develop guidelines in this area, it did so based on Art. 16 (1) EIOPA Regulation in order to ensure consistency in the application of EU law, although Solvency II was not yet applicable.

assessment[142] and in EIOPA's report on first experiences with the ORSA.[143] Because the ORSA is an "own assessment", supervisory authorities should refrain from defining the content of the ORSA report.

3.4.2.1. Objectives and Characteristics

The ultimate objective of the ORSA is to ensure that a (re)insurance undertaking does not engage in business for which it does not have the necessary amount of capital. The ORSA should allow the undertaking to assess the quality and quantity of financial resources available to it, relative to its solvency needs.

The ORSA should help senior management, key staff, the AMSB and supervisory authorities to:

- understand the current and projected risk profile of the undertaking and its key risk drivers;
- understand the adequacy of capital available to support the undertaking's business plan;
- understand any material changes to the risk profile;
- understand risks not covered by regulatory capital;
- understand key drivers of the balance sheet;
- identify potential management actions to mitigate risk.

The ORSA should be a continuous process to ensure that risk and solvency are key factors in the undertaking's decision-making. It should be a key component of the undertaking's risk management culture and it should be a project that is supported by all key stakeholders, based on a clear plan and a clear allocation of responsibilities. It should be a key element of the regular dialogue that must take place under Solvency II between the supervisory authority and key decision-makers in the undertaking (key function holders and members of the AMSB). The AMSB must take an active part in the ORSA, including steering how the assessment is to be performed and challenging the results. Although it may be conducted by the CRO, other key function holders and key staff members should be actively involved in the exercise.

The ORSA *should not* become a compliance-reporting exercise (there should be no box-ticking). It should not be performed solely for the benefit of the supervisory authority. It should not be seen or used as a new capital requirement and it should not replace regulatory capital requirements.

---

142 EIOPA, Guidelines on own risk and solvency assessment, EIOPA-BoS-14/259, 14 September 2015, 8 p.

143 EIOPA, EIOPA's Supervisory Assessment of the Own Risk and Solvency Assessment – First experiences, EIOPA-BoS/17-097, 19 June 2017, 8 p.

3.4.2.2. Regulatory Requirements

The regulatory requirements for the ORSA are included in Art. 45 FD, Art. 262 DA and the EIOPA Guidelines on the own risk and solvency assessment:

- the ORSA is part of the undertaking's risk management system;
- the ORSA forms an integral part of the business strategy and must be taken into account on an ongoing basis in the strategic decisions of the undertaking;
- the way in which the ORSA is carried out in practice must be communicated to the supervisory authority as part of the RSR (Art. 308 (4) DA);
- the ORSA does not require the development of an internal model, nor should it serve to calculate a capital requirement.

The assessment must include at least the following:
- the overall solvency needs, taking into account the specific risk profile, approved risk-tolerance limits and the business strategy of the undertaking;
- the compliance, on a continuous basis, with the capital requirements (SCR and MCR) and with the requirements regarding technical provisions;
- the significance with which the risk profile of the undertaking deviates from the assumptions underlying the SCR calculated on the basis of the standard formula or on the basis of a partial or full internal model.

The ORSA must be an integral part of the business strategy and must be taken into account on an ongoing basis in the undertaking's strategic decisions. The results of the ORSA and the insights gained in the process should be taken into account in capital management, business planning and product development and design.[144]

The ORSA must be performed at least annually and whenever there is a significant change in the risk profile of the undertaking (Art. 45 (5) FD).

3.4.2.2.1. Assessment of the Overall Solvency Needs

The assessment of the overall solvency needs (the relationship between risk and capital) must be forward-looking[145] and based upon processes which are proportionate to the nature, scale and complexity of the risks inherent in the

[144] EIOPA, Guidelines on own risk and solvency assessment, EIOPA-BoS-14/259, 14 September 2015, Guideline 13. See also Art. 25 of Directive (EU) 2016/97 of the EP and of the Council of 20 January 2016 on insurance distribution, *OJ* L 26, 2.2.2016, p. 19 and Commission Delegated Regulation (EU) 2017/2358 of 21 September 2017, supplementing Directive (EU) 2016/97 of the EP and of the Council with regard to product oversight and governance requirements for insurance undertakings and insurance distributors, *OJ* L 341, 20.12.2017, p. 1.

[145] For instance, new business plans, new product development or pricing.

insurer's business and which enable the undertaking to properly identify and assess the risks it faces in the short and long term and to which it is or could be exposed. The undertaking must be able to demonstrate the methods used in the assessment (Art. 45 (2) FD).

In terms of *risk*, the assessment should cover the risks the undertaking is or could be exposed to,[146] taking into account potential future changes in the risk profile due to the undertaking's business strategy or the economic and financial environment, including operational risks, as well as the correlation between risks (Art. 262 (1) (a) DA). The assessment should also look into possible ways and means to mitigate risk, for instance through reinsurance or reduction of risk. Account must be taken of the undertaking's approved risk-tolerance limits and business strategy.

Where appropriate, the undertaking should subject the identified material risks to a sufficiently wide range of stress tests or scenario analyses in order to provide an adequate basis for the assessment of the overall solvency needs.[147] The stress tests applied should reflect the risk profile of the undertaking, taking into account its risk appetite. The stress tests should also consider the possibility of several major events happening at the same time, as well as realistic possible future management actions.[148]

In terms of *capital*, the assessment should examine whether the nature and quality of own fund items or other resources are appropriate to cover the risks that have been identified (Art. 262 (1) (b) DA).

In the assessment, account must be taken of the time periods that are relevant for capturing the risks the undertaking faces in the long term, the bases for valuation and recognition that are appropriate for the undertaking's business and risk profile, and the undertaking's internal control and risk management systems and approved risk-tolerance limits (Art. 262 (2) DA).

3.4.2.2.2. Continuous Compliance with Regulatory Capital Requirements and Technical Provisions

In its assessment of whether the undertaking complies with the Solvency II regulatory capital requirements on a continuous basis,[149] the undertaking must include at least:

(a) the potential future material changes in its risk profile;

---

146 For instance, Brexit or a country leaving the Eurozone.

147 EIOPA, Guidelines on own risk and solvency assessment, EIOPA-BoS-14/259, 14 September 2015, Guideline 7.

148 EIOPA, Supervisory Assessment of the Own Risk and Solvency Assessment – First experiences, EIOPA-BoS/17-097, 19 June 2017, p. 6.

149 As indicated before in Chapter 6, section 4.2.1, continuous compliance with the capital requirements does not mean that the SCR must always be 100% on a permanent basis.

(b) the quantity and quality of its own funds over the whole of its business planning period;
(c) the composition of own funds across tiers and how this composition may change as a result of redemption, repayment and maturity dates during its business planning period.[150]

For the assessment of continuous compliance with technical provisions, the undertaking must ask the actuarial function to:

(a) provide input as to whether the undertaking could comply continuously with the requirements regarding the calculation of technical provisions;[151]
(b) identify potential risks arising from the uncertainties connected to this calculation.[152]

Where the undertaking applies the MA (Art. 77b FD), the VA (Art. 77d FD) or the transitional measures on the risk free interest rate (Art. 308c FD) or on technical provisions (Art. 308d FD), the assessment of compliance must be performed both with and without taking into account these adjustments and transitional measures (Art. 45 (2a) FD).

3.4.2.2.3. Significant Deviations from the Assumptions Underlying the SCR Calculation

The undertaking must assess whether its risk profile deviates from the assumptions underlying the SCR calculation and whether these deviations are significant.[153] This could, for instance, be the case for risks not included in the standard formula or risks that are over- or underestimated by the standard formula compared to the undertaking's own risk profile. The undertaking may, as a first step, perform a qualitative analysis, and if that indicates that the deviation

150 EIOPA, Guidelines on own risk and solvency assessment, EIOPA-BoS-14/259, 14 September 2015, Guideline 10.

151 Undertakings should, for instance, prepare for the scenario that on the withdrawal date the UK becomes a third country and leaves the internal market.

152 EIOPA, Guidelines on own risk and solvency assessment, EIOPA-BoS-14/259, 14 September 2015, Guideline 11.

153 This could, for instance, be the case if the undertaking is carrying out material non-life long-term cross-border business (such as construction defects insurance in France or medical malpractice in Italy) without sufficient knowledge of the local market specificities. See EIOPA, Opinion on non-life cross-border insurance business of a long-term nature and its supervision, EIOPA-BoS-18/527, 21 December 2018, p. 6.

is not significant, a quantitative assessment is not required.[154] In the case of a significant deviation, the undertaking may decide to align its risk profile with the standard formula, to use USPs, to develop a partial or internal model, or to de-risk.

When an internal model is used, the assessment must be performed together with the recalibration that transforms the internal risk numbers into the SCR risk measure and calibration (Art. 45 (3) FD).

3.4.2.3. Some Lessons Learned

In general, (re)insurance undertakings find the ORSA a very useful exercise. It has become an important tool in risk management, particularly when there is the right tone from the top and when the ORSA is a collaborative exercise involving all key function holders.

Discussions with (re)insurance undertakings show the following:

- the AMSB is often not sufficiently aware of its capital management responsibility;
- the process of developing the appropriate "language" in the AMSB takes time;
- a cultural change is often needed, both at the level of the AMSB and within the undertaking;
- a good ORSA process should lead to discussions and improved understanding of the undertaking's future risks in a language that is appropriate and matches the background of the AMSB members;
- the skills needed for an ORSA, i.e. achieving a complete and holistic risk picture, are such that the ORSA should not be outsourced (although doing so is legally possible);
- the first run of an ORSA process is never perfect;
- there is no mechanical way to conduct an ORSA;
- carrying out a good ORSA is not a question of getting experts talking to the AMSB or of asking AMSB members to read a stack of highly technical documents;
- it might be useful to link the ORSA to the capital management plan and to analyse what remedies should be taken if the solvency ratio drops below a certain level;
- the ORSA report is not necessarily voluminous: 40–60 pages for medium-sized undertakings should be enough;
- a very helpful process is to apply a stress scenario and to evaluate what is needed, in terms of capital or other measures, to withstand the stress.

---

154 EIOPA, Guidelines on own risk and solvency assessment, EIOPA-BoS-14/259, 14 September 2015, Guideline 12.

EIOPA has identified a number of areas for improvement:[155]

- small undertakings should further develop the ORSA process, including their ORSA policy and the quality of data used in the assessments;
- the members of the AMSB should play a more active role in the ORSA and should use the ORSA results in their strategic decision-making process to enhance the overall risk management of the undertaking;
- undertakings should widen the scope of their risk assessment and deepen their risk analysis;
- too much reliance on the standard formula prevents undertakings from performing an assessment of their specific risk profile;
- the quality of stress testing, including reverse stress testing, and scenarios used in the ORSA assessments can be further improved. This is probably the greatest weakness in many ORSA assessments. Stress testing based on realistic scenarios is an excellent risk management tool and can help to redefine the limits of risk tolerance.

3.4.2.4. ORSA and Supervision

The SRP must dedicate sufficient attention to assessing the ability of (re)insurance undertakings to identify, measure, monitor and report all material risks the undertaking could be exposed to on a continuous basis.

The ORSA process must give supervisory authorities confidence that the AMSB thoroughly understands the business it is running, that it is aware of which events could trigger a potential problem, and that the undertaking can afford its strategic plan three to five years ahead, even if it comes under pressure.

The ORSA process is there to identify major issues affecting the undertaking's overall solvency needs. If the supervisory authority discovers issues that should have been identified in the ORSA, it should not just take the appropriate supervisory action, but should also examine the reason why the issues were not identified by the undertaking. Non-identification of issues may prove to be of just as much concern as the issues themselves.

3.5. INTERNAL CONTROL AND COMPLIANCE FUNCTION

(Re)insurance undertakings must have in place an effective system of internal control. A system of internal control provides reasonable assurance from a control perspective to the AMSB and senior management that the undertaking is being run consistently with the strategy and risk appetite set by the AMSB,

155 EIOPA, Supervisory Assessment of the Own Risk and Solvency Assessment – First experiences, EIOPA-BoS/17-097, 19 June 2017, p. 2.

with the agreed business objectives, policies and processes, and in compliance with applicable laws and regulations. The system must at least include administrative and accounting procedures, an internal control framework, appropriate reporting arrangements at all levels of the undertaking and a compliance function (Art. 46 (1) FD). Information on the internal control system and on the undertaking's compliance policy must be provided in the RSR submitted to the supervisory authority (Art. 308 (5) DA).

The internal control system must ensure that (re)insurance undertakings comply with applicable laws, regulations and administrative provisions (compliance). It must also ensure the effectiveness and the efficiency of the undertaking's operations in light of its objectives, as well as the availability and reliability of financial and non-financial information.

As stated in ICP 8 – Risk Management and Internal Control (para. 8.2.4), an effective system of internal control will typically include the following, taking account of the nature, scale and complexity of the undertaking:[156]

Segregation of duties and prevention of conflicts of interest (control environment)

- appropriate segregation of duties and controls to ensure such segregation is observed. This includes, amongst others, having sufficient distance between those accountable for a process or policy and those who check if for such a process or policy an appropriate control exists and is being applied. It also includes appropriate distance between those who design a control or operate a control and those who check if such a control is effective in design and operation;
- up-to-date policies regarding who can sign for or commit the undertaking, and for what amounts, with corresponding controls, such as the practice that key decisions should be taken at least by two persons and the practice of double or multiple signatures. Such policies and controls should be designed, among other things, to prevent any major transaction being entered into without appropriate governance review or by anyone lacking the necessary authority and to ensure that borrowing, trading, risk and other such limits are strictly observed. Such policies should foresee a role for control functions, for example by requiring for major matters the review and sign-off by the risk management function and/or approval by the AMSB or a committee within the AMSB.

Policies and processes (internal control activities)

- appropriate controls for all key business processes and policies, including for major business decisions and transactions (including intra-group transactions),

[156] See also, EIOPA, Guidelines on system of governance, EIOPA-BoS-14/253, 14 September 2015, Guideline 38. Both ICP 8 and Guideline 38 are inspired by the Integrated Framework for Internal Control, developed by the Committee of Sponsoring Organizations of the Treadway Commission. See, COSO, *Internal Control – Integrated Framework, Executive Summary*, May 2013, 10 p. (https://na.theiia.org/standards-guidance/topics/documents/executive_summary.pdf).

critical IT functionalities, access to critical IT infrastructure by employees and related third parties, and important legal and regulatory obligations;
- policies on training in respect of controls, particularly for employees in positions of high trust or responsibility or involved in high risk activities;
- a centralised documented inventory of insurer-wide key processes and policies and of the controls in place in respect of such processes and policies, that also may introduce a hierarchy among the policies.

Information and communication

- appropriate controls to provide reasonable assurance over the accuracy and completeness of the undertaking's books, records, and accounts and over financial consolidation and reporting, including the reporting made to the supervisory authority;
- adequate and comprehensive internal financial, operational and compliance data, as well as external market information about events and conditions that are relevant to decision-making. Information should be reliable, timely, accessible, and provided in a consistent format;
- information processes that cover all significant activities of the undertaking, including contingency arrangements;
- effective channels of communication to ensure that all staff fully understand and adhere to the internal controls and their duties and responsibilities and that other relevant information is reaching the appropriate personnel;
- policies regarding escalation procedures.

Monitoring and review

- processes for regularly checking that the totality of all controls forms a coherent system and that this system works as intended and fits properly within the overall corporate governance structure of the undertaking; and provides an element of risk control to complement the risk identification, risk assessment, and risk management activities of the undertaking. As part of such review, individual controls are monitored and analysed periodically to determine gaps and improvement opportunities with senior management taking such measures as are necessary to address these;
- periodic testing and assessments (carried out by objective parties such as an internal or external auditor) to determine the adequacy, completeness and effectiveness of the internal controls system and its utility to the AMSB and senior management for controlling the operations of the undertaking.

The undertaking must establish monitoring and reporting mechanisms within the internal control system that provide the AMSB with relevant information for the decision-making process.[157]

---

157 EIOPA, Guidelines on system of governance, EIOPA-BoS-14/253, 14 September 2015, Guideline 39.

The undertaking must have effective systems and controls to ensure that valuation estimates of its assets and liabilities are reliable and appropriate to ensure compliance with Art. 75 FD (valuation on a market-consistent basis) and must have a process for regularly verifying that market prices or valuation model inputs are appropriate and reliable. The undertaking must establish, implement, maintain and document clearly defined policies and procedures for the process of valuation, including the description and definition of roles and responsibilities of the personnel involved with the valuation, the relevant models and the sources of information to be used.

At the request of the supervisory authority, an external, independent valuation or verification of the value of material assets and liabilities may be required (Art. 267 (3) DA).

Sufficient resources must be provided, both in terms of quality and quantity, to develop, calibrate, approve and review valuation approaches used for solvency purposes. The internal control system must provide for an independent review and verification on a regular basis of the information, data and assumptions that are used in valuing assets and liabilities in the solvency balance sheet, the results of this valuation, and the suitability of using alternative methods of valuation (Art. 263 DA). The internal processes for approval of these valuations and for an external, independent valuation or verification of the value of material assets or liabilities should be subject to oversight by the persons who effectively runs the undertaking (Art. 267 (4) DA).[158]

The FD describes the compliance function as part of the system of internal control. The compliance function includes[159] advising the AMSB on compliance with the laws, regulations and administrative provisions adopted pursuant to the FD. It also includes an assessment of the possible impact of any changes in the legal environment on the operations of the undertaking and the identification and assessment of compliance risk (Art. 46 (2) FD).

The compliance function must establish a compliance policy and a compliance plan. The compliance policy must define the responsibilities, competencies and reporting duties of the compliance function. The compliance plan must set out the planned activities of the compliance function, taking into account all relevant activities of the undertaking and its exposure to compliance risk. The compliance function must also assess the adequacy of measures adopted by the undertaking to prevent non-compliance (Art. 270 DA).

---

158 When the person in charge of the internal control and compliance function is a member of the AMSB, the oversight over the internal control and compliance function must be carried out by the non-executive board members.

159 The compliance function holder is also responsible for monitoring compliance with other legal requirements applicable to insurance undertakings than those following directly from the Solvency II regulatory framework. See DREHER, M., *Treatises on Solvency II*, Springer, Berlin/Heidelberg, 2015, p. 323. For a good description of the compliance function, see the Ageas Group SFCR 2017, pp. 33–34.

The compliance function has a broader role than merely monitoring compliance with laws and regulations and supervisory requirements adopted pursuant to the FD. Monitoring compliance with internal policies and promoting and sustaining a compliance culture within the undertaking are equally important aspects of this control function. Compliance starts at the top. The AMSB is ultimately responsible for establishing standards for honesty and integrity throughout the undertaking and for creating an effective corporate culture that emphasises them. This may include a code of conduct or other appropriate mechanism as evidence of the undertaking's commitment to complying with all applicable laws, regulations, supervisory requirements and internal policies, and to conducting its business ethically and responsibly.[160]

Because of the complex and ever-changing legal environment, the compliance function has become very important. Some (re)insurance undertakings, particularly larger or more complex ones, will have a compliance department led by a chief compliance officer. The person responsible for the compliance function is often a lawyer and the function is sometimes part of the legal affairs department. If the compliance function holder is at the same time the legal director of the undertaking, measures must be taken to avoid conflicts of interest.[161] As Solvency II puts the compliance function within the system of internal control, it may well be better to look at the compliance function as broader than just a watchdog and to bring it closer to the risk management function, requiring the person in charge to also have some risk management and insurance experience.[162]

3.6. INTERNAL AUDIT FUNCTION

3.6.1. Independence of the Internal Audit Function

As a general principle, the internal audit function cannot be performed by the same person or persons who perform any of the other key governance functions, because this could give rise to conflicts of interest since the other key functions are subject to the scrutiny of the internal audit function.[163] This general principle is also recognised under Solvency II, although it is only included in a recital (recital 32) to the FD, which recognises the possibility for an undertaking to

---

160 IAIS, ICP 8 – Risk Management and Internal Controls, paras. 8.5.1 and 8.5.2.

161 See EIOPA, *Peer review of key functions: supervisory practices and application in assessing key functions*, Publications Office of the EU, Luxembourg, 2018, p. 7.

162 In practice, the compliance function is often combined with the risk management function. See EIOPA, *Peer review of key functions: supervisory practices and application in assessing key functions. Executive summary*, Publications Office of the EU, Luxembourg, 2018, p. 6.

163 Art. 271 (1) DA and EIOPA, Final report on the Guidelines on system of governance, EIOPA-BoS-14/253, 28 January 2015, p. 83.

combine all key governance functions, except for the internal audit function. Strong pressures arose, however, during the negotiations on the DA to provide for an exception to this principle, in line with the application of the proportionality principle.[164]

The compromise is laid down in Art. 271 (2) DA. The person carrying out the internal audit function may also carry out other key functions, where:

(a) this is appropriate with respect to the nature, scale and complexity of the risks inherent in the undertaking's business (proportionality principle);
(b) no conflict of interest arises for the person carrying out the internal audit function (general principle);
(c) maintaining a person for the internal audit function that does not carry out other key functions would impose costs on the undertaking that would be disproportionate to the total administrative expenses.

Although the internal audit function can thus be combined with another key governance function under the conditions stated above, it can never be combined with any operational function, such as the role of chief executive officer or chief financial officer.[165] The internal audit function must indeed remain operationally independent and free from influence from the operational functions. A combination with another key function would not be acceptable if such combination could compromise the internal audit function's ability to undertake its duties in an objective, fair and independent manner. In those exceptional cases where combining other key functions with the internal audit function is allowed, the undertaking needs to be able to demonstrate to the supervisory authority, on request, that conflicts of interest are properly dealt with and that no concerns remain that the objectivity and independence of the internal audit function is compromised.[166]

The performance of the internal audit function by the same person or persons who perform the compliance, risk management or actuarial function is only possible where the undertaking has a risk profile that does not involve large or complex risks, i.e. where the undertaking only writes standard lines of business on a limited scale and where the undertaking is not engaged in the sale of complex investment products.[167] The undertaking must explain in its RSR

---

164 A combination of the internal audit function with any other internal control function is not possible in the banking sector. See EBA, Final report on Guidelines on internal governance under Directive 2013/36/EU, EBA/GL/2017/11, 26 September 2017, p. 47.

165 Art. 47 (2) FD. See also EIOPA, *Peer review of key functions: supervisory practices and application in assessing key functions*, Publications Office of the EU, Luxembourg, 2018, p. 7.

166 EIOPA, Final report on the Guidelines on system of governance, EIOPA-BoS-14/253, 28 January 2015, p. 83.

167 EIOPA, Final report on the Guidelines on system of governance, EIOPA-BoS-14/253, 28 January 2015, p. 83.

submitted to the supervisory authority how it can justify the combination of the internal audit function with other key governance functions (Art. 308 (6) DA).

3.6.2. *Tasks of the Internal Audit Function*

The internal audit function must examine and evaluate the functioning, effectiveness and efficiency of the internal control system and all other elements of the system of governance. Any findings and recommendations must be reported to the AMSB, which must determine what actions are to be taken with respect to each of the internal audit findings and recommendations and must ensure that those actions are carried out (Art. 47 (1) and (2) FD).

In its report to the AMSB, the internal audit function must include the envisaged period of time needed to remedy any shortcomings identified, as well as information on whether previous audit recommendations have been successfully carried out.[168] The final decision as to which recommendations to implement and who is responsible rests with the AMSB.

More particularly, the internal audit function has the following tasks (Art. 271 (3), first subparagraph DA):[169]

(a) to establish, implement and maintain an audit plan setting out the audit work to be undertaken in the upcoming years, taking into account all activities and the complete system of governance of the undertaking;
(b) to take a risk-based approach in deciding its priorities;
(c) to report the audit plan to the AMSB;
(d) to issue recommendations based on the result of work carried out and submit a written report on its findings and recommendations to the AMSB on at least an annual basis;
(e) to verify compliance with the decisions taken by the AMSB on the basis of those recommendations.

The internal audit plan should cover all significant activities that are to be reviewed in a reasonable period of time. It should be a relatively flexible tool that needs to be adapted and completed according to the findings.[170] Where necessary, the internal audit function may carry out audits that are not included in the audit plan (Art. 271 (3), second subparagraph DA).

The work of the internal audit function must be documented, allowing for an assessment of the effectiveness of the work for retracing the audits undertaken

---

168 EIOPA, Guidelines on system of governance, EIOPA-BoS-14/253, 14 September 2015, Guideline 45.

169 See also IAIS, ICP 8 – Risk Management and Internal Controls, para. 8.7.

170 EIOPA, Guidelines on system of governance, EIOPA-BoS-14/253, 14 September 2015, Guideline 43.

and the findings they produced.[171] Information on how the internal audit function is operating in practice must be communicated to the supervisory authority in the RSR (Art. 308 (6) DA).

3.7. ACTUARIAL FUNCTION

The importance of a quantitative analysis of risks and probabilities was not always recognised under Solvency I, particularly not for non-life insurance. It can therefore be said that Solvency II put the actuarial profession on the map for both life and non-life insurance. The actuarial profession played an important role in the development of Solvency II, not only through professional organisations, but also through the presence of many actuaries working for supervisory authorities in the CEIOPS Working Party that developed advice (particularly on the standard formula) for the EC. This might explain why the standard formula for the SCR is very much impregnated with actuarial approaches and perhaps rather less with an economic view of the insurance business.

Solvency II introduces the actuarial function as a key control function of any (re)insurance undertaking. The importance of this function is repeated in many EIOPA Guidelines, which show that EIOPA clearly sees this function as being critical.[172] This is in line with Art. 48 (1) FD, which refers to it as "an effective actuarial function". In order to be effective, the person occupying this function must be independent of pressures from management. This needs to be ensured by the way in which the job is organised in practice: direct reporting to top management and to the AMSB, and an independence clause in the employment contract, which the employer is required to respect.

The function must be carried out by a person who has knowledge of actuarial and financial mathematics, commensurate with the nature, scale and complexity of the risks inherent in the business of the (re)insurance undertaking, and who is able to demonstrate his or her relevant experience with applicable professional and other standards (Art. 48 (2) FD). Solvency II does not introduce a monopoly for actuaries, i.e. members of a professional actuarial association. This was done on purpose, as the recognition of a professional qualification would have necessitated the development of common rules on access to the profession, training, supervision and public oversight. The reference to

171 EIOPA, Guidelines on system of governance, EIOPA-BoS-14/253, 14 September 2015, Guideline 44.

172 See, for instance, the EIOPA Guidelines on the valuation of technical provisions, which state in para. 1.5 that the guidelines will be ultimately applied by actuaries and by other professionals who may be appointed to carry out the tasks of the actuarial function. Other Guidelines also contain multiple references to the actuarial function.

"applicable professional and other standards" is a clear recognition of the existence of professional actuarial associations and of the standards developed by them. A person who has obtained an actuarial qualification will therefore in principle meet the conditions for carrying out the actuarial function.

It is not uncommon to combine the actuarial function with the risk management function. There must be a proper justification for doing so if the undertaking cannot invoke the proportionality principle. The actuarial function holder plays a key role in each (re)insurance undertaking as the person who controls the liabilities side of the balance sheet. Sometimes the actuarial function is split between life and non-life business. This organisational solution should not interfere with the responsibility of the actuarial function as such.[173]

In a number of Member States (for instance, Austria and Germany), insurance undertakings are required to nominate a "responsible actuary" whose role consists in protecting policyholders. The "responsible actuary" must see to it that all policyholders are treated equally and fairly and that the insurance undertaking can at all times meet the obligations resulting from insurance contracts. The "responsible actuary" may or may not be the same person as the person in charge of the actuarial function. Solvency II does not recognise or require the existence of a "responsible actuary".[174]

The continued existence of a "responsible actuary" in addition to the actuarial function is confusing and could lead to conflicts of interest. The "responsible actuary" is required to produce a report, and it is not impossible that the "responsible actuary" would in his or her report come to different conclusions from those contained in the report produced by the actuarial function holder.[175] The situation is even worse if both tasks are merged under the presumption that there are no conflicts of interest. In that case, the same person occupying both functions would be required to produce two different reports. It is highly questionable whether this old practice serves any useful purpose under Solvency II, which specifically recognises the actuarial function as an independent

---

173 See EIOPA, *Peer review of key functions: supervisory practices and application in assessing key functions. Executive summary*, Publications Office of the EU, Luxembourg, 2018, p. 7.

174 Reference is made to the "responsible actuary" in the introduction to the EIOPA Guidelines on system of governance, EIOPA-BoS-14/253, 14 September 2015, p. 3. EIOPA indicates that it is up to the supervisory authority to decide on whether to keep the separate function of "responsible actuary". See also IAIS, ICP 8 – Risk Management and Internal Controls, para. 8.5.8.

175 See, for instance, the example given in the BaFin Circular on Governance of Insurance Undertakings (*Rundschreiben 2/2017 (VA) – Mindestanforderungen an die Geschäftsorganisation von Versicherungsunternehmen (MaGo)*, 25 January 2017, under 9.3.7, para. 125: the "responsible actuary" might conclude that a distribution of surplus funds under a life insurance contract is in the interest of policyholders, whilst the actuarial function holder might conclude that such distribution might not be prudent considering the financial position of the undertaking.

control function. The person in charge of this function must also act in the interests of policyholders.[176]

3.7.1. Tasks of the Actuarial Function

The main tasks of the actuarial function are summarised in Art. 48 (1) FD:

- to coordinate the calculation of technical provisions;
- to ensure the appropriateness of the methodologies and underlying models used as well as the assumptions made in the calculation of technical provisions;
- to assess the sufficiency and quality of the data used in the calculation of technical provisions;
- to compare best estimates against experience;
- to inform the AMSB of the reliability and adequacy of the calculation of technical provisions;
- to oversee the calculation of technical provisions in the case of insufficient data of appropriate quality;
- to express an opinion on the adequacy of reinsurance arrangements;
- to contribute to the effective implementation of the risk management system, in particular with respect to the risk modelling underlying the calculation of the SCR and to the ORSA.

3.7.1.1. Coordination of the Calculation of Technical Provisions

This task does not explicitly include the calculation of the technical provisions. There must be a clear allocation and appropriate segregation of responsibilities to ensure independent scrutiny and validation of the calculation. In cases where both calculation and validation of technical provisions is done by the actuarial function, the undertaking must have in place processes and procedures in order to avoid conflicts of interest and ensure appropriate independence. The degree of segregation of duties needs to be proportionate to the nature, scale and complexity of the risks inherent in the calculation of the technical provisions. The undertaking needs to ensure and demonstrate that the processes of calculation and of validation of the technical provisions are independently performed.[177]

---

176 Several respondents to the EIOPA consultation on Guidelines on system of governance questioned why EIOPA accepted that Member States could still choose to keep the requirement to have a responsible actuary. EIOPA's response was that – although the FD introduced maximum harmonisation – this is not the case for the whole Directive. See EIOPA, Final Report on Public Consultation No 14/07 on Guidelines on system of governance, EIOPA-BoS-14/253, 28 January 2015, p. 11.

177 EIOPA, Final report on the Guidelines on system of governance, EIOPA-BoS-14/253, 28 January 2015, p. 87.

In coordinating the calculation of the technical provisions, the actuarial function must carry out the following tasks (Art. 272 (1) DA):

(a) apply methodologies and procedures to assess the sufficiency of technical provisions and to ensure that their calculation is consistent with the legal requirements (Art. 75 to 86 FD);
(b) assess the uncertainty associated with the estimates made in the calculation of technical provisions, for example assess whether the information technology systems used in the calculation of the technical provisions sufficiently support the actuarial and statistical procedures;
(c) ensure that any limitations of data used to calculate technical provisions are properly dealt with;
(d) ensure that the most appropriate approximations for the purposes of calculating the best estimate are used in the cases referred to in Art. 82 FD (insufficient quality of data);
(e) ensure that homogeneous risk groups of (re)insurance obligations are identified for an appropriate assessment of the underlying risks;
(f) consider relevant information provided by financial markets and generally available data on underwriting risks, and ensure that it is integrated into the assessment of technical provisions;
(g) compare and justify any material differences in the calculation of technical provisions from year to year;
(h) ensure that an appropriate assessment is provided of options and guarantees included in (re)insurance contracts.

3.7.1.2. Ensuring Appropriateness of Methodologies

The actuarial function must assess whether the methodologies and assumptions used in the calculation of the technical provisions are appropriate for the specific lines of business of the undertaking and for the way the business is managed, having regard to the available data (Art. 272 (1) and (2) DA).

3.7.1.3. Assessing Sufficiency and Quality of Data

The actuarial function must explain any material effect of changes in data, methodologies or assumptions between valuation dates on the amount of technical provisions. Any inconsistencies with legal requirements must be identified and corrections proposed, where appropriate.[178]

The actuarial function must assess the inconsistency of the internal and external data used in the calculation of technical provisions against the data

178 EIOPA, Guidelines on system of governance, EIOPA-BoS-14/253, 14 September 2015, Guideline 47.

quality standards set in Solvency II. Where relevant, the actuarial function must provide recommendations on internal procedures to improve data quality so as to ensure that the undertaking is in a position to comply with the Solvency II requirements.[179]

3.7.1.4. Comparing Best Estimates against Experience

The actuarial function must review the quality of past best estimates and use the insights gained from this assessment to improve the quality of current calculations. The comparison must include comparisons between observed values and the estimates underlying the calculation of the best estimate, in order to draw conclusions on the appropriateness, accuracy and completeness of the data and assumptions used, as well as on the methodologies applied in their calculation (Art. 172 (4) DA).[180]

3.7.1.5. Informing the AMSB

The information of the AMSB must include at least a reasoned analysis on the reliability and adequacy of the calculation of technical provisions and on the sources and the degree of uncertainty of the estimate of the technical provisions. That reasoned analysis must be supported by a sensitivity analysis that includes an investigation of the sensitivity of the technical provisions to each of the major risks underlying the obligations covered in the technical provisions. The actuarial function must clearly state and explain any concerns it may have about the adequacy of technical provisions.

3.7.1.6. Overseeing the Calculation of Technical Provisions

If there is material uncertainty about the accuracy of the data, the actuarial function must describe the uncertainty and explain any approach taken in light of the uncertainty in the calculation of technical provisions.

3.7.1.7. Expressing an Opinion on the Overall Underwriting Policy

The underwriting policy, the reinsurance arrangements and the technical provisions are interdependent features according to the nature of an undertaking's business.

---

179 EIOPA, Guidelines on system of governance, EIOPA-BoS-14/253, 14 September 2015, Guideline 48.

180 Comparing the best estimate against experience may be difficult for long-term lines of non-life business. In such cases, the actuarial function should try to collect external information to validate the best estimate, such as information provided by industry or actuarial bodies or by the host NSA. See EIOPA, Opinion on non-life cross-border insurance business of a long-term nature and its supervision, EIOPA-BoS-18/527, 21 December 2018, p. 7.

Changes in underwriting policy and practice, for example, may affect not only the calculation of technical provisions, but also the adequacy of reinsurance arrangements. Consequently, the actuarial function is expected to identify any important interrelationships between underwriting policy, reinsurance and technical provisions.[181]

The opinion on the overall underwriting policy must include conclusions regarding the following considerations (Art. 272 (6) DA):

- sufficiency of the premiums to be earned to cover future claims and expenses, notably taking into consideration the underlying risks (including underwriting risks), and the impact of options and guarantees included in (re)insurance contracts on the sufficiency of premiums;
- the effects of inflation, legal risk, change in the composition of the undertaking's portfolio and systems that adjust the premiums policyholders pay upwards or downwards depending on their claims history (bonus-malus systems) or similar systems, implemented in specific homogeneous risk groups;
- the progressive tendency of a portfolio of insurance contracts to attract or retain insured persons with a higher risk profile (anti-selection).

3.7.1.8. Expressing an Opinion on the Adequacy of Reinsurance Arrangements

The opinion must include an analysis on the adequacy of the following (Art. 272 (7) DA):

- the undertaking's risk profile and underwriting policy (consistency of the undertaking's reinsurance arrangements with its risk appetite);
- the credit standing of the reinsurance providers;
- the expected cover under stress scenarios in relation to the underwriting policy;
- the calculation of the amounts recoverable from reinsurance contracts and SPVs.

3.7.1.9. Contributing to the Effective Implementation of the Risk Management System

Although the actuarial function is a key governance function distinct from the risk management function, many tasks of the risk management function can only be performed in close cooperation with the actuarial function.

181 EIOPA, Final report on Guidelines on system of governance, EIOPA-BoS-14/253, 28 January 2015, p. 89.

This close cooperation was also clearly the wish of the co-legislators, as expressed in Art. 269 (2) (c) DA, which states that the risk management function must cooperate closely with the actuarial function.

The distinction between the tasks of both functions has been the subject of debate. The actuarial profession very much wanted the actuarial function to play an important role in internal modelling. After intense debate, it was decided not to assign a specific task relating to internal modelling to the actuarial function because the intention was to put internal modelling clearly in the realm of risk management. However, this does not preclude the risk management function from calling upon the expertise of the actuarial function.[182] Despite the fact that the design, implementation, testing and validation of the internal model is primarily the task of the risk management function, it is expected that the actuarial function assists in this task.[183] The undertaking must describe in its RSR submitted to the supervisory authority how the actuarial function contributes to the effective implementation of the undertaking's management system (Art. 308 (7) DA).[184]

3.7.2. *Actuarial Function Report*

The actuarial function must produce a written report. The report must document all tasks that have been undertaken by the actuarial function and their results, and must clearly identify any deficiencies and give recommendations as to how such deficiencies should be remedied (Art. 272 (8) DA).

Neither the FD, nor the DA, nor the EIOPA Guidelines describe the contents of the actuarial function report. Guidance on the contents can be found in ESAP 2 – Actuarial Function Report under Directive 2009/138/EC, prepared by the Actuarial Association of Europe,[185] which serves as a model standard of actuarial practice that can be adopted by a relevant actuarial standard-setting body.

As a key governance function, the actuarial function must report directly to the AMSB. The actuarial function report must be submitted in written form

---

182 EIOPA, Final report on Guidelines on system of governance, EIOPA-BoS-14/253, 28 January 2015, p. 62.

183 EIOPA, Final report on Guidelines on system of governance, EIOPA-BoS-14/253, 28 January 2015, p. 90.

184 Other provisions in the DA also refer to the cooperation between the risk management function and the actuarial function. See, for instance, Art. 260 (1) (h) (iii) DA, which assigns the task of assessing and validating the underlying assumptions for the projection of future taxable profit for the purpose of the calculation of deferred taxes to either the actuarial function or the risk management function.

185 Actuarial Association of Europe (AAE), *European Standard of Actuarial Practice 2 (ESAP 2) – Actuarial Function Report under Directive 2009/138/EC: Model standard of actuarial practice of the AAE*, 31 January 2016, 15 p. (https://actuary.eu/documents/2016_01_31_ESAP2_final_GA-approved.pdf).

at least once a year. It is good practice for the person who is in charge of the actuarial function to present the report orally to the AMSB. This allows the members of the AMSB to ask questions and forces the actuarial function holder to translate into understandable language the technicalities included in the report. This requires the persons carrying out the actuarial function to develop suitable techniques and skills to communicate with people from outside the profession. As Solvency II attaches great importance to the role of the actuarial function, it is not good to have the CRO present the actuarial function report to the AMSB, as is often the case in practice. Where the risk management function and the actuarial function are two distinct functions, there is no reason why the actuarial function holder should hide behind the CRO.

As indicated by the PRA,[186] the actuarial function can enhance its contribution to the undertaking's system of governance by:

- engaging with the AMSB so that the actuarial function is better understood as a key part of the undertaking's system of governance;
- producing an actuarial function report for the AMSB that gets key messages across in order to support the AMSB's decision-making;
- expressing opinions in the actuarial function report that are supported by a clear rationale and are of value to stakeholders;
- providing evidence in the report that the actuarial function is meeting Solvency II guidelines relating to the validation of technical provisions.

Although the report is addressed to the AMSB, other function holders of the undertaking or of related undertakings and the relevant supervisory authorities might be interested in the report.

3.7.3. Actuarial Standards

The requirements in the FD, the DA and the EIOPA Guidelines deal with what should be done by the actuarial function, rather than how it should be done. There is no doubt that technical guidance, for instance, on the calculation of the best estimate of technical provisions would be very useful. This could be offered by actuarial standards.

The question is who should produce actuarial standards under Solvency II. This matter has not yet been addressed, although it was mentioned during the negotiation of Solvency II. Looking at the development of standards in the

186 See the letter by James Orr, Chief Actuary General Insurance PRA, of 5 February 2018, concerning a review of actuarial function reports: https://www.bankofengland.co.uk/-/media/boe/files/prudential-regulation/letter/2018/review-of-actuarial-function-reports-in-general-insurance-firms.pdf.

areas of accounting and auditing,[187] it is clear that the development of actuarial standards can be carried out neither by supervisory authorities, nor by the actuarial profession alone. It is now recognised in many parts of the world that standards in areas that are considered of public interest, such as accounting and auditing, must be developed by an independent body that represents all relevant stakeholders and that carries out its activities under public oversight. Actuarial standards have not yet reached that stage. In the EEA, the only MS where actuarial standards are developed in this way is the UK, where the task of developing technical actuarial standards was taken over from the Board of Actuarial Standards in 2012 by the Financial Reporting Council, which also carries out public oversight of the regulation of actuaries by the Institute and Faculty of Actuaries (IFoA).

Both the IAA and the AAE[188] produce model actuarial standards, which are known respectively as International Standards of Actuarial Practice (ISAPs) and European Standards of Actuarial Practice (ESAPs). These standards are not binding on individual members of the member associations. However, member associations have agreed to take the necessary steps to ensure that these standards are applied in practice.

In the EEA, the process of developing actuarial standards that could provide guidance to actuaries and other professionals in performing their tasks under Solvency II[189] could be started by EIOPA in collaboration with the AAE. The next step could be the creation of an independent standard-setting body that includes all relevant stakeholders and that should carry out its task under public oversight. The oversight body needs to be independent from the body that sets the standards and should be composed of persons with different backgrounds (multi-stakeholder model).

3.8. REMUNERATION

3.8.1. *Background*

There is widespread consensus that inappropriate remuneration practices in the financial services industry contributed to the financial crisis. These practices, particularly in the banking sector, tended to reward short-term profit and gave staff incentives to pursue unduly risky activities that provided higher income

---

187 In both areas, the standard-setting is carried out by an independent standard-setting body, the International Accounting Standards Board (IASB) in the case of accounting, and the International Auditing and Assurance Standards Board (IAASB) in the case of auditing.

188 See also the very useful work carried out by the predecessor to the AAE, the Groupe Consultatif.

189 And clearly also the tasks performed for occupational pension funds under Art. 27 IORP II.

in the short term while exposing the undertaking to higher potential losses in the longer term. Risk-taking incentives provided by remuneration practices should be consistent with the risk tolerance of the undertaking. Creating appropriate incentives within the remuneration system itself reduces the burden on risk management and increases the likelihood of the risk management system becoming more effective.

In 2009, the EC adopted a recommendation on remuneration policies in the financial services sector.[190] This recommendation is addressed to Member States and applies to all financial services undertakings, including (re)insurance undertakings. Based upon the principles of this recommendation, provisions on remuneration policy for credit institutions and investment firms were included in the CRD.[191] This was not the case for (re)insurance undertakings under Solvency II, as the Solvency II proposal was introduced before 2009. Art. 258 (1) (l) DA remedies this situation, although the FD does not contain a specific authorisation to develop rules on remuneration.[192] This also explains why the rules on remuneration for (re)insurance undertakings are less stringent than those applicable to credit institutions and investment firms.

3.8.2. Remuneration Policy

The AMSB of each (re)insurance undertaking must adopt a written remuneration policy (Art. 258 (1) (l) DA). This policy must comply with the following principles (Art. 275 DA):

(a) the remuneration policy and practices must be established, implemented and maintained in line with the undertaking's business and risk management strategy, its risk profile, objectives, risk management practices and the long-term interests and performance of the undertaking as a whole and must incorporate measures aimed at avoiding conflicts of interest;
(b) the remuneration policy must promote sound and effective risk management and may not encourage risk-taking that exceeds the risk-tolerance limits of the undertaking. For instance, remuneration awards may not threaten the undertaking's ability to maintain an adequate capital base or encourage service providers to take risks that are excessive in view of the undertaking's risk management strategy;
(c) the remuneration policy must apply to the undertaking as a whole, and must contain specific arrangements that take into account the tasks and performance of the members of the AMSB, persons who effectively run

190 Commission Recommendation (2009/384/EC) of 30 April 2009 on remuneration policies in the financial services sector, *OJ* L 120, 15.5.2009, p. 22.
191 Arts. 92–95 CRD.
192 This can be regarded as a form of "gold plating" by the EC.

the undertaking or have other key functions and other categories of staff whose professional activities have a material impact on the undertaking's risk profile;

(d) the AMSB, which establishes the general principles of the remuneration policy for those categories of staff whose professional activities have a material impact on the undertaking's risk profile, is responsible for the oversight of its implementation. This is particularly important if no remuneration committee is established within the AMSB;

(e) there must be clear, transparent and effective governance with regard to remuneration, including the oversight of the remuneration policy;

(f) the remuneration policy must be disclosed to each member of the undertaking's staff.

Art. 275 (1) (f) DA also includes a requirement to create an independent remuneration committee, if appropriate in relation to the significance of the undertaking in terms of size and internal organisation.[193] It is unclear where this independent remuneration committee must be situated. It could be part of the AMSB, as is often the case in financial and non-financial institutions, in order to periodically support the AMSB in overseeing the design of the remuneration policy and remuneration practices, their implementation and operation.

Not all (re)insurance undertakings must create an independent remuneration committee. One can assume that it is only required in large and more complex undertakings.

Where the remuneration includes a variable component or a bonus, the remuneration policy must be structured with an appropriate balance of fixed and variable remuneration. Unlike the CRD,[194] Solvency II does not set a maximum limit on the variable component. However, the following principles must be respected (Art. 275 (2) DA):

(a) the components must be balanced so that the fixed or guaranteed component represents a sufficiently high proportion of the total remuneration to avoid employees being overly dependent on the variable components and to allow the undertaking to operate a fully flexible bonus policy, including the possibility of paying no variable component;

193 From a legal perspective, the "imposition" of a remuneration committee by the DA is particularly questionable, as no other committees are required under the governance system set up by the FD. Art. 95 (1) CRD requires the establishment of a remuneration committee by institutions that are significant in terms of their size, their internal organisation and the nature, the scope and the complexity of their activities.

194 For credit institutions and investment firms, the variable component of the remuneration may not exceed 100% of the fixed component of the total remuneration for each individual, unless the general meeting has approved a higher level, which may in no case be higher than 200% of the fixed component. See Art. 94 (1) (g) CRD.

(b) where variable remuneration is performance-related, the total amount of the variable remuneration must be based on a combination of the assessment of the performance of the individual and of the business unit concerned and of the overall result of the undertaking or the group to which the undertaking belongs;
(c) the payment of a substantial portion of the variable remuneration component, irrespective of the form in which it is to be paid, must contain a flexible, deferred component that takes account of the nature and time horizon of the undertaking's business: that deferral period may not be less than three years and the period must be correctly aligned with the nature of the business, its risks, and the activities of the employees in question;
(d) financial as well as non-financial criteria must be taken into account when assessing an individual's performance;
(e) the measurement of performance, as a basis for variable remuneration, must include a downwards adjustment for exposure to current and future risks, taking into account the undertaking's risk profile and the cost of capital;
(f) termination payments must be related to performance achieved over the whole period of activity and be designed in a way that does not reward failure;
(g) persons subject to the remuneration policy must commit to not using any personal hedging strategies or remuneration and liability-related insurance which would undermine the risk alignment effects embedded in their remuneration arrangement;
(h) the variable part of remuneration of the key governance function holders must be independent from the performance of the operational units and areas that are submitted to their control.

The remuneration policy must be designed in such a way as to take into account the internal organisation of the undertaking, and the nature, scale and complexity of the risks inherent in its business (Art. 275 (3) DA). Information about the remuneration entitlements of the members of the AMSB must be provided in the RSR submitted to the supervisory authority (Art. 308 (1) (c) DA).

3.9. OUTSOURCING

Outsourcing has been popular among (re)insurance undertakings for decades. Its importance is likely to grow with InsurTech. Many core tasks of (re)insurance undertakings are being outsourced to new players in the market, which have developed IT solutions that make it possible to do things more quickly and at lower cost. For an (re)insurance undertaking that outsources core tasks, new operational risks arise. For supervisory authorities, outsourcing means that supervision becomes more difficult, particularly if the service provider is not a financial institution or is situated in a third country.

Information about how the undertaking organises its outsourcing and about the way it ensures that the service providers comply with the legal requirements must be provided in the RSR submitted to the supervisory authority (Art. 308 (8) DA).

3.9.1. Basic Principle

The basic principle underlying outsourcing is that the outsourcing undertaking remains fully responsible for discharging all its obligations under Solvency II when it outsources functions or any (re)insurance activities (Art. 49 (1) FD). In principle, any function or activity of an undertaking can be outsourced, but the AMSB retains ultimate responsibility.

Because the AMSB retains ultimate responsibility, the undertaking needs to include in its system of governance a process for monitoring and reviewing the quality of the service provided. It is not sufficient for the service provider itself to have internal controls and a risk management system that covers the services performed. In order to ensure effective control of outsourced activities and manage the risks associated with the outsourcing, the undertaking needs to maintain the competence and ability within the undertaking to assess whether the service provider has fulfilled its obligations in accordance with what has been agreed.

The service provider is a third party. It may be a supervised entity, an entity from the same group as the undertaking or not, and it may be located inside the EEA or outside. While an outsourcing arrangement may be performed directly by the service provider, the service provider may sub-outsource to another provider if this is permitted by the contract agreed with the undertaking. In the case of sub-outsourcing, the undertaking will not be a party to the sub-outsourcing agreement. It must therefore ensure that it is informed by the service provider of any sub-outsourcing, because the undertaking remains fully responsible for the activity or function outsourced and must ensure that the service provided is performed well.

As part of good management practice, the undertaking is expected to effectively monitor whether its service provider is in compliance with all the terms of the written agreement. If the service provider does not effectively carry out the functions or activities in compliance with the terms of the outsourcing agreement, appropriate actions must be taken. If, for example, a service provider is unwilling to cooperate with the undertaking's supervisory authority, the undertaking will have to terminate the outsourcing agreement. In this context, where a service provider is located outside the EEA, the undertaking needs to pay particular attention to whether the service provider's regulator or local laws and regulations might restrict access to information about the outsourced activity or function or to the service provider's premises.[195]

3.9.2. Written Outsourcing Policy

Before outsourcing or proposing to outsource functions or activities to a service provider, the undertaking must establish a written outsourcing policy that takes into account the impact of outsourcing on its business and the reporting and monitoring arrangements to be implemented in cases of outsourcing. The undertaking must ensure that the terms and conditions of the outsourcing agreement are consistent with the requirements in Art. 49 FD.

The outsourcing policy must cover the undertaking's approach and processes for outsourcing from the inception to the end of the contract. This includes:

- the process for determining whether a function or activity is critical or important;
- how a service provider of suitable quality is selected and how and how often its performance and results are assessed;
- the details to be included in the written agreement with the service provider;
- business contingency plans, including exit strategies for outsourced critical or important functions or activities.[196]

An undertaking needs to decide whether an arrangement falls within the definition of outsourcing. Generally, for example, where an undertaking provides insurance services to its policyholders and certain elements of the delivery of those services are contracted to a third party, the arrangement is likely to be an outsourcing arrangement unless the policyholder has a direct contractual relationship with the third party for the delivery of those services. Any reliance on a third party for functions enabling the undertaking to provide those insurance services is also likely to be outsourcing.

However, not every provision of a function or service to an undertaking by a service provider will fall within the definition of outsourcing. Hiring a specialist consultant, for example, to provide one-off technical advice or one-off support for an undertaking's compliance, internal audit, accounting, risk management or actuarial functions, does not normally constitute outsourcing. However, it may become outsourcing if an undertaking subsequently relies on that consultant to

195 EIOPA, Final report on Guidelines on system of governance, EIOPA-BoS-14/253, 28 January 2015, p. 103. This might also require the prior conclusion of a cooperation agreement with the relevant third country. See Art. 66 FD.

196 EIOPA, Guidelines on system of governance, EIOPA-BoS-14/253, 14 September 2015, Guideline 63.

manage an internal function or service, for example when it is set up or becomes fully operational.

While it is not possible to determine a bright line, it can be expected that, in broad terms, the more substantial or frequent the advice or service provided to an undertaking by a third party is, the more likely it is to fall within the definition of outsourcing.

3.9.3. Outsourcing of Critical or Important Operational Functions and Activities

The requirements for the outsourcing of critical or important functions or activities are very detailed. They aim at reducing the risk for the outsourcing undertaking and at ensuring the possibility for the supervisory authority to carry out its supervisory role.

The principle is that outsourcing critical or important operational functions or activities may not create problems for the outsourcing undertaking. The outsourcing should therefore not lead to:[197]

- a material impairment of the outsourcing undertaking's quality of governance;
- an undue increase in the outsourcing undertaking's operational risk;
- an impairment of the ability of the supervisory authority to monitor the compliance by the outsourcing undertaking with its obligations;
- an undermining of the continuous and satisfactory service to policyholders.

EIOPA had to remind NSAs and (re)insurance undertakings about these requirements in the context of Brexit.[198] There was indeed a risk that UK (re)insurance undertakings might seek to limit the impact of a relocation (from the UK to an EEA30 MS) through an extensive use of outsourcing of functions or activities. Such an approach could result in a depletion of the corporate substance of the relevant EU entities, with repercussions for the adequacy of their management and on the effectiveness of supervision by EEA30 NSAs.

A person within the undertaking must remain responsible for the outsourced key functions on an ongoing basis. Conflicts of interest should be prevented between the undertaking and the service provider. In particular where the service provider is part of the same group, the undertaking's ability to control and influence the actions of the service provider to which critical or important functions or activities are outsourced should remain intact. This means that the undertaking must remain able to access its data and that it must remain involved in decision-making in relation to its business. In particular where the service provider is located in a third country (such as the UK, after Brexit),

[197] Art. 49 (2) FD.

[198] See EIOPA, Opinion on supervisory convergence in light of the UK withdrawing from the EU, EIOPA-BoS-17/141, 11 July 2017, pp. 5–6.

access to information and to the service provider's premises, by the undertaking and supervisor, should be guaranteed. The cooperation between relevant NSAs to guarantee, where relevant, on-site inspections to service providers must be ensured.

The part of key activities or functions that must be retained in the undertaking compared with tasks outsourced must be assessed having regard to the nature, scale and complexity of the business. The undertaking must retain sufficient expertise and resources to monitor and manage its risks. The undertaking must be in a position to resume direct control over an outsourced activity either by insourcing or through an alternative outsourcing arrangement.

While it may be acceptable that undertakings with simple risk-profiles or a small scale of business outsource a significant part of their key functions, it is not acceptable that undertakings with complex risk-profiles or a large scale of business do so.

In order to prevent outsourcing of critical or important operational activities to create problems for the outsourcing undertaking, the undertaking must ensure that (Art. 274 (5) DA):

(a) the service provider's risk management and internal control systems are such that there is no risk of a material impairment of the outsourcing undertaking's quality of governance or an undue increase in operational risk;
(b) the outsourcing is adequately taken into account in its risk management and internal control systems so that there is no risk of a material impairment of the outsourcing undertaking's quality of governance, nor an undue increase in operational risk;
(c) the service provider has the necessary financial resources to perform the additional tasks in a proper and reliable way, and that all staff of the service provider who will be involved in providing the outsourced functions or activities are sufficiently qualified and reliable;
(d) the service provider has adequate contingency plans in place to deal with emergency situations or business disruptions and periodically tests backup facilities where necessary, taking into account the outsourced functions and activities.

The FD does not contain a definition of "critical or important operational functions and activities". However, recital 33 FD clearly states that all key governance functions must be considered important and critical functions. Key governance functions can be outsourced. An example is the actuarial function, which is often outsourced, particularly in the case of small (re)insurance undertakings. The requirements for an outsourcing of key governance functions are stricter than those for the outsourcing of other critical or important operational functions and activities.

If a key governance function is outsourced, the undertaking needs to assess whether all persons performing that function at the service provider are fit and proper. As appropriate, the undertaking can use a service provider's assessment of the fitness and propriety of the relevant staff to help in its own assessment. The undertaking must also designate a person within the undertaking with overall responsibility for the outsourced key function. That person must be fit and proper and possess sufficient knowledge and experience regarding the outsourced key function to be able to challenge the performance and results of the service provider. The designated person will be considered the person responsible for the key function from a supervisory perspective. The fitness of that person is assessed taking into account the fact that, while the oversight role carries ultimate responsibility for the key function, the level of knowledge required would not need to be as high as that of the relevant person(s) at the service provider.[199]

Examples of critical or important functions or activities are the design and pricing of insurance products, the investment of assets or portfolio management, claims handling[200] and settlement, the provision of regular or constant compliance, internal audit,[201] accounting, risk management or actuarial support, the provision of data storage, the provision of ongoing, day-to-day systems of maintenance or support, and the ORSA process.[202]

Underwriting is considered a critical or important operational function or activity. It is common in most Member States or in some lines of business to have insurance intermediaries involved in the underwriting process. If the activity of the intermediary is limited to introducing, proposing or carrying out other preparatory work for the conclusion of insurance contracts, or assisting in the administration and performance of such contracts, in particular in the event of a claim, the activity is not subject to the outsourcing requirements. It may however be subject to the requirements of the IDD.[203]

On the other hand, if an insurance intermediary is mandated by a (re)insurance undertaking to write insurance business or to settle claims

---

199 EIOPA, Guidelines on system of governance, EIOPA-BoS-14/253, 14 September 2015, Guideline 14.

200 To the extent that it is more than claims administration and implies decision-making about the payment of the claim.

201 The internal audit function cannot be outsourced to the statutory auditor. See Art. 6 AR (below, section 3.10.2). See also FINMA, Circular 2017/2 Corporate Governance – Insurers, margin 55, which indicates that the internal audit function can only be outsourced to an audit firm that is independent of the statutory auditor.

202 EIOPA, Final report on Guidelines on system of governance, EIOPA-BoS-14/253, 28 January 2015, p. 100. As indicated above, outsourcing of the ORSA process is not a good idea. However, if it is acceptable to outsource the risk management function in its entirety, it is difficult to object to an outsourcing of the ORSA process.

203 Unless the activity is the professional management of claims, loss adjusting or the expert appraisal of claims, in which case the activity is specifically excluded from the scope of the IDD. See Art. 2 (2) (b) IDD.

on behalf of the undertaking, this is an outsourced service and is therefore covered by the outsourcing requirements for critical or important functions or activities.[204]

Activities that are not considered critical or important functions or activities include the provision of advisory services to the undertaking and other services that do not form part of the undertaking's (re)insurance activities, such as legal advice, the training of personnel and the security of premises and personnel, the purchase of standardised services, including market information services and the provision of price feeds, the provision of logistical support, such as cleaning or catering, and the provision of elements of human resources support, such as recruiting temporary employees and processing payroll.[205]

Where the service provider is a legal entity from the same group as the undertaking that is outsourcing a critical or important operational function or activity, the examination of the service provider may be less detailed, provided that the undertaking's AMSB has greater familiarity with the service provider and the undertaking has sufficient control over, or can influence the actions of, the service provider (Art. 274 (2) DA).

When choosing the service provider for any critical or important operational functions or activities, the AMSB must ensure that (Art. 274 (3) DA):

(a) a detailed examination is performed to ensure that the potential service provider has the ability, the capacity and any authorisation required by law to deliver the required functions or activities satisfactorily, taking into account the undertaking's objectives and needs;
(b) the service provider has adopted all means to ensure that no explicit or potential conflict of interests jeopardises the fulfilment of the needs of the outsourcing undertaking;
(c) a written agreement is entered into between the outsourcing undertaking and the service provider which clearly defines the respective rights and obligations of the undertaking and the service provider;
(d) the general terms and conditions of the outsourcing agreement are clearly explained to the members of the AMSB and authorised by them;
(e) the outsourcing does not entail the breaching of any law, in particular with regard to rules on data protection;
(f) the service provider is subject to the same provisions on the safety and confidentiality of information relating to the (re)insurance undertaking or to its policyholders or beneficiaries that are applicable to the (re)insurance undertaking itself.

204 EIOPA, Guidelines on system of governance, EIOPA-BoS-14/253, 14 September 2015, Guideline 61.

205 EIOPA, Final report on Guidelines on system of governance, EIOPA-BoS-14/253, 28 January 2015, p. 100.

The written agreement that must be concluded between the outsourcing undertaking and the service provider should clearly state (Art. 274 (4) DA):

(a) the duties and responsibilities of both parties involved;
(b) the service provider's commitment to complying with all applicable laws, regulatory requirements and guidelines, as well as policies approved by the outsourcing undertaking, and to cooperating with the outsourcing undertaking's supervisory authority with regard to the outsourced function or activity;
(c) the service provider's obligation to disclose any development which may have a material impact on its ability to carry out the outsourced functions and activities effectively and in compliance with applicable laws and regulatory requirements;
(d) a notice period for the termination of the contract by the service provider which is long enough to enable the outsourcing undertaking to find an alternative solution;
(e) that the outsourcing undertaking is able to terminate the arrangement for outsourcing where necessary without detriment to the continuity and quality of its provision of services to policyholders;
(f) that the outsourcing undertaking reserves the right to be informed about the outsourced functions and activities and their performance by the service provider, as well as the right to issue general guidelines and individual instructions at the address of the service provider, as to what has to be taken into account when performing the outsourced functions or activities;
(g) that the service provider will protect any confidential information relating to the outsourcing undertaking and its policyholders, beneficiaries, employees, contracting parties and all other persons;
(h) that the outsourcing undertaking, its external auditor and the supervisory authority have effective access to all information relating to the outsourced functions and activities, including carrying out on-site inspections of the business premises of the service provider;
(i) that, where appropriate and necessary for the purposes of supervision, the supervisory authority may address questions directly to the service provider, to which the service provider must respond;
(j) that the outsourcing undertaking may obtain information about the outsourced activities and may issue instructions concerning the outsourced activities and functions;
(k) the terms and conditions, where applicable, under which the service provider may sub-outsource any of the outsourced functions and activities;
(l) that the service provider's duties and responsibilities deriving from its agreement with the outsourcing undertaking must remain unaffected by any sub-outsourcing taking place.

Outsourcing of critical or important functions or activities requires prior notice, in writing and in a timely manner, to the supervisory authority (Art. 49 (3) FD).[206] If the outsourcing concerns a key function, the written notification must include the name of the person at the service provider who is in charge of the outsourced function, in order to enable the supervisory authority to approach the service provider directly, as appropriate and necessary.[207]

Written notification in a timely manner presents an opportunity for the supervisory authority to discuss concerns with the undertaking in the event that the outsourcing appears not to comply with the legal requirements, and the opportunity to object to the outsourcing if supervisory concerns cannot be dispelled. "In a timely manner" constitutes a period of time sufficient for the supervisory authority to examine the proposed outsourcing before it comes into force. EIOPA believes that this should be at least six weeks before the outsourcing is due to come into effect.[208]

Written notification is also required for any subsequent material development with respect to the outsourced critical or important functions or activities. This concerns all developments that are relevant for supervisory purposes, i.e. any circumstances that may give supervisors reasons to reassess the undertaking's compliance with legal requirements or adversely affect the undertaking's ability to deliver its services to policyholders. This could, in particular, apply to material changes in the outsourcing arrangements, including any sub-outsourcings; a new service provider; or major problems with the performance of the existing service provider, such as non-performance on account of business disruption, non-compliance with applicable laws and regulations, serious and repeated infringements of guidelines, inadequate risk management, insufficient granting of access to data and information, or anything else that causes significant dissatisfaction with the service to the undertaking or policyholders.[209]

3.10. EXTERNAL AUDIT

3.10.1. Principle

The FD only deals with external audit as a support for the supervisory authority. The statutory auditor who performs the external audit, i.e. the person (or firm) who expresses an opinion on the (general purpose) annual or consolidated

[206] Notification of the outsourcing of other functions or activities is not required.

[207] EIOPA, Guidelines on system of governance, EIOPA-BoS-14/253, 14 September 2015, Guideline 64.

[208] EIOPA, Final report on Guidelines on system of governance, EIOPA-BoS-14/253, 28 January 2015, p. 104.

[209] EIOPA, Final report on Guidelines on system of governance, EIOPA-BoS-14/253, 28 January 2015, pp. 103–104. Another example would be a cybersecurity breach.

financial statements of the (re)insurance undertaking, must immediately inform the supervisory authority in the case of irregularities that might put the future of the undertaking in jeopardy. This whistleblowing role was introduced after the BCCI demise in the banking sector[210] and thus also found its way into the insurance sector.[211] As it was part of the old Insurance Directives, it was recast into the FD with some small changes to reflect the introduction of the new solvency capital regime.

The presence of a statutory auditor as an external independent expert constitutes an important extra line of defence for (re)insurance undertakings. Equally, the existence of an audit committee, which must be set up by each (re)insurance undertaking and which has a privileged relationship with the statutory auditor, allows for many problems to be identified and addressed at an early stage.

Although supervisory authorities can always ask the auditor for ad hoc information that is needed for supervisory purposes (Art. 35 (2) (c) FD and Art. 12 (1), third subparagraph Audit Regulation (AR)), it is useful for the statutory auditor to entertain a more streamlined and well-developed dialogue with the supervisory authority. Although such a dialogue is often seen primarily as a help for the supervisory authority, it adds to the importance of the external audit as an additional line of defence for the undertaking itself. In that sense, the dialogue should be a two-way street and be of interest to both sides. The dialogue should be a true dialogue and not a combination of two monologues.

By virtue of the Insurance Accounts Directive (IAD),[212] each (re)insurance undertaking must have its annual financial statements and, in the case of a group, its consolidated financial statements, audited by a qualified auditor who satisfies the conditions of the Audit Directive (AD).[213] The AD, which deals

210 The Bank of Credit and Commerce International (BCCI) was founded in 1972. It was registered in Luxembourg but had its main activities in London. It became involved in massive money laundering and other financial crimes. The liquidators of the bank, Deloitte & Touche filed a lawsuit against the bank's auditors, Price Waterhouse and Ernst & Young, which was settled in 1998 for US$175 million. The case became famous because it raised questions about prudential supervision (which authority should supervise?) and about statutory audit (what role do auditors have to play and should they inform the supervisory authority in the case of irregularities?).

211 Directive 95/26/EC of the EP and of the Council of 29 June 1995 amending Directives 77/780/EEC and 89/646/EEC in the field of credit institutions, Directives 73/239/EEC and 92/49/EEC in the field of non-life insurance, Directives 79/267/EEC and 92/96/EEC in the field of life assurance, Directive 93/22/EEC in the field of investment firms and Directive 85/611/EEC in the field of undertakings for collective investment in transferable securities (UCITS), with a view to reinforce prudential supervision, *OJ* L 168, 18.7.1995, p. 7.

212 Council Directive 91/674/EEC of 19 December 1991 on the annual accounts and consolidated accounts of insurance undertakings, *OJ* L 374, 31.12.1991, p. 7.

213 Directive 2006/43/EC of the EP Parliament and of the Council of 17 May 2006 on statutory audits of annual and consolidated accounts, amending Council Directives 78/660/EEC

with all statutory audits imposed by EU law, introduces further requirements for public interest entities, including (re)insurance undertakings. As public interest entities,[214] all (re)insurance undertakings and their statutory auditors are also subject to the more stringent requirements for public interest entities introduced by the AR.[215]

3.10.2. Statutory Audit

The statutory auditor or audit firm is in principle appointed by the general meeting of shareholders or members on the recommendation of the AMSB,[216] which receives a recommendation from the audit committee (Art. 16 AR). The duration of the mandate is dealt with in Art. 17 AR, which sets as a principle an appointment of at least one year, with a maximum of 10 years, and introduces requirements on internal rotation (within the audit firm) and external rotation (change of the auditor or audit firm), so as to strengthen the independence of the auditor. Dismissal of the statutory auditor is only possible on proper grounds (Art. 38 AD).

All statutory auditors and audit firms must meet the requirements of the AD in terms of approval (Art. 3), good repute (Art. 4), educational qualifications (Arts. 6–13), registration (Arts. 15–20), professional ethics and professional scepticism (Art. 21), independence and objectivity (Arts. 22, 22a and 24), confidentiality and professional secrecy (Art. 23), internal organisation (Art. 24a), audit fee (Art. 25), auditing standards (Art. 26), annual and consolidated financial statements (Art. 27), audit report (Art. 28), quality assurance (Art. 29), investigations and sanctions (Arts. 30, 30a, 30b, 30c and 30d), whistleblowing to competent authorities (Art. 30e), and public oversight (Arts. 32–36).

Because (re)insurance undertakings are public interest entities under the AD, their statutory auditors and audit firms must also respect the stricter requirements under the AR in terms of audit fees and fees for non-audit services (Art. 6), prohibition on the provision of certain non-audit services to the audit client (for instance, internal audit) (Art. 5), independence (Art. 6), disclosure of

---

and 83/349/EEC and repealing Council Directive 84/253/EEC, *OJ* L 157, 9.6.2006, p. 87. A consolidated version including subsequent changes was published on 16 June 2014: http://data.europa.eu/eli/dir/2006/43/2014-06-16.

214 Although Art. 2 (13) (c) of Directive 2006/43/EC only refers to "insurance undertakings", it is also meant to cover reinsurance undertakings. The reference to the now repealed Directive 91/674/EEC is wrong.

215 Regulation (EU) No 537/2014 of the EP and of the Council of 16 April 2014 on specific requirements regarding statutory audit of public-interest entities and repealing Commission Decision 2005/909/EC, *OJ* L 158, 27.5.2014, p. 77.

216 Reference is made to the "administrative or supervisory body" which is the same as the AMSB under the FD.

irregularities to the AMSB of the audited entity and if no action to the competent authority (Art. 7), engagement in a quality-control review (Art. 8), conditional application of international standards on auditing (ISAs) (Art. 9),[217] additional information to be provided in the audit report (Art. 10), additional report to the audit committee (Art. 11), report to the supervisory authority (Art. 12), transparency report (Art. 13), and record keeping (Art. 15).

The results of the statutory audit must be presented in a written audit report, signed and dated by the statutory auditor or, in the case of an audit firm, by the statutory auditor who has carried out the statutory audit on behalf of the audit firm. The report must include at least the following information:[218]

(a) identification of the entity whose annual or consolidated financial statements are the subject of the statutory audit, with specification of the annual or consolidated financial statements and the date and period they cover, and identification of the financial reporting framework that has been applied in their preparation;
(b) description of the scope of the statutory audit which must, as a minimum, identify the auditing standards in accordance with which the statutory audit was conducted;
(c) an audit opinion, which is either unqualified, qualified or an adverse opinion, and must state clearly the opinion of the statutory auditor or the audit firm as to:
    (i) whether the annual financial statements give a true and fair view in accordance with the relevant financial reporting framework; and,
    (ii) where appropriate, whether the annual financial statements comply with statutory requirements.

    If the statutory auditor or the audit firm is unable to express an audit opinion, the report must contain a disclaimer of opinion;
(d) reference to any other matters to which the statutory auditor or the audit firm draw(s) attention by way of emphasis without qualifying the audit opinion;[219]
(e) an opinion, based on the work undertaken in the course of the audit, whether the management report is consistent with the financial statements for the same financial year, and whether the management report has been prepared in accordance with the applicable legal requirements and a statement, based

[217] Art. 9 empowers the EC to adopt by way of delegated acts the International Auditing Standards (ISAs) developed by the International Auditing and Assurance Standards Board (IAASB) under certain conditions. The EC has not done so yet but in practice all Member States in the EEA require the use of ISAs for statutory audits.
[218] Art. 28 (2) AD.
[219] These are the so-called key audit matters (KAM).

on the work undertaken in the course of the audit, whether, in the light of the knowledge and understanding of the undertaking and its environment obtained in the course of the audit, the auditor or audit firm has identified material misstatements in the management report with an indication of the nature of any such misstatements;
(f) a statement on any material uncertainty relating to events or conditions that may cast significant doubt about the undertaking's ability to continue as a going concern;
(g) the place of establishment of the statutory auditor or the audit firm.

Because (re)insurance undertakings are public interest entities under the AD, the audit report must also include the following information:[220]

(a) a statement by whom or by which body the statutory auditor or the audit firm was appointed;
(b) the date of the appointment and the period of total uninterrupted engagement, including previous renewals and reappointments of the statutory auditor or the audit firm;
(c) a description of the most significant assessed risks of material misstatement, including assessed risks of material misstatement due to fraud, as well as a summary of the auditor's response to those risks and, where relevant, key observations arising with respect to those risks, and a clear reference to the relevant disclosures in the financial statements;
(d) an explanation of the extent to which the statutory audit was considered capable of detecting irregularities, including fraud;
(e) confirmation that the audit opinion is consistent with the additional report to the audit committee;
(f) a declaration that no prohibited non-audit services[221] were provided and that the statutory auditor or the audit firm remained independent of the audited undertaking in conducting the audit;
(g) an indication of any services, in addition to the statutory audit, that were provided by the statutory auditor or the audit firm to the audited entity and its controlled undertaking(s), and which were not disclosed in the management report or financial statements.

The audit report must be worded in clear and unambiguous language[222] and the statutory auditor or the audit firm may not use the name of any competent authority in a way that would indicate or suggest endorsement or approval by that authority of the audit report.

---

220 Art. 10 (2) AR.
221 The services referred to in Art. 5 (1) AR, such as internal audit.
222 Art. 10 (3) AR.

3.10.3. Audit Committee

Each (re)insurance undertaking[223] must set up an audit committee (Art. 39 AD), either as a stand-alone committee or as a committee within the AMSB. At least one member of the audit committee must have competence in accounting and/or auditing.

The audit committee has the following tasks:[224]

(a) to inform the AMSB of the undertaking of the outcome of the statutory audit and explain how the statutory audit contributed to the integrity of financial reporting and what the role of the audit committee was in that process;
(b) to monitor the financial reporting process and submit recommendations or proposals to ensure its integrity;
(c) to monitor the effectiveness of the undertaking's internal quality control and risk management systems and, where applicable, its internal audit, regarding the financial reporting of the undertaking, without breaching its independence;
(d) to monitor the statutory audit of the annual and consolidated financial statements, in particular its performance, taking into account any findings and conclusions from inspections carried out by the competent authority (in the field of statutory audit);[225]
(e) to review and monitor the independence of the statutory auditor or the audit firm in accordance with the legal requirements;[226]
(f) to be responsible for the procedure for the selection of the statutory auditor or audit firm and recommend the statutory auditor or the audit firm to be appointed in accordance with Art. 16 AR.

The statutory auditor or audit firm of the (re)insurance undertaking must submit a written report to the audit committee (Art. 11 AR) no later than the date of submission of the audit report. Where the audit committee is not a committee within the AMSB, Member States may additionally require this written report to be submitted to the AMSB.

The written report must describe the results of the statutory audit carried out and include at least the following:[227]

(a) a declaration of independence;[228]

---

223 There are some exceptions to this principle. See Art. 39 (2), (3) and (4) AD.
224 Art. 39 (6) AD.
225 Art. 26 (5) AR.
226 Arts. 22, 22a, 22b, 24a and 24b AD and Arts. 5 and 6 AR.
227 Art. 11 (2) AR.
228 Stating whether the statutory auditor or audit firm has complied with the independence requirements in Arts. 4 and 5 AR.

(b) where the statutory audit was carried out by an audit firm, an identification of each key audit partner involved in the audit;
(c) where the statutory auditor or the audit firm has made arrangements for any of his, her or its activities to be conducted by another statutory auditor or audit firm that is not a member of the same network, or has used the work of external experts, an indication of that fact and confirmation that the statutory auditor or the audit firm received an independence declaration from the other statutory auditor or audit firm and/or the external expert;
(d) a description of the nature, frequency and extent of communication with the audit committee or the body performing equivalent functions within the undertaking and the AMSB, including the dates of meetings with those bodies;
(e) a description of the scope and timing of the audit;
(f) where more than one statutory auditor or audit firm have been appointed, a description of the distribution of tasks between the statutory auditors and/or the audit firms;
(g) a description of the methodology used, including which categories of the balance sheet have been directly verified and which categories have been verified based on system and compliance testing, including an explanation of any substantial variation in the weighting of system and compliance testing when compared to the previous year, even if the previous year's statutory audit was carried out by other statutory auditor(s) or audit firm(s);
(h) disclosure of the quantitative level of materiality applied to perform the statutory audit for the financial statements as a whole and, where applicable, the materiality level or levels for particular classes of transactions, account balances or disclosures, and disclosure of the qualitative factors which were considered when setting the level of materiality;
(i) a report and explanation of judgements about events or conditions identified in the course of the audit that may cast significant doubt on the undertaking's ability to continue as a going concern and whether they constitute a material uncertainty, and provision of a summary of all guarantees, comfort letters, undertakings of public intervention and other support measures that have been taken into account when making a going-concern assessment;
(j) a report on any significant deficiencies in the undertaking's or, in the case of consolidated financial statements, the parent undertaking's internal financial control system, and/or in the accounting system. For each such significant deficiency, the additional report shall state whether or not the deficiency in question has been resolved by the management;
(k) a report on any significant matters involving actual or suspected non-compliance with laws and regulations or articles of association which were identified in the course of the audit, in so far as they are considered to be relevant in order to enable the audit committee to fulfil its tasks;

(l) a report and assessment of the valuation methods applied to the various items in the annual or consolidated financial statements, including any impact of changes of such methods;
(m) in the case of a statutory audit of consolidated financial statements, explanation of the scope of consolidation and the exclusion criteria applied by the undertaking to the non-consolidated entities, if any, and whether those criteria applied are in accordance with the financial reporting framework;
(n) where applicable, identification of any audit work performed by third-country auditor(s), statutory auditor(s), third-country audit entity(ies) or audit firm(s) in relation to a statutory audit of consolidated financial statements other than by members of the same network as that to which the auditor of the consolidated financial statements belongs;
(o) indication whether all requested explanations and documents were provided by the audited undertaking;
(p) a report on any significant difficulties encountered in the course of the statutory audit, on any significant matters arising from the statutory audit that were discussed or were the subject of correspondence with management and on any other matters arising from the statutory audit that, in the auditor's professional judgement, are significant to the oversight of the financial reporting process.

Upon request by a statutory auditor, an audit firm or the audit committee, the statutory auditor or the audit firm must discuss key matters arising from the statutory audit, referred to in the additional report to the audit committee, and in particular in point (j) above, with the audit committee or the AMSB.

Where more than one statutory auditor or audit firm has been engaged simultaneously, and any disagreement has arisen between them on auditing procedures, accounting rules or any other issue regarding the conduct of the statutory audit, the reasons for such disagreement must be explained in the additional report to the audit committee (Art. 11 (3) AR).

The written report to the audit committee must be signed and dated. Where an audit firm carries out the statutory audit, the report to the audit committee must be signed by the statutory auditors carrying out the statutory audit on behalf of the audit firm (Art. 11 (4) AR).

Upon request, and in accordance with national law, the statutory auditors or the audit firms must make their written report available to the competent authorities without delay (in the field of statutory audit) (Art. 11 (5) AR).

3.10.4. Relationship between the Statutory Auditor and the Supervisory Authority

The statutory auditor or audit firm of a (re)insurance undertaking must report promptly to the supervisory authority any fact or decision concerning the undertaking (or an undertaking that has close links with the (re)insurance undertaking and within which they are carrying out the statutory audit) of which they become aware while carrying out their task and which is liable to bring about the following:[229]

- a material breach of the laws, regulations or administrative provisions which lay down the conditions governing authorisation or which specifically govern the pursuit of the activities of the undertaking;
- the impairment of the continuous functioning of the undertaking;
- a refusal to certify the accounts or an expression of reservations;
- non-compliance with the SCR;
- non-compliance with the MCR.

In order to protect the statutory auditor or audit firm in this whistleblowing role, Art. 72 (2) FD states that any disclosure in good faith to the supervisory authority does not constitute a breach of any restriction on disclosure of information imposed by contract or by any legislative, regulatory or administrative provision and cannot create a liability of any kind.

Although not required under the FD, (re)insurance undertakings will normally be required to submit to the supervisory authority the audit report and the written report for the audit committee, in addition to the audited annual and consolidated financial statements. Sometimes, statutory auditors are required to file an additional report with the supervisory authority on the undertaking's audited annual report and accounts.[230]

There is no requirement under the FD to subject documents that must be transmitted to the supervisory authority to an external audit. The possibility of such a requirement was discussed during the negotiation of the FD and was expressly discarded in the co-decision procedure, as it would have imposed additional costs on (re)insurance undertakings.[231] Nevertheless, some NSAs require external auditors to certify documents that are submitted to them. This is, for instance, the case for parts of the SFCR in the UK[232] or for the semi-annual and annual prudential reporting in Belgium.[233] EIOPA has struggled

---

229 Art. 72 (1) FD and Art. 12 (1) AR.

230 See, for instance, Bank of England, PRA Rulebook, Auditors, Rule 8.3.

231 An amendment tabled by the Shadow Rapporteur, Sylvie Goulard (ALDE, France) to that effect was rejected.

232 See PRA, *Supervisory Statement SS11/16 – Solvency II: external audit of the public disclosure requirement*, September 2016. Following a public consultation, the PRA abolished the audit requirement of the SFCR for small insurers. See PRA Policy Statement 25/18, published on 17 October 2018.

233 See Arts. 332 and 333 (individual undertakings) and Arts. 433 and 434 (groups) of the Belgian Law of 13 March 2016 on the regulation and supervision of (re)insurance undertakings. Only auditors certified by the National Bank of Belgium may audit financial statements of

with this[234] and adopted a "message" on 29 June 2015 dealing with this issue, recognising the usefulness of an external audit of certain parts of the SFCR, without recommending or requiring it.[235]

Although subjecting prudential information to an external audit may provide some assurance to supervisory authorities that the information can be relied upon, it can in no way remove the supervisory authorities' responsibility to examine the documents and forming an opinion on them themselves.

Particularly after the financial crisis, the question was raised why auditors had not warned stakeholders and supervisory authorities about the upcoming difficulties. As indicated in recital 15 AR, "supervisory tasks would be facilitated if supervisors of credit institutions and insurance undertakings and their statutory auditors and audit firms were required to establish an effective dialogue with each other".

Art. 12 (2) AR introduces a requirement for such a dialogue between (re)insurance undertakings and supervisory authorities. Details on how such a dialogue can be arranged are included in guidelines adopted by EIOPA on 2 February 2017, based upon an explicit mandate in Art. 12 (3) AR.[236]

In terms of the objectives of the dialogue, Guideline 1 indicates that the dialogue should be open and constructive, as well as sufficiently flexible. Both sides in the dialogue should respect the rules on confidentiality. The supervised undertaking should remain the main source of information for supervisory and statutory audit purposes and neither party should use the work of the other as a substitute for its own work. A risk-based approach to the frequency and depth of communication should be followed in order to ensure a proportionate approach.

As for the nature of the information to be exchanged, Guideline 2 indicates that the information must be relevant, and that it can be undertaking-specific, industry-specific, current and emerging. Possible topics include the external environment of the undertaking, corporate governance, internal controls, the going-concern assumption, the audit approach, communication with the AMSB, valuation and own funds, investments, financial statements and other audit documentation. If the undertaking is part of a multinational group, the group supervisor should also consider covering relevant group-audit issues.

---

insurance undertakings and groups. These auditors must carry out a restricted review on the periodic information submitted to the Bank.

234 In a document dated 25 May 2010, CEIOPS "urged the EC to adopt some text either through Omnibus II or its level 2 implementing measures to mandate the role of an external audit in the Solvency II pillar 3 process". See CEIOPS, Solvency II Pillar 3: Public Disclosure and Supervisory Reporting – External Audit, CEIOPS-IGSRR-08/10, 25 May 2010, p. 4.

235 EIOPA, Need for high quality public disclosure: Solvency II's report on solvency and financial condition and the potential role of external audit, EIOPA-BoS-15/154, 29 June 2016, 2 p.

236 EIOPA, Guidelines on facilitating an effective dialogue between competent authorities supervising insurance undertakings and statutory auditor(s) and the audit firm(s) carrying out the statutory audit of those undertakings, EIOPA-BoS-16/071, 2 February 2016, 6 p.

In terms of the form of the dialogue, Guideline 3 suggests that the most appropriate and most effective means and channels of dialogue must be chosen in light of the individual circumstances of the dialogue. Channels may include written or oral communication, including phone calls and regular physical meetings. Physical meetings should be promoted in order to facilitate open communication, especially when initiating a dialogue with participants for the first time. A record should be kept of the communication in order to ensure proper follow-up.

It is important to ensure the right level of representation in the dialogue. Guideline 4 suggests that the individuals from both parties invited to the dialogue must be knowledgeable, informed and empowered by their organisation or firm to exchange information relevant to the dialogue. The primary participants should be a representative of the supervisory authority acting as team leader and the key audit partner. It should also be possible to have a trilateral meeting, including a representative of the audit committee.

Regular dialogues should be scheduled as frequently as necessary to ensure that the dialogue is effective and taking into account the planning cycle of supervisory inspections and of the statutory audit (Guideline 5). It should be possible to have an ad hoc dialogue meeting if important issues arise. There should at least be an annual meeting, particularly for (re)insurance undertakings that are highly risky and are likely to have a high impact in the event of failure (risk-based approach).

In order to promote a more efficient dialogue at sectoral and national level, EIOPA recommends that regular dialogues should be held with statutory auditors collectively to allow for an exchange of views on current and emerging developments, at least annually, where relevant (Guideline 6). No undertaking-specific information should be shared during such a meeting and the same confidentiality and professional secrecy requirements as in individual dialogues should apply.

Just such a sectoral dialogue between statutory auditors and audit firms and supervisory authorities is now required by Art. 12 (2) AR, which calls for an effective dialogue to be held between the competent authorities supervising credit institutions and insurance undertakings on the one hand, and the statutory auditor(s) and the audit firm(s) carrying out the statutory audit of those institutions and undertakings on the other hand. The responsibility for compliance with this requirement rests with both parties to the dialogue.

Furthermore, at least once a year, the ESRB and the Committee of European Auditing Oversight Bodies (CEAOB) must organise a meeting with the statutory auditors and the audit firms or networks carrying out statutory audits of all global systemically important financial institutions authorised within the EU, as identified internationally, in order to inform the ESRB of sectoral or any significant developments in those systemically important financial institutions.

The role of the ESRB is to monitor the build-up of systemic risk in the EU. Given the information that statutory auditors and audit firms of systemically important financial institutions have access to, their experience could help the ESRB in its work. Therefore, there should be an annual forum for dialogue between statutory auditors and audit firms on the one hand, and the ESRB on the other, on a sectoral, anonymised basis.[237] This should happen in close cooperation with EBA and EIOPA.

237 Recital 16 AR.

CHAPTER 8

PILLAR 3

Public Disclosure and Supervisory Reporting

Under Solvency I, the insurance sector in the EEA was not characterised by a high level of transparency. Although (re)insurance undertakings had to provide information on a regular basis to supervisory authorities (for instance, to allow them to check whether they had respected the investment rules), and although they were required to publish their annual and consolidated financial statements, neither the information available for supervisory purposes nor the financial information made publicly available were fit for purpose, i.e. allowed supervisory authorities to have a good understanding of what was really going on within the undertaking or provided stakeholders with an insight into the true financial position of the undertaking.

From a supervisory perspective, this was not without problems. When the financial crisis broke out in 2008 and CEIOPS was asked to provide information to the EC and to the Council on the exposure of the insurance sector to Lehman Brothers, it was incapable of doing so because the information that was available was too general and not comparable. The existing requirements were dated and the insurance sector was lagging behind the banking sector, where regular detailed reporting requirements had been in place for a long time.

Finding publicly available, relevant information on insurance for all Member States of the EEA was a difficult challenge. The financial information published by (re)insurance undertakings was not readily comparable, and information on issues such as the exact number of (re)insurance undertakings in the EEA or the type of investments was difficult to obtain as neither CEIOPS nor the main organisation representing the insurance sector, Insurance Europe, possessed that information.[1] It was obvious that it would take a long time before it would be possible to provide interested parties with information on insurance that was as detailed and comparable as that which existed in the banking sector.

1 Insurance Europe, which succeeded CEA in 2012, started to publish statistics on the European (re)insurance sector in 2014 but the statistics were incomplete and only related to their members.

This changed completely with the introduction of Solvency II. Pillar 3 is the area where Solvency II has brought about a revolution. It has brought a lot of new information into the public domain for the first time.

In terms of prudential supervision, it was clear that a solvency regime that was principles-based and that transferred the responsibility for solvency capital management to the management of the undertaking could not be properly supervised without detailed information for supervisory authorities about the choices made and the decisions taken by undertakings. NSAs and EIOPA were very eager to ensure that they would obtain the right amount of information and that the information would be timely and comparable. Contrary to Solvency I, the amount of information to be delivered under Solvency II is massive. The timely delivery of that information has forced all parties concerned (undertakings, NSAs, EIOPA) to invest heavily in IT programs. This was costly and at times heavily criticised, because of the extent of the information required and the cost involved. Some adjustments were made, particularly in favour of small and medium-sized undertakings, through Omnibus II, with a more explicit application of the proportionality principle.

EIOPA has assisted undertakings by providing templates and by organising extensive consultations. The five QIS exercises were also very helpful, as they allowed EIOPA to improve the data requests and helped undertakings to prepare themselves to deliver the information from day one.

Just two years since the first application of Solvency II, the results are already impressive. The work carried out by undertakings, NSAs and EIOPA is remarkable. However, there are obviously still problems. Not all data are perfectly comparable and many NSAs, particularly from new Member States, are struggling to obtain correct data from (re)insurance undertakings that are still having difficulties to produce these data.

Nevertheless, for the first time in European history, detailed and comparable information is now available at European level on many aspects of the insurance sector and the website of EIOPA now includes a specific section on statistical information.

In terms of public disclosure, transparency contributes to market discipline. Market discipline can be defined as the influence customers, insurance intermediaries, auditors, researchers, rating agencies and investors have on the behaviour of undertakings. The underlying idea is that a transparent market will require less overt regulation, as market participants themselves force appropriate behaviour.[2] Undertakings are encouraged to comply with the new solvency requirements when they know that interested parties are able to compare

---

2 ELING, M., The Role of Market Discipline in the Insurance Industry, in LIEDTKE, P.M. and MONKIEWICZ, J. (Eds.), *The Future of Insurance Regulation and Supervision: A Global Perspective*, Palgrave Macmillan, Basingstoke, 2011, p. 131.

their situation with that of their competitors. This is clearly the case with the SFCR, which (re)insurance undertakings had to publish for the first time in 2017 and which provides a wealth of information on issues such as business and performance, the system of governance, capital management, including the amounts of the MCR and the SCR, and valuation for solvency purposes.

On 21 March 2018, the EC published a consultation document[3] for a fitness check on the EU framework for public reporting by companies, including (re)insurance undertakings. The document included an online questionnaire that had to be completed by 21 July 2018. For (re)insurance undertakings, the questionnaire dealt with financial[4] and non-financial[5] information but not with prudential information to be provided on the basis of the Solvency II FD.[6]

1. PUBLIC DISCLOSURE

1.1. FINANCIAL AND NON-FINANCIAL INFORMATION

All (re)insurance undertakings[7] are required to prepare and publish annual and, in the case of groups, consolidated financial statements. The annual and consolidated financial statements comprise a balance sheet, a profit and loss account and notes on the financial statements. The financial statements must be drawn up in accordance with the requirements of the IAD.[8] As indicated above, it was decided not to amend this Directive during the development of Solvency II. Unlike under Solvency I, the financial statements no longer serve as a basis for the calculation of the capital requirements under Solvency II.

---

3 EC, *Consultation Document: Fitness check on the EU framework for public reporting by companies*, 21 March 2018: https://ec.europa.eu/info/sites/infor/files/2018-companies-public-reporting-consultation-document_en.pdf. This fitness check is part of the Action Plan on Financing Sustainable Growth. See EC, Communication to the EP, the European Council, the ECB, the EESC and the CoR – Action Plan: Financing Sustainable Growth, COM (2018) 97 final, 8 March 2018, p. 9.

4 On the basis of the IAD and on the basis of IFRS.

5 On the basis of Directive 2014/95/EU of the EP and of the Council of 22 October 2014 amending Directive 2013/34/EU as regards disclosure of non-financial and diversity information by certain large undertakings and groups, *OJ* L 330, 15.11.2014, p. 1.

6 A fitness check on supervisory reporting took place in 2017. The public consultation was closed on 14 March 2018. A factual overview of the 391 responses was published by the EC on its website (https://ec.europa.eu/info/sites/info/files/2017-supervisory-reporting-requirements-summary-report_en.pdf.). The follow-up will come early 2019 in the form of a Staff Working Document. EIOPA's contribution was sent to the EC on 5 March 2018 (https://eiopa.europa.eu/Publications/Letters/EIOPA-18-072%20Letter%20to%20Olivier%20Guersent%20on%20Fitness%20Check%20on%20Supervisory%20reporting.pdf).

7 This requirement does not apply to branches of third-country (re)insurance undertakings.

8 Council Directive (91/674/EEC) of 19 December 1991 on the annual accounts and consolidated accounts of insurance undertakings, *OJ* L 374, 31.12.1991, p. 7.

The financial statements are accompanied by a management report, which must include a corporate governance statement,[9] including a description of the diversity policy applied in relation to the undertaking's AMSB in terms of, for instance, age, gender or educational and professional backgrounds, the objectives of that diversity policy, how it has been implemented and the results in the reporting period. If no such policy is applied, the statement must contain an explanation of why this is the case. The annual financial statements and, where applicable, the consolidated financial statements must be audited by an external auditor, who must also express an opinion on whether the management report is consistent with the financial statements for the same financial year and whether the management report has been prepared in accordance with the applicable legal requirements.[10]

(Re)insurance undertakings that are listed on a European stock exchange must prepare their consolidated financial statements in conformity with IAS/IFRS adopted by the EC on the basis of the IAS Regulation.[11] Member States may extend this requirement to all financial statements (both annual and consolidated) of all (re)insurance undertakings (as an option or as a requirement).

In its March 2018 consultation document *Fitness check on the EU framework for public reporting by companies*, the EC observes that – for insurance – depending on Member States' use of options, the European accounting and prudential framework requires the preparation of multiple sets of financial statements (statutory annual and/or consolidated financial statements based on national law implementing the IAD, the solvency balance sheet under Solvency II, and IAS/IFRS annual and/or consolidated financial statements). A number of questions are raised, such as whether the IAD is still effective, relevant and efficient, and whether the IAD should be harmonised with the Solvency II requirements and/or with IFRS 17 – Insurance Contracts. This is a highly complex matter and action should only be taken if a clear direction emerges from the consultation. In its response to the public consultation, EIOPA did not advocate a replacement of the IAD by IFRS 17 for all (re)insurance undertakings. EIOPA underlined that the existence of different reporting requirements is

---

9 Because all insurance undertakings are considered as public interest entities. See Arts. 2 (1) (c) and 20 Directive 2013/34/EU of the EP and of the Council of 26 June 2013 on the annual financial statements, consolidated financial statements and related reports of certain types of undertakings, amending Directive 2006/43/EC of the European Parliament and of the Council and repealing Council Directives 78/660/EEC and 83/349/EEC, *OJ* L 182, 29.6.2013, p. 19 (Accounting Directive). It is interesting that the definition of "public interest entity" in Art. 2 (1) (c) AD does not include reinsurance undertakings as it refers to the scope of the IAD.

10 Art. 34 Directive 2013/34/EU.

11 Regulation (EC) No 1606/2002 of the EP and of the Council of 19 July 2002 on the application of international accounting standards, *OJ* L 243, 11.9.2002, p. 1.

not necessarily an expression of inefficiencies, but rather a consequence of the different objectives of financial reporting and public disclosure by (re)insurance undertakings in the EU.[12]

Nevertheless, financial statements published by listed (re)insurance undertakings remain difficult to compare and it would be great progress if more comparability could be achieved. IFRS 17 should achieve this. However, the standard remains controversial and the insurance industry has asked for a two-year delay in its application in order to resolve some outstanding problems and to allow for more time for the industry to prepare.[13] The European Financial Reporting Advisory Group (EFRAG), which is preparing advice for the EC on the endorsement of IFRS 17, has written to the Chairman of the IASB asking for a delay in the application of IFRS while it examines a number of technical issues brought up by the insurance industry.[14] Following these requests, the IASB voted on 14 November 2018 to propose (subject to public consultation) a one-year deferral of the effective date for IFRS 17 to 1 January 2022. The IASB has also decided to propose extending to 2022 the temporary exemption for insurers to apply IFRS 9, the accounting standard for financial instruments, so that both IFRS 9 and IFRS 17 can be applied at the same time.[15] EIOPA is broadly supportive of IFRS 17, as it sees the standard as a means to improve comparability.[16] It is however doubtful whether application of IFRS 17 will lead to a lowering of the cost of capital for listed (re)insurance undertakings. The complexity of insurance as an activity and the uncertainty about its profitability over the long term remains a challenge for any accounting framework. This inevitably decreases its attractiveness as an investment opportunity.[17]

Because they are public interest entities, large (re)insurance undertakings – i.e. undertakings exceeding on their balance sheet dates an average of 500 employees during the financial year – must include in their management report a non-financial statement containing information necessary for an understanding of the undertaking's development, performance, position and impact of its activity, relating to, at a minimum, environmental, social and

---

12 See letter sent by Gabriel Bernardino, Chairman of EIOPA, to Olivier Guersent, Director-General of DG FISMA, on 24 July 2018 (https://eiopa.europa.eu/Publications/Letters/EIOPA-18-072%20Letter%20to%20Olivier%20Guersent%20on%20Fitness%20Check%20on%20Supervisory%20reporting.pdf).

13 See the letter sent by nine insurance associations to the Chairman of the IASB on 16 October 2018 (http://www.insurancecouncil.com.au/assets/submission/2018/Global%20insurance%20industry%20letter%20to%20IASB%20on%20IFRS%2017.pdf).

14 See the information on its website: https://efrag.org.

15 See the press statement on the website of the IASB: https://www.ifrs.org.

16 See EIOPA, Analysis of IFRS 17 Insurance Contracts, EIOPA-18-717, 18 October 2018, 34 p.

17 This was confirmed at the 2018 Insurance Conference organised by S&P in London on 6 November 2018 where at a public Q&A session 80% of the audience responded that they expected IFRS 17 to improve comparability but not to reduce the cost of capital for (re)insurance undertakings.

employee matters, respect for human rights, anti-corruption and bribery matters.[18] A similar requirement applies to large (re)insurance groups for the consolidated management report.[19]

This requirement, which only applies to large public interest entities and groups, is part of the development towards sustainable reporting.[20] The EC has published guidelines in order to help undertakings and groups disclose this non-financial information in a relevant, useful, consistent and more comparable manner.[21]

1.2. SOLVENCY AND FINANCIAL CONDITION REPORT

The tool selected by the co-legislators under Solvency II for communicating with stakeholders is the SFCR.[22] The SFCR aims at establishing market discipline, i.e. making it possible for all stakeholders to see how (re)insurance undertakings subject to Solvency II are applying the new solvency rules. The requirement to publish that information should encourage undertakings to do it right and should allow all interested parties to compare how (re)insurance undertakings are carrying out their legal obligations (market discipline).[23]

The SFCR must be published on an annual basis by all (re)insurance undertakings (Art. 51 FD) and (re)insurance groups (Art. 256 FD) subject

18 Art. 19a Directive 2013/34/EU, introduced by Directive 2014/95/EU of the EP and of the Council of 22 October 2014 amending Directive 2013/34/EU as regards disclosure of non-financial and diversity information by certain large undertakings and groups, *OJ* L 330, 15.11.2014, p. 1.

19 Art. 29a Directive 2013/34/EU, introduced by Directive 2014/95/EU of the EP and of the Council of 22 October 2014 amending Directive 2013/34/EU as regards disclosure of non-financial and diversity information by certain large undertakings and groups, *OJ* L 330, 15.11.2014, p. 1.

20 See also the EC, *Financing a sustainable European economy: Final Report 2018 of the High-Level Expert Group on Sustainable Finance*, January 2018, https://ec.europa.eu/info/sites/info/files/180131-sustainable-finance-final-report_en.pdf and EC, Communication to the EP, the European Council, the ECB, the EESC and the CoR – Action Plan: Financing Sustainable Growth, COM (2018) 97 final, 8 March 2018, 19 p.

21 EC, Communication on Guidelines on non-financial reporting (methodology for reporting non-financial information), *OJ* C 215, 5.7.2017, p. 1. On 20 February 2019, the EC launched a consultation on an update of the Guidelines on non-financial information to include climate related reporting. The consultation document is based on the report produced in January 2019 on climate related reporting by the Technical Expert Group on Sustainable Finance (ihttps://ec.europa.eu/info/sites/info/files/business_economy_euro/banking_and_finance/documents/2019-non-financial-reporting-guidelines-consultation-document_en.pdf).

22 The relevant legal requirements can be found in Arts. 51, 53–56, 256 and 308b (6) FD, Arts. 290–303, 359–371 and Annex XX DA, and EIOPA Guidelines on reporting and public disclosure, EIOPA BoS-15/109, 14 September 2015.

23 Some people question whether the SFCR is capable of establishing market discipline because undertakings are unlikely to disclose that, for instance, their governance regime is weak. See RIEF, W., Marktdisziplinierende Einwirkungen durch Solvency II?, *Kredit & Rating Praxis*, 2017, No 2, 2–3. One should however not overlook the impact of comparability.

to Solvency II.[24] There is no exception for small and medium-sized undertakings. The requirement does not apply to branches established in the EEA by (re)insurance undertakings with head offices situated outside the EEA,[25] nor to branches established by EEA (re)insurance undertakings in another MS.[26]

Subject to supervisory approval, (re)insurance groups may publish a single SFCR, covering the information at the level of the group with that relating to all or some of their subsidiaries (Art. 365 DA). Where the parent undertaking does not publish a single SFCR, the subsidiary (re)insurance undertakings must include in their solo SFCR a reference to the published group SFCR (Art. 370 (2) DA).

Although there is no requirement for third-country insurance undertakings that have established a branch in an EEA MS to disclose an SFCR for the operations of the branch, branch policyholders must be able to obtain any publicly disclosed information concerning the solvency and financial condition of the whole third-country insurance undertaking, if the rules and regulations of the third country prescribe such disclosure.[27]

As there are about 3,000 (re)insurance undertakings applying Solvency II, more than 3,000 SFCRs are published annually, as many (re)insurance groups publish a separate group SFCR in addition to the SFCRs relating to their subsidiaries. EIOPA has analysed a sample of SFCRs published in 2017 and issued some recommendations on how to improve the quality of the reports.[28] Some private firms have also carried out an analysis of published SFCRs, sometimes with recommendations for improvement.[29]

---

24 Including (re)insurance undertakings in run-off, subject to the transitional provision in Art. 308b (1) (a) and (b) FD.

25 As third-country branches are part of a legal person established outside the EEA, it is not possible for the EU to impose the disclosure of an SFCR by that branch as this would constitute an extraterritorial application of EU law.

26 This would constitute a discrimination on the grounds of nationality, as national branches are not required to disclose an SFCR.

27 EIOPA, Guidelines on the supervision of branches of third-country insurance undertakings, EIOPA-BoS-15/110, 23 October 2015, Guideline 36.

28 EIOPA, Supervisory Statement – Solvency II: Solvency and Financial Condition Report, EIOPA-BoS/17-310, 18 December 2017, 11 p. In an article published in September 2018, the German supervisory authority, BaFin, noted that SFCR reporting has further improved although there are still some shortcomings, for instance in the summary section and in references to annexes. See *BaFin Journal*, September 2018, pp. 7–8.

29 See, for instance, Deloitte (study of 61 SFCRs in Ireland, https://www2.deloitte.com/ie/en/pages/financial-services/articles/solvency-and-financial-condition-report.html#), KPMG (study of the top 10 non-life insurers in the Netherlands, https://home.kpmg/content/dam/kpmg/nl/pdf/2017/sector/financiele-dienstverlening/sfcr-analysis-non-life-insurers.pdf), LCP (study of SFCR reporting in UK and Ireland, https://insight.lcp.uk.com/acton/attachment/20628/f-071e/1/-/-/-/-/LCP%20Solvency%20II%20survey%202018.pdf), and ZEB (study of the SFCRs published by the 25 largest German life insurers, https://control.zeb.eu/news/sfcr-initial-experiences-german-insurance-market). These reports relate to the SFCRs published in 2017 and 2018. See also Solvencyiiwire.com, How do you SFCR?,

Although improvement is always possible, it can be said that the first publication of SFCRs in 2017 was a success. Many SFCRs are really interesting to read. They provide an insight into the business strategy of the undertaking, how the undertaking is organised and how the undertaking manages its capital under a risk-based solvency capital regime. It was not easy for (re)insurance undertakings to produce their first SFCR, though a standardised presentation is provided for in Annex XX to the DA.[30] Undertakings and groups are required to follow this structure. They must provide in the SFCR narrative information in quantitative and qualitative form, supplemented, where appropriate, with quantitative templates. Most undertakings provide quantitative reporting templates (QRTs) at the end of the SFCR, sometimes in an annex. In its 2017 supervisory statement on the SFCR, EIOPA recommended that the addition of QRTs by itself should not prevent undertakings or groups from providing quantitative and qualitative information in the body of the SFCR. It is important to provide background information so that the quantitative information in the QRTs can be more easily understood by the reader.

A standardised presentation has the advantage of comparability and ease of research. The disadvantage is a lack of creativity in presenting the undertaking or the group. The SFCR is an important communication tool for (re)insurance undertakings. If the undertaking or group uses boilerplate language or repeats legal requirements rather than providing insights, it is unlikely to be the case that the undertaking or group has a consumer focus. Some undertakings do not follow the structure required by the DA. This makes comparability with other SFCRs more difficult.

There is no prescribed length for the SFCR. The average length of the solo SFCR is 40–70 pages.[31] The group SFCR will obviously be more extensive.[32] This is even more so for a single SFCR covering both group and solo information.[33]

The AMSB must approve the SFCR and is responsible for its disclosure. As soon as the SFCR has been disclosed, it must be submitted to the supervisory authority (Art. 300 (2) DA).

---

http://www.solvencyiiwire.com/how-do-you-sfcr/1586952 and KPMG, *Solvency II public reporting*, December 2017, 11 p. (https://assets.kpmg/content/dam/kpmg/uk/pdf/2017/12/sfcr-benchmarking.pdf).

30 Commission Delegated Regulation (EU) 2015/35 of 10 October 2014 supplementing Directive 2009/138/EC of the European Parliament and of the Council on the taking-up and pursuit of the business of Insurance and Reinsurance (Solvency II), *OJ* L 12, 17.1.2015, p. 1.

31 This may not include the QRTs. In Germany, the average length of the solo SFCR is 90 p. See, GDV, Solvency II: Berichtspflichten grundlegend überarbeiten, *Regulierung und Aufsicht kompakt*, No 14, January 2019, p.3 (https://www.gdv.de/resource/blob/43650/a1618e99abcb7320271b34e1b2d3edc1/regulierung-und-aufsicht-kompakt-14-data.pdf).

32 For instance the 2017 SFCR of Allianz Group, which comprises 189 pages, i.e. 103 pages in the report and an appendix of 86 pages.

33 See, for instance, the 2017 SFCR published by UNIQA (325 pages), which comprises the SFCR of the UNIQA Group, as well as the solo SFCRs of UNIQA Insurance Group AG and UNIQA Österreich Versicherungen AG.

In the event of any major development affecting significantly the relevance of the information disclosed in the SFCR, the undertaking must disclose appropriate information on the nature and effects of that major development and must disclose an updated version of the SFCR. Two examples of such major developments are given in Art. 54 (1) FD.

The first is a situation where there is *non-compliance with the MCR* and the supervisory authority either considers that the undertaking will not be able to submit a realistic short-term finance scheme or does not receive such a scheme within one month of the date when non-compliance was observed. In that case, the undertaking must disclose immediately the amount of non-compliance, together with an explanation of its origin and consequences, including any remedial measure taken. Where, in spite of a short-term finance scheme initially considered to be realistic, non-compliance with the MCR has not been resolved within three months of its observation, this must be disclosed at the end of that period, together with an explanation of its origin and consequences, including any remedial measure taken, as well as any further remedial measures planned.

The second example is a situation where there is *significant non-compliance with the SCR* and the supervisory authority does not obtain a realistic recovery plan within two months of the date when non-compliance was observed. In that case, the undertaking must disclose immediately the amount of non-compliance, together with an explanation of its origin and consequences, including any remedial measure taken. Where, in spite of a recovery plan initially considered to be realistic, a significant non-compliance with the SCR has not been resolved within six months of its observation, this must be disclosed at the end of that period, together with an explanation of its origin and consequences, including any remedial measure taken, as well as any further remedial measures planned.

Updates to any information or explanations in a published SFCR are always possible in an updated version of the report. Without prejudice to any immediate disclosure that the undertaking must make in accordance with the requirements of Art. 54 (1) FD, an updated version of the SFCR must be disclosed as soon as possible after the major development has taken place. The update may take the form of an amendment supplementing the initial report (Art. 302 (3) DA).

Undertakings may also disclose, on a voluntary basis, additional information to that which is required, on the condition that this information is consistent with the information submitted to the supervisory authority (Art. 298 DA).

In order to make the SFCR shorter and to avoid duplication, (re)insurance undertakings may replace information in their SFCR with a reference to the information already made public by virtue of other legal or regulatory requirements, such as the financial statements or the management report (Art. 53 (3) FD). Some undertakings make extensive use of this possibility, meaning that the SFCR reads more like a reference document. This is clearly not user-friendly.

Sometimes, the DA requires information to be provided only where that information is material. Information is considered material if its omission or misstatement could influence the decision-making or the judgement of the users of the SFCR, including the supervisory authority (Art. 291 DA).

1.2.1. Publication of the SFCR

The first SFCRs were published in 2017, relating to information for the financial year 2016.

A solo SFCR must be published 14 weeks after the end of the financial year (Art. 300 (1) DA), with a transitional period of four years, starting on 1 January 2016 and ending on 31 December 2019, during which time the deadline for publication is decreased by two weeks each financial year (from 20 to 14) (Art. 308b (6) FD).

For a group SFCR or a single SFCR covering both group and solo information, the reporting deadline is six weeks later, i.e. 20 weeks after the financial year-end (Art. 362 DA), with a transitional period of four years, starting on 1 January 2016 and ending on 31 December 2019, during which time the deadline for publication is decreased by two weeks each financial year (from 26 to 20) (Art. 308b (8) DA).

Sometimes, undertakings or groups will make the SFCR available in English, in addition to the local language. When groups produce a separate group SFCR or a single SFCR, the report must be disclosed in the language or the languages determined by the group supervisor (Arts. 360 and 366 DA).

For many undertakings, the SFCR can easily be found on the internet, sometimes through a reference to the undertaking's website.

Art. 301 DA prescribes the following means of disclosure:[34]

- disclosure on the website of the undertaking or, in the absence thereof, on the website of the relevant trade association (the report must remain available on that website for at least five years after the disclosure date);
- provision of an electronic copy (if the report is not published on a website) within 10 working days to any person who requests the report within five years of the disclosure date;
- provision of a printed copy (irrespective of whether the report is published on a website) within 20 working days to any person who requests the report within two years of the disclosure date.

In practice, it is easy to obtain the SFCR.[35] That is entirely in line with the intention of the co-legislators. However, EIOPA reports that some undertakings

---

34 This also applies to the disclosure of the group and single SFCR. See Art. 8 Commission Implementing Regulation (EU) 2015/2452 of 2 December 2015.

35 A good example is the Central Bank of Ireland which has created on its website a repository of all publicly disclosed SFCRs (https://www.centralbank.ie/regulation/industry-market-sectors/insurance-reinsurance/solvency-ii/solvency-and-financial-condition-report-repository).

still do not have a website and that broad access may in this case be compromised despite the option to request the document in physical format. On the other hand, some websites of insurance groups give direct access to all the SFCRs published by the group and by major entities in the group.[36]

There are also websites where it is possible to find (against payment) solo and group SFCRs of (re)insurance undertakings and groups. Examples include www.solvencydata.com, which provides solo and group SFCRs of German and Austrian (re)insurance undertakings and groups, and www.solvencyiiwiredata.com, which provides a database of Solvency II public disclosures.

Some SFCRs include a report by the statutory auditors covering certain parts of the SFCR. This is, for instance, the case in the UK, because the PRA requires parts of the SFCR to be audited.[37] As stated above (Chapter 7, section 3.10.3), there is no EU requirement for an audit of the SFCR. EIOPA indicates in its message of 29 June 2015[38] that:

> "to ensure high quality public disclosure for Solvency II purposes, external audit can certainly be a powerful tool. In order to make best use of external audit in the context of the SFCR, EIOPA is of the view that at individual and group level main elements of the SFCR (balance sheet, own funds and capital requirements) of all (re)insurance undertakings could fall within the scope of an external audit."

Although the SFCR is an interesting and informative document, the question remains whether it has achieved its purpose, i.e. market discipline[39] and whether

---

36 See, for instance, the websites of Achmea (all reports in English), Aegon (all reports in English), Nordea (reports available in the languages of the subsidiaries) and Mapfre (all reports only in Spanish).

37 Following a public consultation, the PRA has abolished the audit requirement of the SFCR for small insurers. See PRA Policy Statement 25/18, published on 17 October 2018 (https://www.bankofengland.co.uk/-/media/boe/files/prudential-regulation/policy-statement/2018/ps2518.pdf?la=en&hash=B6F2081E80FB20BADD93AA31320CA0B67FBE53B1). The PRA estimates that about 150 small insurers and groups could benefit from this exemption. See Bank of England, Prudential Regulation Authority, *Solvency II: external audit of the public disclosure requirement*, Consultation Paper 8/18, April 2018, 13 p. (https://www.bankofengland.co.uk/-/media/boe/files/prudential-regulation/consultation-paper/2018/cp818).

38 EIOPA, Need for high quality public disclosure: Solvency II's report on solvency and financial condition and the potential role of external audit, EIOPA-BoS-15/154, 29 June 2015, p. 1.

39 A recent study in Germany shows that, on average, each undertaking's SFCR was downloaded only 33 times a month, immediately following its release. See, GDV, Solvency II: Berichtspflichten grundlegend überarbeiten, *Regulierung und Aufsicht kompakt*, No 14, January 2019, p.3. (https://www.gdv.de/resource/blob/43650/a1618e99abcb7320271b34e1b2d3edc1/regulierung-und-aufsicht-kompakt-14-data.pdf). This could be a cultural issue, limited to Germany. It is contradicted by the experience gathered by EIOPA: investors, analysts and consumer associations confirm the relevance of the SFCR as a tool for market discipline. See, BERNARDINO, G., Insurance and pensions: securing the future, 8th Annual EIOPA Conference, Frankfurt, 20 November 2018, p. 4 (https://eiopa.europa.eu/Publications/Speeches%20and%20presentations/2018-11-20%20KeynoteSpeechAnnualConferenceGabrielBernardino.pdf).

imposing a requirement on all (re)insurance undertakings to produce an SFCR for public disclosure purposes is in line with the proportionality principle. It would certainly help small (re)insurance undertakings to be exempted from preparing and disclosing an SFCR, although it would mean that publicly available information on these undertakings would disappear. Requiring parts of the SFCR to be audited is difficult to justify, particularly for small (re)insurance undertakings. A possible improvement of the present requirement could be to adopt a more targeted approach with short, easy to understand information for the general reader and a more technical annex for professionals. Particularly important are the sources of changes in own funds and in the SCR. It would be useful to carry out a cost-benefit analysis on the usefulness of the SFCR as part of the 2020 review of the FD.

1.2.2. Contents of the SFCR

The SFCR contains narrative information in quantitative and qualitative form, supplemented, where appropriate, with quantitative templates. For the quantitative information, EIOPA has developed templates that are regularly updated.[40] The first update took place in 2017,[41] following an update to the Implementing Regulation that deals with regular supervisory reporting (see below, section 3.2.4). A second update took place in 2018.[42]

1.2.2.1. Summary Section

Because the SFCR might be lengthy and because some of the information is technical, it is important to present the relevant quantitative and qualitative information contained in the various sections in a concise and comprehensible manner in the first section of the SFCR, the "Summary". The summary section must be easy to understand for stakeholders in general and for policyholders and beneficiaries, and must highlight any material changes to the undertaking's

---

40 See Commission Implementing Regulation (EU) 2015/2452 of 2 December 2015 laying down implementing technical standards with regard to the procedures, formats and templates of the solvency and financial condition report in accordance with Directive 2009/138/EC of the EP and of the Council, *OJ* L 347, 31.12.2015, p. 285. This Regulation contains the templates for the SFCR of individual undertakings and groups.

41 Commission Implementing Regulation (EU) 2017/2190 of 24 November 2017 amending and correcting Implementing Regulation (EU) 2015/2452 laying down implementing technical standards with regard to the procedures, formats and templates of the solvency and financial condition report according to Directive 2009/138/EC of the European Parliament and of the Council, *OJ* L 310, 25.11.2017, p. 30.

42 Commission Implementing Regulation (EU) 2018/1843 of 23 November 2018 amending Implementing Regulation (EU) 2015/2452 as regards the scope of application of the template for disclosing premiums, claims and expenses by country, *OJ* L 299, 26.11.2018, p. 2.

business and performance, system of governance, risk profile, valuation for solvency purposes and capital management over the reporting period (Art. 292 DA). Insurance is complex, but it should be possible to explain in simple terms the main elements of the business, the main risks to which the undertaking or the group is exposed, how the company or the group is organised and its capital and solvency position.

In its 2017 supervisory statement on the SFCR, EIOPA indicated that it expects undertakings to be more careful in preparing the summary section in the SFCR so as to ensure that it includes at least the following:

- the key elements and drivers of the undertaking's business model and business strategy;
- key indicators for the undertaking's underwriting performance and investment performance, including material lines of business and material geographical areas where the business is carried out;
- any significant business or other events with material impact on the solvency and financial condition that have occurred over the reporting period;
- the key elements of the system of governance;
- information about the undertaking's/group's key risks;
- the solvency ratio with and without the VA or MA;
- the approach to the use of transitional arrangements, including the solvency ratio without the transitional adjustment to the relevant risk-free interest rate term structure or without the transitional measure on technical provisions;
- the amount of the SCR and the eligible amount of own funds to cover the SCR, classified by tiers;
- the amount of the MCR and the eligible amount of basic own funds to cover the MCR, classified by tiers;
- information about any non-compliance with the MCR or significant non-compliance with the SCR over the last reporting period.

The list provided by EIOPA excludes some of the more technical information, which can be found in the section "Valuation for solvency purposes" and in the QRTs, and which is more directly addressed to experts.

For stakeholders, the information contained under each of the bullet points listed by EIOPA is relevant, as it provides an answer to the following questions (only listed as examples):

- Who owns the undertaking? What is its group structure? What is the main business of the undertaking or group (life, non-life, health, reinsurance, etc.)? What products and services are being offered? Under which brands? How are these products offered to the public (agents, brokers, banks)? What is the strategy going forward? Does the undertaking or group have a specific policy to ensure that policyholders are treated fairly?

- What are the earnings of the undertaking or group? From which line of business do they come? What is the combined ratio (incurred losses + expenses divided by total earned premiums)? Which assets does the undertaking or group invest in and what is the return on these investments?
- Have there been acquisitions, sales of parts of the undertaking or group, significant losses or unexpected events?
- How is the undertaking or group organised? Who is reporting to whom? Have there been any changes in the organisation of the undertaking or group? How is risk management organised? What committees are established within the board? Is there a risk committee? Is the undertaking or group using a partial or full internal model? How is the governance of the model organised in practice?
- What are the specific risks to which the undertaking or group is exposed? Who is in charge of identifying those risks? How are they being monitored? What is the targeted risk profile? Who is in charge of the risk management function? Is there a CRO? To whom does the CRO report?
- What is the solvency ratio? Did it change from the previous year? How was it influenced by the use of the VA or the MA? How is it calculated (standard formula, partial or full internal model)? Is there a different confidence level?
- Has the undertaking or group used any of the transitional measures that influence the level of technical provisions and thus the solvency ratio? What is the impact of these measures on the solvency ratio?
- What is the amount of the SCR? Is there a target level and how does the amount of the SCR relate to this target level? What is the eligible amount of own funds to cover the SCR divided by tiers? What is the level of Tier 1 capital? Are there any changes compared with the previous period and how are they explained?
- What is the amount of the MCR? What is the eligible amount of basic own funds to cover the MCR, classified by tiers? Are there any changes compared with the previous period and how are they explained?
- Has there been any non-compliance with the MCR during the reporting period? Has there been any significant non-compliance with the SCR over the reporting period? Has a recovery plan been put in place and how is it being implemented? This information is particularly important because it shows possible weaknesses in the solvency position of the undertaking or group.

An answer to these questions gives an insight into where the undertaking or group stands in terms of its business strategy, its relationship with policyholders, its capital position, its solvency and its risk management.

In general, few undertakings or groups publish a good summary. For policyholders and beneficiaries, as well as for other stakeholders, such as insurance intermediaries, the summary should be the place to look. If the summary is well prepared, the undertaking or group is likely to have a consumer focus.

1.2.2.2. Business and Performance

Annex XX DA prescribes the following structure for this section of the SFCR:
A. Business and Performance
- A.1 Business
- A.2 Underwriting performance
- A.3 Investment performance
- A.4 Performance of other activities
- A.5 Any other information

This is further specified in Art. 293 DA:
1. *Business of the (re)insurance undertaking*
   (a) the name and legal form of the undertaking;
   (b) the name and contact details of the supervisory authority responsible for financial supervision of the undertaking and, where applicable, the name and contact details of the group supervisor of the group to which the undertaking belongs;
   (c) the name and contact details of the external auditor of the undertaking;
   (d) a description of the holders of qualifying holdings in the undertaking;[43]
   (e) where the undertaking belongs to a group, details of the undertaking's position within the legal structure of the group;[44]
   (f) the undertaking's material lines of business and material geographical areas where it carries out business;
   (g) any significant business or other events that have occurred over the reporting period that have had a material impact on the undertaking.
2. *Underwriting performance*
   Qualitative and quantitative information on the undertaking's underwriting performance, at an aggregate level and by material line of business and material geographical areas where it carries out business over the reporting period, together with a comparison of the information with that reported on the previous reporting period, as shown in the undertaking's financial statements.

[43] EIOPA Guidelines on reporting and public disclosure, EIOPA-BoS-15/109, 14 September 2015, Guideline 1.

[44] EIOPA Guidelines on reporting and public disclosure, EIOPA-BoS-15/109, 14 September 2015, Guideline 1.

3. *Investment performance*
   Qualitative and quantitative information regarding the performance of the investments of the undertaking over the reporting period together with a comparison of the information with that reported on the previous reporting period, as shown in the undertaking's financial statements:
   (a) information on income and expenses arising from investments by asset class and, where necessary for a proper understanding of the income and expenses, the components of such income and expenses;
   (b) information about any gains and losses recognised directly in equity;
   (c) information about any investments in securitisation.
4. *Performance of other activities*
   Other material income and expenses of the undertaking incurred over the reporting period, together with a comparison of the information with that reported in the previous reporting period, as shown in the undertaking's financial statements.[45] Other activities may include fund or asset management.
5. *Any other information*
   Any other material information regarding the business and performance of the undertaking, for instance events happening after the balance sheet date, such as major acquisitions or sales of parts of the business.

Art. 359 DA further requires the group SFCR to include a description of the legal structure and governance and organisational structure of the group, with a description of all subsidiaries, material related undertakings and significant branches, as well as qualitative and quantitative information on relevant operations and transactions within the group.

For a group SFCR, the "A.1 Business" section must also include an explanation of the material differences between the scope of the group used for the consolidated financial statements and the scope of the consolidated data for the group's solvency.[46]

This section of the SFCR can be defined as the passport of the undertaking or group. It also shows the strengths and weaknesses of the business and provides an insight into the business strategy.

The templates that may be included to supplement the narrative information are: balance sheet (S.02.01), premiums, claims and expenses by line of business and by top five countries (S.05.01, S.05.02) and scope of the group (S.32.01).

---

[45] EIOPA, Guidelines on reporting and public disclosure, EIOPA-BoS-15/109, 14 September 2015, Guideline 2.

[46] EIOPA, Guidelines on reporting and public disclosure, EIOPA-BoS-15/109, 14 September 2015, Guideline 14.

1.2.2.3. System of Governance

Annex XX DA prescribes the following structure for this section of the SFCR:
B. System of Governance

- B.1 General information on the system of governance
- B.2 Fit and proper requirements
- B.3 Risk management system including the own risk and solvency assessment
- B.4 Internal control system
- B.5 Internal audit function
- B.6 Actuarial function
- B.7 Outsourcing
- B.8 Any other information

This is further specified in Art. 294 DA:

1. *General information on the system of governance*
   (a) the structure of the undertaking's AMSB, providing a description of its main roles and responsibilities and a brief description of the segregation of responsibilities within these bodies, in particular whether relevant committees exist within them, as well as a description of the main roles and responsibilities of key functions;
   (b) any material changes in the system of governance that have taken place over the reporting period;
   (c) information on the remuneration policy and practices regarding the AMSB and, unless otherwise stated, employees, including:
      (i) principles of the remuneration policy, with an explanation of the relative importance of the fixed and variable components of remuneration;
      (ii) information on the individual and collective performance criteria on which any entitlement to share options, shares or variable components of remuneration is based;
      (iii) a description of the main characteristics of supplementary pension or early retirement schemes for the members of the AMSB and other key function holders;
   (d) information about material transactions during the reporting period with shareholders, with persons who exercise a significant influence on the undertaking, and with members of the AMSB;
   (e) an assessment of the adequacy of the system of governance to the nature, scale and complexity of the risks inherent in the business.
2. *Fit and proper requirements*
   (a) a description of the undertaking's specific requirements concerning skills, knowledge and expertise applicable to the persons who

effectively run the undertaking or have other key functions (for instance, the existence of a skills matrix for board members and key function holders);

(b) a description of the undertaking's process for assessing the fitness and the propriety of the persons who effectively run the undertaking or have other key functions (for instance, the existence of a nomination committee).

3. *Risk management system and ORSA*

(a) a description of the undertaking's risk management system, comprising strategies, processes and reporting procedures, and how it is able to effectively identify, measure, monitor, manage and report, on a continuous basis, the risks, on an individual and aggregated level, to which the undertaking is or could be exposed;

(b) a description of how the risk management system, including the risk management function, is implemented and integrated into the organisational structure and decision-making processes of the undertaking;

(c) a description of the process used by the undertaking to fulfil its obligation to conduct an ORSA as part of its risk management system, including how the ORSA is integrated into the organisational structure and decision-making processes of the undertaking;

(d) a statement detailing how often the ORSA is reviewed and approved by the undertaking's AMSB;

(e) a statement explaining how the undertaking has determined its own solvency needs given its risk profile and how its capital management activities and its risk management system interact with each other.

4. *Internal control system*

(a) a description of the undertaking's internal control system;

(b) a description of how the compliance function is implemented.

5. *Internal audit function*

(a) a description of how the undertaking's internal audit function is implemented;

(b) a description of how the undertaking's internal audit function maintains its independence and objectivity from the activities it reviews.

6. *Actuarial function*

A description of how the actuarial function is implemented, for instance to what extent it is part of the risk management function.

7. *Outsourcing*

A description of the outsourcing policy of the undertaking, the undertaking's outsourcing of any critical or important operational functions or activities and the jurisdiction in which the service providers of such functions or activities are located.

8. *Any other information*
   Any other material information regarding the system of governance of the undertaking, for instance whether a single ORSA document was produced for the group and its subsidiaries (Art. 246 (2) FD) or whether the effectiveness of the governance system is regularly tested by a system of self-assessment.

Art. 359 DA further requires the group SFCR to include: a description of how the risk management and internal control systems and reporting procedures are implemented consistently in all the undertakings within the scope of group supervision; a statement, where applicable, that the group has chosen the option to prepare a single ORSA report for the group; and information on any material intra-group outsourcing arrangements.

The EIOPA Guidelines[47] indicate that the "B.1 General information on the system of governance" section should explain how the key functions have the necessary authority, resources and operational independence to carry out their tasks, and how they report to and advise the AMSB.

Where the undertaking is using a partial or full internal model to calculate the SCR, the "B.3 Risk management system including the own risk and solvency assessment" section should include the following information on the governance of the internal model:

- the responsible roles and specific committees, if any, and their main tasks, position and scope of responsibilities;
- how existing committees interact with the AMSB in order to ensure the proper functioning of the internal model;
- any material changes to the internal model governance during the reporting period;
- a description of the validation process used to monitor the performance and ongoing appropriateness of the internal model.[48]

The governance section of the SFCR is usually very extensive. There is sometimes a tendency to repeat the laws, regulations and administrative provisions. This cannot be the objective of the SFCR. The information should relate to the specific situation of the undertaking or the group.

In terms of the ORSA, EIOPA expects the SFCR to include information on:

- the process for performing and ongoing monitoring of the ORSA, including the involvement of the board;

---

47 EIOPA, Guidelines on system of reporting and public disclosure, EIOPA-BoS-15/109, 14 September 2015, Guideline 3.

48 EIOPA, Guidelines on system of reporting and public disclosure, EIOPA-BoS-15/109, 14 September 2015, Guideline 4.

- the link to the business strategy and how the main areas/risks of the business strategy are considered in the ORSA, namely in the overall solvency needs;
- the timing and frequency of the ORSA and the triggers for performing additional assessments.

The objective of the ORSA is to ensure that a (re)insurance undertaking or group does not engage in business for which it does not have the right amount of capital. It is therefore useful to see how undertakings or groups carry out this legal requirement in practice.

Particularly important is the way the undertaking or group organises its risk management. Some undertakings or groups report extensively in their SFCR about the way in which they organise the so-called "three lines of defence" model and how this is integrated into the governance model of Solvency II, with its four key governance functions.

1.2.2.4. Risk Profile

Annex XX DA prescribes the following structure for this section of the SFCR:
C. Risk Profile
- C.1 Underwriting risk
- C.2 Market risk
- C.3 Credit risk
- C.4 Liquidity risk
- C.5 Operational risk
- C.6 Other material risks[49]
- C.7 Any other information

This is further specified in Art. 295 DA:[50]

1. *Risk profile*
   Qualitative and quantitative information regarding the risk profile of the undertaking, separately for underwriting risk, market risk, credit risk, liquidity risk, operational risk and other material risks.

[49] For instance, regulatory change risk, reputation risk, strategic risk, economic environment risk, other environmental risk, concentration risk, emerging risk and intangible risk. For interesting examples, see the 2017 SFCR of Hannover Re, pp. 59–61 (https://www.hannover-re.com/1265699/2017-solvency-and-financial-condition-report-hannover-ruck-se.pdf).

[50] The information must be given for each of the risks listed.

2. *Risk exposure*
   Qualitative and quantitative information regarding the risk exposure of the undertaking, including the exposure arising from off-balance sheet positions and the transfer of risk to SPVs:
   (a) a description of the measures used to assess these risks within the undertaking, including any material changes over the reporting period;
   (b) a description of the material risks to which the undertaking is exposed, including any material changes over the reporting period;
   (c) a description of how assets have been invested in accordance with the prudent person principle.
3. *Risk concentration*
   A description of the material risk concentrations to which the undertaking is exposed.
4. *Risk mitigation*
   A description of the techniques used for mitigating risks, and the processes for monitoring the continued effectiveness of these risk-mitigation techniques.
5. *Liquidity risk*
   The total amount of the expected profit included in future premiums as calculated in accordance with Art. 260 (2) DA.
6. *Risk sensitivity*
   A description of the methods used, the assumptions made and the outcome of stress testing and sensitivity analysis for material risks and events.
7. *Any other material information*
   Any other material information regarding the risk profile of the undertaking.

Art. 359 DA requires further qualitative and quantitative information in the group SFCR on significant risk concentrations.

The EIOPA Guidelines[51] indicate that special attention needs to be paid to information concerning transfer of risk from the undertaking to SPVs. The undertaking needs to describe whether the SPV has been authorised. It must identify the risks that are transferred to it and explain how the fully funded principle is assessed on an ongoing basis.

In its 2017 supervisory statement on the SFCR, EIOPA indicated that the information on the risk sensitivity to different scenarios or stresses, including the sensitivity of the SCR of the undertaking or group, should be better structured

[51] EIOPA, Guidelines on reporting and public disclosure, EIOPA-BoS-15/109, 14 September 2015, Guideline 5.

and more comprehensive. It expects the reporting of sensitivities to include at least the following:

- description of the methods used, i.e. scenario analysis, stress tests and sensitivity analysis for the different risks;
- adequate information on the underlying assumptions of the methods used, including how the future management actions are taken into consideration;
- the impact of the sensitivity measured as an amount of the SCR for that specific risk and as a percentage of the overall SCR ratio;
- an interpretation of the results considering the strategy and business model of the undertaking or group, and any impact on the management of the most material sensitivities.

The templates that could be included to supplement the narrative information: liabilities are: life, health and non-life technical provisions (S.12.01 and S.17.01) and capital adequacy: SCR (S.25).

1.2.2.5. Valuation for Solvency Purposes

Annex XX DA prescribes the following structure for this section of the SFCR:
D. Valuation for Solvency Purposes

- D.1 Assets
- D.2 Technical provisions
- D.3 Other liabilities
- D.4 Alternative methods for valuation
- D.5 Any other information

This is further specified in Art. 296 DA:

1. *Asset valuation*
   (a) separately for each material class of assets, the value of the assets, as well as a description of the bases, methods and main assumptions used for valuation for solvency purposes;
   (b) separately for each material class of assets, a quantitative and qualitative explanation of any material differences between the bases, methods and main assumptions used by the undertaking for the valuation for solvency purposes and those used for its valuation in the financial statements.
2. *Valuation of technical provisions*
   (a) separately for each material line of business, the value of technical provisions, including the amount of the best estimate and the risk margin, as well as a description of the bases, methods and main assumptions used for its valuation for solvency purposes;
   (b) a description of the level of uncertainty associated with the value of technical provisions;

(c) separately for each material line of business, a quantitative and qualitative explanation of any material differences between the bases, methods and main assumptions used by the undertaking for the valuation for solvency purposes and those used for their valuation in the financial statements;
(d) where the MA is applied,[52] a description of the MA and of the portfolio of obligations and assigned assets to which the MA is applied, as well as a quantification of the impact of a change to zero of the MA on the undertaking's financial position, including on the amount of technical provisions, the SCR, the MCR, the basic own funds and the amounts of own funds eligible to cover the MCR and the SCR;
(e) a statement on whether the VA is used[53] by the undertaking and quantification of the impact of a change to zero of the VA on the undertaking's financial position, including on the amount of technical provisions, the SCR, the MCR, the basic own funds and the amounts of own funds eligible to cover the MCR and the SCR;
(f) a statement on whether the transitional risk-free interest rate term structure is applied[54] and a quantification of the impact of not applying the transitional measure on the undertaking's financial position, including on the amount of technical provisions, the SCR, the MCR, the basic own funds and the amounts of own funds eligible to cover the MCR and the SCR;
(g) a statement on whether the transitional measure on technical provisions[55] is applied and a quantification of the impact of not applying the that measure on the undertaking's financial position, including on the amount of technical provisions, the SCR, the MCR, the basic own funds and the amounts of own funds eligible to cover the MCR and the SCR;
(h) a description of the recoverables from reinsurance contracts and SPVs and of any material changes in the relevant assumptions made in the calculation of technical provisions compared to the previous reporting period.

3. *Valuation of other liabilities*
(a) separately for each material class of other liabilities, the value of other liabilities, as well as a description of the bases, methods and main assumptions used for their valuation for solvency purposes;
(b) separately for each material class of other liabilities, a quantitative and qualitative explanation of any material differences, with the valuation

52 Art. 77b FD.
53 Art. 77d FD.
54 Art. 308c FD.
55 Art. 308d FD.

bases, methods and main assumptions used by the undertaking for the valuation for solvency purposes and those used for their valuation in the financial statements.

4. *Alternative valuation methods*
Information about the use of alternative valuation methods and the assets and liabilities to which that valuation approach has been applied.[56]
5. *Any other information*
Any other material information regarding the valuation of assets and liabilities for solvency purposes.

Art. 359 DA further requires the group SFCR to provide a quantitative and qualitative explanation of any material differences between the bases, methods and main assumptions used at group level for the valuation for solvency purposes of the group's assets, technical provisions and other liabilities, where those differ materially from those used by any of its subsidiaries for the valuation for solvency purposes of its assets, technical provisions and other liabilities.

The EIOPA Guidelines contain further clarifications concerning the information to be provided in the case of aggregation of assets into material classes, the content by material classes of assets (intangible assets, financial assets, financial and operating leases, deferred tax assets, related undertakings), the use of significant simplified methods for the calculation of technical provisions, the information to be provided in the case of aggregation of liabilities other than technical provisions by class, and the content by material classes of liabilities other than technical provisions.[57]

Regarding the description of the bases, methods and main assumptions used for the valuation of assets, liabilities and technical provisions, EIOPA points out that the SFCR should include more relevant undertaking- or group-specific information. The following recommendations are given:

- for the valuation of investments: the focus should be on the entity's specific approaches to investments, the conditions under which each valuation method is applied, the type of investments to which the method is applied and the relative weight of investments valued by each method;
- for the valuation of deferred tax assets and deferred tax liabilities: the information should include the identified relevant differences between

56 Art. 263 DA. Alternative valuation methods are applied when readily observable, external market valuation is not available or when the relevant market is inactive. This may be the case, for instance, for property, infrastructure or private equity holdings. See above, Chapter 6, section 2.

57 EIOPA, Guidelines on reporting and public disclosure, EIOPA-BoS-15/109, 14 September 2015, Guidelines 6–10.

accounting standards and Solvency II and the reason or sources for such differences, any unused tax losses and the maturity date of any losses;
- for the valuation of technical provisions: a description should be provided of the level of uncertainty, by linking it at least to the assumptions underlying the calculation, such as economic and non-economic assumptions, expected profits in future premiums, future management actions and future policyholder behaviour.

The templates that could be used to supplement the narrative information are: balance sheet (S.02.01), liabilities: life, health and non-life technical provisions (S.12.01 and S.17.01), and impact of LTG and transitional measures on the amount of technical provisions, own funds, SCR and MCR (S.22.01).

This section is no doubt the most technical section of the SFCR. It contains important information on the valuation of assets and liabilities in the solvency balance sheet and a comparison with the valuation of the same assets and liabilities for financial reporting purposes. The differences can be very significant.[58]

This section also shows the impact on the solvency ratio of using the MA and the VA. This can also be very significant.[59]

A study by ZEB of the 2016 SFCRs published by the 25 largest German life insurance undertakings shows the importance of applying the VA and the interest rate transitional measure on technical provisions for the solvency ratio: for insurance undertakings that only used the VA, the difference in the solvency ratio with and without the VA was 101%, and for insurance undertakings that used both the VA and the interest rate transitional measure, the difference was 283%.[60]

1.2.2.6. Capital Management

Annex XX DA prescribes the following structure for this section of the SFCR:
E. Capital Management
- E.1 Own funds
- E.2 SCR and MCR

---

58 For instance, the 2017 group SFCR of Aviva plc (p. 4) indicates that the excess of assets over liabilities was £26.1 billion on a Solvency II basis, which was £6.9 billion higher than the value under IFRS, primarily driven by a difference in valuation of technical provisions. Aviva applies the transitional deduction to technical provisions, whilst also applying the MA and VA.

59 For instance, the 2016 group SFCR of Aegon indicated that the combined impact of both adjustments on the group solvency ratio was 26%.

60 For instance, in its 2017 SFCR, Alte Leipziger Lebensversicherung auf Gegenseitigkeit indicated that it was using neither the VA nor the interest rate transitional. Its solvency ratio for 2017 was 302%. If it were to use the VA and the interest rate transitional, its solvency ratio would be 505%.

- E.3 Use of the duration-based equity risk sub-module in calculating the SCR
- E.4 Differences between the standard formula and any internal model used
- E.5 Non-compliance with the MCR and non-compliance with the SCR
- E.6 Any other information

This is further specified in Art. 297 DA:

1. *Own funds*
   (a) information on the objectives, policies and processes employed by the undertaking for managing its own funds, including information on the time horizon used for business planning and on any material changes over the reporting period;
   (b) separately for each tier, information on the structure, amount and quality of own funds at the end of the reporting period and at the end of the previous reporting period, including an analysis of the significant changes in each tier over the reporting period;
   (c) the eligible amount of own funds to cover the SCR, classified by tiers;
   (d) the eligible amount of basic own funds to cover the MCR, classified by tiers;
   (e) a quantitative and qualitative explanation of any material differences between equity as shown in the undertaking's financial statements and the excess of assets over liabilities as calculated for solvency purposes;
   (f) for each basic own-fund item that is subject to a transitional arrangement,[61] a description of the nature of the item and its amount;
   (g) for each material item of ancillary own funds, a description of the item, the amount of the ancillary own-fund item and, where a method by which to determine the amount of the ancillary own-fund item has been approved, that method, as well as the nature and the names of the counterparty or group of counterparties[62] for the following items: unpaid share capital or initial fund that has not been called up, letters of credit and guarantees and any other legal binding commitments received by the undertaking;[63]
   (h) a description of any item deducted from own funds and a brief description of any significant restriction affecting the availability and transferability of own funds within the undertaking;
   (i) information regarding deferred taxes recognised in the balance sheet, their likely use against probable future taxable profit as well as an

61 Art. 308b (9) and (10) FD.

62 The names of the counterparties must not be disclosed where such disclosure is legally not possible or impracticable or where the counterparties concerned are not material.

63 Art. 89 (1) FD.

analysis of net deferred tax assets (for instance, to what extent these net deferred tax assets have been recognised as eligible own funds).[64]

Art. 359 DA requires further information concerning the method used for the calculation of the group solvency capital, on significant restrictions to the fungibility and transferability of own funds eligible for the calculation of the group SCR and on material sources of group diversification effects.

The EIOPA Guidelines contain further clarifications on the information to be disclosed concerning the use of additional solvency ratios, the structure, amount, quality and eligibility of own funds, and the differences between the standard formula and internal models used, as well as on the issue of material own-fund items within a group context.[65]

In its 2017 supervisory statement on the SFCR, EIOPA recommended that the information on the management of own funds be described in the context of the undertaking's/group's strategy and business model, with specific reference to the time horizon used for business planning and any material changes over the reporting period.

2. *SCR and MCR*
   (a) the amounts of the undertaking's SCR and MCR at the end of the reporting period, accompanied, where applicable, by an indication that the final amount of the SCR is still subject to supervisory assessment;
   (b) the amount of the undertaking's SCR split by risk modules where the undertaking applies the standard formula, and by risk categories where the undertaking applies an internal model;
   (c) information on whether and for which risk modules and sub-modules of the standard formula the undertaking is using simplified calculations;
   (d) information on whether and for which parameters of the standard formula the undertaking is using USPs;[66]
   (e) where applicable, a statement that the undertaking's MS has made use of the option not to require the disclosure of capital add-ons or the impact of any USPs that the undertaking is required to use because of significant deviations of the risk profile of the undertaking from the assumptions underlying the standard formula calculation[67] until 2021;[68]

---

64 This point was added in the EC's 2019 amendment of the DA, following the advice of EIOPA in the context of the 2018 review of the DA. See EIOPA, Second set of advice to the EC on specific items in the Solvency II Delegated Regulation, EIOPA-BoS-18/075, 28 February 2018, pp. 333–340.

65 EIOPA, Guidelines on reporting and public disclosure, EIOPA-BoS-15/109, 14 September 2015, Guidelines 11, 12, 13 and 15.

66 Art. 104 (7) FD.

67 Art. 110 FD.

68 Art. 51 (2), third subparagraph FD.

(f) unless the undertaking's MS has made use of the option referred to under (e) above, the impact of any USPs the undertaking is required to use and the amount of any capital add-on applied to the SCR, together with concise information on its justification by the supervisory authority concerned;
(g) information on the inputs used by the undertaking to calculate the MCR;
(h) any material change to the SCR and the MCR over the reporting period, and the reasons for any such change;
(i) the amount by which the SCR has been adjusted for the LAC-DT, as well as a description of deferred tax liabilities, carry-backs (reversals of deferred tax liabilities) and probable future taxable profit used to demonstrate the likely utilisation of deferred taxes and of the underlying assumptions used for the projection of probable future taxable profits, where the amount of deferred tax assets is material.[69]

3. *Use of the duration-based equity risk sub-module*[70]
(a) an indication that the undertaking is using the duration-based equity risk sub-module for the calculation of its SCR, after approval from its supervisory authority;
(b) the amount of the capital requirement for the duration-based equity risk sub-module resulting from such use.

4. *Use of an internal model*
(a) a description of the various purposes for which the undertaking is using its internal model;
(b) a description of the scope of the internal model in terms of business units and risk categories;
(c) where a partial internal model is used, a description of the technique which has been used to integrate any partial internal model into the standard formula, including, where relevant, a description of alternative techniques used;
(d) a description of the methods used in the internal model for the calculation of the probability distribution forecast and the SCR;
(e) an explanation, by risk module, of the main differences in the methodologies and underlying assumptions used in the standard formula and in the internal model;
(f) the risk measure and time period used in the internal model, and where they are not the same as those set for the standard formula,[71]

---

69 This point was added in the EC's 2019 amendment of the DA, following the advice of EIOPA in the context of the 2018 review of the DA. See EIOPA, Second set of advice to the EC on specific items in the Solvency II Delegated Regulation, EIOPA-BoS-18/075, 28 February 2018, pp. 333–340.

70 Art. 304 FD.

71 Art. 101 (3) FD.

an explanation of why the SCR calculated using the internal model provides policyholders and beneficiaries with a level of protection equivalent to that set out for the standard formula;

(g) a description of the nature and appropriateness of the data used in the internal model.

Art. 359 DA further requires a description of the undertakings that fall within the scope of any internal model used to calculate the group SCR, as well as a description of the main differences, if any, between any internal model used at individual undertaking level and any internal model used to calculate the group SCR.

5. *Non-compliance with the MCR or significant non-compliance with the SCR*
   (a) regarding any non-compliance with the MCR: the period and maximum amount of each non-compliance during the reporting period, an explanation of its origin and consequences, any remedial measures taken and an explanation of the effects of such remedial measures;
   (b) where non-compliance with the MCR has not been subsequently resolved: the amount of the non-compliance at the reporting date;
   (c) regarding any significant non-compliance with the SCR: the period and maximum amount of each significant non-compliance during the reporting period, an explanation of its origin and consequences, any remedial measures taken and an explanation of the effects of such remedial measures;
   (d) where a significant non-compliance with the SCR has not been subsequently resolved: the amount of the non-compliance at the reporting date.
6. *Any other information*
   Any other material information regarding the capital management of the undertaking.

The templates that could be used to supplement the narrative information are: impact of LTG and transitional measures on the amount of own funds and liabilities (S.22.01), and capital adequacy: own funds, SCR and MCR (S.23, S.25 and S.28).

Particularly important under the "Capital Management" section is the information concerning the amount of the SCR and the MCR, and the structure, amount and quality of the own funds. Despite being a target ratio, the solvency ratio (own funds/SCR%) has now become important information used to compare the strength of (re)insurance undertakings. The solvency ratio must be at least 100%. A solvency ratio of 100% does not mean that a (re)insurer cannot fail – Solvency II is not a zero-failure regime. It ensures that a (re)insurer with a solvency ratio of 100% can withstand the worst annual loss over the next 200 years.

The SCR, and thus the solvency ratio, will be volatile, as they are based upon a calculation of assets and liabilities in the balance sheet at market value and markets are more volatile today than ever before. In practice, (re)insurance undertakings will aim at a solvency ratio that is higher than 100%, for instance because they want to have more capital (free funds) so as to obtain a higher rating in the market, to protect themselves against the volatility of the SCR and a possible breach of the SCR as a result of this volatility, to make new acquisitions, or to protect themselves against a hostile bid.

In most cases, the SCR will be calculated on the basis of the standard formula introduced by Solvency II. In some cases, the SCR will be calculated on the basis of an internal model developed by the undertaking and approved by the supervisor.

The MCR represents the minimum level of security. It is calculated in a simpler manner and will usually be between 25% and 45% of the SCR.

(Re)insurance undertakings need to hold own funds to cover the SCR and the MCR. The own funds represent the excess of assets over liabilities and include subordinated liabilities. They are classified into three tiers, with Tier 1 representing the highest-quality capital. Own funds should absorb losses and be of sufficient quality. This will be clearly visible under this section of the SFCR.

(Re)insurance groups are also required to calculate a group SCR and a group MCR (when applying the default method) because groups may have risks that are different from the risks to which individual group members are exposed. This means that for a (re)insurance group, a group SCR and a group MCR (when applying the default method) will be available in addition to SCR and MCR amounts for each member of the group (parent and subsidiaries).

If a (re)insurance undertaking has a solvency ratio that is lower than 100% and thus breaches the SCR, it does not mean that the undertaking is insolvent. As the SCR is volatile, a breach of the SCR is not dramatic. The (re)insurance undertaking will have to take measures to restore the SCR within six months.

A breach of the MCR is more serious, as the MCR reflects the minimum level of protection for policyholders and beneficiaries. Breaching the MCR would amount to an unacceptable level of risk. An insurer that breaches the MCR will be put into run-off by the supervisor, unless the MCR is met again within a short period of time.

It should be kept in mind that each SFCR only describes the situation of the undertaking at a specific point in time. Comparative numbers must be available from 2018 onwards, although several (re)insurance undertakings have already provided comparative amounts for the SCR and the MCR for the period prior to 1 January 2016. Comparative numbers allow the reader to better assess the situation of the undertaking over a period of time. This is in particular relevant for the solvency ratio (own funds/SCR%), which may be affected by a number of elements, such as the LTG measures (VA or MA) or transitional measures (the adjustment of the risk-free interest rate or the technical provisions).

Solvency ratios are not yet readily comparable because of these measures, but the evolution of the solvency ratio over time is an important piece of information.

In terms of the solvency ratio, the investment strategy of the undertaking is relevant. Diversification of investments will influence the solvency ratio. Under Solvency II, an investment in sovereign bonds requires no capital charge (in the standard formula) because such an investment is considered to be without risk. This may however not always be true. On the other hand, if a (re)insurance undertaking diversifies its investments, that may have an impact on its solvency ratio: an investment in equity or property requires a capital charge, as opposed to an investment only in sovereign bonds. However, an investment in equity or property might deliver a higher return, which may be more advantageous for policyholders. Just reading the solvency ratio is therefore not enough.

Solvency ratios are sometimes very high. This may not always be in the interest of policyholders, as it may reflect a lack of vision. Capital should be used for investment and not for creating an artificially high capital buffer. An efficient allocation of capital may result in lower premiums for policyholders. An interesting example is Gresham Insurance Company Ltd, a member of the Aviva plc group, which published in its 2016 SFCR a solvency ratio of 1,175% (almost 12 times its regulatory capital) and an MCR of 2,390%. No indication is given in the SFCR of why the solvency ratio is so high, although a reason might be found in the summary section, which indicates that "the majority of written premiums is ceded to the company's immediate parent Aviva Insurance Limited through a quota share reinsurance arrangement." This example shows how important it is to look at the business model and not merely at the solvency ratio.

Low solvency ratios do not mean that the undertaking is experiencing difficulties. What is important is to see what the capital management strategy is. Undertakings will sometimes express their intention in terms of the solvency ratio they want to keep as a target.[72]

1.2.3. Non-Disclosure of Information

The SFCR contains a wealth of information, which may be sensitive in certain cases. Art. 53 FD requires supervisory authorities to permit undertakings not to disclose information, where, by disclosing such information, competitors would gain significant undue advantage or where there are obligations to policyholders

72 See, for instance, the 2016 SFCR of Canada Life Assurance Europe plc, which pointed out that "the Company seeks to manage its total aggregated capital to exceed 125% of the SCR at all times on a Solvency II basis to protect against adverse changes in its overall risk profile, having regard to the risk preferences for material risks in the Company's Risk Strategy. In setting the target range for the solvency ratio, the Board considers the results of capital projections and stress tests produced as part of the ORSA process, which uses a five year projection period".

or other counterparty relationships binding an undertaking to secrecy or confidentiality. Non-disclosure of information relating to the SCR or the MCR is not possible under this exception.[73]

In the interest of transparency, where non-disclosure of information is permitted, the undertaking must make a statement to this effect in its SFCR and must state the reasons. The permission is only valid for as long as the reason for non-disclosure continues to exist. The undertaking must notify the supervisory authority as soon as the reason for any permitted non-disclosure ceases to exist (Art. 299 DA). Information that is not made public must still be submitted to the supervisory authority as part of the RSR (Art. 304 (1) (b) DA).

2. SUPERVISORY REPORTING

2.1. GENERAL PRINCIPLES

The supervisory reporting requirements aim at providing supervisory authorities with the information necessary for them to carry out the supervisory review process. It should allow them:

- to assess the undertaking's system of governance, the business it is pursuing, the valuation rules applied for solvency purposes, the risks faced and the risk management system as well as the capital management;
- to make any appropriate decisions resulting from the exercise of their supervisory rights of duties (Art. 35 (1) FD).

The supervisory authority may specify the nature, the scope and the format of the information to be delivered, as well as when the information must be delivered, which may be for predefined periods (for instance annually or quarterly), on the occurrence of predefined events or in the course of an inspection. The information may relate to contracts held by intermediaries or contracts entered into with third parties and may be obtained from external experts, such as external auditors or actuaries (Art. 35 (2) FD).

In terms of the nature of the information, the information may be qualitative (narrative) or quantitative, it may be historic, current or prospective, and it may originate from internal or external sources (Art. 35 (3) FD).

---

73 Under Solvency I, such information would clearly have been regarded as a business secret. It is remarkable how readily undertakings are prepared to provide this information now. When Solvency II was developed, there was much fear about the possible consequences of disclosing SCR and MCR amounts to the market.

The information required must be proportionate and risk-based. It must be accessible, complete in all material respects, comparable and consistent over time. It must also be relevant, reliable and comprehensible (Art. 35 (4) FD).

As supervisory information is extensive, the AMSB must ensure that it can deliver the information as requested. This means that the AMSB must see to it that the undertaking has appropriate IT systems and structures in place and that there is a written policy indicating how the undertaking ensures that supervisory information satisfying the conditions referred to above can be delivered on time (Art. 35 (5) FD).

Sometimes the DA requires information to be submitted only where that information is material. Information submitted to the supervisory authority is considered material where its omission or misstatement could influence the decision-making or judgement of the supervisory authority (Art. 305 DA).

2.2. ELEMENTS OF REGULAR SUPERVISORY REPORTING

All (re)insurance undertakings subject to Solvency II must provide information to supervisory authorities on a regular basis. Supervisory authorities may require this information if it is necessary for them to carry out the supervisory review process. The information submitted to the supervisory authority is prepared under the responsibility or at the request of the AMSB.

The regular reporting comprises the following (Art. 304 (1) and (3) DA):

- the SFCR, including other publicly disclosed information under other legal or regulatory requirements to which the SFCR refers (for instance, the financial statements or management report), as well as any updates to the SFCR;
- the RSR, including the information which the supervisory authority has allowed the undertaking not to disclose in its SFCR;
- the ORSA supervisory report comprising the results of each regular ORSA, whenever such an assessment is carried out;
- annual and quarterly QRTs, which specify in greater detail and supplement the information presented in the SFCR and in the RSR, with the quarterly QRTs being narrower in scope than the annual QRTs.

Regular reporting for groups follows the same requirements as regular reporting for solo entities (Art. 372 DA).

Supervisory authorities may require regular communication of further information, the so-called national templates. They can for instance request the submission of other quantitative templates, covering products and conditions with particular relevance to local markets and national legal requirements. This is, for instance, the case in the Netherlands (additional national templates on health care, in-kind funeral services, profit and loss account, and windstorms) and in Belgium (additional national submissions on liquidity, interest-rate risk, life assurance and profitability in non-life insurance, per product and per branch).

Third-country insurance undertakings, which have established a branch in an EEA MS, carrying out direct life and non-life insurance business,[74] must submit to the host supervisory authority in the MS where they have established the branch, the following information in respect of branch operations:[75]

- the RSR in relation to branch operations, in narrative form and including quantitative data;
- the ORSA supervisory report in respect of branch operations, comprising the results of each regular ORSA performed by the undertaking and following any significant change in its risk profile;
- completed annual and quarterly QRTs in respect of branch operations, specifying in greater detail and supplementing, where appropriate, the information presented in the RSR;
- a copy of the supervisory reporting documentation of the whole third-country insurance undertaking;
- a summary of any significant concerns which the home supervisory authority has raised with the third-country insurance undertaking, in the official language of the country in which the branch is located.

2.2.1. Solvency and Financial Condition Report

For the contents of the SFCR, see above, section 2.2.

2.2.2. ORSA Supervisory Report

As explained above (Chapter 7, section 3.4.2), each (re)insurance undertaking must carry out at least once a year as part of its risk management, an assessment of its overall solvency needs, its compliance with the capital requirements and requirements on technical provisions and the significance with which its risk profile deviates from the assumptions underlying the SCR. Solvency II does

74 If a third-country insurance undertaking wants to carry out direct life or non-life insurance business in an EEA MS, it is required to establish a branch in the territory of the MS in which it wants to carry out this business (Art. 162 (2) (b) FD). There is no similar EU requirement for third-country reinsurance undertakings, although some Member States (for instance, Germany) require the establishment of a branch for third-country reinsurance undertakings operating in their territory.

75 EIOPA, Guidelines on the supervision of branches of third-country insurance undertakings, EIOPA-BoS-15/110, 23 October 2015, Guidelines 37–50.

not prescribe a specific format for the ORSA. The results of the ORSA must be communicated to the supervisory authority as part of the ORSA supervisory report.

The ORSA supervisory report must contain the following information (Art. 306 DA):

(a) the qualitative and quantitative results of the ORSA and the conclusions drawn by the undertaking from those results;
(b) the methods and main assumptions used in the ORSA;
(c) information on the undertaking's overall solvency needs and a comparison between those solvency needs, the regulatory capital requirements and the undertaking's own funds;
(d) qualitative information on and, where significant deviations have been identified, a quantification of the extent to which quantifiable risks of the undertakings are not reflected in the calculation of the SCR.

2.2.3. *Regular Supervisory Report*

The RSR follows the same structure as that of the SFCR as set out in Annex XX DA (Art. 304 (1) (b) DA). As it is addressed to the supervisory authority, the information is slightly different from that which is made available to the public. For the group RSR, the same structure applies (Art. 372 (1) DA) but some additional group-specific information must be submitted (Art. 372 (2) DA).

The RSR must include a summary which highlights any material changes that have occurred in the undertaking's business and performance, system of governance, risk profile, valuation for solvency purposes and capital management over the reporting period, and which provides a concise explanation of the causes and effects of such changes. The summary must also include information on the results of ORSAs carried out by the undertaking (Art. 304 (2) DA).

2.2.3.1. Business and Performance (Art. 307 DA)

The following information[76] must be included in the RSR regarding the *business* of the (re)insurance undertaking:[77]

(a) the main trends and factors that contribute to the development, performance and position of the undertaking over its business planning time period,

---

[76] See also EIOPA, Guidelines on reporting and public disclosure, EIOPA-BoS-15/109, 14 September 2015, Guidelines 16 and 17.

[77] This section should also include information about the number of employees and the list of all related undertakings and branches. See EIOPA, Guidelines on reporting and public disclosure, EIOPA-BoS-15/109, 14 September 2015, Guideline 16.

including the undertaking's competitive position and any significant legal or regulatory issues;
(b) a description of the business objectives of the undertaking, including the relevant strategies and timeframes.

As the main business of the undertaking is insurance or reinsurance, the RSR must include detailed qualitative and quantitative information concerning its *underwriting performance* as shown in its financial statements:

(a) information on the undertaking's underwriting income and expenses by material line of business and material geographical areas where it writes business during the reporting period, a comparison of the information with that reported on the previous reporting period and the reasons for any material changes;
(b) an analysis of the undertaking's overall underwriting performance during the reporting period;
(c) information on the undertaking's underwriting performance by line of business during the reporting period against projections, and significant factors affecting deviations from these projections;
(d) projections of the undertaking's underwriting performance, with information on significant factors that might affect such underwriting performance, over its business planning time period;
(e) information on any material risk-mitigation techniques[78] purchased or entered into during the reporting period.

In order to assess to what extent the undertaking's investment policy is in line with the nature of its business and respects the prudent person principle, the RSR must include detailed qualitative and quantitative information regarding the *performance of the investments* of the undertaking, as shown in the undertaking's financial statements:

(a) information on income and expenses with respect to investment activities during the last reporting period, a comparison of the information with that reported on the previous reporting period and reasons for any material changes;
(b) an analysis of the undertaking's overall investment performance during the reporting period and also by relevant asset class;

78 Including the impact of these techniques on underwriting performance and the effectiveness of the risk-mitigating techniques. See EIOPA, Guidelines on reporting and public disclosure, EIOPA-BoS-15/109, 14 September 2015, Guideline 17.

(c) projections of the undertaking's expected investment performance, with information on significant factors that might affect such investment performance, over its business planning time period;
(d) the key assumptions which the undertaking makes in its investment decisions with respect to the movement of interest rates, exchange rates, and other relevant market parameters, over its business planning time period;
(e) information about any investments in securitisation, and the undertaking's risk management procedures in respect of such securities or instruments.

The RSR must also include information of *any other material income and expenses*, over the undertaking's business planning time period, as well as any other material information regarding its business and performance.

The group RSR must include in addition (Art. 372 (2) (a) DA):
(a) a list of all subsidiaries, related undertakings and branches;
(b) a description of activities and sources of profits or losses for each material related undertaking and for each significant branch;[79]
(c) a description of the contribution of each subsidiary to the achievement of the group strategy;
(d) qualitative and quantitative information on significant intra-group transactions (as defined in Art. 377 DA, see below Chapter 9, section 9.9.3) by undertakings with the group and the amount of the transactions over the reporting period and their outstanding balances at the end of the reporting period.

2.2.3.2. System of Governance (Art. 308 DA)

Regarding the *system of governance*[80] of the (re)insurance undertaking, the RSR must include the following information:

(a) information allowing the supervisory authority to gain a good understanding of the system of governance within the undertaking, and to assess its appropriateness to the undertaking's business strategy and operations;
(b) information relating to the undertaking's delegation of responsibilities, reporting lines and allocation of functions;

---

79 As defined in Art. 354 (1) DA. See further, Chapter 9, section 11.

80 See also EIOPA, Guidelines on reporting and public disclosure, EIOPA-BoS-15/109, 14 September 2015, Guidelines 18 and 19.

(c) the remuneration entitlements of the members of the AMSB, over the reporting period and a comparison of the information with that reported on the previous reporting period and the reasons for any material changes;
(d) any other material information on the system of governance than that specifically required under this section.

Regarding the *fit and proper requirements*, the RSR must include the following information:

(a) a list of the persons in the undertaking that are responsible for key functions;[81]
(b) information on the policies and processes established by the undertaking to ensure that those persons are fit and proper.

Regarding the *four key governance functions*, the RSR must include the following information:

1. *Risk management function*
   (a) information on the undertaking's risk management strategies, objectives, processes and reporting procedures for each category of risk;
   (b) information on significant risks to which the undertaking is exposed over the lifetime of its insurance and reinsurance obligations, and how these have been captured in its overall solvency needs;
   (c) information on any material risks that the undertaking has identified and that are not fully included in the calculation of the SCR;
   (d) information on how the undertaking fulfils its obligation to invest all its assets in accordance with the prudent person principle;
   (e) information on how the undertaking verifies the appropriateness of credit assessments from ECAIs, including how and the extent to which credit assessments from ECAIs are used;
   (f) results of the assessments regarding the extrapolation of the risk-free rate, the MA and the VA;
   (g) a description of how the ORSA is performed, internally documented and reviewed;
   (h) a description of how the ORSA is integrated into the management process and the decision-making process of the undertaking.

81 This list must be broader than that of the four key governance functions and also include other key function holders.

2. *Internal control system and compliance function*
   (a) information on the key procedures that the internal control system includes;
   (b) information on the activities performed by the compliance function during the reporting period;
   (c) information on the undertaking's compliance policy, the process for reviewing that policy, the frequency of review and any significant changes to that policy during the reporting period.
3. *Internal audit function*
   (a) a description of internal audits performed during the reporting period, with a summary of the material findings and recommendations reported to the undertaking's AMSB, and any action taken with respect to these findings and recommendations;
   (b) a description of the undertaking's internal audit policy, the process for reviewing that policy, the frequency of review and any significant changes to that policy during the reporting period;
   (c) a description of the undertaking's audit plan, including future internal audits and the rationale for these future audits;
   (d) where the persons carrying out the internal audit function assume other key functions, an assessment, in qualitative and quantitative terms, of the extent to which this is appropriate with respect to the nature, scale and complexity of the risks inherent in the undertaking, and the extent to which conflicts of interests are avoided.
4. *Actuarial function*
   An overview of the activities undertaken by the actuarial function in each of its areas of responsibility during the reporting period, describing how the actuarial function contributes to the effective implementation of the undertaking's risk management system.

Regarding *outsourcing*, the RSR must include the following information:
(a) where the undertaking outsources any critical or important operational functions or activities, the rationale for the outsourcing and evidence that appropriate oversight and safeguards are in place;
(b) information on the service providers to whom any critical or important operational functions or activities have been outsourced and on how the undertaking ensures that the service providers have the ability, the capacity and the authorisation to deliver the required functions or activities satisfactorily;
(c) a list of the persons responsible for the outsourced key functions in the service provider.

The group RSR must include in addition (Art. 372 (2) (b) DA):[82]

(a) a description of how the group internal control mechanisms comply with the requirement to have adequate mechanisms as regards group solvency in order to identify and measure all material risks incurred and to appropriately relate eligible own funds to risks, and the requirement to have sound reporting and accounting procedures in order to monitor and manage intra-group transactions and risk concentration;
(b) where applicable, information on the subsidiaries included in the ORSA;
(c) qualitative and quantitative information on material specific risks at group level.

2.2.3.3. Risk Profile (Art. 309 DA)

The RSR must include qualitative and quantitative information regarding the risk profile of the undertaking,[83] separately for underwriting risk, market risk, credit risk, liquidity risk, operational risk and other material risks.[84]

More specifically, the RSR must include the following information regarding the risk exposure of the undertaking, including the exposure arising from off-balance sheet positions and the transfer of risk to SPVs:

(a) an overview of any material risk exposures anticipated over the business planning time period given the undertaking's business strategy, and how these risk exposures will be managed;
(b) where the undertaking sells or re-pledges collateral, the amount of that collateral, valued on a market-consistent basis;
(c) where the undertaking has provided collateral, the nature of the collateral, the nature and value of assets provided as collateral and the corresponding actual and contingent liabilities created by that collateral arrangement;
(d) information on the material terms and conditions associated with the collateral arrangement;
(e) a complete list of assets and how those assets have been invested in accordance with the prudent person principle;

[82] See also EIOPA, Guidelines on reporting and public disclosure, EIOPA-BoS-15/109, 14 September 2015, Guideline 26.

[83] See also EIOPA, Guidelines on reporting and public disclosure, EIOPA-BoS-15/109, 14 September 2015, Guidelines 27–28 for the group RSR.

[84] For other material risks, see EIOPA, Guidelines on reporting and public disclosure, EIOPA-BoS-15/109, 14 September 2015, Guideline 20.

(f) where the undertaking has entered into securities lending or borrowing transactions, repurchase or reverse repurchase agreements,[85] including liquidity swaps, information on their characteristics and volume;
(g) where the undertaking sells variable annuities, information on guarantee riders and hedging of the guarantees.[86]

The RSR must also include information regarding:
(a) the volume and nature of the loan portfolio of the undertaking;
(b) the material risk concentrations to which the undertaking is exposed to and an overview of any future risk concentrations anticipated over the business planning time period given the undertaking's business strategy, and how these risk concentrations will be managed;
(c) the risk-mitigation techniques of the undertaking and more specifically:
   (i) information on the techniques currently used to mitigate risks, and a description of any material risk-mitigation techniques that the undertaking is considering purchasing or entering into over the business planning time period given the undertaking's business strategy, and the rationale for and effect of such risk-mitigation techniques;
   (ii) where the undertaking holds collateral, the value of the collateral and information on the material terms and conditions associated with the collateral arrangement;
(d) information regarding the expected profit included in future premiums for each line of business and a description of the methods and main assumptions used to calculate the expected profit included in future premiums;
(e) information regarding relevant stress tests and scenario analyses carried out by the undertaking including their outcome and a description of the methods used and the main assumptions underlying those stress tests and scenario analyses;
(f) information regarding quantitative data that is necessary for determining dependencies between the risks covered by the risk modules or sub-modules of the BSCR;
(g) any other material information regarding the risk profile of the undertaking.

---

85 As defined in Art. 4 (1) (82) CRR. This information is particularly important because these transactions are of a banking nature and might be the source of systemic risk.

86 Variable annuities are unit-linked life insurance contracts with investment guarantees which, in exchange for single or regular premiums, allow the policyholder to benefit from the upside of the unit but be partially or totally protected when the unit loses value. VAs have been a concern for supervisory authorities because they could be a source of systemic risk and because of the selling practices relating to variable annuities. See EIOPA, Report on Variable Annuities, EIOPA-11/031, 5 April 2011, 74 p. and EIOPA, Report on good practices for disclosure and selling of VA, EIOPA-CP-11/007, 4 April 2012, 16 p.

Groups must also report on significant risk concentrations and significant intra-group transactions (Art. 376 and 377 DA).

Significant risk concentrations are risk concentrations that could threaten the group solvency or liquidity position. For the purposes of identifying significant risk concentrations, participating (re)insurance undertakings, insurance holding companies or mixed financial holding companies must consider, at least, direct and indirect exposures of undertakings in the group to all of the following:

(a) individual counterparties;
(b) groups of individual but interconnected counterparties, for example undertakings within the same corporate group;
(c) specific geographical areas or industry sectors;
(d) natural disasters or catastrophes.

When determining appropriate thresholds in a particular group for significant risk concentrations to be reported, the group supervisor must consider the following elements:

(a) the solvency and liquidity position of the group;
(b) the complexity of the structure of the group;
(c) the importance of regulated entities from other financial sectors or non-regulated entities carrying out financial activities;
(d) the diversification of the group's investments portfolio;
(e) the diversification of the group's insurance activities, in terms of geographical areas and lines of business.

Significant intra-group transactions are intra-group transactions that materially influence the solvency or liquidity position of the group or of one of the undertakings involved in these transactions. For the purposes of identifying significant intra-group transactions, participating (re)insurance undertakings, insurance holding companies or mixed financial holding companies must consider at least all of the following:

(a) investments;
(b) inter-company balances, including loans, receivables and arrangements to centralise the management of assets or cash;
(c) guarantees and commitments, such as letters of credit;
(d) derivative transactions;
(e) dividends, coupons, and other interest payments;
(f) reinsurance operations;
(g) provision of services or agreements to share costs;
(h) purchase, sale or lease of assets.

2.2.3.4. Valuation for Solvency Purposes (Art. 310 DA)

The RSR must include any important information, other than that already disclosed in the SFCR, regarding the valuation of the undertaking's assets, technical provisions and other liabilities for solvency purposes.[87]

It must comprise in particular:
(a) the relevant assumptions about future management actions and the relevant assumptions about policyholder behaviour;
(b) information on the use of alternative valuation methods as part of the fair value valuation hierarchy set out in Art. 263 DA;
(c) where the undertaking values assets or liabilities based on the valuation methods used to prepare its financial statements by virtue of Art. 9 (4) DA, an assessment, in qualitative and quantitative terms, of why the use of IAS/IFRS would impose costs that would be disproportionate with respect to the total administrative expenses.

2.2.3.5. Capital Management (Art. 311 DA)

Actions by the AMSB may have important consequences for the capital position of the undertaking. It is important for supervisory authorities to know the reasons underlying capital management.[88]

The RSR must include the following information:
(a) the material terms and conditions of the main items of own funds[89] held by the undertaking;
(b) the expected developments of the undertaking's own funds over its business planning time period given the undertaking's business strategy and appropriately stressed capital plans, and whether there is any intention to repay or redeem any own-fund items or plans to raise additional own funds;
(c) the undertaking's plans on how to replace basic own-fund items that are subject to the transitional arrangements referred to in Art. 308b (9) and (10) FD (see above, Chapter 6, section 3.2.2);

---

87 See also EIOPA, Guidelines on reporting and public disclosure, EIOPA-BoS-15/109, 14 September 2015, Guidelines 21–23.

88 See also EIOPA, Guidelines on reporting and public disclosure, EIOPA-BoS-15/109, 14 September 2015, Guidelines 24–25.

89 Also showing the amount of distributions to shareholders. See EIOPA, Guidelines on reporting and public disclosure, EIOPA-BoS-15/109, 14 September 2015, Guideline 24.

(d) quantitative information on the undertaking's SCR split by risk modules where the undertaking applies the standard formula, and by risk categories where the undertaking applies an internal model;
(e) a description of the amount of deferred tax assets recognised in the balance sheet and of the amount that is likely to be used against probable future taxable profit taking into account carry-backs (reversions of deferred tax liabilities), as well as the underlying assumptions used for the projection of probable future taxable profit and an analysis of the sensitivity of net deferred tax assets to changes in the underlying assumptions;[90]
(f) the expected developments of the undertaking's anticipated SCR and MCR over its business planning time period given the undertaking's business strategy;
(g) an estimate of the undertaking's SCR determined in accordance with the standard formula, where the supervisory authority requires the undertaking to provide that estimate;
(h) where an internal model is used to calculate the SCR: the results of the review of the causes and sources of profits and losses, required by Art. 123 FD, for each major business unit and how the categorisation of risk chosen in the internal model explains those causes and sources of profits and losses; information on whether, and if so to what extent, the risk profile of the undertaking deviates from the assumptions underlying its internal model; information about future management actions used in the calculation of the SCR;
(i) where USPs are used to calculate the SCR, or a MA is applied to the relevant risk-free interest term structure, information regarding whether there have been changes to the information included in the application for approval of the USPs or MA that are relevant for the supervisory assessment of the application;
(j) information on any reasonably foreseeable risk of non-compliance with the MCR or the SCR and the undertaking's plans for ensuring that compliance with each is maintained;
(k) any other material information regarding the capital management of the undertaking;
(l) for the future projection of profits for the purpose of the LAC-DT, a description and the relevant amount of each of the components used to demonstrate a positive value of the increase in deferred tax assets, a detailed description of the underlying assumptions used for the projection

90 This point was added in the EC's 2019 amendment of the DA, following the advice of EIOPA in the context of the 2018 review of the DA. See EIOPA, Second set of advice to the EC on specific items in the Solvency II Delegated Regulation, EIOPA-BoS-18/075, 28 February 2018, pp. 333–340.

of probable future taxable profits (for the purpose of Art. 207 DA) and an analysis of the sensitivity of the value of the adjustment to changes in the underlying assumptions.[91]

The group RSR must in addition include (Art. 372 (2) (c) DA):

(a) qualitative and quantitative information on the SCR and own funds for each (re)insurance undertaking within the group, in so far as it is included in the calculation of the group solvency;
(b) qualitative and quantitative information on the SCR and own funds for each intermediate insurance holding company, insurance holding company, intermediate mixed financial holding company, mixed financial holding company and ancillary services undertaking within the group, in so far as it is included in the calculation of the group solvency;
(c) qualitative and quantitative information on the solvency requirements and own funds for each related undertaking which is a credit institution, investment firm, financial institution, UCITS management company, alternative investment fund manager or IORP, in so far as it is included in the calculation of the group solvency;
(d) qualitative and quantitative information on the notional solvency requirement and own funds for each related undertaking which is a non-regulated undertaking carrying out financial activities, in so far as it is included in the calculation of the group solvency;
(e) qualitative and quantitative information on the solvency requirement and own funds for each related third-country (re)insurance undertaking, in so far as it is included in the calculation of the group solvency; when the deduction and aggregation method is used in the case of a related third-country (re)insurance undertaking that has its head office in a third country whose solvency regime is deemed to be equivalent, the SCR and the own funds eligible to satisfy that requirement as laid down by the third country concerned must be separately identified;
(f) qualitative and quantitative information on the solvency requirement and own funds for any other related undertaking, in so far as it is included in the calculation of the group solvency;
(g) a description of SPVs within the group which comply with the requirements set out in Art. 211 FD;
(h) a description of SPVs within the group which are regulated by a third-country supervisory authority and comply with requirements equivalent to

[91] This point was added in the EC's 2019 amendment of the DA, following the advice of EIOPA in the context of the 2018 review of the DA. See EIOPA, Second set of advice to the EC on specific items in the Solvency II Delegated Regulation, EIOPA-BoS-18/075, 28 February 2018, pp. 333–340.

those set out in Art. 211 (2) FD, for the purposes of including a description of the verification carried out by the participating (re)insurance undertaking, insurance holding company or mixed financial holding company whether the requirements to which these SPVs are subject to in the third country are equivalent to those set out in Art. 211 (2) FD;

(i) a description of each SPE within the group, other than those referred to under (g) and (h), together with qualitative and quantitative information on the solvency requirement and own funds of these entities, in so far as they are included in the calculation of the group solvency;

(j) where relevant, for all related (re)insurance undertakings which are included in the calculation of the group solvency, qualitative and quantitative information on how the undertaking complies with Art. 222 (2)–(5) FD;

(k) where relevant, qualitative and quantitative information on the own-fund items referred to in Art. 222 (3) FD that cannot effectively be made available to cover the SCR of the participating (re)insurance undertaking, insurance holding company or mixed financial holding company for which the group solvency is calculated, including a description of how the adjustment to group own funds has been made;

(l) where relevant, qualitative information on the reasons for the classification of own-fund items referred to in Arts. 332 and 333 DA.

2.2.4. Annual and Quarterly Quantitative Reporting Templates

The templates for the submission of information to supervisory authorities and the format in which it must be delivered are included in two Commission Implementing Regulations of 2 December 2015, with extensive annexes, dealing respectively with information relating to the RSR[92] and information relating to the SFCR.[93] In most cases only a subset of the templates provided for must be submitted, as not all the templates are applicable to all undertakings. For instance, the undertaking may not be using a full or partial internal model or may not apply the MA. The templates themselves are regularly revised.[94]

---

[92] Commission Implementing Regulation (EU) 2015/2450 of 2 December 2015 laying down implementing technical standards with regard to the templates for the submission of information to the supervisory authorities according to Directive 2009/138/EC of the European Parliament and of the Council, *OJ* L 347, 31.12.2015, p. 1.

[93] Commission Implementing Regulation (EU) 2015/2452 of 2 December 2015 laying down implementing technical standards with regard to the procedures, formats and templates of the solvency and financial condition report in accordance with Directive 2009/138/EC of the European Parliament and of the Council, *OJ* L 347, 31.12.2015, p. 1285.

[94] See Commission Implementing Regulation (EU) 2018/1844 of 23 November 2018 amending and correcting Implementing Regulation (EU) 2015/2450 laying down implementing technical standards with regard to the templates for the submission of information to the supervisory authorities according to Directive 2009/138/EC of the European Parliament and of the Council, *OJ* L 299, 26.11.2018, p. 5; Commission Implementing Regulation

The templates specify in greater detail and supplement the information presented in the RSR and in the SFCR.[95] If the undertaking is exempted from quarterly reporting, it must submit only annual quantitative templates. If the undertaking is exempted from reporting on an item-by-item basis, the annual reporting must not include reporting on an item-by-item basis.

A distinction is made between QRTs for individual undertakings and QRTs for groups. In both cases, simplifications are allowed on quarterly reporting.

2.3. DEADLINES AND MEANS OF COMMUNICATION

2.3.1. Regular Supervisory Report

The RSR must be submitted in electronic form to the supervisory authority at least every three years, no later than 14 weeks after the end of the financial year (Art. 312 (1) (a) DA), with a transitional period of four years, starting on 1 January 2016 and ending on 31 December 2019, during which time the deadline for submitting the information is extended by a decreasing number of weeks (from 20 to 14) (Art. 308b (5) FD). For the group RSR, the deadlines are extended by six weeks to 20 weeks, except for the ORSA supervisory report (Art. 373 DA). Where the college of supervisors comprises supervisory authorities from more than one MS, the group supervisor may require the group RSR to be drawn up in a language most commonly understood by the supervisory authorities concerned, as agreed in the college of supervisors (Art. 374 DA).

Annual submission of the RSR may be required by the supervisory authority, subject to the same deadlines (Art. 312 (2) DA).

Where there is no requirement for an RSR to be submitted in relation to a given financial year, (re)insurance undertakings must nevertheless submit

(EU) 2017/2189 of 24 November 2017 amending and correcting Implementing Regulation (EU) 2015/2450 laying down implementing technical standards with regard to the templates for the submission of information to the supervisory authorities according to Directive 2009/138/EC of the European Parliament and of the Council, *OJ* L 310, 25.11.2017, p. 3; Commission Implementing Regulation (EU) 2016/1868 of 20 October 2016 amending and correcting Implementing Regulation (EU) 2015/2450 laying down implementing technical standards with regard to the templates for the submission of information to the supervisory authorities according to Directive 2009/138/EC of the European Parliament and of the Council, *OJ* L 286, 21.10.2016, p. 35. A next revision is being prepared. See, EIOPA, Consultation on the amendments and corrections to the Implementing Regulation (EU) 2015/2450 with regard to the templates for the submission of information to the supervisory authorities and to the Commission Implementing Regulation (EU) 2015/2452, laying down implementing technical standards with regard to the procedures, formats and templates of the SFCR, EIOPA-CP-19/002, 2 April 2019, 4 p.

95 See also the explanatory notes provided by EIOPA: EIOPA, Explanatory notes on reporting templates – Variation Analysis templates, EIOPA-17-403, 5 July 2018, 81 p.

to their supervisory authority a summary report that sets out any material changes that have occurred in the undertaking's business and performance, system of governance, risk profile, valuation for solvency purposes and capital management over the given financial year, and provide a concise explanation of the causes and effects of such changes. Submission of that report is also subject to the deadlines stated above (Art. 312 (3) DA).

Similar requirements apply to third-country insurance undertakings that have established a branch in an EEA MS in respect of branch operations.[96]

2.3.2. *ORSA Supervisory Report*

The ORSA supervisory report must be submitted in electronic form to the supervisory authority within two weeks of concluding the ORSA (Art. 312 (1) (b) DA). The same requirement applies to groups (Art. 373 DA) and to third-country insurance undertakings that have established a branch in an EEA MS.[97]

2.3.3. *Annual Quantitative Reporting Templates*

The annual QRTs must be submitted in electronic form to the supervisory authority no later than 14 weeks after the end of the financial year (Art. 312 (1) (c) DA), with a transitional period of four years, starting on 1 January 2016 and ending on 31 December 2019, during which time the deadline for submitting the information is decreased by two weeks each financial year from 20 to 14 weeks (Art. 308b (5) FD). The same requirements apply to third-country insurance undertakings that have established a branch in an EEA MS.[98] For groups, the deadlines are extended by six weeks to 20 weeks (Art. 373 DA).

2.3.4. *Quarterly Quantitative Reporting Templates*

The quarterly QRTs must be submitted in electronic form to the supervisory authority no later than five weeks after the end of any quarter, with a transitional period of four years starting on 1 January 2016 and ending on 31 December 2019 during which time the deadline for submitting the information is decreased by one week each financial year from 8 to 5 weeks (Art. 308b (7) FD). The same requirements apply to third-country insurance undertakings that have

---

96 EIOPA, Guidelines on the supervision of branches of third-country insurance undertakings, EIOPA-BoS-15/110, 23 October 2015, Guidelines 51–53 and 59.

97 EIOPA, Guidelines on the supervision of branches of third-country insurance undertakings, EIOPA-BoS-15/110, 23 October 2015, Guideline 54.

98 EIOPA, Guidelines on the supervision of branches of third-country insurance undertakings, EIOPA-BoS-15/110, 23 October 2015, Guideline 60.

established a branch in an EEA MS.[99] For groups, the deadlines are extended by six weeks to 11 weeks (Art. 373 DA).

2.4. TRANSITIONAL INFORMATION REQUIREMENTS

It is obvious that supervisory authorities needed relevant supervisory information as soon as possible from the start date of the new solvency regime, i.e. 1 January 2016. Art. 314 DA therefore required (re)insurance undertakings to submit to the supervisory authority the following information no later than 20 weeks after the first financial year starting on or after 1 January 2016 (but before 1 July 2016):

(a) an opening balance sheet in which assets and liabilities are valued in accordance with the Solvency II valuation principles;
(b) separately for each material class of assets and liabilities, a qualitative explanation of the main differences between the figures reported in the opening balance sheet and those calculated under Solvency I;
(c) the undertaking's MCR, SCR and eligible own funds as of the date of the opening balance sheet.

The same requirements applied to groups and to third-country insurance undertakings that have established a branch in an EEA MS.[100] For groups, the deadline for submission was extended by six weeks to 26 weeks (Art. 375 DA).

2.5. EXEMPTIONS

As indicated before, the information to be submitted to supervisory authorities is quite extensive. Although Art. 35 (4) FD specifically refers to the application of the proportionality principle, it was unclear how this principle would work in practice in the case of supervisory reporting. In particular, quarterly reporting and reporting on an item-by-item basis (for instance, reporting of individual investments) were considered particularly burdensome, especially for small and medium-sized undertakings.

On the other hand, supervisory authorities wanted to avoid exemptions in this area preventing them from having a holistic view of the (re)insurance market in their country.

---

99 EIOPA, Guidelines on the supervision of branches of third-country insurance undertakings, EIOPA-BoS-15/110, 23 October 2015, Guideline 61.

100 EIOPA, Guidelines on the supervision of branches of third-country insurance undertakings, EIOPA-BoS-15/110, 23 October 2015, Guidelines 57–58.

When the issue was debated in the context of Omnibus II on the basis of an amendment tabled by the Rapporteur, Burkhard Balz (EPP, Germany), an urgent plea was sent by EIOPA to the EC and to the EP to ensure that sufficient supervisory information on the local (national) insurance market would remain available. The argument made by EIOPA was that providing sufficiently detailed information at regular intervals to supervisory authorities would reduce the frequency of on-site inspections, which are particularly burdensome for SMEs. The result is a compromise, which is included in Art. 35 (6), (7) and (8) FD. It is the clearest example of application of the proportionality principle under Solvency II.[101]

In the case of *quarterly reporting*, supervisory authorities may limit regular supervisory reporting,[102] where:

(a) the submission of that information would be overly burdensome in relation to the nature, scale and complexity of the risks inherent in the business of the undertaking;
(b) the information is reported at least annually.

In the case of *reporting on an item-by-item basis*, supervisory authorities may limit regular supervisory reporting or exempt an undertaking from reporting on an item-by-item basis, where:

(a) the submission of that information would be overly burdensome in relation to the nature, scale and complexity of the risks inherent in the business of the undertaking;
(b) the submission of that information is not necessary for the effective supervision of the undertaking;
(c) the exemption does not undermine the stability of the financial systems concerned in the EU;[103]
(d) the undertaking is able to provide the information on an ad hoc basis.

The exemption from quarterly reporting or from reporting on an item-by-item basis does not apply when the undertaking is part of a group,[104] unless the undertaking can demonstrate to the satisfaction of the supervisory authority that regular supervisory reporting with a frequency shorter than one year or

---

101 For the exemption of groups from supervisory reporting, see Art. 254 FD.

102 The exemption does not apply to the requirement for (re)insurance undertakings to calculate the MCR at least quarterly and to report the results of this calculation to the supervisory authority.

103 This condition was added because of the experience during the financial crisis in 2008/2009, when it was impossible for supervisory authorities to provide information about the exposure of the insurance sector to Lehman Brothers.

104 See also EIOPA, Guidelines on methods for determining the market shares for reporting, EIOPA-BoS-15/106, 14 September 2015, Guidelines 8–9.

reporting on an item-by-tem basis is inappropriate, given the nature, scale and complexity of the risks inherent in the business of the group.[105] In the case of an exemption from reporting on an item-by-item basis, account must also be taken of the objective of financial stability. In assessing the request for exemption, account must be taken of the opinion of the group supervisor.

An exemption from quarterly reporting or from reporting on an item-by-item basis can only be given to undertakings that do not represent more than 20% of a MS's life and non-life insurance or reinsurance market[106] respectively, where the non-life insurance market share is based on gross written premiums and the life insurance market share is based on gross technical provisions. Supervisory authorities must give priority to the smallest undertakings when determining the eligibility of the undertakings concerned for an exemption from reporting.

In their assessment of whether the submission of information would be overly burdensome in relation to the nature, scale and complexity of the risks of the undertaking, the supervisory authority must take into account at least:

(a) the volume of premiums, technical provisions and assets of the undertaking;
(b) the volatility of the claims and benefits covered by the undertaking;
(c) the market risks that the investments of the undertaking give rise to;
(d) the level of risk concentrations;
(e) the total number of classes of life and non-life insurance for which authorisation is granted;
(f) possible effects of the management of the assets of the undertaking on financial stability;
(g) the systems and structures of the undertaking to provide information for supervisory purposes and the written policy in this respect;
(h) the appropriateness of the system of governance of the undertaking;
(i) the level of own funds covering the SCR and the MCR;
(j) whether the undertaking is a captive (re)insurance undertaking only covering risks associated with the industrial or commercial group to which it belongs.

Undertakings should be informed within a reasonable timeframe by the supervisory authority that they have been granted an exemption. If the undertaking is part of a group, the supervisory authority must inform the undertaking concerned about the process, including the timeframe, to demonstrate that quarterly reporting or reporting on an item-by-item basis is inappropriate, given the

105 Belonging to a group often excludes an undertaking from being considered small.

106 When an insurance or reinsurance undertaking has business in both the non-life and the life insurance market, the undertaking should not be exempted if its business is above the 20% threshold in one of the market shares. See EIOPA, Guidelines on methods for determining the market shares for reporting, EIOPA-BoS-15/106, 14 September 2015, Guideline 5.

nature, scale and complexity of the risks inherent in the business of the group and taking account the objective of financial stability.[107]

A third-country insurance undertaking that has established a branch in an EEA MS may be allowed by the host supervisory authority of the country in which the branch is established to provide quarterly information in a simplified manner or to be exempted from submitting certain information where the submission of that information would be unduly burdensome in relation to the nature, scale and complexity of the risks inherent in the business of the branch.[108]

Where all (re)insurance undertakings in a group are exempted from quarterly reporting, the group RSR includes only annual QRTs. Where all undertakings in the group are exempted from item-by-item reporting, the annual reporting for the group does not include item-by-item reporting (Art. 372 (1) DA).

2.6. REPORTING FOR FINANCIAL STABILITY PURPOSES

In accordance with Art. 35 EIOPA Regulation, EIOPA can ask national competent authorities to provide it with all the necessary information to carry out its duties. One of the duties of EIOPA is to cooperate closely with the ESRB, in particular by providing the ESRB with the information necessary for achieving its tasks (Arts. 8, 32 and 35 EIOPA Regulation). The ESRB has been very eager to obtain more detailed and comparable information on the European insurance sector.[109] The best way to achieve this was via close cooperation with NSAs through EIOPA, which has developed detailed information templates under Solvency II. The advantage of close cooperation with EIOPA is the avoidance of specific data requests by the ESRB, which would impose an additional burden on (re)insurance undertakings. To the extent possible, the information to be collected must be aligned with that which (re)insurance undertakings have to provide under Solvency II.

In order to achieve this, EIOPA has issued Guidelines on reporting for financial stability purposes.[110] The Guidelines apply to individual (re)insurance undertakings and branches of third-country insurance undertakings, which must report individual data, as well as to groups, i.e. participating (re)insurance undertakings, insurance holding companies or mixed financial holding companies, which must report consolidated data.

---

107 EIOPA, Guidelines on methods for determining the market shares for reporting, EIOPA-BoS-15/106, 14 September 2015, Guidelines 7 and 8.

108 EIOPA, Guidelines on the supervision of branches of third-country insurance undertakings, EIOPA-BoS-15/110, 23 October 2015, Guidelines 46 and 48.

109 The ESRB has published a number of research documents on insurance. See, for instance, ESRB, *Report on systemic risk in the insurance sector*, December 2015, 42 p. with annexes.

110 EIOPA, Guidelines on reporting for financial stability purposes, EIOPA-BoS-15, 14 September 2015, 14 p.

Reporting for financial stability purposes is only required for large entities, i.e. (re)insurance groups or solo undertakings and branches of third-country insurance undertakings with more than €12 billion in total assets or the equivalent in the national currency in the solvency balance sheet. No reporting is required for solo undertakings and branches of third-country insurance undertakings if they belong to a group that is already reporting separately (Guideline 2, para. 1.18).

For (re)insurance groups, most of the information requested for financial stability purposes is also required for supervisory reporting under Art. 372 DA. However, the information obtained for financial stability purposes and covered by the Guidelines is requested with earlier deadlines and/or increased frequency (also semi-annual information). The information is used for macro-prudential analysis (by the ESRB and EIOPA).

According to Art. 35 (6) and (7) FD, NSAs may limit regular quarterly supervisory reporting and exempt certain undertakings (including third-country branches) from item-by-item reporting where the submission of that information would be overly burdensome in relation to the nature, scale and complexity of the risks inherent in the business of the undertaking (or branch). (Re)insurance undertakings, parent (re)insurance undertakings, insurance holding companies, mixed financial holding companies and third-country branches that are exempted from quarterly reporting and/or exempted from item-by-item reporting under Art. 35 or 254 FD are also exempted from semi-annual, quarterly and/or item-by-item reporting for financial stability purposes (Guideline 2, para. 1.20).

Reporting entities should provide the information on a best-effort basis, balancing the effort required with the accuracy of the information provided (Guidelines 7 and 8).

The provision of quarterly information on the solvency capital position is considered crucial for financial stability purposes. However, it is acknowledged that a full calculation of the SCR on a quarterly basis may be an unnecessary burden for the entities concerned. Therefore, the aim of the Guidelines is to approximate the development of the overall SCR based on a re-calculation of only the more volatile SCR modules, rather than requiring a full SCR calculation. The method is detailed in Guideline 9. In particular, the market risk module may require a more frequent recalculation due to its more volatile input parameters. Other SCR modules are considered stable enough to accept an extrapolation of yearly figures, unless exceptional circumstances necessitate a recalculation according to the FD.

The deadline for submission of information to the NSAs is seven weeks after the end of the reference period, with a transitional period of three years starting at 10 weeks for submitting quarterly, semi-annual or annual information relating to the year 2016 and finishing at eight weeks for information relating to the year 2018 (Guideline 16).

In order to ensure alignment with the information that undertakings are required to submit under Solvency II, reference is made in the Guidelines to the QRTs to be used for the submission of information to supervisory authorities (see above, section 3.2.4).

2.7. REPORTING TO THE ECB

Like the ESRB, the ECB had also been waiting to collect detailed information on the insurance sector until the finalisation of Solvency II.

The ECB needs to collect data on insurance undertakings in the Member States whose currency is the euro in order to have adequate statistics on the financial activities of the insurance sector. The ECB has the power to impose this by way of regulation.

The ECB Regulation of 28 November 2014[111] introduces the statistical reporting requirement.[112] An attempt has been made to ensure that the information to be collected by the ECB through the national central banks (NCBs) is closely connected with the information collected by NSAs for supervisory purposes under the Solvency II FD. In order to limit the administrative burden and to avoid the duplication of tasks, NCBs may derive the data required to be reported to the ECB from data collected under the FD. This is specifically foreseen in Art. 70 (1) (a) FD, which provides that NSAs may transmit information intended for the performance of their tasks to NCBs and other bodies with a similar function in their capacity as monetary authorities.

The data to be submitted to the ECB through the NCBs are based on the QRTs that must be transmitted by (re)insurance undertakings[113] to NSAs as part of the regular supervisory reporting under Solvency II. The data must be delivered quarterly and annually and deal with individual assets and liabilities, technical provisions, claims, premiums, commissions and financial transactions.

---

111 Regulation (EU) No 1374/2014 of the European Central Bank of 28 November 2014 on statistical reporting requirements for insurance corporations (ECB/201/50), *OJ* L 366, 20.12.2014, p. 36.

112 See also ECB Guideline ECB/2015/44 of the European Central Bank of 4 December 2015 amending Guideline ECB/2014/15 on monetary and financial statistics (2014/810/EU), https://www.ecb.europa.eu/ecb/legal/pdf/en_ecb_2015_44_f_sign.pdf.

113 The Regulation refers to insurance corporation and IC (subsector 128 of the ESA 2010), which are defined in Art. 1 as "a financial corporation or quasi-corporation that is principally engaged in financial intermediation as a consequence of the pooling of risks mainly in the form of direct insurance or reinsurance". The definition covers all undertakings that provide life insurance, non-life insurance and reinsurance. The insurance corporation (parent or subsidiary) is treated as a stand-alone entity and its balance sheet is included in the country data where the entity is legally incorporated. Branches are also included. (Art. 2 (2) ECB Regulation).

Specific tables in the Annex to the Regulation provide the details of the information to be provided.

While a large part of the information required under the ECB Regulation can be derived from the data provided for supervisory purposes, some additional information is still needed. NCBs have the option to develop a single reporting flow for statistical and supervisory data, jointly with the NCAs, using reporting templates prepared by the ECB in close cooperation with EIOPA that consolidate the statistical and supervisory data requirements.

These reporting templates are called "unofficial reporting templates including ECB add-ons" and highlight the information that needs to be provided for statistical purposes over and above the supervisory requirements. These unofficial templates are purely for illustrative purposes and are not subject to mandatory reporting across the Member States of the EU. The templates are called "unofficial" to distinguish them from the reporting templates introduced by the Commission Implementing Regulation of 2 December 2015.[114]

Small insurance undertakings, subject to Solvency II and as defined in Art. 35 (6) FD, may be exempted from providing quarterly information so long as information is available for at least 80% of the total market share of insurance undertakings in each Eurozone MS. Exempted undertakings must provide the information on an annual basis so that the insurance undertakings that contribute to the annual aggregated balance sheet account for at least 95% of the total market share of insurance undertakings in each Eurozone MS. The NCBs must check that the undertakings still meet the conditions for exemption annually and in good time in order to grant or withdraw, if necessary, any derogation with effect from the start of the following calendar year (Art. 7 (1) (d) ECB Regulation).

The required quarterly data must be transmitted to the relevant NCB or the relevant NSA, or both, at the latest eight weeks after the end of the quarter. This deadline is brought forward by one week per year thereafter, so as to be five weeks for quarters ending in 2019.

The required annual data must be transmitted at the latest 20 weeks after the end of the year. This deadline is brought forward by two weeks per year thereafter, so as to be 14 weeks for 2019. The first reporting to the ECB started after the first quarter of 2016.

---

114 Commission Implementing Regulation (EU) 2015/2451 of 2 December 2015 laying down implementing technical standards with regard to the templates and structure of the disclosure of specific information by supervisory authorities in accordance with the FD, *OJ* L 347, 31.12.2015, p. 1224. See also http://www.ecb.europa.eu/stats/financial_corporations/insurance_corporations/html/index.en.html.

CHAPTER 9
GROUP SUPERVISION

Group supervision was one of the most hotly debated issues under Solvency II. It raised some of the most contentious and sensitive issues in the whole Solvency II project, in particular where cross-border groups were concerned. Although the importance of recognising group risks had already been underlined in the Sharma Report,[1] many supervisory authorities in the EEA were still of the view that solo supervision was the only supervision that really mattered. The Insurance Groups Directive (IGD)[2] had been the first attempt to change this attitude and had introduced group supervision as a form of supplementary supervision (so-called "solo plus" approach). This "solo plus" approach was still favoured by many supervisory authorities in the EEA when Solvency II was being developed.

The IGD organised the exchange of information between supervisory authorities in insurance groups. This was further developed by the Helsinki Protocol,[3] which advocated the creation of a Coordinating Committee (Co-Co) to handle the supplementary supervision of insurance groups and described the role of the lead supervisor as the supervisor responsible for carrying out most or all of the supplementary supervision. The Helsinki Protocol was accompanied by Co-Co Guidelines.[4] In practice, the system did not work well. At the start of the negotiation of Solvency II, most insurance groups had not established a Co-Co and when a Co-Co was put in place, it rarely met. Very often no lead supervisor

---

1 Conference of Insurance Supervisory Services of the Member States of the EU, *Report on Prudential Supervision of Insurance Undertakings*, December 2002, section 4.4.5.

2 Directive 98/78/EC of the EP and of the Council of 27 October 1998 on the supplementary supervision of insurance undertakings in an insurance group, *OJ* L 330, 5.12.1998, p. 1, subsequently amended by the FICOD, by the Lamfalussy Directive and by the Reinsurance Directive.

3 Protocol of 11 May 2000 relating to the collaboration of the supervisory authorities of the Member States of the European Union with regard to the application of Directive 98/78/EC on the supplementary supervision of insurance undertakings in an insurance group, 15 p., https://eiopa.europa.eu/CEIOPS-Archive/Documents/Protocols/14.pdf.

4 CEIOPS, Guidelines for Coordination Committees in the context of supplementary supervision as defined by the Insurance Groups Directive (98/78/EC), CEIOPS-DOC-02/05, February 2008, 18 p.

had been appointed.[5] CEIOPS and later EIOPA, pushed by the EC, expended a lot of effort in persuading NSAs to ensure the establishment of a Co-Co in all cross-border insurance groups and to have the Co-Co meet regularly.

The IGD was designed to eliminate "double gearing", i.e. the duplicate use of the same capital to support risks in two or more entities within a group. However, the IGD did not consider an insurance group to be a discrete economic entity within which risks are pooled and diversified. The operation of the IGD in practice was regarded by the insurance industry as very burdensome and the whole system of supplementary group supervision did not correspond to the way large insurance groups were managing their risks and their capital. In 2005, CEIOPS published a consultation paper in which it suggested a number of improvements to the IGD, acknowledging that the IGD would be revised as a result of Solvency II, which was likely to put more emphasis on risk-based methods of supervision.[6]

From the outset, the EC supported the idea of group supervision as a supervisory approach of equal importance to solo supervision. This was already the case in banking (consolidated supervision), but it was also the only possible approach under a risk-based solvency regime. Risks can indeed also arise at group level. Difficulties at subsidiary level might affect the solvency position of the parent. Equally so, problems at the level of the parent might have an impact on the solvency position of the subsidiaries. Subsidiaries may end up bearing risks beyond those that they would normally assume if they were operating as independent entities. Subsidiaries that are poorly capitalised may in fact find themselves in a stronger position than other solo undertakings by virtue of belonging to a group that is well capitalised.[7] Supervisory authorities dealing with group undertakings must take these wider aspects into account in assessing the solvency of the undertaking subject to their supervision, regardless of whether that undertaking is a parent or a subsidiary.[8] This was also the view of a majority of the members of CEIOPS.[9] A minority of supervisory authorities

---

5 CEIOPS, Recommendation on Possible Need for Amendments to the Insurance Groups Directive, October 2005, CEIOPS-DOC-04/05, pp. 10–11, https://eiopa.europa.eu/CEIOPS-Archive/Documents/Recommendations/DOC0504.pdf.

6 CEIOPS, Recommendation on Possible Need for Amendments to the Insurance Groups Directive, October 2005, CEIOPS-DOC-04/05, p. 4.

7 RIEF, W., Marktdisziplinierende Wirkungen durch Solvency II?, *Herbert Frommes Versicherungsmonitor*, 29 September 2016.

8 For a good summary of the potential for adverse dynamics in insurance group networks and the supervisory consequences following from this, see MÄCHLER, M., Insurance Group Supervision: Addressing the Emergence of Adverse Network Dynamics, in LIEDTKE, P.M. and MONKIEWICZ, J. (Eds.), *The Future of Insurance Regulation and Supervision: A Global Perspective*, Palgrave Macmillan, Basingstoke, 2011.

9 This view was also supported by supervisors outside the EU. See, for instance the contribution of the CEO of the Bermuda Monetary Authority: ELDERFIELD, M., Solvency II: Setting the pace for regulatory change, *The Geneva Papers*, 2009, No 34, pp. 35–41.

within CEIOPS was, however, more reluctant to move in the direction of group supervision. This minority, which was very vocal, came not only from smaller Member States, such as Hungary and Luxembourg, but also from larger Member States, such as Poland and Spain.

One of the ideas behind the EC's approach to group supervision was that a higher level of harmonisation of solvency requirements across Member States would reduce the need for supervisory interventions at all levels of the group. The group supervisor should play a key role and cooperate with the supervisory authorities of subsidiary undertakings in the context of a college of supervisors. It had indeed been alleged by the European Financial Services Round Table (EFR), which represents major financial groups within the EEA, that the presence of so many supervisory authorities around the table in the context of cross-border financial groups created an unacceptable regulatory burden for these groups.[10] This message was clearly understood by Commissioner Charlie McCreevy, who stated at the public hearing on Solvency II, organised by the EC in June 2006, that what really matters to policyholders is the soundness of the supervisory method and not the identity of the MS from which it is sourced:

> "By defending their own little turf and habits, supervisors create nightmares for companies and ruin the efforts made at EU level to agree common standards. And frankly, consumers do not care a second whether the supervisory method used comes from country X or Y. He wants the method to be sound and applied effectively, nothing else."

An important reason for the opposition of some supervisory authorities (and their MS) to group supervision as a supervisory approach of equal importance to solo supervision was precisely the transfer of powers to the group supervisor, to the detriment of the local supervisory authorities. It was argued that it was not fair to supervisory authorities in host Member States that part of their powers would be transferred to a supervisory authority (the group supervisor) in another MS, whilst they would still remain responsible in the event of an insurance failure. The separation between *power* on the one hand and *responsibility* on the other hand was an important reason why host Member States were reluctant to transfer responsibilities to the group supervisor.

The opposition to a strong form of group supervision became particularly virulent when the EC decided to include *group support* in its Solvency II proposal. Under the group support regime (see below, section 2), a parent undertaking could replace the solvency capital in a subsidiary with a promise to deliver the capital when needed, under the control of the group supervisor.

---

10 EFR, *On the lead supervisor model and the future of financial supervision in the EU. Follow-up recommendations of the EFR*, June 2005, 44 p. (http://www.efr.be/documents/publication/22676EFRlsvfinal-June2005.pdf).

Even before the EC's proposal was officially tabled, a group of host Member States announced that they would vigorously oppose this approach.

Group supervision is not only politically controversial, as it involves difficult legal (who is responsible for what?) and cultural (intervention of a foreign supervisory authority) issues, it is also *technically complex*, as it introduces an economic approach that cuts through the legal structure of a group. In the end, each individual member of the group is a separate legal entity and whilst groups may be managed as a single entity from an economic perspective, the capital within the group belongs legally to each individual legal entity and can only be used within the boundaries of local company law requirements. A parent undertaking that holds 80% of the capital of a subsidiary undertaking does not own the remaining 20%. A parent undertaking that decides to distribute a dividend and wants to use profits of its subsidiaries for that purpose can only do so after each subsidiary has decided to transfer money to the parent undertaking.

Group supervision is also *legally complex*. The definition of what constitutes a group has preoccupied regulators for a long time, first in accounting[11] and subsequently for supervisory purposes.

With respect to solvency, two different assessment methodologies can be distinguished. Either the undertakings that are part of a group are assessed individually, including their links to the other group members (unconsolidated or granular approach), or the group is considered as one economic entity and the consolidated accounts form the basis of the assessment (consolidated approach). Under the consolidated approach, which is followed under Solvency II, the links to the rest of the group are formally taken into account when the parent or other undertakings in the group enter into commitments for the benefit of local undertakings, or vice versa, such as reinsurance arrangements or guarantees. The risk associated with this approach is that there may be a disconnect between the aspiration of a home supervisor viewing the group holistically and its ability to implement this aspiration as a result of a lack of powers going beyond its borders. This is particularly the case when a smaller jurisdiction is the home supervisor to a large, internationally active group and fails to secure the cooperation of other regulators supervising parts of the group.[12]

---

11 Group definitions were first included in the Seventh Council Directive 83/349/EEC of 13 June 1983 based on Art. 54 (3) (g) of the Treaty on consolidated accounts, *OJ* L 193, 18.7.1983, p. 1. See VAN HULLE, K. and VAN DER TAS, L., European Union – Consolidated Accounts, in ORDELHEIDE, D. and KPMG (Eds.), *Transatlantic Accounting*, second edition, Volume I, Palgrave, Basingstoke, 2001. The definitions are now included in the AD, i.e. Directive 2013/34/EU of the EP and of the Council of 26 June 2013 on the annual financial statements, consolidated financial statements and related reports of certain types of undertakings, amending Directive 2006/43/EC of the EP and of the Council and repealing Council Directive 78/660/EEC and 83/349/EEC, *OJ* L 182, 29.6.2013, p. 19.

12 MÄCHLER, M., Evolution of Insurance Group Supervision, in KEMPLER, C., FLAMEE, M., YANG, C.H. and WINDELS, P. (Eds.), *Global Perspectives on Insurance Today*, Palgrave Macmillan, New York, 2013, p. 110.

When Solvency II was developed, it was decided to adopt the definitions contained in the IGD, as amended by the FICOD. As the FD was merely a recast of existing legal provisions, there was no need to rewrite the existing definitions. This was a mistake. It would have been much better to rewrite the existing texts, as these texts are very complex and difficult to understand. They were also developed in a different context, i.e. Solvency I. It was feared, however, that rewriting the definitions would create even more problems and a risk of dis-harmonisation with the definitions contained in the FICOD and in the CRD.

1. PRINCIPLES

Group supervision under Solvency II is of *equal importance* to solo supervision, although solo supervision remains the cornerstone of prudential supervision. That means that the basic supervisory approach is the same and that the three pillars that apply to solo supervision also apply to group supervision. Groups must draw up a solvency balance sheet and calculate a group solvency. They must establish a system of governance with key governance functions and carry out a group ORSA. They must prepare and publish a group (or single) SFCR and report on the situation of the group to the supervisory authority of the parent undertaking. Initially, the chapter on group supervision in the EC's proposal contained a series of cross-references to the provisions on solo supervision. This approach was slightly changed[13] during the negotiation of the FD and more specific provisions on group supervision were included in Title III of the FD (Arts. 212–266) so as to make the text easier to understand.

The recognition that group supervision is no longer merely supplementary to solo supervision implies that the provisions in the FD dealing with group supervision also directly influence the way in which solo supervision is carried out on entities belonging to a group (for instance, the link between the governance functions or the requirement for the solo supervisor to cooperate closely with the group supervisor). Group supervision under Solvency II rests on the concept of the group as single economic entity rather than a collection of entities.[14]

---

13 The FD still contains a number of provisions which state that the provisions for solo supervision apply mutatis mutandis to group supervision. See, for instance, Art. 246 (1) FD for the system of governance.

14 BORSELLI, A., Insurance Group Supervision in the EU, in MARANO, P. and SIRI, M. (Eds.), *Insurance Regulation in the European Union*, Palgrave Macmillan, Cham, 2017, p. 207; FABER-GRAW, P., Gruppenaufsicht im Wandel? – Die wesentlichen Veränderungen unter Solvency II im Vergleich zu Solvency I, in BENNEMANN, C., OEHLENBERG, L. and STAHL, G., *Handbuch Solvency II*, Schäffer-Poeschel Verlag, Stuttgart, 2011.

Group supervision can only work if all supervisory authorities concerned cooperate closely and exchange relevant information. Art. 247 (1) FD therefore establishes the principle that for all groups a group supervisor must be designated, from among the supervisory authorities of the Member States concerned, who is responsible for group supervision and who cooperates with the other supervisory authorities concerned in a college of supervisors. Group supervision also requires cooperation from the natural or legal persons included within the scope of group supervision. Member States must ensure that these persons are able to exchange any information that is relevant for the purposes of group supervision (Art. 254 (1) FD). The supervisory authorities concerned may obtain the necessary information directly from a (re)insurance undertaking subject to group supervision if the information has not been supplied by it within a reasonable period of time (Art. 254 (2), fourth paragraph FD).

As a principle, group supervision should normally be carried out only at the ultimate level of the group (in the EEA) and all entities belonging to the group should be included in the supervision. This principle also applies if the top of the group is an insurance, mixed-activity insurance or mixed financial holding company. In the case of a group that has one or more national sub-groups, Member States may allow their supervisory authorities to also carry out group supervision at the ultimate (national) level in their MS for the national sub-group. In practice, this reduces the number of levels of supervision to a maximum of three: EEA group, national sub-groups and solo entities.

Group structures allow (re)insurance undertakings to further diversify their risks. The diversification benefits resulting from the spreading of risks across several legal entities in different Member States (and third countries) are taken into account in the calculation of the group solvency capital.

The group definitions are largely[15] based on those contained in the IGD, as amended by the FICOD and the Reinsurance Directive. These definitions are based upon the definitions adopted for financial reporting purposes in the Seventh Company Law Directive, now included in the Accounting Directive (AD) of 26 June 2013, which repealed the Seventh Company Law Directive.

The EP was very supportive of the progress made in the area of group supervision under Solvency II, although it wanted to go even further, as it favoured a European approach to supervision. It therefore required the EC to make an assessment by 31 December 2017 of the application of the provisions in the FD on group supervision and to present a report to the EP and to the Council, accompanied, where appropriate, by proposals for an amendment of the FD (Art. 242 (1) FD).

---

15 See, for instance, the definition of mutual group in Art. 212 (c) (ii) FD, which is new.

The EC presented this report on 5 April 2018,[16] taking into account the comments made by EIOPA.[17] In its report, the EC concluded that there is at present no urgent need to amend the FD in this area and that some of the issues raised by EIOPA can be dealt with when the FD is reviewed in 2020. The only exception is the introduction of an enhanced role for EIOPA in ensuring supervisory convergence in the area of approval of internal models (at solo and group level), which is part of the package of proposals to review the functioning and financing of the ESAs adopted by the EC on 20 September 2017.[18]

2. GROUP SUPPORT: A MISSED OPPORTUNITY

In November 2006, i.e. at the very end of the preparatory work on Solvency II, the UK (HM Treasury and the FSA) tabled a paper in the EC's Solvency Expert Working Group, proposing a radically new approach to group supervision. The main objective of that paper, presented as a discussion paper, was to avoid the introduction of group supervision as a form of supervision of equal importance to solo supervision creating duplicated supervisory processes for the group as a whole and the undertakings within it, and increasing the regulatory burden on insurance groups operating in the EU. The paper suggested that the additional powers following from group supervision should be allocated in an appropriate way between the supervisors responsible for an insurance group, thereby encouraging supervisory cooperation.

The paper submitted by HM Treasury and the FSA can be summarised as follows:

(a) each group is required to hold eligible assets and capital of sufficient quality in each of its subsidiaries equal to the sum of the technical provisions and the solo MCR;

---

16 EC, Report to the EP and the Council on the application of Title III of Directive 2009/138/EC of the EP and the Council of 25 November 2009 on the taking-up and pursuit of the business of Insurance and Reinsurance (Solvency II) as regards the supervision of insurance and reinsurance undertakings in a group, and the assessment of the transitional period for the occupational retirement provision business of life insurance undertakings, COM (2018) 169 final, 5 April 2018.

17 EIOPA, Report to the EC on the application of group supervision under the Solvency II Directive, EIOPA 17-648, 22 December 2017, 13 p.

18 Proposal for a Directive of the EP and of the Council amending Directive 2014/65/EU on markets in financial instruments and Directive 2009/138/EC on the taking-up and pursuit of the business of Insurance and Reinsurance (Solvency II), COM (2017) 537 final. Agreement was reached between the EP and the Council on the proposal in March 2019. The enhanced role for EIOPA with regard to the approval of internal models is included in the new Art. 112 (3a) FD.

(b) a solvency control level, i.e. an intervention point where the supervisory authority will take action to protect the interests of policyholders and beneficiaries, is set only at group level and not in each subsidiary. The sum of the subsidiaries' MCRs provides a floor for the group-wide SCR;
(c) no SCR is set as a solvency control level in each subsidiary, but each subsidiary calculates a (notional) solo SCR as if it were a solo entity as an informational requirement for the group. The amount of this solo SCR needs to be known so that in the event of a loss in a subsidiary that renders it insolvent, the group's obligation to policyholders and beneficiaries is known;
(d) the group must be able to meet a significant unexpected loss in any subsidiary in a timely manner and must be able to transfer capital into any subsidiary equal to the difference of the solo SCR and the amount of capital available in the subsidiary;
(e) because the solo SCR is not applied as a control level in each subsidiary, there is no need to provide for eligible capital at group level in the form of group contingent support;
(f) each group must be able to move capital freely between its subsidiaries as long as eligible capital is held by each subsidiary up to the level of its MCR;
(g) if one or more subsidiaries of the group become insolvent, the group is required to meet its commitments to policyholders in each subsidiary in the same way as if the subsidiary were a solo entity;
(h) if the group as a whole becomes insolvent and is run off or wound up, assets should be allocated to the subsidiaries in order to meet the technical provisions in each subsidiary. If assets are insufficient to achieve this, they should be allocated so that the ratio of assets to technical provisions is the same in each subsidiary.

The paper further dealt with group-wide diversification effects, the role of the group supervisor, the development of a group internal model, and third-country groups and EEA groups operating in third countries.

The EC expressed initial support for the paper, because it would allow for a more efficient use of capital within insurance groups, while at the same time ensuring a robust system of prudential supervision.[19] When Member States were asked for their views on this paper in the context of the EC's Solvency Expert Working Group, it turned out that only few Member States were in principle in favour of the approach proposed. Most Member States expressed reservations, which went from scepticism to outright opposition. Most Member States wanted

19 The position of the EC had been influenced by representations made by members of the CRO Forum alleging that capital in large multinational insurance groups was managed centrally. Later discussions with the CRO Forum showed that this was not entirely true and that some of the complexities around the transferability of capital within groups had been overlooked.

to follow the advice delivered earlier by CEIOPS.[20] They believed that the solo SCR of each subsidiary in the group should remain a control level, as it was the subsidiary that had concluded a contract with the policyholder. The proposed approach entailed a complete change of emphasis: it would turn things upside down by making solo supervision an annex of group supervision and would weaken national supervision of individual undertakings to an unjustifiable extent.

The insurance industry, by contrast, very much welcomed the approach proposed in the paper. This was expressed in numerous letters from the CEA,[21] the CRO Forum[22] and the Pan-European Insurance Forum.[23] Although it was acknowledged that the proposed approach needed further development, there was a strong feeling that it was in line with the risk-based approach of Solvency II and that it would streamline prudential supervision of groups and enhance supervisory cooperation.

CEIOPS was not pleased with the proposed approach, as it had just provided the EC with advice on a number of issues concerning group supervision in Consultation Paper No 14 (October 2006) and expressed its concern to the EC.

The EC nevertheless went ahead and developed its group support proposal based on the paper submitted by HM Treasury and the FSA. After lengthy discussions with Member States and with CEIOPS, a number of safeguards were built into the EC's proposal, which answered some of the concerns that had been expressed both by Member States and by CEIOPS.

The group support regime was an optional regime included in Arts. 234–244 of the Solvency II Proposal. In line with the approach taken in other areas of Solvency II, the EC's group support text was a principles-based text. Art. 245 in the Solvency II Proposal provided for the adoption of implementing measures with a view to ensuring uniform application of the group support regime.

The group support regime, proposed by the EC, can be summarised as follows:

- *Entry conditions*

  A parent undertaking may apply, on a subsidiary-by-subsidiary basis, to use the group support regime, subject to certain conditions being met: in particular, the subsidiary must be included in group supervision and covered by group risk management and internal control and the parent must provide a legally binding declaration in which it guarantees that eligible own funds

---

20 CEIOPS, Draft Advice to the European Commission in the framework of the Solvency II project on sub-group supervision, diversification effects, cooperation with third countries and issues related to the MCR and SCR in a group context, Consultation Paper No 14, CEIOPS-CP-03/06, 16 October 2006, 30 p.

21 Now Insurance Europe (since 2012).

22 A forum of CROs of large multinational (re)insurance companies.

23 A forum of CEOs of major European-headquartered, multinational (re)insurance groups.

will be transferred where necessary to the subsidiary up to the limit of the notional SCR of the subsidiary.

- *Decision on the application*
  Application of the group support regime is subject to a joint decision between the group supervisor and the other supervisory authorities concerned. In the absence of a joint decision, the group supervisor makes its own decision on the application.
- *First key derogation from normal group supervision – setting of the solo SCR*
  The subsidiary to which the group support regime applies must have eligible capital corresponding to its MCR. By derogation from the rules applicable outside the group support regime, the ultimate responsibility for setting the SCR of the subsidiary belongs to the group supervisor.
- *Second key derogation from normal group supervision – own funds eligible to meet the solo SCR*
  By derogation from the rules applicable outside the group support regime, the difference between the MCR and the solo SCR of the subsidiary may be covered either by eligible own funds or group support or by any combination thereof. The capital in excess of the MCR of the subsidiary can be held anywhere within the group, as long as it is transferable.
- *Third key derogation from normal group supervision – limitation of the role of the solo supervisor*
  By derogation from the rules applicable outside the group support regime, the solo supervisor is no longer responsible for enforcing the SCR of the subsidiary (i.e. by taking measures if the SCR is no longer met), as long as any occurring breach is properly addressed (by an increase of the existing group support and/or by a transfer of own funds).
- *Exit provisions*
  The system ceases to apply to a particular subsidiary when the necessary conditions are no longer met (in which case the parent undertaking must transfer eligible capital to the subsidiary in order to meet the liability against policyholders up to the limit of the group support) and to all subsidiaries involved when the conditions applying to the group as a whole are no longer met (for instance, when the group does not have enough capital to meet the sum of all MCRs). In such cases, the solo supervisors concerned recover their entire powers.
- *Equal treatment*
  When the parent does not have enough money to support all subsidiaries in need of a transfer, the declarations of group support are reduced by application of a fair proportional rule. In addition, policyholders of the parent cannot be treated better than policyholders of subsidiaries.

In order to facilitate the discussions in the Council and the EP, the EC asked CEIOPS in a letter of 19 July 2007 for further advice on "practical measures to facilitate the effective supervision of groups and in particular the operation of the group support regime, as it is likely that parties involved in the negotiation will want to have more details about how these topics will be dealt with in practice, even if much of the detail will be left to level 2". The EC emphasised in its letter that "the advice should not put the Commission's Framework Directive Proposal into question, but rather provide technical answers to issues such as group support, cooperation between supervisors and diversification".

Following the EC's request, CEIOPS provided further advice on practical aspects of the group support regime.[24] In his letter of 28 May 2008, accompanying the advice, the Chairman of CEIOPS, Thomas Steffen, pointed out that several members of CEIOPS continued to believe that the supervisory authority that had authorised the subsidiary undertaking should remain responsible for monitoring and enforcing compliance with its solo SCR. Furthermore, it was pointed out that under the group support regime, there would be a different capital treatment of stand-alone undertakings and group subsidiaries, which might have implications in terms of competition.[25]

Because the proposed group support regime was innovative, it raised numerous questions that were difficult to answer, for instance:

- What is the legal nature of a declaration of group support and how can it be enforced in practice?
- Can a group supervisor take a binding decision on the solo SCR of a subsidiary based in another MS? How does this affect the functioning of the supervisory ladder of intervention with respect to the solo SCR in the case of a breach of the solo SCR?
- Is capital freely transferable between the parent and subsidiary undertakings, particularly when the parent is based in a third country?
- Will the parent undertaking provide eligible capital to a subsidiary when it is itself facing difficulties?
- How can equal treatment of policyholders be ensured? Will the parent undertaking give preference to its own policyholders to the detriment of the policyholders of the subsidiaries?

The regime was discussed at length in the Council Working Party and in ECON, as well as during the trilogue with the EP. The discussions were made difficult

24 CEIOPS, Advice to the EC on aspects of the Framework Directive Proposal related to Insurance Groups. Measures to facilitate the effective supervision of groups, CEIOPS-DOC-25/08, May 2008, 77 p.

25 This is debatable: it is not unfair that subsidiaries are required to hold less capital than stand-alone undertakings. The fact that their activities are comparable does not make their situation comparable: subsidiaries subject to the group support regime can count on the support of their parent undertaking where stand-alone companies would have to face any difficulties with their own resources only.

by the fact that Commissioner Charlie McCreevy was not prepared to make any compromise on the EC's proposal, which he considered innovative, and by a blocking minority of 12 host Member States, led by Hungary, Spain, Poland and Luxembourg, which vigorously opposed any form of group support. Several compromise proposals were considered: a limitation of the regime to national groups or to situations whereby all supervisory authorities concerned agreed; an option for Member States; introduction of a total limit on group support; and a transitional local limitation of group support to a certain percentage of the difference between the MCR and the solo SCR.

Under the Slovenian Presidency in the first half of 2008, a compromise proposal was put on the table that could have formed the basis for an acceptable solution. However, the situation completely changed when France (which had initially supported the EC's proposal, together with the UK and the Netherlands) decided under its Presidency in the second half of 2008 to join the blocking minority in the hope of receiving support from that minority group in its quest to reduce the capital charge for investment in equity.

After it became clear that no agreement could be reached in the Council on the group support regime and that no compromise proposal was likely to receive sufficient support, a solution was developed that provided a way out, thereby giving the blocking minority basically what it wanted, i.e. no group support regime. The solution adopted in the trilogue between the EP and the Council contained three elements:

(a) introduction of a special regime for groups with centralised risk management (Arts. 236–241 FD and Arts. 351–353 DA).[26] This regime has not yet been applied by any group in the EEA because it is questionable whether it provides any specific advantage;[27]
(b) introduction of a duration-based equity risk sub-module (Art. 304 FD and Art. 170 DA). This sub-module was introduced to please France and is presently applied by one French insurance group;
(c) a review clause (Art. 242 (2) FD). This review clause requires the EC to examine how group supervision and capital management within (re)insurance groups can be further enhanced. The EC was required to present a report to the EP and to the Council on this issue by 31 December 2018, accompanied, where appropriate, by proposals for an amendment of the FD.[28]

---

26 This was a face-saving proposal introduced by the Czech Presidency in order to help the EP come over the bridge.

27 EIOPA, Report to the EC on the application of group supervision under the Solvency II Directive, EIOPA 17-648, 22 December 2017, p. 9.

28 At the request of the EC, EIOPA provided advice on a number of questions listed in Art. 242 (2) FD and other questions added by the EC. See EIOPA, Report to the EC on Group Supervision and Capital Management with a Group of Insurance or Reinsurance Undertakings and FoS and FoE under Solvency II, EIOPA-BoS-18-485, 14 December 2018, 145 p.

The EC has not yet presented this report and it has not included the question of enhancing capital management within groups as part of its request to EIOPA for technical advice on the 2020 review of the FD.[29]

The review clause was suggested by the EP and contains a reference to the EC's initial proposal for a group support regime and to the comments on this proposal in the Skinner Report.[30] The areas which the EC is required to look into as part of its report reflect the debate on group support in the EP and in the Council:

(a) a harmonised framework on early intervention;
(b) practices in centralised group risk management and functioning of group internal models including stress testing;
(c) intra-group transactions and risk concentrations;
(d) the behaviour of diversification and concentration effects over time;
(e) a legally binding framework for the mediation of supervisory disputes;
(f) a harmonised framework on asset transferability, insolvency and winding-up procedures that eliminates the relevant national company or corporate law barriers to asset transferability;
(g) an equivalent level of protection of policyholders and beneficiaries of the undertakings of the same group, particularly in crisis situations;
(h) a harmonised and adequately funded EU-wide solution for insurance guarantee schemes;
(i) a harmonised and legally binding framework between competent authorities, central banks and ministries of finance concerning crisis management, resolution and fiscal burden-sharing that aligns supervisory powers with fiscal responsibilities.

It is obvious that it will take time before progress is made at EU level on all these issues. It should also be kept in mind that the group support regime was proposed before the financial crisis. After the financial crisis, NSAs have become even more reluctant to rely on each other in crisis situations, notwithstanding the important progress that has been made within EIOPA and on financial stability between EIOPA and the ESRB. An obvious response by the insurance industry to the absence of group support would have been a restructuring of

---

29 See, EC, Request to EIOPA for technical advice on the review of the Solvency II Directive, Ares (2019) 782244, 11 February 2019, 10 p. (https://ec.europa.eu/info/sites/info/files/business_economy_euro/banking_and_finance/documents/190211-request-eiopa-technical-advice-review-solvency-2.pdf).

30 SKINNER, P., Report of the Committee on Economic and Monetary Affairs (ECON) of the EP of 16 October 2008, A6-0413/2008. It is rather unusual to refer in a legal instrument to a report by a Committee of the EP. It shows the frustration of the EP for not having obtained a better result in the negotiations with the Council and for the disappearance of the group support regime from the FD.

groups and a transformation of subsidiaries into branches. However, prudential requirements for branches have become more and more demanding, and branches, particularly of third-country insurance undertakings, are now treated almost in the same way as subsidiaries.[31]

Nevertheless, the deletion of the group support regime from the final text is a missed opportunity. It should have been possible to develop a text that provided for some capital relief in (re)insurance groups, at least in the case of 100% subsidiaries or in the case of domestic groups.[32]

3. DEFINITIONS

As stated above, the group definitions are derived from the IGD, as amended by the FICOD and the Reinsurance Directive. These definitions are based upon the definitions in the AD. They are extremely difficult to read because they cover a wealth of different situations as the group reality is very complex. The definitions are included in Arts. 13 and 212 FD[33] and in Art. 1 DA. There are slight divergences between the definitions in the FD and in the AD. These divergences either expand the definitions in the AD[34] or introduce situations that are not specifically covered by the AD so as to provide more powers to supervisory authorities.[35] They offer the possibility for supervisory authorities to apply group supervision to cases where they believe there is a group situation, even though this is not apparent from the legal structure.

Most groups have a complex structure; it may have grown from simple to complex as the group expanded.[36] The structure often comprises one or more holding companies and mostly has different layers, with a multitude of sub-groups

---

31 See EIOPA, Guidelines on the supervision of branches of third-country insurance undertakings, EIOPA-BoS-15/110, 23 October 2015.

32 EIOPA does not seem to be very excited about restarting a debate on group support. In its 2018 report to the EC on group supervision, EIOPA writes: “It is not adequate to promote a discussion of a group support regime … It is also not clear whether such a regime should be discussed in the near future either, if taking into account that the responsibility remains on the solo supervisors”. See EIOPA, Report to the EC on Group Supervision and Capital Management with a Group of Insurance or Reinsurance Undertakings and FoS and FoE under Solvency II, EIOPA-BoS-18-485, 14 December 2018, p. 8. This is disappointing.

33 The text refers to the provisions in the Seventh Directive (Directive 83/349/EEC) which was repealed by the AD (Directive 2013/34/EU). These provisions are now included in Arts. 2 (9) and (10) and 22 AD and have not been changed in substance.

34 See, for instance, the definition of parent and subsidiary undertaking in Art. 212 (2) FD.

35 See, for instance, the definition of group in Art. 212 (1) (c) FD and in Art. 22 AD.

36 A new Art. 256a FD introduced by Omnibus II requires all (re)insurance undertakings, insurance holding companies and mixed financial holding companies to disclose publicly, at the level of the group, on an annual basis, the legal structure and the governance and organisational structure, including a description of all subsidiaries, material related undertakings and significant branches belonging to the group.

and intermediate holding companies. Insurance groups may also comprise other financial institutions, such as credit institutions or investment firms. In some cases, the group also includes one or more unregulated undertakings, such as asset management companies (which are not UCITSs, AIFMs or investment firms), real estate companies or financial leasing companies. (Re)insurance groups in the EEA may comprise third-country (re)insurance undertakings. They may also be sub-groups of a group that is headquartered in a third country. Some groups are based on relationships that are not built on capital ties.[37] All these situations have to be covered by the definitions.

In its simplest form, a group may be vertical or horizontal. In a vertical group, an undertaking, called the parent undertaking, controls another undertaking, called the subsidiary undertaking. In a horizontal group, several undertakings situated at the same level control other undertakings, called subsidiary undertakings.[38] Another situation is that of mutual groups, which are composed of undertakings that are coordinated centrally, and may have a vertical or horizontal structure.

The most important definitions that are relevant in this chapter on group supervision are described below.

A *parent undertaking* is an undertaking that controls one or more subsidiary undertakings (Art. 2 (9) AD). An undertaking is presumed to control another undertaking where:[39]

- it has a majority of the voting rights[40] in that undertaking;[41]
- it has the right to appoint or remove a majority of the members of the AMSB of that undertaking;[42]
- it has the right to exercise a dominant influence pursuant to a contract entered into or to a provision in the articles of association[43] of that undertaking;[44]
- it holds a majority of the voting rights in that undertaking pursuant to an agreement with other shareholders.[45]

---

37 These are referred to in France as "non-capitalistic groups" ("*groupes non capitalistiques*"). See https://acpr.banque-france.fr/autoriser/procedures-secteur-assurance/regime-administratif/autorisations-relatives-aux-sgam-sgaps-et-umg.

38 For more details, see VAN HULLE, K. and VAN DER TAS, L., European Union – Consolidated Accounts, in ORDELHEIDE, D. and KPMG (Eds.), *Transatlantic Accounting*, second edition, Volume I, Palgrave, Basingstoke, 2001, pp. 910–913.

39 These are all situations where there exists a legal power of control.

40 A parent undertaking may hold a majority of the capital but not of the voting rights, for instance in the case of multiple voting rights. It is the percentage of voting rights that matters.

41 Art. 22 (1) (a) AD.

42 Art. 22 (1) (b) AD.

43 This is in practice only possible in Germany, where these contracts are part of the law on groups of companies and are referred to as "*Beherrschungsvertrag*".

44 Art. 22 (1) (c) AD.

45 Art. 22 (1) (d) (ii) AD.

Control can also exist where an undertaking does not have legal power of control over another undertaking but where it exercises effective control over that undertaking. Three situations of effective control are distinguished:

- the undertaking is able to appoint a majority of the members of the AMSB of that other undertaking, solely as a result of the exercise of its voting rights;[46]
- the undertaking exercises dominant influence or control over that other undertaking;[47]
- the undertaking and that other undertaking are managed on a unified basis.[48]

As indicated above, the FD expands some of the definitions in the AD for supervisory purposes. Supervisory authorities must also treat as a parent undertaking any undertaking which, in their opinion, effectively exercises a dominant influence over another undertaking (even without any capital ties, i.e. without being a shareholder or member).[49] Such a situation is unlikely to arise frequently.

A *subsidiary undertaking* is an undertaking controlled by a parent undertaking, including any subsidiary undertaking of an ultimate parent undertaking (sub-subsidiary[50]). The FD also expands this definition for supervisory purposes. Supervisory authorities must also treat as a subsidiary undertaking any undertaking over which, in their opinion, a parent undertaking effectively exercises a dominant influence.[51] This is the mirror image of the expanded definition of a parent undertaking.

A *participating undertaking* is an undertaking that is either a parent undertaking, an undertaking which holds a participation or an undertaking linked with another undertaking in the context of a horizontal group.[52]

A *related undertaking* is either a subsidiary undertaking, an undertaking in which a participation is held, or an undertaking linked with another undertaking in the context of a horizontal group.[53]

Participation means the ownership, direct or indirect, of 20% or more of the voting rights or capital of an undertaking.[54]

This definition is expanded for supervisory purposes to other holdings, directly or indirectly, of voting rights or capital in an undertaking over which,

---

46 Art. 22 (1) (d) (i) AD. Such a situation can arise when no undertaking has legal power of control and the shares of the subsidiary are widespread.
47 Art. 22 (2) (a) AD.
48 Art. 22 (2) (b) AD.
49 Art. 212 (2), first subparagraph FD.
50 Art. 2 (10) AD and Art. 1 (48) DA.
51 Art. 212 (2), second subparagraph FD.
52 Art. 212 (1) (a) FD.
53 Art. 212 (1) (b) FD.
54 Art. 13 (20) FD.

in the opinion of the supervisory authority, a significant influence is effectively exercised.[55]

Three types of *groups* may be distinguished: vertical groups, horizontal groups and groups not created through capital ties (mutual groups).

A *vertical group* is defined as a group consisting of a participating undertaking, its subsidiaries and the entities in which the participating undertaking or its subsidiaries hold a participation.[56]

A *horizontal group*[57] is defined as a group consisting of undertakings that are not related undertakings (i.e. between which there is no parent–subsidiary relationship) but that are managed on a unified basis in accordance with a contract concluded between them or with a provision in the memorandum or articles of association of the undertakings concerned or whose AMSB members are largely the same.[58]

As a general rule, the parent undertaking is responsible for the fulfilment of the group supervision requirements. If no parent can be identified, an entity within the group needs to be assigned responsibility for the fulfilment of the group supervision requirements. Particularly in the case of a horizontal group, it may be difficult to identify which entity is responsible for the fulfilment of the group supervision requirements. This matter is not specifically dealt with in the FD. It is not unique to group supervision and also came up in the context of financial reporting, where the question arose as to which of the entities that are managed on a unified basis had to prepare the consolidated financial statements. The pragmatic solution in the case of financial reporting is to impose the requirement on both entities, but to allow the entities concerned to decide between themselves which one should carry out the obligation. The other entity would then be exempted from the obligation. A similar solution could be applied here in the context of group supervision requirements. It would not be appropriate to allow the group supervisor to ask each entity to satisfy the group supervision requirements, including reporting; that would not be in line with the proportionality principle.

A *mutual group* is defined as a group of undertakings which is not built on the basis of capital ties but on the basis of strong and sustainable financial relationships. These financial relationships are the result of contractual or other

55 Art. 212 (2), third subparagraph FD.

56 Art. 212 (1) (c) (i) FD.

57 This is referred to in Germany as "*Gleichordnungskonzern*". Examples are the Alte Leipziger-Hallesche group, where Alte Leipziger Lebensversicherung and Hallesche Krankenversicherung are the parent undertakings (https://www.alte-leipziger.de/unternehmen-al/konzern-konzern.htm), and the Signal Iduna group, where Signal Iduna Kranken, Iduna Leben and Signal Unfall are the parent undertakings (https://www.signal-iduna.de/ueber-uns/signal-iduna-gruppe/konzern/vorstand.php).

58 Art. 212 (1) (c) (i) FD.

constructs and the group may include mutual or mutual-type associations. Further conditions are that:

- one of the undertakings (the parent undertaking) effectively exercises, through centralised coordination,[59] a dominant influence over the decisions, including financial decisions, of the other undertakings (related undertakings) that are part of the group; and
- the establishment and dissolution of the financial relationships for the purposes of group supervision are subject to prior approval by the group supervisor.[60]

Dominant influence can be evidenced by representation on the board or equivalent governing body, participation in the policy-making process, material transactions between the investor and the investee, interchange of managerial staff, provision of essential technical information, management on a unified basis or voting rights.[61]

The inclusion of this third type of group is justified in recital 98 FD as follows:

> "Subject to Community and national law, undertakings, in particular mutual and mutual-type associations, should be able to form concentrations or groups, not through capital ties but through formalised strong and sustainable relationships, based on contractual or other material recognition that guarantees a financial solidarity between those undertakings. Where a dominant influence is exercised through a centralised coordination, those undertakings should be supervised in accordance with the same rules as those provided for groups constituted through capital ties in order to achieve an adequate level of protection for policyholders and a level playing field between groups."

Large mutual groups, including horizontal and vertical groups, can be found in Austria, Belgium, Finland, France, Germany, Italy, the Netherlands, Norway, Spain and Sweden.[62] Their organisation in practice differs considerably.[63]

---

59 This may not always be easy to prove. See EIOPA, Report to the EC on the Application of Group Supervision under the Solvency II Directive, EIOPA 17-648, 22 December 2017, p. 6. The coordination can, for instance, take the form of committees in which staff from group undertakings work together on key issues for the group.

60 Art. 212 (1) (c) (ii) FD.

61 CEIOPS, CEIOPS' Advice for Level 2 Implementing Measures on Solvency II: assessment of Group Solvency, CEIOPS-DOC-52/09, October 2009, p. 12.

62 For more information, see the website of AMICE: www.amice-eu.org.

63 For interesting examples, see the mutual groups Covéa in France and Länsförsikringär in Sweden. The latter is an alliance comprising 23 local and customer-owned regional insurance companies and the jointly owned Länsförsikringär AB with subsidiaries. The alliance is not a group in the legal sense of the term. Each of the 23 local and customer-owned regional companies operate independently. They jointly own Länsförsikringär AB. Länsförsikringär AB and its subsidiaries are a classical group. See https://mb.cision.com/Main/152/2474709/807357.pdf.

An *insurance holding company* is a holding company of a (re)insurance group. It is defined as a parent undertaking:

- which is not a mixed financial holding company;
- the main business of which is to acquire and hold participations in subsidiary undertakings, which are exclusively or mainly (re)insurance undertakings, or third-country (re)insurance undertakings;
- where at least one of the subsidiary undertakings is an EEA (re)insurance undertaking.[64]

There is no guidance in the FD on how to decide whether the main business of the holding company is the acquisition or holding of participations in (re)insurance subsidiaries. By analogy to Art. 3 (1) FICOD, a solution could be to look at the proportion of the consolidated balance sheet that is represented by (re)insurance business. If the (re)insurance business makes up more than 50% of the consolidated balance sheet, the holding company can be considered to be an insurance holding company.[65] It is also important to look at the business model of the holding company, in line with the text of Art. 212 (1) (f) FD, which refers to the business of the holding company. If the business model is not specifically oriented towards (re)insurance but rather towards a range of (non-financial) activities, the holding company is not an insurance holding company but must be treated as a mixed-activity insurance holding company, even if in one specific financial year its main activity happens to be (re)insurance.

A *mixed-activity insurance holding company* is a holding company of a group that carries out various activities and comprises one or more (re)insurance undertakings. It is defined as a parent undertaking:

- which is not a (re)insurance undertaking or a third-country (re)insurance undertaking, insurance holding company or mixed financial holding company;
- which has at least one subsidiary that is an EEA (re)insurance undertaking.[66]

The term "mixed-activity insurance holding company" is misleading because the definition specifically states that the mixed-activity insurance holding company is not an insurance holding company, i.e. its exclusive or main business is not the acquisition of participations in (re)insurance undertakings. The intention of the co-legislators was no doubt to capture here a situation where one of the group's main activities is (re)insurance but other (non-financial) activities are equally important.

---

64 Art. 212 (1) (f) FD.

65 This seems to be the approach preferred by EIOPA. See EIOPA, Report to the EC on Group Supervision and Capital Management with a Group of Insurance or Reinsurance Undertakings and FoS and FoE under Solvency II, EIOPA-BoS-18-485, 14 December 2018, p. 88.

66 Art. 212 (1) (g) FD.

A *mixed financial holding company* is a holding company of a group that might comprise a (re)insurance undertaking but includes also other financial undertakings. It is defined as a parent undertaking:

- which is not a regulated entity (credit institution, (re)insurance undertaking or investment firm);
- which has at least one subsidiary that is a regulated entity with its head office in the EEA;
- which constitutes with that subsidiary and with other entities (carrying out banking or investment services) a financial conglomerate.[67]

A *third-country (re)insurance undertaking* is defined in Art. 13 (1) and (6) FD as an undertaking that would require authorisation as a (re)insurance undertaking in accordance with Art. 14 FD if its head office were situated in the EU.

4. WHEN DOES GROUP SUPERVISION APPLY?

Art. 213 FD lists the cases in which group supervision applies. As indicated earlier, group supervision does not take away solo supervision, i.e. the individual undertakings that are part of the group continue to be supervised by the supervisory authority that has authorised them. Solo supervision continues to be the cornerstone of supervision.

Group supervision applies in the following cases.

1. Firstly, in the case of (re)insurance undertakings that are participating undertakings in at least one (re)insurance undertaking in the EEA or in a third country (Art. 213 (2) (a) FD). This is the classic example of an insurance group. Therefore, the principle is that all provisions concerning group supervision (Arts. 218–258 FD) apply. However, where the parent undertaking is subject to supplementary supervision as a financial conglomerate, the group supervisor may, after consulting the other supervisory authorities concerned, decide not to carry out the supervision of risk concentration (Art. 244 FD), the supervision of intra-group transactions (Art. 245 FD) or both (Art. 215 (2) FD), as this would already take place by virtue of the FICOD. The objective is to prevent the duplication of tasks (Art. 212 (3) FD).
2. Secondly, group supervision applies in the case of (re)insurance undertakings where the parent undertaking is an insurance holding company or a mixed financial holding company with its head office in the EEA (Art. 213 (2) (b) FD). In this case, the parent undertaking of the group is not itself an insurance undertaking but a holding company. Nevertheless, all provisions concerning

[67] Art. 212 (1) (h) FD and Art. 2 (15) FICOD.

group supervision (Arts. 218–258 FD) apply in principle. However, as for the previous case, where the parent undertaking is subject to supplementary supervision as a financial conglomerate, the group supervisor may, after consulting the other supervisory authorities concerned, decide not to carry out the supervision of risk concentration (Art. 244 FD), the supervision of intra-group transactions (Art. 245 FD) or both (Art. 215 (2) FD), as this would already take place by virtue of the FICOD. The objective is to prevent the duplication of tasks (Art. 212 (3) FD).

3. Thirdly, group supervision applies to (re)insurance undertakings where the parent undertaking is an insurance holding company, a mixed financial holding company or a (re)insurance undertaking with its head office in a third country (Art. 213 (2) (c) FD).[68] The problem here is that the parent undertaking does not have its head office within the EEA. This means that it is not governed by EU law. In this case, reliance might nevertheless be placed on the group supervision carried out by the group supervisor in the third country if supervision in that country is considered equivalent to supervision under Solvency II (Arts. 260–263 FD). See further, Chapter 10.

   Where a mixed financial holding company is subject to equivalent risk-based supervision under the FD and under the FICOD, the group supervisor may, in agreement with the other supervisory authorities concerned, apply only the relevant provisions of the FICOD to the mixed financial holding company (Art. 213 (4) FD).

   Where a mixed financial holding company is subject to equivalent risk-based supervision under the FD and under the CRD, the group supervisor may, in agreement with the consolidating supervisor in the banking and investment sector, apply only the provisions of the relevant directive relating to the most significant sector (Art. 213 (5) FD).

   As these situations require close cooperation between the supervisory authorities in different financial sectors, it is important that a convergent approach is developed. The group supervisor must therefore inform EBA, EIOPA and ESMA about the decisions taken and the ESAs are tasked with developing guidelines and regulatory technical standards in this area through the Joint Committee (Art. 213 (6) FD).[69]

4. Finally, group supervision applies in the case of (re)insurance undertakings where the parent undertaking is a mixed-activity insurance holding

---

[68] The scope of group supervision will change after Brexit for EEA groups with a UK parent undertaking, as that parent undertaking will become a third-country parent undertaking after the withdrawal date.

[69] See, for instance, Commission Delegated Regulation (EU) 2015/2303 of 28 July 2015 supplementing Directive 2002/87/EC of the EP and of the Council with regard to regulatory technical standards specifying the definitions and coordinating the supplementary supervision of risk concentration and intra-group transactions, *OJ* L 326, 11.12.2015, p. 34, and Joint Committee of the ESAs, Joint Guidelines on the convergence of supervisory

company (Art. 213 (2) (d) FD). Because insurance is not the sole activity of the group, the parent undertaking is not a regulated entity and the group carries out activities that may not be regulated, it is difficult to apply the provisions on group supervision.[70] In this case, calculation of group solvency *does not apply*, but the supervisory authorities responsible for the supervision of the (re)insurance undertakings that are part of the group must exercise general supervision over transactions between these (re) insurance undertakings and the mixed-activity insurance holding company and its related undertakings (Art. 265 FD).[71]

As indicated earlier, the term "mixed-activity insurance holding company" is misleading, because the parent undertaking is described in the definition (Art. 212 (1) (g) FD) as not being itself an insurance holding company. That means that its exclusive or main business is by definition not the acquisition or holding of participations in (re)insurance undertakings.

This would not include the situation where an ultimate parent undertaking is a mixed-activity holding company with direct or indirect (for instance, through a sub-holding company) participations in one or more (re)insurance undertakings but whereby the main activity of the group is not (re)insurance. Art. 213 (2) (d) FD does not apply in this case. It may nevertheless be useful from a supervisory perspective to apply in this case a similar solution, i.e. to exclude that group from the application of group supervision but to exercise supervision over the intra-group transactions between the insurance sub-group and the mixed-activity insurance holding company and its related undertakings in order to have an insight into possible spill-over effects from other parts of the group on the insurance sub-group. In this case, it would clearly make no sense to apply the provisions on group supervision and the calculation of a group SCR at the level of the mixed-activity insurance holding company.

5. SCOPE OF GROUP SUPERVISION

As a principle, all (re)insurance undertakings that are part of a group are subject to group supervision at the level of the group (Art. 213 (1) FD).

In the case of a third-country (re)insurance undertaking, an insurance holding company, a mixed financial holding company or a mixed-activity

practices relating to the consistency of supervisory coordination arrangements for financial conglomerates, JC/GL/2014/01, 22 December 2014, 35 p.

70 The ultimate parent undertaking may itself be the parent of an insurance holding company or a mixed financial holding company, in which case sub-group supervision could be applied at the sub-holding level. See further, Chapter 9, section 6. However, the ultimate parent of the group is not itself subject to supervision (Art. 214 (1) FD).

71 EIOPA, Guidelines on group solvency, EIOPA-BoS-14/181, 2 February 2015, Guideline 6.

insurance holding company, this does not imply that supervisory authorities are required to play a supervisory role in relation to the third-country (re)insurance undertaking, insurance holding company, mixed financial holding company or mixed-activity insurance holding company individually (Art. 214 (1) FD). That would not be possible because the undertaking concerned either does not fall under the jurisdiction of the supervisory authority or is not a regulated entity. However, in the case of an insurance holding company or a mixed financial holding company, the fit and proper requirements for persons who effectively run the insurance holding company or mixed financial holding company apply (Art. 257 (1) FD), because these situations are closer to that of regulated entities.

There may be situations where it is difficult to include an undertaking in the scope of group supervision. These situations are by definition exceptional and the decision to exclude them from group supervision must be taken by the group supervisor on a case-by-case basis, after consulting the other supervisory authorities concerned.

Art. 214 (2) FD lists the following cases of exclusion:[72]

(a) the undertaking is situated in a third country and there are legal impediments to the transfer of the necessary information. The book value of that undertaking in the solvency balance sheet of the participating (re)insurance undertaking is in that case deducted from the own funds eligible for the group solvency calculation (Art. 229 FD);
(b) the undertaking is of negligible interest with respect to the objectives of group supervision. This materiality test does not apply if several undertakings are excluded on that basis and if, taken together, they cannot be considered to be of negligible interest;[73]
(c) inclusion of the undertaking would be inappropriate or misleading with respect to the objectives of group supervision.

As a principle, group supervision should cover the same entities that are included in the scope of the consolidated financial statements, as the same definitions apply for prudential purposes and for accounting purposes.[74] However, as indicated above in section 3, there may be a number of situations in which the supervisory authority might include within the scope of group supervision entities that are either not required to prepare consolidated financial statements

---

72 Where an undertaking is excluded from group supervision in the cases mentioned under points (b) or (c), the supervisory authority of the MS of that undertaking may ask the parent undertaking for any information that may facilitate its supervision of the undertaking concerned (Art. 214 (2), fourth subparagraph FD).

73 This exclusion ground has been applied so far in 46 cases. For the full list, see EIOPA, Report to the EC on Group Supervision and Capital Management with a Group of Insurance or Reinsurance Undertakings and FoS and FoE under Solvency II, EIOPA-BoS-18-485, 14 December 2018, pp. 141–142.

74 This is also the approach in ICP 23 – Group-wide Supervision, which does however recognise (para. 23.1.14) that there are differences in the scope.

or are not normally included in the scope of the consolidation as they are not considered either parent or subsidiary undertakings under the accounting rules. It is also possible for entities that are included in the scope of the consolidated financial statements not to be included in the scope of group supervision, as the cases of exclusion from the scope of the consolidated financial statements have become very exceptional. For instance, materiality is no longer a case for exclusion from the scope of the consolidated financial statements under Art. 23 (9) AD and under IFRS 10 – Consolidated Financial Statements.[75]

6. LEVELS OF GROUP SUPERVISION

Groups may comprise several sub-groups headed by intermediate holding companies. The principle is that group supervision should take place only at the level of the ultimate parent which has its head office in the EEA (Art. 215 (1) FD).

Where the ultimate parent that has its head office in the EEA is itself a subsidiary of an undertaking subject to supplementary supervision as a financial conglomerate, the group supervisor may, after consulting the other supervisory authorities concerned, decide not to carry out the supervision of risk concentration or of intra-group transactions, or both, at that ultimate parent undertaking. The objective is to avoid the duplication of tasks (Art. 215 (2) FD).

Some Member States had difficulties with the principle that group supervision should only take place at the level of the ultimate parent of a group. They felt that sub-group supervision at national level should be possible, particularly if an important sub-group of a group headquartered in another MS was established in their territory. In its advice to the EC,[76] CEIOPS had recommended allowing sub-group supervision in cases where the supervisory authority involved considers this necessary, for instance where the sub-group is in financial distress or where the sub-group is an important actor on the local market. It was however agreed that no unnecessary burden should be placed on groups and that it should be possible to waive sub-group supervision at national level.

Art. 216 FD allows the supervisory authority of the home MS of a sub-group[77] to apply sub-group supervision at national level (including the requirement to calculate a group SCR) under a number of conditions:

- sub-group supervision must be specifically allowed by the MS concerned;
- the group supervisor and the ultimate parent undertaking must be consulted;

---

75 It can be argued that the materiality principle applies in all situations, even when not specifically mentioned.

76 CEIOPS, Advice to the EC in the framework of the Solvency II project on sub-group supervision, diversification effects, cooperation with third countries and issues related to the MCR and SCR in a group context, CEIOPS-DOC-05/06, November 2006, pp. 13–14.

77 The article does not refer to sub-group but to the ultimate parent at national level.

- the supervisory authority of the sub-group must explain its decision to the group supervisor and to the ultimate parent undertaking;
- the group supervisor must inform the college of supervisors;
- the supervisory authority of the sub-group may restrict its supervision to certain aspects of group supervision (see Art. 216 (2)–(6) FD);
- the decision to apply sub-group supervision must be justified by objective differences in the operations, organisation or risk profile of the sub-group and the group (Art. 358 DA).[78]

In order to avoid the multiplication of cases of sub-group supervision with respect to groups that have sub-groups covering several Member States, and in order to allow sub-group supervision on a regional basis (for instance, in Scandinavia), Art. 217 FD requires Member States that have allowed their supervisory authority to apply sub-group supervision to permit their supervisory authority to conclude an agreement with supervisory authorities in other Member States where another related ultimate parent undertaking at national level is present, with a view to carrying out group supervision at the level of a sub-group covering several Member States.

As a result, Solvency II provides for a maximum of three levels of supervision: solo supervision of individual undertakings, sub-group supervision for sub-groups at a national or regional level (optional), and group supervision for the entire group.[79]

Fortunately,[80] only three EEA Member States conduct sub-group supervision on eight cross-border groups. The regime is burdensome and should be seen as a remainder of the past where supervisory authorities were reluctant to trust each other's supervisory capabilities. The cross-reference in Art. 216 (1) FD to Arts. 218–258 FD (virtually all requirements concerning group supervision) in the case of sub-groups has the consequence that an additional college must be set up for each sub-group, with separate coordination arrangements, the development of an emergency plan and double information exchanges, as well as an overlap in the reporting to supervisors by the group and its sub-groups. As pointed out by EIOPA, further maturity of colleges could remove the need for formal sub-group supervision in many cases. In EIOPA's view, it should be possible to achieve effective supervision of a sub-group by using a specialised

---

78 Important elements to consider in this regard may be the unity of decision-making at sub-group level or a significant difference between the business activity of the sub-group and that of the group as a whole, for instance where the group's main business is non-life insurance and the sub-group is focused on life insurance.

79 For examples, see GRÜNDL, H. and KRAFT, M. (Eds.), *Solvency II – Eine Einführung*, Verlag Versicherungswirtschaft, Karlsruhe, 2015, pp. 118–128.

80 Sub-group supervision is not in line with the risk-based approach of Solvency II, which looks at the whole group as one economic entity and therefore situates group supervision at the ultimate level of the group.

team within the college to focus on particular parts of the group with significant differences from the group as a whole. Any specific requirements for reporting or the thresholds for reporting intra-group transactions and risk concentrations needed by the specialist team could be put into the annexes of the group coordination arrangement.[81]

7. CALCULATION OF GROUP SOLVENCY

7.1. GENERAL PRINCIPLES

Participating (re)insurance undertakings, insurance holding companies or mixed financial holding companies must calculate a group SCR.[82] The eligible own funds in the group must always be at least equal to the group SCR (Art. 218 (2) and (3) FD). The group SCR will be lower than the sum of the solo SCRs of its component entities because of the existence of group diversification benefits.[83]

Membership of a group may have positive and negative effects. The positive effect is the diversification benefit resulting from the diversification of risk between different legal entities.[84] Group diversification benefits can be defined as the difference between the sum of the solo SCRs of each related (re)insurance undertaking[85] in the group and the group SCR, as calculated by a standard formula based on consolidated data or by an internal group model, before group-specific risks have been taken into account. These benefits must be confronted with possible negative effects resulting from group risk, i.e. events or factors that relate to being part of a group and might have an adverse financial, legal or reputational effect on individual entities of the group. The overall group diversification effect must also take into account group contagion risks, issues around the fungibility and transferability of capital and any potential weaknesses in the correlation data, particularly under stressed conditions.[86]

---

81 EIOPA, Report to the EC on the application of group supervision under the Solvency II Directive, EIOPA 17-648, 22 December 2017, p. 8.

82 See also CEIOPS, CEIOPS' Advice for Level 2 Implementing measures on Solvency II: Assessment of Group Solvency, CEIOPS-DOC-52/09, October 2009, 59 p. and EIOPA, Guidelines on group solvency, EIOPA-BoS-14/181, 2 February 2015, 15 p.

83 See also above, Chapter 6, section 4.2.2.1.1. See also Art. 222 (4) FD and recital 101 FD.

84 Only in the case of application of the accounting consolidation-based method (default method).

85 Where an insurance group has cross-sectoral holdings, for instance in credit institutions, the relevant sectorial capital requirements are simply added to the group SCR so that no cross-sector diversification benefits are taken into account.

86 CEIOPS, Advice to the EC in the framework of the Solvency II project on sub-group supervision, diversification effects, cooperation with third countries and issues related to the MCR and SCR in a group context, CEIOPS-DOC-05/06, November 2006, p. 16.

The group SCR must be calculated at least annually and the relevant data for and the results of that calculation must be submitted to the group supervisor. The participating (re)insurance undertaking, insurance holding company or mixed financial holding company must monitor the group SCR on an ongoing basis and must recalculate the group SCR without delay where the risk profile of the group deviates significantly from the assumptions underlying the last reported group SCR. A recalculation of the group SCR may also be required by the group supervisor (Art. 219 FD).

The calculation of the group SCR must take account of the proportional share held by the parent undertaking in its related undertakings, as defined in Art. 221 FD. Double use of eligible own funds (double gearing) must be eliminated, for instance shares held by the parent undertaking in a related undertaking (Art. 222 FD). Forms of reciprocal finance must also be eliminated, for instance when a parent undertaking holds shares in, or makes loans to, another undertaking which, directly or indirectly, holds own funds eligible for the SCR of the parent undertaking (Art. 223 FD).

For the calculation of the group SCR, intermediate insurance holding companies or intermediate mixed financial holding companies are treated as if they were a (re)insurance undertaking (Art. 226 FD). Related credit institutions, investment firms or financial institutions, IORPs, UCITS management companies and AIFMs must be included in the group solvency calculation using sectorial requirements (Art. 228 FD and Art. 329 DA). For non-regulated financial undertakings, a notional capital requirement is calculated that corresponds to the capital requirement with which the undertaking would have to comply under the relevant sectorial rules if the undertaking were a regulated entity. SPVs to which risks have been transferred and which satisfy the legal requirements (Art. 211 FD) are excluded from the calculation of the group solvency.

Subsidiary undertakings that are situated in a third country are included in the calculation of the group solvency on the basis of the Solvency II rules, unless the third country's solvency regime has been recognised as equivalent to Solvency II (Art. 227 (1) FD). See further, Chapter 10, section 2.

Where the necessary information for the calculation of the group SCR is not available for a particular related undertaking, the book value of that undertaking must be deducted from the own funds eligible for the group solvency (Art. 229 FD).

The parent undertaking ((re)insurance undertaking or insurance holding company) must immediately inform the group supervisor in the case of deteriorating financial conditions of the group. The same applies when the parent undertaking has observed that the group SCR is no longer complied with or that there is a risk of non-compliance in the following three months. The group supervisor must inform the other supervisory authorities within the college of supervisors, which will then analyse the situation of the group

(Art. 218 (5) FD). The procedure provided in Art. 138 FD applies mutatis mutandis (Art. 218 (4) FD).[87]

7.2. CALCULATION METHODS

The group solvency must be calculated in accordance with the technical principles and one of the methods set out in Arts. 221–233 FD, further implemented by Arts. 328–350 DA. The calculation is complex.[88]

As a principle,[89] the group SCR is calculated on the basis of the accounting consolidation-based method (method 1), which is recognised as the default method. Member States may however allow[90] their supervisory authority (not the parent undertaking!), where it assumes the role of group supervisor with regard to a particular group, to decide that the group SCR for that group should be calculated using the deduction and aggregation method (method 2). The group supervisor may also allow a combination of both methods, for instance when the amount and quality of information available in relation to a related undertaking would not be sufficient for it to be able to apply the default method, where a group internal model is used for the calculation of the group SCR and a related undertaking is not covered by that group internal model, or when the use of the default method in relation to a related undertaking would be overly burdensome (Art. 328 DA).

In deciding whether method 2 or a combination of both methods should be applied, the group supervisor must consult the other supervisory authorities concerned, as well as the group. Where method 2 is applied, no diversification benefits are recognised at group level because they are already recognised in the solo calculations and the group SCR represents the sum of the solo SCRs.

---

87 Since the application of Solvency II, there have been four notifications of deteriorating financial conditions and communications on non-compliance with the group SCR or of a risk of non-compliance within the next three months. See EIOPA, Report to the EC on Group Supervision and Capital Management with a Group of Insurance or Reinsurance Undertakings and FoS and FoE under Solvency II, EIOPA-BoS-18-485, 14 December 2018, p. 25.

88 For a good overview, see the document produced by the Malta Financial Services Authority (MFSA), *Insurance Groups under Solvency II*, November 2013, 21 p. (https://www.mfsa.com.mt/wp-content/uploads/2019/01/18_1441623566_InsuranceGroupsunderSolvencyII.pdf). EIOPA has identified a number of difficulties with the application of the legal requirements, which are partly due to the mutatis mutandis reference in Arts. 218 (4) and 246 (1) FD and has suggested a number of changes. See EIOPA, Report to the EC on Group Supervision and Capital Management with a Group of Insurance or Reinsurance Undertakings and FoS and FoE under Solvency II, EIOPA-BoS-18-485, 14 December 2018, pp. 95–107.

89 Art. 220 (2), first subparagraph FD.

90 Art. 220 (2), second subparagraph FD.

7.2.1. *Method 1 (Default Method): Accounting Consolidation-Based Method*

The accounting consolidation-based method implies that the calculation of the group solvency by the participating (re)insurance undertaking or the insurance holding company is carried out on the basis of the consolidated accounts using the valuation rules prescribed under Solvency II.[91]

The group SCR is the difference between the own funds eligible to cover the SCR, and the SCR calculated at group level. The SCR at group level is calculated using either the standard formula[92] or an approved internal model[93] (Art. 230 FD).

Subject to approval by the group supervisor, the consolidated group SCR may, within the framework of the standard formula, be calculated by replacing a subset of the standard parameters by parameters specific to the group ("group-specific parameters" or GSPs) (Art. 338 DA).[94] The application to use GSPs must be provided in writing to the group supervisor by the parent undertaking, in one of the official languages of the group supervisor's MS or in a language for which the group supervisor has given prior approval. The group supervisor must inform the other supervisory authorities within the college of supervisors without delay of the receipt of the application and must also forward the application to them. Prior to making its final decision, the group supervisor must consult the other supervisory authorities within the college. After this consultation, the group supervisor makes its own decision and provides that decision to the parent undertaking and to the other supervisory authorities within the college. The decision must be written in an official language of the MS of the group supervisor, and in another language most commonly understood by the other supervisory authorities (Art. 356 DA).

Where the consolidated group SCR is calculated, wholly or in part, on the basis of the standard formula, the local currency from which to calculate the currency risk is the currency used for the preparation of the consolidated accounts, unless a material amount of the consolidated technical provisions or the consolidated group own funds is denominated in another currency. In that case, that other currency is used as the reference currency from which to calculate the currency risk in the currency risk sub-module (Art. 337 DA).[95]

---

91 For the calculation of technical provisions in the consolidated balance sheet, see Arts. 339 and 340 DA.

92 The group supervisor might allow the use of GSPs. See Art. 338 DA.

93 The application for the use of an internal model to calculate only the consolidated group SCR is laid down in Arts. 343–346 DA.

94 See above, Chapter 6, section 4.2.2.1.1.a. The same provisions apply mutatis mutandis, although the references are somewhat misleading as Art. 338 (1) DA does not refer to the life, non-life and health underwriting risk modules, while Art. 338 (2) DA does, through its reference to Art. 104 (7) FD.

95 As amended after the 2018 review of the DA, based on a proposal from EIOPA. See EIOPA, Second set of advice to the EC on specific items in the Solvency II Delegated Regulation,

Where an internal model is used only for the calculation of the consolidated group SCR and is not used to calculate the SCR of related (re)insurance undertakings in the group (see below, section 7.3), the procedure to be followed by the group supervisor for the approval of the model is consistent with that which applies for the approval of an internal model at solo level (see above, Chapter 6, section 4.2.3).

The internal model may be full or partial. A partial model should be applied for when only some related undertakings are included in the scope of the internal model, or when the model has a limited scope, for instance in terms of risk modules (Art. 112 (2) FD) or in the case of a combination of both (recital 134 DA). In terms of the use test (Art. 120 FD), the requirement for an internal model to be widely used and to play an important role in the system of governance of the group must be so understood that the output of that internal model is used by those (re)insurance undertakings whose business is fully or partly included in the scope of the internal model and only for the calculation of the consolidated group SCR (recital 135 DA).

Where a group applies for the use of the same internal model to calculate the consolidated group SCR as well as the SCR of (re)insurance undertakings in the group (group internal model), the procedure set out in Art. 231 FD applies. Approval of an internal model used only for the calculation of the consolidated group SCR granted on the basis of Art. 230 FD is different from the approval of a group internal model, which is dealt with in Art. 231 FD. Approval of a group internal model is not bound by an earlier decision relating to the use of an internal model for the calculation of the consolidated group SCR only (recital 133 DA).

The consolidated data for the calculation of group solvency are calculated as follows (Art. 335 DA):

(a) full consolidation of data of all the (re)insurance undertakings, third-country (re)insurance undertakings, insurance holding companies, mixed financial holding companies and ancillary services undertakings[96] which are subsidiaries of the parent undertaking;
(b) full consolidation of data of SPVs to which the participating undertaking or one of its subsidiaries has transferred risk and which are not excluded from the scope of the group solvency calculation pursuant to Art. 329 (3) DA;[97]

EIOPA-BoS-18/075, 28 February 2018, p. 182. This is highly relevant. Based on an analysis of 294 groups, EIOPA found that 38 groups had more than 50% of their assets in foreign currencies, with 25 groups having more than 60% of their assets in foreign currencies.

96 Defined in Art. 1 (53) DA as "a non-regulated undertaking the principal activity of which consists of owning or managing property, managing data-processing services, health and care services or any other similar activity which is ancillary to the principal activity of one or more (re)insurance undertakings".

97 They are excluded if they comply with the requirements in Art. 211 FD or if they are regulated by a third-country supervisory authority. See above, Chapter 6, section 4.2.2.1.1.

(c) proportional consolidation of data of the (re)insurance undertakings, third-country (re)insurance undertakings, insurance holding companies, mixed financial holding companies and ancillary services undertakings managed by an undertaking referred to in point (a), together with one or more undertakings not included in point (a), where those undertakings' responsibility is limited to the share of the capital they hold;[98]
(d) on the basis of the adjusted equity method,[99] data of all holdings in related (re)insurance undertakings, third-country (re)insurance undertakings, insurance holding companies, mixed financial holding companies which are not subsidiaries of the parent and which are not covered by points (a) and (c);
(e) the proportional share of the undertakings' own funds calculated according to the relevant sectorial rules, as referred to in Art. 2 (7) FICOD, in relation to holdings in related undertakings which are credit institutions, investment firms and financial institutions, AIFMs, UCITS management companies and non-regulated undertakings carrying out financial activities and the proportional share of the regulatory own funds in relation to holdings in IORPs;
(f) in accordance with Art. 13 DA,[100] data of all related undertakings, including ancillary service undertakings, collective investment undertakings and investments packaged as funds, other than those referred to in points (a)–(e).

The consolidated group SCR is calculated as the sum of the capital requirements[101] of all the different undertakings that are part of the group based on consolidated data as described above (Art. 336 DA). Related (re)insurance undertakings in the EEA, which are subsidiary undertakings, contribute fully to the diversification effects recognised at group level when calculating the consolidated group SCR.

For related (re)insurance undertakings which are not subsidiary undertakings, the proportional share of the notional SCR is included in the consolidated group SCR as a simple sum without recognition of diversification effects at group level.

Related (re)insurance undertakings situated in a third country are also included in the consolidated group SCR. Their notional SCR to be used for the purpose of the group solvency calculation is determined as if they were

98 For instance, in the case of a joint venture.

99 Valuation of the holdings by the participating undertaking in related undertakings based on the share of the excess of assets over liabilities of these related undertakings. See Art. 13 (3) DA.

100 Setting out the valuation methods for related undertakings.

101 And of the data of collective investment undertakings and investments packaged as funds that are subsidiaries of the parent undertaking.

(re)insurance undertakings situated in the EEA, i.e. on the basis of the Solvency II valuation principles (Art. 336 (a) DA).[102]

Where the related (re)insurance undertakings in a third country are subsidiary undertakings, their notional SCR is fully consolidated into the group SCR and diversification effects can be recognised at group level (Art. 336 (a) DA). Where the related (re)insurance undertakings in a third country are not subsidiary undertakings, the proportional share of their notional SCR is included in the consolidated group SCR as a simple sum without recognition of diversification effects at group level (Art. 336 (b) DA):

- for related undertakings which are credit institutions, investment firms, financial institutions, AIFMs, UCITS management companies and IORPs, the proportional share calculated according to the relevant sectorial rules is included in the consolidated group SCR as a simple sum without recognition of diversification effects at group level (Art. 336 (c) DA);
- for non-regulated undertakings carrying out financial activities, the proportional share of their notional capital is added to the consolidated group SCR as a simple sum without recognition of diversification effects at group level. For these undertakings, which include ancillary service undertakings and SPVs, no calculation of a notional SCR is required as the relevant data are implicitly included in the data used to calculate the group SCR (Art. 336 (d) FD);
- for collective investment undertakings or investments packaged as funds which are not subsidiaries of the parent undertaking and to which the look-through approach (Art. 84 (1) DA) is applied at solo level, the consolidated group SCR includes the amount of the SCR calculated on the basis of each of the underlying assets of the collective investment undertakings and investments packaged as funds (Title I, Chapter V and Art. 84 (1) DA).

No real MCR is calculated at group level. However, a proxy MCR or floor group SCR must be calculated under the default method or in the case of a combination of both methods, for the part of the group which is covered by the default method, in order to define a floor to the group SCR (Art. 230 (2) FD). This proxy MCR is the sum of the MCRs of the participating (re)insurance undertaking or notional MCR of the insurance holding company or mixed financial holding company and the proportional share of the MCRs of the related (re)insurance undertakings. The calculation of the proportional share of the MCR of the related undertakings is based on the proportional share that is included in the consolidated data.

---

102 Unless the undertaking is situated in a third country whose solvency regime has been recognised as equivalent, in which case the SCR of that undertaking is included as calculated in accordance with the third country's requirements. See further, Chapter 10, section 2.1.1.

Regardless of any equivalence decision, the solo MCR with respect to third-country (re)insurance undertakings is the local capital requirement below which authorisation would be withdrawn by the third-country local supervisory authority.[103] Ancillary services undertakings and SPVs are not included in the sum of the MCR since no notional SCR is required for them.

The group MCR must be covered by eligible basic own funds as determined in Art. 98 (4) FD. When the group MCR is no longer complied with, or when there is a risk of non-compliance in the following three months, the supervisory measures referred to in Art. 139 (1) and (2) FD for non-compliance with the individual MCR apply at group level.[104]

The consolidated group own funds are calculated using consolidated data, including the proportional share of own funds in related undertakings in other financial sectors. Consolidated group own funds are calculated net of any intra-group transactions and are subject to the same tiering limits that apply at solo level, to determine the amount of group own funds eligible to cover the group SCR.

For the calculation of the amount of eligible group own funds to cover the group SCR, the group needs to assess the amount of eligible own funds from each related undertaking that is also available at the group level, i.e. the group needs to determine if there are restrictions on the transferability or fungibility of each related undertaking's eligible own funds to the group. Where there are restrictions on the transferability or fungibility of own-fund items, these items are regarded as non-available eligible own-fund items. Where there are no restrictions on transferability or fungibility of own funds to the group, the own funds are considered available and eligible at group level. The restrictions should result from legal or regulatory requirements not from accounting rules.

Fungibility at group level means that an element of own funds can fully absorb any kind of losses within the group, regardless of the undertaking within which those own funds are held or where the commitments arise. Fungibility of own funds at solo level does not automatically imply fungibility at group level.[105]

Transferability refers to the ability to transfer own funds from one undertaking to another within the group. Transferability should not be instantaneous but within a maximum of nine months. Transferability leads to increase/decrease of own funds in a solo entity without increasing/decreasing the group own funds,

103 EIOPA, Guidelines on Group Solvency, EIOPA-BoS-14/181, 2 February 2015, Guideline 21, para. 1.56.

104 EIOPA, Guidelines on Group Solvency, EIOPA-BoS-14/181, 2 February 2015, Guideline 22, para. 1.57.

105 CEIOPS, CEIOPS' Advice for Level 2 Implementing Measures on Solvency II: Assessment of Group Solvency, CEIOPS-DOC-52/09, October 2009, p. 30.

except the likely cost of the transfer.[106] Own funds may be transferable but not fungible and vice versa.[107]

To determine the amount of each related undertaking's eligible own funds that is available at the group level, the amount of eligible own funds for each related undertaking that is not transferable or not fungible to the group is deducted, for the purposes of the calculation, from the related undertaking's eligible own funds. The part of the own funds of related undertakings that is not available to cover the group SCR is deducted from the relevant own-fund items and the relevant tiers of the consolidated group own funds.[108]

Non-available eligible own-fund items are assumed to be but are not limited to the following (Art. 330 DA):

(a) the value of any asset of the participating undertaking or related undertaking representing the financing of own funds eligible for the SCR of any of its related undertakings;
(b) any subscribed but not paid up capital which represents a potential obligation on the part of the participating undertaking, or on the part of any one of the related undertakings;
(c) ancillary own funds;
(d) preference shares;
(e) subordinated liabilities;
(f) net deferred tax assets; and
(g) minority interests.

The non-available eligible own-fund items of the related undertaking which are subsidiary undertakings can be used to cover the group SCR, but only up to the contribution of that related undertaking's SCR to the group SCR. If the amount of non-available eligible own-fund items exceeds the contribution of the solo undertaking to the group SCR, the excess is not available to the group and has to be deducted from the group eligible own funds (Art. 330 (5) DA).

Where the non-available eligible own-fund items of the related undertaking are lower than the contribution of the related undertaking's SCR to the group SCR, then the above limitation does not apply.

The assessment of the availability of own funds in respect of ancillary services undertakings, SPVs and related undertakings that are not subsidiaries

106 For the difficulties in applying this concept, see EIOPA, Report to the EC on Group Supervision and Capital Management with a Group of Insurance or Reinsurance Undertakings and FoS and FoE under Solvency II, EIOPA-BoS-18-485, 14 December 2018, pp. 60–71.

107 CEIOPS, CEIOPS' Advice for Level 2 Implementing Measures on Solvency II: Assessment of Group Solvency, CEIOPS-DOC-52/09, October 2009, pp. 30–31.

108 EIOPA, Guidelines on Group Solvency, EIOPA-BoS-14/181, 2 February 2015, Guideline 16, para. 1.46.

has to be explained to the group supervisor and to the NSA by the participating (re)insurance undertaking or insurance holding company.[109]

When applying the default method or when using a combination of the two methods, the parent undertaking or insurance holding company must consider the amount of minority interest in the eligible own funds as non-available eligible own funds for covering the group SCR.

7.2.2. Method 2 (Alternative Method): Deduction and Aggregation Method

Under this method, rather than applying the standard formula to the consolidated accounts, group solvency is assessed through the sum of the solo SCR and own funds of the participating undertaking and the proportional share of the participating undertaking in the own funds of its related undertakings.

The group SCR under method 2 is the difference between:

- the aggregated group eligible own funds, i.e. the sum of the own funds eligible for the SCR of the participating (re)insurance undertaking and the proportional share of the participating (re)insurance undertaking in the own funds eligible to cover the SCR of the related (re)insurance undertakings, and
- the aggregated SCRs of the group, i.e. the sum of the SCR of the participating (re)insurance undertaking and the proportional share of the SCRs of the related (re)insurance undertakings (Art. 233 (1), (2) and (3) FD).

The aggregated group eligible own funds consist of the sum of the own funds eligible for the SCR of the participating (re)insurance undertaking, the notional own funds of the insurance holding company or mixed financial holding company, the proportional share of own funds of the related undertakings, the proportional share of own funds of related third-country undertakings and the proportional share of own funds of credit institutions, investment firms, financial institutions and IORPs calculated according to the relevant sectorial rules. Own funds are calculated net of intra-group transactions and net of adjustments related to non-available own funds.

The contribution of a subsidiary undertaking to the group SCR when using the deduction and aggregation method is the solo SCR, since diversification effects at group level cannot be recognised.

The aggregated solvency capital requirements of the group consist of the sum of the solo SCRs of the participating (re)insurance undertakings, the notional SCR of the insurance holding company or the mixed financial

[109] EIOPA, Guidelines on Group Solvency, EIOPA-BoS-14/181, 2 February 2015, Guideline 13, para. 1.36.

holding company, the proportional share of the SCR of each related undertaking and the proportional share of the notional SCR of intermediate insurance holding companies, the proportional share of the SCR of related third-country undertakings and intermediate insurance holding companies, and the proportional share of the capital requirements for credit institutions, investment firms, financial institutions and IORPs calculated according to the relevant sectorial rules.

There is no MCR calculation required under the deduction and aggregation method.

7.3. GROUP INTERNAL MODEL

When a group applies for permission to calculate the consolidated group SCR (using the default method), as well as the SCRs of (re)insurance undertakings within the group, on the basis of an internal model, the procedure set out in Art. 231 FD and Arts. 347–350 DA applies.[110] The supervisory authorities concerned must cooperate to decide whether or not to grant that permission and to determine the terms and conditions to which that permission is subject.

Where a group applies for the use of the same internal model to calculate the consolidated group SCR as well as the SCR of one or more related (re)insurance undertakings in the group, the same procedure set out in Art. 231 FD applies. The approval of an internal model used *only* for the calculation of the consolidated group SCR granted on the basis of Art. 230 FD has no influence on decisions taken under Art. 231 FD. Any application for permission to calculate the consolidated group SCR *together* with the SCR of one or more related (re)insurance undertakings in the group on the basis of an internal model already approved under Art. 230 FD must follow the procedure laid down in Art. 231 FD (recital 133 DA).

The procedure for the approval of a group internal model is the same as the procedure set out in Art. 20 CRR for joint decisions on prudential requirements (including the use of an internal model) in the banking sector. This is intentional in order to establish a level playing field. The group supervisor (insurance) or consolidating supervisor (banking) has a very important role to play in this exercise.

---

110 See also above, Chapter 6, section 4.2.3. See BEHRENDT, B. and GRÖNHOFF, E., Interne Modelle nach Solvency II für einen Holding geführten Versicherungskonzern und die hierfür geltenden Rahmenbedingungen, in BENNEMANN, C., OEHLENBERG, L. and STAHL, G., *Handbuch Solvency II*, Schäffer-Poeschel Verlag, Stuttgart, 2011; WAGNER, C., Das interne Risikokapitalmodell der Allianz-Gruppe, in GRÜNDL, H. and PERLET, H. (Eds.), *Solvency II & Risikomanagement*, Gabler Verlag, Wiesbaden, 2005.

The application must be submitted to the group supervisor, who will inform the college of supervisors of the receipt of the application without delay and forward the application to the other supervisory authorities concerned[111] and other supervisory authorities involved in the assessment of the application. The supervisory authorities concerned must do everything in their power to reach a joint decision on the application within six months of the date of receipt of the complete application. This is quite a challenge, as many supervisory authorities may be involved. The group supervisor must determine whether the application is complete within 45 days of the day of receipt of the application (Art. 348 (1) DA). An application is complete if it includes all the documentation that is required by Art. 347 DA. The process for arriving at the joint decision is described in a Commission Implementing Regulation.[112]

The six-month period within which a joint decision must be reached may be extended if the group supervisor or any of the other supervisory authorities concerned decide to consult EIOPA.[113] EIOPA must make a decision within one month, in accordance with Art. 19 EIOPA Regulation. That decision is final and must be respected by all supervisory authorities concerned.[114]

In the absence of the adoption of a joint decision within six months of the date of receipt of the group's complete application (and when none of the supervisory authorities concerned has referred the matter to EIOPA), the group supervisor will make its own decision on the application. The group supervisor also takes the final decision, when EIOPA fails to take a decision. The group supervisor must duly take into account any views and reservations of the other supervisory authorities concerned expressed during that six-month period. The group supervisor must provide the applicant and the other supervisory authorities

---

111 The group supervisor and the supervisory authorities of all the Member States in which the head offices of each related (re)insurance undertaking applying for the use of the group internal model to calculate their SCR are situated (Art. 347 (3) DA). In its 2017 report to the EC on group supervision, EIOPA complains that it is not considered a "supervisory authority concerned" and does therefore not receive the application materials for group internal models. See EIOPA, Report to the EC on the application of group supervision under the Solvency II Directive, EIOPA-17-648, 21 December 2017, p. 10. Following the ESFS review, EIOPA must also be informed of the application and receive the documentation submitted by the undertaking. Upon request from an NSA, EIOPA may provide technical assistance.

112 Commission Implementing Regulation (EU) 2015/461 of 19 March 2015 laying down implementing technical standards with regard to the process to reach a joint decision on the application to use a group internal model in accordance with Directive 2009/138/EC of the EP and of the Council, *OJ* L 76, 20.3.2015, p. 19.

113 EIOPA has not yet been called upon to play its role as a mediator in this case.

114 Where an insurance group with a UK parent undertaking applies an internal model, it will no longer be able use this model after the UK has left the internal market to calculate the SCRs of the (re)insurance undertakings in the group that are located in EEA30 Member States without re-approval by the relevant NSAs. In the absence of any other approved internal model, the SCR for these undertakings will have to be calculated on the basis of the standard formula. See EIOPA, Opinion on the solvency position of insurance and reinsurance undertakings in light of the withdrawal of the UK from the EU, EIOPA-BoS-18/201, 18 May 2018, p. 7.

concerned with a document setting out its fully reasoned decision. That decision is final and must be applied by all supervisory authorities concerned.

The group supervisor and the other supervisory authorities involved must assess the appropriateness of the scope of the internal model upon receiving the relevant application from the group. In that context, they must consider at least:[115]

- the significance of related undertakings within the group with respect to the risk profile of the group;
- the risk profile of related undertakings within the group compared to the overall group risk profile;
- if applicable, a transitional plan by the group to extend the scope of the model at a later stage and the timeframe for doing so;
- the appropriateness of the standard formula or another internal model approved or in the process of approval for the calculation of the SCR of any related undertaking included in the scope of the internal model;
- the appropriateness of the standard formula or another internal model approved or in the process of approval for the calculation of the SCR of any related undertaking within the group but not included in the scope of the internal model for the group.

When assessing the appropriateness of the exclusion of related undertakings within the group from the scope of the internal model, the group supervisor and the other supervisory authorities concerned must assess whether the exclusion of the undertakings could lead to:

- an improper allocation of own funds based on individual undertaking SCRs rather than on its contribution to the risk profile of the group;
- inconsistencies that would derive from the use of the internal model to calculate the group SCR and the use of the standard formula or a different internal model, approved or in the process of approval, of any related undertaking within the group to calculate its SCR;
- weaknesses in risk management of the group and related undertakings within the group resulting from the limited scope of the internal model;
- an inadequate group SCR in relation to the risk profile of the group.

The internal model, which may be full or partial, must satisfy all the conditions required for the approval of an internal model at solo level, such as the use test,[116]

---

115 EIOPA, Guidelines on the use of internal models, EIOPA-BoS-14/180, 2 February 2015, Guideline 58.

116 See also Art. 350 DA, which lists the undertakings that must comply with the use test.

statistical quality standards, calibration standards, profit and loss attribution, validation standards and documentation standards. See above, Chapter 6, section 4.2.3.

If any of the supervisory authorities concerned considers that the risk profile of a (re)insurance undertaking under its supervision deviates significantly from the assumptions underlying the internal model approved at group level, and where the undertaking has not properly addressed the concerns of the supervisory authority, that authority may set a capital add-on to the SCR of that (re)insurance undertaking resulting from the application of the internal model. In exceptional cases where the capital add-on would not be appropriate, the supervisory authority may require the undertaking concerned to calculate its SCR using the standard formula and may impose a further capital add-on. These decisions need to be explained to the (re)insurance undertaking and to all supervisory authorities concerned (Art. 231 (7) FD).

In order to ensure that group internal models could be used from day one (1 January 2016), a pre-application process was organised and Art. 308a (g) required Member States to ensure that their supervisory authorities had the power to decide to approve a group internal model from 1 April 2015. EIOPA has invested a considerable amount of work in promoting supervisory convergence in this area.[117]

In the EEA insurance market, 363 groups apply Solvency II. Of these groups, 322 use the standard formula, 33 groups use a partial internal model and eight groups use a full internal model to calculate the group SCR.[118]

7.4. GROUP CAPITAL ADD-ON

The process for setting a capital add-on for solo undertakings and for groups[119] is identical.[120] Following the SRP, supervisory authorities may in exceptional circumstances decide to set a capital add-on, stating the reasons for doing so (Art. 232 FD).

In determining whether the consolidated group SCR appropriately reflects the risk profile of the group, the group supervisor must pay particular attention to any significant deviation from the assumptions underlying the consolidated

---

117 See above, Chapter 6, section 4.2.3 and EIOPA, Report to the EC on the application of group supervision under the Solvency II Directive, EIOPA 17-648, 22 December 2017, pp. 13–14.

118 EIOPA, Report on long-term guarantee measures and measures on equity risk 2018, EIOPA-BoS-18/471, 18 December 2018, p. 12. Most models use the consolidation method.

119 As indicated in Chapter 7, section 2.4.4. above, only two NSAs (the Netherlands and the UK) have so far applied group capital add-ons.

120 See above, Chapter 7, section 2.4. The same procedure applies mutatis mutandis.

group SCR as calculated using the standard formula or using an internal model, or any significant deviation from the governance standards set out in the FD.[121]

Particular attention should be paid to:
- a specific risk existing at group level that would not be sufficiently covered by the standard formula or the internal model used, because the risk is difficult to quantify;
- a capital add-on that might have been imposed by a supervisory authority on the SCR of a related (re)insurance undertaking.

Where the risk profile of the group is not adequately reflected in the consolidated group SCR, a capital add-on may be imposed on the consolidated group SCR (Art. 232, second subparagraph FD).

In its second report, published on 21 December 2018,[122] which relates to the situation as at year-end 2017, EIOPA indicated that two NSAs (as opposed to one in 2016) have imposed a total of six capital add-ons (as opposed to four in 2016) at group level (four in the UK and two in the Netherlands). Four capital add-ons were imposed because the risk profile of the group deviated significantly from the assumptions underlying the SCR calculated under the standard formula, and two capital add-ons related to cases where the risk profile deviated significantly from the assumptions underlying the SCR calculated under a full or partial internal model.

8. GROUPS WITH CENTRALISED RISK MANAGEMENT

8.1. CONDITIONS

As indicated above, this special regime for groups with centralised risk management is all that remains of the group support regime that was in the end not retained in the FD. As under the group support regime, more powers are given to the parent undertaking and to the group supervisor in the calculation of the SCR of the subsidiary undertakings included in the regime.

It is unclear what the real advantage of this regime is, as it does not go as far as the group support regime.[123] It establishes a closer relationship between the

---

121 A capital add-on may also be imposed in the case of a significant deviation from the assumptions underlying the MA, the VA or the transitional measures on technical provisions or on the risk-free interest rate.

122 EIOPA, *Report on the use of capital add-ons during 2017*, Publications Office of the EU, Luxembourg, 2018, 15 p. The first report was published on 21 December 2017. See EIOPA, Report on the use of capital add-ons during 2016, EIOPA-BoS/17-336, 21 December 2017, 10 p.

123 EIOPA is not aware of any case of application of the centralised risk management regime. See EIOPA, Report to the EC on the application of group supervision under the Solvency II

parent undertaking and the subsidiaries that are included in the regime. Possible positive effects might include a better standing in the market because of a well-documented centralised risk management system, a more detailed decision-making process between supervisors and a better understanding of the group's processes on the part of the supervisory authorities concerned, which might be helpful when the group applies for the approval of an internal model.[124]

Centralisation of risk management can be achieved in different ways. One example is the conclusion of a domination agreement (establishing the right for the parent undertaking to exercise a dominant influence over a subsidiary undertaking) between the parent undertaking and one or more subsidiary undertakings, in which a subsidiary accepts that material tasks are carried out by its parent undertaking. These material tasks may also include tasks regarding risk management.[125] A parent undertaking and a subsidiary undertaking may, however, centralise their risk management in other ways.

The following conditions must be satisfied for the application of the special regime for groups with centralised risk management:

(a) The subsidiaries concerned are included in the group supervision carried out by the group supervisor at the level of the parent undertaking. The regime only applies to subsidiaries as defined in Art. 13 (16) FD and not excluded from group supervision on the basis of Art. 214 (2) FD.
(b) The risk management processes and internal control mechanisms of the parent undertaking cover the subsidiary and the supervisory authorities concerned are satisfied with the prudent management of the subsidiary by the parent undertaking. The fact that the parent undertaking covers the risk management and internal control of the subsidiary does not mean that any responsibility is removed from the subsidiary. It means that material tasks in relation to risk management and internal control are transferred substantially from the subsidiary to the parent. The subsidiary remains responsible for the appropriateness of its governance system including risk management and internal control at solo level.[126]

Directive, EIOPA 17-648, 22 December 2017, p. 9. See also EIOPA, Report to the EC on Group Supervision and Capital Management with a Group of Insurance or Reinsurance Undertakings and FoS and FoE under Solvency II, EIOPA-BoS-18-485, 14 December 2018, pp. 31–33.

124 CEIOPS, Advice for Level 2 Implementing Measures on Solvency II: Supervision of Group Solvency for Groups with Centralised Risk Management, CEIOPS-DOC-62/09, 29 January 2010, p. 19.

125 Such agreements are only allowed in certain jurisdictions. See, for instance, the "*Beherrschungsvertrag*" in the German law on groups of companies (*Konzernrecht*).

126 This is in fact an outsourcing of risk management and compliance, to which all conditions regarding outsourcing apply. See CEIOPS, Advice for Level 2 Implementing Measures on Solvency II: Supervision of Group Solvency for Groups with Centralised Risk Management, CEIOPS-DOC-62/09, 29 January 2010, pp. 24–25.

The establishment of centralised risk management goes beyond the requirement in Art. 246 (1) FD for all groups to establish an effective risk management at group level and to implement risk management and internal control mechanisms consistently in all undertakings included in the scope of group supervision.

In assessing whether the risk management processes and internal control mechanisms of the parent undertaking cover the subsidiary, the group supervisor and the other supervisory authorities concerned must consider whether:

(i) the risk management function in respect of the subsidiary is carried out to a significant extent by the parent undertaking, in such a way that the parent undertaking carries out most of the tasks of the risk management function listed in Art. 269 DA;

(ii) the compliance function is carried out, in respect of the subsidiary, to a significant extent by the parent undertaking, in such a way that the parent undertaking carries out most of the tasks of the compliance function listed in Art. 270 DA;

(iii) the requirements on outsourcing set out in Art. 49 FD are complied with by the subsidiary in relation to the risk management and compliance activities carried out by the parent undertaking.

In assessing whether the subsidiary is managed prudently, the group supervisor and the other supervisory authorities concerned must consider whether the systems of governance of the group and of the subsidiary concerned are sufficiently effective and do not deviate significantly from the legal requirements concerning governance and whether the system of governance of the subsidiary is not impaired by the risk management and compliance functions of the parent undertaking covering the subsidiary.

(c) The group supervisor has agreed on the preparation of a single document covering the ORSA on solo and group level (Art. 246 (4) FD).

(d) The group supervisor has agreed on the preparation of a single SFCR for the whole group (Art. 256 (2) FD).

(e) The permission to be subject to the special regime for groups with centralised risk management has been granted using the process laid out in Art. 237 FD.

8.2. APPLICATION PROCESS

The procedure for the application process is similar to the procedure for the approval of a group internal model in Art. 231 FD, but obviously shorter in time.

The parent undertaking submits an application for each of the subsidiaries that it wants to include in the regime. The application must include all relevant information and is submitted only to the supervisor that has authorised the subsidiary concerned, who must inform the other members of the college of supervisors and forward the complete application to them, without delay. Where several applications for different subsidiaries are submitted by the parent undertaking, the applications are considered jointly by the group supervisor and the other supervisory authorities concerned.[127]

Upon receipt of all applications plus all relevant information, the group supervisor discusses the applications within the college of supervisors and tries to reach a joint decision on the application within three months of the date of receipt of the complete application by all supervisory authorities within the college.

Where the supervisory authorities concerned have reached a joint decision, the supervisory authority that has authorised the subsidiary provides the applicant with a fully reasoned decision The joint decision is final and must be applied by all supervisory authorities concerned.

The decision is deferred when any of the supervisory authorities concerned has referred the matter to EIOPA within the three-month period. EIOPA must take its decision within one month in accordance with the procedure foreseen in Art. 19 EIOPA Regulation. That decision is final and must be applied by all supervisory authorities concerned.

In the absence of the adoption of a joint decision within the three-month period (and when none of the supervisory authorities concerned has referred the matter to EIOPA), the group supervisor makes its own decision on the application. The group supervisor also takes the final decision, where EIOPA fails to take a decision.

In preparing its decision, the group supervisor must duly consider any views and reservations of the supervisory authorities concerned, as well as any reservations of the other supervisory authorities within the college. In its decision, the group supervisor must state the full reasons for its decision and explain any significant deviation from the reservations of the other supervisory authorities concerned. The group supervisor must provide the parent undertaking and the other supervisory authorities concerned with a copy of the decision. The decision is final and must be applied by all supervisory authorities concerned.

8.3. CALCULATION OF THE SCR OF THE SUBSIDIARY

Within the logic of the centralised risk management regime, the SCR of the subsidiary should be calculated on the basis of an approved group internal model.

---

127 "The other supervisory authorities concerned" are defined as "the supervisory authorities of the Member States in which the head office of the subsidiaries for which permission to be subject to Arts. 238 and 239 FD has been submitted are situated" (Art. 352 (1) DA).

Where this is the case, and where the supervisory authority that has authorised the subsidiary considers that the risk profile of the subsidiary deviates significantly from that which results from the group internal model, and the subsidiary does not properly address its concerns, the supervisory authority may[128] propose imposing a capital add-on to the subsidiary's SCR resulting from the application of the group internal model or, in exceptional circumstances where such capital add-on would not be appropriate, propose requiring the subsidiary to calculate its SCR on the basis of the standard formula. The supervisory authority must discuss its proposal within the college of supervisors and communicate the grounds for the proposal to both the subsidiary and the college of supervisors.

The SCR of the subsidiary concerned may also be calculated on the basis of the standard formula. Where this is the case, and where the supervisory authority that has authorised the subsidiary considers that the risk profile of the subsidiary deviates significantly from the assumptions underlying the standard formula, and the subsidiary does not properly address its concerns, the supervisory authority may, in exceptional circumstances, propose that the subsidiary replace a subset of the parameters used in the standard formula calculation with parameters specific to the subsidiary when calculating the life, non-life and health underwriting risk modules,[129] or propose setting a capital add-on[130] to the SCR of the subsidiary. The supervisory authority must discuss its proposal within the college of supervisors and communicate the grounds for the proposal to both the subsidiary and the college of supervisors.

The college of supervisors must do everything within its power to reach an agreement on the proposal of the supervisory authority that has authorised the subsidiary or on other possible measures.

Where the supervisory authority and the group supervisor disagree, either supervisor may, within one month of the proposal of the supervisory authority, refer the matter to EIOPA and request its assistance in accordance with Art. 19 EIOPA Regulation. EIOPA must take its decision within one month of the referral. The supervisory authority that has authorised the subsidiary must defer its decision and await EIOPA's decision. That decision is final and must be applied by all supervisory authorities concerned. It must state the full reasons on which it is based and be submitted to the subsidiary and to the college of supervisors.

In the event of non-compliance with the SCR,[131] the supervisory authority that has authorised the subsidiary must, without delay, forward to the college

128 This would only apply in exceptional cases under the conditions referred to in Art. 37 FD. See above, Chapter 7, section 2.4.

129 As set out in Art. 110 FD.

130 This would only apply in exceptional cases under the conditions referred to in Art. 37 FD. See above, Chapter 7, section 2.4.

131 See also Art. 138 FD. See above, Chapter 6, section 4.2.1.3.

of supervisors a recovery plan submitted by the subsidiary in order to achieve, within six months of the observation of non-compliance with the SCR, the reestablishment of the level of eligible own funds or the reduction of its risk profile to ensure compliance with the SCR (Art. 239 (1) FD).

The college of supervisors must do everything within its power to reach an agreement on the proposal of the supervisory authority regarding the approval of the recovery plan within four months of the date on which non-compliance with the SCR was first observed.

In the absence of an agreement, the supervisory authority that has authorised the subsidiary must decide whether the recovery plan should be approved, taking due account of the views and reservations of the other supervisory authorities within the college of supervisors.

Where the supervisory authority that has authorised the subsidiary identifies, in accordance with Art. 136 FD, deteriorating financial conditions, it must notify the college of supervisors without delay of the proposed measures to be taken. Save in emergency situations, the measures to be taken must be discussed within the college of supervisors. In assessing whether a situation should be considered an emergency situation, the supervisory authority that has authorised the subsidiary must consider whether the time required to cooperate, exchange information and consult within the college would jeopardise the effectiveness of the measures to be taken and whether a delay in the application of the proposed measures is likely to cause the financial conditions of the subsidiary to further deteriorate in such a way that there is a risk that the subsidiary will not comply with its MCR in the following three months (Art. 353 DA).

The college of supervisors must do everything within its power to reach an agreement on the proposed measures to be taken within one month of the notification. In the absence of such agreement, the supervisory authority that has authorised the subsidiary must decide whether the proposed measures should be approved, taking due account of the views and reservations of the other supervisory authorities within the college of supervisors (Art. 239 (2) FD).

In the event of non-compliance with the MCR,[132] the supervisory authority that has authorised the subsidiary must, without delay, forward to the college of supervisors the short-term finance scheme submitted by the subsidiary in order to achieve, within three months of the date on which non-compliance with the MCR was first observed, the re-establishment of the level of eligible own funds covering the MCR or the reduction of its risk profile to ensure compliance with the MCR. The college of supervisors must also be informed of any measures taken to enforce the MCR at the level of the subsidiary (Art. 239 (3) FD).

---

132 See also Art. 139 FD. See above, Chapter 6, section 4.3.4.

The supervisory authority that has authorised the subsidiary or the group supervisor may refer the matter to EIOPA and request its assistance in accordance with Art. 19 EIOPA Regulation, where there is disagreement on the approval of the recovery plan, including any extension of the recovery period or on the approval of the proposed measures in the case of deteriorating financial conditions. The supervisory authority must in that case defer its decision and await a decision by EIOPA. That decision is final and must be applied by all supervisory authorities concerned. It must state the full reasons on which it is based and be submitted to the subsidiary and to the college of supervisors (Art. 239 (4) FD).

8.4. END OF THE DEROGATION FOR THE SUBSIDIARY

The rules provided for in Arts. 238 and 239 FD cease to apply where the conditions stated in Art. 236 FD are no longer complied with (Art. 240 FD).

Where the group supervisor decides, after consulting the college of supervisors, to no longer include the subsidiary in the group supervision it carries out at the level of the parent undertaking, it must immediately inform the supervisory authority concerned and the parent undertaking.

With respect to the other conditions in Art. 236 FD, the parent undertaking is responsible for ensuring that the conditions are complied with on an ongoing basis. In the event of non-compliance, it must inform the group supervisor and the supervisor of the subsidiary concerned without delay. The parent undertaking must present a plan to restore compliance within an appropriate period of time.

The group supervisor must verify at least annually, on its own initiative, that the other conditions referred to in Art. 236 FD continue to be complied with. The group supervisor must also perform such verification upon request of the supervisory authority that has authorised the subsidiary, where the latter has significant concerns related to the ongoing compliance with those conditions. Where the verification performed identifies weaknesses, the group supervisor must require the parent undertaking to present a plan to restore compliance within an appropriate period of time.

Where, after consulting the college of supervisors, the group supervisor determines that the plan to restore compliance is insufficient or subsequently that it is not being implemented within the agreed period of time, the group supervisor must conclude that the conditions referred to in Art. 236 (b), (c) and (d) FD are no longer complied with and it must immediately inform the supervisory authority that has authorised the subsidiary.

The regime provided for in Arts. 238 and 239 FD is applicable again where the parent undertaking submits a new application and obtains a favourable decision in accordance with the procedure set out in Art. 237 FD.

9. RISK CONCENTRATION AND INTRA-GROUP TRANSACTIONS

9.1. RELEVANCE AND KEY CONCEPTS

Risk concentrations and intra-group transactions can affect the financial position of (re)insurance undertakings. Supervisory authorities must therefore be able to exercise supervision over such risk concentrations and intra-group transactions, taking into account the nature of the relationships between regulated entities as well as non-regulated entities, including insurance holding companies and mixed-activity insurance holding companies. They must be able to take appropriate measures where the solvency of a (re)insurance undertaking is being or may be jeopardised (recital 109 FD). The importance of risk concentration and intra-group transactions was highlighted during the financial crisis.

Risk concentration is not defined in the FD. It is defined in Art. 2 (19) FICOD as exposures with a loss potential borne by entities within a financial conglomerate that are large enough to threaten the solvency or the financial position in general of the regulated entities in the financial conglomerate. Such exposures may be caused by counterparty risk (credit risk), investment risk, insurance risk, market risk, other risks, or a combination or interaction of these risks. Risk concentration is a broad term that covers single risk exposures and combinations of risk exposures that may arise in a group. Concentrated exposures may arise with reference to specific counterparties or specific industry sectors or countries.

Concentration risk is defined in Art. 13 (35) FD as all risk exposures with a loss potential that is large enough to threaten the solvency or the financial position of a (re)insurance undertaking.

Intra-group transactions are defined in Art. 13 (19) FD as any transaction by which a (re)insurance undertaking relies, either directly or indirectly, on other undertakings within the same group or on any natural or legal person that has close links to undertakings within that group for the fulfilment of an obligation, whether or not contractual, and whether or not for payment. Although the definition does not explicitly refer to transactions with an insurance holding company, a mixed financial holding company or a mixed-activity insurance holding company or between these holding companies, there can be no question that all transactions between group entities are covered. This also includes transactions with natural or legal persons that have close links with group undertakings in any capacity, i.e. as private persons or as board members. The definition does not go so far as to also cover related parties that are not part of the group or have no direct links with group entities, such as family members of the person that has close links with group undertakings.[133]

9.2. SUPERVISION OF RISK CONCENTRATION

Supervision of the risk concentration at group level is exercised by the group supervisor. (Re)insurance undertakings, insurance holding companies or mixed financial holding companies must report on a regular basis and at least annually to the group supervisor any significant risk concentration at the level of the group. The group supervisor may decide not to carry out the supervision of significant risk concentrations where the (re)insurance undertaking, insurance holding company or mixed financial holding company has its head office in the EEA and is itself a subsidiary undertaking of an undertaking that is subject to supplementary supervision in accordance with Art. 5 (2) FICOD, in which case supervision of significant risk concentrations would already take place by virtue of the FICOD. Duplication of tasks should in that case be avoided (Art. 244 FD).

In identifying significant risk concentrations, participating (re)insurance undertakings, insurance holding companies or mixed financial holding companies must consider, at least, direct or indirect exposures of undertakings in the group to individual counterparties, groups of individual but interconnected counterparties (for example, undertakings within the same corporate group), specific geographical areas or industry sectors, and natural disasters or catastrophes (Art. 376 (2) DA).

The necessary information must be submitted to the group supervisor by the (re)insurance undertaking which is at the head of the group or, where the group is not headed by a (re)insurance undertaking, by the insurance holding company, the mixed financial holding company or the (re)insurance undertaking in the group identified by the group supervisor after consulting the other supervisory authorities concerned and the group.[134]

The group supervisor, after consulting the other supervisory authorities concerned and the group, must identify the type of risks (re)insurance undertakings in a particular group must report in all circumstances. When defining or giving their opinion about the type of risks, the group supervisor and

---

133 See, for a discussion of the definition, EIOPA, Report to the EC on Group Supervision and Capital Management with a Group of Insurance or Reinsurance Undertakings, and FoS and FoE under Solvency II, EIOPA-BoS-18-485, 14 December 2018, pp. 44–45.

134 For the quantitative templates for groups on significant risk concentrations, see Art. 36 Commission Implementing Regulation (EU) 2015/2450 of 2 December 2015 laying down implementing technical standards with regard to the templates for the submission of information to the supervisory authorities according to Directive 2009/138/EC of the EP and of the Council, *OJ* L 347, 31.12.2015, p. 1.

the other supervisory authorities concerned must take into account the specific group and the risk management structure of the group.

In order to identify significant risk concentration that needs be reported, the group supervisor, after consulting the other supervisory authorities concerned and the group, must impose appropriate thresholds, whereby particular attention should be paid to the solvency and liquidity position of the group, the complexity of the group structure, the importance of regulated entities from other financial sectors or non-regulated entities carrying out financial activities, the diversification of the group's investments portfolio and the diversification of the group's insurance activities in terms of geographical areas and lines of business (Art. 376 (3) DA).

When reviewing the risk concentrations, the group supervisor must in particular monitor the possible risk of contagion in the group, the risk of a conflict of interests, and the level or volume of risks.

9.3. SUPERVISION OF INTRA-GROUP TRANSACTIONS

Intra-group transactions play a key role in group supervision. Intra-group transactions are designed, among other purposes, to reallocate risk within a group. For instance, through an intra-group guarantee, one legal entity of the group may back certain risks of another entity in the group, or through a group internal reinsurance contract, risks from one insurance undertaking may be assumed by another undertaking in the group.[135]

Supervision of intra-group transactions at group level is exercised by the group supervisor. (Re)insurance undertakings, insurance holding companies or mixed financial holding companies must report to the group supervisor on a regular basis, and at least annually, all significant intra-group transactions by (re)insurance undertakings within a group, including those performed with a natural person with close links to an undertaking in the group (Art. 245 FD).

Significant intra-group transactions are intra-group transactions that materially influence the solvency or liquidity position of the group or of one of the undertakings involved in these transactions (Art. 377 (1) DA).

The group supervisor may decide not to carry out the supervision of the intra-group transactions where the (re)insurance undertaking, insurance holding company or mixed financial holding company has its head office in the EEA and is itself a subsidiary undertaking of an undertaking that is subject to

135 MÄCHLER, M., Insurance Group Supervision: Addressing the Emergence of Adverse Network Dynamics, in LIEDTKE, P.M. and MONKIEWICZ, J. (Eds.), *The Future of Insurance Regulation and Supervision: A Global Perspective*, Palgrave Macmillan, Basingstoke, 2011, p. 155.

supplementary supervision in accordance with Art. 5 (2) FICOD, in which case supervision of the intra-group transactions would already take place by virtue of the FICOD. Duplication of tasks should in that case be avoided.

Very significant intra-group transactions must be reported as soon as practicable.[136] The necessary information must be submitted to the group supervisor by the (re)insurance undertaking which is at the head of the group or, where the group is not headed by a (re)insurance undertaking, by the insurance holding company, the mixed financial holding company or the (re)insurance undertaking in the group identified by the group supervisor having consulted the other supervisory authorities concerned and the group.

The group supervisor, after consulting the other supervisory authorities concerned and the group, must identify the type of intra-group transactions that (re)insurance undertakings in a particular group must report in all circumstances. When defining or giving their opinion about the type of transactions, the group supervisor and the other supervisory authorities concerned must take into account the specific group and risk management structure of the group.

In order to identify significant intra-group transactions to be reported, the group supervisor, after consulting the other supervisory authorities concerned and the group, must impose appropriate thresholds, whereby particular attention must be paid to investments, inter-company balances (including loans, receivables and arrangements to centralise the management of assets or cash), guarantees and commitments (such as letters of credit), derivative transactions, dividends, coupons and other interest payments, reinsurance operations, provision of services or agreements to share costs, and purchase, sale or lease of assets (Art. 377 (2) DA).

When reviewing the intra-group transactions, the group supervisor must in particular monitor the possible risk of contagion in the group, the risk of a conflict of interests, and the level or volume of risks.

10. SYSTEM OF GOVERNANCE

10.1. PRINCIPLES

The Pillar 2 provisions on the system of governance that apply at solo level, also apply (mutatis mutandis) at group level (Art. 246 (1) FD).[137] This implies that the ultimate parent undertaking is – without prejudice to its own obligation to

[136] For the quantitative templates for groups on significant and very significant intra-group transactions, see Art. 36 Commission Implementing Regulation (EU) 2015/2450 of 2 December 2015 laying down implementing technical standards with regard to the templates for the submission of information to the supervisory authorities according to Directive 2009/138/EC of the EP and of the Council, *OJ* L 347, 31.12.2015, p. 1.

[137] See above, Chapter 7, section 3.

have in place a robust governance system at solo level – required to establish an effective system of governance at the level of the group, which provides for sound and prudent management of the business of the group. The reference to "mutatis mutandis" is unclear, as groups may have different structures. It is obvious that the system of governance will be different when the ultimate parent is a holding company rather than an operational (re)insurance undertaking. But even where the parent undertaking is a holding company, it must have its own governance system, in addition to the governance system of the group.

Art. 246 (1), second subparagraph FD requires the risk management and internal control systems and reporting procedures to be implemented consistently in all undertakings included in the scope of group supervision so that those systems can be controlled at the level of the group. It is the responsibility of the ultimate parent undertaking to ensure consistent implementation and ongoing monitoring of the risk management systems in all individual undertakings of the group. Appropriate tools and procedures must be put in place to enable the parent to oversee and steer the functioning of risk management systems at solo level.

The group-wide risk management system must be suitable, effective and proportionate to the nature, scale and complexity of the group's business and the risks inherent in the business. Special focus must be given to group-specific risks, as well as to the impact of intra-group transactions and risk concentrations. Decisions taken by the risk management at group level must always consider the impact on the group's risk situation to ensure that the group's solvency and financial situation are not jeopardised.

As the requirements for a system of governance at solo level apply mutatis mutandis at the level of the group, key governance functions must also exist at group level and the persons who effectively run the group or have other key functions in the group must be fit and proper.[138] The FD does not specifically repeat these provisions, but does add some clarifications, particularly in the area of risk management and internal control (Art. 246 FD). Furthermore, the EIOPA Guidelines on the system of governance contain a number of guidelines that deal specifically with group situations (Guidelines 65–70).

10.2. SYSTEM OF GOVERNANCE AT GROUP LEVEL

The entity responsible for meeting the governance requirements at group level is usually the ultimate parent undertaking,[139] but depending on the structure

---

[138] Although the holding company or mixed financial holding company is not individually subject to supervision, the persons who effectively run the undertaking must be fit and proper (Art. 257 FD).

[139] See also CEIOPS, Advice for Level 2 Implementing Measures on Solvency II: Supervision of Group Solvency for Groups with Centralised Risk Management, CEIOPS-DOC-62/09, 29 January 2010, pp. 11–18.

and organisation of the group, this entity may be another undertaking than the parent undertaking (for instance, in a horizontal group or a mutual group). The group supervisor must be notified of the identity of the responsible entity.

The ultimate parent undertaking ((re)insurance undertaking, insurance holding company or mixed financial holding company) must set adequate internal governance requirements across the group which are appropriate to the structure, business model and risks of the group and of its related entities. The parent must also consider the appropriate structure and organisation for risk management at group level, setting out a clear allocation of responsibilities at all entities that are part of the group.[140]

In particular, the parent undertaking must:
- have in place appropriate and effective tools, procedures and lines of responsibility and accountability to enable it to oversee and steer the functioning of the risk management and internal control systems at individual level;
- have in place reporting lines within the group and effective systems for ensuring that information in the group flows from the bottom up and from the top down;
- document and inform all the entities that are part of the group about the tools used to identify, measure, monitor, manage and report all risks to which the group is exposed;
- take into account the interests of all the entities belonging to the group and how these interests contribute to the common purpose of the group as a whole over the long term.[141]

When setting up its own system of governance for the group, the AMSB of the parent undertaking must respect the responsibilities of the AMSB of other undertakings in the group. When an undertaking in the group outsources a key function within the group, the parent undertaking must document which functions relate to which legal entity within the group. The parent undertaking must ensure that the performance of the key functions at the level of solo undertakings is not impaired by such intra-group arrangements. The solo undertaking remains responsible for the outsourced function, has to manage the outsourcing arrangement effectively and must have in place suitable business contingency plans.

140 EIOPA, Guidelines on system of governance, EIOPA-BoS-14/253, 14 September 2015, Guideline 65.

141 EIOPA, Guidelines on system of governance, EIOPA-BoS-14/253, 14 September 2015, Guideline 66.

The ultimate parent undertaking must consider in its risk management system the risks both at individual and group level, as well as their interdependencies. Of particular importance are:

- reputational risk and risks arising from intra-group transactions and risk concentrations, including contagion risk, at the group level;
- interdependencies between risks stemming from conducting business through different entities and in different jurisdictions;
- risks arising from third-country entities;
- risks arising from non-regulated entities;
- risks arising from other regulated entities.[142]

The ultimate parent undertaking must provide for a risk management function at group level. It must have a comprehensive group-wide risk management strategy, which lays out the objectives and key risk management principles of the group's risk management and has to be consistent with the group's overall business strategy. Although each individual group undertaking remains responsible for its risk management strategy at solo level, it is the responsibility of the ultimate parent to ensure the alignment of the individual risk management strategies with the group-wide risk management strategy.

Written policies must exist at group level which ensure that the definition, categorisation and assessment of material risks, as well as the reporting procedures, are harmonised within the group. Appropriate processes and procedures must enable the ultimate parent to identify, measure, manage and monitor the risks the group is or might be exposed to, providing for a sufficient link with corresponding reporting processes and procedures at solo level. In order to ensure consistent implementation of risk management systems, the ultimate parent undertaking must have access to all relevant information. Management of liquidity risk should be supported by clear agreements that govern the use of excess funds, supervision of each undertaking's financial position and regular stress and transferability testing.

An important element of group-wide risk management is adequate emergency planning and business continuity management. This must ensure that essential business processes are not interrupted in a serious manner in the case of internal or external threats and that the economic existence and business continuity of the group is safeguarded.

The group-wide risk management system must be supported by a suitable, comprehensive and consistent internal control system. The internal control

142 EIOPA, Guidelines on system of governance, EIOPA-BoS-14/253, 14 September 2015, Guideline 67.

mechanism must include adequate mechanisms as regards group solvency to identify and measure all material risks incurred and to appropriately relate eligible own funds to risks, as well as sound reporting and accounting procedures to monitor and manage intra-group transactions and risk concentrations (Art. 146 (2) FD).

A group internal audit function must be established at the highest level of the group. The internal audit function must be objective and independent of all operational functions at solo and group level. It must produce a written report on its findings at least annually. The report must cover any deficiencies in the efficiency and suitability of the internal control system, as well as major shortcomings in the compliance with internal policies, procedures and processes. The report must include recommendations on how to remedy the deficiencies identified and also address past points of criticism.

The group must also set up a group compliance function, which should advise the AMSB of the ultimate parent undertaking on compliance with applicable laws and regulations adopted on the basis of the FD and have a close relationship with the compliance function holders in the solo undertakings of the group.

The group actuarial function must look specifically at the group-specific risks as far as they relate to technical provisions and must, where applicable, assist the risk management function in the development of a group internal model.

10.3. GROUP ORSA

As part of its group-wide risk management, the ultimate parent undertaking must carry out an ORSA at the level of the group, which is subject to review by the group supervisor (Art. 246 (4), first subparagraph FD). The group ORSA should reflect the nature of the group's structure and its risk profile. The material risks arising from all undertakings that are part of the group must be included in the group ORSA.[143]

Where the calculation of the solvency at the level of the group is carried out in accordance with the default method (accounting consolidation-based method), the parent undertaking must explain to the group supervisor the difference between the sum of the SCRs of all the related undertakings of the group and the group consolidated SCR (Art. 246 (4) second subparagraph FD), in order to allow the group supervisor to assess the impact of diversification effects within the group.

When using an internal model for calculating the group solvency, the ultimate parent undertaking must indicate in the group ORSA the related undertakings

143 EIOPA, Guidelines on own risk and solvency assessment, EIOPA-BoS-14/259, 14 September 2015, Guideline 15.

included in the scope of group supervision that do not use the internal model for the calculation of their solo SCR and the underlying reasons for not using the internal group model.

The group ORSA should highlight the impact on the group solvency and on related undertakings of all material risks that the group is facing which cannot be identified at individual level. Group-specific risks include, at least, contagion risk, risks arising from intra-group transactions, risk concentrations, interdependencies within the group and their impact on the group's risk profile, currency risk, and risks arising from the complexity of the group structure.

The group ORSA should include the overall solvency needs of the group in quantitative terms, including a qualitative description of the major risks surrounding the group. It should also provide a description of the materiality and contribution of each related undertaking, together with a comparison of the group overall solvency needs and the sum of the solo overall solvency needs. The group ORSA report must contain an assessment of any diversification effects assumed at group level.[144]

The group ORSA is an important document to be discussed in the college of supervisors. On the basis of its experience as an observer in colleges of supervisors, EIOPA has identified a number of issues for further improvement:[145]

- a greater commitment from top management to embed the ORSA results in strategic and operational decision-making processes;
- the need for stronger links with the undertaking's risk appetite and risk tolerance;
- the appropriateness and severity of stress scenarios and sensitivity analysis;
- the need for more sophisticated forward-looking approaches;
- the inclusion of non-EEA entities in the group ORSA and comparability of ORSA-like reports of non-EEA entities;
- the need to improve the assessment of deviations from the standard formula.

The record of the group ORSA should at least include a description of how the following factors were taken into consideration for the assessment of overall solvency needs and of continuous compliance with regulatory capital requirements:

(a) identification of possible sources of capital within the group and possible needs for additional capital;

144 Malta Financial Services Authority (MFSA), *Insurance Groups under Solvency II*, November 2013, p. 20.

145 EIOPA, *Year-end report 2016 on functioning of colleges of supervisors and priorities for 2017*, 1 March 2017, p. 13.

(b) assessment of the availability, transferability or fungibility of capital;[146]
(c) any envisaged transfer of capital within the group that might have a material impact on any entity of the group, and its consequences;
(d) alignment of individual strategies with those established at group level;
(e) specific risks the group could be exposed to.[147]

The parent undertaking may decide, subject to prior approval from the group supervisor, to undertake an ORSA at the level of the group and at the level of any subsidiary in the group at the same time and produce a single document covering all the assessments. Before approving the request, the group supervisor must consult the members of the college of supervisors and duly take into account their views or reservations. The single document must be submitted to all supervisory authorities concerned at the same time (Art. 246 (4), third to fifth subparagraphs FD).

In the case of a single ORSA document, the parent undertaking should provide the group supervisor in particular with a list of the undertakings the individual ORSA of which is covered in the single ORSA document, including the reason for the choice made and a description of how the AMSBs of the subsidiaries have been involved in the assessment process and approval of the outcome.[148]

11. GROUP SUPERVISOR

Although the IGD did not require a lead or consolidating[149] supervisor to perform the supplementary group supervision to be appointed or identified, it could be inferred from Art. 4 (2) IGD that a single supervisor was to be identified with responsibility for carrying out this task. The Helsinki Protocol[150] was introduced

146 This is particularly important where the group includes third-country (re)insurance undertakings.
147 EIOPA, Guidelines on own risk and solvency assessment, EIOPA-BoS-14/259, 14 September 2015, Guidelines 17 and 18.
148 EIOPA, Guidelines on own risk and solvency assessment, EIOPA-BoS-14/259, 14 September 2015, Guideline 19.
149 Consolidating supervisor is the term used in the CRD/CRR. See Art. 4 (1) (41) CRR.
150 Protocol relating to the collaboration of the supervisory authorities of the Member States of the EU with regard to the application of Directive 98/78/EC on the supplementary supervision of insurance undertakings in an insurance group, 11 May 2000, 15 p. The protocol was developed before the creation of CEIOPS. See https://eiopa.europa.eu/Publications/Protocols/CEIOPS-DOC-07-08%20General%20Protocol%20on%20Collaboration%20of%20Insurance%20Supervisory%20Authorities.pdf.

to deepen the cooperation between supervisory authorities, in order to carry out supplementary supervision. In section 2.2, the Helsinki Protocol states:

> "Although the supervisors involved share a mutual duty to co-operate as far as the supplementary supervision is concerned, in practice it will often be useful to strive for one of the supervisors to carry out most or all of the supplementary supervision, and assume the responsibility to do so, whenever the Directive leaves a choice in that respect. This supervisor will be called the lead supervisor for supplementary supervision (further: lead supervisor)."

The lead supervisor under the IGD was seen as a key coordinator.[151] The tasks of the lead supervisor were described in more detail in the Co-Co Guidelines published by CEIOPS in February 2005.[152] These guidelines distinguished between the key coordinator and the lead supervisor, although it was pointed out that if a lead supervisor were appointed, this person should, for the sake of good order, also be chosen to act as the key coordinator. While the key coordinator's role was seen as one of coordination of the activities necessary to carry out the supplementary supervision, the role of the lead supervisor was to play a key role in pulling together relevant information, analysing it and disseminating the conclusions to the other members of the Co-Co.

Solvency II completely changes this approach, because more importance is attached to group supervision, which is no longer supplementary. The appointment of a key coordinator or a lead supervisor can therefore no longer be considered optional or useful; it is now *necessary* to put somebody in charge of group supervision. In the design of group supervision under Solvency II, careful attention had to be paid to the natural reluctance – particularly of host Member States – to accept that one of the supervisory authorities concerned in a group situation would receive decision-making powers. Solvency II introduces the concept of the group supervisor, who chairs the college of supervisors and who is in charge of group supervision. The group supervisor is more than a key coordinator or a lead supervisor. He can be described as the *primus inter pares* i.e. the first among equals. The emphasis is put on the cooperation of the supervisory authorities concerned in a college of supervisors, which must strive at taking joint decisions. Only in exceptional cases can the group supervisor take the final decision, and this only after the mediation role played by EIOPA, at the request of one of the supervisory authorities concerned, has failed. EIOPA has

---

151 See CEIOPS, Statement on the role of the lead supervisor, CEIOPS-DOC-07/06, December 2006, 7 p.

152 CEIOPS, Guidelines for Co-ordination Committees in the context of supplementary supervision as defined by the Insurance Groups Directive (98/78/EC), CEIOPS-DOC-02/05, February 2005, 18 p.

indicated that it has not yet received a request to play a formal mediation role for colleges.[153]

11.1. DESIGNATION OF THE GROUP SUPERVISOR

The principle under Solvency II is that a single supervisor – the group supervisor – is responsible for the coordination and execution of group supervision and that this person is designated from among the supervisory authorities of the Member States concerned (Art. 247 (1) FD).

As indicated above, group structures can be complex. It is therefore not always evident where the top of the group is situated. As group supervision under Solvency II takes place at the level of the ultimate parent, it is logical that the group supervisor is also situated at that level.

Different situations can be distinguished:

1. *National (domestic) group*: where the same supervisory authority is the NSA for all (re)insurance undertakings in a group, the role of group supervisor is exercised by that NSA (Art. 247 (2), first subparagraph FD).
2. *Cross-border group headed by a (re)insurance undertaking*: where the group is headed by a (re)insurance undertaking with its head office in any EEA MS, the role of group supervisor is exercised by the supervisory authority which has authorised that undertaking (Art. 247 (2), second subparagraph, (a) FD).
3. *Cross-border group not headed by a (re)insurance undertaking, with a (re)insurance subsidiary in an EEA MS*: where the parent of a (re)insurance undertaking is an insurance holding company (or a mixed financial holding company) with its head office in any EEA MS, the role of group supervisor is exercised by the supervisory authority which has authorised that (re)insurance undertaking (Art. 247 (2), second subparagraph, (b) (i) FD).
4. *Cross-border group not headed by a (re)insurance undertaking, with (re)insurance subsidiaries in several EEA Member States*: where more than one (re)insurance undertaking with their head offices in the EEA have as their parent the same insurance holding company (or mixed financial holding company) and one of those undertakings has been authorised in the MS in which the insurance holding company (or mixed financial holding company) has its head office, the role of group supervisor is exercised by the supervisory authority of the (re)insurance undertaking authorised in that MS (Art. 247 (2), second subparagraph, (b) (ii) FD).

---

[153] EIOPA, Report to the EC on the application of group supervision under the Solvency II Directive, EIOPA 17-648, 22 December 2017, p. 9.

5. *Cross-border group headed by more than one insurance holding company (or mixed financial holding company) with head offices in different EEA Member States*: where the group is headed by more than one insurance holding company (or mixed financial holding company) with head offices in different EEA Member States and there is a (re)insurance undertaking in each of those Member States, the role of group supervisor is exercised by the supervisory authority of the (re)insurance undertaking with the largest balance sheet total (Art. 247 (2), second subparagraph, (b) (iii) FD).
6. *Cross-border group headed by an insurance holding company (or mixed financial holding company) with (re)insurance subsidiaries in another MS than that where the holding company has its head office*: where more than one (re)insurance undertaking in the EEA have as their parent the same insurance holding company (or mixed financial holding company) and none of those undertakings has been authorised in the MS in which the insurance holding company (or mixed financial holding company) has its head office, the role of group supervisor is exercised by the supervisory authority which has authorised the (re)insurance undertaking with the largest balance sheet total (Art. 247 (2), second subparagraph, (b) (iv) FD).
7. *Cross-border group without parent undertaking or with a structure different from those described above*: where the group does not have a parent undertaking (for instance, a horizontal group or a mutual group), or where the group has a structure that is different from any of the structures described above, the role of group supervisor is exercised by the supervisory authority which authorised the (re)insurance undertaking with the largest balance sheet total (Art. 247 (2), second subparagraph, (b) (v) FD).

The situations described above may not be appropriate in particular cases, taking into account the structure of the group and the relative importance of the (re)insurance undertakings' activities in different countries. In that case, the supervisory authorities concerned may, at the request of any of the other supervisory authorities, take a joint decision to derogate from the criteria set out above and designate a different supervisory authority as group supervisor. For that purpose, any of the supervisory authorities concerned may request that a discussion be opened on whether the criteria referred to above are appropriate. Such a discussion may not take place more often than once a year.

The supervisory authorities concerned must do everything within their power to reach a joint decision on the choice of the group supervisor within three months from the request for discussion. Before taking their decision, the supervisory authorities concerned must give the group an opportunity to state its opinion. The designated group supervisor must submit the joint decision to the group stating the full reasons (Art. 247 (3) FD).

If, within the three-month period, any of the supervisory authorities concerned has referred the matter to EIOPA in accordance with Art. 19 EIOPA

Regulation, the supervisory authorities concerned must defer their joint decision until EIOPA has taken a decision. EIOPA must do so within one month of the referral. Once EIOPA has decided, the supervisory authorities concerned must take their joint decision in conformity with EIOPA's decision. That joint decision is final and must be complied with by all supervisory authorities concerned. The three-month period is considered to be the conciliation period within the meaning of Art. 19 (2) EIOPA Regulation. The designated group supervisor must submit the joint decision to the group and to the college of supervisors, giving the full reasons for that decision (Art. 247 (4) and (5) FD).

In the absence of a joint decision (and when none of the supervisory authorities concerned has referred the matter to EIOPA), the role of group supervisor is exercised by the supervisory authority identified in accordance with the criteria set out above (Art. 247 (6) FD).

As it was unclear when Solvency II was developed whether the criteria set out in the FD for the designation of a group supervisor would allow for the appointment of a group supervisor in most cases, Art. 247 (7) FD instructs EIOPA to inform the EP, the Council and the EC of any major difficulties with the application of these criteria in practice, on at least an annual basis. The EC would then have to provide more guidance in an Implementing Regulation. This has not been the case and the system seems to work well. EIOPA must also report regularly on the process for the nomination of the group supervisor, the number of group supervisors and the geographical spread (Art. 259 (2) FD).[154]

11.2. RIGHTS AND DUTIES OF THE GROUP SUPERVISOR

The group supervisor has the following rights and duties with regard to group supervision (Art. 248 FD):

(a) coordination of the gathering and dissemination of relevant or essential information for going-concern and emergency situations, including the dissemination of information that is of importance for the supervisory task of a supervisory authority;
(b) supervisory review and assessment of the financial situation of the group;
(c) assessment of the compliance of the group with the rules on solvency and of risk concentration and intra-group transactions;

[154] See, for instance, EIOPA, *List of identified insurance groups for which a college of supervisors is in place*, which reflects the situation as per 31 December 2017, dated April 2018 (https://eiopa.europa.eu/Publications/Administrative/List%20of%20groups%202017.pdf). The list includes 87 groups for which a college has been established. Most of the group supervisors come from France (20), Germany (15) and the UK (10). The European supervisory arrangements do not preclude the organisation of additional colleges on a worldwide level.

(d) assessment of the system of governance of the group and of whether the members of the AMSB of the participating undertaking (in the case of an insurance holding company or a mixed financial holding company) meet the fit and proper requirements;
(e) planning and coordination, through regular meetings held at least annually or through other appropriate means, of supervisory activities in going-concern as well as in emergency situations, in cooperation with the supervisory authorities concerned and taking into account the nature, scale and complexity of the risks inherent in the business of all undertakings that are part of the group;
(f) other tasks, measures and decisions assigned to the group supervisor, in particular leading the process for validation of any internal model at group level and leading the process for permitting the application of the regime for groups with centralised risk management.

The coordination arrangements between the group supervisor and the other supervisory authorities for the establishment and functioning of the college of supervisors may entrust additional tasks to the group supervisor.

In practice, the group supervisor takes the lead in the college's activities, chairs the meeting and establishes an appropriate mechanism to facilitate its operational functioning. The group supervisor:

- updates the contact details of members and participants;
- informs the other members and participants that a college meeting will be held;
- prepares the agenda of the college meetings with clearly defined objectives;
- records the minutes of the college meeting;
- formalises and follows up agreed action points;
- develops the college work plan in cooperation with the other members;
- performs the supervisory review and assessment of the financial situation of the group;
- reviews the organisational structure and the coordination arrangements;
- engages in a discussion regarding the need to designate a new group supervisor in the event of a change in the group structure.[155]

Where the group supervisor fails to carry out the tasks attributed to it, any of the supervisory authorities concerned may refer the matter to EIOPA and request its assistance in accordance with Art. 19 EIOPA Regulation. EIOPA cannot itself replace the group supervisor in such case.

---

155 EIOPA, Guidelines on operational functioning of colleges, EIOPA-BoS-14/146, 2 February 2015, Guideline 10.

Close cooperation between the group supervisor and the authorities responsible for the supervision of individual (re)insurance undertakings in the group is particularly necessary in cases where a (re)insurance undertaking encounters financial difficulties (Art. 249 (1), first subparagraph FD). The authorities responsible for the supervision of the individual (re)insurance undertakings[156] and the group supervisor must each of them call immediately for a meeting of all supervisory authorities involved in the supervision of the group (Art. 249 (2) FD):

- where they become aware of a significant breach of the SCR or a breach of the MCR of an individual (re)insurance undertaking;
- where they become aware of a significant breach of the SCR at group level;
- where other exceptional circumstances are occurring or have occurred.

The supervisory authorities concerned and the group supervisor must communicate to one another without delay all relevant information as soon as it becomes available, or exchange information on request (Art. 249 (1), second subparagraph FD). The group supervisor must provide the supervisory authorities concerned and EIOPA with information regarding the group, in particular regarding the legal structure and the governance and organisational structure of the group (Art. 249 (1), third subparagraph FD).[157]

The group supervisor must transmit to EIOPA information on the functioning of the college of supervisors and on any difficulties encountered. That information must help EIOPA to carry out a review on the functioning of the colleges of supervisors at least every three years (Art. 248 (6), first subparagraph FD).[158]

The group supervisor may invite the supervisory authority of the MS in which a parent undertaking has its head office but which does not carry out the group supervision to request from the parent undertaking any information that would be relevant for the exercise of its coordination rights and duties and to transmit that information to the group supervisor (Art. 251 FD).

The group supervisor may limit supervisory reporting at a frequency shorter than one year or grant an exemption at the level of the group from reporting on an item-by-item basis where all (re)insurance undertakings within the group benefit from the exemption from quarterly reporting or from the exemption to report on an item-by-item basis, taking into account the nature, scale and complexity of the risks inherent in the business of the group (Art. 254 (2) FD).[159]

---

156 This does not include EIOPA, although EIOPA is a member of the college. EIOPA does not however carry out direct supervision and might therefore not be aware of the situation of a particular (re)insurance undertaking.

157 Information about the group structure and governance must also be disclosed publicly on an annual basis by the parent undertaking (Art. 256a FD).

158 The last report on the operational functioning of colleges was published by EIOPA in 2017.

159 See above, Chapter 8, section 3.5.

12. COLLEGE OF SUPERVISORS

In order to facilitate the exercise of group supervision, a college of supervisors must be established for each cross-border group.[160] The college is chaired by the group supervisor and must ensure that cooperation, exchange of information and consultation processes among the supervisory authorities that are members of the college of supervisors are effectively applied, with a view to promoting the convergence of their respective decisions and activities (Art. 248 (2) FD). In its Report to the EC on the application of group supervision under the Solvency II Directive, EIOPA states that there are currently 92 colleges in existence, which vary considerably in their size and nature.[161]

12.1. COMPOSITION OF THE COLLEGE

The members of the college are the group supervisor, the supervisory authorities of the EEA Member States in which the head offices of the subsidiary undertakings are situated, and EIOPA (Art. 248 (3), first subparagraph FD).

Supervisory authorities of significant branches may participate in any relevant activity of the college, following a reasoned request by them or on the initiative of the group supervisor. The same applies to the supervisory authorities of related undertakings where the group supervisor considers their participation appropriate to enhance the efficient exchange of information and to facilitate the exercise of group supervision, and after consultation with the other supervisory authorities in the college (Art. 354 (1) and (2) DA). The effective functioning of the college may require that some activities are carried out by a reduced number of supervisory authorities in the college (Art. 248 (3) FD). The group supervisor may also invite the supervisory authority responsible for the supervision of a credit institution or investment firm that is part of the group to participate in the college meeting (Art. 252 FD).

A significant branch of a (re)insurance undertaking is defined in Art. 354 (1) DA as a branch for which at least one of the following conditions is met:

(a) the annual gross written premium of the branch exceeds 5% of the annual gross written premium of the group, measured with reference to the last available consolidated financial statements of the group;

---

160 If the group is made up of a (re)insurance undertaking and one or more branches in other Member States, no college must be set up, as the prudential supervision of the branches is carried out by the NSA of the (re)insurance undertaking.

161 EIOPA, Report to the EC on the application of group supervision under the Solvency II Directive, EIOPA 17-648, 22 December 2017, p. 4. The most recent list of colleges can be found at https://eiopa;europa.eu/Pages/Supervision/Insurance/Collges.aspx. In April 2018, EIOPA reported the existence of 87 groups as at the end of 2017.

(b) the annual gross written premium of the branch exceeds 5% of total annual gross written premiums for the life activity, the non-life activity or both in the MS in which the risk is situated, measured with reference to the last available financial statements.

Guideline 2 of the EIOPA Guidelines on the operational functioning of colleges[162] establishes criteria for the assessment of the significance and materiality of related undertakings and branches. It is the group supervisor who maps all the related undertakings and branches of the group in order to determine the group structure and to identify all members and participants of the college. When assessing the significance of a related undertaking or branch, the following criteria are considered: the ratio of the balance sheet of the undertaking to the total balance sheet of the group, its proportional contribution to the group SCR, to the group's own funds and to the performance and earnings of the group as a whole, its role within the group's organisational structure, the level of influence exercised over the undertaking, and the interactions between undertakings.

When assessing the materiality of undertakings in the local market, the following factors are considered: the market share of the undertaking and its role in specific markets, the ratio of the total balance sheet of the group to the total balance sheet of all groups in a particular MS or third country, the level of risk to which the undertaking is exposed and the potential effect on the local market, and the role of the undertaking in the infrastructure of the financial system.

Third-country supervisory authorities may only be invited to join the college as participants if they sign the coordination arrangements and demonstrate that they can comply with the coordination arrangements under their national legislation. It is particularly important that the professional secrecy requirements are at least equivalent to those applicable to EEA supervisory authorities. This may be the subject of a cooperation agreement concluded with the third country or supervisory authority concerned.[163]

EIOPA is a member of all colleges of supervisors.[164] However, it is not involved in the day-to-day supervision of the undertakings concerned.

---

162 EIOPA, Guidelines on operational functioning of colleges, EIOPA-BoS-14/146, 2 February 2015, p. 5.

163 EIOPA, Guidelines on operational functioning of colleges, EIOPA-BoS-14/146, 2 February 2015, Guideline 4. See Art. 264 FD and further in Chapter 9, section 12.3. EIOPA has carried out 11 professional secrecy and exchange of confidential information assessments regarding third countries that are not the subject of an equivalence decision. See BERNARDINO, G., Statement on third-country equivalence at the ECON meeting of 9 March 2017, p. 3 (https://eiopa.europa.eu/Publications/Speeches%20and%20presentations/Third-Country Equivalencespeech.pdf).

164 In its Report to the EC on the application of group supervision under the Solvency II Directive, EIOPA 17-648, 22 December 2017, p. 4, EIOPA indicated that it had attended the majority of the colleges of supervisors for cross-border groups in recent years. EIOPA's engagement in each college is risk-based. The engagement may be direct involvement in

This is the sole responsibility of NSAs. EIOPA assists the group supervisor and the college of supervisors by providing information, advice, practical examples and sharing best practices upon request and on its own initiative. EIOPA also uses its presence in the college of supervisors to promote the implementation of its action plan and strategy for colleges of supervisors.[165] EIOPA also facilitates delegation of tasks within the college by identifying those tasks that can be delegated or jointly exercised, following the principle of allocating supervisory competence to the supervisor that is best placed to take action on a particular issue.[166]

12.2. OPERATIONAL FUNCTIONING OF THE COLLEGE

Subject to specific provisions in the FD or in implementing measures, the establishment and functioning of the college of supervisors is based on coordination arrangements concluded by the group supervisor and the other supervisory authorities concerned.[167] Where diverging views concerning the coordination arrangements arise, any member of the college may refer the matter to EIOPA and request its assistance in accordance with Art. 19 EIOPA Regulation. Where EIOPA has decided, the group supervisor must act in conformity with that decision and transmit it to the other supervisory authorities concerned (Art. 248 (4) FD).

The coordination arrangements must be in writing and must, with regard to both going-concern and emergency situations, specify the following:

(a) the minimum information to be transmitted to the group supervisor by the other supervisory authorities in the college or to be disseminated by the group supervisor to the other supervisory authorities in the college;
(b) the language and frequency of the information to be transmitted to the group supervisor by the other supervisory authorities in the college or to be disseminated by the group supervisor to the other supervisory authorities in the college;
(c) the language and frequency of the information to be exchanged with any other authorities concerned;

---

the college on an ongoing basis, engagement only at a certain frequency or a follow-up of developments using a desk-based review approach.

165 See EIOPA, *Colleges Strategy 2016–2019*.

166 EIOPA, Guidelines on operational functioning of colleges, EIOPA-BoS-14/146, 2 February 2015, pp. 2–3. See also Guidelines 22 and 23.

167 A template for the coordination arrangements is included in Annex 1 to the Guidelines on operational functioning of college. These coordination arrangements which include, for instance, the calendar of college meetings are unfortunately not public and are sometimes not shared with the supervised group concerned.

(d) the obligation to adopt a work plan revised at least annually and agreed by the college for coordinating the supervisory activities of the college in the following 12 months;
(e) an emergency plan[168] agreed by the college of supervisors.

In the context of the emergency plan, the following information must be exchanged between the supervisory authorities within the college as soon as it becomes available:

(a) a description of the emergency situation, with an indication of any impact on policyholders and on financial markets;
(b) an identification of the undertakings in the group which are affected by the emergency situation, with relevant information on their financial situation;
(c) an overview of any measures taken by the group in relation to the emergency situation;
(d) an overview of any measures taken by any of the supervisory authorities concerned in relation to the emergency situation and a description of any existing national measures relevant to the management and resolution of the crisis.

The coordination arrangements must be regularly tested and reviewed by the college of supervisors (Art. 355 DA).

Specific procedures must be included for the approval of group internal models, the imposition of a group capital add-on, the designation of a group supervisor, disagreements concerning the coordination arrangements and a breach of the group SCR. The coordination agreements can entrust additional tasks to the group supervisor, the other supervisory authorities or EIOPA where this would result in a more efficient supervision of the group and would not impair the supervisory activities of the members of the college in respect of their individual responsibilities.

The coordination arrangements may also set out procedures for the numerous cases in which the group supervisor is required to consult the other supervisory authorities concerned.[169] Art. 248 (5), third subparagraph FD lists the following cases:

(a) cases of application of group supervision and levels of supervision (Arts. 213–217 FD);
(b) frequency and method for calculating the group solvency (Arts. 219–221 FD);

---

168 See also the template included in Annex 1.E. to the EIOPA Guidelines on operational functioning of colleges, EIOPA-BoS-14/146, 2 February 2015.

169 For the procedure to be followed for the consultation, see EIOPA, Guidelines on operational functioning of colleges, EIOPA-BoS-14/146, 2 February 2015, Guideline 16.

(c) equivalence relating to third-country (re)insurance undertakings (Art. 227 FD);
(d) supervision of risk concentration, intra-group transactions supervision and system of governance (Arts. 244–246 FD);
(e) decisions of importance for the supervisory tasks of other supervisory authorities (Art. 250 FD);
(f) production of a single SFCR (Art. 256 FD);
(g) equivalence in the case of a parent undertaking outside the EEA (Art. 260 FD);
(h) absence of equivalence in the case of a parent undertaking outside the EEA (Art. 262 FD);
(i) cooperation with other supervisory authorities.

The following information must be exchanged by the supervisory authorities that are members of the college on a systematic basis with the group supervisor for each related (re)insurance undertaking falling within the scope of group supervision (Art. 357 (2) DA):

(a) the SFCR, unless the group supervisor has agreed to the inclusion of subsidiaries within the group in a single SFCR;
(b) the RSR, as well as relevant annual and quarterly quantitative templates;
(c) the conclusions drawn by the supervisory authority concerned following the SRP carried out at the level of the individual undertaking.

The group supervisor must exchange with the other supervisory authorities within the college on a systematic basis the following information (Art. 357 (3) DA):[170]

(a) regarding the parent undertaking: the group SFCR, the group RSR, as well as relevant group annual and quarterly QRTs and the conclusions drawn by the group supervisor following the SRP carried out at group level;[171]
(b) for each related (re)insurance undertaking falling within the scope of group supervision: the SFCR, the RSR and the conclusions drawn following the SRP.[172]

---

170 See also Commission Implementing Regulation (EU) 2015/2014 of 11 November 2015 laying down implementing technical standards with regard to the procedures and templates for the submission of information to the group supervisor and for the exchange of information between supervisory authorities in accordance with Directive 2009/138/EC of the EP and of the Council, *OJ* L 296, 12.11.2015, p. 11.

171 For more details concerning the information that must be provided by the group supervisor, see EIOPA, Guidelines on exchange of information on a systematic basis within colleges, EIOPA-BoS-15/112, 14 September 2015, Technical Annex II.

172 For more details concerning the information that must be provided by the other supervisory authorities to the group supervisor, see EIOPA, Guidelines on exchange of information on a systematic basis within colleges, EIOPA-BoS-15/112, 14 September 2015, Technical Annex I.

The group supervisor takes the lead in the activities of the college, chairs its meetings and establishes an appropriate mechanism to facilitate its operational functioning. This means in particular: updating the contact details of members and participants, informing the members and participants within a reasonable time about the dates of the college meetings, preparing the agenda, keeping a record of the meeting, formalising and following up that action points, developing the work plan, performing the supervisory review and assessing the financial situation of the group, reviewing the organisational structure and the coordination arrangements, and engaging a discussion regarding the need to designate a new group supervisor in the case of a change in the group structure.[173]

12.3. SUPERVISORY COOPERATION

Supervisory cooperation is essential to make group supervision work in practice. The FD therefore requires close cooperation between the authorities responsible for the supervision of the individual (re)insurance undertakings in a group and the group supervisor. This is particularly necessary in cases where a (re)insurance undertaking in the group is experiencing financial difficulties.

Close cooperation is only possible if the supervisory authorities concerned and the group supervisor have the same amount of relevant information. They must therefore provide one another with relevant information in order to allow and facilitate the exercise of their supervisory tasks. They must communicate to one another without delay all relevant information as soon as it becomes available, or exchange information on request. Relevant information includes, at least, information about actions of the group and of the supervisory authorities and information provided by the group itself (Art. 249 (1), second subparagraph FD).

Where a supervisory authority has not communicated relevant information or where a request for cooperation, in particular to exchange relevant information, has been rejected or has not been acted upon within two weeks, the supervisory authorities may refer the matter to EIOPA, which might take action on the basis of Art. 19 EIOPA Regulation (Art. 249 (1a) FD).

In order to also ensure cooperation between supervisory authorities in cases where decisions are taken that are not of direct relevance for the undertaking under their supervision, supervisory authorities are required to consult each

173 EIOPA, Guidelines on operational functioning of colleges, EIOPA-BoS-14/146, 2 February 2015, Guideline 10.

other in the college of supervisors where a decision is of importance for the supervisory tasks of other supervisory authorities, in the following situations:

(a) changes in the shareholder, organisational or management structure of (re)insurance undertakings in a group that require the approval or authorisation of supervisory authorities;
(b) a decision on the extension of the recovery period in the case of non-compliance with the SCR;
(c) major sanctions or exceptional measures taken by supervisory authorities, including the imposition of a capital add-on to the SCR and the imposition of any limitation on the use of an internal model for the calculation of the SCR.

For the purposes of points (b) and (c) above, the group supervisor must always be consulted.

In addition, the supervisory authorities concerned must, where a decision is based on information received from other supervisory authorities, consult each other prior to that decision.

A supervisory authority may decide not to consult other supervisory authorities in cases of urgency or where such consultation could jeopardise the effectiveness of the decision. In that case, the supervisory authority must, without delay, inform the other supervisory authorities concerned.

Where a (re)insurance undertaking and either a credit institution or an investment firm, or both, are directly or indirectly related or have a common participating undertaking, the supervisory authorities concerned and the authorities responsible for the supervision of those other undertakings must cooperate closely. Without prejudice to their respective responsibilities, the authorities must provide one another with any information likely to simplify their task, in particular in the context of group supervision.

Member States must authorise the exchange of information between their NSAs and between their supervisory authorities and other authorities (for instance EIOPA). Information received in the framework of group supervision, and in particular any exchange of information between supervisory authorities and between supervisory authorities and other authorities, is subject to professional secrecy (Art. 253 FD).

A supervisory authority may carry out within its territory, either directly or through the intermediary of a person whom it appoints for that purpose (for instance, an actuary or an auditor), on-site verification of relevant information for group supervision at the premises of a (re)insurance undertaking that is subject to group supervision, a related undertaking of that (re)insurance undertaking, the parent undertaking of that (re)insurance undertaking, or a related undertaking of that parent undertaking (Art. 255 (1) FD).

Where the information relates to an undertaking, whether regulated or not, which is part of a group and is situated in another MS, the supervisory authority must ask the supervisory authorities of that other MS to have the verification carried out. The authorities which receive such a request must, within the framework of their competences, act upon that request either by carrying out the verification directly, by allowing, for example, an auditor or expert to carry it out, or by allowing the authority which made the request to carry it out itself. The group supervisor must be informed of the action taken. The supervisory authority that made the request may, where it so wishes, participate in the verification even if it does not carry out the verification directly.

Any supervisory authority or participant in the college who wishes to verify information which it deems relevant to the supervision of the group or entities within the group can request a joint on-site examination. The request must mention the scope and the objective of the on-site examination and take into account the need to avoid duplication of effort between supervisory authorities. The supervisory authority requesting the joint on-site examination must inform the group supervisor, who should then notify EIOPA,[174] as well as the other members and participants that may be affected by or interested in participating in the on-site examination or its outcome.[175]

Where a request to another supervisory authority to have a verification carried out has not been acted upon within two weeks, or where the supervisory authority is unable in practice to exercise its right to participate in the verification, the requesting authority may refer the matter to EIOPA and may request its assistance in accordance with Art. 19 EIOPA Regulation in order to settle the disagreement.

In most situations, the cooperation between supervisory authorities seems to work well. There could however be enforcement problems. They are dealt with in Art. 258 FD.

Where a (re)insurance undertaking in a group does not comply with the requirements concerning cooperation in the context of group supervision or where the requirements are met but solvency may nevertheless be jeopardised, or where the intra-group transactions or the risk concentrations are a threat to the financial position of a (re)insurance undertaking that is part of the group, the measures necessary to rectify the situation must be adopted as soon as possible by either the group supervisor, in the case of an insurance holding company or mixed financial holding company, or by the supervisory authorities concerned, in the case of a (re)insurance undertaking.

Where the group supervisor is not one of the supervisory authorities of the MS in which the insurance holding company or mixed financial holding

174 EIOPA is entitled to participate in joint on-site examinations (Art. 255 (2) FD).

175 EIOPA, Guidelines on operational functioning of colleges, EIOPA-BoS-14/146, 2 February 2015, Guideline 20.

company has its head office, the group supervisor must inform these supervisory authorities of its findings, with a view to enabling them to take the necessary measures.

Where the group supervisor is not one of the supervisory authorities of the MS in which the (re)insurance undertaking has its head office, the group supervisor must inform these supervisory authorities of its findings, with a view to enabling them to take the necessary measures.

The supervisory authorities concerned, including the group supervisor, must, where appropriate, coordinate their measures. In carrying out group supervision, problems of enforcement may arise in practice in the case of insurance holding companies, mixed financial holding companies or persons who effectively manage these companies, as these companies and persons are not subject to direct supervision by an insurance supervisory authority. Art. 258 (2) FD therefore requires Member States to impose sanctions (including criminal sanctions) on these companies or persons if they infringe laws, regulations or administrative provisions adopted in the context of group supervision. Supervisory authorities must cooperate closely to ensure that such sanctions or measures are effective, in particular where the central administration or main establishment of an insurance holding company or mixed financial holding company is not located in the same MS as its head office.

In order to establish cooperation with third-country supervisory authorities, Art. 264 FD provides for the possibility for the EU to negotiate agreements with one or more third countries regarding the means of exercising group supervision over (re)insurance undertakings that have a parent undertaking with its head office in a third country or third-country (re)insurance undertakings that have a parent undertaking with its head office in the EU, with a view to facilitating an exchange of information between supervisory authorities. Only one such agreement has been concluded so far: the Covered Agreement between the EU and the USA on prudential measures regarding insurance and reinsurance. This bilateral agreement includes a provision on group supervision (Art. 4) and on exchange of information (Art. 5). It also includes in an annex a Model Memorandum of Understanding on Exchange of Information between Supervisory Authorities.[176]

The co-legislators attached great importance to effective cooperation between supervisory authorities in the context of groups.[177] This is not only apparent

176 Bilateral Agreement between the EU and the USA on prudential measures regarding (re)insurance, dated 18 September 2017, *OJ* L 258, 6.10.2017, p. 4.

177 The need for supervisory cooperation in the context of group supervision is also recognised at international level where the IAIS has developed a Multilateral Memorandum of Understanding which is being joined by an increasing number of IAIS members. See BRAUMÜLLER, P. and WARZILEK, A., IAIS Multilateral Memorandum of Understanding, in KEMPLER, C., FLAMEE, M., YANG, C.H. and WINDELS, P. (Eds.), *Global Perspectives on Insurance Today*, Palgrave Macmillan, New York, 2013.

from the number of articles in the FD dealing with supervisory cooperation and exchange of information between supervisory authorities in the context of group supervision, but also from the obligation placed on EIOPA to report regularly on all relevant and significant experiences concerning supervisory activities and cooperation between supervisors in the context of group supervision (Art. 259 (2) FD). EIOPA must in particular report on:

- the process of nomination of the group supervisor, the number of group supervisors and the geographical spread;
- the work of the colleges of supervisors and the involvement and commitment of supervisory authorities where they are not the group supervisor.

EIOPA has produced annual reports on the functioning of colleges. In its last published report, EIOPA identified the priorities for 2017: further development of the effectiveness, efficiency and impact of information exchange and joint risk assessment in colleges, and ensuring the robustness and reliability of the Solvency II balance sheet.[178] In its Colleges Strategy 2016–2019, EIOPA focuses on those areas where a potential failure of a supervised group would have significant impact on the financial market from a European perspective, and where EIOPA's support is needed in order to coordinate the cross-border supervision of EEA undertakings belonging to groups based in non-EEA countries with no formal sub-group structures at EEA level.[179]

13. PUBLIC DISCLOSURE AND SUPERVISORY REPORTING

The Pillar 3 requirements concerning public disclosure and supervisory reporting at solo level also apply at group level. Groups must publish a group (or single) SFCR and must report regularly to the group supervisor. The detailed provisions are discussed in Chapter 8; this chapter only includes special provisions that have not been dealt with in Chapter 8.

---

178 EIOPA, *Year-end report 2016 on functioning of colleges of supervisors and priorities for 2017*, 1 March 2017, p. 16.

179 EIOPA, *Year-end report 2016 on functioning of colleges of supervisors and priorities for 2017*, 1 March 2017, p. 5. In two situations where there are several insurance undertakings authorised in different EEA Member States owned by the same or several related undertakings located in a third country, a proto-college was set up with all NSAs concerned to exchange information and assess potential risks stemming from activities and uncertainties on the strategy of the ultimate parent. See EIOPA, Report to the EC on Group Supervision and Capital Management with a Group of Insurance or Reinsurance Undertakings and FoS and FoE under Solvency II, EIOPA-BoS-18-485, 14 December 2018, p. 15.

13.1. PUBLIC DISCLOSURE

All groups must publish a group SFCR on an annual basis (Art. 256 FD). The report is published by the parent undertaking (participating (re)insurance undertaking, insurance holding company or mixed financial holding company).

The group SFCR is published in the language or languages determined by the group supervisor. Where the college of supervisors comprises supervisory authorities from more than one MS, the group supervisor may, after consulting the other supervisory authorities concerned and the group itself, require the parent undertaking to also disclose the report in another language most commonly understood by the other supervisory authorities concerned, as agreed in the college of supervisors (Art. 360 DA).

Subject to the agreement of the group supervisor, the parent undertaking may provide a single SFCR comprising the group information and the information about one or more subsidiaries within the group. Information about that or these subsidiaries must be individually identifiable. Before granting the agreement, the group supervisor must consult and duly take into account any views and reservations of the members of the college of supervisors.

In the single SFCR, the information at group level and the information for any subsidiary covered by the report must follow the structure set out in Annex XX DA. However, the parent undertaking may decide, when providing any part of the information to be disclosed for a subsidiary covered by the report, to refer to information at group level, where that information is equivalent in both nature and scope (Art. 365 DA). Where the single SFCR fails to include information which the supervisory authority that has authorised a subsidiary within the group requires comparable undertakings to provide, and where the omission is material, the supervisory authority concerned may require the subsidiary concerned to disclose the necessary additional information.

The single SFCR is published in the language or languages determined by the group supervisor. Where the college of supervisors comprises supervisory authorities from more than one MS, the group supervisor may, after consulting the other supervisory authorities concerned and the group itself, require the parent undertaking to also disclose the report in another language most commonly understood by the other supervisory authorities concerned, as agreed in the college of supervisors (Art. 366 DA).

Where only some subsidiaries are included in the single SFCR, the other subsidiaries must include in their solo SFCR a reference to the single SFCR. Similarly, the single SFCR must include a reference to the solo SFCRs of those other subsidiaries (Art. 370 (1) DA).

Art. 256a FD, introduced by Omnibus II, also requires parent undertakings to disclose publicly, at the level of the group, on an annual basis, the legal structure and the governance and organisational structure of the group, including a description of all subsidiaries, material related undertakings and significant branches belonging to the group. There is no indication of where this information must be disclosed. It is often found in the group SFCR, sometimes with a reference to the management report.

13.2. SUPERVISORY REPORTING

As for solo undertakings, the supervisory reporting for groups is very extensive. The parent undertaking must report to the group supervisor. The information is basically the same as that required for solo undertakings, with additional information concerning the group as stated in Art. 372 DA.

Where all (re)insurance undertakings in the group are exempted from quarterly reporting obligations on the basis of Art. 35 (6) FD, the group regular supervisory report must only include annual quantitative templates. Reporting on an item-by-item basis may also be omitted where all undertakings in the group are exempted from it on the basis of Art. 35 (7) FD.[180]

Where the college of supervisors comprises supervisory authorities from more than one MS, the group supervisor may, after consulting the other supervisory authorities concerned and the group itself, require the parent undertaking to report the group regular reporting in a language most commonly understood by the supervisory authorities concerned, as agreed in the college of supervisors (Art. 374 DA).

[180] Art. 254 (2) FD indicates that it is for the group supervisor to decide whether the exemption applies at group level, while Art. 372 (1) DA makes this exemption apply automatically.

CHAPTER 10
EQUIVALENCE

1. PRINCIPLES

(Re)insurance groups in the EEA may have subsidiaries in third countries. As the FD requires each EEA group to calculate a group SCR, the question arises how the solvency position of these third-country subsidiaries can be integrated in the group solvency calculation.

(Re)insurance undertakings in the EEA may have an ultimate parent situated in a third country. As the FD requires all groups to be subject to group supervision, the question arises how the group supervision can be organised when the ultimate parent undertaking is not situated in the EEA.

(Re)insurance undertakings in the EEA may conclude a reinsurance contract with a (re)insurance undertaking situated in a third country. The question arises how such contracts should be dealt with under Solvency II.

To resolve these three issues, the FD introduces the concept of equivalence. As soon as the solvency regime of a third country is recognised as equivalent, undertakings from that third country are treated as if they were an EEA undertaking. The concept of equivalence had already been used extensively in other areas of EU (financial services) regulation.[1] It makes it possible to resolve complex problems without having to use the instrument of an international agreement, which usually takes more time.

For each of the three situations described above, an equivalence regime has been developed: Art. 172 (third-country reinsurers); Art. 227 (group solvency calculation in the case of a third-country subsidiary); and Art. 260 (group supervision in the case of a third-country parent).

Equivalence must be distinguished from market access. Undertakings from third countries whose solvency regime has been recognised as equivalent to Solvency II do not automatically benefit from market access.[2] For instance, it is

1 For an overview, see EC, Commission Staff Working Document: EU equivalence decisions in financial services policy: an assessment, SWD (2017) 102 final, 27 February 2017, 18 p.

2 An example is Brexit. Even if an equivalence decision is taken with regard to the solvency regime in the UK after Brexit, UK (re)insurers will still have to apply for authorisation in each EEA MS if they want to conduct business there.

not because the solvency regime of a third-country reinsurance undertaking has been deemed equivalent that this third-country reinsurance undertaking has direct access in all EEA Member States. Additional requirements, such as the establishment of a branch may have to be met.

Equivalence does not mean that the third country must have a solvency regime that is exactly the same as Solvency II. The assessment looks at the substance rather than the form. For instance, for the solvency regime of a third country to be considered equivalent to Solvency II, there is no requirement to have the same confidence level as Solvency II. The third-country solvency or supervisory regime must provide a similar level of policyholder/beneficiary protection as that provided under Solvency II. In that sense, the equivalence assessment follows an outcome-based approach.[3]

In order to provide legal certainty, equivalence decisions at EU level are taken by the EC or by the group supervisor, in both cases assisted by EIOPA. Initially, it was envisaged that the EC would take these decisions, after consultation with the EIOPC, without the specific intervention of the EP.[4] During the negotiation of the FD, the EP insisted that equivalence decisions by the EC should take the legal form of a delegated act, which involves a right of scrutiny for the EP (and for the Council). This underlines the political nature of an equivalence decision. Reciprocity and other criteria might play a role in the ultimate decision. The decision can be reviewed, for instance if the legal situation in the third country or in the EU changes fundamentally. The decision can also be limited in time, for instance in the case of provisional or temporary equivalence. In practice, the delegated acts indicate that the EC can undertake a specific review at any time outside the general review, where relevant developments make it necessary to re-assess the recognition granted. The EC monitors the evolution of the third country's solvency regime and the fulfilment of the conditions, with the technical assistance of EIOPA.

Equivalence decisions are based upon assessment criteria included in the DA. The EC can only adopt an equivalence decision if these criteria are fulfilled. The criteria are sufficiently broad to allow for judgement to be exercised. For the assessment, it is also important to verify to what extent the rules and regulations in the third country are actually applied in practice. The assessments

---

3 In fact, equivalence assessment leads to a "circular process" of harmonisation of insurance regulation. Transnational sources, such as the ICPs, affect Solvency II. The EU in turn incites third countries to meet an equivalence test based upon EU rules, thus helping to disseminate rules complying with international standards around the world. See MARANO, P., Sources and tools of insurance regulation, in MARANO, P. and SIRI, M. (Eds.), *Insurance Regulation in the European Union: Solvency II and Beyond*, Palgrave Macmillan, Cham, 2017, p. 10. See also KADING, B. and MADEIROS, L., Insurance Regulation: Mutual Recognition, Equivalence and International Standards, in LIEDTKE, P.M. and MONKIEWICZ, J. (Eds.), *The Future of Insurance Regulation and Supervision: A Global Perspective*, Palgrave Macmillan, Basingstoke, 2011, p. 395.

4 See, for instance, Art. 227 (3) of the initial proposal tabled by the EC.

follow a risk-based approach and proportionality is used in the application of the equivalence criteria in order to take account of the specific features of each individual case.[5]

It is impossible to take equivalence decisions for all relevant third countries. The EC is not required to take an equivalence decision and may well prefer to leave the decision to the group supervisor and to EIOPA. A choice must be made based upon priorities defined after consultation with stakeholders and with EIOPA.

The ability to exchange information with relevant third-country supervisors is fundamental to equivalence determinations. Confidential information exchanged between supervisory authorities must be protected by rules of professional secrecy. This requirement is specifically included in the assessment criteria (Arts. 378 (r) and (s), 379 (h) and (i), and 380 (v) and (w) DA).

Equivalence decisions by the EC are based upon advice provided by EIOPA. The initial advice on the technical criteria for assessing equivalence was provided to the EC by CEIOPS on 1 April 2010.[6] On 31 August 2010, CEIOPS provided advice on the third countries to be assessed for equivalence.[7] Both documents were subject to a transparent, open process and dialogue with stakeholders before being finalised. In its advice, CEIOPS underlined the need for transitional measures in order to integrate the international operations of groups into the Solvency II regime and to allow for the development of a harmonised approach across Europe to internationally active groups.

In its request for advice to CEIOPS, the EC had identified the following factors to be examined by CEIOPS when considering third countries to be included in the first wave of equivalence decisions:

- existence of a supervisory regime that is fully risk-based[8] or of measures to move towards such a system;
- materiality of an equivalence finding to EU (re)insurance undertakings and their policyholders;
- number of related undertakings held by EU (re)insurance undertakings situated in the third country;
- importance of an equivalence finding for the insurance market in the third country;
- existence of mutual recognition or equivalent arrangements, such as memoranda of understanding between third countries and Member States.

---

5 See EC, Commission Staff Working Document: EU equivalence decisions in financial services policy: an assessment, SWD (2017) 102 final, 27 February 2017, p. 8.

6 CEIOPS, Advice for Level 2 Implementing Measures on Solvency II: Technical criteria for assessing 3rd country equivalence in relation to Arts. 172, 227 and 260, CEIOPS-DOC-78/10, March 2010, 52 p.

7 CEIOPS, Advice to the EC: Equivalence assessments to be undertaken in relation to Arts. 172, 227 and 260 of the Solvency II Directive, CEIOPS-DOC-92-10, 31 August 2010, 16 p.

8 CEIOPS advised the EC not to use this terminology as it sets a standard that is too absolute.

CEIOPS added the following considerations:

- willingness of the third country to engage in the process;
- realistic possibility for individual third countries to meet the criteria ultimately agreed for equivalence;
- capacity to carry out an equivalence assessment;
- proposed evolution of the regulatory regime to a model akin to Solvency II.

On the basis of these considerations, CEIOPS advised the EC to include Bermuda and Switzerland in the first wave of equivalence decisions, for each of the situations described above, i.e. Art. 172 (third-country reinsurers), Art. 227 (group solvency calculation in the case of a third-country subsidiary), and Art. 260 (group supervision in the case of a third-country parent). Once the FD was adopted in its final form, the EC asked EIOPA to carry out an equivalence assessment for the following countries: Australia, Bermuda, Brazil, Canada, Japan, Mexico, Switzerland and the USA.

The procedure to be followed for an assessment of equivalence is the same for the three equivalence articles:

- EC call for advice to EIOPA;
- advice delivered by EIOPA to the EC after consultation of stakeholders;
- adoption of a delegated act by the EC, which is subject to scrutiny by the EP and by the Council;
- regular review of the delegated act in order to take account of any significant changes to the supervisory regime of the third country or to Solvency II. In practice, the delegated acts adopted by the EC indicate that the EC must monitor, with the technical assistance of EIOPA, the evolution of the solvency regime in the third country and the fulfilment of the conditions on the basis of which the equivalence decision has been taken.

Carrying out an assessment of equivalence is a time-consuming exercise and is taken very seriously. It involves an intense dialogue with the supervisory authorities of the third countries concerned based upon answers provided to a detailed questionnaire, which is followed up by a meeting with the third-country supervisory authority. EIOPA uses a number of indicators for its assessment. Its draft advice is published for comments by stakeholders. Before a final decision is taken, a gap analysis is carried out comparing the third country's solvency regime with Solvency II. This gap analysis, which is different from the assessment report, is not made public but is communicated to the EP.

Following the entry into force of Omnibus II, there are now three types of equivalence decisions: full equivalence, temporary equivalence and provisional equivalence. The EC does not have to grant the same type of equivalence decision in all three situations in the same third country (reinsurance, parent undertaking in a third country, subsidiary in a third country). For instance, in the case of Japan, the EC has granted a temporary equivalence decision for reinsurance activities carried out by Japanese reinsurers in the EEA and a provisional equivalence decision for insurance activities carried out by Japanese insurers with a subsidiary undertaking in the EEA.

Full equivalence is granted for an indefinite period (subject to regular review) and can relate to three situations: third-country reinsurance undertakings with activities in the EEA; EEA (re)insurance groups with subsidiaries in a third country; and third-country (re)insurance groups with subsidiaries in EEA Member States. Two countries have been assessed so far for full equivalence, Bermuda and Switzerland. In both cases, full equivalence has been granted in all three situations.

Temporary equivalence is granted for a very limited (non-renewable) period, as it is based on the assumption that the third country concerned is in the process of developing a solvency regime that will eventually become equivalent to Solvency II. Extension of the period is limited to one year. A temporary equivalence decision can be granted in the case of third-country reinsurance undertakings with activities in the EEA or in the case of third-country groups with subsidiaries in the EEA. Only one country has so far received a temporary equivalence decision: Japan (for reinsurance), until 31 December 2020.

Provisional equivalence can be granted for a less limited (renewable) period. It is based on the premise that the third country concerned has a risk-based solvency regime in place that has not yet been assessed for (full) equivalence. Provisional equivalence has been granted to Australia, Brazil, Canada, Mexico, the USA and Japan. The period can be extended for further periods of 10 years.

EIOPA publishes on its website an updated list of all third countries whose solvency regime has been recognised as equivalent (whether full, temporary or provisional) to Solvency II (Arts. 172 (2), third subparagraph and (4), third subparagraph, 227 (4), third subparagraph, and 260 (3), third subparagraph and (5), third subparagraph FD).

2. GROUP SOLVENCY CALCULATION WHEN THE GROUP INCLUDES A SUBSIDIARY SITUATED IN A THIRD COUNTRY

2.1. FULL EQUIVALENCE

2.1.1. Principle

When a participating (re)insurance undertaking holds a participation in a (re)insurance undertaking which has its head office in a third country and that undertaking is subject to a solvency regime which is at least equivalent to Solvency II,[9] it can include the SCR and the eligible own funds of that undertaking as calculated in accordance with the requirements of that third country in the group SCR without the need to recalculate them on the basis of the Solvency II requirements (Art. 227 (1), second subparagraph FD).[10] This means in practice that the third-country subsidiary of an EEA parent is treated, for the purpose of calculating the group SCR, as an EEA undertaking.[11]

This only applies where the parent undertaking is applying the deduction and aggregation method to that subsidiary, i.e. the parent considers the third-country subsidiary to be operating independently (see above, Chapter 9, section 7.2.2). If the parent undertaking were applying the default method, i.e. the accounting consolidation-based method, the data relating to the third-country subsidiary undertaking would be included in the consolidated accounts of the parent undertaking, which automatically means that these data must be harmonised with those of the parent undertaking and the other undertakings in the group. It is for the group supervisor to decide whether the deduction and aggregation method can be applied to the third-country subsidiary.

The verification of whether the third country's solvency regime is at least equivalent is carried out by the group supervisor at the request of the participating undertaking or on its own initiative, with the assistance of EIOPA.[12] The group supervisor must inform EIOPA whether it wishes to undertake the assessment at national level, assisted by EIOPA and after consulting the other NSAs concerned, or whether it wants EIOPA to carry out the assessment. The decision must be based on the assessment criteria included in Art. 379 DA.[13]

In order to establish a harmonised approach, the group supervisor cannot take any decision in relation to a third country's solvency regime that contradicts any decision taken vis-à-vis that third country previously (for instance by

---

9 The legal text refers to Title I, Chapter VI FD, which contains the Solvency II regime.

10 This is only relevant when using the deduction and aggregation method. When using the default method (accounting consolidation-based method), the verification of equivalence is not required, as the parent undertaking prepares consolidated accounts that include the third-country subsidiary.

11 One of the possible consequences is that the capital contribution by the third-country subsidiary is lower than if that subsidiary would have been based within the EEA. See KRAFT, M., Auswirkungen von Solvency II und der neuen EU-Finanzaufsichtsarchitektur auf die Kapitalallokationsstrukturen von Versicherungsgruppen, *Zeitschrift für Versicherungswissenschaft*, 2012, No 101, p. 665.

12 If the group SCR is calculated in accordance with the default method (accounting consolidation-based method), the verification of equivalence is not required, as the parent undertaking prepares consolidated accounts that include the third-country subsidiary.

13 For the procedure to be followed, see EIOPA, Guidelines on the methodology for equivalence assessments by national supervisory authorities under Solvency II, EIOPA-BoS-14/182, 2 February 2015. The Guidelines include a template questionnaire to be submitted to the third-country supervisor in Technical Annex I.

another group supervisor or by the EC via a delegated act), save where significant changes have been made to either the Solvency II regime or to the supervisory regime[14] in the third country.

Where the other supervisory authorities disagree with the decision taken by the group supervisor, they may refer the matter to EIOPA and request its assistance in accordance with Art. 19 EIOPA Regulation, within three months of notification of the decision by the group supervisor (Art. 227 (2) FD). EIOPA's decision is binding for all supervisory authorities concerned. So far, EIOPA has not taken any decision on equivalence.

On the basis of the assessment criteria in Art. 379 DA, the EC may, assisted by EIOPA, adopt a delegated act determining that the solvency regime of a third country is equivalent to Solvency II.

2.1.2. Assessment Criteria

Art. 227 (3) FD allows the EC to develop criteria for the assessment of a third country's solvency regime. Assessment criteria are useful for developing a harmonised approach and for providing legal certainty. They are also helpful for the group supervisor (and EIOPA) in the assessment of the solvency regime of those third countries for which the EC has not yet taken an equivalence decision. The assessment criteria in Art. 379 DA are based upon advice provided to the EC by CEIOPS.

The assessment criteria deal not only with technical solvency aspects, but also with aspects relating to prudential supervision, including professional secrecy and the treatment of confidential information. In that sense, the reference in the legal text to an assessment of the "solvency regime" is somewhat misleading.

In accordance with Art. 379 DA, the following criteria must be taken into account in assessing whether the solvency regime of a third country is equivalent to Solvency II:[15]

(a) whether the assessment of the financial position of domestic (re)insurance undertakings relies on sound economic principles and whether solvency requirements are based on an economic valuation of all assets and liabilities;
(b) whether the solvency regime requires domestic (re)insurance undertakings to hold adequate financial resources, including all of the following:
    (i) technical provisions must be established with respect to all (re)insurance obligations towards policyholders and beneficiaries;
    (ii) assets held to cover technical provisions must be invested in the best interests of policyholders and beneficiaries, taking into account any disclosed policy objective;

[14] The legal text sometimes refers to "supervisory regime" where it should read "solvency regime".
[15] Reference is made to Title I, Chapter VI FD, which includes the Pillar 1 requirements.

(iii) investments can only be made in assets and instruments whose risks the undertaking concerned can properly identify, measure, monitor, manage, control and report (prudent person principle);

(iv) the capital requirements to be met must be set at a level equivalent to the confidence level established under Solvency II, which ensures that in the event of significant losses policyholders and beneficiaries are adequately protected and continue to receive payments as they become due;

(v) a minimum level of capital must be maintained and non-compliance with this must trigger immediate and ultimate supervisory intervention;[16]

(vi) the capital requirements must be met with own funds that are of sufficient quality and are able to absorb significant losses, and the own-fund items considered by the supervisory authorities to be of a high quality must be able to absorb losses both as a going concern and in the event of a winding-up;

(c) whether the capital requirements are risk-based,[17] with the objective of capturing quantifiable risks, and where a significant risk is not quantifiable and cannot be captured in the capital requirements, whether that risk is addressed through another supervisory mechanism;

(d) whether the solvency regime ensures timely intervention by supervisory authorities of the third country in the event that the solvency capital requirement applicable in the third country is not complied with;

(e) whether the solvency regime provides that all persons who are working or who have worked for the supervisory authorities of that third country, as well as auditors and experts acting on behalf of those authorities, are bound by obligations of professional secrecy and whether such obligations of professional secrecy extend to information received from all supervisory authorities;

(f) whether the solvency regime provides that, without prejudice to cases covered by criminal law, any confidential information received by all persons who are working or who have worked for the supervisory authorities of that third country is not divulged to any person or authority whatsoever, except in summary or aggregate form, such that individual (re)insurance undertakings cannot be identified;

(g) whether the solvency regime of the third country provides that, where a (re)insurance undertaking has been declared bankrupt or is being compulsorily wound up, confidential information that does not concern third parties involved in attempts to rescue that undertaking may be divulged in civil or commercial proceedings;

---

16 There is no requirement to have an MCR as this is dealt with in Title I, Chapter VII FD.

17 Following the advice of CEIOPS, the EC did not retain the requirement for the solvency regime to be "fully risk based". This allows for the exercise of judgement and flexibility.

(h) whether third-country supervisory authorities that receive confidential information from supervisory authorities may only use that information in the course of their duties and for any of the following purposes:
   (i) to check that the conditions governing the taking-up of business, system of governance and public disclosure and solvency assessment have been met;
   (ii) to impose sanctions;
   (iii) in administrative appeals against decisions of the supervisory authorities;
   (iv) in court proceedings relating to the solvency regime in that third country;
(i) whether third-country supervisory authorities are permitted to exchange information received from supervisory authorities, in the discharge of their supervisory functions or the detection and investigation of breaches of company law, with other authorities, bodies or persons where that authority, body or person is subject to the obligation of professional secrecy in the relevant third country and whether that information may only be disclosed once the express agreement of the supervisory authority from which it originates has been obtained and, where appropriate, has been obtained solely for the purposes for which the authority gave its agreement.

The assessment criteria must be met before the EC, assisted by EIOPA, will develop a delegated act determining the equivalence of a third country's solvency regime. On the basis of the assessment criteria in Art. 379 DA, the EC has taken two full equivalence decisions, on Bermuda and Switzerland.[18] Each preamble to the delegated act adopted by the EC contains an extensive justification of how each country meets the assessment criteria.

In the case of a positive determination of equivalence, the calculation of the group solvency takes into account, in relation to the third-country undertaking, the solvency capital requirement applicable in that third country and the own funds eligible to satisfy that requirement, as laid down by the third country concerned (Art. 227 (2) FD).[19]

18 Commission Delegated Decision EU2016/309 of 26 November 2015 on the equivalence of the supervisory regime for insurance and reinsurance undertakings in force in Bermuda to the regime laid down in Directive 2009/138/EC of the EP and of the Council and amending Commission Delegated Decision EU2015/2290, *OJ* L 58, 4.3.2016, p. 50 and Commission Delegated Decision EU2015/1602 of 5 June 2015 on the equivalence of the solvency and prudential regime for insurance and reinsurance undertakings in force in Switzerland based on Articles 172 (2), 227 (4) and 260 (3) of Directive 2009/138/EC of the EP and of the Council, *OJ* L 248, 24.9.2015, p. 95.

19 See EIOPA, Opinion on the group solvency calculation in the context of equivalence, EIOPA-BoS-15/201, 25 September 2015, 7 p.

2.2. PROVISIONAL EQUIVALENCE

Recalculating the solvency capital and eligible own funds of a subsidiary in a third country in the context of the group solvency calculation is complex. In addition, if the solvency regime in a third country is less stringent than Solvency II, requiring EEA (re)insurance undertakings with a subsidiary in that country to recalculate the solvency capital of the subsidiary using the more stringent Solvency II requirements is not without problems. Will the supervisory authority in the third country allow the subsidiary to operate with less capital when it appears that – following the Solvency II approach – it actually should have more capital? On the other hand, recalculating the solvency capital of the third-country subsidiary on the basis of Solvency II might result in a level of capital that makes the subsidiary no longer competitive in the local environment.[20]

The need to find a solution in this area was particularly high and industry made strong representations to the co-legislators and to the EC that equivalence should provide a way out for multinational groups headquartered in the EEA. For the EP, this was the priority for the work to be undertaken in the area of equivalence, as it should enable EU groups to do business outside the EU in a capital-efficient manner.[21]

On the other hand, even though many countries in the world are upgrading their solvency regime in the direction of a risk-based capital regime, this does not mean that there is equivalence with Solvency II. In its earlier advice to the EC, CEIOPS had already suggested that some kind of transitional regime would be useful in order to allow the gradual integration of international groups into the Solvency II regime.

The USA in particular was a difficult case. Several large (re)insurance undertakings in the EEA have important operations in the USA. Capital requirements in the USA are generally[22] considered much lower than those

---

20 This is the reason why major European insurance groups, such as Allianz and Aegon, with life insurance operations in the USA treat these operations as separate from those of the European parent and use the (provisional) equivalence provisions to include these operations into the group solvency balance sheet using data calculated on the basis of the local solvency requirements.

21 See the letter dated 19 December 2014 from the Chair of ECON to the EC. Although the Chair of ECON underlined the urgency for the EC adopting a delegated act in this area, it asked for an extension of the scrutiny period by three months. See the letters dated 16 July 2015 from the Chair of ECON to the EC and to the Council.

22 As insurance regulation is state-based, the situation differs from state to state. This is tempered by the NAIC's Financial Regulatory Standards Accreditation Program, whereby states that meet a wide range of legal, financial, functional and organisational standards are certified or "accredited" by the NAIC. This ensures that states meet minimum baseline standards of solvency regulation. See VAUGHAN, T., Improving Regulatory Capital Requirements, in KEMPLER, C., FLAMEE, M., YANG, C.H. and WINDELS, P. (Eds.), *Global Perspectives on Insurance Today*, Palgrave Macmillan, New York, 2013, p. 26.

required by Solvency II.[23] It was unlikely that the USA – where insurance is regulated at state level – would change its solvency regime, although there was some hope of this when the Federal Insurance Office (FIO) was created as a result of the 2010 Dodd–Frank Wall Street Reform and Consumer Protection Act[24] and when the Solvency Modernization Initiative (SMI) was launched by the National Association of Insurance Commissioners (NAIC) in December 2012.[25] Although a dialogue had started between the EC (assisted by EIOPA) and the USA (FIO and NAIC), it was unlikely that quick progress would be made.[26] Furthermore, the dialogue with the USA had shown that there was no interest in the USA in becoming engaged in an equivalence discussion. The USA believed that its solvency regime was at least as good as Solvency II[27] and that it was not for the EU to pass any judgement on insurance regulation in the USA.[28] On the other hand, both sides agreed that it would be strange for two of the largest insurance markets in the world not to be able to agree on a solution that would work for both sides.

---

23 Although the risk-based capital (RBC) regime in the USA was more advanced than Solvency I. When the risk-based capital system was introduced in the USA in 1994, based on a multi-risk factor approach, it was the most advanced set of insurance regulation in the world. See SINGH, R., Toward a Global Approach to Regulating Insurers and Reinsurers, in KEMPLER, C., FLAMEE, M., YANG, C.H. and WINDELS, P. (Eds.), *Global Perspectives on Insurance Today*, Palgrave Macmillan, New York, 2013, p. 83. For a critical analysis, see Federal Insurance Office, US Department of the Treasury, *How to modernise and improve the system of insurance regulation in the United States*, December 2013, 71 p.

24 The equivalence discussions were indirectly responsible for the creation of the Federal Insurance Office (FIO) in the USA. During the discussions of the Dodd–Frank Act in Congress, extensive reference was made to Solvency II and to the impact that Solvency II might have for the insurance industry in the USA. The FIO was empowered to represent the USA in international discussions, for instance within the IAIS, and for preparing a covered agreement to be concluded with the EU. See HARRINGTON, S.E., The Dodd–Frank Act, Solvency II, and US insurance regulation, *The Journal of Financial Perspectives*, 2013, Vol 1, No 1, pp. 1–12.

25 One of the results of this reform was the introduction of an ORSA requirement, although the ORSA in the USA is different from the ORSA under Solvency II as – contrary to the ORSA under Solvency II – there is no compliance check with the capital requirements in the USA. For the origins and the contents of the SMI, see KLEIN, R.W., The Modernization of Insurance Company Solvency Regulation in the US: Issues and Implications, Networks Financial Institute Policy Brief PB-2012-01, Indiana State University, March 2012, 58 p. (available at http://ssrn.com/abstract=2026898) and VAUGHAN, T., Improving Regulatory Capital Requirements, in KEMPLER, C., FLAMEE, M., YANG, C.H. and WINDELS, P. (Eds.), *Global Perspectives on Insurance Today*, Palgrave Macmillan, New York, 2013.

26 Information on this dialogue which is still ongoing can be found on the websites of the EC and of EIOPA.

27 See VAUGHAN, T., The Implications of Solvency II for US Insurance Regulation, *Networks Financial Institute Policy Brief PB*-2009-03, Indiana State University, February 2009, 26 p.

28 Because the USA did not want to discuss equivalence, the dialogue which had started between the EC and the FIO/NAIC in January 2012 did not refer to equivalence but to "enhancing understanding and cooperation for the benefit of insurance consumers, business opportunity and effective supervision". The dialogue led to the adoption of a Covered Agreement between the EU and the USA in 2017.

The magic solution that came out of the Omnibus II negotiations was the introduction of the concept of "provisional equivalence", which is dealt with in Art. 227 (5) FD.

Even where the third country has not met the assessment criteria for equivalence, the EC, assisted by EIOPA, may adopt a delegated act determining that the third country's solvency regime applicable to undertakings with their head office in that country is *provisionally equivalent* to Solvency II, where:

(a) it can be shown that a solvency regime capable of being assessed as equivalent in accordance with the assessment criteria is currently in place or may be adopted and applied by the third country;
(b) the third country has a solvency regime that is risk-based and establishes quantitative and qualitative solvency requirements and requirements relating to supervisory reporting and transparency;
(c) the third country's law in principle allows cooperation and exchange of confidential supervisory information with EIOPA and supervisory authorities;
(d) the third country has an independent system of supervision; and
(e) the third country has established obligations on professional secrecy for all persons acting on behalf of its supervisory authorities.

Provisional equivalence is granted for a period of 10 years,[29] unless before the expiry of that period:

(a) the delegated act has been revoked; or
(b) a delegated act has been adopted determining that the supervisory regime of that third country has been deemed to be equivalent to Solvency II (full equivalence).

Applying the French proverb "*il n'y a que le provisoire qui dure*" (only provisional things last for ever), provisional equivalence can be renewed for further periods of 10 years as long as the criteria for provisional equivalence continue to be met.

Provisional equivalence provides a solution for third countries that are in the process of modernising their risk-based capital solvency regime, as well as for third countries (like the USA) that have a well-functioning solvency regime that is unlikely to be updated very soon.[30]

---

29 The EC had initially proposed three years. Some Member States wanted five years and the EP went for 10 years.

30 See, however, the recent introduction in the USA of the aggregation method for the calculation of group solvency. This development may have been influenced by the discussions within the IAIS concerning the development of ICS (international capital standards).

Once provisional equivalence has been determined, the subsidiaries of EEA parent undertakings in the third country concerned are exempted from a recalculation of their solvency capital for the purposes of calculating the group solvency capital (Art. 227 (7) FD).

As in the case of a full equivalence decision, a decision on provisional equivalence is taken by the EC by way of a delegated act. In taking a decision on provisional equivalence, the EC needs to take account of the way in which EEA (re)insurance undertakings are treated in the third country concerned, in terms of freedom of establishment, the acquisition of holdings in (re)insurance undertakings, the pursuit of (re)insurance activities and the provision of cross-border (re)insurance services. The EC must periodically report to the Council and the EP on such treatment (Art. 227 (6), third subparagraph FD). This is a remainder from the reciprocity clause that is usually included in international agreements.

Two decisions on provisional equivalence have been taken so far applying to five countries: Australia, Brazil, Canada, Japan, Mexico and the USA.[31] The decisions have been granted for a period of 10 years from 1 January 2016. They can be renewed for further periods of 10 years, which would require a new decision by the EC.

In the case of a positive determination of equivalence, the calculation of the group solvency takes into account, in relation to the third-country undertaking, the solvency capital requirement applicable in that country and the own funds eligible to satisfy that requirement, as laid down by the third country concerned (Art. 227 (2) FD).[32]

2.3. ABSENCE OF EQUIVALENCE

In the absence of a decision on equivalence (full or provisional), or if the group supervisor has come to the conclusion that there is no equivalence, the solvency capital and the eligible own funds of the third-country (re)insurance undertaking must be recalculated as if it were an EEA undertaking, i.e. on the basis of Solvency II (Art. 227 (1), first subparagraph FD).

---

31 Commission Delegated Decision (EU) 2015/2290 of 12 June 2015 on the provisional equivalence of the solvency regimes in force in Australia, Bermuda, Brazil, Canada, Mexico and the United States and applicable to insurance and reinsurance undertakings with head offices in those countries, *OJ* L 323, 9.12.2015, p. 22 and Commission Delegated Decision (EU) 2016/310 of 26 November 2015 on the equivalence of the solvency regime for insurance and reinsurance undertakings in force in Japan to the regime laid down in Directive 2009/138/EC of the EP and of the Council, *OJ* L 58, 4.3.2016, p. 55. Bermuda has meanwhile been granted full equivalence status.

32 See EIOPA, Opinion on the group solvency calculation in the context of equivalence, EIOPA-BoS-15/201, 25 September 2015, 7 p., which includes an example relating to the USA and to Brazil.

3. GROUP SUPERVISION WHERE THE ULTIMATE PARENT UNDERTAKING IS SITUATED IN A THIRD COUNTRY

3.1. FULL EQUIVALENCE

3.1.1. Principle

Group supervision applies by default at the ultimate level of the group in the EEA. This can be waived if the ultimate parent undertaking[33] of (re)insurance undertakings authorised in the EEA is situated in a third country with equivalent group supervision to that provided for by Solvency II.[34] In that case, the third-country group is exempted from group supervision at the ultimate level in the EEA. The exemption is automatic (Art. 261 (1) FD), once equivalence has been established.

In accordance with Guideline 5 of the EIOPA Guidelines on Group Solvency,[35] the decision whether to exempt the third-country group from group supervision at the ultimate level in the EEA should be taken on a case-by-case basis and should depend on whether global supervision would result in more efficient supervision of the group and would not impair the supervisory activities of the supervisory authorities concerned in terms of their individual responsibilities. In the view of EIOPA, this means that the following criteria must be met:

- the worldwide group supervision allows for a robust assessment of the risks to which the EEA sub-group and its entities are exposed, considering the structure of the group, the nature, scale and complexity of the risks, and the capital allocation within the group;
- the cooperation currently in place between the third country's group supervisor and the EEA supervisory authorities for the group concerned is structured and well managed through regular meetings and appropriate exchange of information within a college of supervisors to which the EEA supervisory authorities and EIOPA are invited;
- an annual work plan, including joint on-site examinations, is agreed upon in these regular meetings by the supervisory authorities involved in the supervision of the group.

This guideline is slightly misleading. It should not be read as adding a condition to the automatic exemption following from the application of Art. 261 (1) FD,

33 (Re)insurance undertaking, insurance holding company or mixed financial holding company. See Art. 213 (2) (c) FD.

34 Reference is made in Art. 260 (1) FD to Title III FD, which deals with group supervision.

35 EIOPA, Guidelines on group solvency, EIOPA-BoS-14/181, 2 February 2015, pp. 3–4.

but should rather be understood as a reference to the normal application of the group supervision requirements in Arts. 247–258 FD. These requirements also apply in the case of group supervision carried out by a third-country supervisory authority. In the exceptional situation where the third-country group supervisor does not establish a college of supervisors or refuses to cooperate with the EEA supervisory authorities, there can be no exemption from group supervision at the ultimate level in the EEA because there is no equivalence.

The verification of equivalence must be made by the supervisory authorities concerned and is carried out by the EEA supervisory authority that would be the group supervisor if the criteria set out in Art. 247 (2) FD were to apply (the "acting group supervisor"),[36] with the assistance of EIOPA, at the request of the parent undertaking or of any of the (re)insurance undertakings authorised in the EEA or on its own initiative. The group supervisor must inform EIOPA whether it wishes to undertake the assessment at national level, assisted by EIOPA and after consulting the other NSAs concerned, or whether it wants EIOPA to carry out the assessment. The decision must be based on the assessment criteria included in Art. 380 DA.[37]

The acting group supervisor, assisted by EIOPA, must consult the other supervisory authorities concerned,[38] before taking a decision on equivalence. In order to establish a harmonised approach, the acting group supervisor cannot take any decision in relation to a third country that is in opposition to any previous decision taken vis-à-vis that third country (for instance by another group supervisor or by the EC via a delegated act), save where significant changes have been made to either the Solvency II regime or to the supervisory regime in the third country.

Where the other supervisory authorities disagree with the decision taken by the acting group supervisor, they may refer the matter to EIOPA and request its assistance in accordance with Art. 19 EIOPA within three months of notification of the decision by the acting group supervisor (Art. 260 (1) FD). EIOPA's decision is binding on all supervisory authorities concerned. So far, EIOPA has not taken any decision on equivalence.

On the basis of the assessment criteria in Art. 380 DA, the EC may, assisted by EIOPA, adopt a delegated act determining that the prudential regime of a third country is equivalent to Solvency II.

---

36 As the ultimate parent is situated in a third country, the group supervisor would be the third-country supervisory authority. Therefore, it is necessary to identify an acting group supervisor, i.e. the supervisory authority that is situated at the top of the EEA sub-group.

37 For the procedure to be followed, see EIOPA, Guidelines on the methodology for equivalence assessments by national supervisory authorities under Solvency II, EIOPA-BoS-14/182, 2 February 2015. The Guidelines include a template questionnaire to be submitted to the third-country supervisor in Technical Annex I.

38 These would be the supervisory authorities of the EEA subsidiaries, as well as of significant branches and third-country entities that belong to the European sub-group.

The third-country parent undertaking may itself be an intermediate holding company of an ultimate parent undertaking situated in the same or in another third country. In that case, group supervision should take place in principle at the level of the ultimate parent undertaking. In the absence of equivalent group supervision at that level, the supervisory authorities concerned may carry out a new verification at a lower level where a parent undertaking exists, whether at the level of a third-country insurance holding company, a third-country mixed financial holding company or a third-country (re)insurance undertaking. The acting group supervisor must in that case explain its decision to the group (Art. 263 FD).

3.1.2. Assessment Criteria

Art. 260 (2) FD allows the EC to develop criteria for the assessment of the equivalence of a third country's prudential regime for the supervision of groups. Assessment criteria are useful for developing a harmonised approach and for providing legal certainty. They are also helpful for the acting group supervisor (and EIOPA) in the assessment of the prudential regime for group supervision of those third countries for which the EC has not yet taken an equivalence decision. The assessment criteria in Art. 380 DA are based upon advice provided to the EC by CEIOPS. They are extensive because the whole group supervision chapter must be looked at, including the cooperation and exchange of information between supervisory authorities.

In accordance with Art. 380 DA, the following criteria must to be taken into account in assessing whether the prudential regime in a third country for the supervision of groups is equivalent to the group supervision regime under Solvency II:[39]

(a) whether the supervisory authorities have the necessary means, relevant expertise, capacities (including financial and human resources) and mandate to effectively protect policyholders and beneficiaries, regardless of their nationality or place of residence;
(b) whether the supervisory authorities are empowered by law or regulation to:
    (i) determine which undertakings fall under the scope of supervision at group level;
    (ii) supervise (re)insurance undertakings which are part of a group;
    (iii) impose sanctions or take enforcement action where necessary;
(c) whether the supervisory authorities are able to effectively assess the risk profile and solvency and financial position of (re)insurance undertakings which are part of a group, as well as that group's business strategy;

[39] Title III FD, which deals with group supervision.

(d) whether the scope of supervision at group level at least includes all undertakings over which a participating undertaking exercises dominant or significant influence, except where this would be inappropriate for the objectives of group supervision;
(e) whether the supervisory authorities, in the exercise of their general duties, duly consider the potential impact of their decisions on the stability of financial systems globally, particularly during emergency situations, on the basis of the information available at the time;
(f) whether the supervisory authorities take into account the potential pro-cyclical effects of their actions where exceptional movements in the financial markets occur;
(g) whether the prudential regime requires an effective system of governance at the group level which provides for sound and prudent management of the business and prescribes all of the following:
  (i) the existence of an adequate, transparent organisational structure with a clear allocation and appropriate segregation of responsibilities;
  (ii) requirements for ensuring that persons who effectively run the undertaking are fit and proper;
  (iii) the existence of effective processes to ensure the timely transmission of information both within the group and to the relevant supervisory authorities;
  (iv) requirements for ensuring that the outsourced functions or activities are effectively supervised;
(h) whether the prudential regime of that third country requires an effective risk management system in place at the group level comprising at least all of the following:
  (i) strategies, processes and internal reporting procedures necessary to identify, measure, monitor, manage and report risks on a continuous basis to which the group is or could be exposed, and their interdependencies;
  (ii) an effective internal control system;
(i) whether the prudential regime requires the group to have sound reporting and accounting procedures to monitor and manage intra-group transactions and risk concentrations;
(j) whether the prudential regime requires that effective risk management, compliance, internal audit and actuarial functions are established and maintained by the group;
(k) whether the prudential regime requires the group to do all of the following:
  (i) to provide supervisory authorities with any information necessary for the purposes of supervision;
  (ii) to report significant risk concentration at the level of the group and significant intra-group transactions, on at least an annual basis;
  (iii) to disclose publicly, on at least an annual basis, a report on the solvency and financial condition of the group;

(l) whether the prudential regime requires that proposed changes to the business policy or management of the group, or to qualifying holdings in the group, are consistent with the sound and prudent management of the group;
(m) whether the assessment of the financial position of the group relies on sound economic principles and whether the assessment of solvency is based on an economic valuation of all assets and liabilities;
(n) whether the prudential regime requires the group to hold adequate financial resources, including all of the following:
 (i) technical provisions are established by the group with respect to all of its (re)insurance obligations towards policyholders and beneficiaries of (re)insurance undertakings which are part of the group;
 (ii) assets held to cover technical provisions are invested in the best interests of all policyholders and beneficiaries, taking into account any disclosed policy objective;
 (iii) the group only invests in assets and instruments whose risks it can properly identify, measure, monitor, manage, control and report;
 (iv) the group must meet capital requirements set at a level equivalent to that achieved under Solvency II, which ensures that in the event of significant losses policyholders and beneficiaries are adequately protected and continue to receive payments as they become due;
 (v) (re)insurance undertakings which are part of the group must maintain a minimum level of capital, non-compliance with which triggers immediate and ultimate supervisory intervention;
 (vi) the group capital requirement is met with own funds that are of sufficient quality and are able to absorb significant losses, and own-fund items considered by the supervisory authorities to be of high quality must be able to absorb losses both as a going concern and in the event of a winding-up;
(o) whether the capital requirements of the prudential regime are risk-based, with the objective of capturing quantifiable risks, and where a significant risk is not quantifiable and cannot be captured in the capital requirements, whether that risk is addressed through another supervisory mechanism;
(p) whether the prudential regime ensures timely intervention by supervisory authorities in the event that the capital requirement is not complied with;
(q) whether the supervisory authorities restrict the use of own-fund items of a related (re)insurance undertaking where they consider that they cannot effectively be made available to cover the capital requirement of the participating undertaking for which the group solvency is calculated;
(r) whether the calculation of group solvency produces a result that is at least equivalent to the result achieved by either one of the calculation methods set out in Arts. 230 and 233 FD or a combination of them, and that calculation ensures that there is no double use of own funds to meet the group capital

requirement, and that the intra-group creation of capital through reciprocal financing is eliminated;

(s) whether the prudential regime provides that all persons who are working or who have worked for the supervisory authorities of that third country, as well as auditors and experts acting on behalf of those authorities, are bound by obligations of professional secrecy and whether such obligations of professional secrecy extend to information received from all supervisory authorities;

(t) whether the prudential regime provides that, without prejudice to cases covered by criminal law, any confidential information received by all persons who are working or who have worked for the supervisory authorities of that third country is not divulged to any person or authority whatsoever, except in summary or aggregate form, such that individual (re)insurance undertakings cannot be identified;

(u) whether the prudential regime of the third country provides that, where a (re)insurance undertaking has been declared bankrupt or is being compulsorily wound up, confidential information that does not concern third parties involved in attempts to rescue that undertaking may be divulged in civil or commercial proceedings;

(v) whether third-country supervisory authorities that receive confidential information from other supervisory authorities only use that information in the course of their duties and for any of the following purposes:
    (i) to check that the conditions governing the taking-up of business, system of governance and public disclosure and solvency assessment have been met;
    (ii) to impose sanctions;
    (iii) in administrative appeals against decisions of the supervisory authorities;
    (iv) in court proceedings relating to the solvency regime in that third country;

(w) whether third-country supervisory authorities are permitted to exchange information received from supervisory authorities, in the discharge of their supervisory functions or the detection and investigation of breaches of company law, with other authorities, bodies or persons where that authority, body or person is subject to the obligation of professional secrecy in the relevant third country and whether that information is only disclosed once the express agreement of the supervisory authority from which it originates has been obtained and, where appropriate, has been obtained solely for the purposes for which the authority gave its agreement.

The assessment criteria must be met before the EC, assisted by EIOPA, will develop a delegated act for determining the equivalence of a third country's prudential regime for the supervision of groups to the group supervision regime under Solvency II.

A decision on full equivalence of the regime for group supervision has been taken so far for two countries: Bermuda and Switzerland.[40]

Where a third country's supervisory regime on group supervision has been determined to be equivalent to the group supervision regime under Solvency II, Member States must rely on the equivalent group supervision exercised by the third-country supervisory authority, and the provisions on supervisory cooperation and the college of supervisors apply mutatis mutandis (Art. 261 FD). The application of these provisions can be facilitated by the conclusion of an agreement with the third country on the means of exercising group supervision (Art. 266 FD).[41]

3.2. TEMPORARY EQUIVALENCE

The ultimate objective is that as many third countries as possible develop a supervisory regime for group supervision that is equivalent to the group supervision requirements of Solvency II. Group supervision is a key element of Solvency II. Where the ultimate parent of a (re)insurance undertaking or group has its head office outside the EEA, it is not possible for the EU to impose its rules on the country in which the head office of the parent is situated. In order to encourage third countries to adopt an equivalent group supervision regime, Omnibus II introduces the concept of "temporary equivalence", which is included in Art. 260 (5) FD.

Even where the assessment criteria in Art. 380 DA have not been met, the EC, assisted by EIOPA, may, for a limited period of time (until 31 December 2020),[42] adopt delegated acts determining that the prudential regime of a third country applicable to undertakings the parent undertaking of which has its head office

40 Commission Delegated Decision (EU) 2016/309 of 26 November 2015 on the equivalence of the supervisory regime for insurance and reinsurance undertakings in force in Bermuda to the regime laid down in Directive 2009/138/EC of the EP and of the Council and amending Commission Delegated Decision (EU) 2015/2290, *OJ* L 58, 4.3.2016, p. 50 and Commission Delegated Decision (EU) 2015/1602 of 5 June 2015 on the equivalence of the solvency and prudential regime for insurance and reinsurance undertakings in force in Switzerland based on Articles 172 (2), 227 (4) and 260 (3) of Directive 2009/138/EC of the EP and of the Council, *OJ* L 248, 24.9.2015, p. 95.

41 See, for instance, the Bilateral Agreement between the EU and the USA on prudential measures regarding insurance and reinsurance, in particular Art. 4.

42 The limited period ends on 31 December 2020 or on the date on which the prudential regime of the third country has been deemed to be equivalent, whichever is earlier. The period may be extended by a maximum of one more year where such time is necessary for EIOPA and the EC to carry out the equivalence assessment (Art. 260 (6) FD).

outside the EEA on 1 January 2014[43] is temporarily equivalent to the group supervision regime under Solvency II, if that third country has complied with at least the following criteria:

(a) it has given a commitment to the EU to adopt and apply a prudential regime that is capable of being assessed as equivalent in accordance with the assessment criteria in Art. 380 DA before 31 December 2020, and to engage in the equivalence assessment process;
(b) it has established a work programme to fulfil the commitment under point (a);
(c) it has allocated sufficient resources to fulfil the commitment under point (a);
(d) it has a prudential regime that is risk-based and establishes quantitative and qualitative solvency requirements and requirements relating to supervisory reporting and transparency and to the supervision of groups;
(e) it has entered into written arrangements to cooperate and exchange confidential supervisory information with EIOPA and supervisory authorities in EEA countries;
(f) it has an independent system of supervision;
(g) it has established obligations on professional secrecy for all persons acting on behalf of its supervisory authorities, in particular on the exchange of information with EIOPA and supervisory authorities in the EU.

As in the case of a full equivalence decision, a decision on temporary equivalence is taken by the EC by way of a delegated act. The delegated act may impose further conditions, such as a timeline or additional supervisory reporting requirements during the period of temporary equivalence. The delegated act must be reviewed regularly by the EC, on the basis of progress reports by the relevant third country, which must be presented to and assessed by the EC annually, with the assistance of EIOPA.

In taking a decision on temporary equivalence, the EC needs to take account of the way in which EU (re)insurance undertakings are treated in the third country concerned, in terms of freedom of establishment, the acquisition of holdings in (re)insurance undertakings, the pursuit of (re)insurance activities and the provision of cross-border (re)insurance services. The EC must periodically report to the Council on such treatment (Art. 177 (2) FD). This is a remainder from the reciprocity clause that is usually included in international agreements.

Where a third country's supervisory regime on group supervision has been determined to be temporarily equivalent to the group supervision regime under

[43] A date was inserted in order to prevent groups from reorganising themselves in order to benefit from temporary equivalence.

Solvency II, Member States must rely on the equivalent group supervision exercised by the third-country supervisory authority, unless there is a (re)insurance undertaking in the EEA with a balance sheet total that exceeds the balance sheet total of the parent undertaking situated outside the EU. In that case, the supervisory authority of the undertaking with the larger balance sheet total must act as the group supervisor.

The provisions on supervisory cooperation and the college of supervisors apply mutatis mutandis (Arts. 260 (7) and 261 FD).

No decision on temporary equivalence has yet been taken in the case of third-country parent undertakings with subsidiaries in EEA countries.

3.3. ABSENCE OF EQUIVALENCE

In the absence of equivalent group supervision, the Solvency II provisions on group solvency are applied to the extent possible at the level of the ultimate third-country parent undertaking by the EEA supervisory authorities concerned through the EEA insurance undertakings supervised by them (Art. 262 (1) FD). The same applies where there is temporary equivalence but a MS does not rely on the equivalent group supervision exercised by the third-country supervisory authority because the balance sheet total of the (re)insurance undertaking under its supervision is larger than that of the third-country parent (Art. 260 (7) FD).

Alternatively,[44] other methods may be applied, with the agreement of the group supervisor following consultation of the other supervisory authorities concerned. The most obvious solution is the requirement for the third-country parent undertaking to establish an insurance holding company or a mixed financial holding company in the EEA and to apply the group supervision provisions to the (re)insurance undertakings in the group controlled by that holding company. The method chosen must allow the objectives of group supervision to be achieved and must be notified to the other supervisory authorities concerned and to the EC (Art. 262 (2) FD).

4. THIRD-COUNTRY REINSURANCE UNDERTAKINGS

Reinsurance is by definition an international activity. Reinsurance allows risk to also be diversified geographically.[45] This is the reason why Art. 50 Reinsurance

[44] For instance, where there is no group as defined in Art. 213 (2) (a) or (b) FD within the EEA.

[45] The importance of reinsurance for managing catastrophe risk is underlined in a recent report from the OECD, which observes that "rather than to impose regulatory or supervisory burdens on reinsurers (such as the imposition of a requirement to post collateral), other approaches, such as ensuring that reinsurers are appropriately supervised in their home jurisdiction and

Directive already provided for the possibility for the EU to conclude agreements with one or more third countries in order to facilitate reinsurance operations internationally.

Art. 175 FD includes a similar provision allowing the EC to submit proposals to the Council for the negotiation of agreements with one or more third countries regarding the means of exercising supervision over third-country reinsurance undertakings that conduct reinsurance business in the EU and EU reinsurance undertakings that conduct reinsurance business in the territory of a third country.

The objective of these agreements is to ensure, under conditions of equivalence of prudential regulation, effective market access for reinsurance undertakings in the territory of each contracting party and to provide for mutual recognition of supervisory rules and practices on reinsurance. The agreements should also seek to ensure that NSAs of the Member States are able to obtain the information necessary for the supervision of reinsurance undertakings that have their head offices situated in the EU and conduct business in the territory of third countries, and that the supervisory authorities of third countries are able to obtain the information necessary for the supervision of reinsurance undertakings that have their head offices situated within their territories and conduct business in the EU.[46]

One such international agreement has so far been concluded: the Covered Agreement between the EU and the USA on prudential measures regarding insurance and reinsurance (see above, Chapter 9, section 12), which includes provisions (Art. 3) requiring the states within the USA to adopt reinsurance reforms which will remove collateral or local presence requirements (establishment of a branch) for EU reinsurers that meet the prescribed minimum conditions within 60 months (five years). The agreement also involves the abolition by EU Member States of collateral[47] or local presence requirements[48] for US reinsurers operating in the EU.

---

enhancing supervisory cooperation and information exchange across jurisdictions, might offer a better means to ensuring that counterparty and execution risks related to cross-border reinsurance are properly managed while reflecting the global nature of reinsurance markets". OECD, *The Contribution of Reinsurance Markets to Managing Catastrophe Risk*, www.oecd.org/finance/the-contribution-of-reinsurance-markets-to-managing-catastrophe-risk.pdf, 2018, p. 3.

46 Reference is made to "the Community" because the article has been copied from the Reinsurance Directive, which referred to "the Community" instead of "the European Union".

47 Portugal requires the posting of collateral for reinsurers from non-equivalent jurisdictions, such as the USA.

48 Austria, Belgium, Germany and Poland require reinsurers from non-equivalent jurisdictions, such as the USA, to establish a branch in their country. See Global Reinsurance Forum, *Reinsurance trade barriers and market access issues worldwide*, July 2018, 39 p., http://www.grf.info/images/Publications/TradeBarriers/300718_GRF-Reinsurance-Trade-Barriers.pdf. This requirement will have to be abolished as part of the implementation of the Covered Agreement.

The importance of this bilateral agreement cannot be underestimated. For years, the EC discussed with US authorities, including the NAIC, the possibility of abolishing the collateral requirement imposed on non-US reinsurers, which was seen by many EU reinsurers as an unjustified regulatory burden, particularly for those reinsurers that were well capitalised. US ceding insurers opposed the abolition of the collateral requirement, arguing that maintaining this requirement was in the interest of policyholders, as the collateral was a guarantee in case the reinsurer were to fail to honour its commitments. Although some states in the USA had already reduced the collateral requirement for EU reinsurers, and although in 2011 the NAIC had adopted revisions to the Credit for Reinsurance Model Law and the Credit for Reinsurance Model Regulation that reduced collateral requirements for certified reinsurers licensed and domiciled in qualified jurisdictions, it was clear that it would be a long time before collateral requirements for EU reinsurers would ultimately be abolished by all states in the USA.[49] It now appears that even the Covered Agreement is more difficult to implement than expected, as the agreement is not self-implementing and requires action from the 50 states through amendments to their local credit for reinsurance regulations. If the laws for each state do not meet the terms of the Covered Agreement before 22 September 2022, the US Treasury will have to call on Congress to pass legislation that would pre-empt state law.[50]

4.1. FULL EQUIVALENCE

4.1.1. Principle

The EC, assisted by EIOPA, may determine that the solvency regime of a third country that applies to reinsurance activities of undertakings[51] with their head office in that country is equivalent to Solvency II. Such determination is only possible if the solvency regime of that third country meets the assessment criteria included in Art. 378 DA.[52] The assessment criteria in Art. 378 DA are

[49] For background information on the issue of collateral requirements imposed on non-US reinsurers, see HALL, D.J. and BERSET, J., Toward Global Reinsurance Regulation, in KEMPLER, C., FLAMEE, M., YANG, C.H. and WINDELS, P. (Eds.), *Global Perspectives on Insurance Today*, Palgrave Macmillan, New York, 2013, pp. 93–96.

[50] THIND, S., US-EU covered agreement: a rocky road to implementation, *Insurance ERM*, 27 November 2018. See also, the press statement by the NAIC of 28 January 2019, https://www.naic.org/cipr_topics/topic_covered_agreement.htm.

[51] The undertaking may be an insurance undertaking that is authorised to carry out reinsurance activities or a reinsurance undertaking.

[52] As the assessment can only be made by the EC and not by a supervisory authority as is the case in the other situations where equivalence is assessed, the development of assessment criteria at EU level was mandatory. See Art. 172 (1) FD.

based upon advice provided to the EC by CEIOPS. The determination is made in a delegated act adopted by the EC.

Where the solvency regime of a third country has been determined to be equivalent to Solvency II, reinsurance contracts concluded with undertakings with their head office in that third country are treated in the same manner as reinsurance contracts concluded with undertakings authorised in accordance with the FD (Art. 172 (3) FD).[53] This makes the conclusion of such reinsurance contracts cheaper, as capital requirements in the counterparty default risk module are lower. Member States are also forbidden from imposing a collateral requirement on reinsurance undertakings from that third country (Art. 173 FD).

4.1.2. *Assessment Criteria*

The following criteria must be considered in assessing whether the solvency regime that applies to reinsurance activities carried out by undertakings with their head office in a third country is equivalent to Solvency II:[54]

(a) whether the supervisory authorities have the power, by law or regulation, to effectively supervise domestic insurance undertakings carrying out reinsurance activities or reinsurance undertakings and to impose sanctions or take enforcement action where necessary;
(b) whether the supervisory authorities have the necessary means, relevant expertise, capacities (including financial and human resources) and mandate to effectively protect policyholders and beneficiaries, regardless of their nationality or place of residence;
(c) whether the supervisory authorities of that third country, in the exercise of their general duties, duly consider the potential impact of their decisions on the stability of financial systems globally, particularly during emergency situations, on the basis of the information available at that time;
(d) whether the supervisory authorities of that third country take into account the potential pro-cyclical effects of their actions where exceptional movements in the financial markets occur;
(e) whether the taking-up of the business of reinsurance in that third country is subject to prior authorisation conditional on a clear, objective and publicly available set of written standards;
(f) whether the solvency regime of that third country requires domestic (re)insurance undertakings carrying out reinsurance activities to have

---

[53] See, for instance, Art. 199 (6) DA.

[54] Reference is made to Title I FD, which is very broad and covers all general rules on the taking-up and pursuit of direct insurance and reinsurance activities, including the provisions on solvency, including the three pillars. This explains the length of the assessment criteria.

an effective system of governance in place which provides for sound and prudent management of the business and prescribes all of the following:
- (i) the existence of an adequate, transparent organisational structure with a clear allocation and appropriate segregation of responsibilities;
- (ii) requirements for ensuring that persons who effectively run the undertaking are fit and proper;
- (iii) the existence of effective processes to ensure the timely transmission of information both within the undertaking and to the relevant supervisory authorities;
- (iv) requirements for ensuring that the outsourced functions or activities are effectively supervised;

(g) whether the solvency regime requires domestic (re)insurance undertakings carrying out reinsurance activities to have an effective risk management system in place comprising all of the following:
- (i) strategies, processes and internal reporting procedures necessary to identify, measure, monitor, manage and report risks, to which the undertaking is or could be exposed, at an individual and an aggregated level and on a continuous basis, and their interdependencies;
- (ii) an effective internal control system;

(h) whether the solvency regime requires domestic (re)insurance undertakings carrying out reinsurance activities to establish and maintain effective risk management, compliance, internal audit and actuarial functions;

(i) whether the solvency regime requires domestic (re)insurance undertakings carrying out reinsurance activities to:
- (i) provide third-country supervisory authorities with any information necessary for the purposes of supervision;
- (ii) disclose publicly, on at least an annual basis, a report on their solvency and financial condition;

(j) whether the solvency regime requires that proposed changes to the business policy or management of domestic (re)insurance undertakings carrying out reinsurance activities, or to qualifying holdings in such undertakings, are consistent with maintaining a sound and prudent management of those undertakings;

(k) whether the assessment of the financial position of domestic (re)insurance undertakings carrying out reinsurance activities relies on sound economic principles and whether solvency requirements are based on an economic valuation of all assets and liabilities;

(l) whether the solvency regime of that third country requires domestic (re)insurance undertakings carrying out reinsurance activities to hold adequate financial resources, including all of the following requirements:
- (i) technical provisions are established with respect to all reinsurance obligations towards policyholders and beneficiaries of reinsurance contracts;

(ii) assets held to cover technical provisions are invested in the best interests of policyholders and beneficiaries, taking into account any disclosed policy objective;
(iii) investments are only made in assets and instruments whose risks the undertaking can properly identify, measure, monitor, manage, control and report;
(iv) capital requirements are set at a confidence level equivalent to that established under Solvency II, which ensures that in the event of significant losses policyholders and beneficiaries are adequately protected and continue to receive payments as they become due;
(v) a minimum level of capital is maintained and non-compliance with it triggers immediate and ultimate supervisory intervention;
(vi) capital requirements are met with own funds that are of sufficient quality and are able to absorb significant losses, and own-fund items considered by the supervisory authorities to be of high quality must be able to absorb losses both as a going concern and in the event of a winding-up;

(m) whether the capital requirements are risk-based, with the objective of capturing quantifiable risks, and where a significant risk is not quantifiable and cannot be captured in the capital requirements, that risk is addressed through another supervisory mechanism;
(n) whether the solvency regime ensures timely intervention by supervisory authorities in the event that the solvency capital requirement applicable in the third country is not complied with;
(o) whether the solvency regime provides that all persons who are working or who have worked for the supervisory authorities of that third country, as well as auditors and experts acting on behalf of those authorities, are bound by obligations of professional secrecy and whether such obligations of professional secrecy extend to information received from all supervisory authorities;
(p) whether the solvency regime provides that, without prejudice to cases covered by criminal law, any confidential information received by persons who are working or who have worked for the supervisory authorities of that third country is not divulged to any person or authority whatsoever, except in summary or aggregate form, such that individual (re)insurance undertakings cannot be identified;
(q) whether the solvency regime provides that, where a (re)insurance undertaking has been declared bankrupt or is being compulsorily wound up, confidential information that does not concern third parties involved in attempts to rescue that undertaking may be divulged in civil or commercial proceedings;

(r) whether third-country supervisory authorities that receive confidential information from supervisory authorities only use that information in the course of their duties and for any of the following purposes:
    (i) to check that the conditions governing the taking-up of business of reinsurance, system of governance and public disclosure and solvency assessment have been met;
    (ii) to impose sanctions;
    (iii) in administrative appeals against decisions of the supervisory authorities;
    (iv) in court proceedings relating to the solvency regime in that third country;
(s) whether third-country supervisory authorities are permitted to exchange information received from supervisory authorities, in the discharge of their supervisory functions or the detection and investigation of breaches of company law, with other authorities, bodies or persons where that authority, body or person is subject to the obligation of professional secrecy in the relevant third country and whether that information is only disclosed once the express agreement of the supervisory authority from which it originates has been obtained and, where appropriate, has been obtained solely for the purposes for which the authority gave its agreement.

The EC can only adopt a delegated act determining that a third country's solvency regime applicable to reinsurance activities of undertakings with their head office in that country is equivalent to Solvency II when the assessment criteria are met.

Two full equivalence decisions have been taken so far, for Bermuda and Switzerland.[55]

4.2. TEMPORARY EQUIVALENCE

Even where the assessment criteria in Art. 378 DA have not been met, the EC, assisted by EIOPA, may, for a limited period of time (until 31 December 2020),[56]

---

55 Commission Delegated Decision (EU) 2016/309 of 26 November 2015 on the equivalence of the supervisory regime for insurance and reinsurance undertakings in force in Bermuda to the regime laid down in Directive 2009/138/EC of the EP and of the Council and amending Commission Delegated Decision (EU) 2015/2290, *OJ* L 58, 4.3.2016, p. 50 and Commission Delegated Decision (EU) 2015/1602 of 5 June 2015 on the equivalence of the solvency and prudential regime for insurance and reinsurance undertakings in force in Switzerland based on Articles 172 (2), 227 (4) and 260 (3) of Directive 2009/138/EC of the EP and of the Council, *OJ* L 248, 24.9.2015, p. 95.

56 The limited period ends on 31 December 2020 or on the date on which the prudential regime of the third country has been deemed to be equivalent, whichever is earlier. The period may be extended by a maximum of one more year where such time is necessary for EIOPA and the EC to carry out the equivalence assessment (Art. 172 (5) FD).

adopt delegated acts determining that the solvency regime of a third country applicable to reinsurance activities carried out by undertakings with their head office in that country is temporarily equivalent to Solvency II, if that third country has complied with at least the following criteria:

(a) it has given a commitment to the EU to adopt and apply a solvency regime that is capable of being assessed as equivalent in accordance with the assessment criteria in Art. 378 DA before 31 December 2020, and to engage in the equivalence assessment process;
(b) it has established a work programme to fulfil the commitment under point (a);
(c) it has allocated sufficient resources to fulfil the commitment under point (a);
(d) it has a solvency regime that is risk-based and establishes quantitative and qualitative solvency requirements and requirements relating to supervisory reporting and transparency and to the supervision of groups;
(e) it has entered into written arrangements to cooperate and exchange confidential supervisory information with EIOPA and supervisory authorities in EEA countries;
(f) it has an independent system of supervision;
(g) it has established obligations on professional secrecy for all persons acting on behalf of its supervisory authorities, in particular on the exchange of information with EIOPA and supervisory authorities in the EU.

As in the case of a full equivalence decision, a decision on temporary equivalence is taken by the EC by way of a delegated act. The delegated act may impose further conditions, such as a timeline. The delegated act must be reviewed regularly by the EC, on the basis of progress reports provided by the relevant third country, which must be presented to and assessed by the EC annually, with the assistance of EIOPA.

In taking a decision on temporary equivalence, the EC needs to take account of the way in which EU (re)insurance undertakings are treated in the third country concerned, in terms of freedom of establishment, the acquisition of holdings in (re)insurance undertakings, the pursuit of (re)insurance activities and the provision of cross-border (re)insurance services. The EC must periodically report to the Council on this treatment (Art. 177 (2) FD). This is a remainder from the reciprocity clause that is usually included in international agreements.

Where the solvency regime of a third country has been deemed to be temporarily equivalent to Solvency II, reinsurance contracts concluded with undertakings with their head office in that third country are treated in the same manner as reinsurance contracts concluded with undertakings authorised in accordance with (EEA) (re)insurance undertakings (Art. 172 (6) FD).[57] Member States are also forbidden from imposing a collateral requirement on reinsurance undertakings from that third country (Art. 173 FD).

A temporary equivalence decision has been taken so far for one country: Japan.[58] It ends on 31 December 2020, unless before that time the Japanese solvency regime is recognised as fully equivalent to Solvency II. The decision can be extended by one year, where necessary for EIOPA and the EC to carry out a full equivalence assessment (Art. 172 (5) FD). This would cover the scenario in which Japan were to adopt new legislation towards the end of 2020 and that legislation were to be so close to Solvency II that a full equivalence assessment would make sense.

The Japanese (re)insurance market is the second largest in the world (and the largest in terms of a market overseen by a single supervisor).[59] It is therefore not surprising that Japan was from the beginning a candidate for an equivalence assessment. The presence of Japanese (re)insurers in the EEA is increasing. This is particularly important for reinsurance. The recognition of (provisional) equivalence provides EEA (re)insurers with additional opportunities for risk diversification.

4.3. ABSENCE OF EQUIVALENCE

Reinsurance contracts concluded with a third-country undertaking carrying out reinsurance activities without equivalence recognition (full or temporary equivalence) are not dealt with under EU law but are a matter for Member States. Member States may decide that reinsurance undertakings established in non-equivalent countries may only conduct reinsurance business in the MS through a local branch.[60] In any case, the reinsurance transaction will incur a higher capital charge in the counterparty default risk module.

Member States may not apply to third-country reinsurance undertakings provisions which result in more favourable treatment than that granted to EU reinsurance undertakings (Art. 174 FD). They can continue to impose a collateral requirement (Art. 173 FD).[61]

As indicated above, Art. 175 FD provides for the possibility for the EU to conclude international agreements with one or more third countries to open up

---

57 See, for instance, Art. 199 (6) DA.

58 Commission Delegated Decision (EU)2016/310 of 26 November 2015 on the equivalence of the solvency regime for insurance and reinsurance undertakings in force in Japan to the regime laid down in Directive 2009/138/EC of the EP and of the Council, *OJ* L 58, 4.3.2016, p. 55.

59 EIOPA, Advice to the EC. Equivalence assessment of the Japanese supervisory system in relation to Art. 172 of the Solvency II Directive, EIOPA-BoS-11/029, p. 6.

60 This is the case in Austria, Belgium, Germany and Poland.

61 This is the case in Portugal.

the reinsurance market in cases where no equivalence decision has been taken. The bilateral agreement between the EU and the USA, referred to above, is the only international agreement concluded so far.

Figure 18. Overview of different equivalence regimes

	Full equivalence	Temporary equivalence	Provisional equivalence
EEA (re)insurance group with subsidiaries in third countries	Art. 227 (4) FD	NA	Art. 227 (5) FD
Third country (re)insurance group with EEA subsidiaries	Art. 260 (3) FD	Art. 260 (5) FD	NA
Third country reinsurance undertaking with EEA activities	Art. 172 (2) FD	Art. 172 (4) FD	NA

Source: Produced by the author.

5. BERMUDA AND SWITZERLAND

It is not possible within the context of this book to examine in detail the relevant insurance regulation in Bermuda and in Switzerland. However, these two countries, which are so far the only countries that have obtained a full equivalence decision under each relevant article in the FD, merit at least some comments.

5.1. BERMUDA

For people not familiar with the international insurance market, it might seem strange that a country as small as Bermuda should be one of two third countries whose solvency regime has been considered equivalent to Solvency II.

However, Bermuda's role in (re)insurance cannot be underestimated. Thirteen of the world's top 40 reinsurers are based in Bermuda. As early as 2008, Bermuda reinsurers assumed approximately half of the insurance ceded cross-border by US insurers, and over a quarter of Lloyds' premiums. For the period between 1997 and 2016, claims paid by Bermuda (re)insurers to EU policyholders and ceding insurers amounted to $72.8 billion.[62] There are

62 BMA, *Market Wide Survey on EU Claims History*, 2017. 96 Bermuda legal entity (re)insurers participated in the sample. In 2017, eight of the largest 50 reinsurance groups in the world were domiciled in Bermuda. See AM Best's Ranking of Top 50 World's Largest Reinsurance Groups by Premiums Written, 2017.

a number of reasons for this: a favourable tax regime, an environment with a high standard of living, a good location (less than two hours away by plane from New York and approximately six hours away from London) and an environment that enables the development of innovative ideas that have proven to be long-lasting, spanning from products such as captive insurance or insurance securitisations to risk management tools, such as economic capital and catastrophe models. Bermuda's insurance market has a strong focus on captive insurers and is a rapidly growing jurisdiction for insurance-linked securities (ILS).[63] Its market expertise lies in low frequency, high severity business lines. In addition to reinsurance, Bermuda's (re)insurance undertakings are active in professional liability insurance, including Directors and Officers (D&O) insurance, energy, natural disasters and terrorism risks.

Being strategically placed between the USA and Europe, the supervisory authority of Bermuda, the Bermuda Monetary Authority (BMA), wanted to establish a good relationship with the US supervisory authorities and with the EU. For the relationship with the USA it was important to obtain the status of qualified jurisdiction,[64] and for the relationship with the EU it was important to obtain equivalence status. The BMA worked hard to obtain this. In 2010, the BMA published a roadmap to regulatory equivalence with Solvency II, recognising the important relationship that existed between the Bermuda market and the insurance sector in Europe.[65] The BMA succeeded in its efforts, thanks to support from its government and from industry,[66] but also thanks to the leadership role played by its successive CEOs[67] and to the efforts of a highly qualified staff, many of whom are also very active within the IAIS. The pragmatism and accessibility of the BMA are often mentioned as key reasons that make Bermuda an attractive jurisdiction.[68]

---

63 See RAMELLA, M., The Regulatory Future of International Insurance Centres: Balancing Sound Supervision, Innovation and Competition, in LIEDTKE, P.M. and MONKIEWICZ, J. (Eds.), *The Future of Insurance Regulation and Supervision: A Global Perspective*, Palgrave Macmillan, Basingstoke, 2011, pp. 409–410. Catastrophe reinsurance is particularly important in Bermuda. See BMA, *Catastrophe risk in Bermuda. BSCR stress testing and modelling practice analysis: 2017 Report*, 30 November 2018, 51 p.

64 It has obtained this status. See the press statement by the NAIC of 28 January 2019: https://www.naic.org/cipr_topics/topic_covered_agreement.htm.

65 BMA, *Bermuda's Insurance Solvency Framework. The Roadmap to Regulatory Equivalence*, September 2010, 20 p.

66 The Association of Bermuda Insurers and Reinsurers (ABIR) has been very supportive throughout the equivalence discussions and has been an active respondent to all consultations issued by the EC and EIOPA in the context of Solvency II. ABIR organises a well-attended annual regulatory dialogue in Brussels for senior people from the regulatory and business community from EEA countries, from the USA and from Bermuda and this already more than 10 years.

67 Matthew Elderfield and Jeremy Cox.

68 See Insurance ERM, *The drivers behind Bermuda's thriving life re/insurance business*, 4 December 2018.

Obtaining equivalence status required amendments to the Insurance Act, the Insurance Code of Conduct, the Insurance Regulations and the Prudential Rules adopted by the BMA.[69] The whole process was carried out in close cooperation between the BMA and CEIOPS/EIOPA.

Because of its strategic importance for the EU, Bermuda was identified as one of three countries for which the EC asked CEIOPS to provide advice on whether its supervisory regime satisfied the general criteria for third-country equivalence. In a letter of 29 October 2010, the EC asked EIOPA to assess the Bermudian supervisory regime for equivalence under Arts. 172, 227 and 260 FD.[70] Following full consultation with stakeholders, EIOPA provided its advice to the EC in October 2011.[71] As the negotiations on Omnibus II were still ongoing, final conclusions on equivalence could not be drawn as the EU legislation was not yet in its final form. As soon as the debate on Omnibus II reached its final stage, the EC requested by letter of 25 February 2014 an update to the equivalence advice for Bermuda. In its updated advice delivered on 30 January 2015,[72] EIOPA concluded that Bermuda met the criteria set out in EIOPA's methodology for equivalence assessments under Solvency II, but with certain caveats. These caveats related primarily to the valuation standards (economic balance sheet),[73] which had not yet been fully implemented. By letter of 4 May 2015, the EC came back to EIOPA with a request for a further review, as Bermuda was making substantial amendments to its supervisory regime in order to address the issues raised by EIOPA in its earlier advice. Meanwhile, Bermuda was included in the list of third countries that had obtained provisional equivalence status under Art. 227 FD.[74]

In its final advice delivered to the EC on 31 July 2015,[75] EIOPA concluded that the caveats mentioned in its earlier advice had been suitably addressed.

---

69 In Bermuda, the Insurance Act lays down two capital requirements: the minimum solvency margin (MSM) and the enhanced capital requirement (ECR). The ECR is determined from the relevant Bermuda SCR standard formula or from the insurer's approved internal capital model provided that the ECR is at least equal to the insurer's MSM.

70 See CEIOPS, *Annual Report 2010*, pp. 34–35.

71 EIOPA, Advice to the EC. Equivalence assessment of the Bermudian supervisory system in relation to Arts. 172, 227 and 260 of the Solvency II Directive, EIOPA-BoS-11-029, 55 p.

72 EIOPA, Final Report on Public Consultation No 14/041. EIOPA Advice to the EC: Equivalence assessment of the Bermudian supervisory system in relation to Arts. 172, 227 and 260 of the Solvency II Directive, EIOPA-BoS-15/042, 30 January 2015, 89 p.

73 Other issues concerned outsourcing, public disclosure, the internal audit function, the actuarial function and the treatment of currency and concentration risk.

74 Commission Delegated Decision (EU) 2015/2290 of 12 June 2015 on the provisional equivalence of the solvency regimes in force in Australia, Bermuda, Brazil, Canada, Mexico and the United States and applicable to insurance and reinsurance undertakings with head offices in those countries, *OJ* L 323, 9.12.2015, p. 22.

75 EIOPA, Progress Report: Equivalence assessment of the Bermudian supervisory system in relation to Arts. 172, 227 and 260 of the Solvency II Directive, EIOPA-BoS-15/176, 31 July 2015, 19 p.

Bermuda was therefore granted full equivalence status under Arts. 172, 227 and 260 FD from 1 January 2016 onwards.[76]

From the EU point of view, two issues needed special consideration, i.e. the status of Bermuda as a British Overseas Territory and the multi-licence regime that categorises life and non-life insurers into classes. It was decided that the status of Bermuda as a British Overseas Territory did not prevent Bermuda from being considered a third country under the FD. Bermuda has its own government and its own legal framework. It is authorised to negotiate and conclude trade agreements related to the treatment of goods and services, as well as agreements for technical assistance or of a cultural or scientific nature. As far as the different classes of insurers are concerned, equivalence status was only granted for the solvency regime applicable to (re)insurance undertakings (Classes 3A (small commercial insurers), 3B (large commercial insurers), 4 (very large insurers and reinsurers), C (small long-term insurers), E (large long-term insurers) and D (very large long-term insurers)), with the exclusion of captives and special-purpose insurers.[77]

On 17 January 2017, EIOPA and the BMA signed a Memorandum of Understanding that provides the framework for regular exchanges of information, and sets forth the basis for further cooperation and increased mutual understanding with a view to ensuring optimal supervision for (re)insurance groups with international activities in the EU and Bermuda. The Memorandum is shorter than that concluded with the Swiss Financial Market Supervisory Authority (FINMA) and goes into less detail, both in terms of requests for assistance and confidentiality. EIOPA supports BMA's participation in the activities of the European supervisory colleges formed by the competent authorities in the EU when a Bermudian insurance undertaking is concerned. Similarly, the BMA supports EIOPA's participation in BMA's supervisory colleges where European (re)insurance undertakings are concerned.[78]

5.2. SWITZERLAND

The Swiss (re)insurance industry is very closely integrated with the EEA (re)insurance market.[79] Switzerland started the development of a new solvency

---

76 Commission Delegated Decision (EU) 2016/309 of 26 November 2015 on the equivalence of the supervisory regime for insurance and reinsurance undertakings in force in Bermuda to the regime laid down in Directive 2009/138/EC of the EP and of the Council and amending Commission Delegated Decision (EU) 2015/2290, *OJ* L 58, 4.3.2016, p. 50.

77 In 2017, 126 insurers were registered under Class 3A, 25 under Class 3B, 40 under Class 4, 94 under Class C, 10 under Class D, and 31 under Class E. There were 739 captives and 126 special purpose insurers. See BMA, *Annual Report 2017*, p. 54.

78 See the joint press release issued by EIOPA and the BMA on 17 January 2017: *EIOPA and the BMA sign a Memorandum of Understanding*.

79 This was the reason why an agreement was already concluded in 1989 between the EEC and Switzerland on opening up the market in direct insurance. This agreement allows non-life

regime, called the Swiss Solvency Test (SST), in 2003.[80] This new regime was based on the same principles underlying Solvency II, i.e. a total balance sheet approach with market-consistent valuation of assets and liabilities, risk-based capital requirements and a fully organised system of group supervision. The SST was introduced gradually and became mandatory in 2011.

It is therefore not surprising that Switzerland was one of the two third countries for which the EC asked CEIOPS to provide advice on whether its supervisory regime satisfied the general criteria for assessing third-country equivalence. In a letter of 29 October 2010, the EC asked EIOPA to assess the Swiss supervisory regime for equivalence under Arts. 172, 227 and 260.[81] Following full consultation with stakeholders, EIOPA provided its advice to the EC in October 2011. As the negotiations on Omnibus II were still ongoing, final conclusions on equivalence could not be drawn as the EU legislation was not yet in its final form. As soon as the debate on Omnibus II reached its final stage, the EC requested by letter of 25 February 2014 an update to the equivalence advice for Switzerland. In its updated advice delivered on 30 January 2015,[82] EIOPA concluded that Switzerland met the criteria set out in EIOPA's methodology for equivalence assessments under Solvency II, but with certain caveats. These caveats related mainly to the public disclosure requirements, which were not as extensive as those under Solvency II. The remaining issues were addressed by a revision of the Insurance Supervisory Ordinance (ISO), and Switzerland

insurance undertakings to branch into one jurisdiction from the other with greater ease, for instance, through mutual recognition of each other's solvency requirements. See, Agreement of 10 October 1989 between the EEC and the Swiss Confederation on direct insurance other than life assurance, *OJ* L 205, 27.7.1991, p. 3. The annexes and protocols to this agreement were amended in 2018, reflecting the accession of new Member States since 1989 and the adoption of Solvency II and of the Swiss Solvency Test. See, Decision No 1/2018 of the EU-Switzerland Joint Committee of 3 July 2018 amending the Annexes and Protocols to the Agreement between the EEC and the Swiss Confederation on direct insurance other than life assurance and finding that the domestic legislation of the Contracting Parties is compatible with that Agreement, *OJ* C 255, 20.7.2018, p. 9. With a view of Brexit, a bilateral agreement was signed between the UK and CH on 25 January 2019 which replicates the terms of the existing agreement between the EU and CH (https://www.gov.uk/government/publications/joint-statement-united-kingdom-and-the-swiss-confederation-sign-agreement-on-direct-insurance-other-than-life-assurance/joint-statement-on-signing-the-agreement-between-the-united-kingdom-and-the-swiss-confederation-on-direct-insurance-other-than-life-assurance).

80 See Swiss Federal Office of Private Insurance, *White Paper of the Swiss Solvency Test*, November 2004, which indicates on p. 8 that "it is an aim of the SST to be compatible with the future European Solvency II framework. This entails in particular that both a minimal solvency level and target capital have to be calculated and that internal models – provided they satisfy regulatory requirements – can be used for target capital calculation".

81 See CEIOPS, *Annual Report 2010*, pp. 34–35.

82 EIOPA, Final Report on Public Consultation No 14/041. EIOPA Advice to the EC: Equivalence assessment of the Swiss supervisory system in relation to Arts. 172, 227 and 260 of the Solvency II Directive, EIOPA-BoS-15/041, 30 January 2015, 70 p.

was granted full equivalent status under Arts. 172, 227 and 260 FD from 1 January 2016 onwards.[83]

Obtaining equivalence required amendments to the Swiss regulatory requirements on solvency, which are included in the following legal acts:[84] the Financial Market Supervisory Act (FINSAMA), the Insurance Supervision Act (ISA), the Ordinance on the Supervision of Private Insurance Companies, and the Insurance Supervision Ordinance (ISO-FINMA), and in circulars published by FINMA. In general, the requirements are less detailed[85] than those under Solvency II and there are some differences, such as the confidence level, which is set at 99% tail VaR instead of 99.5% VaR under Solvency II. Insurers are encouraged to use an internal model and reinsurers and groups are required to develop an internal model. Operational risk is not quantified but is addressed qualitatively through the Swiss Quality Assessment (SQA). The MCR for insurers varies under the SST, depending on the insurance business line.

The equivalence assessment was facilitated by excellent contacts between CEIOPS/EIOPA and the insurance department of the Swiss supervisory authority, FINMA.[86] Also useful was the informal regulatory dialogue held yearly between the EC and FINMA, very often in cooperation with EIOPA.[87] The Swiss insurance industry[88] strongly supported the equivalence discussions.

As early as 21 September 2012, EIOPA and FINMA signed a Memorandum of Understanding in order to ensure optimal cooperation in supervision, in particular for insurance groups with international activities in the EEA and in Switzerland. The Memorandum is more detailed than the Memorandum

---

83 Commission Delegated Decision 2015/1602/EU of 5 June 2015 on the equivalence of the solvency and prudential regime for insurance and reinsurance undertakings in force in Switzerland based on Arts. 172 (2), 227 (4) and 260 (3) of Directive 2009/138/EC of the European Parliament and of the Council, *OJ* L 248, 24.9.2015, p. 95.

84 *Bundesgesetz über die Eidgenössische Finanzmarktaufsicht*, 22 June 2007; *Bundesgesetz betreffend die Aufsicht über Versicherungsunternehmen (VAG)*, 17 December 2004; *Verordnung über die Beaufsichtigung von privaten Versicherungsunternehmen (AVO)*, 9 December 2005; and *Verordnung der Eidgenössisches Finanzmarktamt über die Beaufsichtigung von privaten Versicherunguntemehmen (AVO-FINMA)*, 9 November 2005.

85 See, for instance, FINMA Circular 2017/2, *Corporate governance – insurers*, 7 December 2016, which is only 7 pages, as compared with the EIOPA Guidelines on governance which is a document of 25 pages with a full report of over 100 pages.

86 An important role in the equivalence discussions was played by Monica Mächler, who was Vice-Chair and member of the FINMA Board of Directors and was Director of the Federal Office of Private Insurance before it was incorporated into FINMA.

87 See MÄCHLER, M., Versicherungsaufsicht in europäischer Dynamik, in NOTTER, M., WEBER, R.H., HEINEMANN, A. and BAUMGARTNER, T. (Eds.), *Europäische Idee und Integration – mittendrin und nicht dabei? Liber amicorum für Andreas Kellerhals*, Schulthess, Zürich/Basel/Geneva, 2018, pp. 352–353 and VAN HULLE, K., Rückblick und Ausblick auf die Versicherungsregulierung in der EU, in KELLERHALS, A. (Ed.), *Bilateralismus im multilateralen Europa. Referate zu Fragen der Zukunft Europas 2013*, Zürich, 2014, p. 78.

88 Many Swiss (re)insurers actively participated in the development of Solvency II by responding to consultations from the EC or EIOPA.

with the BMA. It creates a formal basis for cooperation in group supervision, sets out the participation in the activities of EEA colleges formed by the EEA authorities and Swiss colleges formed by FINMA, and deals with the exchange of information for macro-prudential (financial stability) purposes, such as monitoring and assessment of risks, interconnectedness and stress testing. It includes a procedure for requests for information and assistance and a chapter on permissible use of information and on confidentiality.[89]

6. COMMENTS ON THE EQUIVALENCE PROCESS

Because (re)insurance groups from EEA countries are important players in third countries and because the presence of third-country (re)insurance groups in EEA countries is increasing,[90] it is important to find an approach that allows supervision to take place under conditions that protect the rights of policyholders, without at the same time creating undue burdens on (re)insurance groups. Obviously, an international approach, whereby all major players in the world would apply the same standards, would provide the optimal solution. The IAIS has been working on a Common Framework for the Supervision of Internationally Active Insurance Groups (IAIGs) (ComFrame). It is also in the process of developing an international capital standard (ICS) that would be part of ComFrame and would apply to all IAIGs and G-SIIs. Version 2.0 of the ICS will be field-tested in 2019 and should be adopted together with ComFrame at the general meeting of the IAIS in November 2019. It will then be monitored for a period of five years before being fully adopted as a group-wide consolidated prescribed capital requirement (PCR). However, there are still a lot of concerns in the insurance industry about the proposed Version 2.0 of the ICS – as can be seen from some of the responses to the consultation launched by the IAIS[91] – and it remains to be seen whether all major economies in the world will adopt the ICS and ComFrame.[92]

---

89 See the joint press release issued by EIOPA and FINMA on 21 September 2012: *EIOPA and FINMA sign a Memorandum of Understanding.*

90 See, for instance, the acquisitions by Chinese insurers in Belgium, Germany, the Netherlands and Portugal.

91 IAIS, *Risk-based Global Insurance Capital Standard Version 2.0*, Public Consultation Document, 31 July 2018, 158 p., for which comments were due by 30 October 2018 (https://www.iaisweb.org/page/supervisory-material/insurance-capital-standard/file/76133/ics-version-20-public-consultation-document). See, for instance, the contributions from Insurance Europe (https://www.insuranceeurope.eu/sites/default/files/attachments/Response%20to%20IAIS%20consultation%20ICS%20version%202.0.pdf) and from the Geneva Association (https://www.genevaassociation.org/sites/default/files/research-topics-document-type/pdf_public//ga2013-ga-response-to-consultation-on-iais-comframe-for-supervision-of-iaigs.pdf).

92 Extensive information on ICS and ComFrame can be found on the website of the IAIS. Critical comments were made both in the EP and in the US Congress about the work of the

Equivalence might provide a temporary solution, but some improvements to the system are needed. This was no doubt the underlying thinking of the EC when it produced a paper on equivalence decisions in financial services.[93]

In its report on third countries and financial services,[94] adopted on 11 September 2018, ECON underlines the political nature of equivalence decisions and seems to give preference to international agreements over equivalence decisions as such agreements provide for reciprocity which is absent[95] in the case of unilateral equivalence decisions.[96] ECON emphasises that one of the key objectives of equivalence is to promote regulatory convergence on the basis of international standards and calls for the active involvement of the EC, the Member States and the ESAs in global standard-setting in order to work towards international consistency in financial regulation and to maximise financial stability, prevent regulatory loopholes between jurisdictions and develop an efficient international financial system.

6.1. NEED TO BE MORE PROACTIVE

Equivalence decisions are taken by the EC on the advice of EIOPA. EIOPA becomes active as soon as it has received a call for advice from the EC. EIOPA has developed a methodology that is very resource-intensive, using a large number of indicators (up to 300).[97]

IAIS on ComFrame and on ICS, as that work might result in standards that are in conflict with the regulatory framework in the EU and in the USA. See EP, Report on stocktaking and challenges of the EU Financial Services Regulation: Impact and the way forward towards a more efficient and effective EU framework for Financial Regulation and a Capital Markets Union, 2015/2106 (INI), 9 December 2015, presented by Burkhard Balz, which calls (para. 39) on "the Member States, the Council, the Commission and ESAs to streamline the EU position, with a view to increasing its influence and promoting the legislation it has adopted through a democratic process", http://www.europarl.europa.eu/sides/getDoc.do?pubRef=-//EP//TEXT+PV+20160118+ITEM-018+DOC+XML+V0//EN&language=EN. See also, EP, The EU's role in international economic for a, Paper 8: the IAIS, Study for the ECON Committee (author Lieve Lowet), August 2015, 88 p. (http://www.europarl.europa.eu/RegData/etudes/STUD/2015/542197/IPOL_STU(2015)542197_EN.pdf).

93 EC, Commission Staff Working Document: EU equivalence decisions in financial services policy: an assessment, SWD (2017) 102 final, 27 February 2017, 18 p.

94 See, the Report by Brian Hayes of 18 July 2018 on relationships between the EU and third countries concerning financial services regulation and supervision, A8-0263/2018, 4 p. (http://www.europarl.europa.eu/doceo/document/A-8-2018-0263_EN.html?redirect).

95 This is not entirely true, as indicated above. The EC is required to keep an eye on possible discriminations by third countries when taking its equivalence decisions. See also Art. 177 FD.

96 One should keep in mind that not all negotiations will go as smoothly as that concerning the bilateral agreement between the EU and the USA, which was the result of many years of discussions between the EC, EIOPA and the US authorities.

97 See Statement by Gabriel Bernardino, Chairman of EIOPA, before ECON on 9 March 2017, *Third-country equivalence: exchange of views with the EC and the ESAs*, p. 3 (https://eiopa.europa.eu/Publications/Speeches%20and%20presentations/Third-CountryEquivalencespeech.pdf).

An equivalence assessment may take up to 40/42 weeks and it is not easy for EIOPA to find the right experts from NSAs to devote the necessary time for carrying out the assessment. This may be one of the reasons why no further assessments have been conducted since the first wave of equivalence decisions. Another reason may of course be that the EC did not ask EIOPA to carry out further assessments. A wait and see attitude is not without problems. There are other countries in the world that have a solvency regime that is ready to be assessed for equivalence. These countries must of course be relevant from an EU point of view. Examples can be found in Latin America (Argentina, Chile), Asia (China,[98] Hong Kong, Singapore, South Korea) or even in Europe (the Balkan countries that are candidates for accession). Unless equivalence assessments are carried out, particularly for Asian countries, there is a risk that EEA operators will change their structures so as not to find themselves in a situation that is anti-competitive.[99]

6.2. NEED TO ADOPT A PARTNERSHIP APPROACH

Only two third countries have been granted full equivalence. It is astonishing that this has not led to these countries being treated as real partners, as belonging to the same family.[100] It is obviously in the interest of the EU and of the third countries concerned that optimal relationships be established between EIOPA and the NSAs of these countries and that regular meetings take place between EIOPA, FINMA and the BMA to exchange experience, to learn from each other and to think about improvements in the regulatory and supervisory regime.[101]

The assessment is particularly resource-intensive when solvency regimes are examined from third countries whose language is different from that of any EEA MS (for instance, Japan).

98 EIOPA has concluded a Memorandum of Understanding with the CIRC. See Memorandum of Understanding between the China Insurance Regulatory Commission (CIRC) and EIOPA, June 2016, 4 p. (https://eiopa.europa.eu/Publications/Protocols/2016-06-15%20EIOPA-CIRC%20MoU-EN.PDF). China has developed a risk-based solvency regime, called C-Ross. See VAN HULLE, K., *China is candidate for provisional equivalency under Solvency II*, Swiss Re Centre for Global Dialogue, 2014, 10 p.

99 See, for instance, the UK insurer Prudential, which moved to Hong Kong after a demerger. RALPH, O., Prudential to switch its main regulator to Hong Kong, *Financial Times*, 8 August 2018. See also, TANNER, C., *UK insurers emphasise post-Brexit opportunity*, Insurance ERM, 26 January 2017, 2 p. (https://www.insuranceerm.com/analysis/uk-insurers-emphasise-post-brexit-opportunity.html).

100 See also the Report by Brian Hayes of 18 July 2018 on relationships between the EU and third countries concerning financial services regulation and supervision, A8-0263/2018, para. 18 (http://www.europarl.europa.eu/doceo/document/A-8-2018-0263_EN.html?redirect).

101 The Memorandums of Understanding between EIOPA and FINMA and between EIOPA and the BMA foresee a joint annual meeting. However, a Memorandum of Understanding is not sufficient in this respect. As can be seen from the annual reports, EIOPA holds every year regulatory dialogues with third-country supervisory authorities, such as NAIC (USA), CIRC (China), JFSA (Japan) and ASSAL (Latin America).

The equivalence regime is set up as a one-way mechanism, i.e. only to serve the interests of the EU. This is too short-term an approach and is unlikely to be sustainable in the long term. When the EU is adapting the standard formula, as is presently the case, and even more so when work on a more substantial revision of Solvency II starts, as is now the case with the revision of the FD, the EU should liaise at least with the third countries that have been granted full equivalence, in order to see what the implications will be for those countries and which modifications they would favour.[102] After all, these countries apply a solvency regime that is to a large extent the same, meaning that common experiences can be shared.[103] The UK will occupy a particular position in this regard, once it will have become a third country after Brexit. This was already the subject of a debate in the House of Commons, during which a number of topics relating to Solvency were listed that could usefully be reviewed by the PRA in close collaboration with the UK insurance industry (including issues such as the risk margin, the MA, the VA, the transitional measures on technical provisions, contract boundaries, proportionality and internal model approval).[104] If the UK's solvency regime were to move away from Solvency II, it might become difficult to grant the UK full equivalence after Brexit. It would therefore be of interest to include the UK authorities in the discussions about the reform of the FD.

Full equivalence involves more than just a regular review of the third country's solvency regime.[105] It is also about cooperation and mutual trust. Art. 75 EIOPA Regulation includes the possibility for EIOPA to cooperate with third-country supervisory authorities and even for third-country supervisory authorities to be represented as an observer in meetings of the Board of Supervisors of EIOPA. Reference is made to those third countries whose regulatory regime has been recognised as equivalent. The text however seems to suggest that close cooperation with EIOPA requires the conclusion of an international agreement between the EU and the third country. This should not, however, prevent EIOPA from upgrading its relationship with full-equivalence third countries, even in the absence of such an international agreement.

---

102 In the same way, MÄCHLER, M., Versicherungsaufsicht in europäischer Dynamik, in NOTTER, M., WEBER, R.H., HEINEMANN, A. and BAUMGARTNER, T. (Eds.), *Europäische Idee und Integration – mittendrin und nicht dabei? Liber amicorum für Andreas Kellerhals*, Schulthess, Zürich/Basel/Geneva, 2018, p. 361.

103 In the case of the UK leaving the EU, it would be ill-conceived not to continue building on the good relationship that exists between EIOPA, its members and the UK supervisory authority (PRA).

104 See, House of Commons, Treasury Committee, *The Solvency II Directive and its impact on the UK Insurance Industry*, Third Report of Session 2017–2019, 25 October 2017, p.55 (https://publications.parliament.uk/pa/cm201719/cmselect/cmtreasy/324/324.pdf).

105 EIOPA has started its three-year re-assessment of the Bermudian and Swiss solvency regimes.

6.3. NEED FOR MORE TRANSPARENCY

It is unclear what strategy that the EC is pursuing in terms of equivalence and whether preference is given to a multilateral approach within the context of organisations such as the IAIS or to a bilateral approach with individual third countries.[106] Furthermore, a number of financial services regulatory dialogues take place regularly between the EC and third countries, such as China, India, Russia and the USA. Are topics such as equivalence assessments on the agenda? Is there an action plan?

Under Arts. 227 and 260 FD, the group supervisor or acting group supervisor, assisted by EIOPA, must assess the equivalence of the third country's solvency regime, in the absence of an equivalence decision by the EC. There is no information available on whether such assessments have taken place and what decision EIOPA has taken in this area. In the absence of an equivalence decision by the EC, an assessment by EIOPA at the request of the group supervisor might provide a flexible way forward.

106 See also the Report by Brian Hayes of 18 July 2018 on relationships between the EU and third countries concerning financial services regulation and supervision, A8-0263/2018, para. 12 (http://www.europarl.europa.eu/doceo/document/A-8-2018-0263_EN.html?redirect).

CHAPTER 11

EIOPA

EIOPA and its predecessor, CEIOPS, played a major role in the development and implementation of Solvency II. A detailed description of the role and competences of EIOPA goes beyond the objectives of this book.[1] However, a good understanding of Solvency II is not possible without having an insight in how EIOPA operates in the context of Solvency II and how EIOPA helps to shape the practical implementation and further development of Solvency II.[2]

1. FROM CEIOPS TO EIOPA

Following the proposals made by the Committee of Wise Men, chaired by Alexandre Lamfalussy,[3] the EC set up CEIOPS in 2003.[4] It was CEIOPS that was involved in the first development of Solvency II by offering technical advice to the EC (see above, Chapter 3). The members of CEIOPS were the NSAs of the EU Member States. The NSAs of the three EEA countries (Iceland, Liechtenstein and Norway) participated as observers.

The first chairman of CEIOPS was Henrik Bjerre-Nielsen, the Director-General of the Danish Financial Supervisory Authority (2003–2007), followed by Thomas Steffen, the Director of Insurance Supervision at BaFin (2007–2009), and then by Gabriel Bernardino, the Director-General of the Instituto de Seguros de Portugal (2009–2011). CEIOPS was established as an independent

---

1 For a description of the origin of EIOPA and its competences under the EIOPA Regulation, see HAGEN, B., *Ist die EU für eine zentrale Versicherungsaufsicht bereit?*, Dike, Zürich/St. Gallen, 2014, 362 p. Of particular importance is the role of EIOPA in consumer protection, for which it has received a specific mandate in the EIOPA Regulation. Another important task is the supervision of occupational pension funds (IORPs).

2 EIOPA publishes answers to questions from stakeholders on the application of the Solvency II regulatory framework on its website under the heading "Q&A Regulation".

3 *Final Report of the Committee of Wise Men on the Regulation of European Securities Markets*, 15 February 2001, 117 p.

4 Commission Decision 2004/6/EC of 5 November 2003 establishing the Committee of European Insurance and Occupational Pensions Supervisors, *OJ* L 3, 7.1.2004, p. 30.

body whose main role was to advise the EC. In 2009, its mandate was expanded.[5] CEIOPS had its seat in Frankfurt, initially in a building made at its disposal by BaFin. For members' meetings, CEIOPS had to move each time to another location in the region of Frankfurt, offered by the City of Frankfurt or by the State of Hessen until it was able to move to a proper building.[6] The EC was an observer at the meetings of the Managing Board and at the members' meetings. The working language was English.

The (part-time) Chairman was assisted by a (full-time) Secretary-General. The first Secretary-General was Alberto Corinti, a Director at the Italian Insurance Supervisory Authority (ISVAP) (2003–2007), who was succeeded by Carlos Montalvo, an insurance supervisor with the Spanish supervisory authority (DG SFP) (2007–2011). CEIOPS had a secretariat, initially comprised of four members. The number of staff increased to a total of 16 members in 2010.

In order to further transparency, CEIOPS was assisted by a Consultative Panel composed of representatives of stakeholder organisations. It also had a Review Panel, which organised peer reviews.

From its creation in 2003 until the transition to EIOPA in 2011, CEIOPS spent most of its time assisting the EC in the development of Solvency II.[7] An important event in that context were the annual conferences organised in Frankfurt at which an exchange of views took place with stakeholders about key issues relating to Solvency II.

Following a proposal from the EC on 23 September 2009 (see above, Chapter 3), EIOPA was established by a Regulation of 24 November 2010.[8] EIOPA started its work on 1 January 2011. Whilst in 2003 CEIOPS' main role had been to advise the EC, the EIOPA Regulation creates an independent body with a great deal of powers that is directly accountable to the EP and to the Council (Art. 3 EIOPA Regulation).

EIOPA has a full-time Chairman (Gabriel Bernardino) and Executive Director (Fausto Parente).[9] It has a Board of Supervisors, comprising high level

---

5 See Commission Decision 2009/79/EC of 23 January 2009, *OJ* L 25, 29.1.2009, p. 28, which repealed and replaced the Commission Decision of 2003.

6 Initially, some members' meetings were also held in other locations, such as the capital of Member States. Finding a suitable location was not easy as a normal members' meeting easily brings about 120 people around the table.

7 For more information, see the annual reports published by CEIOPS.

8 Regulation (EU) No 1094/2010 of the EP and of the Council of 24 November 2010 establishing a European Supervisory Authority (European Insurance and Occupational Pension Authority) amending Decision 716/2009/EC and repealing Commission Decision 2009/79/EC, *OJ* L 331, 15.12.2010, p. 8. A similar regulation was adopted for EBA and ESMA. Because the same basic text was used for the three ESAs, the text is sometimes fairly general and not specifically geared to the specific role of EIOPA.

9 Fausto Parente, Director of the Italian Insurance Supervisory Authority (IVASS), succeeded Carlos Montalvo in 2016.

representatives[10] of the NSAs[11] of the Member States of the EU.[12] The EC, as well as a representative from the ESRB and from EBA and ESMA, attend the meetings as observers (Art. 40 EIOPA Regulation). The Management Board is composed of the Chairman and six other members of the Board of Supervisors. The EC attends the meetings of the Management Board as an observer (Art. 45 EIOPA Regulation). Appeal against EIOPA decisions is possible under the conditions set out in Art. 60 EIOPA Regulation. The Board of Appeals, which is a joint body of the ESAs, is composed of six members and six substitutes (Art. 58 EIOPA Regulation). The NSAs of the three EEA countries (Iceland, Liechtenstein and Norway) participate in the work of EIOPA, without voting rights.

Cooperation between the ESAs takes place in the Joint Committee, which is composed of the Chairpersons of the ESAs (Art. 55 EIOPA Regulation). The Joint Committee is established as a joint forum in which the ESAs cooperate regularly and closely and ensure cross-sectoral consistency, for instance with regard to financial conglomerates. Positions of the Joint Committee can be of relevance for Solvency II.[13]

EIOPA is assisted by two Stakeholder Groups: the Insurance and Reinsurance Stakeholder Group (IRSG) and the Occupational Pensions Stakeholder Group (OPSG), which each comprise 30 members representing various stakeholders. The Stakeholder Groups must be consulted before the adoption of regulatory or implementing technical standards, guidelines and recommendations. They may also submit opinions or advice on any issue related to the tasks of EIOPA. The opinions and advice of the Stakeholder Groups are published on the website of EIOPA (Art. 37 EIOPA Regulation). This is also the case for the activity reports that the Stakeholder Groups produce at the end of their two-and-a-half-year mandates.

---

10 Art. 40 (1) EIOPA Regulation refers to "the head of the national public authority competent for the supervision of financial institutions in each Member State". This person must attend the meetings at least twice a year. This has proven difficult in practice, particularly for those authorities that are responsible for banking and insurance. Even the EC rarely sends a person of an equivalent level (that would have to be the Director-General of FISMA) to the meetings. The requirement is clearly unrealistic.

11 The EIOPA Regulation uses the term "competent authorities" because this is the term that was used in the IMD and in IORP I (see Art. 4 (2) EIOPA Regulation). In this book, we use the term "supervisory authorities" as this is the term used in the FD.

12 Representatives of the three EEA countries participate in the meetings but have no voting rights. This is based upon Art. 75 (1) EIOPA Regulation, which also provides the possibility for full equivalence third countries to participate in the work of EIOPA and to be represented in the Board of Supervisors.

13 See, for instance, the Consultation Paper on a draft implementing technical standards amending Implementing Regulation (EU) 2016/1800 on the allocation of credit assessments of external credit assessment institutions to an objective scale of credit quality steps in accordance with Directive 2009/138, JC/CP/2017/37, 18 July 2017, 23 p.

As the competences of EIOPA have expanded considerably, its staff has also increased. Starting with 27 members of staff in 2011, by 31 December 2017 EIOPA had 100 members of staff, 34 contract agents and 17 seconded national experts.

EIOPA has established itself as the technical adviser to the European institutions on matters concerning insurance and pensions. For instance, during the difficult discussions between the Council and the EP in the context of Omnibus II, the EP asked EIOPA (rather than the EC) to carry out an impact assessment of the LTG package. Similarly, the EC has turned to EIOPA for advice in a large number of cases, even when not specifically required to do so under the Solvency II FD. In turn, EIOPA has not hesitated to intervene when it felt that action was needed. The clearest example is the adoption of preparatory guidelines for Solvency II,[14] which followed an opinion issued on 20 December 2012 on interim measures regarding Solvency II,[15] urging NSAs to already put in place certain important aspects of Solvency II. This action was the follow-up to a letter written on 4 October 2012 by the Chair of EIOPA to the Omnibus II trilogue parties, setting out EIOPA's concerns about the status of the Omnibus II negotiations, which risked further delaying the application of the new solvency regime.[16]

The ESAs founding Regulations[17] required the EC to publish a general report early in 2014 on the experience acquired as a result of the operations of the ESAs and the procedures laid down in these Regulations. This report was presented by the EC on 8 August 2014,[18] based upon broad consultations with stakeholders, a self-assessment carried out by the ESAs,[19] a resolution of the EP on the ESFS review,[20] and studies undertaken by the IMF[21] and the EP.[22] The EC's review showed that overall the ESAs performed well. Nevertheless, a number of areas for improvement were identified. For instance, on financing, the report proposed reviewing the existing funding model, which is based upon a 60% contribution from the NSAs and a 40% contribution from the EU budget,

---

14 EIOPA, Guidelines on forward looking assessment of own risks (based on the ORSA principles), EIOPA-CP-13/09, 31 October 2013, 12 p.; EIOPA, Guidelines on pre-application of internal models, EIOPA-CP-13/011, 31 October 2013, 35 p.; EIOPA, Guidelines on system of governance, EIOPA-CP-13/08, 31 October 2013, 21 p.

15 EIOPA, Opinion on interim measures regarding Solvency II, EIOPA-12-388, 20 December 2012, 4 p.

16 https://eiopa.europa.eu/publictions/other-documents/index.html.

17 See, for instance, Art. 81 EIOPA Regulation.

18 EC, Report to the EP and the Council on the operation of the ESAs and the ESFS, COM (2014) 509 final, 8 August 2014, 14 p.

19 Joint Committee (JC 2012-100), *Self-Assessment Report of the ESAs*, 21 December 2012 (not public).

20 EP Resolution of 11 March 2014 with recommendations to the EC on the ESFS Review, 2013/2166 (INL), 18 p.

21 IMF, *Financial Sector Assessment Program at EU Level*, March 2013.

22 See PE 507.490 (on the ESRB) and PE 507.446 (on the ESAs), both of October 2013.

ideally by abolishing EU and national contributions and obtaining funding through direct payment from the supervised entities.

In a Communication of 20 September 2017,[23] the EC elaborated on a number of changes which it proposes to make to the ESA Regulations. These proposals were presented on the same day as the Communication and are commonly referred to as the ESFS review package. The package consists of four legislative proposals, i.e. three proposals for a regulation and one proposal for a directive, amending in total 13 existing legislative instruments:

- Proposal for a Regulation of the EP and of the Council amending Regulation (EU) No 1093/2010 of the EP and of the Council of 24 November 2010 establishing EBA; Regulation (EU) No 1094/2010 of the EP and of the Council of 24 November 2010 establishing EIOPA; Regulation (EU) No 1095/2010 of the EP and of the Council of 24 November 2010 establishing ESMA; Regulation (EU) No 345/2013 on European venture capital funds; Regulation (EU) No 346/2013 on European social entrepreneurship funds; Regulation (EU) No 600/2013 on markets in financial instruments; Regulation (EU) 2015/760 on European long-term investment funds; Regulation (EU) 2016/1011 on indices used as benchmarks in financial instruments and financial contracts or to measure the performance of investment funds; and Regulation (EU) 2017/1129 on the prospectus to be published when securities are offered to the public or admitted to trading on a regulated market;[24]
- Proposal for a Regulation of the EP and of the Council amending Regulation (EU) No 1092/2010 on European Union macro-prudential oversight of the financial system and establishing a ESRB;[25]
- Amendment of pending proposal for a Regulation amending Regulation (EU) No 1095/2010 establishing ESMA and amending Regulation (EU) No 648/2012 as regards the procedures and authorities involved for the authorisation of CCPs and requirements for the recognition of third-country CCPs (EMIR II Commission proposal);[26]
- Proposal for a Directive of the EP and of the Council amending Directive 2014/65/EU on markets in financial instruments and Directive 2009/138/EC on the taking-up and pursuit of the business of Insurance and Reinsurance (Solvency II).[27]

---

23 EC, Communication to the EP, the European Council, the Council, the ECB, the Economic and Social Committee and the Committee of the Regions on Reinforcing integrated supervision to strengthen Capital Markets Union and financial integration in a changing environment, COM (2018) 645 final, 20 September 2017, 13 p.

24 COM (2017) 536 final, 20 September 2017, 283 p.

25 COM (2017) 538 final, 20 September 2017, 11 p.

26 COM (2017) 539 final, 20 September 2017, 3 p.

27 COM (2017) 537 final, 20 September 2017, 14 p.

On 12 September 2018, the EC published an amendment to the pending 2017 proposal in order to adapt the ESA regulations to recent developments in the area of anti-money laundering and counter-terrorist financing.[28]

As far as insurance is concerned, the EC wants to give EIOPA a stronger role in promoting convergence in the validation of internal models that (re)insurance undertakings use to calculate the SCR. This will help overcome fragmentation and ensure better and more integrated supervision of large cross-border insurance groups. Despite ongoing work by EIOPA on supervisory convergence in internal models, major inconsistencies remain in the requirements of NSAs for internal models across the EU. The proposed Directive gives EIOPA a greater role with regard to internal model application and comprises changes to the FD with respect to information sharing regarding internal model applications, the possibility for EIOPA to issue opinions in relation to internal model application, as well as the possibility for EIOPA to assist in the settlement of disputes in this area between NSAs, either at their request, on its own initiative or, in certain circumstances, at the request of the undertakings concerned. EIOPA is also asked to prepare annual reports on internal model applications which should allow close monitoring of the situation regarding internal model applications, including bringing to light any outstanding concerns with regard to supervisory convergence in this area. Based upon an amendment from the EP and in line with a specific request from EIOPA,[29] it is also envisaged that EIOPA's oversight of cross-border business will be strengthened (see below, section 2.2.3).

---

28 Amended Proposal for a Regulation of the EP and of the Council amending Regulation (EU) No 1093/2010 of the EP and of the Council of 24 November 2010 establishing a European Supervisory Authority (European Banking Authority); Regulation (EU) No 1094/2010 of the EP and of the Council of 24 November 2010 establishing a European Supervisory Authority (European Insurance and Occupational Pension Authority); Regulation (EU) No 1095/2010 of the EP and of the Council of 24 November 2010 establishing a European Supervisory Authority (European Securities and Markets Authority); Regulation (EU) No 345/2013 on European venture capital funds; Regulation (EU) No 346/2013 on European social entrepreneurship funds; Regulation (EU) No 600/2013 on markets in financial instruments; Regulation (EU) No 2015/760 on European long-term investment funds; Regulation (EU) 2016/1011 on indices used as benchmarks in financial instruments and financial contracts or to measure the performance of investment funds; Regulation (EU) 2017/1129 on the prospectus to be published when securities are offered to the public or admitted to trading on a regulated market; and (EU) Directive 2015/849 on the prevention of the use of the financial system for the purposes of money-laundering or terrorist financing, COM (2018) 646 final, 12 September 2018, 288 p.

29 See, for instance, EIOPA, Report to the EC on Group Supervision and Capital Management with a Group of Insurance or Reinsurance Undertakings, and FoS and FoE under Solvency II, EIOPA BoS-18-485, 14 December 2018, pp. 108–120 and BERNARDINO, G., *Insurance and pensions: securing the future*, 8th Annual Conference, Frankfurt, 20 November 2018, p.6, listing the detection of unsustainable cross-border business models, the sufficiency of technical provisions in cross-border business and fit and proper analysis, as priorities for cross-border supervision (https://eiopa.europa.eu/Publications/Speeches%20and%20presentations/2018-11-20%20KeynoteSpeechAnnualConferenceGabrielBernardino.pdf).

All ESAs, including EIOPA will have to set EU-wide priorities for supervision in the form of a strategic supervisory plan against which all NSAs will be assessed. NSAs will be required to draw up annual work programmes in line with the strategic plan. Regarding funding, the EC proposes that for each ESA a maximum of 40% of the funding should come from the general budget of the EU, while the rest should come from industry through fees, voluntary contributions and charges for publications and training. In terms of governance, it is proposed to create in each ESA an independent executive board with full-time members that should ensure effective, impartial and EU-oriented decisions with regard to the coordination of supervisory practices.

The ESFS review package has been discussed in trilogue between the EP[30] and the Council.[31] An agreement was reached in March 2019, which confirms the enhanced role of EIOPA in the approval of internal models and in the oversight of cross-border business.

2. POWERS OF EIOPA

The tasks and powers of EIOPA are set out in Art. 8 EIOPA Regulation:[32]

- to contribute to the establishment of high-quality common regulatory and supervisory standards and practices;
- to contribute to the consistent application of legally binding EU acts;
- to stimulate and facilitate the delegation of tasks and responsibilities among supervisory authorities;
- to cooperate closely with the ESRB;
- to organise and conduct peer review analyses of supervisory authorities;[33]
- to monitor and assess market developments in the area of its competence;
- to undertake economic analyses of markets;
- to foster the protection of policyholders and beneficiaries;
- to contribute to the consistent and coherent functioning of colleges of supervisors, the monitoring, assessment and measurement of systemic risk,

30 The position of ECON was adopted on 14 January 2019 and constitutes the basis for the negotiations with the Council in trilogue. See, Report by Othmar Karas and Pervenche Berès, A8-0013/2019, http://www.europarl.europa.eu/doceo/document/A-8-2019-0013_EN.pdf?redirect, 320 p.

31 The Council adopted its general approach in December 2018.

32 Art. 9 EIOPA Regulation includes other specific tasks related to consumer protection and financial innovation.

33 The EIOPA Regulation refers to "competent authorities" because this is the term used in the IDD, in FICOD, in IORP II and in other relevant legislative acts, such as Directive 2002/65/EC of the EP and of the Council of 23 September 2002 concerning the distance marketing of consumer financial services, *OJ* L 271, 9.10.2002, p. 16 and Directive 2005/60/EC of the EP and of the Council on the prevention of the use of the financial system for the purpose of money laundering and terrorist financing, *OJ* L 309, 25.11.2005, p. 15. See Art. 4 (2) EIOPA Regulation.

and the development of recovery and resolution plans, providing a high level of protection to policyholders and beneficiaries;
- to fulfil any other specific tasks set out in the EIOPA Regulation or in other legislative acts;
- to publish on its website, and to update regularly, information on (re)insurance undertakings in order to ensure information is easily accessible to the public;
- to take over, as appropriate, all existing and ongoing tasks from CEIOPS.

It is not possible, within the scope of this book, to cover in detail all of EIOPA's responsibilities. The emphasis is placed on EIOPA's tasks in relation to Solvency II. These tasks were considerably increased by Omnibus II, through an amendment of the FD, and they may be further expanded as part of the ongoing review of the ESFS, which is expected to be completed during the course of 2019.

2.1. REGULATORY POWERS

2.1.1. Regulatory and Implementing Technical Standards

An important task of EIOPA is the development of technical standards in the form of draft RTS and ITS, which become legally binding upon endorsement by the EC.

Art. 290 TFEU allows the EP and the Council to delegate to the EC the power to adopt "non-legislative acts of general application to supplement or amend certain non-essential elements of a legislative act". Non-legislative acts adopted by the EC in this way are called "delegated acts". As explained above (Chapter 3, section 4.3.6.1.1), the FD contains a number of provisions that empower the EC to adopt RTS by means of delegated acts under Art. 290 TFEU in order to ensure consistent harmonisation. As technical standards, RTS do not involve strategic decisions or policy choices (such decisions or choices must be made by the co-legislators) and the scope is clearly defined in the legislative act upon which they are based (for instance the FD).

Responsibility for implementing legally binding EU acts lies primarily with the Member States. However, where EU legislation requires uniform conditions for the implementation of an EU act, Art. 291 TFEU allows the EP and the Council to empower the EC to adopt an implementing act. Acts adopted by the EC on this basis are also called "delegated acts". As explained above (Chapter 3, section 4.3.6.1.2), the FD contains a number of provisions that empower the EC to adopt ITS by means of delegated acts under Art. 291 TFEU.

The difference between RTS and ITS is that RTS supplement or amend non-essential elements of the FD, whilst ITS aim at a uniform application of provisions in the FD (for instance, common templates or procedures).

RTS and ITS take the form of a Commission regulation so as to make them directly applicable (no transposition by Member States is necessary), thereby contributing to the creation of a single European rulebook.

Draft RTS and ITS are prepared by EIOPA, within the time set in the FD.[34] The procedure for the development of RTS and ITS is included in Arts. 10–15 EIOPA Regulation. In both cases, EIOPA must conduct an open consultation and carry out an impact analysis before submitting the draft text to the EC. The IRSG must give its opinion. The EC must forward the draft to the Council and to the EP and must decide within three months of receipt of the draft whether to endorse it.[35]

Once the EC has adopted an RTS, the EP and the Council may raise objections within a period of three months from the date of notification of its adoption by the EC. This period may be extended by three months on the initiative of the EP or the Council. In order to speed up the process, the co-legislators may agree a flexible procedure for early non-objection. This was the case for the DA, which had to enter into effect on 1 January 2016.

The situation is different in the case of ITS, as these are considered of a very technical nature. As soon as an ITS has been adopted by the EC, it can enter into effect and neither the EP nor the Council can raise objections.[36]

As explained above (Chapter 3, section 4.2), all RTS, which the FD required the EC to adopt, are included in the DA. The text is based on advice from EIOPA but was written by the EC.

EIOPA prepared a number of draft ITS, which were subsequently adopted by the EC as implementing regulations on the following topics:

- procedure for the approval of an internal model (Art. 114 (2) FD);[37]
- process to reach a joint decision on the application to use a group internal model (Art. 231 (4) FD);[38]
- procedures for supervisory approval to establish SPVs, for the cooperation and exchange of information between supervisory authorities regarding SPVs as well as to set out formats and templates for information to be reported by SPVs (Art. 211 (2) (a) and (b) FD;[39]

---

34 If EIOPA does not produce a draft RTS or ITS within the time limits set in the FD, the EC sets a new time limit or can produce the RTS without a draft from EIOPA. See Arts. 10 (2) and (3) and 15 (2) and (3) EIOPA Regulation. This has not happened yet.

35 The EC can decide not to endorse a draft RTS or ITS. It cannot change the content of a draft RTS or ITS without prior coordination with EIOPA. See Arts. 10 (1) and 15 (1) and (3) EIOPA Regulation.

36 As soon as the EC has received a draft ITS, it must send the draft to the EP and to the Council.

37 Commission Implementing Regulation (EU) 2015/460 of 19 March 2015, *OJ* L 76, 20.3.2015, p. 13.

38 Commission Implementing Regulation (EU) 2015/461 of 19 March 2015, *OJ* L 76, 20.3.2015, p. 19.

39 Commission Implementing Regulation (EU) 2015/462 of 19 March 2015, *OJ* L 76, 20.3.2015, p. 23.

- supervisory approval procedure to use USPs (Art. 111 (2) FD);[40]
- procedures to be used for granting supervisory approval for the use of ancillary own-fund items (Art. 92 (3) FD);[41]
- procedures to be followed for the supervisory approval of the application of an MA (Art. 86 (3) FD);[42]
- lists of regional governments and local authorities, exposures to whom are to be treated as exposures to the central government (Art. 109a (2) (a) FD);[43]
- procedures for decisions to set, calculate and remove capital add-ons (Art. 37 (8), third subparagraph FD);[44]
- standard deviations in relation to health risk equalisation systems (Art. 109a (4), third subparagraph FD);[45]
- procedures and templates for the submission of information to the group supervisor and for the exchange of information between supervisory authorities (Art. 249 (4) FD);[46]
- procedures for assessing external credit assessments (Art. 44 (4a), fourth subparagraph FD);[47]
- equity index for the symmetric adjustment of the standard equity capital charge (Art. 109a (2) (b) FD);[48]
- adjusted factors to calculate the capital requirement for currency risk for currencies pegged to the euro (Art. 109q (2) (c) FD);[49]
- templates for the submission of information to the supervisory authorities (Arts. 35 (10), third subparagraph, 244 (6), third subparagraph, and 245 (6), second subparagraph FD[50]);

---

40 Commission Implementing Regulation (EU) 2015/498 of 24 March 2015, *OJ* L 79, 25.3.2015, p. 8.

41 Commission Implementing Regulation (EU) 2015/499 of 24 March 2015, *OJ* L 79, 25.3.2015, p. 12.

42 Commission Implementing Regulation (EU) 2015/500 of 24 March 2015, *OJ* L 79, 25.3.2015, p. 18.

43 Commission Implementing Regulation (EU) 2015/2011 of 11 November 2015, *OJ* L 295, 12.11.2015, p. 3.

44 Commission Implementing Regulation (EU) 2015/2012 of 11 November 2015, *OJ* L 295, 12.11.2015, p. 5.

45 Commission Implementing Regulation (EU) 2015/2013 of 11 November 2015, *OJ* L 295, 12.11.2015, p. 9.

46 Commission Implementing Regulation (EU) 2015/2014 of 11 November 2015, *OJ* L 295, 12.11.2015, p. 11.

47 Commission Implementing Regulation (EU) 2015/2015 of 11 November 2015, *OJ* L 295, 12.11.2015, p. 16.

48 Commission Implementing Regulation (EU) 2015/2016 of 11 November 2015, *OJ* L 295, 12.11.2015, p. 18.

49 Commission Implementing Regulation (EU) 2015/2017 of 11 November 2015, *OJ* L 295, 12.11.2015, p. 21.

50 Commission Implementing Regulation (EU) 2015/2450 of 2 December 2015, *OJ* L 347, 31.12.2015, p. 1.

- templates and structure for the disclosure of specific information by supervisory authorities (Art. 31 (5), third subparagraph FD);[51]
- procedures, formats and templates for the SFCR (Arts. 56, fourth paragraph, and 256 (5) FD);[52]
- procedures for the application of the transitional measure for the equity risk sub-module (Art. 308b (13), sixth subparagraph FD);[53]
- allocation of credit assessments of external credit assessment institutions to an objective scale of CQSs (Art. 109a (1) FD);[54]
- amendment and correction of the templates for the submission of information to the supervisory authorities (Arts. 35 (10), third subparagraph, 244 (6), third subparagraph, and 245 (6), second subparagraph FD);[55]
- amendment and correction of the templates for the submission of information to the supervisory authorities (Arts. 35 (10), third subparagraph, 244 (6), third subparagraph, and 245 (6), second subparagraph FD);[56]
- amendment and correction of the procedures, formats and templates for the SFCR (Arts. 56, fourth paragraph, and 256 (5) FD);[57]
- amendment of the allocation of credit assessments of external credit assessment institutions to an objective scale of CQSs (Art. 109a (1) FD);[58]
- amendment and correction of the procedures, formats and templates of the SFCR as regards the scope of application of the template for disclosing premiums, claims and expenses by country (Arts. 56, fourth paragraph, and 256 (5) FD);[59]
- amendment and correction of the templates for the submission of information to the supervisory authorities (Arts. 35 (10), third subparagraph, 244 (6), third subparagraph and 245 (6), second subparagraph FD).[60]

---

51 Commission Implementing Regulation (EU) 2015/2451 of 2 December 2015, *OJ* L 347, 31.12.2015, p. 1224.

52 Commission Implementing Regulation (EU) 2015/2452 of 2 December 2015, *OJ* L 347, 31.12.2015, p. 1285.

53 Commission Implementing Regulation (EU) 2016/1630 of 9 September 2016, *OJ* L 243, 10.9.2016, p. 1.

54 Commission Implementing Regulation (EU) 2016/1800 of 11 October 2016, *OJ* L 275, 12.10.2016, p. 19.

55 Commission Implementing Regulation (EU) 2016/1868 of 20 October 2016, *OJ* L 286, 21.10.2016, p. 35.

56 Commission Implementing Regulation (EU) 2017/2189 of 24 November 2017, *OJ* L 310, 25.11.2017, p. 3.

57 Commission Implementing Regulation (EU) 2017/2190 of 24 November 2017, *OJ* L 310, 25.11.2017, p. 30.

58 Commission Implementing Regulation (EU) 2018/633 of 24 April 2018, *OJ* L 105, 25.4.2018, p. 6.

59 Commission Implementing Regulation (EU) 2018/1843 of 23 November 2018, *OJ* L 299, 26.11.2018, p. 2.

60 Commission Implementing Regulation (EU) 2018/1844 of 23 November 2018, *OJ* L 299, 26.11.2018, p. 5.

2.1.2. *Guidelines and Recommendations*

EIOPA can issue guidelines and recommendations addressed to NSAs or to (re)insurance undertakings,[61] with a view to establishing consistent, efficient and effective supervisory practices (Art. 16 (1) EIOPA Regulation). It can do so on its own initiative or at the request of the co-legislators.

The FD provides for the adoption of guidelines by EIOPA only in very few instances, for example the specification of the methods to determine the market share in the case of an exemption from quarterly or item-by-item reporting (Art. 35 (11) FD),[62] or the specification of the regime to be applied in the case of a mixed financial holding company that is subject to equivalent provisions concerning risk-based supervision under the FICOD (Art. 213 (6) FD)[63] and the operational functioning of colleges of supervisors (Art. 248 (6) FD).[64]

This was intentional, as the co-legislators were afraid that the principles-based approach of Solvency II would be infringed by an overload of guidelines.[65] Most of the guidelines issued by EIOPA under Solvency II are therefore own-initiative guidelines. The guidelines are published on the website of EIOPA in all 24 official languages of the EU.

In order to facilitate the entry into force of the new solvency regime, to further supervisory convergence and to help ensure a uniform application of Solvency II, EIOPA decided to issue a large number of own-initiative guidelines. Although this is understandable, it nevertheless substantially increases the amount of "rules" with which undertakings and supervisory authorities have to comply. In a number of cases, the IRSG, which has to be consulted about each draft guideline proposed by EIOPA, referred to the risk of issuing so many

---

61 None of the guidelines developed by EIOPA under Solvency II specifically state that they are also addressed to (re)insurance undertakings, although it is clear that some guidelines (such as the guidelines on system of governance) are actually applicable to the undertakings themselves.

62 EIOPA, Guidelines on methods for determining the market shares for reporting, EIOPA-BoS-15/106, 14 September 2015.

63 These guidelines had to be developed by the Joint Committee. See Joint Committee of the ESAs, Guidelines on the convergence of supervisory practices relating to the consistency of supervisory coordination arrangements for financial conglomerates, JC/GL/2014/01, 22 December 2014.

64 EIOPA, Guidelines on operational functioning of colleges, EIOPA-BoS-14/146, 2 February 2015.

65 See EP, Report on stocktaking and challenges of the EU Financial Services Regulation: impact and the way forward towards a more efficient and effective EU framework for Financial Regulation and a Capital Markets Union, 2015/2106 (INI), 9 December 2015, presented by Burkhard Balz, which calls (para. 54) on "the ESAs to adopt a careful approach to the extent and number of guidelines, particularly where they are not explicitly empowered in the basic act", http://www.europarl.europa.eu/sides/getDoc.do?pubRef=-//EP//TEXT+PV+20160118+ITEM-018+DOC+XML+V0//EN&language=EN.

guidelines at the start of the new solvency regime. It was argued that it would be better to take stock of the experience in applying Solvency II before issuing detailed rules. This would allow all parties concerned to learn from experience. Particularly for the guidelines on governance, it was suggested that best practice guidance be issued first, before issuing detailed guidelines.

EIOPA decided to adopt a similar approach to the issuance of guidelines as that adopted for the preparation of draft ITS. The guidelines were therefore adopted in stages, with stage one comprising those guidelines that EIOPA considered particularly urgent in order to facilitate the transition to Solvency II and stage two comprising the other guidelines. The guidelines that were part of stage one were published in February 2015. The guidelines that were part of stage two were published in September 2015.

The following guidelines have been adopted in the context of Solvency II:
- contract boundaries (2 February 2015);
- valuation of technical provisions (2 February 2015);
- ancillary own funds (2 February 2015);
- classification of own funds (2 February 2015);
- ring-fenced funds (2 February 2015);
- treatment of related undertakings, including participations (2 February 2015);
- look-through approach (2 February 2015);
- basis risk (2 February 2015);
- application of outwards reinsurance arrangements to the non-life underwriting risk sub-module (2 February 2015);
- treatment of market and counterparty risk exposures in the standard formula (2 February 2015);
- health catastrophe risk sub-module (2 February 2015);
- LAC-DT (2 February 2015);
- USPs (2 February 2015);
- the SRP (2 February 2015);
- use of internal models (2 February 2015);
- group solvency (2 February 2015);
- methodology for equivalence assessments by NSAs under Solvency II (2 February 2015);
- reporting for financial stability purposes (14 September 2015);[66]
- extension of the recovery period in exceptional adverse situations (14 September 2015);
- reporting and public disclosure (14 September 2015);
- implementation of the LTG measures (14 September 2015);

66 These guidelines were amended twice: on 18 June 2017 and 25 June 2018.

- exchange of information on a systematic basis within colleges (14 September 2015);
- recognition and valuation of assets and liabilities other than technical provisions (14 September 2015);
- system of governance (14 September 2015);
- the ORSA (14 September 2015);
- supervision of branches of third-country insurance undertakings (23 October 2015);[67]
- facilitation of an effective dialogue between competent authorities supervising insurance undertakings and statutory auditor(s) and the audit firm(s) carrying out the statutory audit of those undertakings (2 February 2017).[68]

In developing guidelines, EIOPA must, where appropriate, conduct open public consultations and prepare an impact assessment, which must be proportionate to the scope, nature and impact of the guidelines. The IRSG must also be consulted (Art. 16 (2) EIOPA Regulation).

Guidelines are not legally binding. However, the NSAs to whom the guidelines are addressed must make every effort to comply with the guidelines (Art. 16 (3) EIOPA Regulation).[69] Within two months of the issuance of a guideline, each NSA must confirm that it complies or intends to comply with the guideline. In the event that a supervisory authority does not comply or does not intend to comply, it must inform EIOPA, stating the reasons (comply or explain).[70] For all guidelines issued by EIOPA in the context of Solvency II, NSAs have confirmed that they comply or intend to comply with the guidelines.[71] For each guideline, the website of EIOPA indicates whether NSAs have confirmed that they comply or intend to comply with the guideline (Art. 16 (3) EIOPA Regulation). Where an NSA has declared that it intends to comply with a guideline, it is unclear whether it has in the meantime complied, as no updates are given by EIOPA.[72]

Although guidelines are not legally binding, (re)insurance undertakings are in fact required to comply with them when they are enforced by NSAs, via administrative circulars or via transposition into national law.

---

67 These guidelines were amended twice: on 18 June 2017 and 12 July 2018.

68 These guidelines were issued on the basis of the specific mandate in Art. 12 (2) AR.

69 In accordance with Art. 71 (2) (b) FD, Member States must ensure that their supervisory authorities make every effort to comply with the guidelines issued by EIOPA.

70 See also Art. 71 (2) (b) FD.

71 An exception is, for instance, the guidelines on system of governance, where the ACPR (France) indicates that it does not comply with Guideline 14 on outsourcing of key functions.

72 See, for instance, the guidelines on system of governance, where for most of the guidelines the Danish supervisory authority indicated (13 November 2015) that it intends to comply and where the PRA (UK) indicated (12 November 2015) that it intends to comply with the guidelines on behalf of Gibraltar.

CEIOPS/EIOPA has only published a limited number of recommendations. Particularly relevant for Solvency II are the following recommendations:

- Recommendations (CEIOPS) regarding the implications of the IAS/IFRS introduction for the prudential supervision of insurance undertakings (September 2005);[73]
- Recommendations (CEBS and CEIOPS) on the supplementary requirements of the FICOD for supervisory colleges of financial conglomerates (21 December 2010);[74]
- Recommendations (EIOPA) for the insurance sector in light of the UK withdrawing from the EU (19 February 2019).[75]

2.2. SUPERVISORY POWERS

2.2.1. Representation in Colleges of Supervisors

As indicated above in Chapter 9, section 12, EIOPA has been a member of all colleges of supervisors since 1 January 2011 and participates in the activities of the colleges of supervisors, including on-site examinations, carried out jointly by two or more supervisory authorities. For that purpose, EIOPA is considered a supervisory authority (Art. 21 (1) and (2) EIOPA Regulation). The fact that EIOPA is considered a supervisory authority for the purpose of its participation as a member of the college does not mean that EIOPA carries out direct supervision. This is the task of the NSAs. EIOPA participates in the direct oversight of cross-border groups and plays a coordinating role. EIOPA has developed annual action plans for colleges since 2010.[76] The representative of EIOPA in the college of supervisors does not lead the debate. This is the task of the group supervisor. EIOPA's role is to advise the group supervisor and the other members of the college and to contribute to a convergent approach in the supervision of cross-border groups. In the case of formal voting, EIOPA will give its opinion but does not take part.[77]

---

73 CEIOPS-DOC-05/05, 19 p. with 3 annexes (https://eiopa.europa.eu/CEIOPS-Archive/Documents/Standards/recommendations_DOC0505.pdf).

74 https://eiopa.europa.eu/CEIOPS-Archive/Documents/Standards/Recommendations.pdf, 10 p.

75 EIOPA-BoS-19/040, 19 February 2019, 7 p.

76 Prior to the application of Solvency II, EIOPA carried out a peer review on the governance of colleges. See EIOPA, Peer review on the NCAs' governance of colleges (reference period: Sept. 2012–Sept. 2013), EIOPA-RP-15-297, 8 January 2016, 21 p.

77 EIOPA, Guidelines on operational functioning of colleges, EIOPA-BoS-14/146, 2 October 2015, para. 1.9.

EIOPA can ask a college to deliberate further in cases where it considers that a group supervisor's decision would result in an incorrect application of EU law or would not contribute to the objective of convergence of supervisory practices. EIOPA can also require the group supervisor to schedule a meeting of the college or add a point to the agenda of the meeting (Art. 21 (2) (e) EIOPA Regulation). EIOPA has a legally binding mediation role in resolving disputes between members of the college upon their request, and it may, under certain conditions, require a (re)insurance undertaking to take a specific action or to stop a practice in order to ensure compliance with EU law (Art. 21 (4) EIOPA Regulation).

As EIOPA may be part of a college that includes third-country supervisory authorities, it is important for EIOPA to be recognised as a full member of the college, with whom information can also be shared by third-country supervisory authorities, because EIOPA is bound by the same rules of professional secrecy. To achieve this, in 2016 EIOPA signed the IAIS Multilateral Memorandum of Understanding.[78]

In 2017, EIOPA participated in 49 cross-border colleges and in 14 colleges on internal models. It engaged with 60% of all cross-border colleges in the EEA. EIOPA also increased the number of interactions with group supervisors outside college meetings, to assist them on supervisory activities and risk reviews. EIOPA also actively interacted with some third-country colleges of (re)insurance undertakings that conduct major activities in the EEA and which have their head offices in equivalent countries, in particular Switzerland and Bermuda. Meriting particular attention in 2017 have been the use of the group ORSA as a key source of information in assessing a group's risk profile, the effectiveness, efficiency and impact of information exchange, and joint risk assessment, as well as the robustness of the Solvency II balance sheet and raising awareness of intra-group transactions and risk concentrations.[79]

As observed by the European Court of Auditors (ECA) in its 2018 report on EIOPA, problems sometimes arise in colleges because NSAs do not always share important information with other members of the college (for instance, the ORSA report) or do not implement recommendations made by EIOPA (for instance, on an improvement of risk management practices).[80]

---

78 http://www.iaisweb.org/page/supevisory-material/mmou-signatories.

79 EIOPA, *Oversight activities in 2017*, Publications Office of the EU, Luxembourg, 2018, pp. 14–15. See also EIOPA, *Year-end report 2016 on functioning of colleges of supervisors and priorities for 2017*, 1 March 2017, 17 p. (https://eiopa.europa.eu/Publications/Administrative/Year-end%20report%202016%20on%20functioning%20of%20colleges%20of%20supervisors%20and%20priorities%20for%202017.pdf).

80 ECA, *Special Report: EIOPA made an important contribution to supervision and stability in the insurance sector, but significant challenges remain*, Publications Office of the EU, Luxembourg, 2018, para. 36.

2.2.2. *Development of a Common Supervisory Culture*

In accordance with Art. 29 (1) EIOPA Regulation, EIOPA plays an active role in building a common European supervisory culture. EIOPA defines the European supervisory culture as a common understanding of the way supervisors think, behave and work within their community. This culture manifests itself in processes and procedures, but also in behaviour. In arriving at a common culture, processes and procedures are easier to align than behaviour.[81]

Establishing a common supervisory culture requires a common understanding of supervisory objectives and a common view on the key characteristics of high-quality and effective supervision.

Building a common European supervisory culture should not disregard the motto of the EU, i.e. "unity in diversity". The existence of different cultures within the EEA is at the same time a strength and a weakness. It would be naïve to believe that it is sufficient to impose a common supervisory culture from above (through common rules and guidelines) upon NSAs. Culture is a sticky thing.[82] On the one hand, a common supervisory culture requires NSAs to embrace the European idea, i.e. to be open to different approaches and receptive to new ideas and best practices in other Member States. On the other hand, it also requires NSAs and EIOPA to be respectful of different traditions and cultures. It is only through mutual respect that real progress towards a common supervisory culture can be made. This means that it is not enough for Member States to ensure that the mandate of NSAs takes into account, in an appropriate way, a European dimension (Art. 71 (1) FD). It presupposes that NSAs move away from a "think national first" approach, for example when they have to judge whether board members or other key function holders of (re)insurance undertakings in other Member States, which intend to acquire an undertaking in their country, are fit and proper. NSAs should not be allowed to put into question the fit and proper analysis carried out by another NSA unless there are specific reasons to do so, for instance required knowledge of local rules and regulation (fitness) or unlawful behaviour (proper). Board members and key function holders should be able to take up positions in another MS without being required to pass an entirely new fit and proper test. They should in that sense also benefit from a European passport.

The main objective of supervision is the protection of policyholders and beneficiaries across jurisdictions, regardless of the location of the (re)insurance

---

81 EIOPA, *A common supervisory culture. Key characteristics of high-quality and effective supervision*, Publications Office of the EU, Luxembourg, 2017, p. 3.

82 LAUTENSCHLÄGER, S., *European banking supervision – towards a common culture*, statement made at the Eurofi Financial Forum 2018, Vienna, 6 September 2018 (https://www.ecb.europa.eu/press/key/date/2018/html/ecb.sp180906_1.en.html).

undertaking's head office (Art. 27 FD). It is also an objective of supervision to duly consider the potential impact of supervisory decisions on the stability of the broader financial system, especially in times of exceptional movements in financial markets (Art. 28 FD).

The protection of policyholders and beneficiaries needs to be seen from a broad perspective, as there is a close relationship between market conduct and prudential issues. The role of supervisors is to ensure that (re)insurance undertakings are soundly managed and have an effective system of governance and a robust solvency position (current and prospective) in order to make sure that they can fulfil all their commitments while also acting honestly, fairly and professionally in accordance with the best interests of policyholders and beneficiaries.[83]

The principles and key characteristics of high-quality and effective supervision are defined by EIOPA as:[84]

- risk-based and proportionate;
- forward-looking, preventive and proactive;
- challenging, sceptical and engaged;
- comprehensive;
- conclusive.

The implementation by NSAs of appropriate decision-making processes and procedures, including documentation, supported by a clear rationale, should lead to a predictive and forward-looking judgement. This should be accompanied by flexibility in the SRP to reflect the fact that the environment is constantly evolving. One challenge – but one that is also a goal – is to ensure that the treatment of all (re)insurance undertakings is consistent. NSAs should be able to assess the consistency of supervisory outcomes over time and between undertakings.

The regular review of the SRP that has been implemented, including an assessment of the efficiency of the methodologies and tools used to identify risks, is of the utmost importance. The sharing of experiences and lessons learned from this regular review with other NSAs and with EIOPA is key.[85]

---

83 EIOPA, *A common supervisory culture. Key characteristics of high-quality and effective supervision*, Publications Office of the EU, Luxembourg, 2017, pp. 3–4 and EIOPA, Strategy towards a comprehensive risk-based and preventive framework for conduct of business supervision, EIOPA-16/015, 11 January 2016, 10 p.

84 EIOPA, *A common supervisory culture. Key characteristics of high-quality and effective supervision*, Publications Office of the EU, Luxembourg, 2017, pp. 5–13. For more details, see above, Chapter 7, section 1.2.

85 EIOPA, *A common supervisory culture. Key characteristics of high-quality and effective supervision*, Publications Office of the EU, Luxembourg, 2017, p. 14.

A common supervisory culture requires basic tools to be available in any NSA:

- *legal standing*: NSAs should have the authority and appropriate powers to fulfil their tasks;
- *proper governance structure*: NSAs should set themselves high governance standards with respect for the principles of independence, transparency and accountability;
- *clear, defined strategy*: NSAs should have a clear strategy and work plan, allowing for proper planning and setting of priorities and timelines;
- *proper processes for cooperation* with other competent authorities and EIOPA.

NSAs should have in place processes that ensure a proper dialogue with other supervisory authorities, at both the national and the international level, and ensure that common European practices are duly considered when making interpretations and decisions and exercising supervisory powers. NSAs must also have adequate resources from both a human and a financial perspective.[86]

EIOPA monitors supervisory developments as part of its oversight activity.[87] This involves a number of things, including carrying out balance sheet reviews,[88] issuing supervisory opinions (Art. 29 EIOPA Regulation), carrying out consistency projects on internal models, carrying out peer reviews of supervisory authorities (Art. 30 EIOPA Regulation), participating in supervisory colleges (Art. 21 EIOPA Regulation), engaging with cooperation platforms,[89] agreeing

86 EIOPA, *A common supervisory culture. Key characteristics of high-quality and effective supervision*, Publications Office of the EU, Luxembourg, 2017, pp. 15–16.

87 This oversight role is not specifically foreseen by the FD, nor by the EIOPA Regulation. It is a delicate issue as EIOPA should not be seen as the supervisor of the supervisors. That would not be in its interest. On the other hand, EIOPA can contribute to spreading best supervisory practice among NSAs.

88 See the balance sheet review of the Bulgarian insurance sector: *Final Report on Insurance Balance Sheet Review of the Bulgarian Insurance Sector*, February 2017, 73 p. (https://eiopa.europa.eu/Publications/Other%20Documents/Balance%20Sheet%20Review%20of%20the%20Bulgarian%20Insurance%20Sector.pdf#search=Final%20report%20on%20insurance%20balance%20sheet%20review%20of%20the%20bulgarian%20insurance%20sector%202017). An earlier balance sheet review was carried out on the Romanian insurance sector: see *Balance Sheet Review and Stress Test of the Romanian Insurance Sector*, July 2015, 121 p. (https://asfromania.ro/files/engleza/comunicate/20150715%20BSR%20-%20Final%20Report%20-engl-logo.pdf).

89 Cooperation platforms are a new tool developed by EIOPA in 2018 to tackle issues relating to cross-border business activities provided by groups and solo undertakings through the freedom to provide services regime. This is a follow-up to the EIOPA Decision on the collaboration of the supervisory authorities, EIOPA-BoS-17/014, 30 January 2017, 59 p. As part of the ESFS reform, it is now envisaged that the practice of cooperation platforms will be formalised by inserting a specific article in the FD to that effect. See, Presidency compromise proposal for a Directive of the EP and of the Council amending Directive 2014/65/EU on

structured bilateral engagements with national supervisors, providing technical assistance, and independently assessing troubled undertakings.[90]

As part of its task of developing a common supervisory culture, Art. 29 (1) (a) EIOPA Regulation provides for the adoption by EIOPA of supervisory opinions addressed to NSAs. During the course of the development and implementation of Solvency II, a number of important supervisory opinions were published:[91]

- Opinion on external models and data (20 April 2012);[92]
- Opinion on interim measures regarding Solvency II (20 December 2012);[93]
- Opinion on supervisory response to a prolonged low interest rate environment (28 February 2013);[94]
- Opinion on the use of a common application package for internal models (27 March 2014);[95]
- Opinion on the preparation for internal model applications (14 April 2015);[96]
- Opinion on the group solvency calculation in the context of equivalence (25 September 2015);[97]
- Opinion on the application of a combination of methods to the group solvency calculation (27 January 2016);[98]
- Opinion on disclosure of information related to the use of transitional measures in the calculation of technical provisions (21 December 2016);[99]
- Opinion on supervisory convergence in light of the UK withdrawing from the EU (11 July 2017);[100]
- Opinion on monetary incentives and remuneration between providers of asset management services and insurance undertakings (11 December 2017);[101]
- Opinion on service continuity in insurance in light of the withdrawal of the UK from the EU (21 December 2017);[102]
- Opinion on the supervisory assessment of internal models including a dynamic volatility adjustment (30 November 2017);[103]

---

markets in financial instruments and Directive 2009/138/EC on the taking-up and pursuit of the business of insurance and reinsurance (Solvency II), Council document 5835/19, 4 February 2019. pp. 14–15.

90 EIOPA, *Oversight activities in 2017*, Publications Office of the EU, Luxembourg, 2017, 20 p.

91 All supervisory opinions are published on the website of EIOPA.

92 EIOPA-BoS-12/156, 3 p.

93 EIOPA-BoS-12/388, 4 p.

94 EIOPA-BoS-12/110, 6 p. See also, EIOPA, *Low interest rate environment stock taking exercise*, -BoS-14/103, 28 November 2014, 36 p.

95 EIOPA-BoS-14/035, 2 p.

96 EIOPA-BoS-15/083, 3 p.

97 EIOPA-BoS-15/201, 7 p.

98 EIOPA-BoS-16/008, 4 p.

99 EIOPA-BoS-16/243, 3 p.

100 EIOPA-BoS-17/141, 7 p.

101 EIOPA-BoS-17/295, 7 p.

102 EIOPA-BoS-17/389, 5 p.

103 EIOPA-BoS-17/366, 3 p.

- Opinion on the solvency position of (re)insurance undertakings in light of the withdrawal of the UK from the EU (18 May 2018);[104]
- Opinion on disclosure of information to customers about the impact of the withdrawal of the UK from the EU (28 June 2018);[105]
- Opinion on non-life cross-border insurance business of a long-term nature and its supervision (21 December 2018).[106]

EIOPA also published a supervisory assessment on the ORSA,[107] on the SFCR and on the application of the proportionality principle in the supervision of the SCR.[108]

Peer reviews are carried out periodically on some of the activities of NSAs in order to further strengthen the consistency in supervisory outcomes (Art. 30 (1) EIOPA Regulation). A peer review is an evaluation of the work of supervisory authorities by other supervisory authorities. Peer reviews are a means to evaluate (Art. 30 (2) EIOPA Regulation):

- the adequacy of resources and governance arrangements of NSAs;
- the degree of convergence reached in the application of EU law and in supervisory practice;
- best practices developed by some NSAs that might be of benefit for other NSAs;
- the effectiveness and degree of convergence with regard to the enforcement of EU law.

Peer reviews are based on the methodology adopted by EIOPA[109] and are organised and conducted by the Review Panel, which consists of representatives of the NSAs who possess the necessary independence, objectivity, seniority, knowledge of EU legislation and EIOPA measures, and expertise in supervisory practices to guarantee the credibility and the effectiveness of the peer review. For matters concerning Solvency II, peer reviews have been organised on the following topics:

- supervisory practices for the pre-application of internal models for NSAs and colleges;[110]

---

104 EIOPA-BoS-18/201, 8 p.

105 EIOPA-BoS-18/119, 4 p., with a Q&A document, EIOPA-BoS-18/217, 3 p.

106 EIOPA-BoS-18/527, 25 p.

107 EIOPA, Supervisory Assessment of the Own Risk and Solvency Assessment – First experiences, EIOPA-BoS/17-097, 19 June 2017, 8 p. EIOPA, Supervisory Statement - Solvency II: Application of the proportionality principle in the supervision of the SCR, EIOPA-BoS-19-033, 11 March 2019 9 p.

108 EIOPA, Supervisory Statement – Solvency II: Solvency and Financial Condition Report, EIOPA-BoS/17-310, 18 December 2017, 11 p.

109 EIOPA, Decision adopting the methodology for the conduct of peer reviews, EIOPA-BoS-15-301, 29 January 2016, as amended by Decision of 28 September 2018, EIOPA-BoS-18-354, 16 p.

110 EIOPA, Peer review on supervisory practices for pre-application of internal models for NCAs and colleges, EIOPA-RP-13-096a, 18 July 2013, 17 p.

- follow-up of the peer review on pre-application of internal models;[111]
- supervisory practices for NSAs' governance of participation in colleges;[112]
- supervisory practices for freedom to provide services;[113]
- supervisory practices and application in assessing key functions;[114]
- propriety of administrative, management or supervisory body members and qualifying shareholders.[115]

Lastly, structured bilateral engagements with NSAs are carried out by EIOPA to ensure common understanding of effective supervision. These bilateral engagements are tailored to the national specificities, following a diagnosis and analysis of national markets, and where necessary deal with cross-border issues. As an outcome of these bilateral engagements, EIOPA may update its risk assessment on the market and the level of supervision, provide independent and challenging feedback, deliver recommendations for improvements or define follow-up measures, including further visits addressing the implementation of EIOPA's recommendations and taking preventive and remedial actions.

2.2.3. *Supervisory Convergence*

In a single market with cross-border activities and a European passport system supervised by the home country, the supervisory system is as strong as its weakest link.[116] The development of a common supervisory culture should lead to supervisory convergence. However, supervisory convergence should not lead to a full harmonisation of the supervisory framework. Proper account must be taken of the national specificities of local markets.[117] Supervisory convergence should not lead to the adoption by all NSAs of the strictest regulatory or supervisory approach.

---

111 EIOPA, Follow up to peer review on pre-application of internal models, EIOPA-BoS-14-248, 17 December 2014, 15 p.

112 EIOPA, Peer review on supervisory practices for NCAs' governance of participation in colleges of supervisors, EIOPA-RP-15-297, 8 January 2016, 21 p.

113 EIOPA, Peer review on supervisory practices for freedom to provide services, EIOPA-BoS-16-072, 29 April 2016, 30 p.

114 EIOPA, *Peer review of key functions: supervisory practices and application in assessing key functions. Executive summary*, Publications Office of the EU, Luxembourg, 2018, 12 p.

115 EIOPA, *Results of the peer review on propriety of administrative, management or supervisory body members and qualifying shareholders*, Publications Office of the EU, Luxembourg, 2018, 50 p.

116 BERNARDINO, G., *Solvency II review, proportionality and supervisory convergence*, International Conference on Insurance Regulation, Berlin, 18 October 2018, p. 5 (https://eiopa.europa.eu/Publications/Press%20Releases/2018-10-18%20InternationalGdVConference InsuranceRegulationGabrielBernardino.pdf).

117 See also EIOPA, *Supervisory Convergence Plan 2018–2019*, Publications Office of the EU, Luxembourg, 2018, p. 5.

Supervisory convergence requires active cooperation between the NSAs in the context of EIOPA. Member States must therefore ensure that the mandates of supervisory authorities take into account, in an appropriate way, the EU dimension (Art. 71 (1) FD). They must ensure that, in the exercise of their duties, supervisory authorities have regard to the convergence of supervisory tools and practices in the application of the European regulatory framework. More specifically, Member States must ensure that (Art. 71 (2) FD):

- their supervisory authorities participate in the activities of EIOPA, for instance by attending the meetings of the Board of Supervisors and by participating in the various working groups;
- their supervisory authorities make every effort to comply with the guidelines and recommendations issued by EIOPA and that they state the reasons if they do not do so;
- national mandates conferred on their supervisory authorities do not inhibit the performance of their duties as members of EIOPA or under the FD.

With the application of Solvency II, there has been a shift in EIOPA's activities from regulation to supervisory convergence. Consistency and convergence of supervisory practices in the EU is a key element in ensuring that EU regulation is applied in all Member States to guarantee a level playing field and prevent regulatory arbitrage in the internal market, and ultimately to safeguard a similar level of protection for all policyholders and beneficiaries in the EU.[118]

An important tool for supervisory convergence is the Supervisory Handbook, which is presently being developed by EIOPA. It includes recommendations and good practices for the supervision of (re)insurance undertakings, with examples and case studies. The most important areas of Solvency II have already been covered in the Handbook: risk assessment framework, the AMSB, key functions, the prudent person principle, the ORSA, technical provisions, own funds, the SCR, group supervision, and ongoing supervision of internal models.

Going forward, it would be good for EIOPA to share this Handbook with the (re)insurance industry, which has the right to know how NSAs interpret and intend to apply Solvency II. It should not remain a secret, as proper supervision and application of the regulatory framework are in the interest of all stakeholders.

EIOPA has also developed a supervisory convergence plan for 2018–2019, which focuses on the implementation of Solvency II. It includes actions in the following three priority areas[119] – implementation of a common supervisory

---

118 BERNARDINO, G., *Solvency II implementation – beyond compliance*, IVASS Conference, Rome, 3 March 2016, p. 3 (https://eiopa.europa.eu/Publications/Speeches%20and%20presentations/2016-03-03%20IVASS%20Solvency%20II%20Conference.pdf).

119 EIOPA, *Supervisory Convergence Plan 2018–2019*, Publications Office of the EU, Luxembourg, 2018, pp. 9–11.

culture and further development of supervisory tools, risks to the internal market and to the level playing field which may lead to supervisory arbitrage, and supervision of emerging risks:

1. *Implementation of a common supervisory culture and further development of supervisory tools*
   (a) *Development of common supervisory tools and benchmarks:* The focus of attention here is the application in supervisory practice of the proportionality principle. Peer reviews should show how proportionality is used in supervisory reporting and in the requirements regarding key governance functions.[120] These examinations should result in recommendations to NSAs.
   (b) *Common benchmarks for the supervision of internal models:* Convergence of supervisory practices in the approval of internal models is a high priority for EIOPA. The objective is the development of a supervisory plan for internal models. The ESFS review package, when adopted, provides for more powers for EIOPA in this area.
   (c) *Supervisory assessment of conduct risks:* This area is particularly important because of the shift in life insurance towards unit-linked and index-linked products whereby the investment risk is transferred to policyholders. This puts more pressure on business conduct risk, i.e. the risk of mis-selling with the consequential reputational and financial damage for the insurer and for policyholders and the insurance market as a whole.[121]
   (d) *Group supervision:* Focus of attention are the supervisory practices on the treatment of own funds of related undertakings that belong to another financial sector and for which sectorial rules apply, for instance the FICOD, with the objective to develop good practices on the supervision of intra-group transactions and risk concentrations.
   (e) *Remuneration policies:* The objective is the development of convergent practices on Solvency II remuneration requirements.
2. *Risks to the internal market and to the level playing field which may lead to supervisory arbitrage*
   (a) *Calculation of technical provisions:* EIOPA is analysing the consistency of technical provisions' best estimate calculations, with a special emphasis on the practical implementation of contract boundaries, economic scenario generators, management actions, expenses projection and expected profits in future premiums.

---

120 See EIOPA, *Peer review of key functions: supervisory practices and application in assessing key functions*, Publications Office of the EU, Luxembourg, 2018, 11 p.

121 See EIOPA, Strategy towards a comprehensive risk-based and preventive framework for conduct of business supervision, EIOPA-16/015, 11 January 2016, 10 p.

(b) *Cross-border business:* EIOPA has set up cooperation platforms with home and host supervisors to look at concrete cases of undertakings carrying out cross-border business through the FoS regime. So far, 13 platforms have been set up involving NSAs from different countries. For each platform, EIOPA has provided concrete supervisory recommendations to the home supervisor. In some cases, home supervisory authorities were encouraged to initiate intrusive interventions in relation to insurers offering cross-border services, such as a prohibition on writing new business in order to limit the risk to prospective policyholders. One of the objectives of this exercise is to do away with unsustainable cross-border business models.[122] For insurance undertakings, it is not always easy to control how their products are being sold on an FoS basis. In order to have a better overview and avoid problems of mis-selling, it may be advisable to set up a branch in the MS in which the products are being sold.

EIOPA is also looking at how the provisions on exchange of information between supervisory authorities of home and host countries regarding authorisation, notification and supervision on a continuous basis are applied in practice as a follow-up to its decision on the collaboration between insurance supervisory authorities.[123] As part of the ESFS review package – and based upon an amendment introduced by the EP, it is envisaged that EIOPA's oversight of cross-border business will be strengthened. A new Art. 152a FD, which was proposed by the EP, would require the NSA of a home MS that intends to authorise a (re)insurance undertaking whose scheme of operations indicates that a significant part of its activities will be based on FoS or FoE in another MS to notify EIOPA and the NSA of the relevant host MS. This requirement would only apply where the scheme of operations of the (re)insurance undertaking that will be authorised also indicates that the FoS or FoE activities are likely to be of relevance with respect to the host MS's market. The home MS will also be required to notify EIOPA and the NSA of the relevant host MS where it identifies deteriorating financial conditions or other emerging risks posed by a (re)insurance undertaking carrying out activities based on FoS or FoE that may have a cross-border effect. The NSAs concerned may also request the assistance of EIOPA in case no bilateral solution can be found. This would be combined with the formal recognition in a new Art. 152b FD of cooperation

122 On cooperation platforms, see EIOPA, *Oversight activities in 2017*, Publications Office of the EU, Luxembourg, 2018, pp. 15–17.

123 EIOPA, Decision on the collaboration of the insurance supervisory authorities, EIOPA-BoS-17/014, 30 January 2017, 59 p.

platforms which can help to improve the exchange of information and the collaboration between the NSAs of the home and host Member States.[124]

(c) *Assessment of internal model outcomes:* EIOPA is carrying out an annual comparative study on market and credit risk modelling.[125] This is part of EIOPA's work on the development and testing of sound ongoing appropriateness indicators and benchmarking for internal models, which EIOPA regards as fundamental to avoiding internal models becoming a capital optimisation tool, "because a race to the bottom will kill the underlying idea of an internal model".[126]

(d) *Authorisations, fitness and propriety:* EIOPA has carried out a peer review on the supervisory assessment of propriety of board members and key governance function holders[127] and has issued recommendations to NSAs following the results of this review. Another focus of attention was the way in which NSAs carry out the authorisation process of (re)insurance undertakings, in particular how they examine the viability of the business model and assess the fitness and propriety of key managers and/or owners.

(e) *Consistent implementation of the EU–USA Covered Agreement:* EIOPA monitors the implementation by NSAs of the provisions of the covered agreement relating to reinsurance collateral and group supervision.[128]

3. *Supervision of emerging risks*

(a) *Supervision of data and IT-related risks, including cyber risk:* EIOPA is working on the development of good practices on the supervision of

---

124 See, Presidency compromise proposal for a Directive of the EP and of the Council amending Directive 2014/65/EU on markets in financial instruments and Directive 2009/138/EC on the taking-up and pursuit of the business of insurance and reinsurance (Solvency II), Council document 5835/19, 4 February 2019. pp. 13–15. This proposal was agreed in March 2013.

125 EIOPA, Decision of the Board of Supervisors on the annual market and credit risk modelling comparative study, EIOPA-BoS-18/062, 12 February 2018, 3 p. and EIOPA, First Comparative Study on Market and Credit Risk Modelling, EIOPA-BoS/18-180, 22 May 2018, 13 p.

126 BERNARDINO, G., *EIOPA and supervisory convergence – The beginning of a new journey*, EIOPA 5th Annual Conference, Frankfurt, 18 November 2015, p. 5 (https://eiopa.europa.eu/Publications/Speeches%20and%20presentations/2015-11-18%20EIOPA%20Annual%20Conference.pdf). See also EIOPA, Update on Internal Model Consistency Projects, EIOPA-BoS-17/269, 25 October 2017, 2 p. The possible increase of the powers of EIOPA in the area of internal model approval was the subject of debate between the EP and the Council as part of the ESFS review package. The role of EIOPA in internal model approval will be strengthened in order to achieve greater supervisory convergence in this area, in particular for insurance groups present in several Member States. The power to approve the application will, however, remain with the group supervisor and the college of supervisors.

127 EIOPA, *Peer review of key functions: supervisory practices and application in assessing key functions*, Publications Office of the EU, Luxembourg, 2018, 9 p.

128 Bilateral Agreement between the European Union and the United States of America on prudential measures regarding insurance and reinsurance, dated 18 September 2017, *OJ* L 258, 6.10.2017, p. 4. See above, Chapter 9, section 12.

data management, data quality and IT security and governance. It is also looking at practices of (re)insurance undertakings in the area of cybersecurity and exploring efficient ways to perform a cyberattack test.[129]

(b) *InsurTech:* EIOPA is carrying out a thematic review of the insurance industry's use of Big Data covering underwriting, pricing, marketing, claims management and sales. It is also monitoring NSAs' approaches to innovation, including the use of sandboxes and innovation hubs.[130]

(c) *Brexit:* EIOPA is closely following the consequences of Brexit for the insurance and pension markets, with a view to ensuring consistency in supervisory approaches by the EEA30 NSAs.[131]

2.2.4. Binding Mediation

Art. 19 EIOPA Regulation provides for a legally binding mediation role for EIOPA in order to facilitate the impartial settlement of disagreements between NSAs in cross-border and/or cross-sectorial situations. It is obvious that this task conferred to EIOPA is very delicate. Art. 41 EIOPA Regulation therefore specifically requires the Board of Supervisors of EIOPA to set up an independent Mediation Panel. This Panel consists of the Chairman of EIOPA, who also chairs the Panel, two members of the Board of Supervisors and four substitutes. These substitutes are necessary to ensure that members of the Panel are not party to the disagreement and have no interest in the conflict nor any direct links to the NSAs concerned.

Any NSA may take the initiative in bringing a matter to the attention of EIOPA in order to seek its assistance in settling a disagreement in the situations specified in the FD. EIOPA may also intervene on its own initiative in order to assist NSAs in reaching an agreement. The time limit for conciliation between the NSAs is either set by EIOPA or specified in the FD (Art. 19 (2) and (3) EIOPA Regulation).

---

129 See EIOPA, *Understanding Cyber Insurance – A structured dialogue with insurance companies*, Publications Office of the EU, Luxembourg, 2018, 32 p. and the questionnaire launched by EIOPA on cyber risk at the occasion of the 2018 stress test; see also, IAIS, *Issues paper on cyber risk to the insurance sector*, August 2016, 38 p. See also, Joint Committee, Joint Advice of the ESAs to the ECON on the need for legislative improvements relating to the ICT risk management requirements in the EU financial sector, JC 2019/26, 10 April 2019, 42 p.

130 See EIOPA, InsurTech Roundtable. How technology and data are reshaping the insurance landscape, Summary from the roundtable organised by EIOPA on 28 April 2017, EIOPA-BoS/17-165, 5 July 2017, 17 p.; *Big Data thematic review. NCA Survey*, 29 June 2018, 10 p.; *Big Data thematic review. Consumer Associations Survey*, 29 June 2018, 6 p.; EIOPA, *InsurTech Insight Survey*, 2018.

131 See the four opinions adopted by EIOPA in this area listed above.

If the NSAs concerned fail to reach an agreement within the conciliation phase, EIOPA may take a decision itself. The decision is prepared by the Mediation Panel and its proposal is normally adopted if approved by a simple majority of the Board of Supervisors (Art. 44 (1) EIOPA Regulation).

Although EIOPA's decision is final (Art. 19 (4) and (5) EIOPA Regulation), there always is the possibility of a supervisory authority refusing to accept that decision. This matter is also dealt with in Art. 19 EIOPA Regulation: where a supervisory authority does not comply with the decision of EIOPA and thereby fails to ensure that a (re)insurance undertaking complies with the requirements of EU law, EIOPA may adopt an individual decision addressed to the undertaking concerned, requiring the necessary action to comply with its obligation under EU law, including the cessation of any practice (Art. 19 (4) EIOPA Regulation). Reference is also made in Art. 19 to the possibility for the EC to start an infringement case against the MS concerned on the basis of Art. 258 TFEU, in the case of a breach of EU law. It is indeed up to Member States to ensure that their supervisory authorities act in accordance with EU law.

Omnibus II has specified the cases where EIOPA may be asked to intervene so as to settle a disagreement between NSAs. As indicated in recital 20 Omnibus II, the binding procedure for the settlement of disagreements is designed to solve situations where NSAs cannot resolve procedural or substantive issues relating to compliance with EU law among themselves. Recital 21 Omnibus II specifies that in cases where EU law confers discretion on Member States, decisions by EIOPA should not replace the exercise of discretion by NSAs, where that exercise is in accordance with EU law. It should however be possible for disagreements to be resolved and cooperation to be strengthened before a final decision is taken by an NSA or issued to an insurance undertaking. EIOPA should resolve disagreements by mediating between the conflicting views of NSAs (recital 22 Omnibus II). The listing of a number of areas for binding mediation through EIOPA does not mean that EIOPA should not try to resolve disagreements in other areas through non-binding mediation. This is clearly part of EIOPA's role in contributing to a more effective functioning of the internal market and a more effective implementation of micro-level supervision (Art. 31 (c) EIOPA Regulation).[132]

The FD provides for binding mediation in the case of disagreement between supervisory authorities in the following circumstances:

1. *On-site verifications in the case of supervision of branches*
   The supervisory authority of a home MS may want to carry out on-site verifications of the information necessary to ensure the financial supervision

[132] For an example, see the Opinion of EIOPA's Mediation Panel, dated 25 June 2018, EIOPA-BoS-18-279, 7 p. The mediation concerned the classification of an insurance product sold in France on the basis of FoS.

of the undertaking which it has authorised and which is carrying out business in a host MS through a branch. Where that supervisory authority has informed the supervisory authority of the host MS that it intends to carry out such on-site verifications and where it is prohibited from exercising this right, or where the supervisory authority of the host MS that wants to participate in these verifications is unable in practice to exercise this right, the supervisory authorities concerned may refer the matter to EIOPA and request its assistance as a mediator (Art. 33, third subparagraph FD).

2. *Supervision of outsourced functions and activities*
The supervisory authority of a (re)insurance undertaking may want to carry out on-site inspections at the premises of a service provider located in another MS. Where that supervisory authority has informed the competent authority of the MS of the service provider that it intends to carry out an on-site inspection or where it carries out an on-site inspection but is in practice unable to do so because of a lack of support from the competent authority of the MS of the service provider, the supervisory authority of the (re)insurance undertaking may refer the matter to EIOPA and request its assistance as a mediator (Art. 38 (2), third subparagraph FD).
3. *Insurance undertakings not complying with the law of the host MS*
Where an insurance undertaking that is operating in a host MS through a branch or through the provision of cross-border services is not complying with the law of that MS and fails to comply with the measures taken by the supervisory authority of the home MS at the request of the supervisory authority of the host MS, the supervisory authority of the home or the host MS may refer the matter to EIOPA and request its assistance as a mediator (Art. 155 (3), second subparagraph FD).
4. *Reinsurance undertakings not complying with the law of the host MS*
Where a reinsurance undertaking that is operating in a host MS through a branch or through the provision of cross-border services is not complying with the law of that MS and fails to comply with the measures taken by the supervisory authority of the home MS at the request of the supervisory authority of the host MS, the supervisory authority of the home or the host MS may refer the matter to EIOPA and request its assistance as a mediator (Art. 158 (2), second subparagraph FD).
5. *Decision by the group supervisor concerning the equivalence of a third-country solvency regime*
The EC may decide that a third country's solvency regime is equivalent to Solvency II for the purpose of the treatment of subsidiaries of EEA groups in that third country in the context of the calculation of the group SCR. Where no equivalence decision has been taken by the EC, the verification of whether a third country's solvency regime is at

least equivalent to Solvency II is carried out by the group supervisor at the request of the parent undertaking or on its own initiative, with the assistance of EIOPA. The group supervisor, assisted by EIOPA, must consult the other supervisory authorities concerned before taking a decision on equivalence.

Where supervisory authorities disagree with the decision of the group supervisor on equivalence, they may refer the matter to EIOPA and request its assistance as a mediator within three months of the notification of the group supervisor's decision (Art. 227 (2), third subparagraph FD).

6. *Decision by the group supervisor on the use of a group internal model*
Within six months of the date of receipt by the group supervisor of a complete application for the permission to calculate the consolidated group SCR, as well as the SCR of (re)insurance undertakings belonging to a group, any of the supervisory authorities concerned may voice its concerns to EIOPA and request its assistance as a mediator. The group supervisor must in that case defer its decision and await the decision by EIOPA, which must be taken within one month. The group supervisor must follow the decision of EIOPA, which is final and must be applied by all supervisory authorities concerned (Art. 231 (3) FD).

It may well be that the panel of supervisors set up by EIOPA's Board of Supervisors to deal with this matter comes to a decision, but that this decision is rejected by EIOPA's full Board of Supervisors. In order to facilitate the use of a group internal model in such a situation, Art. 231 (3), third subparagraph FD states that when EIOPA fails to take a decision the group supervisor will take the final decision, which must then be applied by all supervisory authorities concerned. The fact that the ultimate decision might rest with the group supervisor will create additional pressure on EIOPA's Board of Supervisors to follow the advice of the panel of supervisors.

7. *Application of the specific regime for groups with centralised risk management*
A parent undertaking may apply for the specific regime for groups with centralised risk management. The group supervisor will in that case seek the agreement of all supervisory authorities concerned within the college of supervisors (Art. 236 (e) FD). Within three months of the date of receipt of the complete application by all supervisory authorities concerned, any of the supervisory authorities concerned may refer the matter to EIOPA and request its assistance as a mediator. The group supervisor must in that case defer its decision and await the decision by EIOPA, which must follow within one month. The group supervisor must follow the decision of EIOPA, which is final and must be applied by all supervisory authorities concerned (Art. 237 (3) FD).

It may well be that the panel of supervisors set up by EIOPA's Board of Supervisors to deal with this matter comes to a decision, but that this decision is rejected by EIOPA's full Board of Supervisors. In order to facilitate the decision-making in such a situation, Art. 237, third subparagraph FD states that when EIOPA fails to take a decision the group supervisor will take the final decision, which must then be applied by all supervisory authorities concerned. The fact that the ultimate decision might rest with the group supervisor will create additional pressure on EIOPA's full Board of Supervisors to follow the advice of the panel of supervisors.

8. *Calculation of the SCR for subsidiaries that are part of a group with centralised risk management*

Where the SCR of a subsidiary that is part of a group with centralised risk management is calculated on the basis of an internal model approved at group level and the supervisory authority that has authorised the subsidiary considers that its risk profile deviates significantly from the assumptions underlying this internal model, and as long as that undertaking does not properly address the concerns of the supervisory authority, that authority may propose setting a capital add-on to the SCR of that subsidiary resulting from the application of such model or, in exceptional circumstances where such a capital add-on would not be appropriate, require that undertaking to calculate its SCR on the basis of the standard formula. The supervisory authority must discuss its proposal within the college of supervisors and communicate the grounds for such proposals to both the subsidiary and the college of supervisors.

Where the SCR of a subsidiary that is part of a group with centralised risk management is calculated on the basis of the standard formula and the supervisory authority that has authorised the subsidiary considers that its risk profile deviates significantly from the assumptions underlying the standard formula, and as long as that undertaking does not properly address the concerns of the supervisory authority, that authority may, in exceptional circumstances, propose that the undertaking replace a subset of the parameters used in the standard formula by USPs or set a capital add-on to the SCR of that subsidiary. The supervisory authority must discuss its proposal within the college of supervisors and communicate the grounds for its proposal to both the subsidiary and the college of supervisors.

In both cases, the possibility exists for EIOPA to act as a mediator in the case of disagreement between the supervisory authorities concerned. Within one month of the date of receipt of the proposal from the supervisory authority of the subsidiary concerned, either the group supervisor or the supervisory authority of the subsidiary may refer the matter to EIOPA and request its assistance as a mediator. The supervisory authority that authorised the subsidiary must in that case defer its decision and await the decision by EIOPA, which must follow within one month. The supervisory authority's decision must be in conformity with EIOPA's decision. The decision is final and must be applied by all supervisory authorities concerned (Art. 238 (5) FD).

9. *Non-compliance with the SCR by a subsidiary belonging to a group with centralised risk management*
   In the event of non-compliance with the SCR, the supervisory authority that has authorised the subsidiary must, without delay, forward to the college of supervisors the recovery plan submitted by the subsidiary in order to achieve, within six months of the observation of non-compliance with the SCR, the re-establishment of the level of eligible own funds or the reduction of its risk profile to ensure compliance with the SCR. Where the supervisory authority that has authorised the subsidiary identifies deteriorating financial conditions, it must notify the college of supervisors without delay of the proposed measures to be taken.
   Within four months of the date on which non-compliance with the SCR was first observed or within one month of the notification to the college of supervisors of the proposed measures to be taken in the case of deteriorating financial conditions, the supervisory authority that authorised the subsidiary or the group supervisor may refer the matter to EIOPA and request its assistance as a mediator where they disagree over either the approval of the recovery plan or the proposed measures. The supervisory authority that authorised the subsidiary must in that case defer its decision and await the decision by EIOPA, which must follow within one month. The supervisory authority's decision must be in conformity with EIOPA's decision. The decision is final and must be applied by all supervisory authorities concerned (Art. 239 (4) FD).
10. *Designation of the group supervisor*
   In particular cases, the supervisory authorities concerned may decide to depart from the criteria established in Art. 247 (2) FD for the designation of a group supervisor where application of these criteria would be inappropriate, taking into account the structure of the group and the relative importance of the (re)insurance undertakings' activities in different countries, and may designate a different supervisory authority as that group supervisor (Art. 247 (3) FD).
   Within three months of the request by any of the supervisory authorities to discuss the appropriateness of the criteria for the choice of the group supervisor, any of the supervisory authorities concerned may refer the matter to EIOPA and request its assistance as a mediator. The supervisory authorities concerned must in that case defer their joint decision and await the decision by EIOPA, which must follow within one month. The joint decision must be in conformity with EIOPA's decision. The decision is final and must be applied by all supervisory authorities concerned (Art. 247 (4) FD).
11. *Operational functioning of the college of supervisors*
   In order to facilitate group supervision, a college of supervisors is established, chaired by the group supervisor (Art. 248 (2) FD).

Where the group supervisor fails to carry out the tasks specified in Art. 248 (1) FD, or where the members of the college of supervisors do not cooperate to the extent referred to in Art. 248 (2) FD, any of the supervisory authorities concerned may refer the matter to EIOPA and request its assistance as a mediator. EIOPA's decision must be complied with by all supervisory authorities concerned (Art. 248 (2) FD).

The establishment and functioning of the college of supervisors is based upon coordination arrangements concluded by the group supervisor and the other supervisory authorities in the college of supervisors (Art. 248 (4) FD).

Where diverging views arise concerning the coordination arrangements between the group supervisor and the other supervisory authorities in the college, any member of the college of supervisors may refer the matter to EIOPA and request its assistance as a mediator. The group supervisor must take its final decision in conformity with EIOPA's decision (Art. 248 (4) FD).

Art. 21 (4) EIOPA Regulation also foresees a legally binding mediation role for EIOPA to resolve all other disputes between NSAs within the context of a college of supervisors. The same procedure provided for in Art. 19 EIOPA Regulation applies in this case.[133]

12. *Cooperation and exchange of information between supervisory authorities*
The authorities responsible for the supervision of individual (re)insurance undertakings in a group and the group supervisor must cooperate closely, in particular in cases where a (re)insurance undertaking encounters financial difficulties (Art. 249 (1) FD).

Where a supervisory authority has not communicated relevant information or where a request for cooperation, in particular to exchange relevant information, has been rejected or has not been acted upon within two weeks, the supervisory authorities may refer the matter to EIOPA and request its assistance as a mediator. EIOPA's decision must be complied with by all supervisory authorities concerned (Art. 249 (1a) FD).

13. *On-site verification of information*[134]
Exchange of information between supervisory authorities is crucial within the context of group supervision. That information may be verified through on-site verifications (Art. 255 (1) FD).

Where the request to another supervisory authority to have an on-site verification carried out has not been acted upon within two weeks, or where the supervisory authority that wishes to verify the information

---

133 Art. 248 (4), third subparagraph still refers to the old dispute settlement procedure with CEIOPS. It will be removed as part of the ESFS review package, which implies an amendment of the FD.

134 For branches, see above under point 1.

concerning a group undertaking is unable in practice to exercise its right to participate in the on-site verification, the requesting authority may refer the matter to EIOPA and request its assistance as a mediator. The decision by EIOPA must be complied with by all supervisory authorities concerned (Art. 255 (2), fourth subparagraph FD).

14. *Decision by the group supervisor concerning the equivalence of a third country's group supervision regime*
In the case of a parent undertaking which has its head office outside the EEA and which has subsidiary (re)insurance undertakings situated in the EEA, the supervisory authorities of the (re)insurance undertakings must verify whether the undertakings are subject to a regime of group supervision by a third-country supervisory authority that is equivalent to the group supervision provided under Solvency II. In the absence of an equivalence decision by the EC, the verification of equivalence is carried out by the acting group supervisor within the EEA, assisted by EIOPA. The acting group supervisor, assisted by EIOPA, must consult the other supervisory authorities concerned before taking a decision on equivalence.
Where supervisory authorities disagree with the decision of the acting group supervisor, they may refer the matter to EIOPA and request its assistance as a mediator within three months of the notification of the acting group supervisor's decision (Art. 260 (1), fourth subparagraph FD).

2.3. REPORTING OBLIGATIONS UNDER SOLVENCY II

For the implementation of Solvency II, EIOPA has been given the task of publishing technical information that is crucial for the functioning and monitoring of the new solvency regime. The information is based upon data provided by NSAs to EIOPA on the basis of Art. 35 (1) EIOPA Regulation.[135]

The following reporting obligations for EIOPA apply under Solvency II:

1. *Publication on an annual basis of information on capital add-ons and on limitations and exemptions from reporting (Art. 52 (2) FD)*
For *capital add-ons*, EIOPA must provide:
(a) for all Member States together, the total distribution of capital add-ons, measured as a percentage of the SCR, for (re)insurance undertakings, life insurance undertakings, non-life insurance undertakings, insurance

[135] See Decision of the Board of Supervisors on Collection of Information by EIOPA under Solvency II, EIOPA-BoS-15/198, 3 November 2015, 6 p.

undertakings pursuing both life and non-life activities and reinsurance undertakings;

(b) for each MS separately, the distribution of capital add-ons, measured as a percentage of the SCR, covering all (re)insurance undertakings in that MS.[136]

In relation to *exemptions from reporting*, EIOPA must provide:

(a) for all Member States collectively, the total of (re)insurance undertakings and groups benefiting from the limitation from regular supervisory reporting and the total number of (re)insurance undertakings and groups benefiting from the exemption of reporting on an item-by-item basis, together with their volume of capital requirements, premiums, technical provisions and assets, respectively measured as percentages of the total volume of capital requirements, premiums, technical provisions and assets of all (re)insurance undertakings and groups;

(b) for each MS separately, the number of (re)insurance undertakings and groups benefiting from the limitation from regular supervisory reporting and the number of (re)insurance undertakings and groups benefiting from the exemption of reporting on an item-by-item basis, together with their volume of capital requirements, premiums, technical provisions and assets, respectively measured as percentages of the total volume of premiums, technical provisions and assets of the (re)insurance undertakings and groups of the MS.[137]

2. *Publication at least on a quarterly basis of information concerning the relevant risk-free interest rate term structure (Art. 77e (1) FD)*

EIOPA must provide:

(a) a relevant risk-free interest rate term structure to calculate the best estimate without any MA or VA;

(b) for each relevant duration, credit quality and asset class, a fundamental spread for the calculation of the MA;

(c) for each relevant national insurance market, a VA to the relevant risk-free interest rate term structure.

In practice, EIOPA publishes on a monthly basis technical information relating to the relevant risk-free interest rate term structures on its website. It also regularly publishes technical information on the methodology to derive risk-free interest rate term structures. In order to provide legal

---

136 EIOPA, Report on the use of capital add-ons 2016, EIOPA-BoS/17-336 rev2, 21 December 2017, 10 p.; EIOPA, *Report on the use of capital add-ons during 2017*, Publications Office of the EU, Luxembourg, 2018, 15 p.

137 EIOPA, *Report on the use of limitations and exemptions from reporting during 2017 and Q1 2018*, Publications Office of the EU, Luxembourg, 2018, 14 p.; EIOPA, Report on the use of limitations and exemptions from reporting 2017, EIOPA-BoS/17-340 rev2, 21 December 2017, 20 p.; EIOPA, Report on the use of limitations and exemptions regarding the submission by (re)insurance undertakings of regular supervisory reporting 2016, EIOPA-BoS/16-293, 23 December 2016, 14 p.

certainty, this information is published by the EC on the basis of Art. 77e (2) FD on a quarterly basis by way of an implementing regulation.[138]

EIOPA must inform the EC of any substantial change in the data used for determining the technical information on the relevant risk-free interest rate term structure and may in that case submit to the EC appropriate modifications of the techniques, data specifications or parameters. Modifications may also be requested by the EC to ensure that the rates of the relevant risk-free interest rate term structure are determined in a transparent, prudent, reliable and objective manner that is consistent over time.[139]

3. *Publication on an annual basis, until 1 January 2021, of a report to the EP, the Council and the EC about the impact of the LTG measures and measures on equity risk based upon information provided by NSAs (Art. 77f (1) FD)*
The annual reports published by EIOPA about the impact of the LTG measures and measures on equity risk deal with the extrapolation of the risk-free interest rates, the MA, the VA, the transitional measures on the risk-free interest rate and technical provisions, the duration-based equity risk sub-module, the symmetric adjustment to the equity risk charge and the extension of the recovery period for the SCR in extreme adverse situations. They describe the use of the measures and their impact on the financial position of undertakings, on policyholder protection, on the investments of undertakings, on consumers and products, on competition and the level playing field in the EU insurance market, and on financial stability. These reports will form the basis for an opinion to be provided by EIOPA to the EC for a report to be delivered by 1 January 2021 to the EP and to the Council on the effects of these measures on policyholder protection, the functioning and stability of European insurance markets, the internal market and in particular the competition and the level playing field in European insurance markets, the extent to which (re)insurance undertakings continue to operate as long-term investors, the availability and pricing of annuity products, the availability and pricing of competing products, the long-term investment strategies by (re)insurance undertakings in relation to products to which the MA and VA are applied relative to those in relation to other long-term guarantees, consumer choice and consumer awareness of risk, the degree of diversification in the insurance business

138 See, for instance, Commission Implementing Regulation (EU) 2018/1078 of 30 July 2018 laying down technical information for the calculation of technical provisions and own funds for reporting with reference dates from 30 June 2018 until 29 September 2018 in accordance with Directive 2009/138/EC, *OJ* L 194, 31.7.2018, p. 47.

139 See Art. 43 (3)–(5) DA, as replaced by the EC's 2019 amendment of the DA, C(2019) 1900 final, 8 March 2019 (not yet published in the OJ).

and asset portfolio of (re)insurance undertakings and financial stability (Art. 77f (3) FD).

4. *Publication on at least a quarterly basis of technical information concerning the symmetric adjustment to the equity capital charge in the equity risk sub-module (Art. 109a (3) FD)*
   In practice, EIOPA publishes an update to the symmetric adjustment of the equity capital charge on its website on a monthly basis.
5. *Declaration, following a request by the supervisory authority concerned, of the existence of exceptional adverse situations affecting (re)insurance undertakings representing a significant share of the market or of the affected lines of business (Art. 138 (4) FD)*
   No such declaration has taken place yet.
6. *Publication of an up-to-date list on its website of all third countries whose solvency regime applicable to reinsurance activities of undertakings with their head office in that third country has been considered equivalent or temporarily equivalent to Solvency II (Art. 172 (2), third subparagraph and (4) third subparagraph FD)*
7. *Publication of an up-to-date list on its website of all third countries whose supervisory regime applicable to third-country (re)insurance undertakings has been considered equivalent or provisionally equivalent to Solvency II (Art. 227 (4), third subparagraph and (5), second subparagraph FD)*
8. *Information on an annual basis of the EP, the Council and the EC of any major difficulties with the application of the provisions concerning the designation of a group supervisor (Art. 247 (7) FD)*
   No specific disclosure has been made by EIOPA on this issue.
9. *Report on an annual basis to the EP on all relevant and significant experiences of the supervisory activities and cooperation between supervisors in the context of group supervision*
   In particular (Art. 259 FD), EIOPA must report on:
   (a) the process of the nomination of the group supervisor, the number of group supervisors and their geographical spread;[140]
   (b) the work of the college of supervisors, in particular the involvement and commitment of supervisory authorities where they are not the group supervisor;
   (c) the main lessons drawn from the review of the work of the colleges of supervisors.[141]

---

[140] See the latest report: EIOPA, *List of identified insurance groups for which a college of supervisors is in place*, April 2018, 5 p.

[141] See EIOPA, *Year-end report 2016 on functioning of colleges of supervisors and priorities for 2017*, 1 March 2017, 17 p. (https://eiopa.europa.eu/Publications/Administrative/Year-end%20report%202016%20on%20functioning%20of%20colleges%20of%20supervisors%20and%20priorities%20for%202017.pdf); EIOPA, *Year-end report 2015 on functioning of*

10. *Publication of an up-to-date list on its website of all third countries whose prudential regime for the supervision of groups has been considered equivalent or temporarily equivalent to Solvency II (Art. 260 (3), third subparagraph and (5), third subparagraph FD)*

2.4. FINANCIAL STABILITY AND MACRO-PRUDENTIAL SUPERVISION

2.4.1. Financial Stability Reporting

Financial stability is one of the objectives of insurance supervision. EIOPA carries out comprehensive biannual economic analyses of risks and vulnerabilities facing the insurance sector in order to assess its financial stability. The financial stability reports are based on a range of qualitative and quantitative data drawn from supervisory and market sources. They also describe key developments and their likely impact on the insurance sector. For instance, the financial stability report published in June 2018 looks at climate risk and sustainable insurance, cyber risk and InsurTech.[142] EIOPA also publishes a quarterly risk dashboard based on a common set of quantitative and qualitative indicators used to identify and measure systemic risks. The data are based on the QRTs provided by (re)insurance undertakings in the context of Solvency II.

2.4.2. Cooperation with the ESRB

EIOPA cooperates closely and on a regular basis with the ESRB (Art. 36 EIOPA Regulation). A representative of the ESRB attends the meetings of the Board of Supervisors of EIOPA and the ESRB cooperates with EIOPA in the organisation of stress tests. The objective of this cooperation is to mitigate the likelihood and the impact of a systemic crisis in insurance.[143]

2.4.3. EIOPA Stress Tests

EIOPA regularly organises stress tests. A stress test is an important risk management tool (for instance, as part of the ORSA). It is also a supervisory tool to explore vulnerabilities and to assess the resilience of (re)insurance

---

colleges and accomplishments of action plan and priorities for 2016, 4 May 2016, 8 p. (https://eiopa.europa.eu/Publications/Administrative/Year-End-Report_Functioning_Colleges_and_Accomplishment.pdf).

142 EIOPA, *Financial Stability Report*, June 2018.

143 See ESRB, *Report on systemic risk in the EU insurance sector*, December 2015, 42 p. with 6 annexes.

undertakings and whole systems (for example, the insurance sector) to severe but plausible external shocks. Stress tests assess adverse outcomes under a variety of risks. They provide an indication of the impact and potential losses on materialisation of these risks, and help to indicate areas where further supervisory actions are needed. It is important to observe that Solvency II in itself is already a stress test. The stress tests organised by EIOPA test different scenarios and their impact on (re)insurance undertakings. They are not a pass or fail test, i.e. their outcome is not intended to result in an increase in capital requirements. The results of the stress tests should therefore be looked at with caution. Even if a number of (re)insurance undertakings or groups do not meet the SCR or the MCR threshold as a result of the stress test, this does not necessarily mean that the undertakings or groups concerned are at risk from a solvency point of view. It means that there are potential vulnerabilities that need to be considered as part of the undertaking's or group's risk management. The first three stress tests were carried out before the official start of Solvency II.

The first EU-wide stress test was carried out by CEIOPS in early 2010. The goal of the stress test was to evaluate the overall resilience of the insurance sector to the economic and financial markets environment under several stress scenarios. The exercise included 28 large and important European insurance groups, covering above 60% of premiums of the European insurance market. Participating insurance groups were asked to calculate the impact of stresses on their solvency ratios under three scenarios: an adverse scenario and two additional severe scenarios (a deep recession and an inflation scenario). The results indicated that the large and important European insurance groups would remain resilient even in severe scenarios. In all scenarios, the aggregated level of available capital exceeded the regulatory requirements.[144]

EIOPA carried out a second stress test in 2011. The stress test was completed by 221 (re)insurance groups and undertakings from the EEA. The stress test included three main scenarios. The baseline scenario was defined as a severe stress, while the adverse scenario included an even more severe deterioration in the main macro-economic variables. The inflation scenario assumed an increase in inflation, which forced central banks to rapidly increase interest rates. A supplementary test to evaluate sovereign bond exposures was also performed. The result of the stress test showed that overall the (re)insurance groups and undertakings concerned were well prepared for potential future shocks as tested in the exercise. Some participating groups and undertakings would not meet the MCR under either the adverse scenario or the inflation scenario. The main risk drivers identified in the stress test were adverse developments in equity prices, interest rates and sovereign debt markets.

---

144 CEIOPS, *Annual Report 2010*, p. 43.

On the liability side, non-life risks were more critical, triggered by increased claims inflation and natural disasters.[145]

The third stress test was carried out in 2014. The stress test included a core module and a low-yield module with a Japanese-like scenario of a persistent low interest rate environment. Participation in the stress test went beyond EIOPA's target of covering at least 50% of the insurance market in each country. The results of the stress test showed that the insurance sector would be more vulnerable to a "double hit" stress scenario that combines decreases in asset values with a lower risk-free rate. A continuation of the current low-yield conditions could see some insurers having problems in fulfilling their promises to policyholders in the medium term (8–11 years). Based on the results of the stress test, EIOPA issued a number of recommendations to NSAs in order to address the identified vulnerabilities in a coordinated way:

- to engage in a rigorous assessment of the preparedness of insurance undertakings to implement Solvency II;
- to put in place the necessary procedures to operate the transitional provisions relating to non-compliance with the MCR (Art. 131 FD) and the SCR (Art. 308 (b) (14) FD);
- to engage with insurance undertakings to ensure that they are able to make informed choices on the use of the LTG and transitional measures;
- to put in place efficient processes to support robust decision-making in relation to the use of the LTG and transitional measures;
- to engage with relevant insurance undertakings to ensure that they have in place a robust system of governance, including the capacity to prepare the required progress report in the case of non-compliance with the SCR (Art. 308 (b) (14) FD);
- to engage with insurance undertakings to ensure that they have a clear understanding of their risk exposures and the vulnerability to given stress scenarios as a result of this and that they have the capacity to take recovery actions to deal with those vulnerabilities;
- to engage with relevant insurance undertakings to ensure that they properly assess the sustainability of the guaranteed rates that they offer;
- to take the necessary supervisory measures to deal with undertakings deemed to be operating unsustainable business models.[146]

---

[145] EIOPA, Specifications for the 2011 EU-wide stress test in the insurance sector, EIOPA-FS-11/012, 23 March 2011, 24 p.; Press Release, 4 July 2011 (https://eiopa.europa.eu/Publications/Press%20Releases/Stress-Test-Results-Release.pdf).

[146] EIOPA, Insurance Stress Test 2014, EIOPA-BoS-14-203, 28 November 2014, 244 p.; *EIOPA announces results of the EU-wide insurance stress test 2014*, Press Release, 30 November 2014; Recommendations EIOPA Stress Test 2014, EIOPA-BoS-14/209, 27 November 2014, 7 p.

The fourth stress test was carried out in 2016. Two scenarios were tested, i.e. a low-for-long yield scenario and a "double-hit" scenario. The low-for-long scenario covered a situation of entrenched secular stagnation where a lack of long-term investment opportunities and permanently low productivity growth was combined with a prolonged scarcity of risk-free assets that drove down yields at all maturities. The "double-hit" scenario was set up by EIOPA in cooperation with the ESRB. It reflected the prevailing systemic risks of the European financial system, i.e. an abrupt increase in risk premiums combined with a prolonged low yield environment. The exercise included 236 undertakings at solo level, from 30 countries. It confirmed the vulnerability of the insurance sector to a low interest rate environment and to a pronounced reassessment of risk premiums.[147] Based on the results of the stress test, EIOPA issued a number of recommendations to NSAs in order to address the vulnerabilities identified during the exercise:

- to ensure that undertakings align their internal risk management processes to the external risks faced as part of their ORSA;
- to review and assess undertakings' models regarding future management actions and policyholder behaviour;
- to review the clauses of the guarantees, their typologies and the options associated with them to assess whether the valuation of the technical provisions can be considered proportionate and prudent;
- to request a reduction in the maximum guarantees or in unsustainable profit participations offered;
- to request a cancellation or deferral of dividend distribution when the viability of the business model is at risk;
- to ensure that the vulnerabilities identified at solo level are appropriately recognised and dealt with at group level.[148]

The fifth stress test was carried out in 2018.[149] Whilst the 2016 stress test was at solo level, this stress test focused on the impact of adverse scenarios on 42 large insurance groups from 12 EEA countries representing a market coverage of around 75% based on total consolidated assets. The reference date was 31 December 2017. Three stress scenarios were tested:

- a yield curve up shock combined with lapse and provisions deficiency shocks, implying a sudden and sizeable repricing of risk premiums and a significant increase in claims inflation;

---

147 EIOPA, Insurance Stress Test Report 2016, EIOPA 16/302, 15 December 2016, 74 p.

148 EIOPA, Insurance Stress Test 2016. Recommendations, EIOPA 16/297, 15 December 2016, 5 p.

149 EIOPA, *2018 Insurance Stress Test Report*, Publications Office of the EU, Luxembourg, 2018, 40 p.; EIOPA, *2018 Insurance Stress Test. Frequently asked questions & answers*, 14 December 2018, 9 p.; EIOPA, *EIOPA announces results of the 2018 insurance stress test*, Press Release, 14 December 2018, 2 p.

- a yield curve down shock combined with longevity stress, implying a protracted period of extremely low interest rates accompanied by an increase in the life expectancy;
- a series of natural catastrophes where European countries were hit in quick succession by four windstorms, two floods and two earthquakes.

The impact of the different scenarios on the balance sheet position (assets over liabilities) and on the capital position (SCR ratio) of the participating groups was assessed. Given the operational and methodological challenges related to the recalculation of the group SCR post-stress, participating groups were allowed to use approximations and simplifications as long as these provided a fair reflection of the direction and magnitude of the impact.

In the pre-stress (baseline) situation, participating groups reported an aggregate ratio of assets over liabilities of 109.5% and a pre-stress SCR coverage of 202.4%.

In the yield curve up scenario, the excess of assets over liabilities is reduced by 32.2%, from 109.5% to 107.6%, because of a significant drop in the value of assets that is not compensated by decreasing liabilities, and the aggregate post-stress SCR ratio drops from 202.4% to 145.2%. Six groups reported a post-stress SCR ratio below 100%.

In the yield curve down scenario, the excess of assets over liabilities is reduced by 27.6% from 109.5% to 106.7%, driven by an increase in technical provisions, and the aggregate post-stress SCR ratio drops from 202.4% to 137.4%. Seven groups reported a post-stress SCR below 100%.

In the natural catastrophe scenario only a small decrease of assets over liabilities (0.3 percentage points) was reported. Overall, the participating groups demonstrated a high resilience to the series of natural catastrophes tested, because 55% of the losses were transferred to reinsurance. As a result, the most affected groups were reinsurers and those direct insurers largely involved in reinsurance activities.

It was the first time that participating groups were asked to have their individual results disclosed (as is now commonly the case in the banking sector). Four of the 42 participating groups[150] agreed to have their individual results disclosed.

In its conclusions, EIOPA noted the importance of the LTG and transitional measures. In the first scenario, almost half of the groups reported SCR ratios below 100% when these measures were excluded. In the second scenario, half of the groups reported SCR ratios below 100%.

150 Vienna Insurance Group, PFA Pension, Forsikringsselskabet Danica and Mapfre.

2.4.4. Macro-Prudential Supervision

Of particular importance is the work which EIOPA is carrying out on macro-prudential supervision, which is consistent with the work carried out by the IAIS in this area.[151] The financial crisis has shown that it is important for supervisory authorities to also consider the way in which systemic risk[152] is created and/or amplified and to have proper policies in place to address those risks. So far, the discussion on macro-prudential supervision has mainly concentrated on the banking sector.[153] EIOPA has initiated a number of papers on systemic risk and macro-prudential policy[154] in insurance with the aim of contributing to the debate and ensuring that any extension of this debate to the insurance sector reflects the specific nature of the insurance business.

In its first paper,[155] EIOPA examines and analyses the sources of systemic risk insurance from a conceptual point of view. The first part of the paper provides an overview of the status of the discussion on systemic risk and macro-prudential policies in insurance and depicts the most important lessons learned from the financial crisis and their relevance for insurance:

- it is widely acknowledged that traditional insurance is generally less systemically important than banking;[156]

---

151 See, for instance, IAIS, *Macro-prudential policy and surveillance in insurance*, 18 July 2013, 56 p., and IAIS, *Holistic Framework for systemic risk in the insurance sector*, Public Consultation Document, 14 November 2018, 72 p. See also IAIS, ICP 24 – Macro-prudential Surveillance and Insurance Supervision.

152 Systemic risk is defined as "a risk of disruption in the financial system with the potential to have serious negative consequences for the internal market and the real economy". See Art. 2 (c) Regulation (EU) No 1092/2010 of the EP and of the Council of 24 November 2010 on EU macro-prudential oversight of the financial system and establishing a European Systemic Risk Board, *OJ* L 331, 15.12.2010, p. 1.

153 See, for instance, ESRB, *Flagship report on macro-prudential policy in the banking sector*, March 2013, 26 p.; *Handbook on operationalising macro-prudential policy in the banking sector*, March 2014, 264 p; *Final report on the use of structural macro-prudential instruments in the EU*, December 2017, 106 p. For a review of the literature, see GALATI, G. and MOESSNER, R., *Macro-prudential policy – a literature review*, BIS Working Paper No 337, February 2011, 40 p., and CLAESSENS, S., *An overview of macro-prudential policy tools*, IMF Working Paper WP/14/214, 2014, 38 p.

154 Macro-prudential policy is defined by EIOPA as "a framework that aims at mitigating systemic risk (or the build-up thereof), thereby contributing to the ultimate objective of the stability of the financial system and, as a result, the broader implications for economic growth".

155 EIOPA, *Systemic risk and macro-prudential policy in insurance*, Publication Office of the EU, Luxembourg, 2017, 77 p. This paper also includes an extensive list of references to the academic literature on the subject.

156 See, for instance, the Geneva Association, *Systemic risk in insurance: an analysis of insurance and financial stability, Special Report of the Geneva Association Systemic Risk Working Group*, March 2010, 129 p. The report underlines that the insurance business model – encompassing both insurers and reinsurers – has specific features that make it a source of stability in the financial system. Insurance is funded by upfront premiums, giving insurers strong operating

- insurance can potentially create or amplify systemic risk; therefore, a macro-prudential approach also seems justified in insurance;
- macro-prudential policies for insurance can help to prevent a financial crisis but they should be tailored to insurance;
- a balance between an entity-based and an activity-based approach needs to be struck in insurance, whereby special attention should be paid to the systemic risk arising from certain activities or products;[157]
- sufficient tools need to be in place to address the sources of systemic risk;
- there could be a risk of regulatory arbitrage if insurance is not included within the wider macro-prudential framework.

Macro-prudential and micro-prudential approaches to policy and supervision are two sides of the same coin: the financial crisis has demonstrated that the actions of individual undertakings may be optimal at the level of the undertaking but suboptimal from a macro-prudential standpoint, and thus solvency of individual undertakings is not, on its own, adequate to protect against the risk of financial instability.[158] In this way, the micro-prudential approach to supervision is complemented by the macro-prudential approach. Forward-looking macro-prudential supervision endeavours to identify those risks to individual insurers arising from interconnections with other parts of the financial system and the real economy. By properly identifying these interconnections, as well as identifying the vulnerabilities and risks that may arise therefrom, macro-prudential supervision contributes to financial system stability.

Although Solvency II is a micro-prudential supervisory regime, it already contains elements of macro-prudential supervision. This was analysed in the second paper published by EIOPA.[159] Most of the measures relate to the LTG package. However, Solvency II also includes other tools that may have an indirect effect on macro-prudential policy. These tools include the prudent person principle in investment, the ORSA and the possibility for supervisory

cash flow without requiring wholesale funding. Insurance policies are generally long-term, with controlled outflows, enabling insurers to act as stabilisers to the financial system. During the crisis, insurers maintained relatively steady capacity, business volumes and prices. Those few insurers who experienced serious difficulties, most notably AIG, were brought down not by their insurance business but by their quasi-banking activities.

157 Often referred to as non-traditional, non-insurance activities (NTNI), such as derivative trading and securities lending. On this issue, see HUFELD, F., A regulatory framework for systemic risk in the insurance industry, in HUFELD, F., KOIJEN, R.S.J. and THIMANN, C. (Eds.), *The Economics, Regulation and Systemic Risk of Insurance Markets*, Oxford University Press, New York, 2017.

158 IAIS, *Macro-prudential policy and surveillance in insurance*, 18 July 2013, p. 10.

159 EIOPA, *Solvency II tools with macro-prudential impact*, Publications Office of the EU, Luxembourg, 2018, 58 p.

authorities to impose a capital add-on in exceptional situations.[160] In addition, the design of Solvency II, with its forward-looking approach and its introduction of two capital requirements, also has a positive impact on macro-prudential policy. Finally, the risk-free interest rate term structure and the extrapolation towards an ultimate forward rate have a clear macro-prudential impact, as they affect the calculation of the technical provisions, as well as the investment and risk management behaviour.[161]

In its paper, EIOPA identifies and analyses the following tools with macro-prudential impact that are available under Solvency II:

- symmetric adjustment to the equity risk sub-module;[162]
- VA to the relevant risk-free interest rate;[163]
- MA to the relevant risk-free interest rate;[164]
- extension of the recovery period in case of non-compliance with the SCR;[165]
- transitional measures on technical provisions;[166]
- prohibition or restriction by EIOPA or by an NSA for (re)insurance undertakings to carry out certain types of financial activities;[167]
- measures in the case of a breach of the SCR;[168]
- other measures at the disposal of NSAs.[169]

EIOPA concludes that Solvency II in itself is designed to ensure sufficient loss-absorbing capacity and provisioning, and that it puts significant emphasis on the identification, measurement and proactive management of risks, which discourages risky behaviour and excessive levels of direct and indirect exposure concentrations.

160 EIOPA, *Solvency II tools with macro-prudential impact*, Publications Office of the EU, Luxembourg, 2018, pp. 3–6.

161 EIOPA, *Solvency II tools with macro-prudential impact*, Publications Office of the EU, Luxembourg, 2018, p. 6.

162 See above, Chapter 6, section 4.2.2.2.4.

163 See above, Chapter 6, section 2.3.4.

164 See above, Chapter 6, section 2.3.3.

165 See above, Chapter 6, section 4.2.1.4.

166 See above, Chapter 6, section 2.3.6.

167 This tool is not foreseen under Solvency II but is available under Art. 9 (5) EIOPA Regulation and under Arts. 16 and 17 of Regulation (EU) No 1286/2014 of the EP and of the Council of 26 November 2014 on key information documents for packaged retail and insurance-based investment products (PRIIPS), *OJ* L 352, 9.12.2014, p. 1.

168 See above, Chapter 6, section 4.2.1.4.

169 This includes measures such as a limitation or restriction on certain business lines and operations, additional provisioning or a requirement to use net profits to strengthen own funds. See, for instance, National Bank of Belgium, *Financial Stability Report 2018*, p. 19: insurance undertakings are required to set up additional annual provisions (called "flashing-light provisions") to ensure that they can meet their future obligations.

However, Solvency II did not specifically address systemic risk and macro-prudential policy. The question therefore arises as to whether other tools than those which are already present in the FD are needed to enhance the current framework from a macro-prudential perspective. This is the subject of the third paper developed by EIOPA, which looks at four categories of tools: capital and provisioning-based tools; liquidity-based tools; exposure-based tools and pre-emptive planning. It examines whether these tools should be used for enhanced reporting and monitoring or as intervention powers, and proposes to further consider a number of specific tools as part of the revision of Solvency II in 2021.

The following (micro- and macro-prudential) tools are listed as part of enhanced reporting and monitoring:

- leverage ratio: monitoring at market level the ratio of capital to assets and the non-insurance liabilities to capital might add value to identify potential risks;
- enhanced monitoring against market-wide under-provisioning: gathering additional data on the actuarial assumptions and monitoring them with the actual developments to identify structural deviations might help to avoid market-wide under-provisioning;
- additional reporting on liquidity risk: enhanced quantitative reporting on liquidity risk would allow a better monitoring of liquidity risk at sector level;
- liquidity risk ratios: a risk assessment framework based on prudential liquidity indicators could be developed that captures the level of liquidity risk at market level;
- enhancement of the prudent person principle and of the ORSA: allowing supervisory authorities to make specific requests from a macro-prudential perspective;
- recovery and resolution plans and liquidity risk and systemic risk management plans: enhancement of financial stability by imposing pre-emptive plans that address sources of systemic risk.

The following tools are listed as part of further intervention powers:

- capital add-on for systemic risk: a macro-prudential capital surcharge on top of the existing micro-prudential capital surcharge for systemically relevant (re)insurers;
- temporary freeze on redemption rights: avoid life insurers being over-impacted by a run on insurance. This tool should only be used in very exceptional circumstances, to prevent risks that represent a strong threat to the financial health of the whole insurance market or to the financial system, and for a limited period of time;

- concentration thresholds: avoiding excessive exposures (for instance, government or corporate bonds, equity, real estate, etc.) through enhanced risk management practices as part of the prudent person principle.

In its report,[170] which follows the three reports issued by EIOPA, the ESRB highlights a number of options that could help to strengthen the macro-prudential framework for the (re)insurance sector:

- a power for supervisory authorities to impose entity-based and/or activity/behaviour-based market-wide capital increases and dividend restrictions in situations in which (re)insurance market developments could generate systemic risk;
- symmetric capital requirements for cyclical risks;
- liquidity requirements for (re)insurers with a vulnerable liquidity profile;
- a discretionary power for supervisory authorities to intervene in cases of mass lapses;
- instruments to target bank-like activities to ensure cross-sectoral consistency of macro-prudential policy.

The three papers developed by EIOPA and the paper published by the ESRB are a good start for the discussion on how to enhance the current solvency framework as part of the Solvency II review in 2021, in line with developments taking place at international level within the context of the IAIS.[171]

---

170 ESRB, *Macro-prudential powers, measures and instruments for insurance*, November 2018, 79 p.

171 See also, EIOPA, Discussion paper on Systemic Risk and Macroprudential Policy in Insurance, EIOPA-BoS-19/131, 29 March 2019, 46 p.

CHAPTER 12
CONCLUSION

It cannot be denied that Solvency II has been a success. Although it is the most far-reaching change in insurance regulation in the EU for 30 years, and although it was introduced in the middle of a financial crisis that created the worst possible environment for (re)insurers, with a prolonged period of low interest rates, the introduction of Solvency II happened smoothly and the very large majority of (re)insurance undertakings in the EU are still well capitalised. Failures, where they have occurred, have been fairly well contained.[1]

Nevertheless, it has been alleged that Solvency II has made it more difficult for insurers to continue to provide long-term guarantees, with the consequence that risks have been transferred back to policyholders. This has had an impact on the possibility for insurers to continue their role as long-term investors, providing stability in the market.[2]

This criticism must be taken seriously. It is very much linked to the debate about sustainability. The insurance industry will have to play an important role in helping to resolve major societal problems, such as climate change, health care, longevity and pension financing. This will not be possible unless the insurance industry can operate in a regulatory framework that fully recognises its unique business model.

This raises difficult questions for which there is no ready answer. Accounting standard-setters have struggled for a long time with the valuation of long-term liabilities. So have insurance regulators. The debate about how to do this right has not yet led to unanimous conclusions. On the one hand, accountants and actuaries warn against an overly prudent treatment of long-term liabilities. On the other hand, insurance supervisors caution against an approach that might end up hurting policyholders. As insurance liabilities can have a very long duration and as nobody knows exactly how interest rates and inflation might fluctuate over a long period, much of the debate will remain a question of agreeing on a treatment that is acceptable to most parties concerned at a particular point in

1 CUNDY, C., Solvency II: what reforms can we expect? *Insurance ERM*, 27 December 2018, p. 1.

2 See, for instance, EC, *Financing a sustainable European Economy: Final Report 2018 by the High-Level Expert Group on Sustainable Finance*, January 2018, pp. 70–72. See also JONES, O., Solvency II. Review views, in Insurance Europe, *Annual Report 2017–2018*, pp. 15–17.

time and in a particular environment. It is not possible to find a solution that is absolutely correct, as we are trying to predict the future.

In terms of Solvency II, there are two basic questions: how should insurance liabilities, which can be very predictable and can therefore be qualified as illiquid, be valued, and what capital charge should apply to the assets (bonds, equities, property) that are invested by (re)insurers in order to match these liabilities?

These questions were already on the table in the context of Omnibus II and led to the development of the LTG package. Although this package offered a solution, I have never liked it, because it did not address the specificities of the insurance business model and was basically a compromise that helped the co-legislators move forward and agree so that Solvency II could come into force.[3] The co-legislators were well aware of the limitations inherent in the LTG package and therefore provided for regular reporting by undertakings and by EIOPA on its application and for a review of the package in 2020. EIOPA has already been asked by the EC to start preparing this review[4] and has issued a consultation paper on the treatment of illiquid liabilities.[5] That paper clearly sets the scene for the start of the debate. Meanwhile, the EC has, in the context of the 2018 review of the DA, introduced a new category of long-term equity investments with a lower capital charge. Although this is not a bad idea, it is doubtful whether such a quick-fix remedy could be a solution to a problem that is far more complex, i.e. how to better align the regulatory framework with the long-term business model of (re)insurers. This is an issue that needs to be addressed in a holistic manner.

One of the objectives of the review of the FD in 2020 should be to find a solution that better recognises the long-term business model of (re)insurers and that can work independently of the development of financial markets, i.e. in all circumstances. It should take account of the way in which (re)insurers operate in reality and contain at the same time the necessary prudence, because the ultimate objective remains the protection of policyholders and beneficiaries.

---

3 A good example is the MA, whose scope was defined very narrowly. It was not considered on its merits but as a mechanism that might potentially distort the internal market. See, Towers Watson, Solvency II. The matching adjustment and implications for long-term savings, 2012, 14 p. (https://www.towerswatson.com/en/Insights/IC-Types/Survey-Research-Results/2012/08/Solvency-II-The-matching-adjustment-and-implications-for-long-term-savings).

4 See the letter of 27 April 2018 from the Director-General of DG FISMA, Olivier Guersent, to Gabriel Bernardino asking EIOPA to provide information about insurance liabilities, about asset management of (re)insurers, about the impact of the LTG-measures and about the market valuation of insurance liabilities (https://eiopa.europa.eu/Publications/Letters/COM%20request%20for%20info%20on%20impact%20of%20SII%20on%20long%20term%20insurance%20and%20reinsurance%20activities.pdf). EIOPA needs to provide the information by 16 December 2019 in order to contribute to the 2020 review of the FD.

5 EIOPA, Request for Feedback on Methodological Considerations regarding Illiquid Liabilities, EIOPA-PSC-18/093, 29 October 2018, 30 p.

Discussions on this issue have also taken place in the context of the development of an ICS. Account must be taken of these discussions and of the various solutions that have been advanced in that context. The idea of introducing a spread risk adjustment, i.e. to remove from the risk-free rate the volatility created by movements in spreads, seems attractive. Equally so, the possibility of lowering the capital requirement for assets held to match long-term "illiquid" liabilities is tempting, on the condition that it can be shown that such an investment is less risky. More research is however needed.[6] A solution must be found that limits pro-cyclical behaviour by (re)insurers and that does not send the message that a market-consistent valuation of assets means that all assets held by (re)insurers are ready for sale in the short term.

The co-legislators have provided for a number of reviews in the FD. These reviews are different from the 2018 review of the DA. The reviews that are now on the table relate to the FD itself, with spill-over effects for the DA, various ITS and the guidelines of EIOPA. The reviews that are explicitly foreseen concern the following issues:

- the LTG package, for which the EC is asked to submit a report based on an opinion submitted by EIOPA, by 1 January 2021 (Art. 77f (3) FD);
- the standard formula for the calculation of the SCR, for which the EC is asked to submit a report, after making an assessment, by 31 December 2020 (Art. 111 (3) FD);
- the enhancement of group supervision and capital management within groups, for which the EC is asked to make an assessment by 31 December 2018 and to present a report afterwards (Art. 242 (2) FD);
- temporary equivalence in the case of parent undertakings outside the EU, for which there is a deadline of 31 December 2020 (Art. 260 (6) FD);
- the calculation of the MCR, on which the EC must submit a report to the EP and to the Council by 31 December 2020 (Art. 129 (5) FD).

In addition to these reviews, there is also the implementation of the Action Plan on Financing Sustainable Growth,[7] which calls for:

- a reorientation of capital flows towards sustainable investment in order to achieve sustainable and inclusive growth;

---

6 For instance: Should there be ring-fencing? Can the long-term portfolio also include equities and property? Can we learn something about the debate in accounting about the banking book and the trading book? How should forced sales of assets be dealt with?

7 See the proposals from the EC, dated 24 May 2018 on sustainable finance, including a proposal for a regulation on disclosures relating to sustainable investments and sustainability risks and targeted amendments to increase disclosures of environmental, social and governance (ESG)-related information and to integrate ESG-related preferences into the suitability assessment under the IDD and MiFID II.

- an assessment and management of relevant financial risks stemming from climate change,[8] resource depletion, environmental degradation and social issues;
- the fostering of transparency and long-termism in financial and economic activity.

The debate on sustainable finance will profoundly affect the insurance sector. It will have an impact on risk management (the need to apply a longer time horizon in looking at risk and to consider risks that are not only financial),[9] on investment (reorientation of investments towards environmental, social and governance (ESG) investments with the related transition risks following from the move towards a more sustainable economy), on prevention (risk mitigation), and on product design and insurance distribution. Sustainable insurance is defined as a strategic approach where all activities in the insurance value chain, including interaction with stakeholders, are done in a responsible and forward-looking way by identifying, assessing, managing and monitoring risk and opportunities associated with ESG issues. Sustainable insurance aims to reduce risk, develop innovative solutions, improve business performance and contribute to ESG sustainability.[10] It also requires a fresh look at some prudential rules, such as the restrictive treatment of intangible assets in the solvency balance sheet.

On 24 July 2018,[11] EIOPA was asked by the EC to provide technical advice by 30 April 2019 on the possibility of explicitly requiring the integration of sustainable risks, i.e. ESG risks, in the investment decisions of (re)insurance undertakings. The EC wants to ensure that sustainability concerns are sufficiently taken into account by (re)insurance undertakings in their investment decisions.[12] This was followed by a further request from the EC on 28 August 2018[13] to provide advice

[8] See CRO Forum, The heat is on. Insurability and resilience in a changing climate, 2019, 51 p. (https://www.thecroforum.org/wp-content/uploads/2019/01/CROF-ERI-2019-The-heat-is-on-Position-paper-1.pdf).

[9] See KIVISAARI, E., Risk management should be one of the cornerstones when insurers consider their role in sustainability, *Insurance ERM*, 2 January 2019.

[10] United Nations Environment Programme (UNEP) Finance Initiative, *Principles for Sustainable Insurance*, 2012, http://www.unepfi.org/fileadmin/documents/PSI_document-en.pdf.

[11] Letter of 24 July 2018 from the Director-General of DG FISMA, Olivier Guersent, to Gabriel Bernardino (https://ec.europa.eu/info/sites/info/files/business_economy_euro/banking_and_finance/documents/180828-letter-eiopa-solvency-2_en.pdf) and EIOPA, Consultation Paper on Technical Advice on the integration of sustainability risks and factors in the delegated acts under Solvency II and IDD, EIOPA-BoS-18/483, 26 November 2018, 48 p.

[12] There is a need to proceed cautiously in this area. The importance attached to sustainable investment may not result in higher risks for policyholders. See GRÜNDL, H., *Sustainable Finance: Nicht auf Kosten der Versicherungskunden*, Absolut Impact, 2018, No 4, p. 15 (http://www.icir.de/fileadmin/Documents/Policy_Platform/AI_04-2018_Prof_Gruendl_Kommentar.pdf).

[13] See the letter of 28 August 2018 from the Director-General of DG FISMA, Olivier Guersent, to Gabriel Bernardino (https://eiopa.europa.eu/Publications/Requests%20for%20advice/signed_letter_28_08_18.pdf#search=sustainability).

by 30 September 2019 on: the impact of prudential rules on insurers' sustainable investments; the integration of sustainability factors with particular regard to climate in underwriting practice; the impact of climate-related developments on the calibration of the standard formula and on internal model design and calibration; and the extent to which the calculation of the best estimate captures sustainability and climate-related developments.

Whilst the first request will potentially lead to an amendment of the DA (for instance, by integrating sustainability risks in the prudent person principle and by including sustainability risk as one of the risk management areas to consider by the risk management function[14]), the second request will directly impact the FD and will therefore more likely be integrated into the review of the FD in 2020. Of particular importance for insurance is the general request from the EC addressed to the ESAs in January 2019 to collect evidence of undue short-term pressure from financial markets on undertakings in the financial sector and to provide advice by mid-September 2019 on possible remedial actions by regulators. This request is part of the increased attention paid to sustainability. In insurance, short-term pressures might result from too much reliance on capital markets in credit risk evaluation, from a market consistent valuation of assets and liabilities, from too much insistence on the SCR as a hard threshold that should never be breached, from the application of the tiering structure in own funds, from the governance structure but also from supervisory actions.

Each of these reviews is important, but there is no need for a Solvency III, nor is there a need for revolutionary changes to the FD. However, improvements can certainly be made, as long as the basic principles of Solvency II are respected, such as the existence of three pillars that are of equal importance and are interlinked, the connection between risk and capital, the market-consistent valuation of assets and liabilities, the existence of two capital requirements, with the SCR as an early-warning signal, and the importance of group supervision.

In preparing for these changes, account must be taken of new developments that have occurred since the adoption of Solvency II:

- the adoption in the near future (end 2019) of an ICS: it would not be responsible to disregard the debate that has taken place within the context of the IAIS and in which many supervisory and regulatory authorities of EU MS, including EIOPA, have taken an active role;
- the adoption (at last) of IFRS 17 – Insurance Contracts: some consistency between the two frameworks would be in the interest of all parties concerned;
- the work on macro-prudential supervision that has been carried out at the level of the FSB and the IAIS, and which EIOPA and the ESRB have already

[14] See the proposals made by EIOPA in its Technical Advice on the integration of sustainability risks and factors in the delegated acts under Solvency II and IDD, EIOPA-BoS-19/172, 30 April 2019, 288 p.

picked up: the proper treatment of macro-prudential issues is in the interest of policyholders and financial stability;
- the decision by the EU to move in the direction of a more sustainable society: in order to allow the insurance industry to play its critical role in this area, the regulatory framework must attach more importance to long-term business;
- the adoption of a full equivalence decision for Bermuda and Switzerland: it would be unfair not to include these two countries in the discussions regarding amendments to a framework in which they also strongly believe.[15]

As this is the first major review of the FD, it might be useful to also consider a number of other changes, including:

- Pillar 1 issues;
- simplifications and proportionality;
- group supervision;
- governance;
- macro-prudential issues.

As far as *Pillar 1 issues* are concerned, the risk margin in the valuation of technical provisions needs to be looked at, both the methodology and the cost of capital rate. Things have changed since the adoption of Solvency II and the valuation of technical provisions on a transfer value basis should not provide an excuse for the introduction of an additional layer of prudence.

The calibrations in the standard formula should receive an update, as new data might have become available that warrant an amendment of the capital charges. This should be done not only from an actuarial perspective but also taking into account other considerations, such as the business model of (re)insurers and sustainability.

A fresh look at some calibrations is also necessary after Brexit, as many calibrations were directly or indirectly based upon data collected from the UK market. Considering the importance of that market, the impact of those data on the overall calibration of many risks should not be underestimated. This is particularly the case for property risk, but also for lapse risk, natural catastrophe risk, premium and reserve risk and mortality and longevity risk.

There is also a need to look at the capital treatment of sovereign bonds. This is a thorny issue, but looking at (re)insurance undertakings' investment portfolios, the amount of investment in sovereign bonds is disproportionate.

---

15 This would also have to include, in one way or another, the UK after Brexit, before or after the withdrawal date and depending on whether an equivalence decision is adopted. See, CHEONG, C., EU could weaponise Solvency II to damage UK post-Brexit, ABI warns, Insurance ERM, 25 February 2019 (https://www.insuranceerm.com/news-comment/eu-could-weaponise-solvency-ii-to-damage-uk-post-brexit-abi-warns.html).

As indicated by the ESRB in its report, any change in this area might require a transitional period. It must also be carried out for the whole financial sector, thus including credit institutions and investment firms, and cannot be restricted to the insurance sector.

As far as *simplicity and proportionality* are concerned, even after the 2018 review of the DA, the Solvency II regulatory framework remains too complex. It must be possible to simplify the regime by making better use of the proportionality principle.

For less complex (re)insurers, it should be possible to apply a simplified calculation in the standard formula even when not specifically authorised in the DA, for instance where the undertaking has no exposure (the SCR is zero) or where the undertaking can show that there is no material difference between setting a fixed amount and applying the standard formula.

Not all (re)insurance undertakings should be required[16] to publish a full SFCR or do so on an annual basis and, where small and medium-sized (re)insurers publish an SFCR, Member States should be forbidden from requiring the audit of parts of the SFCR. As a matter of principle, the SFCR should be retained because it is an excellent communication tool. However, for those undertakings that must publish a full SFCR, a better balance must be established between the information that is of interest to the non-expert reader and the information that is relevant for expert readers, such as academics, financial analysts or rating agencies.

As a follow-up to the EC's fitness check on supervisory reporting, it would be useful to examine to what extent the various supervisory reporting obligations can be further streamlined, for instance in terms of deadlines for the submission of the information, reduction of the amount of information and overlaps between the various reports.

The proportionality principle also requires giving proper consideration to the nature of the business. This has only partially been done for captive (re)insurers and for reinsurers. Particularly for reinsurance, there is a need to further clarify how the various types of reinsurance should be treated under Solvency II. This will help (re)insurance undertakings to further optimise their capital position.

Although *group supervision* is of equal importance to solo supervision, it is not treated well under Solvency II. The IGD, which served as the basis for parts of Title III FD, is beyond any doubt the most convoluted text ever produced by the EU. Some of the definitions in the IGD that were incorporated word-for-word into the FD are simply impossible to understand. It was a mistake to copy these articles into the FD. Title III should be reformulated using a bottom-up approach, rather than an approach that mixes parts that are written out in full with other parts which contain a "mutatis mutandis" reference to the solo supervision articles.

---

16 Voluntary publication might also be an option for small and/or medium-sized (re)insurers.

There is no need to change the requirements in substance, but the text should be more clearly drafted so that it becomes easier to understand. In the same way as the basic principles of solo supervision are set out in Title I, it should be possible to lay down the principles of group supervision in Title III. This would also help resolve the problems that EIOPA has identified in its report to the EC on group supervision. At the same time, the relationship between Solvency II, FICOD and the CRD, in terms of who should supervise what in the context of mixed financial groups, should be better explained.

Finally, an attempt should be made to reintroduce parts of the group support regime proposed by the EC in its initial proposal. There is no need to overload all (re)insurance groups with unnecessary levels of capital.

As for *governance*, some of the governance provisions included in the CRD would also be useful in Solvency II. This is particularly true for the provisions concerning the role and composition of the AMSB, the establishment of board committees, the number of directorships and the remuneration committee.

It would also be of interest to take another look at the requirement for all (re)insurance undertakings to establish four separate key governance functions and at how these functions relate to other governance functions in the undertaking. This matter is dealt with under Solvency II in far more detail than in the CRD and has led to a complex regulatory framework. As some of these key functions are exercised in practice by the same person, the question should be raised as to whether more flexibility can be built into the system so as to allow undertakings to set up the governance regime that suits them best.

Furthermore, there is a need to clarify some of the concepts, such as "persons who effectively run the undertaking" and "persons that have other key functions".

Finally, with regard to *macro-prudential issues*, Solvency II was developed before the financial crisis and before the debate on systemic risk and macro-prudential policy. This was to some extent corrected in the context of Omnibus II, as underlined in the papers produced by EIOPA on macro-prudential policy.

Issues such as a capital charge for systemic risk and some resolution tools and competences, both at solo and at group level, which would help to alleviate the effects of an insolvency in the interests of protecting policyholders and of financial stability, should receive proper attention in this review. It is important here not to create a whole new area of regulation but to make maximum use of existing mechanisms, such as risk management and the ORSA.[17]

In that context, it may be useful to reintroduce the debate on a possible harmonisation of insurance guarantee schemes. From an internal market perspective, it is important to ensure a level playing field for policyholders in cross-border business. On the other hand, if all MS have an insurance guarantee scheme that compensates policyholders in the case of an insurance failure, it is

---

17 See, CRO Forum, Insurers' Risk Management Systems – Preparing for Recovery, July 2012, 17 p. (https://www.thecroforum.org/2012/08/01/recovery-and-resolution-2/).

also necessary to look at the calibration in the standard formula in a different perspective. Although the present regime does not guarantee that there won't be insurance failures, the confidence level was set at a level that was considered to be sufficiently high, independent from the existence of an insurance guarantee scheme. The introduction of a fall-back mechanism means that this confidence level might have to be looked at again, so as to avoid the system from becoming too costly for policyholders.

On 11 February 2019,[18] the EC sent a specific request to EIOPA for technical advice on the review of the FD. EIOPA must deliver its advice by 30 June 2020, accompanied by a holistic and robust impact assessment. Many of the aspects mentioned above are included in the request for advice.

In summary, the request for advice refers to the following issues:

- *Pillar 1 issues*

  On *technical provisions*, EIOPA is requested to examine the following issues:
  - the determination of the last liquid point in the context of the extrapolation of the risk-free interest rate term structure;
  - the functioning of the MA and the VA;
  - the modelling of the dynamic VA;
  - the divergent supervisory practices with regard to the calculation of the best estimate;
  - the appropriateness of the design of the risk margin.

  On *own funds*, EIOPA is asked to examine the tiering structure of own funds and particularly the difference with the approach in banking.

  On *the standard formula for the calculation of the SCR*, EIOPA is asked to look at a number of risk modules and sub-modules:
  - the calibration of the interest rate risk sub-module, taking into account the low interest rate environment;
  - a possible simplification of the counterparty default risk module;
  - a possible further simplification of the life and SLT health underwriting risk modules as well as the non-life lapse risk sub-module;
  - the calibration of the underwriting risk modules based on more representative data, that might have become available;
  - the calibration of the natural catastrophe risk sub-module;
  - the equity risk sub-module, including the correlation matrices.

  On *risk-mitigating techniques and other techniques used to reduce the SCR*, EIOPA is asked to examine possible solutions for:
  - non-proportional reinsurance;
  - adverse development covers;

[18] See the letter of 11 February 2019 from the Director-General of DG FISMA, Olivier Guersent, to Gabriel Bernardino (https://ec.europa.eu/info/sites/info/files/business_economy_euro/banking_and_finance/documents/190211-request-eiopa-technical-advice-review-solvency-2.pdf).

- finite reinsurance covers;
- financial risk-mitigating techniques.

On *external ratings*, EIOPA is requested to examine additional methods allowing for a wider use of alternative credit assessments in order to reduce reliance on external ratings.

On *the MCR*, EIOPA is asked to report on the experience with the methodology for the calculation of the MCR, and in particular on:

- whether the rules governing the calculation of the MCR continue to be consistent with a VaR approach subject to a confidence level of 85% over a one-year period;
- potential divergences in supervisory practices in cases of non-compliance with the MCR;
- potential issues with regard to the identification of eligible basic own funds for composite insurers.

- *Pillar 3 issues*

  EIOPA is asked to assess the ongoing appropriateness of the requirements relating to supervisory reporting and public disclosure and whether the volume, frequency and deadlines of reporting and disclosure are appropriate and proportionate.

- *Group supervision issues*

  EIOPA is asked to advise on how to remedy the main issues identified in its Report on group supervision and capital management of (re)insurance undertakings:

  - the scope of application of group supervision and the supervision of intra-group transactions;
  - the rules governing the calculation of group solvency and the interaction with FICOD;
  - the appropriateness of the rules governing the calculation of the minimum consolidated group SCR, including their impact on the level of diversification benefits that may be allowed within a group;
  - uncertainties and gaps related to the application of governance requirements at group level.

- *Macro-prudential issues*

  EIOPA is asked to assess whether the existing provisions allow for an appropriate macro-prudential supervision. Where EIOPA concludes that this is not the case, EIOPA is asked to advise on how to improve the following closed list of items:

  - the ORSA;
  - the drafting of a systemic risk management plan;
  - liquidity risk management planning and liquidity reporting;
  - the prudent person principle.

  EIOPA is also asked to assess whether the Solvency II rules on the recovery of undertakings in stressed situations should be further developed, including harmonised early intervention powers and preventive recovery planning. EIOPA should also advise on which tools should be created to address the failure or the risk of failure of (re)insurance undertakings as well as on what the scope of resolution planning should be.

EIOPA is asked to advise on whether there is a need for minimum harmonisation of national insurance guarantee schemes. For policies sold cross-border through FoS or FoE, EIOPA is asked to examine whether harmonised rules on insurance guarantee schemes could enable recourse to the scheme of the home MS in order to protect policyholders in host Member States.

- *Proportionality*

  EIOPA is asked to examine a further enhancement of the proportionality principle, particularly in the following areas:
  - the appropriateness of the thresholds for exclusion from the scope of the FD;
  - the possibility to waive certain requirements relating to any of the three pillars;
  - rules for the simplified calculation of sub-modules that form an immaterial part of the SCR of an individual (re)insurance undertaking.
- *Transitional measures*

  EIOPA is asked to assess the ongoing appropriateness of the transitional provisions and should examine, in particular, the following measures:
  - the transitional measures concerning the concentration, the spread-risk and the equity risk sub-modules;
  - the transitional measure on the risk-free interest rates;
  - the transitional measure on technical provisions.
- *Long-term investments under Solvency II*

  EIOPA is asked to assess whether the methods, assumptions and standard parameters underlying the calculation of the market risk module appropriately reflect the long-term nature of the insurance business and to:
  - identify the characteristics of insurance business and liabilities that enable insurers to hold their investments for the long term;
  - advise, where appropriate, on revised methods, assumptions and standard parameters for the purpose of calculating the market risk module, reflecting the behaviour of (re)insurers as long-term investors.

The EC's request for advice submitted to EIOPA does not surprise. Many of the issues listed had been identified for review before, or are the subject of specific review clauses. It is, however, remarkable that EIOPA is not asked to look at pillar 2 issues, such as governance, nor at capital management issues within groups. Both issues are important and a review might help to alleviate the regulatory burden, as indicated above.

In terms of timing, this first review of the FD will take a lot of time. This is unavoidable. A proposal from the EC can only come forward some time in 2021.

It will then have to be negotiated between the EP and the Council. Adoption of the proposal is unlikely before the end of 2022. A further two years will be needed for the transposition of the new legislation in Member States. This will be necessary as care must be taken that all follow-up changes in the DA, in the implementing regulations and in the EIOPA Guidelines will be ready in time. A transposition date that is set too early runs the risk that the follow-up changes will not be ready in time, a problem that occurred in other cases, for instance in the case of the IDD, whose transposition date had to be extended as the implementing measures were not ready in time.[19] This makes it unlikely that the changes following from this review of the FD will enter into effect before 2025.

Before the finalisation of the review, other changes may take place in the FD and in the DA as a result of the ESFS review package and the work on sustainability. It is important to carefully plan these changes so as to ensure that (re)insurance undertakings will not be faced with continuous amendments in the regulatory framework. It will also be important to remind all parties concerned (the co-legislators, the (re)insurance industry, EIOPA and NSAs) that a principles-based approach is more likely to be sustainable in the long term.

19 See, Directive (EU) 2018/411 of the EP and of the Council of 14 March 2018 amending Directive (EU) 2016/97 as regards the date of application of Member States' transposition measures, *OJ* L 76, 19.3.2018, p. 28.

BIBLIOGRAPHY

Accountancy Europe, *Standard setting in the 21st century*, Cogito, Brussels, June 2017

ACHARYA, V., PHILIPPON, T. and RICHARDSON, M., Measuring Systemic Risk for Insurance Companies, in HUFELD, F., KOIJEN, R.S.J. and THIMANN, C. (Eds.), *The Economics, Regulation and Systemic Risk of Insurance Markets*, Oxford University Press, New York, 2017

Actuarial Association of Europe (AAE), *European Standard of Actuarial Practice 2 (ESAP 2) – Actuarial Function Report under Directive 2009/138/EC: Model standard of actuarial practice of the AAE*, 31 January 2016

AIGRAIN, J., How do we square the circle between accounting and solvency?, *The Geneva Papers*, 2009, No 34

AISAM, *Governance of Mutual Insurance Companies: the current state of legislation*, Massoz, Liège, October 2006

ANDERSON, D. and EUBANKS, G., *Leveraging COSO across the three lines of defence*, COSO, July 2015

Association of Financial Mutuals (AFM), *Corporate governance for mutual insurers*, Guidance published by AFM in response to the requirements contained in the Myners *Revue of the Governance of Life Mutuals*, January 2015

BaFin, *Government bonds: Treatment of risk under Solvency*, 1 August 2016

BALUCH, F., MUTENGA, S. and PARSONS, C., Insurance, Systemic Risk and the Financial Crisis, *The Geneva Papers on Risk and Insurance – Issues and Practice*, Vol. 36, No 1, January 2011

BALZ, B., Lessons learnt from Solvency II: more rules than principles, *Eurofi Newsletter*, 31 March 2014

Bank of England, *Prudential Regulation Authority, Liquidity risk management for insurers*, Consultation Paper 4/19, March 2019

——, Prudential Regulation Authority, *Solvency II: external audit of the public disclosure requirement*, Consultation Paper 8/18, April 2018

BEHRENDT, B. and GRÖNHOFF, E., Interne Modelle nach Solvency II für einen Holding geführten Versicherungskonzern und die hierfür geltenden Rahmenbedingungen, in BENNEMANN, C., OEHLENBERG, L. and STAHL, G., *Handbuch Solvency II*, Schäffer-Poeschel Verlag, Stuttgart, 2011

BENNEMANN, Ch., OEHLENBERG, L. and STAHL, G., *Handbuch Solvency II*, Stuttgart, Schäffer-Poeschel Verlag, 2011

BERDIN, E., and GRÜNDL, H., The Effects of a Low Interest Rate Environment on Life Insurers, *The Geneva Papers on Risk and Insurance – Issues and Practice*, Vol. 40, No 3, July 2015

BERDIN, E., GRÜNDL, H. and KUBITZA, C.H., *Rising Interest Rates, Lapse Risk and the Stability of Life Insurers*, ICIR Working Paper Series No 29/17, July 2017

BERDIN, E. and SOTTOCORNOLA, M., *Insurance Activities and Systemic Risk*, ICIR Working Paper Series No 19/15, December 2015

BERNARDINO, G., *EIOPA and supervisory convergence – The beginning of a new journey*, EIOPA 5th Annual Conference, Frankfurt, 18 November 2015

——, *Implementation of Solvency II: The dos and the don'ts*, International Conference, Ljubljana, 2 September 2015

——, Infrastructure projects – Improved data is needed to support the reassessment of risk, *Eurofi Newsletter*, 31 March–1 April 2014

——, Insurance and pensions: securing the future, 8th Annual EIOPA Conference, Frankfurt, 20 November 2018

——, Keynote speech at the 3rd Annual FinTech and Regulation Conference in Brussels, 26 February 2019

——, *Milestones of preparation for Solvency II*, European Insurance Conference, London, 2 June 2015

——, *Solvency II implementation – beyond compliance*, IVASS Conference, Rome, 3 March 2016

——, *Solvency II review, proportionality and supervisory convergence*, International Conference on Insurance Regulation, Berlin, 18 October 2018

BMA, *Bermuda's Insurance Solvency Framework. The Roadmap to Regulatory Equivalence*, September 2010

——, *Catastrophe risk in Bermuda. BSCR stress testing and modelling practice analysis: 2017 Report*, 30 November 2018

——, *Market Wide Survey on EU Claims History*, 2017

BORSELLI, A., Insurance Group Supervision in the EU, in MARANO, P. and SIRI, M. (Eds.), *Insurance Regulation in the European Union*, Palgrave Macmillan, Cham, 2017

BRAUMÜLLER, P. and WARZILEK, A., IAIS Multilateral Memorandum of Understanding, in KEMPLER, C., FLAMEE, M., YANG, C.H. and WINDELS, P. (Eds.), *Global Perspectives on Insurance Today*, Palgrave Macmillan, New York, 2013

——, Insurance and Financial Stability, in LIEDTKE, P.M. and MONKIEWICZ, J. (Eds.), *The Future of Insurance Regulation and Supervision: A Global Perspective*, Palgrave Macmillan, Basingstoke, 2011

BUI, D. and EL JAHOUAIRI, K., *Mettre en place les 4 fonctions clés sous solvabilité 2*, Paris, Editions L'Argus de l'Assurance, 2018

BURKHART, T., REUSS, A. and ZWIESLER, H.-J., *Allowance for surplus funds under Solvency II: Adequate reflection of risk sharing between policyholders and shareholders in a risk-based Solvency framework?*, Institute for Finance and Actuarial Science, University of Ulm, 26 June 2016

CADONI, P. and KERFRIDEN, C., Internal Models and Solvency II, in DOFF, R. (Ed.), *The Solvency II Handbook. Practical Approaches to Implementation*, Incisive Media, London, 2014

CASTRO CARVALHO, A.P., HOLL, S., RASKOPF, R. and RUHNAU, S., Proportionality in banking regulation: a cross-country comparison, *FSI Insights on Policy Implementation*, No 1, August 2017

CEA and Groupe Consultatif, *Solvency II Glossary*, March 2007

CEA, *CEA welcomes European Parliament committee vote on Solvency II*, Press Release, 7 October 2008

——, *Solvency II – Frequently asked questions*, February 2007
——, *Solvency II: Making it workable for all*, January 2011
——, *Why excessive capital requirements harm consumers, insurers and the economy*, March 2010
CEBS and CEIOPS, Recommendations on the supplementary requirements of the FICOD for supervisory colleges of financial conglomerates, 21 December 2010
Central Bank of Ireland, *Additional requirements for non-life finite reinsurance*, 2012
——, *Corporate Governance Requirements for Captive Insurance and Captive Reinsurance Undertakings*, 2015
CEPS, *The Future of Insurance Regulation and Supervision in the EU. New developments, new challenges*, Brussels, CEPS, 2006
CHANDELLE, F., *Assurances et Solvabilité II*, Brussels, Larcier Business, 2017
CHELLY, D., GILDAS, R., Gérer les risques sous Solvabilité II, Paris, Editions l'Argus de l'Assurance, Second edition, 2017
CHEONG, C., EU could weaponise Solvency II to damage UK post-Brexit, ABI warns, Insurance ERM, 25 February 2019
CLAESSENS, S., *An overview of macro-prudential policy tools*, IMF Working Paper WP/14/214, 2014
CLEMENT, P., The term "macroprudential": origins and evolution, *BIS Quarterly Review*, March 2010
CLUNE, D., *Topsy-turvy SCR ratios*, http://www.solvencyiiwire.com/topsy-turvy-scr-ratios/1587586, 4 July 2017
COELHO, H., The twists and turns of Solvency II negotiations, *Insurance ERM*, 22 December 2015
COSO, *Internal Control – Integrated Framework, Executive Summary*, May 2013
COUSY, H., Changing Insurance Contract Law: An Age-Old Slow and Unfinished Story, in MARANO, P. and SIRI, M. (Eds.), *Insurance Regulation in the European Union*, Palgrave Macmillan, Cham, 2017
CRO Forum, *Liquidity Risk Management. Best Risk Management Practices*, October 2008
CUNDY, C., Solvency II: what reforms can we expect? *Insurance ERM*, 27 December 2018
CURTIS, R., Solvency as a Focal Point of Prudential Regulation, in LIEDTKE, P. M. and MONKIEWICZ, J. (Eds.), *The Future of Insurance Regulation and Supervision: A Global Perspective*, Palgrave Macmillan, Basingstoke, 2011
DE MAESSCHALCK, N., The Insurance Distribution Directive: What Does It Change for Intermediaries and for Others?, in MARANO, P. and SIRI, M. (Eds.), *Insurance Regulation in the European Union*, Palgrave Macmillan, Cham, 2017
DEGENAAR, T., Managing Model Risk, in DOFF, R. (Ed.), *The Solvency II Handbook. Practical Approaches to Implementation*, Incisive Media, London, 2014
DHAENE, J., STASSEN, B., BARIGOU, K., LINDERS, D. and CHEN, Z., Fair valuation of insurance liabilities: merging actuarial judgement and market-consistency, *Insurance Mathematics and Economics*, 2017, No 76
DOFF, R., A critical analysis of the Solvency II proposals, *The Geneva Papers on Risk and Insurance – Issues and Practice*, 2008, No 33/2, 193–206
——, The final Solvency II framework, *The Geneva Papers on Risk and Insurance – Issues and Practice*, Vol 41, No 4, October 2016
—— (Ed.), *The Solvency II Handbook*, London, Incisive Media, 2014

DREHER, M., *Treatises on Solvency II*, Springer, Berlin/Heidelberg, 2015

DREHER, M. and WANDT, M. (Eds.), *Solvency II in der Rechtsanwendung*, Karlsruhe, Verlag Versicherungswirtschaft, 2009

DREYFUSS, M.-L., *Comprendre et appliquer la gouvernance sous Solvabilité II*, Paris, Editions l'Argus de l'Assurance, 2016

——, *Les grands principes de Solvabilité 2*, Paris, Editions l'Argus de l'Assurance, 2012

DRUMMOND, C., *MCR shock – testing the strength of the SCR coverage ratio*, http://www.solvencyiiwire.com/category/articles 30 October 2017

EBA, *Proportionality in bank regulation: Report by the EBA Banking Stakeholder Group*, 30 June 2014

——, *Report on qualifying securitisation*, July 2015

EC, *A European Framework for Simple and Transparent Securitisation: Fact Sheet*, 30 September 2015

——, *Commissioner Barnier welcomes trilogue agreement by Council and Parliament on the "Omnibus II" Directive*, Press Release, 14 November 2013

——, *Consultation Document – Fitness check on supervisory reporting*, 1 December 2017

——, *Consultation Document: Fitness check on the EU framework for public reporting by companies*, 21 March 2018

——, *Final Report of the Committee of wise men on the regulation of European securities markets*, 15 February 2001

——, *Financing a sustainable European economy: Final Report 2018 by the High-Level Expert Group on Sustainable Finance*, January 2018

——, *Report of the High-Level Group on financial supervision in the EU, chaired by Jacques de Larosière*, 25 February 2009

——, *Request to EIOPA for technical advice on the review of specific items in the Solvency II Delegated Regulation as regards unjustified constraints to financing*, 21 February 2017

——, *Request to EIOPA for technical advice on the review of the Solvency II Directive*, Ares (2019) 782244, 11 February 2019

——, *Solvency II: EU to take global lead in insurance regulation*, Press Release, 10 July 2007

——, *Solvency II: European Parliament's approval of proposed directive brings modern insurance regulation nearer*, Press Release, 22 April 2009

——, *Study into the methodologies to assess the overall financial position of an insurance undertaking from the perspective of prudential supervision*, May 2002

ECB, *Potential impact of Solvency II on financial stability*, July 2007

ECIROA, *Position Paper on Solvency II – the Principle of Proportionality and its Application*, 2010

EID, T.K., *Solvency II: The Political Process*, Master's Thesis, Department of Political Science, University of Oslo, autumn 2014

EIOPA, *2018 Insurance Stress Test Report*, Publications Office of the EU, Luxembourg, 2018

——, *2018 Insurance Stress Test. Frequently asked questions & answers*, 14 December 2018

——, *A common supervisory culture. Key characteristics of high-quality and effective supervision*, Publications Office of the EU, Luxembourg, 2017

——, *Bankruptcy of Qudos Insurance A/S – Equal treatment of European policyholders*, 20 December 2018

——, *Big data analytics in motor and health insurance: a thematic review*, Publications Office of the EU, Luxembourg, 2019

——, *Common Application Package for Internal Models: Explanatory Note*, November 2014
——, *Decision on the collaboration of the insurance supervisory authorities*, EIOPA-BoS-17/014, 30 January 2017
——, *Discussion Paper on resolution funding and national insurance guarantee schemes*, EIOPA-BoS-18/003, 30 July 2018
——, *Discussion paper on Systemic Risk and Macro-prudential Policy in Insurance*, EIOPA-BoS-19/131, 29 March 2019
——, *EIOPA and its Members agree on No-deal Brexit Memoranda of Understanding with the Bank of England and the Financial Conduct Authority*, Press release, 5 March 2019
——, *EIOPA announces results of the 2018 insurance stress test*, Press Release, 14 December 2018
——, *European Insurance Overview 2018. Solo undertakings. Year-end 2017*, Publications Office of the EU, Luxembourg, 2018
——, *Failures and near misses in insurance. Overview of the causes and early identification*, Publications Office of the EU, Luxembourg, 2018
——, *Financial Stability Report*, June 2018
——, *Framework for assessing conduct risk through the product lifecycle*, Publications Office of the EU, Luxembourg, 2019
——, *Guidelines on system of governance*, EIOPA-BoS-14/253, 14 September 2015
——, *List of identified insurance groups for which a college of supervisors is in place*, April 2018
——, *Low interest rate environment stock taking exercise*, EIOPA-BoS-14/103, 28 November 2014
——, *Other potential macro-prudential tools and measures to enhance the current framework*, Publications Office of the EU, Luxembourg, 2018
——, *Oversight activities in 2017*, Publications Office of the EU, Luxembourg, 2018
——, *Peer review of key functions: supervisory practices and application in assessing key functions. Executive summary*, Publications Office of the EU, Luxembourg, 2018
——, *Peer review of key functions: supervisory practices and application in assessing key functions*, Publications Office of the EU, Luxembourg, 2018
——, *Report on Supervisory Activities in 2018*, Publications Office of the EU, Luxcembourg, 2019
——, *Report on the use of capital add-ons during 2017*, Publications Office of the EU, Luxembourg, 2018
——, *Report on the use of limitations and exemptions from reporting during 2017 and Q1 2018*, Publications Office of the EU, Luxembourg, 2018
——, *Results of the peer review on propriety of administrative, management or supervisory body members and qualifying shareholders*, Publications Office of the EU, Luxembourg, 2018
——, *Seventh Consumer Trends Report*, Publications Office of the EU, Luxembourg, 2018
——, *Solvency II tools with macro-prudential impact*, Publications Office of the EU, Luxembourg, 2018
——, *Supervisory Convergence Plan 2018–2019. How EIOPA is building supervisory convergence*, Publications Office of the EU, Luxembourg, 2018
——, *Systemic risk and macro-prudential policy in insurance*, Publications Office of the EU, Luxembourg, 2017

——, *Understanding Cyber Insurance – A Structured Dialogue with Insurance Companies*, Publications Office of the EU, Luxembourg, 2018

——, *Year-end report 2015 on functioning of colleges and accomplishments of action plan and priorities for 2016*, 4 May 2016

——, *Year-end report 2016 on functioning of colleges of supervisors and priorities for 2017*, 1 March 2017

ELING, M., The Role of Market Discipline in the Insurance Industry, in LIEDTKE, P.M. and MONKIEWICZ, J. (Eds.), *The Future of Insurance Regulation and Supervision: A Global Perspective*, Palgrave Macmillan, Basingstoke, 2011

ELING, M., SCHMEISER, H. and SCHMIT, J.T., The Solvency II Process: Overview and Critical Analysis, *Risk Management and Insurance Review*, 2007, No 1

EP, *Solvency II: Economic Committee MEPs concerned about preparation of SCR review*, Press release, 22 January 2019

ESRB, *Macro-prudential powers, measures and instruments for insurance*, November 2018

——, *Recovery & resolution for the EU insurance sector: a macro-prudential perspective*, August 2017

——, *Report on systemic risks in the EU insurance sector*, December 2015

——, *Report on the regulatory treatment of sovereign exposures*, March 2015

European Court of Auditors, *Special Report: EIOPA made an important contribution to supervision and stability in the insurance sector, but significant challenges remain*, Publications Office of the EU, Luxembourg, 2018

FABER-GRAW, P., Gruppenaufsicht im Wandel? – Die wesentlichen Veränderungen unter Solvency II im Vergleich zu Solvency I, in BENNEMANN, C., OEHLENBERG, L. and STAHL, G., *Handbuch Solvency II*, Schäffer-Poeschel Verlag, Stuttgart, 2011

FCA, *Brexit: information for general insurers and intermediaries in the UK*, 11 March 2019

Federal Insurance Office, US Department of the Treasury, *How to modernise and improve the system of insurance regulation in the United States*, December 2013

FINMA, *Circular 2017/3: Swiss Solvency Test*, 7 December 2016

FLAMEE, M. and WINDELS, P., International Insurance Supervision, in KEMPLER, C., FLAMEE, M., YANG, C.H. and WINDELS, P. (Eds.), *Global Perspectives on Insurance Today*, Palgrave Macmillan, New York, 2013

FLOREANI, A., Risk Measures and Capital Requirements: A Critique of the Solvency II Approach, *The Geneva Papers on Risk and Insurance – Issues and Practice*, Vol. 38, No 2, April 2013

FSB, *Developing Effective Resolution Strategies and Plans for Systemically Important Insurers*, 6 June 2016

G20/OECD, *Principles of Corporate Governance*, September 2015

GALATI, G. and MOESSNER, R., *Macro-prudential policy – a literature review*, BIS Working Paper No 337, February 2011

GATZERT, N. and KOSUB, Th., *Insurers' Investment in Infrastructure: Overview and Treatment under Solvency II*, The Geneva Papers, 2014, No 39

GATZERT, N. and WESKER, H., A comparative assessment of Basel II/III and Solvency II, *The Geneva Papers on Risk and Insurance – Issues and Practice*, 2012, No 37/3

GDV, Solvency II: Berichtspflichten grundlegend überarbeiten, *Regulierung und Aufsicht kompakt*, No 14, January 2019

Geneva Association, *Insurance and Resolution in Light of the Systemic Risk Debate*, February 2012
GIEGOLD, S., *EU insurance rules (Solvency II): Industry lobby pays off, as EU fails to protect policyholders*, Press Release, 14 November 2013
——, *Solvency II/Omnibus II: Lobby Festival in the European Parliament*, 21 March 2012
——, Solvency II: Durchmarsch der Versicherungslobby aufgehalten, 12 July 2012
Global Reinsurance Forum, *Reinsurance trade barriers and market access issues worldwide*, July 2018
GRÜNDL, H., *Sustainable Finance: Nicht auf Kosten der Versicherungskunden*, Absolut Impact, 2018, No 4
GRÜNDL, H. and KRAFT, M. (Eds.), *Solvency II - Eine Einführung*, Verlag Versicherungswirtschaft, Karlsruhe, 2015
——, (Eds.), *Solvency II - Eine Einführung*, Karelsruhe, Verlag Versicherungswirtschaft, Second Edition, 2016
——, (Eds.), *Solvency II - Eine Einführung*, Verlag Versicherungswirtschaft, Karlsruhe, Third Edition, 2019
GRÜNDL, H. and PERLET, H. (Eds.), *Solvency II & Risikomanagement*, Wiesbaden, Gabler Verlag, 2005
GUINE, C., Global Systemically Important Insurers, in EIOPA (Ed.), *Financial Stability Report 2014*, 14 May 2014
HAGEN, B., *Ist die EU für eine zentrale Versicherungsaufsicht bereit?*, Dike, Zürich/St. Gallen, 2014
HALL, D.J. and BERSET, J., Toward Global Reinsurance Regulation, in KEMPLER, C., FLAMEE, M., YANG, C.H. and WINDELS, P. (Eds.), *Global Perspectives on Insurance Today*, Palgrave Macmillan, New York, 2013
HARRINGTON, S.E., The Dodd–Frank Act, Solvency II, and US insurance regulation, *The Journal of Financial Perspectives*, 2013, Vol 1, No 1
HERZOG, Th., *Summary of CEIOPS calibration work on standard formula*, 5 January 2011, https://www.naic.org/documents/index_smi_solvency_ii_calibration.pdf
HEUKAMP, W., *Das neue Versicherungsaufsichtsrecht nach Solvency II. Eine Einführung für die Praxis*, C.H. Beck, München, 2015
House of Commons, Treasury Committee, *The Solvency II Directive and its impact on the UK Insurance Industry*, Third Report of Session 2017–2019, 25 October 2017
HUFELD, F., A Regulatory Framework for Systemic Risk in the Insurance Industry, in HUFELD, F., KOIJEN, R.S.J. and THIMANN, C. (Eds.), *The Economics, Regulation and Systemic Risk of Insurance Markets*, Oxford University Press, New York, 2017
HUFELD, F., KOIJEN, R.S.J. and THIMANN, C. (Eds.), *The Economics, Regulation and Systemic Risk of Insurance Markets*, Oxford University Press, New York, 2017
HUMPHRY, D., Solvency II in the UK: evolution rather than revolution, in MARANO, P. and SIRI, M. (Eds.), *Insurance Regulation in the European Union: Solvency II and beyond*, Palgrave Macmillan, Cham, 2017
IAIS, *Application paper on the regulation and supervision of captive insurers*, November 2015
——, *Application paper on the regulation and supervision of mutuals, cooperatives and community-based organisations in increasing access to insurance markets*, September 2017

——, *Guidance Paper No 11 on Risk Transfer, Disclosure and Analysis of Finite Reinsurance*, October 2006

——, *Holistic Framework for systemic risk in the insurance sector*, Public Consultation Document, 14 November 2018

——, ICP 2 – Supervisor and CEIOPS, Recommendations on Independence and Accountability, CEIOPS-DOC-04/06, May 2006

——, *Issues Paper on conduct of business risk and its management*, November 2015

——, *Issues Paper on supervision of cross-border operations through branches*, October 2013

——, *Macro-prudential policy and surveillance in insurance*, 18 July 2013

——, *Risk-based Global Insurance Capital Standard Version 2.0*, Public Consultation Document, 31 July 2018

——, *Systemic Risk from Insurance Product Features (previously referred to as Non-Traditional Non-Insurance activities and products)*, 16 June 2016

IMF, *Belgium FSAP. Technical Note: Banking, Insurance and Financial Conglomerate Supervision*, March 2018

——, *Financial Sector Assessment Program at EU Level*, March 2013

INREV, *Real estate investment under Solvency II*, May 2017

Institute of Internal Auditors, *The three lines of defence in effective risk management and control*, January 2013

Insurance Europe, *How insurance stimulates growth*, 2014

——, *Impact assessment results should be reflected in Omnibus II*, Press Release, 20 September 2012

——, *Insurance Europe comments on amendments to Solvency II Delegated Regulation*, Position Paper, 11 December 2018

——, *Insurance Europe welcomes EU agreement on Omnibus II*, Press Release, 14 November 2013

——, *Insurers seek further improvements to Omnibus II text*, Press Release, 21 March 2012

——, *Testing of Solvency II measures welcomed*, Press Release, 28 January 2013

——, *The benefits of insurance*, 2015

——, *The matching adjustment – Theory and practice*, 8 February 2013

——, *The package of measures to avoid artificial volatility and pro-cyclicality*, 8 February 2013

Insurance Europe and Oliver Wyman, *Funding the future: Insurers' role as institutional investors*, June 2013

IVERSEN, A., Solvency II and sovereign bonds, in ADENAS, M., AVESANI, R., MANES, P., VELLA, F. and WOOD, P. (Eds.), *Solvency II: A dynamic challenge for the insurance market*, Il Mulino, Bologna, 2017

Joint Committee (JC 2012-100), *Self-Assessment Report of the ESAs*, 21 December 2012

JONES, O., Solvency II. Review views, in Insurance Europe, *Annual Report 2017–2018*

——, Solvency II: sophisticated but excessive, in Insurance Europe, *Annual Report 2016–2017*

KADING, B. and MADEIROS, L., Insurance Regulation: Mutual Recognition, Equivalence and International Standards, in LIEDTKE, P.M. and MONKIEWICZ, J. (Eds.), *The Future of Insurance Regulation and Supervision: A Global Perspective*, Palgrave Macmillan, Basingstoke, 2011

KELLER, P., *Risk based supervision and the Swiss Solvency Test*, Federal Office of Private Insurance, 1 December 2006

KELLERMANN, J., DE HAAN, J. and DE VRIES, F. (Eds.), *Financial Supervision in the 21st Century*, Springer, Heidelberg, 2013

KEMPLER, C., FLAMEE, M., YANG, CH. And WINDELS, P. (Eds.), *Global Perspectives on Insurance Today*, New York, Palgrave Macmillan, 2013

KESSLER, D., DE MONTCHALIN, A. and THIMANN, C., The Macroeconomic Role of Insurance, in HUFELD, F., KOIJEN, R.S.J. and THIMANN, C. (Eds.), *The Economics, Regulation and Systemic Risk of Insurance Markets*, Oxford University Press, New York, 2017

KIVISAARI, E., Risk management should be one of the cornerstones when insurers consider their role in sustainability, *Insurance ERM*, 2 January 2019

KLEIN, R.W., The Modernization of Insurance Company Solvency Regulation in the US: Issues and Implications, Networks Financial Institute Policy Brief PB-2012-01, Indiana State University, March 2012

KRAFT, M., Auswirkungn von Solvency II und der neuen EU-Finanzaufsichtsarchitektur auf die Kapitalallokationsstrukturen von Versicherungsgruppen, *Zeitschrift für Versicherungswissenschaft*, 2012, No 101

KWON, W.J., The Economic Rationale for Insurance Regulation, in LIEDTKE, P.M. and MONKIEWICZ, J. (Eds.), *The Future of Insurance Regulation and Supervision: A Global Perspective*, Palgrave Macmillan, Basingstoke, 2011

LAUTENSCHLÄGER, S., *European banking supervision – towards a common culture*, statement made at the Eurofi Financial Forum 2018, Vienna, 6 September 2018

LEADBETTER, D. and SYODOLAK, P., *Why insurers fail: inadequately pricing the promise of insurance*, Property and Casualty Insurance Compensation Corporation, Toronto, 1999

LIEDTKE, P. and MONKIEWICZ, J. (Eds.), *The Future of Insurance Regulation and Supervision*, A global perspective, Basingstoke, Palgrave Macmillan, 2011

LINDER, U. and RONKAINEN, V., Solvency II – towards a new insurance supervisory system in the EU, *Scandinavian Actuarial Journal*, 2004, No 6

LOWET, L., De grootste Europese verzekeringsgroepen (the largest European insurance groups), *Tijdschrift voor Bank- en Financiewezen*, 2010, No 6

——, De minimis not curat praetor: how the Solvency II Directive exempts the very small insurers, *Tijdschrift voor Bank- en Financiewezen*, 2010, No 5

——, *European Solvency II Law*, Knops Publishing, Antwerp, 2016

MÄCHLER, M., Evolution of Insurance Group Supervision, in KEMPLER, C., FLAMEE, M., YANG, C.H. and WINDELS, P. (Eds.), *Global Perspectives on Insurance Today*, Palgrave Macmillan, New York, 2013

——, Insurance Group Supervision: Addressing the Emergence of Adverse Network Dynamics, in LIEDTKE, P.M. and MONKIEWICZ, J. (Eds.), *The Future of Insurance Regulation and Supervision: A Global Perspective*, Palgrave Macmillan, Basingstoke, 2011

——, Versicherungsaufsicht in europäischer Dynamik, in NOTTER, M., WEBER, R.H., HEINEMANN, A. and BAUMGARTNER, T. (Eds.), *Europäische Idee und Integration – mittendrin und nicht dabei? Liber amicorum für Andreas Kellerhals*, Schulthess, Zürich/Basel/Geneva, 2018

MARANO, P. and SIRI, M., Cross-Border Insurance Groups: Towards a Comprehensive Supervision under Solvency II, *The Geneva Papers on Risk and Insurance – Issues and Practice*, Vol. 43, No 4, October 2018

——, (Eds.), *Insurance Regulation in the European Union*, Cham, Palgrave Macmillan, 2017

MARANO, P., Sources and tools of insurance regulation, in MARANO, P. and SIRI, M. (Eds.), *Insurance Regulation in the European Union: Solvency II and Beyond*, Palgrave Macmillan, Cham, 2017

MASCIANDARO, D. and QUINTYN, M., The Architecture of Insurance Supervision Before and After the Financial Crisis, in LIEDTKE, P.M. and MONKIEWICZ, J. (Eds.), *The Future of Insurance Regulation and Supervision: A Global Perspective*, Palgrave Macmillan, Basingstoke, 2011

MONTALVO, C., Risk management under Solvency II: Solvency capital requirements, in DREHER, M. and WANDT, M. (Eds.), *Solvency in der Rechtsanwendung*, Verlag Versicherungswirtschaft, Karlsruhe, 2009

——, The (re)calibration dilemma, *Eurofi Newsletter*, 31 March–1 April 2014

——, *Understanding a breach of the SCR*, 29 January 2012, solvencyiiwire.com/understanding-a-breach-of-the-SCR/7928

NEVILLE, P., Growth and Diversification of the Captive Insurance Market, in KEMPLER, C., FLAMEE, M., YANG, C.H. and WINDELS, P. (Eds.), *Global Perspectives on Insurance Today*, Palgrave Macmillan, New York, 2013

OECD, *The Contribution of Reinsurance Markets to Managing Catastrophe Risk*, www.oecd.org/finance/the-contribution-of-reinsurance-markets-to-managing-catastrophe-risk.pdf, 2018

OPPERMANN, R. and OSTERMEIER, S., *Solvency II visuell. Die Anforderungen von Solvency II in strukturierten übersichten*, Stuttgart, Schäffer-Poeschel Verlag, 2018

PATEL, C. and DAYKIN, C.D., *Actuaries and Discount Rates – A Discussion Paper*, Institute of Actuaries and Faculty of Actuaries, London, May 2010

PERSAUD, A., *How not to regulate insurance markets: the risks and dangers of Solvency II*, Peterson Institute for International Economics Policy Brief PB15-5 April 2015

PRADIER, P.-C. and CHNEIWEISS, A., *The evolution of insurance regulation in the EU since 2005*, Documents de travail du Centre d'Economie de la Sorbonne, 2016

QUAGLIA, L., The European Union, the USA and International Standard Setting by Regulatory Fora in Finance, *New Political Economy*, 2014, No 3

——, The politics of insurance regulation and supervision in the European Union, *Comparative European Politics*, 2011, No 9

RAMELLA, M., Securitization and Insurance, in KEMPLER, C., FLAMEE, M., YANG, C.H. and WINDELS, P. (Eds.), *Global Perspectives on Insurance Today*, Palgrave Macmillan, New York, 2013

——, The Regulatory Future of International Insurance Centres: Balancing Sound Supervision, Innovation and Competition, in LIEDTKE, P.M. and MONKIEWICZ, J. (Eds.), *The Future of Insurance Regulation and Supervision: A Global Perspective*, Palgrave Macmillan, Basingstoke, 2011

RIEF, W., Marktdisziplinierende Einwirkungen durch Solvency II?, *Kredit & Rating Praxis*, 2017, No 2

SANDSTRÖM, A., *Handbook of Solvency for Actuaries and Risk Managers. Theory and Practice*, Chapman & Hall/CRC, Boca Raton, 2011

——, *Solvency: Models, Assessment and Regulation*, Chapman & Hall, Boca Raton, 2006

SCHLUDE, H., The EEC solvency rules for non-life insurance companies, *Nordisk Försäkrings Tidskrift*, 1979, No 1

SCHOENMAKER, D., European Insurance Union and how to get there, Bruegel Policy Brief, 2016, Issue 4, December 2016

SCHUERMANS, P., Solvency II: A Balancing Act, in KEMPLER, C., FLAMEE, M., YANG, C.H. and WINDELS, P. (Eds.), *Global Perspectives on Insurance Today*, Palgrave Macmillan, New York, 2013

SHARMA, P. and CADONI, P., Solvency II: A New Regulatory Frontier, in KEMPLER, C., FLAMEE, M., YANG, C.H. and WINDELS, P. (Eds.), *Global Perspectives on Insurance Today*, Palgrave Macmillan, New York, 2013

SINGH, R., Toward a Global Approach to Regulating Insurers and Reinsurers, in KEMPLER, C., FLAMEE, M., YANG, C.H. and WINDELS, P. (Eds.), *Global Perspectives on Insurance Today*, Palgrave Macmillan, New York, 2013

SINGH, R. and JONES, O., *Solutions to major issues for Solvency II, Joint Submission by the CRO Forum and CEA*, CEIOPS Consultative Panel, Frankfurt, 11 January 2006

SIRI, M., Corporate governance of insurance firms after Solvency II, *ICIR Working Paper Series*, 2017, No 27, 39 p

——, Corporate governance of insurance firms after Solvency II, in MARANO, P. and SIRI, M. (Eds.), *Insurance Regulation in the European Union: Solvency II and beyond*, Palgrave Macmillan, Cham, 2017

Solvency II Wire, *Solvency II News: Omnibus II trialogue calls for impact assessment on long-term guarantee measures*, 13 July 2012

——, *Solvency II News: Omnibus II trilogue in disarray*, 9 October 2012

SPITZ, B., Europe's Risky Insurance Regulation, *The Wall Street Journal Europe*, 18 March 2009

STEFFEN, T., Solvency II and the work of CEIOPS, *The Geneva Papers*, 2008, No 33

STÖLTING, R., *Auf dem Weg zu Solvency II: Aktueller Stand*, 8 November 2004, http://www.mi.uni-koeln.de/jost/stoelting2.pdf

SWAIN, R. and SWALLOW, D., The prudential regulation of insurers under Solvency II, *Bank of England Quarterly Bulletin*, 2015

Swiss Re, Digital distribution in insurance: a quiet revolution, *Sigma*, 2014, No 2

——, Mortality improvement: understanding the past and framing the future, *Sigma*, 2018, No 6

——, Solvency II: an integrated risk approach for European insurers, *Sigma*, 2006, No 4

——, Strategic reinsurance and insurance: the increasing trend of customised solutions, *Sigma*, 2016, No 5

TANNER, C., *UK insurers emphasise post-Brexit opportunity*, Insurance ERM, 26 January 2017

The Geneva Association, *Insurance in the Digital Age: a view of key implications for the economy and society*, September 2018

——, *Insurance Sector Investments and Their Impact on Financial Stability*, June 2016

——, *Modernising Insurance Solvency Regimes – Key Features of Selected Markets*, August 2016

——, *Systemic Risk in Insurance: An analysis of insurance and financial stability*, March 2010

——, *The nature and role of capital in insurance*, November 2016

THIMANN, C., What Is Insurance and How Does It Differ from General Finance?, in HUFELD, F., KOIJEN, R.S.J. and THIMANN, C. (Eds.), *The Economics, Regulation and Systemic Risk of Insurance Markets*, Oxford University Press, New York, 2017

THIND, S., US-EU covered agreement: a rocky road to implementation, *Insurance ERM*, 27 November 2018

TROWBRIDGE, J., The Architecture of Group Supervision, in KEMPLER, C., FLAMEE, M., YANG, C.H. and WINDELS, P. (Eds.), *Global Perspectives on Insurance Today*, Palgrave Macmillan, New York, 2013

VAN HULLE, K., *China is candidate for provisional equivalency under Solvency II*, Swiss Re Centre for Global Dialogue, 2014

——, Do not wait until new regulation is introduced, *Insurance ERM*, 28 December 2018

——, From Accounting Directives to International Accounting Standards, in LEUTZ, C., PFAFF, D. and HOPWOOD, A. (Eds.), *The Economics and Politics of Accounting*, Oxford University Press, New York, 2004

——, Regulatory challenges in the European Union, in LIEDTKE, P. and MONKIEWICZ, J. (Eds.), *The Future of Insurance Regulation and Supervision: A Global Perspective*, Palgrave Macmillan, Basingstoke, 2011

——, Rückblick und Ausblick auf die Versicherungsregulierung in der EU, in KELLERHALS, A. (Ed.), *Bilateralismus im multilateralen Europa. Referate zu Fragen der Zukunft Europas 2013*, Zürich, 2014

——, Solvency II: Reasonable Expectations, in MARANO, P. and SIRI, M. (Eds.), *Insurance Regulation in the European Union*, Cham, Palgrave Macmillan, 2017

——, Solvency II: State of play and perspectives, *Zeitschrift fur die gesamte Versicherungswirtschaft*, 2011, No 100/2

——, Solvency II: What is good for the goose, is good for the gander, *Bipar Academy*, Brussels, 2016

——, The Challenge of Solvency II, *British Actuarial Journal*, 2008, No 14/1

——, The EU is taking the lead with Solvency II, *The European Actuary*, 2010, No 1

——, The Solvency and Financial Condition Report, *Bipar Academy*, Brussels, 2018

VAN HULLE, K. and VAN DER TAS, L., European Union – Consolidated Accounts, in ORDELHEIDE, D. and KPMG (Eds.), *Transatlantic Accounting*, second edition, Volume I, Palgrave, Basingstoke, 2001

VAUGHAN, T., Improving Regulatory Capital Requirements, in KEMPLER, C., FLAMEE, M., YANG, C.H. and WINDELS, P. (Eds.), *Global Perspectives on Insurance Today*, Palgrave Macmillan, New York, 2013

——, The Implications of Solvency II for US Insurance Regulation, *Networks Financial Institute Policy Brief PB*-2009-03, Indiana State University, February 2009

WAGNER, C., Das interne Risikokapitalmodell der Allianz-Gruppe, in GRÜNDL, H. and PERLET, H. (Eds.), *Solvency II & Risikomanagement*, Gabler Verlag, Wiesbaden, 2005

WANDT, M., *Prinzipienbasiertes Recht und Verhältnismässigkeitsgrundsatz im Rahmen von Solvency II*, Mannheimer Vorträge zur Versicherungswissenschaft Vol. 91, VVW, Karlsruhe, 2012

WEBER-REY, D. and RHIEL, J., Perspectives on ORSA, Frankfurt, Clifford Chance, 2013

WYMEERSCH, E., How to make Europe's financial regulatory and supervisory system more efficient?, *Revue trimestrielle de droit financier*, 2016, No 2

ZUBOR, Z., Volatility capital buffer to prevent the breach of the Solvency II capital requirements, *Financial and Economic Review*, 2016, Vol. 15, No 1

INDEX

ABOUT THE AUTHOR

In his function as Head of Insurance and Pensions at the European Commission (until March 2013) Professor Karel Van Hulle played an essential role in the development of the new risk-based solvency capital regime for (re)insurers that led to the Solvency II Directive. In that capacity he also represented the EC within EIOPA and was a member of the Technical Committee of the IAIS. He was an academic member and Chair of the Insurance and Reinsurance Stakeholder Group of EIOPA and is currently a member of the Public Interest Oversight Board and of the Board of the Bermuda Monetary Authority. He started his professional career with the Belgian Banking Commission and the Belgian Accounting Standards Commission and served 30 years with the European Commission with responsibilities in the areas of financial reporting and auditing, company law and corporate governance, and insurance and pensions. He studied law at the KU Leuven and at the Marquette University Law School in Milwaukee (USA). In 2013, he was nominated Distinguished Fellow of the IAIS and in 2014, he was elected Honorary Fellow of the UK Institute and Faculty of Actuaries.

Today, Professor Van Hulle lectures at the Economics and Business Faculty of KU Leuven (Belgium) and at the Economics Faculty of Goethe University in Frankfurt (Germany), where he is also Executive Director of the International Centre for Insurance Regulation.

www.ingramcontent.com/pod-product-compliance
Ingram Content Group UK Ltd.
Pitfield, Milton Keynes, MK11 3LW, UK
UKHW051917100926
8556IPUK00021B/1227

9 781780 68177